# YOUR
# SUCCESSFUL
# REAL ESTATE
# CAREER

# YOUR SUCCESSFUL REAL ESTATE CAREER
## Third Edition

## Kenneth W. Edwards

## amacom
### American Management Association
New York • Atlanta • Boston • Chicago • Kansas City • San Francisco • Washington, DC
Brussels • Mexico City • Tokyo • Toronto

Library of Congress Cataloging-in-Publication Data

Edwards, Kenneth W., 1928–
    Your successful real estate career / Kenneth W. Edwards. — 3rd.
ed.
        p.   cm.
    Includes bibliographical references and index.
    ISBN 0–8144–7931–6
    1. Real estate business—Vocational guidance—United States.
I. Title.
HD1375.E33    1997
333.33′023′73—dc21                                        96-51466
                                                              CIP

Printing number

10 9 8 7 6 5 4 3 2 1

# Contents

# *Preface*

Few things you can do to earn a living are as challenging and exciting as a career in real estate. It is an activity with widely diverse opportunities and exceptional income potential. There has been a continuing interest in it among people searching for meaningful and well-paying work and among educators who respond to such trends. Almost every community college in the country, for example, offers courses in real estate, as do an increasing number of four-year colleges and universities. Several states sponsor major real estate education and research centers. In every part of the United States, scores of private real estate schools present quality instruction. Each year thousands of individuals receive their licenses to sell real estate.

Many who enter the field enjoy long, satisfying careers. Unfortunately, many others do not. Historically, the dropout rate has been extremely high, primarily because all too often people enter the field with an inaccurate or distorted perception of what the business is all about and what it takes to do well in it on a long-term basis.

## WHO THIS BOOK IS FOR

If you are considering real estate as an occupation, this book is written for you. If you have recently entered the field, the book should help get you headed in the right direction and ensure that you stay on track. If you have been in the profession for a while, it can provide a helpful "return to the basics" review. It is a comprehensive, candid, and practical career guide that will assist you in deciding whether to enter the field and will help you be successful if you do. It deals with the opportunities and obstacles you are likely to face, presented in the order you are likely to face them. I describe an effective method of conducting your business affairs that emphasizes professionalism, long-term achievement, and personal satisfaction.

The overwhelming majority of people who work in real estate concentrate their efforts on listing and selling residential property, because that is where most of the opportunities for employment exist. Therefore, I have organized this book to be of maximum assistance to those of you starting out as residential sales agents in general real estate brokerage companies. In all states, that means you will have to be licensed, which entails passing a written examination, and, in most cases, formal course work as well. I provide detailed guidance on getting your license and starting your career, and I discuss extensively the opportunities available to you for specializing or broadening your career as you gain some experience.

One thing that makes real estate such an interesting field in which to work is the widely divergent backgrounds of those who enter the profession. Real estate is truly a melting pot of practitioners. You will encounter everyone from former plumbers to Ph.D.s. At the outset, however, everyone needs reliable career information. If you have extensive previous business experience, you may not require as much information as I present on some topics, but my aim is to be as thorough and helpful as possible and take nothing for granted.

I had three specific groups in mind as I wrote. One is composed of those who are entering the general job market for the first time. I have tried to be particularly sensitive to the needs of these individuals. Although they represent a distinct minority of the total work force in the profession, more and more new workers are choosing careers in real estate as a result of the general upgrading of the profession and the expanding availability of quality licensing programs.

The second group consists of women reentering the work place after an absence, often one of an extended duration. For these individuals, real estate has traditionally been a very popular occupation. Licensing programs can be rigorous, but otherwise the field of real estate is comparatively easy to enter, offers true equality of opportunity, permits a flexible work schedule, and promises good income potential. In writing for women readers, I drew heavily on knowledge of my wife's experiences as a real estate professional and those of several of my women associates.

The final group for whom I wrote this book includes those who are in some other occupation and are now considering real estate as a career change or as a second career after retirement. Real estate was a second career for me, so I have a good understanding of the attraction it holds for people looking for a new field to enter.

In Chapter 15, "Special Messages for Special People," I offer specific suggestions to individuals from each of these groups in order to make their entry into real estate as smooth and productive as possible.

While the book is written as a career guide for people considering real estate as a profession, or already in it, I've received positive feedback from some readers who simply want to learn as much as they can about the real estate profession and how it operates to make them better investors, but who do not want a real estate license. That's a plan I've seen implemented very successfully, and I'll also elaborate on that in Chapter 15.

## HOW TO USE THIS BOOK

First, I suggest you skim the entire book. This will give you a good overview of typical job-related activities and long-term opportunities. Do not become overly involved with specific details. Concentrate on subjects that are of the most immediate interest to you and will help you to make a sound career decision. If you then enroll in a license training course, use the book to help you understand how the subject matter you are studying relates to "real-life real estate." It is widely used as a supplementary licensing text for that specific purpose. When you start looking for a company with which to affiliate, study Chapter 3 thoroughly *before* you begin your search. If there is no formal training program where you work, you can use this book to structure a very effective one of your own. If there is a training program, it can serve as a valuable adjunct, offering a perspective and alternatives you are not likely to encounter elsewhere. However you use the book, I trust you will come to regard it as your "career companion."

## WHY THERE ARE A FEW DISCOURAGING WORDS

As I thought about the content and tone of *Your Successful Real Estate Career*, my challenge was to be candid enough to be helpful, yet positive enough to reflect my genuine enthusiasm for real estate as a career. When I focus on disadvantages of the job and on disagreements among those in the field about the professionalism of certain practices, my intent is to be constructive. If you have a clear idea of what to expect in the work place, good and bad, you will be much more likely to adapt successfully and be better prepared to develop your own personal philosophy of doing business by having been exposed early to divergent ideas. Leigh Robinson, author of the best selling book *Landlording*, put it in these colorful terms: " . . . *Your Successful Real Estate Career* portrays the work just as it is, hemorrhoids and all." One publisher turned down my original manuscript with the comment: "I really doubt there's a market for an honest book about selling real estate." Fortunately, he was wrong.

My objective is certainly not to discourage people who are suited for real estate from entering it. On the contrary, it is to encourage serious-minded, career-oriented individuals who appreciate candor and objectivity. From the standpoint of those in the profession, it is expensive and time-consuming to recruit and train real estate agents. It is clearly in everyone's best interests to provide information that is balanced and is effective in attracting those who are most suited for the field.

## RESEARCH METHODS AND WRITING STYLE

My primary research methodology was that of direct personal observation. I was a very successful residential real estate sales agent for several years, after a career in the Air Force. My wife was also a licensed salesperson, and we worked together as a team in the same office.

To secure background information, and to help me achieve a national perspective, I conducted a written survey of several hundred real estate brokers and salespeople from around the country (see Appendix A). I wanted to find out why people leave the profession prematurely. If I knew what caused difficulties for some, I believed, I could do a better job of advising prospective salespeople. I refer to the results of the survey and quote survey respondents throughout the book.

At the present time, there are approximately two million four hundred thousand real estate licensees in the United States. Of those roughly 750,000, or just over 30 percent, are members of the National Association of Realtors (NAR). The word Realtor is a registered trade name that may only be used by those who are members of NAR. While comprising a minority of the total force, the Realtor organization is the dominant professional real estate force in the country. They publish a series of statistical reports on the status of their members to which I refer frequently in the book.

I have included a few real estate "war stories" and personal experiences to illustrate some particularly important points. Real estate is an exciting and dynamic profession, and any book describing it that does not capture that spirit does not do the profession justice. What you will *not* find are lists of sure-fire success techniques and formulas guaranteed to produce instant fame and untold riches. What specific advice I include I have followed myself, or I have watched others follow, and the suggestions do work. However, only you can decide what is best for your situation and your personality.

I have tried to cover the subject matter itself in a way that applies to all areas of the country. But although there are marked similarities in the practice of real estate in all states, there are also important differences. What is permissible in one place might be improper or illegal in another. Because no one can be licensed to sell real estate without demonstrating a knowledge of local rules and regulations, you should be able to judge where practices I discuss differ from what is followed in your state. In all matters covered in this book, your current state law is your absolute guide. Although this is not a formal research report, you will find an extensive bibliography in the References section for use in your further study.

Real estate prices also vary markedly from one region to another. What buys a mansion in your hometown may purchase only a modest bungalow (or a lot upon which to build a modest bungalow) somewhere else. When I present examples that mention home prices or income levels adjust the figures as necessary to bring them in line with what you know to be the case where you live.

## A FARMER'S PHILOSOPHY

One fellow outside of the profession who read my manuscript made this comment: "You certainly do expect a lot out of a new real estate agent!" At first reading you may have the same impression, but if you take the contents one small chunk at a time, you will find that it is not all that imposing. And, of course, there is the argument that anything worth doing, is worth doing well. When I was on the faculty at Cal Berkeley I had a student from Nebraska who was studying to be an attorney. His father was not thrilled with his son's choice of occupations. The boy said that as he left the family farm, his hard working dad's last words to him were, "Son, if you are determined to be a lawyer, be an honest one and be a good one." That's not bad advice, no matter what profession you enter.

## YOUR INPUT IS WELCOME

I have received excellent feedback from readers to previous editions and I am anxious to have yours. I am particularly interested in suggestions from those of you who are new to the field, as you face the challenges that I discuss in the book. I would also like to hear from brokers about what might be included to be of more help to you in working with new agents. If you are using the book in teaching formal real estate courses, I would be grateful for suggestions on how the material might be expanded or altered. Please direct your comments to: Dr. Kenneth W. Edwards, Professional Associates, 7990 NW Ridgewood Drive, Corvallis, OR 97330.

# *Acknowledgments*

I had two primary objectives when I was in real estate. The first was to succeed, using the type of business practices I describe in this book. The second was to gather the research material and gain the practical experience I needed to write a real estate career guide. I had a lot of help in achieving both goals.

My wife, Judith McVay Edwards, was my real estate business partner. She did most of the hard, unglamorous work, while I generally got the credit. In my writing efforts, she has been my constructive and gentle critic and has given the loving support I needed to see the project through. My broker, W. Dale Dyer and his partner wife Carolyn Dyer, provided the perfect environment for learning about the real estate profession. The experience was made a lot more enjoyable by their constant and friendly encouragement.

For the past several years, I have taught courses in real estate through the Extended Learning Division of Linn-Benton Community College in Albany, Oregon. Many of my students have gone into the real estate profession and continue to give me extremely valuable feedback on the challenges and opportunities they are encountering.

I am grateful to these organizations for assisting me in my research: the Real Estate Educators Association, the National Association of Realtors, the National Association of Real Estate Editors, and the Retired Officers Association.

Finally, special thanks to my past clients, customers, and former associates, all of whom contributed to making my time in real estate such a pleasant, memorable, and profitable experience.

# YOUR SUCCESSFUL REAL ESTATE CAREER

# 1

# *Is Real Estate for You?*

*It's a Great Life...If It's the Life You're Suited For*

Choosing your occupation is one of the toughest decisions you will ever make, and clearly one of the most important. That is true whether you're a young person looking for your first full-time job, or someone embarking on a second or third career later in life. For you to make the best choice you need to find out as much as you can about your possibilities from reliable and unbiased sources. You will want to know what kind of person is most likely to succeed, and you will surely want to find out how much money you can expect to make. It isn't always easy to get the kind of information you require. In real estate, for example, my research indicated that *lack of objective information about the career field before they enter it* is a major reason why people drop out of the profession. (See Appendix A.)

There is no question that residential real estate sales can be exciting and tremendously rewarding—for the right person. My purpose in this chapter is to help you decide whether or not *you* are that person.

## THE NATURE OF THE JOB

First, let's take a brief look at some of the basics. In legal terms an agent is someone empowered to transact business for another person. Real estate agents perform that function. I discuss the subject of agency as it relates to real estate in depth in Chapter 5. As a *licensed real estate salesperson* (the most widely accepted official term) you will work for a *real estate broker*. A broker has spent a prescribed amount of time in the profession, has received additional training, and is subject to separate licensing procedures. Your broker will provide you with desk space and certain support items, and is obliged to supervise your professional real estate activities for as long as you are together. In return, you share your income with him or her. Some states are considering a single licensing system, in which the salesperson designation would be eliminated, everyone would be licensed as brokers, and supervisory relationships altered. Colorado is the only state that has so far adopted such a system. If you plan to become licensed there, you can get guidance by writing the Colorado Real Estate Commission at the address listed in Appendix B.

Almost all real estate agents are paid solely from commissions (brokerage fees paid to their supervising brokers and shared with the agents) that result either from property they sell or from the sale of their listings (contractual agreements with owners to market property) by other agents. This is true whether they are among the approximately 95 percent who are "independent contractors" or whether they are "employees." In real estate sales, employee is used to describe the nature of the supervisory relationship between broker and agent, and has specific legal and tax implications. Rarely are real estate salespeople who are employees paid a set salary. I describe these basics more fully in Chapter 3.

The point is that selling real estate is a job in which you survive and prosper by producing results. How you do that will be left largely to you. Whatever works, within the bounds of common sense, legality, and reason, will be acceptable. Within the profession, even among co-workers in the same office, there can be a remarkable diversity in the ways the role of real estate agent is interpreted. Many very successful agents rely heavily upon the traditional sales techniques, such as door-to-door solicitation and telephone canvassing. Others who are equally productive either do not employ any "standard" approaches or modify them greatly. One of the real attractions of the occupation is that you are able to pursue your career in a manner that is compatible with your own personality and values.

## TRAITS AND SKILLS YOU'LL NEED

How well you do as a real estate agent will be determined by how well adapted you are to the demands of the profession. Here are some of the personality traits and job skills you will need in real estate. No one will possess all of them, nor is everyone equally thrilled with all parts of the job. Further, a real strength in one area can compensate for average abilities in another.

■ *You need to like the lifestyle.* Most successful agents I know treat real estate more as a fascinating hobby than a job. They're never happier than when they are in the middle of putting a transaction together. They do not watch the clock and they are ready to spring into action when the bell rings (or the beeper beeps), whether it's day or night, weekday or weekend. The more astute discipline themselves to ensure they have a balance in their lives, but the fact remains that they love their work and typically immerse themselves in it. You don't have to be quite that passionate about the whole thing to succeed, but it will have to be more than "just a job" for you to put up with the demands upon your time. People expect you to respond at *their* convenience, not yours. For many, evenings and weekends are the only time they can look at property or talk to you about selling their home. If you are the type who dislikes a nine-to-five, Monday-through-Friday routine, then the real estate lifestyle will appeal to you.

■ *You need to be a self-starter.* If the concept of individual accountability for achievement, judged almost exclusively by the number of business transactions you successfully consummate attracts you, you will find real estate an invigorating experience. You will either succeed or fail almost entirely on the basis of your own individual efforts. You need to understand that fact very clearly. No matter how effective the training program of the company with which you affiliate, and no matter how enlightened and supportive the broker with whom you work, you must have the desire and the ability to do it on your own. In my survey, *lack of "self-starter" and "self-motivator" personality* emerged as *the* most important reason people leave real estate prematurely (see Appendix A). A national franchise broker from California summed it up well in his survey reply: "Unless you are strong on self-discipline and do your own motivation, you should forget about real estate." Many people thrive in this atmosphere and would be uncomfortable in a more traditional environment. Others feel neglected, become lost and discouraged, and give up. You need to have a whole lot of the rugged individualist in you.

■ *You need to be a hard worker.* It is not uncommon to encounter someone prospering in real estate who seems to lack all the prerequisites generally thought to be essential for success. Examples abound of people who violate every widely held sales precept and yet do quite well—sometimes amazingly well. But big money without hard work? No. Read my words. Absolutely, positively not. Hard work is an indispensable, unconditional prerequisite. Formal research by the National Association of Realtors reveals what common sense would suggest: a direct, positive correlation exists in real estate sales between average hours worked per week and income. Those mavericks making the big bucks may be marching to a different drummer, but they're all working hard in their own way. A Wisconsin broker summed it up well in this survey comment: "Those who don't do well are those who just can't seem to get to work early and stay late, working effectively while there. Many new people think real estate is an easy job with easy money. Real estate success takes training, dedication, and an ability to work long hours, weekends, and during summer vacation periods." Just to put some numbers to it, NAR research reveals that the median hours worked per week by Realtor salespeople is 45, with 47 percent working more than 50. That's a pretty impressive work ethic.

My guess is that I am preaching to the choir with this sermon on hard work. If you're like many agents, your problem will be just the opposite. You will have to be dragged away from your desk at night and threatened with bodily harm by your broker or your mate to get you to take a vacation. You could even develop some very detrimental personal habits. For example, I frequently encounter a friend of mine, one of the most successful agents in our community, hastily wolfing down a fat-laden hot bratwurst at the stand in front of our local supermarket. He figures he can't afford to take the time for a sit-down lunch.

- *You need to be a smart worker.* Although hard work is essential, you get paid for the results you achieve, not the hours you put in. This means that you must spend your time doing those specific things that have the highest potential for paying off. It also means that you should organize your business affairs to be efficient and productive. (I deal with each aspect in depth in later chapters.) The ability to "work smart" has very little to do with native intelligence. Fortunately for most of us, you do not need to be intellectually gifted to be a successful real estate agent. It is far more important to have common sense and a knowledge of human nature.

- *You need to enjoy solving "people problems."* Excuse the old cliche, but you absolutely must be good at "working with people." You must enjoy the challenge of helping people solve very complex, often highly emotional, problems. Every transaction in which you will be involved will have difficulties. You will try to ensure that nothing serious goes wrong, but without fail you will have to deal with situations you could neither foresee nor forestall. Those who do well acknowledge the inevitability of obstacles and appreciate the fact that they will get paid in direct proportion to their ability to anticipate and resolve them. They are also able to detach themselves enough from the situation to maintain the objectivity that is vital to effective problem solving, and they seem to genuinely enjoy the challenge of handling situations that are particularly complex or sensitive.

▪ *You need to be able to work with all kinds of people.* The longer you are in real estate and the more successful you are, the more you will be able to control your clientele. Your reputation will tend to attract people who share your general business philosophy. But that will not be the case initially, and you will have to be prepared to work with all types of people. When I counsel prospective students for my real estate licensing classes, I typically ask what attracts them to the real estate profession. One of the most frequent responses is: "I like to work with people." What would probably be more accurate is: "I like to work with people I like." If you have never had the experience of dealing with the general public in a service or sales job, it will be difficult for you to fully appreciate how challenging it can be. Humility, an ability to keep things in perspective, and a healthy sense of humor are vital.

▪ *You need to be a good listener.* If you are worried that you are not all that good with words, relax. The perception that the effective real estate salesperson is one who overwhelms the prospect with a steady stream of clever conversation is seriously inaccurate. Experienced brokers agree that the most important communicative skill an agent can have is the ability to keep the mouth closed and listen—I mean really listen. There is a big difference between effective and truly empathetic listening (putting yourself in the position of the other person) and simply remaining silent while someone else is talking. If you are interested in a successful career you must have this talent, or be willing to develop it.

▪ *You need to be emotionally stable and mature.* You have to be able to gain the trust and confidence of others while maintaining your own sense of balance and fairness. More often than not, the people you encounter will be honest and forthright, but there will be enough exceptions to try the patience of the most steadfast and optimistic person. The purchase or sale of a home is typically the largest single monetary transaction that a buyer or seller will ever be involved in, and in dealing with such large sums of money you may rustle up the dark and seamy side of an otherwise sweet and sunny disposition. You will have to be the emotional bellwether.

■ *You need to know your product.* You will not be expected to be an expert electrician, plumber, or carpenter, nor to have an intimate knowledge of architecture or construction. But you do need to be familiar with the practical matters that are of primary concern to homeowners. If you are a homeowner yourself, that helps immensely. If not, I strongly recommend that you place "buy my own home" at the top of your "economic goals" list. Whether you educate yourself through self-study, formal courses, or a combination of the two, you will list and sell more homes—and make more money—if you know your product and can talk intelligently about it.

■ *You need to be convinced of your product's value.* For most people home ownership remains the best investment they will ever make. It also fulfills a basic human need for shelter. It is hard to overstate the economic and social value that real estate ownership provides for the community and the nation. It should be easy to be enthusiastic about your product—but if you are *not*, that will become very clear to those with whom you work. There are those who can sell anything, whether they believe in it or not, but most of us must first be honestly convinced ourselves.

■ *You need to know the territory.* For practical considerations, each real estate company has what it considers a normal geographic area of operation. In some small communities, it may be the whole town and the surrounding countryside. In large metropolitan areas, it may be a particular section of the city. Wherever you work, you must know intimately the structure of the community. You must be knowledgeable not only about residential housing, but also of shopping centers, hospitals, and schools. It may be trite, but it's definitely true, that "you gotta know the territory."

■ *You need to be flexible.* The profession of real estate has undergone tremendous change in the past few years and the future looks just as challenging. Part of the upheaval has been as the result of technological advances and part has been caused by fundamental challenges to traditional ways of doing business. We will cover the more important issues throughout the book, but at this point suffice it to say that you have to be willing to adapt to new technologies and to new methods of operation. It's not always easy.

■ *You have to persevere.* I am familiar with several very successful agents in our local community (I'm talking about roughly $100,000 net income per year) who, if you asked me to name the character trait most responsible for their success, I would unhesitatingly respond: dogged perseverance. Yes, they work hard, they have integrity, and they relate well to people, but they would be the first to admit that they are not inherently gifted. I worked with them in the early 1980s when I was actively selling and the average price of homes in our community was in the $60,000 range. Here we are almost twenty years later and the average price of a home is around $140,000. They stuck it out when mortgage interest rates hit double digits and qualified buyers were as rare as a sunny day in Oregon, and they are now reaping the harvest. The word "quit" is simply not in their vocabulary.

## EXTERNAL FACTORS THAT INFLUENCE SUCCESS

The environment in which you work will make a big difference in how well you do in real estate sales. Here are three factors that will play important roles.

■ *The state of the nation's economy.* Those who work in salaried jobs, particularly in the public sector, can generally expect a reasonably stable income history. In the business world it's different, and as an independent contractor in real estate your income can fluctuate with the health of the economy in general and the housing market in particular. Of course, there are agents who continue to do well when things start to go sour (there are even special opportunities in such an environment), but the fact remains that there is a relationship between your potential income and national economic factors.

■ *The part of the country in which you work.* It doesn't take any more ability or effort to sell a $300,000 house than it does to sell one that costs $100,000 (often it takes far less), but you make three times as much when you do. If you successfully sell residential real estate in an area where housing prices are traditionally high, you will earn a very impressive income. The obvious counterpoint is that it will cost you a lot to live there. Where you work will make a big difference in how much money you make. In most instances, you will be much better off working where you know the territory (and are known in the territory), but there are green, high-paying pastures if you have wanderlust. If you do consider relocating, get current on your demographics. Those areas with healthy growth tend to have robust real estate markets. Those with economic woes will have many sellers and few buyers—not a fun or profitable environment in which to work.

▪ *The quality of the company for which you work.* Given the individualistic nature of the business, it is entirely possible for a strong agent to do well with almost any company,. However, if the office you choose is vigorous and successful and has a genuine commitment to the training and development of its new people, your income potential (not to mention your longevity) will be substantially enhanced. Activity generates activity, success is contagious, and positive role models will be there for you to observe and emulate. It doesn't necessarily have to be a large office or one that has been in business a long time, but when you are new and striving mightily for direction and business contacts, it helps greatly to be part of an energetic and caring brokerage.

## HOW MUCH MONEY CAN YOU MAKE SELLING REAL ESTATE?

There are few fields in which people doing essentially the same work earn such widely divergent incomes. The saying in real estate sales is: "10 percent of the agents do 90 percent of the business." That generalization is essentially correct. A minority of agents do extremely well, during the best of times and during the worst of times. The idea, of course, is to be among the 10 percent. If you are right for the job, if you are willing to work, and if you will persevere, it is an entirely realistic and achievable goal.

When you hear that "your earnings potential in real estate is unlimited," it's not really all hype. The elite among the top producers earn whopping incomes—several hundred thousand per year. But super achievers aside for a moment, let's consider some numbers about average earnings. The best income information is published periodically by the National Association of Realtors (See "Real Estate Industry Statistics and History" in the References). Their most recent information revealed that median (half above and half below) net income (after they paid their expenses) for all full time Realtor salespersons was $23,100 ($38,000 for brokers)—hardly the stuff from which lifestyles of the rich and famous are made. And I hope you're sitting down for this one: the median net income for full time *first year* Realtor salespersons was less than $10,000—they didn't say how much less, but based upon previous surveys it's probably below minimum wage. Don't stop reading.

A closer look suggests that the news is not all bad. First, when you use a median income figure it means that half make less than that and half make more. Further, those in the top 10 percent (the ones doing 90 percent of the business) earn a very decent income. Second, it is almost certain that many who say they are full time are really not in spirit and motivation. For example, in many households the money earned in real estate is a second income. Although the spouse earning it may work hard, the pressure to produce is not the same as if a family-supporting wage had to be earned. Some retirees with incomes from their previous professions also fit this category. Rest assured that if real estate provided their only source of income, most would earn a lot more at it.

We have to acknowledge, however, that many people enter real estate sales who are simply not suited for it. They earn an embarrassingly low income, become discouraged, and quit. In addition, a small minority apparently look upon real estate as a way to earn a lot of money in a glamorous job without much effort. They're history in a hurry. Of course it is disheartening that a large number of people are in real estate sales who should not be. Viewed very selfishly, however, if you *are* suited for the profession you may conclude that it is to your distinct advantage to compete in such an environment.

How much can *you* make your first year? It's probable that it will take about six months for you to hit the break even point—where your income is paying for your expenses—so we'll allow that time as a "break-in" period. From that point on, if you are temperamentally suited for a real estate career, have affiliated with an active company, and approach your job in a businesslike and entrepreneurial manner, you can far exceed normal income expectations. For someone with the right qualities and attitudes, between $20,000 and $30,000 net would not be an unrealistic first year expectation.

Not spectacular, but comparable to entry-level jobs in some very reputable professions. If you have been successful in another field and have extensive local contacts you should be able to earn substantially more, again allowing for break-in. As a successful agent, the longer you stay in the business, the more money you can anticipate earning, for your referrals will increase, your contacts will expand, and you will be able to better identify where to direct your efforts to get results.

Finally, if you get established in one of the areas of the country with high housing costs, you can upgrade all my estimates dramatically. For example, I sold real estate in a small university town in Oregon where housing costs at the time were very modest. In my first year, after that initial training and shakedown period, I earned about what a professor at a mid-size college would make. If I had sold exactly the same number of comparable properties in, let's say, the San Francisco Bay area, I would have made about what the president of the college would have earned. My income increased each year.

Looking far down the road, you might consider some data NAR put together from a survey done of top producers—agents who had closed over $3 million in sales and/or had a minimum of 30 closed transactions in 1994. The median gross income: $130,600. As I said, that's down the road a ways—the average time in the business for the survey respondents was 13 years. (See "Real Estate Industry Statistics" in the References.)

## THE PART-TIME OPTION

For those who wish to choose a middle path and enter real estate part-time, there are some special considerations. First, it will be substantially more difficult to find a broker with whom to affiliate, since many do not accept agents who are not prepared to work at it full-time. The brokers' rationale seems to be that the field is complex and demands total attention. Further, many brokers believe that they invite potential legal difficulties by having part-time agents, since they fear that those who do not constantly stay in touch with the marketplace are more likely to overlook legal requirements.

However, many brokers throughout the country do accept part-time salespeople—roughly one quarter of all Realtor salespersons, for example, are part-time. Among non-Realtors I'm guessing it's higher than that. Many have worked out satisfactory relationships by carefully defining their roles and making themselves available on a predictable, but reduced, schedule. I had one broker tell me: "I've had a few part-time agents who accomplished more in an abbreviated work week than some of my full-time people."

There are even some spectacular part-time success stories. A fellow named Ron Rush, while still on active duty with the U.S. Air Force, reportedly closed over $7 million in transactions one year while working as a part-time agent with Long & Foster Realtors in Fairfax, Virginia. He really got hot after he retired from the Air Force and started selling full-time.

Despite such impressive examples, it would be unwise to get lured by the work part-time and make big money pitch. It just doesn't usually work out that way. As should be expected, those who work an abbreviated schedule earn substantially less, on the average, than their full-time counterparts. Of course, if that fits your monetary and personal goals, fine.

## DECISION TIME

Is real estate for you? If you truly enjoy solving "people problems," if you like running your own affairs, if you are genuinely excited about having the amount of money you make directly related to how hard and how creatively you work, and if you're ready, willing, and able to withstand those predictably lean first six months or so, then the answer is yes. I suspect that for many of you, it is not a case of, "Is it for me?" but rather, "How do I get started?" Step one is to get your license.

# 2

# *Getting Your License*

*Fun or Folly: Your Choice*

Getting your real estate salesperson's license can be either an invigorating experience that you will recall fondly for as long as you are in the profession or a stupefying, mind-numbing bore. The difference will depend not so much on the particular licensing program you choose as on your attitude toward that program.

Some look upon the whole process as a necessary evil, to be concluded with as little pain, strain, and expense as possible. That's unfortunate, because it is incontestably the most important step you will take in pursuing your real estate career. No matter how talented you are, no matter how enthusiastic you might be, no matter what your potential, you must meet this challenge to enter the field.

My purposes in this chapter are to help you understand the testing and licensing procedure, to assist you in selecting the program that best fits your needs and your personality, to suggest some study techniques, and to encourage you to participate in the entire affair in a way that will help you get the most out of it.

## REQUIREMENTS OF INDIVIDUAL STATES

In all fifty states and the District of Columbia, you must have a license issued by the state (or the District) before you can engage in "professional real estate activity." That's a broad term that most states define to include anything from selling real estate to counseling—presuming you do it with the expectation of being compensated. You need to determine the requirements of the state in which you wish to work, for there are substantial differences. Most require the completion of specific course work, while a few permit a plan of self-study. Many have provisions for a waiver of course requirements for those with special backgrounds. *All* require that you pass a written, objective test (multiple choice). Sorry, sociology majors, no essay questions. There is an office in each state that supervises all real estate activity, including licensing. I have included a list of these with the address and phone number of each as Appendix B.

Please understand that the states take their real estate licensing and testing responsibilities *very* seriously. It is definitely not a fill-in-the-square type of operation. Even if you have a Ph.D. in real estate from Prestige U., you will have to take, and pass, the test to sell real estate. Just to motivate you to take the whole process seriously, let me quote a couple of the most recent year's statistics from various states on the percentage of applicants who pass the real estate salesperson licensing exam. This information is taken from a publication titled *1996 Digest of Real Estate License Laws*, published by the Association of Real Estate License Law Officials (see *Real Estate Industry Statistics and History* in the References). In California the pass rate was 50 percent (they tested over 28,000 applicants!), in South Dakota it was 45 percent, in Maryland 34 percent, and Vermont took the prize for the toughest test with a pass rate of 30 percent! Retesting is possible, but it would clearly be preferable to recognize the magnitude of the challenge early and prepare accordingly.

## THE NATURE OF THE TESTS

Some states prepare their own tests while others use national testing services. There is a great deal of similarity among all of them in terms of test construction and subject matter. All have two major parts: one covering national material and one dealing with subject matter related specifically to the state. A certain percent of the entire test requires arithmetic computations. The exact percentage varies, but 15 to 20 percent is the norm. These questions are scattered throughout the test. (I offer some guidance on handling the math in this chapter's section on study techniques.) The state portion will contain material that pertains to their specific laws, rules, regulations, and procedures. It is not unusual for the failure rate of the state section to be higher than that for the national, since the material is typically very specific and sometimes a bit obscure. My advice, therefore, is to bear down hard there, since you have to pass both portions.


## YOUR STUDY OPTIONS

When I was studying for my salesperson license, our state used a national testing service. I found that its *Applicant's Bulletin* was very useful in structuring my own self-study program to supplement my formal training. A recent review of current material from the various testing services and states convinces me that this is still the case. I strongly recommend, therefore, that you secure everything available. Some provide practice tests, for which there is a charge. Oregon may be setting a trend, in that they sell a *Question and Answer* book that contains over 3,000 questions from its official test bank (there's plenty more in their test bank that they don't provide).

Even if specific courses are not mandated by your state, you will almost certainly be better prepared for the examination if you participate in a formal, structured program. A variety of alternatives are available.

Almost all community colleges and many four-year institutions offer courses in real estate. You will need to investigate to determine the actual relationship of each to the licensing requirements. Many institutions have programs tailored to satisfy state standards and prepare students for the exam. They may even be offered in the evenings to permit maximum community participation. These courses may be taught by permanent members of the faculty or by active real estate professionals with acceptable academic credentials.

As real estate has become more and more popular as a profession, a whole industry of private real estate schools has developed. Some are educational franchises, while others are independent activities run by educators, attorneys, real estate brokers, or real estate companies themselves. Many are small "mom and pop" operations, while others are large complex businesses. These private schools are typically very closely monitored by the real estate regulatory agency, both as to course content and instructor qualifications. As private businesses, the schools must keep informed about what is going on in the field in order to survive. In most instances, they have a neatly packaged and lively program, taught by highly qualified instructors, often in modern facilities. Quality and cost do vary, however, so it's smart to check them out thoroughly before you commit yourself.

You can do some investigation over the telephone. Call the sales managers at several local real estate companies and explain that you are planning to enter real estate and would appreciate advice concerning the best way to study for your license, including an assessment of specific local options. You will most likely get a helpful, enthusiastic response, for brokers naturally see prospective licensees as the prime source of new agents. At this point, don't get caught up too much in the quality of various real estate companies, for it will all be academic if you don't pass the test. Your personal interviews will come after you clear your first hurdle—getting your license.

In some states it is permissible for real estate brokerages to run their own real estate licensing schools. Some even offer tuition assistance (or even free tuition) if you will commit to come to work at that brokerage after you pass the exam. That practice has been criticized by some, since they maintain the major motivation of the school is to provide a recruitment pool of new agents for the brokerage. Keep an open mind if that's an option available to you. I recommend that you judge the schools based upon the quality of the instruction you believe you are likely to receive, rather than any monetary incentive.

If you have tentatively decided to go into real estate, but still have some unresolved doubts, you may want to test the waters by enrolling in a single course at a local community college or take a specific segment of a real estate school's curriculum, if that's possible. A taste of real estate practices, real estate law, or real estate finance may be just what you need to help you decide. In my own case, I took a course in real estate practices at the local community college while I was still on active duty with the Air Force. The instructor was an active local broker. He did an excellent job of teaching the material and I also learned about practical job-related matters. After that, I enrolled in a private real estate school taught by an attorney for my formal license training.

Programmed learning courses in real estate are becoming quite popular, and many have enjoyed a high degree of success, as measured by the pass rate of their students. They come in a variety of formats from audio tapes to videos to computer programs. They offer flexibility in scheduling and permit you to work at your own pace. They also eliminate one of the most troublesome aspects of classroom teaching, the inordinate amount of time often spent on tangential discussions. Such courses may be ideal for you, particularly if you have a considerable amount of self-discipline and willpower. For others, it may be that the stimulus of a classroom situation as well as the built-in demands of a regularly scheduled class meeting will prove more practical. You should also be aware that in some states it is permissible for individuals to operate real estate licensing schools that offer programmed instruction who actually have no real estate experience themselves. That would make it difficult to get real time answers to your questions as you proceed through your course work. Some states even permit correspondence study, so check that out if it interests you.

## YOUR IMMEDIATE GOAL: PASS THE TEST!

Regardless of the choice you make, you need to reach peace with yourself on one important matter. You will study some theoretical material that you will almost certainly never use in your active real estate career, and you will not cover a lot of specific matters that you could use. A common sentiment among my survey participants was that licensing courses often fell short in providing immediately useful information. As a matter of fact, almost 60 percent of the respondents felt that *inadequate preparation in practical real estate matters during licensing courses* was *very important* or *important* in explaining high attrition. This comment by a broker-builder from Michigan was typical: "Schools should instruct people on how to conduct their business as well as how to pass the examination. Too many youngsters simply do not know the mechanics of a real estate transaction."

I make this point not to denigrate the quality of the instruction in real estate licensing programs. In both private real estate schools and college classrooms, you will frequently find dedicated instructors who teach not only the theoretical material thoroughly, but relate it to "real world" real estate. But you should be prepared for some disparity between what you must know to pass the licensing test and what you must know to succeed in the profession.

It will be much better for your mental health and peace of mind if you do not fight the problem. The content of these programs is typically very tightly controlled by state regulatory agencies. The schools can teach only what they are told to teach, so if you don't like the message, don't fuss at the messenger. The theoretical background will give you a better perspective of the whole field and confidence in your role as a professional in it. Even if that were not true, you have to master the material to pass the test, and you have to pass the test to get the license. If you understand that, and proceed accordingly, you will be less likely to share the frustrations of the survey respondent who complained: "Real estate school was an exercise in futility. No nuts and bolts!" If it is any consolation to you, students of law and medicine, and every other known profession have always had the same kind of complaints. These requirements of dubious utility are know as "rites of passage," so take a deep breath, swallow hard, and press on.

## STUDY TECHNIQUES: BACK TO BASICS

If you have been away from the books for a few years, don't worry. A lot of people with *very* average academic aptitudes pass the real estate test every year. Taken one small bite at a time, and presuming a fair amount of grit and gizzard on your part, it will not be all that difficult. On the other hand, I have known people with advanced degrees who have failed the exam, at least the first time. A knowledge of quantum physics won't help you a bit in answering questions about the Federal Fair Housing Law. If you have a study system that works for you, then use it. But if you don't have a system, or if it has been a while, consider these suggestions:

A few hours of study each day is preferable to longer, infrequent sessions. Find a quiet place that is conducive to study—preferably somewhere *without* a TV, radio, stereo, or bed. If you are a morning person, two hours of study before the rest of the household starts rustling about will be better than twice that amount of time later. Some people concentrate better and accomplish more late at night, so do whatever works best for you.

I have found that group study sessions are highly overrated. They will be helpful only if the number of participants is kept small and everyone is prepared to contribute. It is tempting to think otherwise, for they can be such enjoyable social events.

An individual study technique that has proved quite successful for some people involves preparing sample test questions. From the course material and study guides you will quickly become familiar with the format of exam questions. (For ease of scoring, questions are of fairly standard construction.) As a culmination of your study efforts and in preparation for the test itself, you might try your hand at preparing some questions on your own. You will be surprised at how well you have to understand the material to be able to write questions about it. If you find yourself getting bogged down with the process, rather than the material, switch to more traditional approaches.

There is one area of real estate licensing preparation that strikes terror into the hearts of many: mathematics. For some people, the fear of anything to do with numbers induces an emotional and mental paralysis. Let's face it: math *is* a requirement, and it *is* difficult for some people. But it is manageable. Here is a suggestion. First, find out exactly what your math skills are. You may know a great deal more than you give yourself credit for. On the other hand, your fears may be well-founded. You can get a copy of a basic real estate text or a real estate math book at the local library or bookstore (see the References for suggested titles). Almost all will have enough information in them to let you know exactly where you stand in math. If you need to, you can then devise a study plan to bring yourself up to speed.

You also need to become adept at using a hand-held calculator. It is impractical to consider taking real estate licensing courses without that skill, even if you use it only for basic arithmetic functions. It is even more impractical to think you could compete effectively as a sales agent without knowing how to do such things as compute monthly mortgage payments on a home loan, for example. There are several moderately priced instruments on the market. You can learn to operate a calculator with just a moderate amount of self-study, using nothing more than the manufacturer's instruction manual. Additional study, individual or formal, will be time well spent.

## SELF-STUDY: PROCEED WITH A PLAN

In the event you decide to pursue a study program on your own, either as a self-directed effort in preparation for the licensing examination (if permitted by your state), or simply to supplement the instruction you get in a formal program, you will find a list of reference books in the References. I have indicated which are the basic, standard texts that are in widespread use. I've used several of them in teaching real estate myself, and have reviewed most of the others in conjunction with my job as Book Review Editor for *The Real Estate Professional* magazine. There is a marked similarity in basic content among the books. If you are just browsing to decide whether or not to start the whole process, some time spent with one of these books will give you a good idea of what to expect in the classroom.

A particularly useful book to give you a preview of what to anticipate and to help you in your course work, no matter what basic text you use, is *SuperCourse for Real Estate Licensing* by Julie Garton-Good (see the References under *Examination Preparation Guides*). It's about the size of a large telephone directory, but don't let that scare you off—it's decidedly "user friendly." Look for it in the "self-help" section of a bookstore rather than the real estate section. *The Language of Real Estate* by John Reilly, an attorney/real estate broker with an ability to communicate, is the definitive basic real estate reference book (see *Real Estate Reference* in the References). If you have only one real estate reference book in your library, I recommend it be this one. I refer to it more than any other.

No self-study program would be complete without coverage of state rules and regulations. Your state agency can provide study references. Often, there are commercial guides available.

## IF AT FIRST . . .

It is not at all unusual for some people who turn out to be very successful real estate professionals to have trouble passing the licensing examination. If you fail on the first try don't get discouraged, get determined. Retrench and try again. Sit down in a brainstorming session with other classmates who took the test with you and try to recall as many specific questions as you can. Then review your course notes and isolate the areas that caused you difficulty. Bear down on those and give it another shot—preferably on the next testing cycle while the information is still fresh in your mind.

## THE LIGHT AT THE END OF THE TUNNEL

If you pursue your goal with a seriousness of purpose and persevere, you will enjoy the academic program, make some good friends and great contacts, and pass the test. When the excitement of receiving the good news subsides, you will be ready to step out into the glare of the "real world." How well you actually do in it will be greatly influenced by the quality of the company with which you affiliate. That's the challenge I look at in Chapter 3.

# 3

# *Choosing a Company*

*For Better or Worse, for Richer or Poorer . . .*

Deciding where you are going to "hang your license" may not be *as* important as selecting a mate, but it ranks right up there. If you work in an environment in which you are comfortable and for a broker with whom you are compatible, you are likely to have a long, happy, and prosperous career there. If you make a hasty emotional choice, it could mean an early split because of irreconcilable differences. The key is to research carefully and decide ahead of time what it is you are looking for.

First, don't worry about getting a job in real estate once you get your license. The personnel situation is volatile, so most companies are constantly recruiting. However, there are wide differences among offices in structure, operation, and philosophy, and the most successful are, of course, the most sought after. Your goal is basic—to find the company and broker with whom you would like to affiliate and who in turn wants you. How do you begin? Whom do you see? What questions do you ask?

## JUDGE AND BE JUDGED

Your first step is to package your most important product—the one and only you—in the best possible way. The outcome you want to achieve is to have every broker in town anxious to have you join his or her team. Don't be surprised if that happens. If you come across as someone who is

20

going to succeed in real estate, brokers will be looking at you, but they'll be seeing dollar signs, for if you make money they make money.

I had a boss once whose advice to those junior executives who wanted to become senior executives was: "Keep your mouth shut and your shoes shined." He was half right. Appearances do count, and you will want to put your best foot forward (with a shined shoe on it). You will also want to be dressed in neat, conservative business clothes and drive up in a freshly washed car. If it has been a while since you've interviewed for a job (or if you never have), do a little research on how to prepare a resume and how to handle interviews.

When interviewing, put yourself in the position of the person on the other side of the desk and try to see yourself as others see you. Real estate brokers are looking for results-oriented individualists who can also function effectively as team players. Your resume need not be elaborate, but it should be typed and free of errors. One page is long enough. There's plenty of literature on how to prepare resumes, and several easily followed computer software programs available.

When you are ready to be judged, you can start doing some judging of your own. As you read what follows, I think it only fair to point out that if you follow my advice you will be in a distinct minority. Few other fledgling real estate agents who are looking for that first broker with whom to affiliate will conduct their search as seriously and conscientiously as you conduct yours. From your standpoint, I would think that would be a *very* encouraging sign.

## STARTING THE SEARCH

You can learn a lot about a company on the basis of some simple observations. Assume you are a buyer from out of town. Drive around the community and inspect the real estate offices from the outside. Ask these questions about each: Does it present the type of appearance that would motivate you to stop and do business? Is it conveniently located and is there ample room to park? On the inside, does the office present an orderly, pleasing appearance, and does it have the look of a successful business operation? That's how potential clients and customers will evaluate the firm, so it is critical that you develop that perspective. Second, review the company's print advertising. You can get a good feel for the broker's business philosophy by the tone. Would you feel comfortable having your name listed in the ads as a salesperson? Many brokerages prominently feature the sales staff in their ads, including pictures and such features as "Our agent of the week." Others rarely even mention the names of the agents.


## TALK IS CHEAP—AND HELPFUL

The next step is to talk to people, the more the better. Start by talking to active agents in different companies—not the supervising broker at this point, but someone who is "in the trenches" doing the same basic things you will be doing. It helps if you already have some contacts, but that isn't really necessary. On several occasions people called our office and asked if it would be possible to meet with an agent to discuss a possible career in real estate. You will likely meet with an agent who is successful, enthusiastic, and articulate. These informal, open exchanges with a working professional will be invaluable to you. The direct, honest approach is best. Tell the agent you have passed your real estate exam and that you are looking for a broker with whom to affiliate. Plan to spend only about 20 to 30 minutes in such a meeting, for a good agent's time is valuable. Find out which companies, other than the one the agent is working for, he or she considers the best in town. If you hear the same two or three mentioned in several interviews, you will know that they enjoy a favorable reputation among those who know them best—their competitors.

At some point in your investigative process, you will also want to talk to people outside of real estate who can give you an idea of the reputation of the various companies within the community. This can be a little awkward for they may be reluctant to express an adverse opinion, but you will be able to learn as much by what they don't say as what they do. If possible, talk to local attorneys who specialize in real estate, real estate loan officers at banks and savings and loans, officers at local escrow and title companies, and insurance agents. They know which of the local firms are the most respected. Ask them whom they would go to work for if they were getting into real estate sales.

Finally, you will need to talk with the broker, for that is the person under whose supervision you will actually work, and who decides how the company will operate. In some instances the broker has an ownership interest. Among NAR brokers, for example, 46 percent have some type of ownership interest in the firm with which they are affiliated. Brokers vary in managerial style just as salespeople vary in selling style. Some are detail-oriented people who also sell, while others are strictly "big picture" managers. Some have characters that are, as they say, above reproach. Others have characters that are definitely reproachable. It would be hard to overstate the importance of working with a broker with whom you can develop personal and professional compatibility. On occasion former students of mine, whom I thought would unquestionably succeed big time in real estate, get off to a fast start, but then after about a year become disillusioned and drop out of the profession altogether or change offices. When possible I follow up to see if I can determine the reason. A recurrent theme: "I just couldn't work for that broker—his business philosophy and mine were just not compatible."

How many companies should you contact? Talk to as many as is practical, but try for a minimum of three or four. As you interview have specific questions in mind and be prepared to take notes, for after several meetings things will begin to blur. Figure 1 is a sample checklist that you can adapt to your own situation. If you talk to a sales agent in the company, do not assume that the answers you get commit the company. That's not likely to be a problem if you are dealing with a firm with a good internal system of communication, but remember that the broker is the boss and sets policy.

There's another outcome you will wish to achieve as a result of your interviews. You can obviously go to work for only one broker, but you will be working on cooperative transactions with all of them at some time in the future. In real estate, unlike most other professions, you have to be able to work in harmony with your fiercest competitors. You therefore certainly don't wish to cause any hard feelings when you go through your interview process. A friendly note to the brokers you did not select thanking them for their time and indicating you look forward to working with them in the future would be appropriate.

Don't be surprised, and don't take it personally, if you occasionally encounter brokers who treat you rather brusquely when you make your initial contact. For example, there are occasions in which I will contact several local brokers on behalf of students of mine who might have either very special talents or a unique set of circumstances to inquire as to the possibility of a job interview. "No, we simply don't have any empty desks so I really don't even want to talk to any prospective agents" is the response I once got when engaged in such a mission. Like if you were the coach of a basketball team and Michael Jordan called asking for a job interview you would say: "Sorry, Michael, I'd love to chat, but we don't have an empty locker." Right.

On the other hand, when you do get an interview, and when you

**Figure 1.** Checklist for evaluating a real estate firm.

Company _____
Broker _____

1. *Before the interviews*

   **A.** Drive by the office.
      (1) Convenient location? _____
      (2) Ample parking? _____
      (3) Attractive exterior? _____
   **B.** Visit the office.
      (1) Businesslike atmosphere? _____
      (2) Diverse, high-quality sales staff? _____
   **C.** Tone, quality, and quantity of ads? _____

2. *Interview with the active agent*

   **A.** General guidance offered: _____
   _____

   **B.** Comments about other companies: _____

3. *Interview with the broker*

   **A.** Share of market/range of agent incomes? _____
   _____

   **B.** Written office instructions? Clear? Comprehensive? _____
   _____

   **C.** Independent contractor or employee? Copy of contract? _____
   **D.** Training program? _____
   **E.** Multiple Listing Service (MLS) membership? _____
   **F.** Facilities support? _____
   **G.** Realtor affiliation? _____
   **H.** Office ethics? _____
   **I.** Commission splits? _____
   **J.** Errors and omissions insurance? _____
   **K.** Obligations to firm? _____
   **L.** Special functions (property management, escrow, building)? ___
   _____

4. *Overall impressions and remarks*

   _____
   _____
   _____

come across as a desirable possible addition to the team, here's a final word of friendly caution about talking to successful real estate salespeople and brokers. They are incurable optimists and are simply not wired to say anything negative about the profession. Most are masters at the art of putting the best face on things. Be an attentive and discriminating listener.

## FACTORS TO CONSIDER IN CHOOSING A COMPANY

There are a number of important factors that you should take into account as you decide where you'll best fit in and where you'll be the most successful. The following are the most critical.

▪ *Local market share and agent income.* Most brokers maintain a detailed accounting of how they are doing in relationship to their competition. They also know how much each sales agent in their organization is earning now, and how much each earned in past years. Don't expect to be given company secrets or to be told exactly what each person in the office is making, but it is not unreasonable to anticipate being told how the company stacks up in the marketplace and the general range of agent incomes.

▪ *Composition and quality of sales staff.* If practical, most brokers try to maintain a mix of ages, races, sexes, and experience levels among their staff. Diversity is an advantage, for they will want exposure to as many ideas and perspectives as possible. If the company is large enough, and successful, it is quite likely that some of the more experienced agents will be specializing in areas like investments, exchanging, or rural and farm property. This is an ideal environment. Nothing is more stimulating and educational than being exposed to a variety of transactions actually being consummated in the marketplace.

Some brokers who run small offices make up for a lack of numbers by injecting their own personality, background, and expertise through a "hands on" managerial style, particularly with new agents in need of guidance, direction, and encouragement.

Pay attention, too, to the ability of the office secretary or office manager. If you are treated with courtesy, good cheer, and efficiency when arranging for your interview, your clients will most likely receive the same kind of welcome. On the other hand . . .

One sign of how well an office is managed is the length of employment of the sales staff. Large office or small, if there has been an extremely high turnover rate, be cautious. There may be a logical explanation, but it pays to investigate.

■ *Recruiting and retention philosophy.* A few brokers subscribe to the "cannon fodder" method of recruiting. They enlist more salespeople than they can reasonably expect to accommodate, train them intensely in the art of pressure selling, send them into battle, and keep the occasional survivor. One of my survey participants called these firms "body shops." Unless you are fully combat-ready, you are well advised to steer clear of them.

A veteran broker explained his personal recruiting philosophy to me this way: "Some real estate companies will bring aboard ten new agents, throw them all hard against the wall, and keep the one who sticks. We screen carefully, select one, and keep throwing her against the wall *until* she sticks."

■ *Agent status (independent contractor or employee?).* Ninety-five percent of all real estate Realtor salespeople are classified as independent contractors, and that's probably typical of the entire industry. There are considerable advantages to both the company and to you in such an arrangement. For the company, it means a simpler accounting and tax procedure, and it is much less costly because they don't have to contribute to such things as Social Security. For you, it means that you basically operate your own business within the framework of the company, and under the supervision of the broker.

Infrequently, there are companies that want the best of both worlds. They want the advantages they derive by their agents being considered independent contractors, but they want to treat them as employees. This is definitely an area you need to cover with the broker. Whether you're an independent contractor or an employee, you will be paid only from your own commissions. Wherever you work, and whatever your status, you will sign a contract (ordinarily a standard form) that specifies your legal classification and your obligations, as well as those of your broker. Ask for a copy to read over and study in advance.

■ *Training programs.* These vary markedly among companies. In some firms, training consists of giving you work space, a telephone, and a pat on the back (pat optional). In others, you have to attend company seminars on listing, selling, and related matters before you can face a prospect alone. If you join a national franchise or a very large independent, you can count on attending a very structured, standardized orientation program, probably at some type of training center. I recently reviewed a product developed by one of the nation's largest franchise companies for training their new agents. They've got the whole training program on one dinky little CD Rom! Even with such a convenient format, there's still need for personal interaction, but you are likely to encounter more and more of these high-tech training products that put the primary responsibility on you—the newcomer. If the company has some type of a formal training course, consider it an asset. You may not wish to use all of the material you encounter (remember, you will undoubtedly be an independent contractor), but it is good to have as many choices as possible. There is also a possibility that there may be a charge for the initial training program, depending upon how complex and extensive it is. A student of mine, who interviewed with a national franchise brokerage that ostensibly did charge for their training was informed that in her case it would be "waived" if she decided to come to work with them.

▪ *Support facilities.* There will likely be written office procedures that describe what the broker provides and what you provide. Typically, you will get work space, a telephone, and some secretarial support, although policies vary widely. For the most part, you will be required to pay for all expenses that relate to your specific activities, such as long-distance phone calls, postage, business cards, and other personal promotional material.

Several philosophies prevail relative to office planning. One is that agents' desks should be grouped together in large open spaces. The rationale is that this arrangement enhances the communicative process. Another view is that private offices are the most desirable. A third holds that individual desks in a common area, with private rooms available for special occasional use, is the best. Don't be disappointed if you are given less than an executive suite when you start. You may even be required to share a desk with another agent. In my own case, I was given a small desk near the rear exit, next to the Coke machine. That didn't do much to boost my ego, but then again, there was nowhere to go but up (or out the back door). Be patient. If there is a particular office or desk you have your eye on, you may inherit it—if you stay around long enough and prove your mettle. Yes, I eventually got a much nicer office.

▪ *Multiple Listing Service (MLS) membership.* MLS is a cooperative arrangement in which member firms make their listings available to all subscriber companies in their area. It is a well-developed, tightly-controlled marketing system. As a member agent you will have use of the lock-box system most MLSs employ, thereby assuring you of convenient entry to most listed properties. I don't know of any MLS that is not now computerized. That means you have convenient access to all listing information. There are also typically printouts in the form of MLS books that make it easy to carry around in the car. Generally, updates are provided on a daily basis. It is hard to conceive of any circumstance in which you would be better off working in an office that was not a subscriber to MLS, or a comparable service. You will need all the help you can get, and having ready-made access to hundreds of listings is about as helpful as anything you could devise. It also gets your own listings immediate, maximum exposure.

■ *Realtor affiliation.* As I pointed out in the preface, just over 30 percent of all real estate licensees in the United States are Realtors. They are, however, the dominant organizational force in the real estate profession. Some segments of the public erroneously think that "Realtor" is synonymous with "real estate agent," much to the understandable dismay of Realtors. An office may not use the logo or the term in advertising unless all those in the organization have some form of Realtor membership. The Association has a comprehensive code of ethics that all members agree to follow, and a procedure for arbitrating disputes between members. It also conducts an extensive educational program, which I cover in more detail in the next chapter, and a well-funded national advertising program. Its official publication, *Today's Realtor*, which is provided to all members, is clearly one of the best periodicals of its kind in the nation.

When I sold real estate I was an active member of the local Realtor organization and participated extensively in their educational programs and other activities. I found the quality of the entire organization exceptional.

For all these reasons, plus the fact that it will provide you an ideal way to develop your critically important personal business network, I strongly recommend that, if at all possible, you join an office with a Realtor affiliation, and that you become an active and contributing member.

■ *Office ethics.* The office should have an internal set of rules and courtesies that govern business conduct among its sales agents. It is important that everyone understand and follow standards of conduct necessary to foster a feeling of cooperation and mutual respect. If a group of physicians were in business together in the same office, each would establish a practice composed of specific clientele. One physician would not think of attempting to entice a patient away from an associate. Attorneys observe similar ethical standards, as do accountants and all other professions of standing. In the best-run real estate offices, agents adhere to the same strict courtesies. In others, it is "catch as catch can," and whoever gets the name on the dotted line wins. The broker's philosophy will prevail, so find out what it is. If it's a survival of the pushiest office, or the broker can't understand why you are concerned about such a subject, I would strongly suggest you keep looking—unless you feel comfortable swimming with sharks.

▪ *Commission splits.* Each broker has written instructions on how commissions are divided within the firm. There will be differences among companies, but the broker who takes a larger share of the commission dollar might provide more support in terms of advertising and facilities, so consider the whole picture. The general rule is that new agents earn a smaller percentage than experienced agents because they require a greater investment of supervisory time and effort. While this is valid, remember that as you become more successful you can legitimately expect to retain more of the dollar you bring to the company. Even though the office may have a standard, published structure detailing percentages, bonuses, and incentives, you can negotiate directly and individually for yourself. It's to your broker's distinct advantage to keep high-volume producers and reward them appropriately. Early in your career you will not be in a strong bargaining position, but keep these thoughts tucked away in the back of your mind for future use.

▪ *Errors and omissions (E&O) insurance.* This form of liability insurance protects you from claims made against you as a result of your activities as a real estate professional. An increasing number of states (11 at this writing) make E&O insurance mandatory. Many observers feel that is the trend for the future. However, at the present time there are offices in the United States that "self insure," which is a fancy way of saying they have no E&O coverage.

If E&O insurance is mandated in your state, the procedure for obtaining it will be well developed. If not, you have a number of options. One approach is for the company to contract for it and pay for the coverage on an annual basis, with the premiums being determined by the number of sales agents and the sales volume. Each salesperson typically contributes a monthly amount toward the premium. Some brokers buy insurance on an individual transaction basis. Another option may be for individual agents to purchase their own coverage. It is not cheap.

Regardless of how conscientious and sincere you might be, you can be a prime target for a lawsuit. Quite often, after all the dust has settled in a controversy, the real estate agent is the only individual left in the locality where the problem occurred. The agent may also be the one with "deep pockets"—the only person really capable of paying a judgment.

Many agents happily go through their entire career with not even a hint of litigation, but the fact is that the frequency of lawsuits has been increasing at an alarming rate over the past few years. In today's (and tomorrow's) environment, I simply would not sell real estate without E&O insurance. Not one transaction. None.

• *Your obligations to the firm.* No matter how the office is organized you will be expected to contribute in various ways to the operation. For example, there will be "floor" days when you will be the agent on call in the office to handle real estate inquiries. As an independent contractor, you technically must volunteer, but floor duty is one you should enthusiastically perform. It can be an excellent source of income. Not all duties, however, are so eagerly anticipated. In your discussions with the broker, make sure you are clear as to what will be expected of you. You will want to do your fair share, but the mark of a well-managed company is that licensed agents perform duties that only they can perform by virtue of holding that license. If it is clear that you will be expected to do a lot of routine clerical chores that anyone, licensed or not, can do, then you are probably dealing with a poorly run firm. You *will* be expected to do the basic clerical tasks in matters related to your own real estate transactions; in fact, you will probably have to do most of them.

• *Special functions.* Some real estate brokers are also builders and market their homes through their own company. This will offer an interesting dimension to your activities—the opportunity to sell new houses. However, you may be expected to give these homes preferential treatment in your sales efforts. Be sure you are clear on the ground rules.

It is also not unusual for real estate companies to have a property management department. This is an advantage, since renters often turn into buyers and the more buyers the better. There are also some companies with affiliated insurance, title and escrow, and appraisal activities. While having all these functions available within a single organization can be convenient for consumers (and profitable for the company) care must be exercised to ensure that a genuine freedom of choice does exist, and that full disclosure is made. There are those who would say that all of these functions would be best left in completely independent hands.

## FRANCHISE VERSUS UNAFFILIATED BROKER

National real estate franchises have become very powerful components of the country's real estate makeup, currently making up about 29 percent of all real estate brokerages—and growing. Forty-one percent of all Realtor salespersons belong to a franchise office. It is difficult to find a city of any size that does not have them. Is working in a franchise office different from working in an unaffiliated office? The answer is a qualified *yes*. Franchises have the advantage of national recognition and ordinarily have standardized training programs in which all new agents are expected to participate. You are also less likely to be left to shift for yourself, at least initially. Remember, however, that most of these companies are independent operations within the franchise structure. It is quite possible to have a wide difference in philosophies of operation among different offices in the same franchise.

You will probably feel more pressure within some franchises to follow standardized procedures, such as wearing distinctive clothing (blazers) and displaying ad signs on your car. If these things bother you, find out in advance how much latitude you will have to operate as you see fit.

## SMALL CAN BE BEAUTIFUL

Small offices, those having ten or fewer agents may have some advantages. For example, you will likely have closer contact with your broker and the rest of the sales staff. It also generally takes less time to get things done in a small organization and ideas are translated into programs and policies more quickly. While formal training may be of the "home-grown" variety, and more independent study may be required of you, there is no reason it cannot be effective.

Size is not the sole determinant of quality. Tremendous opportunities may be found in larger firms, particularly in the area of initial training. On the other hand, a concerned and knowledgeable broker on one side of the desk and you on the other may be just as effective.

## DISORGANIZED ISN'T ALL BAD

Conventional wisdom would advise you to steer clear of any office that appears disorganized and confused. For most people, and for most offices, that is sound advice. However, it is possible to find some real potential for success in such an environment. If the company is basically solvent (that is, has been around for a while), and you are the type of person who thrives on taking advantage of opportunities unrecognized by others, you might prosper in an organization where rules and procedures are not so clearly defined. I should advise you that this particular bit of advice has not been enthusiastically endorsed by other members of the real estate community.

## HOME IS WHERE YOU HANG YOUR LICENSE

By the time you finish your investigation and interviews, you will have a reasonably clear idea where you would like to go to work. Identify your top three or four selections and make yourself available to the first broker on your list. What happens if that broker does not offer you a position? If you need to get started immediately, you simply progress through the list until you are successful. If your first choice is head and shoulders above your second, check out the possibility of future placement. If the broker is encouraging about bringing you on board within two or three months, it could be worth the wait.

Take heart—your hard work will pay off. The strong likelihood is that you will have several offers. Your task will be to choose from among them and then to start what will hopefully be a long and prosperous career in real estate.

# 4

# *Getting Started on the Job*

## *Getting Organized and Beating the Drums*

If you are like most new agents, you will have mixed feelings as you begin work. On the one hand, you will be eager to get on with it and commence doing the things that will earn you some money. On the other hand, you will feel the natural anxiety that comes with anything as important in life as starting a new career. It is essential that you clearly understand the nature of the challenge and that you be aware of what you can do to prepare.

### WHAT YOU NEED TO KNOW UP FRONT

Your first year in real estate will likely be your toughest. That's how it was for most of us. Consider the story of Dorcas T. Helfant, past president of the National Association of Realtors and the first woman to hold that post. In an interview with a Realtor trade magazine shortly after she took office as NAR president, Helfant revealed that she entered real estate sales when she was 21 years old, facing a divorce, and raising an infant. A year went by with no business, which prompted her to apply for a job selling appliances for Sears. By the time Sears called, Helfant had put together five sales, and "from there I never looked back." I'll provide guidance in this chapter designed to get you some early paydays, but be prepared to hang in there.

## KINDS OF ON-THE-JOB TRAINING

Initial on-the-job training is designed to ease your transition from student to practitioner. It may be very formal or extremely casual, depending upon where you work. If it is highly structured, you can expect to spend your early days mastering the basics of the trade. While licensing courses deal mainly with factual information, company sessions will devote substantial time to traditional real estate sales and listing techniques. You can also expect a healthy amount of motivational material. You will be exposed to an array of ideas, techniques, and suggestions, most of which will be time-tested and valuable.

My strong recommendation is that you be open-minded and receptive. Some of the material may be difficult for you and some of it uncomfortable, but withhold judgment. Your broker will be satisfied if you master the techniques and modify them to accommodate your own individual style and philosophy. Even if that were not his or her basic inclination, successful brokers are practical enough not to try to make you into something you are not.

## THAT'S RIGHT: TODAY YOU DEFINITELY GET ORGANIZED

If you have been a successful business person, particularly in a commissioned sales job in which you worked with the general public, you know what it takes to do the job. Whatever worked for you before will work again. However, real estate is just different enough to make it worth your while to consider some of these ideas. If you have had little or no previous work experience, or none in sales, you will want to pay particular attention.

### *Pick a Partner*

In every office there seems to be at least one agent who is exceptionally well organized. He or she always has the latest information on interest rates and loan programs, better property files than the local multiple listing service, and a personal data card for every person with whom he or she has ever done business. His or her closed-deal files are masterpieces of organization, showing who said what to whom, and when. Find out early who this is in your office, and ask if you can look over this agent's system. Generally, someone like this takes a great deal of justifiable pride in how their work is organized, and will probably be happy to share the information.

Even if your office does not have quite the paragon of virtue I have described, *any* established agent will know more about the practical aspects of administration than you will, so pick the person who seems to be the best qualified and with whom you are the most compatible. Some offices have a formal "buddy system" that pairs off each newcomer with an experienced agent, so the contact may be made for you. Make sure that you also find out how the official office files are maintained and learn how to locate things for yourself. You will become very popular if you can find what you need without always asking for help.

### Organize Your Work Space

Whether you have a private office, a cubicle, or simply a desk in a common area, you will want to arrange your space to be efficient and to reflect your personality. Often you will need to locate something in a hurry as someone waits on the phone. You'll become frantic if you have to sort through piles of unrelated information in the classic paper shuffle. The familiar, "I'll have to get back to you on that one," is the inevitable result. As a start, set up three or four desk-top file baskets, each reserved for specific types of material. When your "action pending" basket starts to exceed the volume of all others combined (it will happen—it's a rule), you need to discipline yourself to act on items immediately. The file drawer in your desk (or a file cabinet, if you are lucky enough to have one) should be used for folders of individual clients, customers, prospects, and closed transactions, arranged alphabetically. Be optimistic: Reserve a big drawer for "closed deals." Beyond that, do what works best for you and watch carefully how the successful "old heads" do it.

If you have walls on which you can post personal material, a display of city and county maps will be useful to you and to those who visit your office, many of whom will be new to the area. After you close several transactions you may wish to indicate each such property with a pin on the map along with a small card to identify the people involved and the type of property. With different colored pins you could show your current listings. After a while it will be impressive. I developed this kind of display (after I moved up to an office with a non-portable wall), and when prospects visited for our initial interview, that was inevitably the major focus of their attention. If you can locate a relief map of your state (the kind showing actual topography), your out-of-state visitors will find that particularly interesting.

On a professional note, frame documents showing your Realtor affiliation, membership in other professional organizations, and your diplomas from major real estate courses. If you receive any special awards, don't be bashful, display them. The first year you close $1 million in transactions, hang your Million Dollar Club emblem on the wall. One of my survey correspondents had "Three Million Dollar Agent" on his business card. There is no point in being modest.

### Organize Information

One of the greatest practical problems of organization that new agents traditionally face is keeping all the information about one transaction or one person in one place. If you make separate notes on different pieces of paper for each phone call or contact, you will invariably misplace one or more of them, and you will spend a lot of panicky moments searching.

One solution is to prepare an all-purpose form for each client, customer, or prospect on which you make a chronological record of all contacts and all pertinent actions. This accomplishes several things, in addition to giving you a single-source reference. There are times when disputes arise as to who took what action, when. Unfortunately, such disagreements sometimes result in litigation. If you have a formal record of your actions made at the time they occurred, you will be in an infinitely stronger position than would be the case if you simply assert, "To the very best of my recollection . . ." You will also find that months or even years might go by between contacts with a particular individual. It will be very comforting to you, and impressive to others, to be able to recount past contacts accurately. Your office may have a form for keeping such records, but the format you use is not important—the discipline to use some one-source system is. For general guidance on the importance of documenting everything you do, refer to *The Real Estate Book (The Ultimate Paper Trail)* by Colorado attorney/real estate broker Oliver Frascona and real estate broker Katherine Reece (see the References under "Real Estate Reference").

### Organize Your Time

It's easy to get carried away on this subject and you could spend most of your time organizing your time. But since 72 percent of the respondents in my survey indicated that an *inability to plan and manage time* was *very important* or important in causing real estate agents not to succeed (see Appendix A), it is apparent that time management is a serious matter.

There is general agreement on the basics. First, you need to organize your schedule each day in some fashion; second, you have to establish priorities. There are all sorts of calendars and planners on the market. You need to get one with which you are comfortable, have it with you all the time, and use it religiously. When the year is over save them. Never throw one away. Ever.

Each evening, or *very* early in the morning, you need to formally plan your day *in writing* and identify those items that are the most important. My suggestion is to put at the top of your list tasks necessary to close a transaction (buyer and seller have agreed to terms, but such things as title check, removing contingencies, loan application and approval, pest inspection, and so on are yet to be done). These are paydays ready to happen, but Murphy's Law (whatever can go wrong, will go wrong) is alive and prospering in real estate. Approach each pending transaction with this question: "What could possibly go wrong with this deal today to keep it from closing, and how can I prevent that from happening?" Your job will be to avert the dreaded "fall through"—a term with which I hope you will not become too familiar.

As you establish priorities on how to spend your time, keep in mind the way you earn money in real estate. Forgive the repetition, but the *only* way you get paid is for one of your listings to sell or for you to sell a property. It is remarkable how much time some real estate agents spend on fringe activities. The fact that I advocate a high degree of professionalism should not obscure the fact that I also believe passionately that the only really happy real estate agent is a well-paid one. That is not to say that you should not perform community service activities, help decorate the office for the Halloween party, keep your individual space looking impressive, or engage in enjoyable hobbies. Just remember how the bills get paid.

### Set Goals for Yourself

Again, you can spend an inordinate amount of time deciding what it is you want to accomplish. For most people, the first few months are best spent learning the profession and becoming aware of the various long-range opportunities. The more you know about what is available, the easier it will be to establish short-term and long-term career goals.

Some folks simply opt not to establish formal goals at all. If you don't really care where you're going in your career, then I suppose they are not necessary. Others may have goals, but have rather unique methods of achieving them. Those with a more mystic bent put pictures of expensive cars, lavish mansions, and sleek yachts on their walls and have faith that positive thinking will make it so (although as far as I know, the young bachelor in my office who put a picture of a voluptuous young Hollywood starlet on his wall has yet to hear from her).

### Learn the Nuts and Bolts

It can be a frightening experience to realize that, after all the time you have spent getting your license and in participating in initial training, you wouldn't know how to write up an actual sales agreement should someone walk up to your desk and ask to buy a specific home. I didn't. Fortunately for me, there was about a 24-hour period between the time the young couple decided they wanted the property and the time they made their formal offer. I spent that time frantically going over closed-deal files and preparing to write the actual offer to purchase. The amount of printed information on that form that I had not really read (or understood) before was astonishing. I also relied very heavily on the experienced salesperson on the staff who had agreed to be my "big sister." Most agents who have been in the business for a while remember the paralyzing experience of getting started and are more than willing to help you out.

### Organize for Uncle Sam

There are at least two excellent reasons for knowing as much as possible about federal, state, and local income taxes and for arranging your business and personal affairs with taxes always in mind. First, a substantial portion of your income every year for as long as you live (and beyond) will be subject to taxes. Second, those to whom you provide professional services will expect you to know something about the subject. There are substantial income tax consequences involved with every real estate transaction. You will have to understand basic concepts well enough to be able to discuss them intelligently, and to be able to recognize those questions you need to refer to a professional who specializes in taxes.

Tax time can be a genuinely mind-numbing nightmare if you have not planned ahead and kept informed. Here are some suggestions:

1. *Know who you are.* Although your license may say "salesperson," you are really a self-employed entrepreneur who owns and runs a small

business as a sole proprietor. Maybe only a one-person small business, but a small business nonetheless. You need to develop a total business plan with specific goals and strategies and a profit-oriented, no-nonsense philosophy in which you know your rights and obligations regarding taxes.

2. *Learn as much as you can on your own.* You can get a good basic overview by simply reading official IRS publications, which you can get free at your local IRS office. The one to start with is IRS publication 17, *Your Federal Income Tax.* In that publication, you will find listed dozens of additional free publications dealing with specialized tax matters. There are always several on various aspects of home ownership and small businesses. For example, IRS publication 334, "Tax Guide for Small Business," discusses a variety of tax issues that will be pertinent to you.

The only national level book of which I am aware that deals specifically with tax matters as they relate to real estate professionals is *The Realtor's Bible of Personal Tax-Reduction Strategies* by Albert J. Ayella, a CPA and a real estate broker. You'll find information about it under "Real Estate Taxes" in the References, along with several references to other tax books that relate to real estate in general.

3. *Work your business plan—and document your efforts.* The key to keeping good records is to establish a basic system and stick with it. Central to this is the maintenance of your daily planner. Jot down all appointments and meetings, thereby substantiating your general level of activity. Take the planner with you when you use your auto and record all of your mileage and transportation activity. An envelope in the glove compartment for gas credit card receipts will reduce the clutter. Another large envelope that you keep in your desk drawer marked *Business Receipts—Year XXXX* will also be useful. As you expand your activities, you will need several large envelopes, each to contain receipts for specific functions. My wife and I bought a software program this year to help in preparing our taxes, and assuming we ever find the time to enter the basic information, it looks as though it will be very useful.

Pay for everything by check or credit card so you will automatically have a receipt. If you pay cash, ask for a receipt, and make a note on the back of it indicating what the item was for. If it is not possible to get a receipt, or if your forget, jot down the amount, the date, and the purpose in your planner or on a piece of paper and put it in your business receipts envelope.

4. *Know your legitimate business expenses.* As the sole proprietor of your own business you will be filing a "Profit or Loss From Business"

schedule with your federal tax return. The critical thing to remember here is that your business expenses are deducted from income. If you have an annual gross income of $65,000 and you incur expenses necessary to conduct your business in the amount of $10,000, you will pay taxes (including state and local income taxes as well as Social Security and Medicare) on the net—$55,000. The key is that your business expenses must be legitimate and you must be able to prove them.

Let's say that, through ignorance or faulty record-keeping, you fail one year to claim legitimate deductions in the amount of $2,000 and your tax bracket is 28 percent. You will pay Uncle Sam $560 more in federal tax out of your own pocket than he deserves or expects—but there is no case on record where he has turned it down. But hold it. What about Social Security and the other taxes I mentioned? Together they could easily add another 20 to 30 percent. That means that the $2,000 in deductions you forgot to take could cost you $1,000 or more! As they say, a thousand here and a thousand there adds up in a hurry.

The checklist shown in Figure 2 provides a general guide to expenses commonly incurred by real estate professionals. As in all information pertaining to income taxes, you need to verify everything for yourself by referring to current IRS material. The checklist is simply designed to help you set up an accounting system of your own and to aid you in recognizing those areas in which deductions might be permissible.

5. *Get professional help.* If you develop the uneasy feeling that you are about to get in over your head, seek professional assistance. I did that my first year in real estate and never regretted it. As you generate more activity, your business affairs will get more complicated. An old war horse (his term for himself) in my office put it this way: "Doing your own taxes makes about as much sense as doing your own surgery. Get a pro." My personal preference is a certified public accountant (CPA) who has extensive experience in working with real estate agents and real estate investors. Scout around before you choose, ask for referrals from other successful agents, and discuss fees ahead of time. When a CPA quotes you an hourly rate, it could result in a mild case of cardiac arrest, but with computers they can get a lot done in a short period of time, particularly if you present them with well-organized basic information. The idea is that in the long run they will actually save you money and, just as important, keep you out of trouble. Understand also that (as is the case with attorneys) when you call your CPA with a question, you will likely get a bill for the advice.

Even if you hire a CPA you will still need to be an active participant in the process. In his words, here is how Albert J. Ayella, the CPA/real estate broker to whom I referred earlier suggested I make the point to you: "Would you leave all your health concerns up to your doctor? Of course not! It's your health and your taxes and it is up to *you* to take care of it. Professionals such as doctors and CPAs are there for periodic review and the more difficult problems. You have to take care of everyday matters."

6. *Be scrupulously honest.* The tax authorities are fond of saying that they don't want you to pay any more tax than necessary. Be assured, however, that they will not tolerate it if you pay anything less—either through ignorance or intent. Even if honesty were not the best policy (and it is), it is incredibly foolish to incur the wrath of the federal (and/or state) government. Don't complicate the issue by using your own style of creative tax accounting. If it's creativity you want, secure professional counsel and then decide upon a course of action that suits your tolerance for uncertainty.

### Become a Professional

Become active in your local chapter of the National Association of Realtors, and investigate its professional education offerings. The one with which you will be initially concerned is the Realtors Institute, which is composed of three separate courses: when you successfully complete all three, you earn the right to use the term *GRI* (Graduate Realtors Institute). It is a designation that is well recognized, particularly by others in the business. Try to complete it sometime during your first two years. The course material will be helpful in your job, you will start to get a wider perspective of the profession, and you will meet energetic and career-minded professionals from other offices and other cities. The contacts will be invaluable in establishing your professional network, so cultivate and keep track of them.

You will also be inundated with offerings of real estate-oriented seminars and lectures. Most will be extremely well-researched presentations given by individuals who are professional in every sense of the word. But beware, because some are "high hype" sessions given by people with monumental egos whose main goal seems to be to impress you as to their own superstar status. Until you have been around for a while, you might wish to stick to the Realtors Institute offerings.

**Figure 2.** Checklist of potential income tax deductions.

| | |
|---|---|
| Advertising | |
| Business cards | Picture will cost extra—count it. |
| Telephone listing | To identify yourself as real estate agent. Block type possible. |
| Career apparel | If it has company logo. |
| Car signs (door) | |
| Client follow-up | Files, greeting cards, and so on. |
| Automobile expenses | All expenses deductible to the extent (percentage) your auto is used for business purposes. Mileage to and from office not deductible. |
| Gas and oil | |
| Repairs | |
| Driver's license | |
| Parking and tolls | Don't forget parking meters. They can add up. |
| Wash and polish | |
| Motor club dues | Get emergency start/tow service. |
| Insurance | Get adequate liability coverage. |
| Depreciation | Special rules—investigate. |
| Dues | |
| Realtor dues | |
| Multiple Listing Service | |
| Chamber of Commerce | Clear/documented business purpose. |
| Rotary, Elks, etc. | See above. Athletic, social and sporting clubs do not qualify under any circumstance. |
| Education | Seminars/convention registration. Continuing education only. Expenses to get real estate license not deductible. |
| Entertainment | Special restrictive rules apply. Area of abuse, hence special IRS interest. Review IRS entertainment publication. |
| Gifts to clients | Permissible and advisable, but IRS has strict rules. |
| Office supplies | The cost of pencils, paper, pens, staples, clips, and so on adds up over a year. Keep track. |

When children come along you will be faced with a special challenge, for most youngsters would rather go to the dentist than look at houses. You may wish to keep a "kids' kit" in your car and stock it with reading material to occupy them for at least part of the time. (Do not provide crayons and a coloring book, or you may find purple marks on your beige upholstery, and do not leave anything within reach that could be ingested by a curious and hungry toddler.)

## THINK SUCCESS AND RATE YOUR PROGRESS

How does a successful and professional real estate agent act? It will be hard for you to know before you even start, but you probably will have formed some kind of mental image. Sharpen that perception as you gain experience and through observation of others whom you admire. Here is a suggestion: Establish a rating guide for yourself, in which you list factors you conclude are important for success. Periodically evaluate your own progress, since it is unlikely that anyone else ever will, in a formal way.

To help you, I have prepared a hypothetical evaluation on a fictitious agent who has been in the business for two years. (See Figure 3.) It contains rating factors that most real estate professionals would agree are critical, and the comments are descriptive of an agent who has done a superior job. It is based upon both my own personal observations and discussions with brokers who have had extensive experience supervising new salespeople, and it may be useful to you in establishing your goals and grading yourself.

## SPREADING THE WORD

Now you are finally licensed, trained, organized, well-dressed, and motivated. You have established realistic goals, have become a Realtor, and have a well-running car purring in the parking lot ready to take off. You lack only one thing: people willing to do business with you. The cupboard may not be quite as bare as you think. Here are some suggestions:

1. *Personally let people know you are in the business.* Being a professional in real estate does not mean that you sit and wait for people to beat a path to your door. That may happen after you are established, but you won't

**Figure 3.** Job evaluation: Priscilla Perfect.

---

*Job title:* Real estate salesperson. *Job description:* Specializes in residential sales and listings, with occasional transactions in related general real estate. *Time in profession:* 24 months.

*Attitude:* Has a positive, enthusiastic attitude. Is not a complainer and does not make excuses. Constructively critical of programs and ideas with which she does not agree. Not a "yes person."

*Work habits:* Is a self-starter and a hard worker. Has day planned before she arrives. Has assigned a priority to all tasks. Spends only enough time at her desk to handle administration; spends the remainder in productive activities out of the office.

*Judgment:* Directs her efforts to areas that have the largest potential payoff for herself and for the firm. Wastes little time in nonessential fringe activities.

*Appearance:* Keeps physically fit and trim. Dresses to standards of other successful professionals in the community.

*Professionalism:* Observes highest ethical standards in working with her clients, customers, and associates. Member of National Association of Realtors and very active in the local chapter.

*Job knowledge:* Keeps current on all trends relating to her profession. Completed Realtors Institute (GRI). Thoroughly familiar with the community and its resources. Keeps up-to-date on total housing inventory and office listings.

*Creative ability:* Is able to devise innovative ways of solving problems. Respects tradition, but is not bound by obsolete concepts.

*Human relations:* Gets along well with individuals of every background. Genuinely committed to equal opportunity for all. Enjoys solving "people problems." Associates appreciate her willingness to help when needed. Able to maintain professional objectivity in dealing with problems; does not overidentify.

*Communicative ability:* Speaks and writes in a clear, concise, and personalized manner. Has mastered the important art of listening.

*Growth potential:* Has the leadership ability to be an outstanding broker and the technical skills to excel in any specialized field she selects. Will be well prepared to achieve future goals because of diversity of activities in which she has engaged as a residential sales agent.

| Bottom-line Record | | (Last 12 Months) | |
|---|---|---|---|
| Total listings | 16 | Total listings sold | 11 |
| Other closed sales | 13 | Fall-throughs | 0 |
| Outgoing referrals | 12 | Gross income | $79, 600 |

*Sarah Success*

---

Sarah Success, Broker/Owner, Professional Realty, Inc.

---

be able to depend upon it immediately. Start by making a list of friends and associates. Prepare a brief letter in which you inform them that you are in the business, indicate where you are located, and invite them to call upon you if you can be of service. A form letter may be the only practical alternative, but computer generated products can make form letters look very personalized, and always include a brief personal note. Enclose your business card. If you have your picture on the card, make sure the photograph is professionally done and it is recognizable as you.

2. *Announce your entry into the field in the local newspaper.* This will probably mean taking out a paid ad. Even physicians and attorneys use this procedure, so don't feel shy. The most appropriate method is for the broker to announce your affiliation with the company. Some newspapers have a "New Faces in Business," or some such related column. If so, make sure you take advantage of any free coverage.

3. *Have your listing in the telephone white pages changed.* It will cost some money, but use whatever options the phone company has available to make your name stand out and to identify you as a real estate agent. In some areas, your name can be printed in slightly bolder type than that used for regular listings.

4. *Let your old classmates know.* If you're a college graduate, send a note to your college alumni magazine. Some of your former classmates may know someone moving to your area. Some old friends may even turn out to be prosperous and influential and be in a position to refer substantial business to you. In any event, it is good to make it a matter of public record that you are in real estate and plan to be in it for a while.

## THE NEWBEE BLUES

In a military combat assignment overseas, people who have been at the station a while are respectfully called the "old heads," while the new arrivals are much less respectfully known as the "newbees." A newbee is not hard to spot: His combat fatigues will not have been washed yet and will be several shades darker than everyone else's. The newly issued boots will not have been broken in, causing him to walk with a gait called the "newbee shuffle."

As a new real estate agent, you may feel that you are being treated like a newbee and that you are not getting the respect you deserve. You may believe that people, particularly those in managerial positions, should pay a whole lot more attention to you. A new agent in our office, frustrated at not being able to get in to see the sales manager as quickly as he thought he should, commented: "Man, you have to stand in line around here just to get ignored."

Here are my suggestions for curing the real estate newbee blues. First, make certain that you really need advice and guidance when you ask for it. There are some new agents (and a few old ones who should know better) who have to run to the boss at every turn, ostensibly for help in making the crucial decision that will permit further progress on that megabuck transaction. In reality, what is often being said is, "Look at how good I'm doing, chief. Aren't I just about the best little old rookie real estate agent you ever did see?" Develop the reputation as someone who needs constant head-patting and stroking, and it will be hard to find anyone to talk to when you really have something important to discuss.

Second, close a few deals. I assure you that nothing will get you respect and admiration more quickly than starting to pay part of your broker's overhead. After you have brought in a few commission checks, try this little experiment to see how far your respect quotient has risen. Gather together a stack of papers that looks like an offer to purchase. Stroll casually by your broker's office. Hesitate. Make sure he sees the papers. Study them. Look puzzled. Chances are he will strike like a catfish after a worm and rush to your side to offer guidance.

Eventually, you will even start to notice that he is beginning to visit you at your desk a whole lot more with questions like: "Hey, how's it going this morning? Got anything I can help you with?" At that point, people will accurately say of you: "When Sarah Smith speaks, people listen." Your boots will be broken in, your fatigues faded, and you will have achieved the revered "old head" status.

# 5

# *In the Beginning There Was . . . Agency*

### *The Real Estate Profession's Identity Crises*

I served tours in two combat zones while in the U.S. Air Force. One was in Vietnam and the other was at the University of California at Berkeley, were I commanded the Air Force ROTC unit. One day in the Spring of 1970, in the wake of the Cambodian invasion and the tragedy at Kent State, the campus erupted. Rampaging crowds of students and street people, pursued by police, were everywhere, torching vehicles and generally wreaking havoc. I watched—from a safe distance and in civilian clothes—as U.C. Berkeley's riot de jour really got out of hand. At the epicenter in the middle of Sproul Plaza, apparently oblivious to what was going on around him, I noticed a lonely, solitary figure, sitting in a Ghandi-like pose and clothed only in cut off jeans. His hands were stretched skyward and he was plaintively wailing: "Who am I? Who am I?" That's the question now being asked by a lot of people in the real estate business. I'll do my best to answer it for you, since you need to know before you can fully appreciate your role as a real estate professional, and before we launch into our discussion of the specifics of listing and selling real estate.

## AGENCY: WHERE WE'VE BEEN

In legal terminology, an agent is someone who represents another person in a business transaction. There are different types of agents, ranging from a "universal agent," in which the agent has the power to act in any and all matters, to a "special agent," in which the agent is authorized to act for the principal in a limited set of clearly prescribed activities. The agent assumes a fiduciary responsibility to the principal. Textbooks define the list of obligations that make up that responsibility as: confidentiality, obedience, accountability, loyalty, and disclosure. In essence, it simply means that the agent puts the client's interests ahead of everyone else's in the transaction—including the agent's.

I can best illustrate the concept of agency as it relates to real estate if we fast-forward a bit and assume that you now have your license. Your first real shot at actually earning some money occurs when you list the home of Ed and Mary Johnson. They are highly motivated to sell, since they are re-locating the family business and want to get to their new home in New Jersey to get their children in school for the fall term. That listing agreement between you and the Johnsons is a legally binding contract, in which you pledge your best efforts to secure a ready, willing, and able buyer. If you do that, the Johnsons agree to compensate you with a brokerage fee, typically five, six, or seven percent of the eventual selling price. It's really an employment contract that creates an agency relationship in which the Johnsons actually hire your broker, for you are an agent of your broker. The listing you secure is called an "exclusive right to sell" listing, which means that no matter who sells the property you earn a commission.

Your broker is the Johnson's special agent, who is authorized to act for them in this limited set of circumstances. The contract typically gives the agent the authority to advertise the property, put a lock-box on it, submit it to the local Multiple Listing Service, and cooperate with other real estate brokers in finding a buyer. You are a sub-agent to the Johnsons. Both the agent, your broker, and the sub-agent, you, owe that fiduciary duty to the Johnsons. Again, in its basic terms it means placing their interests above everyone else's in any matter. The Johnsons are your *clients*. Your legal duty to third parties—buyers—is to deal honestly and reveal material facts. They are referred to as *customers*.

In the past the standard procedure has been for the home sellers to authorize the listing broker to submit the listing to the MLS, along with a unilateral offer of subagency, which meant that anyone who accepted that offer would represent the seller. The typical split on the brokerage fee

would be 50 percent to the listing office and 50 percent to the selling office. The practical implication was that legally everyone represented the
seller and no one legally represented the buyer. Your broker submitted the
listing to the local MLS, and in the information describing the listing included the phrase: "Sellers highly motivated—must be in New Jersey in
time for school this fall."

Here's the problem that developed. Let's say Sam Snerdly, the broker
at Sunset Realty and a member of the local MLS, noticed the Johnson listing and concluded it was just right for the Browns, a young couple whom
he had been working with on finding a home for several months. He accepted that unilateral offer of subagency. Snerdly has never met the Johnsons. He has become very good friends with the Browns. He met them at
the airport when they came to town for a house-hunting trip. He made
hotel reservations for them. He got them preapproved for a mortgage loan.
He took them to dinner. He offered advice on how to negotiate when buying a home. He gave them a six-month gift subscription to the local paper.
He shows the Browns the Johnson house. They love it. He shares with them
the fact that the sellers are really anxious to move. Because of Snerdly's advice, they offer four thousand less than full price. Even though that's substantially less than comparable homes are selling for, the Johnsons accept,
since they are so anxious to wrap it up and move on. The deal is done.

Question. Whom did Snerdly legally represent in this transaction?
Answer: the Johnsons. He was required to put their interests first. They
were his clients. He was their sub-agent, by virtue of accepting that unilateral offer of subagency. Question: Did he do that when he counseled
the buyers to offer substantially less than full price, because he knew the
Johnsons were "highly motivated"? Answer: Absolutely not. Question.
Whom do you think the Browns thought Snerdly represented? Answer:
Them, of course. What Snerdly did was enter into an undisclosed dual
agency, since by his actions it was obvious that he was, in fact, representing the Browns, while legally and contractually obligated to represent the
Johnsons. Acting as an undisclosed dual agent is illegal.

If everyone was happy with the outcome, then there was typically no
adverse reactions. But let's suppose that after the Browns move in they discover that the road bordering their home is going to be widened dramatically, which will substantially increase traffic noise. That information was
not disclosed to them. They want out. They consult an attorney wise in the
ways of agency. He asks the Browns to describe Snerdly's actions in the
transaction. It's clear there has been a violation of the laws of agency, so
that's what the attorney focuses on. All sorts of interesting things could re-

sult, including a revocation of the contract and perhaps even damages being levied against the sellers and the real estate agents involved. In an interesting sidelight, it became apparent that although agency violations were not typically the reasons that buyers were unhappy (generally it was non-disclosure of material facts), it became the focal point of the majority of lawsuits.

On the national level how serious a problem was this? In 1984 the Federal Trade Commission conducted a study which revealed that:

- Of buyers (the Browns) who worked with cooperating agents (Snerdly, the sub-agent), 71 percent believed the agent represented them.
- Of the buyers who worked with the listing agent (if the Browns came directly to you and bought the Johnson listing), 31 percent felt that the agent (you) represented them (the Browns).
- 74 percent of the sellers (the Johnsons) thought that the selling agent (Snerdly) represented the buyers.

As a result, states started passing laws that made agency disclosure mandatory. It is very likely that eventually all states will have such a law.

## AGENCY: WHERE WE ARE

There is not near the unanimity of practice now that there once was, but here's how things are sorting out in most parts of the country. The unilateral offer of subagency is not completely a thing of the past, but it is rapidly disappearing. Increasingly, selling agents are now representing buyers as buyers' agents. In most instances, they are not entering into a formal agreement, but are simply using an agency disclosure form as the basis for the buyer's agency role. There's real doubt that this is legally sufficient to establish a legitimate agency relationship, but, for the most part, that's how it's being done. By working as a buyer's broker, the selling agent owes the fiduciary duty to the client buyer, and the duty of fair dealing and disclosure to the customer seller.

Traditionally, licensees who work with buyers have not secured the same type of contractual agreement with them to represent them exclusively in house hunting that licensees who secure listings have. Buyers are completely free to work with anyone they choose and change agents as often as they wish. You can see that if you were a buyer's broker you would like that to change, but that's just not how it's being done in most places now.

Who pays the commission to the buyer's agent? In the vast majority of instances it "comes from the transaction," which simply means that it's done the way it always was—out of the commission the seller agrees to pay the listing broker. Why would a seller agree to pay a broker to represent the buyer? Because in the long run that increases the chances that they will sell their property by giving it the widest exposure, and besides the listing broker is representing their best interests. And in actual practice that's essentially what was being done under the old system.

What happens if you list a property and then find a buyer for it yourself? Can you still sell your own listing and satisfy the agency laws? In most instances, yes, if you enter into an agreement in which you disclose to both parties that you are acting as a "disclosed dual agent." You obviously could not put either party's interests first, since you would be representing both.

As you might suspect, when the old order (everyone representing the seller with the unilateral offer of subagency) broke down, there was (and is) some degree of turmoil in the ranks of the real estate profession. The concept of buyer agency was not warmly embraced by many in the business. One of the real problems developed as a result of the business practices of the advocates of this new way of doing business—the buyer's brokers. Several national level buyers brokerage organizations were formed that recruit real estate agents to act exclusively as buyers agents. A few of them have engaged in what many label as "scare tactics." Their advertising makes it clear that if the consumer does not use a firm that offers buyer brokerage exclusively, then they are not going to get the kind of honest and efficient service that they deserve. Some of it I've heard and read clearly goes well beyond what would be considered ethical by any impartial observer.

## AGENCY: THE FUTURE

As lawmakers wrestle with this problem, one of the alternatives to the traditional concept of agency that has developed is that of "transaction broker" or "facilitator." The idea here is that agency as it exists in common law is not really appropriate for the real estate profession, since the goal of the real estate licensee is to bring parties together and negotiate a mutually satisfactory solution—not to represent one party in a formal agency relationship. There's resistance to the idea, some based upon philosophical convictions, some based upon vested interests.

## AGENCY: THE BOTTOM LINE

Now let's take a step back and focus on the essentials. How do you get paid in real estate? You get paid when the transaction closes. The transaction will close when all parties are satisfied. You are not likely to reach that kind of an agreement if there is an adversarial relationship between the real estate licensees involved. How much do you get paid? You typically get a percentage of the sales price. That's great for the listing agent, since interests are compatible. The more you get for the home the more you make. But how about the buyer's agent? The more his client (the buyer) pays, the more he makes. That's a little inconsistency that hasn't been fully sorted out yet. If you are working with a buyer as a buyer's agent I believe it would be wise to address this openly and honestly and counsel them to come up with an offering price that is within their means and fair to all parties. As with all other matters, the final decision is theirs.

Here are my recommendations:

1. As you participate in your licensing training, pay very close attention to the subject of agency as it is practiced in your state and your local area. If you want to delve into the subject more deeply, read the book *Agency Relationships In Real Estate* by Attorney/Realtor John Reilly (see "Real Estate Reference," References). It's one of the few devoted to the topic that is balanced, unbiased, and authoritative.

2. Make absolutely certain that if your state has mandatory agency disclosure that you understand completely the formal requirements and that you make the necessary agency disclosures when called for—typically at the first substantive contact with a potential client. This can admittedly become burdensome, since the technical requirements of many agency disclosure laws means that the typical house hunter, for example, could end up signing dozens of such disclosure forms.

3. Try to convince everyone that unless the transaction is fair to everyone it's fair to no one. (Those who are proponents of a more adversarial form of agency don't agree with me on this one. They maintain you

represent your client in the best manner possible, strike the best deal, and it's up to the other side to watch out for their interests. If they make a bad deal, that's their problem.)

4. Understand that in some circles in the profession the depth of feeling runs deep on this issue. Most of the troops in the field have rolled with the flow and continue to try to do business legally and ethically while continuing to earn a living, but passions among some are intense—particularly those with vested interests. Do a lot of listening, studying, and asking questions before you become too generous with your personal opinions.

5. Don't be disappointed if, after you've completed your licensing training, you have the nagging feeling that you don't fully understand the subject of agency completely. A member of my network is one of the leading national authorities on this subject. I occasionally call him when I need guidance. His reaction the last time I called: "The more I learn about agency, the less I know."

## WHEN THE DEAL IS DONE

You've listed the Johnson's home. What is the best possible outcome for them? They get a fair price from a qualified buyer, with no unpleasant aftertaste (like a lawsuit). They get their check at close and move happily on to their new life in New Jersey. What is the best possible outcome for the buyers, the Browns? They pay a fair price and get a home that meets their needs. All material facts about the property are disclosed to them before they buy. What's the best possible outcome for you? In addition to that nice commission check, the Johnsons and the Browns are *both* so impressed by your consummate professionalism, hard work, creative problem solving ability, and integrity that they say nice things about you to all their friends and associates and vow that in the future they would never work with anyone but you.

Don't get so involved with fighting the agency alligators that you forget that your primary job is to tidy up the swamp.

# 6

# Listing Residential Property

*Finding the Sellers and Moving the Merchandise*

"If you list, you last" sums up the sentiment of most brokers. It's not hard to appreciate why they feel that way. Listings are the basic inventory of the real estate business. They are what's for sale up on the shelf. It's been said: "When your last listing is gone, you've had your going-out-of-business sale." That's not much of an overstatement. Even though there are now some brokerages who are specializing in working exclusively with buyers, it's clear that unless there's something to sell, everything grinds to a halt.

Lots of positive things happen when a good listing comes into the office. First, everyone, including all those using the local multiple listing service, can start to look for a buyer. In most cases, no matter who finally sells a listing, the listing agent and broker collect their fees. Second, the listing can be advertised, and that will generate activity that benefits the whole staff. Finally, a "For Sale" sign can be placed in the yard—and having those in front of dozens of prime properties (with a rider with your name prominently displayed on many of them as the listing agent) is one of the best forms of advertising possible.

Your broker will also want you to have a "success experience" early—a desire you will share passionately. It's generally easier to get a listing than to make a sale because there are typically more people who want to sell than there are qualified buyers who want to purchase. For all of these reasons, expect to be encouraged to develop your listing skills as your first order of business.

## FINDING THE SELLERS

If, as they say, "old salespeople never die, they just become listless," then here are some suggested sources of listings to keep you alive and perky. In the discussion that follows, I am assuming a traditional relationship between the licensee (you) and seller in which the owner who lists a property is the client, pays the commission, and is owed a fiduciary responsibility.

### Customers of Agents No Longer in the Office

All offices have some turnover of agents, and not every broker does what would be in his or her best interest—that is, assign someone to take over abandoned accounts. For example, the Pearsons bought a home through your brokerage eight years ago from an agent long since gone. No one is keeping in touch with them. Research the situation. You would do that by reviewing the "deal files" that all brokerages maintain (after letting your broker know what you're up to, of course). When you locate such cases, ask to handle them. Send the prospects a letter with your card and any other appropriate promotional material, and follow up with a phone call or a personal visit.

### Builders and Remodelers

Be selective in cultivating this source. Builders differ greatly in their perception of how business should be conducted. Naturally, you will want to list the homes of builders who share your philosophy. If you are fortunate enough to establish rapport with one who does quality work and who will market his homes through you, it will add an interesting and profitable dimension to your activities. Of course, you could really strike it rich if you happen to land the account of a large-scale builder who is developing subdivisions of homes.

### Absentee Owners

People who own real estate in your community, but who live out of the area, are excellent prospects. This is especially true if they are absentee landlords, since the aggravation associated with that arrangement can provide a terrific motivation to sell. The first step is to pick an area and research a manageable number of properties. There are public records in the assessor's or tax collector's office that you can use, and there is probably

a reverse directory for your community, published annually, that lists residences by address and indicates the occupants' names, along with a no-
tation as to whether they are owners or renters.

After you get the addresses of the owners, prepare a letter to them in
which you introduce yourself and your company and offer your marketing assistance, should they wish to sell. Personalize it with a handwritten
note and call the particularly promising prospects. It is remarkable how
positively most people react to long distance business calls, properly handled. Don't ever call before 9 A.M. or after 10 P.M. (*their* time, not yours). It
is hard to establish rapport with someone you have just awakened.

### For Sale by Owner (FSBO)

Every new real estate agent has probably been advised or required to
call people who are attempting to sell their homes themselves. The reason
for pursuing homes for sale by owner (FSBO—or "fizzbos," as they are
fondly known) is simple. History shows that a large percentage of them
find the whole process so daunting that they eventually list with a broker.
If you can convince them that you can do a better job than they can and
net them as much money (or more), they are likely to list with you.

Calling fizzbos gets mixed reviews from agents. Some very successful ones do it as a matter of routine and develop a real knack for it. Others abandon the effort after they secure other sources. Some never do it at
all. No matter what course you select, there is one instance when you
should definitely call. If you are working with a buyer for whom a particular fizzbo listing looks promising, call and ask for a one-party listing.
This is a listing that would be valid for only the person to whom you
showed the property. Be prepared for skepticism when you call, however,
for one of the gimmicks some unethical agents use is to call and indicate
they have a buyer and would like to preview the property. The buyer is
fictitious, but, for some agents, the chance to get their foot in the door
seems to justify the dishonesty. Once they've been taken (or hear from
someone who has), sellers understandably become wary, so when you approach them with the genuine article they are hard to convince. However,
if you have a legitimate prospect, it is definitely worth your effort.

### Expired Listings

If a property has been on the open market for an extended period and
has not sold, ask yourself why. If it was because the listing agent did not
handle the marketing properly, or did not try to get price reductions when

it did not sell, then there is a good chance that a fresh, more professional approach will get better results. If it was because the sellers were not motivated, or some other factor you cannot change, it probably will not be worth your time.

Whether or not you work expired listings, keep track of them. You may encounter a buyer who is looking for exactly the kind of property that was previously on the market. Very unique listings, especially extremely high-priced ones, may go unsold, so it is worth keeping tabs on them. In working expired listings, be circumspect in dealing with the owners, for they will have had an unsuccessful experience with another real estate agent. Out of professional courtesy, resist any temptation (no matter how well justified) to criticize your predecessor's efforts. Never, under any circumstances, contact a seller *before* a listing has expired, in anticipation of being able to secure the listing later. That is unethical and could get you in serious difficulty.

### Ads Generated by Buyer Contacts

Some buyers are in no hurry. They will describe an ideal property to you, whether it be a home, a small acreage, or a business. If you can find what they are looking for, fine. Otherwise, they will stay put. If you occasionally run short newspaper ads indicating that you have a potential buyer for a specific type of property, you may be able to generate some excellent listings. Again, you will probably encounter skepticism, for an ad for a prospective buyer is a ploy used by those few who are willing to bend the truth to make the phone ring.

### Farming

The prospecting technique known as "farming" is covered in almost all real estate training programs. In its classic form it involves an agent deciding upon a specific area of town (typically a section with 200 to 300 homes in a homogeneous, contiguous neighborhood) and "farms it" for listings. The tactic most usually advocated is a series of personal visits to each home on the farm, spaced throughout the year. The objective is to become so well known to the homeowners that they will automatically think of you when it is time to sell.

Suggested farming procedures include leaving gifts (calendars, pens, pot holders, memo pads—all with your name and phone number on them), writing a newsletter (including neighborhood information, such as who baby-sits, who is moving out or in, and so on), and organizing neighborhood activities (get-togethers for newcomers, block parties). The recommended initial contact is through a door-to-door "cold call" (no previous contact), using a rehearsed, introductory speech.

Some agents have gotten rich farming and stay rich by doing it faithfully. Others are not comfortable with the door-to-door solicitation (in some places there are laws against it) and remain unconvinced that it is a wise expenditure of time. If you do farm, do your homework. While I was in real estate sales, we owned a modest condominium that we rented out. An eager real estate agent decided to farm that neighborhood. He never did bother to check to see who owned the property. Our tenant was delighted to keep receiving the gifts, but the potential payoff for the agent was nonexistent, unless the tenant decided to move out and buy (which was unlikely, since it was my mother-in-law).

### Cold-Call Telephone Canvassing

This is another traditional prospecting device. Homeowners are called (sometimes at random, other times with a plan) and asked if they are considering selling their home or if they know anyone who might be. Specific scripts are generally used, with recommended answers to just about any conceivable homeowner question or objection. As was the case with farming, cold-call canvassing has its share of both converts and detractors. Some swear by it, others at it.

It will be impossible for you to follow completely all of the suggestions for getting listings that will be given in your training program (or, for that matter, in this discussion). Much will be dictated by local circumstances and by your personality. Simply become familiar with all the potential sources and concentrate your efforts on those that appear to have the greatest potential. It is entirely possible that you may end up spending most of your time on one specific program that turns out to be particularly productive. When you are considering the alternatives, don't be too quick to write off procedures because you react adversely to the basic concept. For example, you could conclude that traditional farming does not suit you, but with some adaptation and refinement it might have real possibilities. Whatever system you decide upon, give it some time before you expect it to start paying dividends. Finally, don't be discouraged. Remember, getting started is the hardest part.

## WORKING WITH SELLERS

After you get well established, people will often simply call and tell you they want to sell their property and they want you to handle it for them. It may be a family you sold a house to or sold a house for, or it may be someone who was referred to you. That is when real estate becomes really satisfying and profitable. In these cases you merely prepare ahead of time by coming up with pricing information and a marketing plan and meet with the people to take the listing. It won't be quite that easy in the beginning.

Most people, when they decide they want to list, call several different real estate companies. That way they get three or four estimates of an asking price and they have a chance to evaluate the real estate agent who would handle the listing. To be competitive in such an environment, you have to convince the owners that you are a highly competent practitioner who is quite capable of selling the property.

### *Preparing for the Listing Appointment*

Let's assume you have secured an appointment to discuss listing a residential home. Here are some of the steps you can take to make sure you do a professional job in making your presentation, taking the listing, marketing it, and seeing the transaction through to a successful close.

1. *Research the property thoroughly.* The first step is to secure a listing packet. In some areas, the local title company will provide you with one free that includes such things as the legal description, a plat map (showing property boundaries), assessor's tax information, and ownership data. If you have to do the research yourself, all the information will generally be available in public records. Increasingly, such information is available via computer, but however you get it, the information is obviously essential.

2. *Visit the residence.* Remember, this is *before* the formal listing appointment. At this point, you are gathering information. Inspect the neighborhood and the home, take measurements, become familiar with the amenities, ask questions about how things work, and get a feel for the general area. The listing form your office uses will provide guidelines. When you visit the home, take along one or two other agents from your office. It is always good to get a balanced input. Each agent should give

you suggestions on pricing. You will do the same for them on their list-ings, so don't feel you are imposing.

Be sure to become fully aware of all immediate neighborhood prop-erties currently or recently on the market, whether they're for sale by owners or are listed. Homeowners are generally very familiar with what is going on around them. If you do not include this information in your market analysis, you will lose credibility.

3. *Complete a market analysis.* A Competitive Market Analysis (CMA) is simply a process in which you do research to determine your estimate of the market value of a property. Your office will have forms to help you prepare yours, but you may eventually want to adapt these to meet your needs. Your first few will take some time, but soon you will perform them quickly, as a matter of routine. With the advent of computers, it's now more a matter of knowing the right buttons to push, and being able to in-terpret the results.

Your goal is to present the home owners with information upon which they may make their pricing decision—how much they will ask for their home. To do this you will compare their home to similar properties in the same area that sold recently. You will also include information on unsold homes currently on the market and homes that were on the mar-ket, but did not sell. It's basically the process an appraiser uses in arriving at an estimate of value for residential properties. It will be tempting to suggest a specific asking price, and many agents do just that (I will admit I did). However, it is probably wiser to present the information and let the homeowner make the decision on a specific asking price. It won't be a big secret what you think a reasonable figure would be.

4. *Bring your listing folder up-to-date.* You need to make certain that you have all the forms that the sellers need to review, descriptive mater-ial about you and your office, and information (including pictures and fly-ers) about other listings you have. A display binder with plastic inserts is often used. Many agents also now carry along laptop computers that can plug in to the local Multiple Listing Service to display pictures and infor-mation on other current listings. You wouldn't stand before an audience to deliver a 30-minute speech without having prepared an outline ahead of time. Neither should you go to a listing appointment without some idea as to how you would like to proceed when you get there. I do not, however, recommend reciting canned presentations, for the same reason that speech instructors do not recommend presenting memorized speeches. If you forget your lines, you'll come across as a mumbling, in-

competent novice. Work out an approach you are comfortable with, make sure you cover the major items that any seller needs to know, and be flexible.

Before you arrive, confirm that all the decision makers will be on hand for the appointment. Also suggest as tactfully as possible that non-decision makers not be there. Friends and relatives kibitzing from the sidelines can complicate the situation for everyone.

### During the Listing Appointment

Here are some things to consider during the listing appointment. Make sure you have all the information and forms handy.

1. *Go over the market analysis.* The logical order of events suggests itself if you understand what is uppermost in the minds of the sellers. They want to know how much you think their home is worth. They also want to judge you.

Most training programs advocate going through a long ritual before you share pricing information with the poor folks. That always seemed artificial and self-defeating to me, but do what works for you. The first figure I discussed with them was the price range I thought their home was in, based upon *closed sales* of comparable properties. Emphasize that where in that range *they* decide to establish the asking price will be determined largely by their motivation to sell. As you would suspect, the lower in the price range, the more likely the home will move quickly, although determining real estate value is an art, not a science, so be very conservative in how you phrase your statements.

The second item on the agenda is for the home owners to decide upon a suggested asking price, which is almost always somewhat higher than the anticipated selling price (in recognition of the universal procedure among buyers to offer less than full price). It's at this point you need to suggest that your sellers look at the transaction through the eyes of potential buyers. It's quite likely that if the asking price is inflated well beyond what the owners would actually sell for, many excellent prospects will never even bother to look at the home, assuming that it's out of their price range.

Be sensitive to feedback. You should be able to tell whether you are gaining the seller's confidence or not, but do not be afraid to ask questions. Not even the most experienced real estate agent is infallible, so if it is apparent that they think their home is worth a lot more than your analysis seems to indicate (rarely do they think it's worth less), agree to review it and seek still another agent's opinion.

2. *Provide information about yourself and your company.* You can use your listing folder for this and maybe some snappy computer graphics. Some agents even have a short promotional video. You want the sellers to see you for what you are—a skilled professional. You also want your company to come across as an aggressive, wide-awake organization that is respected within the community. If you have letters of appreciation and diplomas from educational programs such as GRI, have copies displayed in the plastic inserts. Modesty will dictate a low-key approach when extolling your own virtues, but people do want to know something about you.

Explain how the multiple listing service works and describe in detail any special marketing techniques you use, such as ads, flyers, and contacts with special groups of buyers. Describe your company. If there are successful agents who work there, that will enhance the likelihood that a listed property will be sold.

3. *Show them the actual forms they will sign.* Use the listing form itself to explain the various ramifications of listing a property, including the formal agency relationship, the role of your broker, the obligations they incur, and the actions you pledge. Leave the forms with them to review and study, unless they want to proceed with the listing immediately.

4. *Go over a "net proceeds to seller" computation.* Sellers are interested in the bottom-line amount they will get from the sale. It is what they walk away with at closing that concerns them. At this time you can give only a rough idea, because there are as yet so many unknown factors. Despite the limitations you can provide a pretty good estimate, with the major variable being the final sales price. After outstanding mortgage and other financial encumbrances are paid, the largest single cost is generally the commission (be ready to describe all the things you do to earn those big bucks). The simplest way of presenting the net proceeds to seller information is as part of the market analysis, on the same form, although some offices use separate forms. When the actual offer is presented, you will do a more detailed "sellers net" sheet.

In most cases, property owners will thank you for your time and tell you that they will think it over and give you their decision later. There is a whole series of techniques designed to forestall that and to convince them to list immediately. Chances are they will have encountered this approach if they have talked to other agents. There are those who believe a low-key, no-pressure approach actually works better. They realize that it is probably a good idea for the sellers to take a little time; after all, the homeowner is making a very important decision. Those agents maintain that sellers are generally so relieved not to be hassled that they become very receptive to doing business.

### Taking the Listing

You call to follow up and are informed you've got the listing. You will then return for another appointment to get the signed contract.

1. *Complete the listing agreement.* The homeowners will have had the documents to review and you will have gone over it with them, but this time it's for the record, and they will have questions. Make certain that you fill in all the items (don't skip something and say "we'll fill that in later") and ensure the listing has an expiration date.

Almost all listing forms have something about "known defects." Most states now have mandatory property condition disclosure forms. No home is perfect, even a new one, and if there are defects that the owners know of, they must disclose them.

2. *Discuss hidden defects.* Selling real estate is more complicated and much riskier than it once was. The concept of *caveat emptor* (let the buyer beware) is rapidly changing. Courts are ruling that sellers and agents are liable to buyers for defects they should have known about, but did not. Even in the states where there are no mandatory disclosure laws, many brokers will not take a listing without a formal written property disclosure. That's a very sound practice.

An independent inspection will help. It would be better for the sellers to have the inspection done and to correct any deficiencies before putting the property on the market, but it's not always easy to convince them of that. If the sellers do order an inspection, advise them to hire a company that does not also do structural repair, for they have a disconcerting habit of finding a lot of work that needs to be done. Sellers may be reluctant to get an early inspection, but if there is bad news it is better for them to know about it up front than to wait for the issue to surface later.

3. *Agree on the asking price.* What happens if the sellers inform you that they have decided to list their home for substantially more than the highest range you documented? Should you take the listing? You will quickly learn that there are few things more frustrating and time-consuming than servicing an overpriced listing. However, if you make the sellers aware of

the dangers inherent in listing above the market and if the price is not fla-grantly excessive, you will probably want to take the listing. During your first year or so in the business, you would probably take a listing at almost any price. Be sensitive to market conditions, however, and recommend a price reduction if the listing has not generated interest after a reasonable period.

4. *Provide a checklist for the homeowners.* The final step is to give the owners a standardized checklist on how to prepare their home to show. In many localities, the multiple listing service will provide such a checklist. If it's not available from MLS, someone in your office may have one, or you can make one up yourself with just a little thought. There are even videos on the market that present the information in an entertaining way.

The advantage of giving your clients a preprinted form or a video suggesting such steps as cleaning, painting, and keeping the house neat is that you will not be perceived as criticizing their house or yard—you are simply providing generalized guidance. Be prepared, however, to diplo-matically bring up any specific problems that may detract from showing the home. The family dog often poses a particular difficulty, especially if, like most dogs, he is very unreceptive to strangers tromping around on his turf. If the owners are not home, the dog should be left in a secure area so the showing can take place with a minimum of disruption to Rover's tranquillity and your prospects' nerves.

## AFTER GETTING THE LISTING

To "move the merchandise," you have to be aggressive and creative in developing a marketing plan for each of your listings, and you have to follow up to keep your clients informed. Perhaps the most common com-plaint among homeowners who have listed is that "after all the sweet talk, we never heard from the agent again." You can help forestall that by en-listing their efforts in calling you each time the home is shown by an agent. Here are some specific things you need to get done in carrying out your marketing strategy.

1. *Prepare the multiple listing entry.* Review listings as they appear in your multiple listing. You will find that many are pretty sparse. Make yours complete. Although MLS formatting requirements now have made most entries pretty standardized, there is still typically room for some

comments. Remember that the users are other real estate agents, so answer the questions that they will have. Include measurements of major rooms, indicate the size of the lot, describe unique features, and by all means outline the terms upon which the house may be purchased. If there is an assumable loan, verify with the lender in writing under what conditions it may be assumed. If the seller will help with financing, point that out. In a tough market, terms often sell houses.

2. *Place signs on the property.* In many locales "For Sale" signs sell more property than any other marketing device. In some exceptional instances, your client may not permit a sign, but most relent when they learn how effective they are. A rider on the sign that says "Ask for Sarah Smith" will give you good exposure. As you service the listing, drive by periodically to make sure the sign is still up and visible. When an offer has been accepted place a sold or sale pending sticker on it—that's great free advertising.

3. *Arrange for access to the property.* Lock-boxes are effective and convenient, but using them can pose problems. Real estate agents are busy and the easier a home is to show the more likely they are to show it. A lock-box contains a key to a home and members of the local multiple listing service are the only people who have keys to the lock-boxes, so you would think that security would be pretty effective. Unfortunately, carelessness and downright dishonesty have resulted in some home owners being very wary of relying on the lock-box technique. If a lock-box is not used and if the key is left in your office, it is crucial that a foolproof and responsive system be implemented that will permit the property to be shown easily and at the same time provide owners the safety and security they deserve.

4. *Advertise the property.* All advertising must be done under your broker's supervision. If you are asked to prepare copy on your listings, keep it simple, honest, and interesting. There are some things you can do on your own that are very effective.

First, prepare a one-page flyer for each of your listings. You can do it with a typewriter, a computer, or have it done by a printer. Secure a picture of the property (generally, you can use the one from your multiple listing service) for the flyer and then simply list features that prospective purchasers will probably be interested in, including price and terms. Place your business card at the bottom and clearly indicate your broker affiliation. Include a disclaimer on the bottom making it clear that, although you believe the information is correct, you cannot guarantee it. However it's prepared, make the flyer look professional.

Place copies in a prominent place at the home itself for agents and prospects who look at the property. If you are working any type of marketing program in which you correspond with prospects, send some copies along. You will want to put one up on your office wall for visitors to see, and you should give other agents in your office as many as they require.

More and more real estate companies, as well as individual agents, are using home pages on the Internet to get additional exposure for their listings. It couldn't hurt.

5. *Hold an open house.* Although it is rare for an open house to result in a sale for that specific listing, it does happen. Even if it doesn't, the exposure you get from conducting an open house is beneficial. Most homeowners will probably want you to hold one so it is a good idea to establish a routine that will allow you to achieve maximum results. First, ask the homeowners whether they would object to your sending the immediate neighbors a flyer about the listing and an invitation to the open house. Some clients don't want their neighbors to know anything about what they are doing, but most will think it's a good idea. If any family in the neighborhood is thinking about selling their home later, be assured they will pay very close attention to how you do your job.

Maintain a log of who visits, both as a record for the homeowner and for you, and as a way of maintaining security. If you indicate to your visitors that the owners have asked for the information, most will comply willingly. Pay attention to each individual. Introduce yourself and attempt to fix name and face. Invite them to look at the home and give them a flyer. Many will be browsers, but some will likely be immediate prospects for a purchase—perhaps not for that home, but for another. The more you know about the visitors and their motivations, the better you can meet their needs. If they are noncommunicative, don't push. Be friendly, businesslike, and unobtrusive. If any appear suspicious, keep an attentive eye on them and be particularly wary if two people arrive and one of them occupies you in conversation while the other disappears.

After the open house, send all visitors a note thanking them for stopping by, along with your card. Try to prepare the notes right after the open house and mail them from the post office so they will be delivered the next day. If you judged anyone to be strong potential prospects (buyers or sellers), prepare a card on each one for your prospect file, and follow up.

6. *Follow up on visits by real estate agents.* Agents who either preview or show a listing are obligated to leave their business cards as a record of their visit. You will want to follow up with each agent personally. Get each one's reaction to the home, and secure feedback on pricing. If an agent noticed things that detract from the listing, discuss it with the owners.

## HANDLING THE OFFER

Unless you sell your own listing to a prospect you are working with, the ball will typically get rolling by a telephone call from another agent, informing you: "I've got an offer on the Jones listing."

1. *Present the offer.* Procedures vary around the country as to what is good form in presenting offers, so local custom and courtesies will prevail. In many instances, agents will want to be with you when you meet with the Joneses. Some might not want to go over the offer with you before it is formally presented, but unless you preview everything there is no way you can do your job properly. For example, verify that the other agent has made certain the prospective buyers are qualified. Sellers are concerned about both the motivation of the buyers and their financial capability.

2. *Compute a net-proceeds sheet.* One of the most important documents that sellers consider when they make their decision is the "net proceeds to seller" form. Because all of the costs of the sale can now be accurately estimated based upon a proposed sale price and exact terms (including a projected closing date), you can give your sellers a reasonably precise breakdown.

The first few forms you complete will be tough and you will need help. Prorating expenses can be tricky and time-consuming. I received a lot of patient tutoring from a bright young escrow agent in a local title company. Computer programs are also available that offer a convenient and helpful format.

It is always best to estimate potential expenditures on the high side, so the sellers will end up getting no less than they expect. If you overlook or underestimate an expense and actual net proceeds are less than projected, you will have disgruntled sellers. They might even suspect you of inflating their expectations intentionally to get them to accept the offer so you could earn a quick commission.

3. *Let the sellers decide.* After the offer has been presented, you should discuss it with the sellers privately and they should be given time to consider their decision. However, there are some advantages to accepting a good offer from highly qualified buyers when it's presented. Until an offer is accepted by the sellers, and the buyers are informed of that acceptance, they are under no obligation to consummate the transaction.

## FOLLOWING UP TO CLOSE

After the sellers accept and that's communicated to the buyers, the whole transaction enters its most crucial stage, and you need to stay on top of it to make sure that the things that need to be done, get done, and on time.

1. *Make a list.* Write down every task that has to be accomplished, who has to do it, and when it has to be done. Some offices have a prepared checklist. Do not *assume* that something will be done. Make sure it *has* been done. Check on it yourself. Put it on the top of your daily schedule under number one priority. Do not accept evasive answers such as, "To the best of my knowledge the loan application has been submitted," or, "I am reasonably sure the credit check has been ordered." Your clients do not get their money until the transaction closes and neither do you. Be tough. Eliminate fall-throughs.

2. *Give advice judiciously.* Your sellers may ask for your advice in choosing other professionals, such as CPAs, attorneys, and title companies to handle specialized phases of the transaction. It is wise to suggest two or three possibilities, particularly in the case of attorneys and CPAs, and let people make their own choices. If you steer a client toward someone specific and it does not work out, there could be repercussions.

3. *Follow up doggedly.* It is very important to establish a personal working relationship with all other professionals involved in the transaction. At times, they will need prodding to get a job done expeditiously, for they will be paid whether the transaction closes or not. Tact and good-natured persistence will be your best tools. Never recommend any company or individual who may have a vested interest in the outcome of the trans-

action without making that interest very clear to all parties. Real estate brokers, for example, sometimes have partial ownership of title, escrow, and insurance companies.

## "PLEASE LADY, DON'T INTERRUPT"

About a year after I joined the firm, our broker decided to affiliate with a national franchise. That meant all the agents had to go to a regional center for week-long training sessions on listing and selling. The facility, the staff, and the training techniques were all impressive. The center had the latest in instructional aids, including a videotaping device that allowed us to tape our listing presentations and play them back for critique. Instructors strongly believed in a structured, practiced approach to selling real estate and had very little use for the more casual "do what the situation demands" method that had been my style.

Although my listing appointments had always seemed to work out pretty well, I decided that I should be open-minded and learn their system. That meant using charts and graphs to accompany a step-by-step rehearsed presentation that included answers for every possible objection. Depending upon how many of those answers you had to use, the entire script was designed to last about 45 to 50 minutes and to ensure that you walk out of the house with a signed listing agreement.

My first chance to use it for real came when a woman called the office one day when I was on floor duty. She wanted someone to "come and tell me how much I can get for my house." The next day I went by to look at it and to make measurements to prepare for the actual listing appointment. The owner, Bonnie, was a young, single parent who worked to support herself and her little boy. She wanted to move to a larger town where job opportunities were better.

I spent almost an hour looking at the house and the grounds and asking questions. It was a lovely home, and I was particularly impressed with the number of bearing fruit trees and the ornamental shrubs she had, and made a diagram of the yard with her help. We talked at length, but I was careful to save the "good stuff" for my upcoming presentation. An associate of mine went by later for a quick look of her own to help me arrive at a suggested price range.

The next day I returned for the listing appointment, bringing my entire arsenal of paraphernalia and ready to deliver a sales pitch that could have convinced King Tut to list his pyramid with me. I was dazzling as I tripped lightly and confidently from one point to the next, pausing only long enough to get her to answer set-up questions (called minor closes).

But after about 15 minutes, I noticed a shift in mood. She became a bit less attentive and that pained "Lord, will this never end?" look became evident in her face. (I recognized it from the days when I used to practice my school-assignment speeches in front of my wife.) Maybe she needs to go to the bathroom, I thought, so I stopped momentarily to ask if everything was all right. "Oh yes, Mr. Edwards, but would it be OK with you if I went ahead and signed those papers now?" Sign now?! But I have charts I haven't shown you, accomplishments I haven't bragged about, and marketing programs I haven't explained. Worst of all, you have not come up with a *single* objection for me to counter! Sign now?! "Sure, Bonnie, that would be great. Right here. Press hard."

It was a fine listing. We sold it quickly and Bonnie moved to a larger city. She still calls when she visits. She later confided to me that she really wanted to sign that first day I came out, but that I seemed so intent upon doing things my way that she didn't want to bring it up.

The training I received at the listing seminar was excellent. It was logical, orderly, and convincing. I used much of it later on during other listing appointments. I still have the padded simulated-leather listing folder that opens up for use as a visual aid on a table. The obvious point is that any training you receive will have to be adapted to your style and to the situation, and that nothing replaces common sense and good judgment. You will also find that if you show a genuine and knowledgeable interest in the property and the people, the personal rapport you achieve will overcome shortcomings in other areas.


## IS IT WORTH ALL THE EFFORT?

It may occur to you that there is a lot of hard work involved in listing and marketing residential property. There is, if you do it right. There is also a great deal of satisfaction to be gained from it and excellent money to be made. Remember, when you secure a listing and put it on the MLS, every other agent in town immediately starts to work trying to find a buyer. If you have several realistically priced properties on the market at any one time, you will have a lot of help making a living.

# 7

# *Selling Residential Property*

*Finding the Buyers, Listening to Them, and Satisfying Their Needs*

If hitting a home run is the magic moment in baseball, then selling a house is the glamour event in residential real estate. Just find qualified buyers, match them with the home they want, and touch all the bases on your way to the bank. It's no wonder that new agents are chomping at the bit to go out there and sell houses.

Of course, selling real estate isn't that easy, but it does have special appeal. First, it can be extremely profitable. For what is often a comparatively short investment of your time, there is the potential for a very substantial commission. Second, working with motivated, qualified buyers can be pure joy—for them, when they move into the home of their choice; for the sellers, when they collect their check at closing; and for you, when you get paid in satisfaction and money.

"Motivated" and "qualified" are the critical words when applied to buyers. If an agent can continually come face-to-face with people who are ready to buy and who have the means (called "belly-button-to-belly-button contact" in less genteel circles), it would be hard not to succeed. Although you will have plenty of competition in your quest for these prizes, you will win more than your fair share if you approach your task systematically and creatively.

As you consider this material, keep in mind our discussion of agency in Chapter 5. In keeping with what seems to be the trend, we will assume that in working with buyers you are representing them as their agent and that you owe them a fiduciary duty. We will also assume, however, that you do not have an exclusive contract with them and that they remain free to work with whomever they wish. Although there's a strong movement among buyer agent groups to reach the point where buyers sign exclusive contracts with buyer's agents, we're not there yet, and there are those who say it's unlikely we ever will be.

## ARE BUYERS LIARS?

So, under our scenario, your potential buyers have no legal obligation to any agent. They can work with whomever they chose, whenever they chose. Some salespeople are devastated when they learn that buyers with whom they were in contact bought through someone else. If you are doing things correctly that will not happen often, but it will happen. When it does, you will want to analyze what you did wrong, or someone else did better, but there is nothing to gain by feeling betrayed. Buyers are concerned with their best interests, not yours, and that is perfectly understandable. You will thoroughly enjoy working with almost all of them, and most will display a remarkable loyalty to you—but there will be losses. Most buyers are not liars, although they may sometimes tell you what they think you want to hear to avoid hurting your feelings, or to take the pressure off themselves. Reverse the roles and we would quite likely do the same.

## CATEGORIES OF HOME BUYERS

Home buyers fall into rather broad, identifiable groups, each with somewhat different motivations and capabilities. What follows are the major segments of the buying public as they are most often classified. Some agents become so adept at working with certain types of buyers that they spend most of their time doing just that.

▪ *First-time buyers.* Whether they're single or married with a small family, or DINKS (double, income, no kids) first-time buyers generally have less money for a down payment and a smaller monthly income. By necessity they are more likely to accept small homes and attached homes. Those who are handy look for older, cheaper homes to buy and repair, but financing on such projects can be tricky. Be prepared to work with parents and older friends who are often called in to inspect potential purchases. Relatives often chip in for a portion of the down payments.

■ *Move-up buyers*. Most buyers in this category are married with children. They can come up with a hefty down payment because they have typically sold a home and are looking for something larger in which to raise the family. They tend to see detached housing as essential, and are often drawn to homes in the suburbs with large yards or small acreage.

■ *Empty-nesters*. Generally empty-nesters have a substantial amount to put down, because they have sold a house that became too large for them once their children left. They are experienced buyers. Listen carefully when they describe what they want, for they know. Depending upon individual circumstances and preference, they will accept attached or detached housing.

■ *Retirees*. Like empty-nesters, retirees probably have a sizable down payment, but monthly cost will be important if they are on a fixed income. They most often prefer a single-level house, because climbing stairs may pose a problem. Having lived through the golden years of the American dream of home ownership, they look upon owning a home as a solid financial investment as well as a fulfilling emotional experience. Most seniors with whom I worked responded best to unhurried, uncomplicated house hunting and viewed with suspicion gimmicky financing. In some cases, you will work with sons and daughters who will want to look at the parents' choice before a final commitment is made.

The following suggestions are intended to help you keep your "Prospects" file full of one of the most coveted of all assets—willing and able buyers. You can never have too many of them.

## MAKING THE MOST OF FLOOR DUTY

In most real estate offices, each day (or portion of it) one agent is designated the "floor agent" and is required to be in the office to handle telephone inquiries and "walk-ins." In some offices, the person "on the floor" also handles that day's correspondence in which someone requests information. If you are new, most brokers will require that you complete all the training programs before you perform floor duty.

Take floor duty as often as you can. In an active office, it could result in several excellent contacts each day. Almost 20 percent of my total income while I was in real estate came as a direct result of days on the floor. There's an adage among the troops in the military you should "never volunteer for anything!" Floor duty is definitely an exception to that rule.


## TYPES OF INQUIRIES


You will most commonly deal with two types of inquiries when you are on floor duty—call-ins and walk-ins. Here are some tips for handling these prospects.

■ *Call-ins.* If an individual calls on a "home for sale" ad, he or she generally wants just one piece of information: the location of the property (assuming the price is stated in the ad). What he or she wants to do is what you would probably want to do under similar circumstances—drive by to see if it looks interesting.

No training program or text on real estate with which I am familiar advocates giving out the addresses in such instances. Some brokers absolutely refuse to let their agents do so. The fear is that the caller will drive by and, if he likes it, contact some other real estate company and buy through it.

There is an alternative approach that works well for some agents. Unless the homeowners have specifically requested that the address of their home not be given out for "drive-bys" (rare, but possible), give the callers the information they want. Proponents of this approach maintain that callers are so relieved that they don't have to agree to an appointment to get the information that they become very easy to work with. In addition, there can be no argument that it certainly gets exposure for the seller's home.

With any call, your basic objective is to get to know the caller and sound like what you are: an informed real estate professional. You also need information, so try to finish each telephone conversation with the person's name, address, phone number, the type of home they are looking for, and a good idea of the caller's financial status. That may seem ambitious and even pushy, but you can't effectively solve housing problems unless you know the capabilities and limitations of the people involved.

If they do not wish to immediately share such information, do not persist. Never antagonize a caller—it's mighty easy for them to hang up and deal with someone who is more congenial. At some point, ask if it would be acceptable for you to call later if you encounter a listing that seems particularly well suited for them. With just a little experience and confidence, you can expect a very high percentage of "yes" answers. If that doesn't happen, you're doing something wrong.

When you do get names and addresses, immediately send a note with your card thanking the person for calling. If your conversation progresses beyond a simple exchange of information, inquire as to whether the caller has been working with anyone else in your office. If so, professional courtesy dictates that you inform that salesperson and turn the follow-up over to them.

It is not unusual for someone who calls on one of your broker's ads to be calling several other real estate companies about their ads at the same time. The person may be in town on a house-hunting trip, sitting in a motel room with the real estate section of your local paper spread out. Ask if there is any other ad they would like information about. Information on most properties is in multiple listings and thus immediately available to you; if the house is not multiple listed you can get the information with a quick phone call to the listing broker. Assure the caller that you can show any house in which he or she has an interest, or you can put the caller in touch with someone who can.

Further, tell the caller that if he or she drives past a house with any real estate company's "For Sale" sign in front of it and wants to know the price, to call you. Many people think that the only company that can show or sell a house is the one whose sign is in front of it. (OK, I admit it. That's what I thought before I got my real estate license.) If a caller judges you to be honest and you are responsive, it is likely that you will turn out to be his or her sole real estate contact. The ultimate compliment will occur when one of your prospects calls and wants you to check on a "For Sale by Owner," for you may be able to get a one-party listing in such an instance.

▪ *Walk-ins.* As the name implies, walk-ins are people who visit your office unannounced, wanting real estate information. When you talk to them your goal will be to gain their confidence and gather as much information as possible. Occasionally, however, walk-ins will have done so to look at a specific property with the intention of buying it if they like it, or listing a piece of property they own. If that's the case, naturally you will not waste time with a lot of formalities.

## PREPARING FOR FLOOR DUTY

Given the importance of floor duty, there are several things you should do to prepare for it. Make sure that you know well in advance when it is to be your turn "up." Mark the date on your calendar and make no other commitments for that day. Arrange for a back-up to be on call if you have to leave the office for an extended period. Most agents have slipped up once, arriving at work unaware that they have floor duty. The ensuing panic is generally adequate to ensure that it does not happen again.

On the day you are actually on duty, get to your desk even earlier than usual so you will be prepared if you get a call or a walk-in right at the opening of business. Some house hunters are very early starters. Because many of the inquiries you receive will be in response to ads, make certain you are thoroughly familiar with those of your company, both the current ones and those from the immediate past. There is no substitute for firsthand knowledge, so try to personally visit each of the properties advertised.

Most companies discuss upcoming ads during staff meetings, with the listing agents presiding. Current ads will represent only a portion of your brokerage's total listings, so it is essential that you bring yourself completely up-to-date on all the listings. Try to visit each property with the listing salesperson when the home is listed. Otherwise, you will have to hustle to catch up by looking at the ones you have missed, for it is crucial that you know the total inventory. If there are "listing caravans" in your locality where specific days are set aside to visit new listings try hard to take advantage of them.

It is also important to read the ads of the other real estate companies in the area so you can respond intelligently if you are asked about their listings. Using all the information you have from all sources, prepare a short list of select properties, similar to the ones in your ad. You will then be prepared to suggest alternatives if the advertised property does not meet the buyer's needs.

Have a form ready on which to record each call-in and walk-in. Your office will likely have a log for this. When you actually answer the phone, a simple and confident, "Professional Realty, Sally Smith" gives the caller all the information needed to proceed. Some agents insist upon answering with a mini-filibuster ("Good morning! Thanks for calling Professional Realty, where service makes the difference. This is Sally Smith. How may I help you solve your housing problems?"), but that technique seems a little contrived. An effective way of handling calls you receive at home is to answer with just your name. Simply saying "Hello" doesn't really help much.


## RECOGNIZING SPECIAL TARGETS

Certain groups of home buyers have exceptional potential. The better you understand them, the better the possibility of doing business with them.

### *Incoming Job Transfers*

People moving to your area because their company has transferred them will probably have sold homes elsewhere and will have sizable amounts of money to put down. If they made a profit on the sale of their last home, they will be motivated to reinvest in another to defer any capital gains tax. You could hardly ask for a better group with which to work.

Identify the companies, businesses, federal and state agencies, hospitals, universities, and other schools that have large numbers of employees. Those that are expanding or have high turnover rates have the greatest potential for generating customers for you. If you live near a military installation, you have the ingredients for sustained activity, for the military rotates its personnel every few years as a matter of policy. Be aware when you sell to a military family, however, that they will, in all likelihood, be moving in three or four years. Make sure the home is one you think you can resell for the family later.

Some agents work exclusively in corporate or organizational relocation and do very well, once they have established their procedures and contacts. Check with your broker to see if there is a program in your firm. Chances are there will be some gaps. Identify those and determine the best way to fill them. If your broker is established within the community, he or she may be able to arrange a meeting with personnel directors, but don't depend upon this, and be prepared to do the leg work yourself.

What you are after are the names of people who are coming in for either jobs or job interviews. You would like to be able to send them material, refer them to your home page on the Internet, contact them by phone, and meet with them when they are in town. If you have prepared a professional looking information packet that includes maps and information about real estate, weather, schools, shopping, medical facilities, transportation, churches, recreation, and the like, there is a chance that the personnel director might be willing to work with you. Done properly, your efforts could save the company time and expense, for this is the kind of service they would normally provide.

Do not, however, discount the importance of informal contacts. Department heads, foremen, and supervisors provide the kinds of grassroots sources that are generally built up over a period of time as a result of personal referrals.

The potential of working with a corporate program can be impressive. In our local community, for example, there is a division of an internationally successful electronics firm. As a result of various programs and referrals, I sold homes to sixteen of their employees (mostly engineers). Without exception, they knew what they wanted, knew what they could afford, recognized it when they saw it, and acted decisively. If you can locate and cultivate a similar source, I can assure you that you will enjoy real estate sales.

### Buyers Who Qualify for Specialized Programs

Any agent who has worked with a veteran in processing a Veterans Administration (VA) loan is well aware that it takes both specialized knowledge and a general appreciation of how large bureaucracies work. There are a variety of such federal and state programs; some have been around for years, while others come and go. All have very precise eligibility requirements. If you become an expert in who qualifies for what, you can develop a reputation that will attract potential participants to you. Some agents announce their expertise right on their business cards ("Specialist in Veterans' Affairs").

Knowing the eligibility requirements, however, is only part of the equation, and not the hardest part at that. You must appreciate how things get done in a bureaucracy (and at what pace) and what motivates program administrators and what does not.

First, there will be a series of specific steps that must be taken and an abundance of forms that must be filled out in a very explicit way. There is no point in fussing about the foolishness or redundancy of any task or any part of the paperwork. It is written in stone. Do the drudge work cheerfully and exactly as required.

Second, bureaucrats are not excited by the profit motive. They will get paid the same amount whether your loan application is processed or not. The finest among them are dedicated public servants trying to do the best job they can with an often overwhelming workload. The worst defy rational analysis. Bad-tempered badgering will get you nowhere, except perhaps to have your loan application end up at the bottom of the pile. Make everyone's job as easy as possible by doing things the way they have to be done. (Not everyone is temperamentally able to follow this advice. One of my survey participants seemed thoroughly convinced that his local VA representative was an operative of an unfriendly government planted there to sabotage our capitalistic system.)

If you can master the intricacies of any specialized program and know how to work within the system, it will provide you with a valuable source of income. But you will earn every penny you make.

## BEING CREATIVE

Your local situation and your imagination will dictate what possibilities exist. Let me describe how my wife and I turned our company's arrangement with the Chamber of Commerce into a program that resulted in ten to twelve home sales a year.

When people are considering moving into a new community, they quite often write the Chamber of Commerce for information. Our chamber maintained a file of those letters and shared them with local real estate agents who were members. That file turned out to be a gold mine of prospects. Once each week my wife reviewed incoming letters. During some weeks there might be 30 or 40 (and ours is a community of only about 40,000). She read each letter and jotted down the essential information, such as name and address, along with any pertinent statements from the letters, such as, "We hope to be able to move to your city as soon as our home here sells." We would then prepare a cover letter and a packet of information that showed samples of listings currently on the market. Primarily, we used flyers from listings in our office (mostly my own). I wrote a personal note at the bottom of each letter, included a housing questionnaire, a stamped, addressed envelope, and my business card, and promptly mailed the entire package out to the prospect.

We mailed all the packets out by Tuesday of each week and Saturday morning I followed up with phone calls to the most promising prospects. Although the same information was available to every other real estate office in town, ours was the only one with a centralized program handled by a single agent. The result was that we accounted for the majority of all sales in the community from this source.

If your chamber does not have a program of this kind, start one. If they do, do not be afraid of the competition, for you will be going after a lucrative market. People who write ahead to a community in advance of their move are quite often well-organized problem solvers. They gather all the information available before making a decision. Chances are good that they have used these same skills in solving other problems, such as how to amass enough money to afford the home of their choice.

### QUALIFYING BUYERS

Qualifying a buyer simply means finding out how much the buyer can afford. It is your most critical immediate task. If you don't do this correctly, you do not pass "Go" and you do not collect any money. Qualifying buyers is a step that is awkward for some real estate agents, even experienced ones. It should not be, for it will be impossible for you to work productively with buyers if you do not have the information. You do not want to waste their time or yours by showing them properties out of their price range, or by showing them anything, if they can't afford to buy at all. If they do make an offer and need financing, a steely-eyed, no-nonsense loan officer at a lending institution will ask the same hard questions in conjunction with a loan application, so why not get the information at the start? Of course, the ideal situation would be for the buyers to prequalify with a lending institution before they even start looking at homes.

Do not judge buyers without investigation, for looks can be deceiving. The couple who drives up in the clanking pickup truck dressed like refugees from Skunk Hollow may be cash customers for the spendiest item in your inventory. On the other hand, I once spent almost a week showing the most expensive homes in town to a couple who dazzled me with their big talk, wardrobe, car, and $100 dollar hairdo (his). To be charitable, let's just say that as it turned out, their tastes exceeded their financial capabilities—by a very wide margin. The key is to ask the right questions and do some discreet checking of your own.

### ARE PURCHASERS PREVARICATORS?

Buyers generally have a pretty good idea of what they want. It is wise to ask them, take notes, and show them the kind of property they say they are after. All of this assumes, of course, that they can afford what they say they want. For some reason I do not yet fully understand, it is hard for many agents to listen to buyers. They seem almost compelled to dominate the conversation and tell folks what they *should* want. This is not to say that you should not be flexible, for everyone who has sold real estate has a story about people who say they are interested in one type of home and end up falling in love with and buying something quite different (in a worst case scenario from another agent, after you have spent untold hours showing them what they *said* they wanted). It would be dangerous to conclude, however, that buyers do not know their own minds, or are somehow being less than honest with you. In the normal course of events, they typically select something very close to what they indicated they prefer, assuming it is available.

It is particularly bad form to try to manipulate buyers toward specific listings in which you, your broker, or some other agent in your office has a vested interest. This does not mean you should not show your own listings, but it does mean that you will lose a lot of sales if your judgment is clouded by any factor other than selecting properties that best meet the buyers' expressed interests and qualifications. There are plenty of very competent real estate agents who have the good sense to show buyers what they want, not what the agent or broker wants to sell them.

## GETTING IT FINANCED

When mortgage money is plentiful, and when it can be borrowed at reasonable interest rates, financing is a comparatively easy step in the home-buying process. When interest rates soar, as they have an aggravating habit of doing periodically, lenders become nervous and buyers have trouble qualifying. When that happens, the type of financing available on a particular property often becomes the most important factor in the whole process. To ensure your long-term success, you must continually stay on top of what is going on in the home financing market. These are the basic options.

▪ *Fixed rate loans.* Long-term fixed rate loans will continue to be available, but they will command the premium interest rate. Because this is the type of financing that most consumers understand and have experience with, it is by far their first choice. Know what the current rates are and use them as your standard of comparison for other options.

■ *Adjustable Rate Mortgages (ARMs).* In the past, lenders were badly burned when changing economic circumstances forced them to start paying more for their money while their assets were tied up in long-term, low-yielding real estate loans. To protect themselves, they have searched for alternative forms of home financing. The problem has been to find a solution that lenders like and that consumers will accept.

The program that has emerged as the leading contender is the ARM. In this loan the interest rate is adjusted periodically (up and down) using as a basis some objective "cost of funds" standard. There will typically be a limit on how much a loan can go up during a year or over the life of the loan (called "caps"). The main problem with the ARM is that people do not as a rule consider "worst case scenarios" and realistically assess their capability of making ends meet if their ARM goes to the limit. Lenders like ARMs, since the rate fluctuation risk is passed on to the borrower, so they offer ARMs at an attractive rate. Just make sure your buyers are fully educated.

■ *Federal Housing Administration (FHA) and Veterans Administration (VA).* These two programs have been in existence through good times and bad and have provided sorely needed stability to the home financing industry. Each will likely continue to offer traditional fixed rate loans as well as many of the newer options. Because of their widespread familiarity, and because of their built-in, consumer-protection features, buyers will want to know what is available through the FHA and VA, so you need to be well informed about them.

■ *Creative Financing.* When traditional ways of solving problems no longer work, and where large sums of money are involved, ingenious solutions emerge. In home buying, these solutions are called "creative financing." Although it is a term that covers a broad range of techniques, owner-assisted financing is one of the most common. Let's say a seller has a $100,000 equity in a $300,000 home, along with a very attractive, low-interest, assumable loan of $100,000. For $20,000 down and promissory for $80,000 (secured by a second mortgage) at "interest only" payments of 10 percent, with a three-year balloon, he or she will sell the home. The buyer assumes the underlying loan. The idea is that this will make the home affordable to the buyer, and during the three-year period it can be refinanced. There will be no problem if the buyer can find affordable refinancing. If he or she cannot, there may be trouble.

Owner-assisted financing is a legitimate and accepted means of facilitating a real estate transaction, but great care has to be exercised to ensure that it is fair to all parties, and particularly to the buyer, whom you represent. All too often, creative financing has simply meant that buyers end up getting in over their heads because a transaction was made too easy for them, or they buy a piece of property that could not have qualified for financing through standard methods.

You see here a practical application of the principal of agency and real world ethics. You are legally and ethically required to put your client buyer's interests first, certainly above your own. If you arrange shaky creative financing that gets the deal done and earns you a payday, that's in your best interests. But if down the road it comes back to bite your buyer, then you've obviously violated your fiduciary responsibility. It's also very bad business. Word gets around.

As noted in the above example, an element of creative financing may involve assuming a loan that already exists on the property. The only safe way to determine whether or not a loan may be assumed, and on what terms, is to contact the lending institution in writing. A lot of innocent (and some not-so-innocent) buyers have been led to believe by unscrupulous sellers (and, regrettably, by real estate agents) that a loan was assumable when that was not the case. If the buyers do not plan to openly contact the lender and follow their instructions about assuming the loan, urge them to consult a real estate attorney for advice before proceeding. Make your recommendation in writing so it will be a matter of record.

## SHOWING PROPERTIES

Although you will be current on the general inventory, you will have to revisit properties you have selected to show a specific prospect. You will also want to review your files on expired listings and fizzbos to see if there are any possibilities for a one-party listing. When looking at the material on the multiple listing service, read the information carefully. If it says to show only in the afternoons, that is when you need to make the appointment. If it says not to let the cat out of the garage or not to pet Fang the Doberman, take notes.

It is unrealistic to show more than five or six properties in one outing, unless the buyers have limited time and must work at an accelerated pace. To make the job easier, provide them with a form on which they can make notes about the houses they see. After a while even the most veteran house hunters start to confuse properties. It is also wise to give them a copy of the sales agreement they will use when they make an offer, so they can study it.

Geographic convenience will likely dictate the order in which you show homes. I do not advocate showing less desirable houses first to "set up" the remainder so they look good by comparison. That technique, although still used, is so transparent that it will cost you in credibility. At the close of (or during) each house-hunting session, ask for feedback to see if you are on the right track.

## HORROR STORY (PG-13)

Let me tell you a brief little horror story, designed to convince you to do your homework thoroughly before you show property. It is embarrassingly true.

I was working with a couple from Los Angeles with whom I had made contact as a result of our Chamber of Commerce prospecting program. Both were executives in a large company. They were articulate, affluent, and an absolute delight to work with. Their daughter, who was a nurse, was moving to our city to work in the local hospital. They were interested in locating a duplex or fourplex for her to live in and as an investment for them.

The choices in our small town were rather limited, but there were four properties I thought might have potential. Far and away my first choice was a beautiful duplex that had just come out on multiple listing. I had visited it when it was brand new a year or so earlier, and it was classy—just like the people from L.A.

The showing instructions said that no appointment was necessary and that the keys were in the mailbox. The three of us arrived and I looked in the mailbox. No keys. "Maybe they put them under the doormat," my resourceful prospect volunteered. He was right.

I let us in and it was apparent I had made the right choice. They were dazzled. It was exactly what they were looking for. You just love moments like that, when it all comes together.

"Oh, it even has a wood stove!" the wife says. Wood stove? I didn't recall the listing saying anything about a wood stove. I got nervous and started checking other features against my listing book.

"We may have a little trouble here folks," I announced as I ran out to the front door to check the house number. "We are in the wrong duplex. The one across the street is for sale."

When I saw the blurry picture with the familiar street name in the multiple listing book, I incorrectly assumed the duplex was the nifty one I had visited earlier. (The one across the street was not nifty.)

The story does have a happy ending, for we found another property that fit my prospects' needs. They never even told my broker about my shortcomings as an address finder, but if the tenant had been home and had suffered cardiac arrest when three well-dressed intruders burst in, I would just about now be qualifying for a work-release program.

## CLOSING A SALE

In sales terminology, a sale is "closed" when customers sign their names to whatever documents are necessary to approve the transaction. In real estate, it happens when a buyer signs the offer to purchase. (Do not confuse this with the "closing" that takes place later when all legal documents are signed and the ownership of property is formally transferred.) There can be no argument as to the importance of the closing step in the initial sales process, for without it the commissioned salesperson never makes any money. There are, however, basic philosophical differences among those in the profession about how salespeople should conduct themselves in working with customers in reaching the critical buying decision.

The most prevalent theory, encountered in almost all sales training programs, is that folks need to be helped along in the decision-making process. To do this, a whole series of closing techniques have been devised, named, cataloged, and taught. Each is designed to facilitate the process as you guide your prospects smoothly and efficiently toward the major "close" by achieving a series of "minor closes" (less important decisions the client makes along the way).

One overly simplified technique, using a setting outside of real estate, will illustrate. It is called the "alternative-of-choice close." Assume you are in a store looking at suits. After some time the clerk asks, "Do you want the blue suit or the brown?" Either choice is acceptable to him, when in fact you may not want either one, or for that matter, anything he has in the store. Books on real estate and training programs routinely cover closing techniques as though there was no argument about whether or not they fulfill the spirit of the agency relationship, or whether they are ethical.

Those who question the appropriateness of the procedures such as this do so on the grounds that they are manipulative and hence unprofessional. They maintain that the only acceptable closing technique is to provide people all the information they need to make an informed choice, and then permit them the courtesy of reaching their decision in their own time.

## HANDLING OFFERS

One of the most exciting moments in real estate occurs when prospective purchasers do, in fact, decide to buy. How you handle the offer influences greatly whether or not it will be accepted.

■ *The offering price.* Since we are assuming that you are representing the buyers as "buyers" agent, your fiduciary responsibility is to them. That means you should attempt to negotiate the best possible price. "How much do you think they will take?" is the inevitable question.

Even the least sophisticated first-time buyers seem to have been told never to offer full price for a home. All parties ordinarily expect some give and take, and that's generally what happens, but the buyers must ultimately determine what their offering price will be. How much can they afford? How much do they want the house? Is it a buyer's market or a seller's market? Is the home priced competitively with other similar properties on the market? Do let your buyers know that they are not operating in a vacuum, and that as long as the owners have not accepted an offer, the house is on the market.

■ *The amount of earnest money.* "Earnest money" is a deposit made by the buyer as evidence of good faith. It is customary for the buyer to give the seller earnest money when the offer is made. Some buyers do not seem very earnest. If they want to put up $100 earnest money on a $200,000 house, counsel them to reconsider. I know it's hard to believe, but some buyers do not realize that their earnest money is applied against the expenses of their purchase. They think it is an extra charge, so make it clear.

■ *Preparation of estimated buyer costs.* Before buyers actually sign an offer to purchase, they should be given a written estimate of the total costs involved, including their one-time expenses incident to closing and their recurrent monthly payments. In some jurisdictions, the form you use is prescribed for you. Whatever the case, the objective is to inform the buyers before they make a commitment. Some brokers think that introducing a form such as this just when the buyers have reached the decision to sign takes the bloom off an otherwise rapturous moment, but it is best if cool and objective heads prevail throughout.

▪ *Presenting the offer.* Once buyers have signed the offer and delivered an earnest money check, the operative term becomes "time is of the essence!" In other words, *hustle!* "You snooze, you lose" is the term those in the trade use. Contact the listing broker immediately, tell him or her that you have an offer, and ask for the earliest opportunity to present it. Rest assured that the sellers are intensely interested in seeing all offers as soon as possible. If you get an offer at 6 P.M., try to get together with the sellers at 7 P.M. or 8 P.M. Try to secure permission to present the offer yourself (with the listing agent present), local rules and courtesies permitting. Remember that you have buyers who have emotionally committed to a house and who are anxiously awaiting a decision. Get the ball out of your court immediately. The first time you lose a sale because you dawdled, it will make a believer out of you. There are times in real estate when you need to push, and this is one of them.

▪ *Negotiating the offer.* The more complex the transaction, the more likely it is that some negotiation will be required. In residential sales, negotiations are ordinarily straightforward and relate mainly to price. If the sellers want to counter the offer, there is a simple form that permits that, listing their specific counter proposal. The important thing to remember in any negotiation process is to keep it as businesslike and unemotional as possible. Isolate areas of disagreement and quantify them, if possible. It is amazing how excited people often become over matters that may amount to a comparatively few dollars. Put in the proper context (how much does it cost?), such issues often evaporate.

▪ *Using your commission to resolve conflicts.* Two generally accepted rules regarding the brokerage fee are: (1) do not give away any part of your fee to hold a transaction together until and unless absolutely necessary, and (2) something is better than nothing. If, early in the negotiation process, you volunteer to pay for certain items out of your brokerage fee, it is amazing how the participants will then look to you to resolve future conflicts in the same way. Remember also that you need your broker's approval to commit any portion of the commission, but if it means kicking in $100 to solve a problem and save a $5,000 fee, you know what the answer will be.

COUNTDOWN TO PAYDAY

After you have an accepted offer the painstaking, unglamorous work begins. Whether or not you eventually get paid for all your efforts depends upon your ability and willingness to follow through.

■ *The loan application.* Assuming they have not already prequalified, go with your buyers to make a formal loan application. Let them know exactly the kind of information the loan officer will need, such as savings account numbers, credit references, and so on. As a matter of fact, give them a copy of the loan application itself ahead of time to prepare them for their meeting. When the appointment takes place, remember that this is the loan officer's moment, not yours. Volunteer information, if needed, but generally keep an amiable low profile.

The buyers will want to know how long it will take for loan approval and so will you, so ask if they do not. Make notes about any items the buyers might have to research and produce later, and follow up to make sure they do. As part of the loan application process, the lender is required by federal law to give the applicants a good faith estimate of the settlement charges that they will likely incur. The information should be essentially the same as the estimate you prepared when the earnest money was signed. If there are significant differences, determine why and explain the reasons to the buyers.

You will know by the conclusion of the meeting whether you can anticipate problems. Unless you have made a serious error in qualifying the buyers, the loan application meeting is ordinarily short, businesslike, and cordial. Every four or five days after the meeting, call the loan officer and see if everything is progressing well. If something needs to be done, volunteer your services, if appropriate. Keep in constant contact with the buyers and let them know everything you know. "Buyers remorse" (when buyers are unhappy with their decision) seems mainly to afflict buyers who were hustled through the buying process and then left to fend for themselves.

■ *Closing.* Procedures vary around the country as to who chooses the title company or attorney who will do the title research and the closing itself. No matter who chooses and who pays, you need to establish immediate contact with the "action officer"—the person who will do the actual work. Provide anything needed and follow up every few days.

At the closing itself (in most areas there's a formal meeting), you will again be a guest, but if you have done your job properly you will know more about the entire transaction than anyone at the table. (In most states, sellers and buyers have separate closings, although in some states, it is combined.) Because closing is the time when all final documents are signed and money changes hands, it can be tense and small misunderstandings can escalate. It is a good policy to go over the official documents with the closing officer *well before* the buyers arrive to make sure you understand everything fully.

In most areas, buyers will have to show up at the close with some kind of negotiable instrument, such as a certified check or bank draft in a specific amount. Be sure they know that amount and that they are aware that a personal check will not do. As a final action, some type of gift to the buyers is appropriate. If your local multiple listing service has taken a photo of the home, you can use that, or an enlargement of it, in a nice frame.

▪ *After closing.* If your buyers will give you permission, send notices to their new neighbors that they are moving in. Most people think this is a great idea, but there are those who do not. Not only is it a good ice-breaker for the newcomers, it is good exposure for you. You should also call a "Welcome Wagon" if the folks are new to the community.

## IT IS WORK—BUT IT GETS EASIER

Your first exposure to the whole residential selling process could well make you want to sit down and have a good cry, because it sounds so hopelessly complex. It is work and there are details to be taken care of, but much of it will become a smooth-running routine after the first few sales. You will waste less time bogged down on dead-end missions with unqualified buyers (the terminal scourge of so many agents) and you will know who to contact to get things done and where to go to get straight answers to your questions. Remember, too, that only a small percentage of your competition will be working as hard and as smart as you. Finally, you will feel real personal satisfaction when you help people solve one of the most important problems they will ever face—how to buy a home.

# 8

# Listing and Selling Specialized Properties

### Custom-Built Homes, Investment Properties, Rural Properties, and More

Even as you are busily getting established in residential real estate, it will become clear to you that there is a lot more to the profession than just listing and selling homes. You may see another salesperson in your office list and market a $750,000 farm (it will make you giddy just to think about what your share of a commission like that would be). At the local Realtors meeting, you might hear about a multi-million-dollar commercial deal put together by several agents you know (now we are talking big money). Or you could read about a 40-year-old ex-housewife in Indiana who, after only a year in the business, is earning a high six-figure annual income structuring real estate exchanges. Your interest will definitely be piqued.

## BYPASSING "HARD KNOCKS U."

If you are accustomed to earning a $2,000 or $3,000 commission on your real estate transactions, and you suddenly see an opportunity to earn five or ten times that much, you'll be tempted to drop everything and concentrate on the big money. That's a fine idea—if you know what you are doing. The sad fact of the matter is that much too often the novice develops delusions of grandeur ("Good Lord, that would mean a $15,000 commission!"), gets in over his or her head, attempts to bluff and bluster the way through, and ends up with nothing but a very costly lesson in the real estate facts of life. My purpose in this chapter is to look at some of the possibilities for career broadening that you will be exposed to just as a result of being active in general real estate, and to offer some counsel on how to best take advantage of them.

First, here are a few friendly suggestions.

1. *Don't cut yourself off from other income.* If you have developed a reasonably stable income from listing and selling residential real estate, it is a good idea to maintain at least a minimal level of activity in those functions. You will want to retain your residential sales expertise and stay in touch with previous contacts to take advantage of their follow-up business. You may also need the money. Before you burn any bridges behind you, make sure you won't have to go back over the river now and then.

2. *Get help from professionals.* A true professional knows the limits of his or her own knowledge and seeks assistance when it's needed. Just as some few real estate agents have trouble listening, there are others, I am told, who consider it a sign of weakness to admit there are a few areas in which they are not expert. That could be a fatal flaw. It will be time and money well spent to get help when you need it.

Let's say, for example, that you are going to list a home on a large acreage that also has marketable trees on it. Chances are that it would be a hard property for you to price, but there are professionals you could consult who specialize in appraising the value of standing timber. Any prospective purchaser who is even slightly cautious would insist upon some proof of estimated value. Ordinarily, the cost of professional service will be borne by either the sellers or buyers, although it is not always easy to convince them of that. Whoever pays, it is a wise investment. Be particularly wary when you enter the murky waters of law and tax accounting.

3. *Get help from the home front.* There may be an experienced agent within your office who concentrates activities in some narrow segment of real estate, such as investments or rural properties. If so, you will need to check with your broker on the ground rules, for some insist that only certain agents become involved in the specialized fields. Even if that is the case, it is not always easy to precisely categorize each potential transaction.

Let's say a former client of yours from a residential transaction comes to you and asks for your help in putting together a complex real estate investment venture. You immediately recognize two things: One, whoever puts the deal together will make a whole lot of money, and two, you are in over your head. What you may wish to do is secure your broker's permission to work with an agent in the office who has experience in such transactions. An agreed-upon split in the commission that recognizes the relative contribution of effort would be appropriate. You gain valuable experience, retain your client for the long term, and make some money. Your clients get the type of professional attention they deserve, and the other agent is compensated for technical expertise.

4. *Watch your backside.* You should realize that when you first begin to deal in these specialized activities you will encounter many buyers, sellers, and other real estate agents who will know a great deal more about what is going on than you do. It is an environment that demands caution. A prospective client, for example, can quickly find out how informed you are by asking you a question to which he or she already knows the answer. You may not think such a tactic is particularly nice, but it is very common and very effective. Some people will simply write you off and not do business with you if they judge you to be uniformed. Others (particularly those on the other side of the bargaining table) may relish the idea of working with someone whose zeal and ambition exceeds their skill and judgment, but it would be the type of relationship you would want to avoid.

## TYPES OF SPECIALIZED PROPERTIES

Here is an overview of some specialized areas of real estate that may have an attraction for you, while you are still active in a general brokerage.

■ *Speculation homes.* In a brisk, fast-moving real estate market, many professional homebuilders construct what they call "spec" (speculation) homes. This simply means that they build the homes before they have a buyer and gamble that they will sell before costs associated with construction and financing eat away the potential profit. The ultimate example of this can be seen in large subdivisions, where a builder will have several model homes constructed for purchasers to inspect, and replicas of these models in the subdivision to purchase. It is a pretty straightforward transaction to sell a home that is already completed or one that will be built to emulate a preexisting structure that the buyer can examine.

Some builders employ a sales staff of their own and do not work with other real estate brokerages. Others have a sales staff, but will "co-op" (split the commission with the selling agent). Still others have no sales staff and list their homes with a real estate broker. Those are typically put on Multiple, making them available for sale by all members.

- *Custom-built homes.* Another alternative is the custom-built home. In this arrangement the buyer purchases a lot and then looks for a builder to construct the individualized home. Very frequently you may be involved in not only locating the lot, but also in recommending a builder with whom to work. In those cases, you would collect a referral fee from the builder (it could be a flat fee or a small percentage of the sales price), and then let the buyers and builder proceed with the project.

- *Residential multi-family investment properties.* It is quite common for an agent specializing in residential sales to encounter a prospect who wishes to buy a small investment property such as a duplex, fourplex, or sixplex. With just a little research and practice, you should be able to handle these transactions with confidence.

There are straightforward and generally agreed upon guidelines that you can apply to any income-producing residential property to determine the quality of the investment for a particular individual. Standard forms are readily available in all states, and with just a moderate amount of training you can complete them quickly and explain them to others. There are computer programs that let you perform the same type of analyses, only a lot faster.

Whether you do it manually or with a computer, the expenses of ownership are compared to rents received to come up with a before-tax monthly cash flow. The individual's specific tax status would determine the after-tax position. This approach can be used whether you are considering an individual house that a buyer might wish to purchase as an investment property, or a two-hundred-unit apartment complex.

A word of caution: Some owners of residential investment property have been known to inflate their income figures when trying to sell. No buyer should commit himself without verifying the information by reviewing the owner's latest federal income tax return, which lists each property separately. The owner's motivation when filling out a tax return is to list all expenses and to not report income not received. If you are working with an owner on a potential listing, diplomatically let him or her know that buyers are going to want to see basic documents. He or she may be inclined to be more conservative when deciding how much to ask for the property.

■ *Businesses.* Somewhere along the line, you are likely to encounter someone who has a yen to buy or establish a small business. It's the dream of a lot of people.

The sobering fact about businesses, particularly the small ones, is that they fail at an alarming rate. My experience in dealing with people who are thinking of setting up their own reveals a startling amount of naivete and innocence on their part. Your first chore in dealing with them is to determine their depth of knowledge and their financial capability. If they are very experienced in business matters, you will probably learn from them. If they are not, recommend that they enlist the services of both an accountant and an attorney and that they talk with the business loan officer at the local bank before you begin a serious search for possible opportunities. You may have to take the initiative in arranging the meeting. Make certain everyone has a clear understanding of intentions, capabilities, and limitations.

■ *Investment property exchanges.* As you become experienced in listing and selling investment property, you may find you have a flair for it. If so, you may wish to consider putting together exchange transactions.

People exchange investment properties for two major reasons. First, there are substantial income tax advantages. Rules have changed through the years, but the basic concept has remained intact: Taxes on a profit realized upon the disposition of investment real estate can be deferred if the property is exchanged for like property of higher value.

Let's say someone bought a duplex from you five years ago and has built up a huge equity in that property. If the investor were to sell the duplex now, he or she would face a tax on the profit. If he or she exchanges it, say for a sixplex, however, the tax payment can be delayed (not avoided). At the same time, your investor's continuing year-to-year tax advantage would almost certainly be improved by acquiring a larger property.

The second major reason for exchanging property is to use the built-up equity in much the same manner as cash. If owners sold the property to get at their money, not only will they trigger tax consequences, they may encounter substantial transaction fees and might have to carry back part of their equity in the form of a contract with the purchaser.

An agent who becomes really skilled in exchange techniques is rare.

Those who do so are so sought after that they are among the best-paid agents in the industry. Because several properties are generally involved in an exchange, there is excellent income potential. It is possible to become well versed enough to handle comparatively simple exchanges and still conduct other real estate activities, but if you really get serious you will be compelled to do it on a full-time basis.

■ *Investment groups.* Large, high-priced investments often present the best opportunities, but the small investor is generally not able to participate. However, if several small investors band together into an investment group, they would have the assets needed to go after more expensive properties; a group of, say, ten people with $30,000 each to invest has a lot of clout and staying power. If you can structure such a group, the potential is there for you to handle acquisition and disposition of properties for the group.

As you are getting established, keep track of people with whom you have worked who might be logical candidates for an investment group, and keep in mind that compatibility of investment objectives is critical. You might not need a lot of cash to participate in the group yourself, for there will be a commission paid on the transactions, part of which will be yours to use as a portion of your contribution. No matter how successful you become, remember that you need to discuss forming an investment group with your broker before you proceed. Your activities could be subject to Securities and Exchange Commission rules as well as real estate laws.

■ *Rural properties.* The desire for "five acres and independence in the country" is a bug that has bitten a lot of people. You could be dealing with buyers who want "a place in the country," or sellers *with* a place in the country who have tried it and desperately want something else instead. Before you lace up your boots and slip into your Levis, a few matters unique to rural property need to be mentioned.

Any acreage, whether small or large, should be surveyed and marked prior to a sale. Ideally, that will have been done by the owners when they listed the property, but not always, since it can be expensive. The consequences of finding that the beautiful knoll on which the buyers want to build their dream house is actually on the neighbor's property are dire, so it is better to resolve the issue early. Don't rely on fences to accurately indicate property lines. Take it from someone who made that mistake— once.

You also need to be sure that you understand state and federal tax rules as they pertain to rural and farm property. In many states, tax advantages are given to those who use their land for certain agricultural purposes. To be eligible, the owners must meet specific qualifications. If they sell to someone and the property use changes, the land may not continue to qualify for the favored tax treatment. In fact, the new owners could be liable for deferred taxes from *before they owned the land!* Get the tax information from the owners, verify it with the county tax assessor, and ensure that the buyers (and you) know exactly what is going on. Include the information on the sales documents so it is a matter of written agreement.

Zoning is another subject about which you need to be clear. In many areas, land use laws are quite restrictive. If you locate a beautiful twenty-acre parcel in the hills with a magnificent view and building site, don't automatically assume that a residence can be built on it, although that *might* be the case. There's a chance that the zoning laws may preclude it from being used for residential purposes. Even more restrictive are prohibitions against dividing large parcels of land. Many buyers are under the mistaken impression that they can pretty well partition their land any way they wish. In most places that is just not true any longer.

Building a house in the country is different from building one in the city. If you list or sell a residential lot in a subdivision inside the city limits, you can be reasonably confident that a house can be built on it. Even so it is a good idea to check with local authorities to determine the costs associated with hooking up city water and sewer services, and to find out whether or not any major improvement projects (such as road widening) are planned for which property owners would be financially liable.

Outside the city limits there are other things to think about. First and most important, determine what conditions have to be met before a building permit can be issued. Generally, the owner must have a water source and a sewage disposal capability. Septic systems and wells will no doubt be used. There is a great deal to know about each, so educate yourself before you get too involved. City and county officials possess the most up-to-date, unbiased information. If you did not meet with these people as part of your office training program, arrange with your broker to invite them to a staff training session.

## WHEN YOU RUN INTO A CLOSED DOOR

If you like diversity in your job, you will love real estate. Your problem will be to restrain yourself from running off in all directions at once to take advantage of what are clearly great opportunities. As you are learning the basics of your trade, and as you start to expand your activities, it is inevitable that you will get your nose bloodied occasionally. One response is to pull into a shell, become less adventurous, and avoid unfamiliar situations. In real estate, that is a formula for disaster. The preferred reaction is to shake it off and press on with a somewhat more seasoned brand of enthusiasm.

# 9

# *Avoiding Problems*

## *Things to Watch Out For From Day One*

Precautionary paralysis is a common affliction. You see it in the teenage driver who, after conscientiously studying the driver's manual and practicing diligently for months, freezes at the wheel during the driving test and is unable to get out of the parking lot. The primary symptom is an unwillingness or inability to act for fear of making a mistake; a mistake with consequences too dire to contemplate. In real estate, such paralysis is most prevalent among two groups of new agents: those who have been told so many things *not* to do that they are afraid to do anything, and those who have tried something new and have been burned.

To combat the effects of this stupor-inducing ailment, the positive approach is best. First, make peace with yourself. Understand that you will make mistakes and that not everyone will always be happy with what you do. If you educate yourself, follow sound and ethical business practices, keep up-to-date about what's going on in the profession, and temper it all with just a moderate amount of prudence, you will develop the confidence you need to relax and do your job. Of course, it's a given that you will have adequate errors and omissions insurance. If you missed that discussion in Chapter 3, now's a particularly appropriate time to review it.

### WHERE THE ICE GETS THIN

It also helps if you know what specific things really can cause you trouble. That way you can concentrate on avoiding the real pitfalls, rather than worrying about the imaginary ones. (Or, "Don't sweat the small stuff.") The trouble spots are reasonably easy to identify. Each state has a set of administrative rules and regulations that govern the conduct of those who have real estate licenses. Typically, 15 to 20 violations are cited that could result in some sort of disciplinary action. In most states, the list has grown over the years, largely in response to adverse public reaction to transgressions by those who sell real estate.

## LESSONS FROM THE GOLDEN STATE

It's instructive to look at California's rules. Because of the huge numbers involved, if a problem in putting together a real estate transaction can occur, it has happened in California, a law suit has been filed, it has gone to the Supreme Court, a mini-series has been produced, and it's all encapsulated into the next edition of the state publication, Real Estate Law (see "Real Estate Reference" in the References). Their list of "no-no's" is titled "Unlawful Conduct in Sale, Lease, and Exchange Transactions." I'm including it not to intimidate you, but to give you an excellent primer on prohibited activities. The information will be more meaningful to you after you've had some practical experience in the field, but at this point it provides a very helpful overview.

1. Knowingly making a substantial misrepresentation of the likely value of real property to:
A. Its owner either for the purpose of securing a listing or for the purpose of acquiring an interest in the property for the licensee's own account.
B. A prospective buyer for the purpose of inducing the buyer to make an offer to purchase the real property.

2. Representing to an owner of real property when seeking a listing that the licensee has obtained a bona fide written offer to purchase the property, unless at the time of the representation the licensee has possession of a bona fide written offer to purchase.

3. Stating or implying to an owner of real property during the listing negotiations that the licensee is precluded by law, by regulation, or by the rules of any organization, other than the broker firm seeking the listing, from charging less than the commission or fee quoted to the owner by the licensee.

4. Knowingly making substantial misrepresentations regarding the licensee's relationship with an individual broker, corporate broker, or

franchised brokerage company, or that entity's/person's responsibility for the licensee's activities.

5. Knowingly underestimating the probable closing costs in a communication to the prospective buyer or seller of real property in order to induce that person to make or to accept an offer to purchase the property.

6. Knowingly making a false or misleading representation to the seller of real property as to the form, amount, and/or treatment of a deposit toward the purchase of the property made by an offeror.

7. Knowingly making a false or misleading representation to a seller of real property, who has agreed to finance all or part of a purchase price by carrying back a loan, about a buyer's ability to repay the loan in accordance with its terms and conditions.

8. Making an addition to or modification of the terms of an instrument previously signed or initialed by a party to a transaction without the knowledge and consent of the party.

9. As a principal or agent, making representations to a prospective purchaser of a promissory note secured by real property about the market value of the securing property without a reasonable basis for believing the truth and accuracy of the representation.

10. Knowingly making a false or misleading representation or representing, without a reasonable basis for believing its truth, the nature and/or condition of the interior or exterior features of a property when soliciting an offer.

11. Knowingly making a false or misleading representation or representing, without a reasonable basis for believing its truth, the size of a parcel, square footage of improvements or the location of the boundary lines of real property being offered for sale, lease, or exchange.

12. Knowingly making a false or misleading representation or representing to a prospective buyer or lessee of real property, without a reasonable basis to believe its truth, that the property can be used for certain purposes with the intent of inducing the prospective buyer or lessee to acquire an interest in the real property.

13. When acting in the capacity of an agent in a transaction for the sale, lease, or exchange of real property, failing to disclose to the prospective purchaser or lessee facts known to the licensee materially affecting the value or desirability of the property, when the licensee has reason to

believe that such facts are not known to nor readily observable by a prospective purchaser or lessee.

14. Willfully failing, when acting as a listing agent, to present or cause to be presented to the owner of the property any written offer to purchase received prior to the closing of a sale, unless expressly instructed by the owner not to present such an offer, or unless the offer is patently frivolous.

15. When acting as the listing agent, presenting competing written offers to purchase real property to the owner in such a manner as to induce the owner to accept the offer that will provide the greatest compensation to the listing broker without regard to the benefits, advantages, and/or disadvantages to the owner.

16. Failing to explain to the parties or prospective parties to a real estate transaction for whom the licensee is acting as an agent the meaning and probable significance of a contingency in an offer or contract that the licensee knows or reasonably believes may affect the closing date of the transaction, or the timing of the vacating of the property by the seller or its occupancy by the buyer.

17. Failing to disclose to the seller of real property in a transaction in which the licensee is an agent for the seller the nature and extent of any direct or indirect interest that the licensee expects to acquire as a result of the sale. The prospective purchase of the property by an entity in which the licensee has an ownership interest, or purchase by any other person with whom the licensee occupies a special relationship where there is reasonable probability that the licensee could be indirectly acquiring an interest in the property, shall be disclosed to the seller.

18. Failing to disclose to the buyer of real property in a transaction in which the licensee is an agent of the buyer the nature and extent of a licensee's direct or indirect ownership interest in such real property. The direct or indirect ownership interest in the property by a person related to the licensee by blood or marriage, by an entity in which the licensee has an ownership interest, or by any person with whom the licensee occupies a special relationship shall be disclosed to the buyer.

19. Failing to disclose to a principal for whom the licensee is acting as an agent any significant interest the licensee has in a particular entity when the licensee recommends the use of services or products of such entity.

## WAIT, THERE'S MORE!

As hard as it may be to believe, the foregoing list is far from inclusive. To round out the picture somewhat, and to expand upon a few areas that have traditionally caused licensees particular difficulties, here are a few more observations. In most instances, good business practice alone justifies observing these cautions, whether or not they are legally prohibited.

### The Broker-Agent Relationship

Loyalty, common sense, and law dictate that as a salesperson or associate broker, you work under your broker's direct, personal, and continuing supervision. This is true whether you are an independent contractor or an employee. Keep your broker informed of all your plans, programs, and activities. Even though he or she will expect you to vigorously pursue your own personal goals, do not become careless about the special relationship that exists.

Regarding compensation: You are paid in one way, and one way only. The commission, when you earn it, is paid to your broker, who pays you in accordance with your contractual agreement. You may not accept compensation from anyone else for your services as a real estate agent. Does that mean you cannot accept a modest "bonus" directly from a satisfied client? Yes, it means just that. It must come through your broker.

### Practicing Law

It is always wise to recommend that principals seek legal counsel when the situation warrants. Never recommend that an attorney *not* be consulted. Each state has guidelines indicating what you can do as a licensed real estate agent, and what represents the unauthorized practice of law. In many cases, there is a fine line of distinction, but it is one you need to recognize and honor.

### Guarantees

Never use the word *guarantee* (or similar words, such as *promise*) when describing future profits from the sale of real estate. As a matter of fact, I recommend that you never use such words at all unless you are, in fact, willing to guarantee results. Even such seemingly innocent phrases as: "I guarantee this duplex will be a money-maker for you" could cause difficulty.

### Prizes and Contests

You will be on safe ground if you completely avoid any type of activity of this nature, designed to induce prospective clients to buy or sell real estate. Almost all states have restrictions, most of which were enacted to prevent past excesses from recurring.

### Fair Housing Laws

Few things will get you on the griddle more quickly than failing to abide by both the letter and the spirit of the Fair Housing laws. As you are aware, in your role as a real estate licensee you have a legal obligation not to discriminate based upon race, color, religion, national origin, ethnic group, sex, familial status, or handicap. Some states and local communities have laws that are even more restrictive than federal laws. Even if you are genuinely and honestly committed to equal treatment for all, you will have to work hard to implement that approach. Finally, it is an area where humor, no matter how well intentioned, is dangerous. Sensitivities are so keen that even the most innocently intended remark could offend.

### Representations to Lenders

Make no verbal or written representations to any lender indicating anything but the true sales price and terms in any transaction. This is a matter of particular concern, as it seems to have become an accepted practice in some circles to present an inflated, erroneous sales price in order to secure a higher loan amount. Do not be misled by the "everyone does it" argument. Everyone doesn't do it.

### Advertising

Misleading or untruthful advertising is specifically forbidden almost everywhere. As a salesperson, all of your advertising has to be done in the name of your broker. The broker will probably prepare the formal media advertising, or have a specialist on the staff do it. However, flyers you may prepare on your listings are also considered advertising, as would be information on the Internet. The fact that there appears to be widespread tolerance of abuses in this activity is not likely to help if you get carried away with your descriptions or claims, and someone complains.

### Conflicts With Other Agents

In the course of your real estate career, you will inevitably become involved in business disagreements with other real estate agents. Hopefully, they will be infrequent and rapidly resolved. Most are likely to be misunderstandings caused by breakdowns in communication, which can be cleared up by you or through your broker. If all parties to the dispute are Realtors, a binding arbitration apparatus is in place at the local level. No matter what else transpires, do not let any controversy jeopardize, delay, or interfere with any phase of a real estate transaction. Get the job done of satisfying the needs of the principals, and then fuss about the less important issues. It's inexcusable, but there have been cases in which arguments between agents over who is entitled to the commission have resulted in whole deals falling apart.

### Contracts

Real estate is a competitive business, but the competition must take place *before* contracts are signed. Any action by you that could be construed as an attempt to induce a buyer or seller to break a contractual agreement will be viewed as grounds for disciplinary action. Eager agents who work expired listings often run afoul of this rule. They often contact sellers *before* the owner's listing with another broker actually expires. Some agents even present an offer directly to the sellers after contracts have been finalized, but before the transaction closes. Give it your best shot before papers are signed—then back off and respect the legal relationship.

### Money

As you might suspect, each state is very particular about how you handle money in any transaction. You and your broker can get into serious difficulties if you ignore or inadvertently overlook the rules. Know what is required, give written receipts in acceptable legal format, do not commingle money from business transactions with personal funds, and get all money to your broker immediately to be placed in an approved holding account.

## GETTING NUMB?

The length of this "better not try it" and "do it and you're dead" discussion may have induced a mild numbness. That can be encouraging if it's a symptom of your increased sensitivity to potential problems and not a prelude to inertia. While on the subject of symptoms, I thought you may be interested in my list of the "Top Ten Ways to Tell When Your Real Estate Career Is in the Dumps." It has proven to be a popular feature in Realtor publications around the country, which proves that folks in the profession do have a healthy (or weird) sense of humor.

Real estate has no more dangers for its practitioners than any other profession—and it's a lot more enjoyable than most of them. What makes it so interesting are the diversity of the people you will meet and the challenging nature of the situations you face. You can appreciate it all more if you have a preview of what to expect, so that's the subject of Chapter 10.

## *TOP TEN WAYS TO TELL WHEN YOUR REAL ESTATE CAREER IS IN THE DUMPS*

10. The Errors and Omissions insurance carrier will only issue you a policy with a million dollar deductible.

9. When you ask your sales manager where your invitation to the company picnic is, she keeps replying: "It's in the mail."

8. The state Real Estate Commissioner continues to send you "Be All You Can Be" U.S. Army recruiting literature.

7. Your only listing has been on the market so long that it has qualified for the national roster of historic homes.

6. Rodney Dangerfield won't let you join his fan club.

5. Your broker changes the locks on the office door and does not give you a key.

4. Your spouse buys a used bike and gets an early morning paper route as a second job.

3. The IRS sends you a sympathy card along with a credit voucher for a thousand dollars.

2. A family of vultures starts following your car as you are showing properties to clients.

1. Your mother lists her home with another agent.

# 10

# *Dealing With Difficult People and Difficult Situations*

## *Challenges—Not Problems*

If everyone with whom you worked each day shared essentially the same perception of reality, and if the business situations you faced all had a certain gray sameness, things would get pretty boring, wouldn't they? I personally guarantee that whatever else you may ever say about your real estate career, you will *never* say it's dull. Let's take a look at a few of the people and some of the situations that provide the stimulants.

### DEALING WITH DIFFICULT PEOPLE

A couple of qualifiers are in order. First, there is absolutely no requirement that you become friends with everyone involved in every transaction. The best escrow officer in town may not be the type of person with whom you would like to associate socially, but you would be foolish to steer people away because of that. You want the job done right, period. Second, because some of the people you have to deal with may be pursu-

109

ing an agenda somewhat different from your own, or may be following slightly different business practices, don't cast them as bad guys who are out to make things difficult for you and scuttle your deals. I've seen agents who develop a real paranoia and find it essential to blame others for the inevitable problems that arise in every transaction. ("Well, *they* did it to me again!") So even though we discuss them under the heading of "difficult people," it might be more accurate to refer to the following as "real estate's most unforgettable characters."

### The Deal Killers

Everyone involved in a real estate transaction is normally quite anxious for the details to be worked out and for it to close. Some, however, are more anxious than others. There are two categories of participants who have caused real estate agents particular anxiety: lawyers and relatives.

■ *Lawyers.* You may encounter an attorney at just about any stage of your transaction. In some jurisdictions, attorneys provide title services and act as settlement agents, while in others their main role may be to review offers and prepare contracts. If you understand their role, and learn how to work with them, there should seldom be any real problem.

Understand, first, that lawyers are representing their clients and, second, that they are searching for potential problems. If they find one, the process stops until it is resolved. If it cannot be resolved to their satisfaction, they will likely recommend that their client pull out. Their attitude is one of caution and conservatism. It's probably the attitude you would want in an attorney who represented you.

Real estate people generally have two major gripes about attorneys: They too often offer financial advice when that's not why they were retained ("You really think this is a fair price for your home?"), and they take too long to do whatever it is that they do (the fact that they get paid by the hour fuels speculation in this area). As an agent, you need to make absolutely certain that price and terms have been agreed to by all parties and spelled out in writing before attorneys get involved. Then, establish a reasonable time for attorney reviews to be completed and include those deadlines in your agreement.

I enjoyed working with lawyers. When all participants in a transaction knew one was going to be reviewing the proceedings, it seemed to keep everyone on their toes and on their best behavior. If a lawyer kills your deal, perhaps it deserved to die.

I should point out that my benevolent attitude concerning lawyers was shaped by my experience in selling mainly residential real estate in a small university town where everyone in the professions pretty much knew everyone else. If an attorney got the reputation as someone who intentionally prolonged negotiations simply to keep the high price meter running, it would have been, in the long run, bad for business. An attorney member of my network in another part of the country (who, for obvious reasons, shall remain anonymous), after reviewing my manuscript offered the opinion that "deal killer" was much too polite a term for attorneys who scuttle complex transactions simply because they don't fully understand them and are unwilling to admit it. Unfortunately, he observed, it is not an infrequent occurrence. You are now forewarned.

- *Veto-wielding relatives.* I once worked with a young bachelor who was looking for a first home. We located a modest condo that seemed to fit his needs. He made an offer to purchase contingent upon his father's inspection. Dad found fault not only with the condo, but also with the seller, the real estate agent, and the financing. I felt for the young fellow, because it seemed clear that Dad was simply asserting control. I really doubt that anything the boy could afford would have passed inspection. On the other hand, I have worked successfully with children who passed on their parents' choice, and with parents who were concerned, but reasonable, participants in the process (and who often came up with a big chunk of the down payment). It is important to know early who all the decision makers are, and whether any out-of-town experts will be flown in. Get to know all the players early.

There are other types of difficult people you're sure to meet eventually. Let's consider them.

### The Lowballers

Some buyers will, no matter what, offer significantly less (like a whole lot less) than the asking price for a property. If you are dealing with sophisticated sellers who are accustomed to bargaining, there is really no problem; everyone understands what is going on, and enters into the spirit of negotiation. Most home owners, however, are generally so appalled at a low ball offer that they become insulted and make all sorts of creative suggestions as to what the buyer can do with the offer.

When working with a lowballer who is shopping for a home, try to

(1) get him or her to make a decent offer that will not alienate the sellers (good luck!), (2) prepare the sellers for what to expect (good luck!), and (3) work hard for a counter offer. If, by whatever fortuitous circumstance, a lowballer comes into contact with a seller who is asking 30 percent to 40 percent more for his property than it's worth, or he really expects to get, you have the potential for a match made in Heaven. Lowballers are not always astute buyers. Some incorrectly assume that any property they can get at a huge discount has to be a good deal.

### The Boy Scout Rejects

Will Rogers may have never met a person he didn't like, but, as far as I know, Will never sold real estate for a living. You will meet at least a few unsavory characters, and on rare occasions, you will encounter buyers or sellers you judge to be flat out dishonest. It is not always easy to just walk away.

In one of my several moves within our office, I shared a large room with my wife. Her desk was on the other side of a divider and we could hear each other's conversations clearly. I was frequently critiqued at home (at my request, of course) about how I handled certain situations. In one instance, she was dumfounded at how difficult I made it for a prospect to make an offer on a house. "The poor man was almost begging you to write up the offer!" It wasn't that I didn't want the business, it was just that I was getting very disturbing signals and was having trouble believing everything I was being told.

Later events proved my intuition was correct (or I wouldn't be telling the story, right?), but we did end up doing business with no difficulty on that transaction, and a couple of years later listed and sold the home he bought. The point is to be on the lookout for indications of serious character flaws. When you spot them, document every step of the transaction in writing, check and double check all information you are given, take absolutely nothing on its face value, and generally cover yourself. It's much better that you be overly cautious than end up trying to explain to a disgruntled broker why you were naive enough to get conned.

### The Lookers

Some people like to look at houses as a hobby. Others do it just to keep harmony in the household. In one instance, over a span of three years, I spent untold hours each summer with a couple from out of state who said they wanted to locate a nice place with a mother-in-law setup in the house. The wife had an elderly mother who would move with them. They were lovely people, and I thoroughly enjoyed each visit. It became clear to me, however, after finding almost exactly what they said they were looking for, that the husband was going through the whole exercise just to pacify his mate. There was no way he was ever going to sell the place he was in and move. As he had it arranged, his mother-in-law had a separate, detached cottage on their property. ("Separate" and "detached" were the key words.)

When you are working with any prospect it's good to ask these questions:

"How long have you been looking?"

"What is the closest thing you have found to what you are looking for?"

"Are you prepared to make an offer on the property when you find it?" (Judge for yourself the answer to this question: "Will you know it when you see it?")

In working with buyers, I did the best job I could of determining motivation and qualifications and of finding the type of property they said they wanted. If I found it, or as near to it as I judged reasonably possible, and if they didn't buy, I stopped spending a lot of time with them. You can remain cordial and keep in touch, and call them if something happens along that seems particularly promising. You will lose a few with this policy, but it is not a wise expenditure of your time to keep showing property to people who are either not motivated or not capable of making a buying decision.

### The Seminar Attenders

I just hated it when a prospective buyer would call and say something like: "I just attended this great seminar on how to get rich in real estate without using any of my own money. I'm really anxious to get started buying houses. When can we meet?"

Some of these schemes are really quite incredible, so it's best if you become familiar with the most popular ones just for self-defense. Do any of these get-rich-quickers really work? I suppose that under just the right set of conditions some of them may, but it's very unlikely that you, as the real estate agent, would ever realize much out of the deal. You would have to spend most of your time searching for the perfect set of circumstances, and then you'd have to try to structure a transaction in which you are paid in a timely manner with readily negotiable instruments. You should know that a common element in these maneuvers is to make the real estate agent wait for the commission, or to offer something in lieu of money—like a bale of cotton.

If you are dealing with otherwise reasonable people, you may sometimes be able to convert them into legitimate buyers. It generally becomes clear to them that, for the seminar's scheme to work, the moon has to be in its seventh high, Jupiter has to be aligned with Mars, and Halley's Comet has to be clearly visible in the southern sky at high noon. Then, they must locate sellers with IQs that would prohibit them from going outside unattended and bank loan officers gullible enough to loan money to an alligator. Of course, anything is possible. Early in your relationship you might try to work in a reference to the old Russian proverb: "The only free cheese is in the mousetrap."

### The Tenants

Now, renters, on the whole, are every bit as nice and just as honorable as homeowners. But renters who occupy homes that are put on the market sometimes develop a nasty streak when their residence is about to be sold out from under them. They are not ordinarily the least bit motivated to make your job easy. If you sell the property, they have to move. If they happen to be present while prospects are being shown the home, it is not at all unusual for them to criticize the property, the neighbors, and the landlord, sometimes in very colorful language. I tried my best to be as considerate of renters as possible, and to show property when they were not at home. Here's why.

*Shock Therapy!* Let's say you are previewing a cozy little bungalow rented by a young woman and her little boy. You call the tenant and make an appointment to inspect the house at 10 A.M. for a noon showing. The woman informs you that she and her child will be going shopping so that would work out fine. You arrive a few minutes before they are to leave, wait for them to come out of the house, introduce yourself, and thank her for her cooperation. They leave and you let yourself in with the key you had received from the listing agent. You hear water running upstairs, investigate, and find the shower has carelessly been left on. You reach in and turn the first knob you come to. At that point, you hear a bloodcurdling scream.

The lady's male house guest is taking a shower, and you have just cut off his hot water. The renter later informs you that she thought Tyrone would sleep through the showing, and it wasn't any big deal anyway. You may correctly conclude that the foregoing illustration is based upon a personal experience.

Moral: It pays to be very cautious when working with renters. That sweet little lady to whom you were planning to show the house may have been shocked to bump into Tyrone, the wet male streaker.

## DEALING WITH DIFFICULT SITUATIONS

Look at it this way. If every real estate transaction were uncomplicated and trauma-free, there would be little demand for your services, right? Don't worry. Even the most routine situation has the potential to be complex and stressful enough to make the majority of people anxious to enlist your services and happy to pay your fee. The more difficult ones separate the journeymen from the real pros, for they will require not only your professional competence, but unusual interpersonal skills as well. Here are just a few that will enliven your career and enhance your bank account.

### *Where There's a Will, There Are Relatives*

A death in the family brings out the best and the worst in people. In the ideal circumstance, the survivors are interested only in paying their respects to the deceased and comforting each other. When there is even a modest amount of property left behind, however, there is quite often a regrettable scramble for it, generating intensely bitter feelings. You may become the listing agent for a piece of real property for the estate, either through your contract with an attorney or with the executor of the will.

In such cases, your first and most important step is to know exactly for whom you are working and who has the legal authority to make decisions. Next, make arrangements for a professional appraiser to evaluate the property, for a routine market analysis won't be enough. Every relative who stands to collect a percentage of the net proceeds from the sale will be intensely interested and will be quick to criticize. Self-appointed experts on real property value will emerge from the woodwork in numbers you never thought possible.

Personal property can be a particular problem. Often there will be personal effects left in the house. Some items will have a monetary value and any item will no doubt have emotional value to someone. Establish clearly what personal property, if any, is to be included in the sale, and do your best to have the remainder removed by responsible parties before showing the home to prospective buyers. Otherwise, if the family Bible or the rare coin collection comes up missing, you will be in big trouble.

Finally, be prepared to deal with attorneys and courts and to document exhaustively what you've done. Your hard work can pay off, for if you do a professional job on an estate sale, it's quite probable that there will be others.

### Divorce, American Style

A year after you sell that cute little Cape Cod in the suburbs to that nice young couple, you could get a call from one of them telling you they are splitting and want you to list the house. They both still like you; they just can't stand each other. If they are desperate, it is likely to be a quick (albeit unpleasant) transaction. They will frequently agree to almost anything to end the relationship. In more acrimonious situations, you may have to deal with attorneys almost exclusively. Sometimes no one trusts anyone enough to move faster than a snail's pace, and principals are often separated by a distance of several thousand miles. In any case, tact, diplomacy, compassion, and patience will be your best allies. Resist any temptation to take sides, for that's a no-win proposition.

### Clutching at Straws—the Lease Option

In this arrangement a potential buyer leases a home for a specific period of time (perhaps a year) with a portion of the monthly payment being credited toward an eventual down payment. During the period of the agreement, the person leasing the home has the option of buying it at a price that has been agreed upon up front. In theory it sounds fine, and in fairness I have to admit that many mutually beneficial lease options have probably resulted in sales. I've just never seen one.

What you often have is a desperate owner who has already tried unsuccessfully to sell the property and is clutching at straws, and a buyer who doesn't have enough money for a down payment and may not be able to qualify for a loan. That is not a great combination.

Remember also that an option is a legal document with specific rights and obligations for all principals. Because lease options are fairly uncommon in many markets, people frequently enter into them without adequate legal counsel. Finally, if an option agreement is signed money will change hands and you deserve to be compensated at that point, as well as when (and if) the option is exercised. Do your homework on this one before you get deeply involved.

### Honeymoon First, Vows Later—Possession Prior to Close

In some instances, buyers are anxious to move into a home before the actual close of the transaction. Closing may be days or even weeks away, because such things as appraisals, employment verification, and credit checks take time. Normally, the buyer pays a daily rental fee based upon the new mortgage payment, or something slightly less. It's an arrangement that lets buyers get in and get settled without having to worry about securing temporary housing, and it gives the seller some unanticipated income. I moved in early once when I was buying a home, and I have been involved in several other early move-ins, both as the listing and selling agent. If you are dealing with reasonable buyers and understanding sellers, it can work to everyone's advantage, but be advised that it does have explosive potential.

People who have closed the deal have a different attitude toward small household problems than "renters" do. If the faucet leaks or the window sticks, they fix the problem and go their happy way. But if they haven't yet made that final payment at the closing and everyone has not finally signed on dotted lines, they may not be as content. Perhaps a neighbor who fancies himself an expert on area property values reacts in shocked disbelief when he finds out how much they paid. "You paid what!? Too bad you didn't deal through my niece, 'Honest Angelica'. She could have saved you $10,000 easy. I know those people were desperate to sell." Or maybe the wind changes and they get a whiff of the onion-processing plant over the hill—and the wife gets nauseous when she smells onions. (Never mind that you can't live anywhere in the county without smelling onions.) Then, there is also the matter of liability and insurance and responsibility for potential loss. Finally, if the buyers make improvements on the property and then the transaction falls apart before it closes, the situation becomes even more muddled.

On the whole, it is best for the delights and privileges of home ownership to be reserved for that time when everyone has said "I do," and all the other legal niceties have been concluded.

### Loathe to Leave: Possession After Close

A less frequent, but equally dangerous practice, involves the sellers staying in the house for a short period of time after the close of the transaction. For the buyers, this poses a couple of serious potential problems. First, they will not be able to inspect the home after the buyers have vacated and before close. That's standard in some parts of the country. It really motivates sellers to leave things shipshape. Second, at the point the transaction closes and the house becomes theirs, they legally become landlords and the sellers become tenants. In a worst case scenario, the sellers refuse to vacate on time. They then become "holdover tenants" and it could take formal eviction action to get them out. I admit this rarely happens, but the elements are there for some serious headaches.

### *"There May Be Another Buyer. Really. I'm Not Kidding!"*

Absolutely nothing will cause people to buy more quickly than the belief that someone else is interested in the same property and may get it before they can.

The quickest reversal of field I ever saw occurred when I was working with a young engineer and his wife who were looking for a home. I showed them a wide variety, but they kept coming back to the same one, a brand-new home on a large wooded city lot. It was clear that it was their first choice. They loved it and it was within their price range, but they were hesitant because I had told them that the builder was adamant on price and she would accept nothing but a full-price offer. No negotiating. (I had sold several of her homes before. I knew she was a rock.)

As we concluded our third or fourth visit to the house, they said they would go back to the motel and consider it, but they also wanted to continue the search the next day. Just as we were leaving, another agent (a successful agent who looked the part) drove up in her shiny new car with the real estate sign on the door and out stepped two of the most affluent-looking people you would ever want to see. The man had a briefcase that easily could have been full of thousand-dollar bills. My prospects looked at each other, looked at me, and looked back at the smiling couple as they disappeared into the house. "Say, I think we've probably seen enough houses. What do you say we head back to your office and write up an offer? A full-price offer. Now." (I was kissed only once at closing. It was when they gave the wife the keys to her new home.)

I often found it difficult to make it clear to buyers that we were not operating in a vacuum. They seemed to believe that they were the only ones looking and that the property would always be available to them. I always made my little speech before we looked at the first house. I pointed out that I took my work very seriously and that the homes I showed them represented what I thought were the very best on the market for what they said they wanted and what they could afford. I told them that all the other agents in town were doing the same thing for their prospects, and that the most desirable properties go the fastest. Maybe I was too low-key, but I rarely got the idea that buyers felt much of a sense of urgency. People have heard the there-may-be-another-buyer pitch so often that they tend to tune it out. You need to continue to make the effort, because there are other buyers and the more successful agents seem attracted to the same properties. I regularly crossed paths with a handful of the same salespeople.

### Unfulfilled Dreams—the Unsold Listing

Of all the difficult situations you will face, the unsold listing has the potential to do the greatest harm to your mental health. Let me illustrate.

My wife and I were very friendly with an older gentleman who owned one of the most beautiful homes in our city. It was over 4,000 square feet, on a hill, in an exclusive neighborhood, with a magnificent view of the Cascade Mountains. When our friend decided he wanted to sell and move to a luxury apartment in the city, he called me to list his home. The only problem was that he wanted about $30,000 more than our estimate of market value. We took the listing at his price, after we informed him that we thought we were substantially above the market. We never worked harder on a listing, and although we generated a lot of traffic, four months went by without a sale.

I attempted to convince him that a price reduction was in order, but he was cordially insistent upon staying the course. Three months later he took it off the market and said he would try again when conditions were better. A very short time after that he died suddenly and unexpectedly.

In most respects my friend was an astute businessman, and he had his overall estate in good order, but he went to his grave with one major unresolved financial problem: the sale of his house. Shortly after his death, the executor of his estate listed the home with another company at a realistic price. In a month it was sold to a family that had visited one of our many open houses when we had the listing.

Property owners have to make their own decisions when it comes to setting a price. You can only give advice based upon your best professional judgment. But try hard not to let extraneous factors cloud your thinking, and remember that you always have the option of walking away from a potential listing, if you believe you should. You will end up with one or two less listings, but you will also have fewer haunting memories.

### One Person's Meat, Another's Poison—Negotiating

I recall a rookie agent in our office who was working on one of his first transactions. He had written up an offer to purchase a home and had presented it the night before. He had just received the owner's counteroffer from the listing agent. After she left, and after he had a chance to go over the documents, he came slowly out of his office, visibly shaken. Our broker, who was in the lobby, spotted him and asked what was wrong. "Awful news," he whispered through an obviously tight throat. "The Smedleys just countered the Whimpsters' offer. They'll be devastated. It looks like the whole thing is dead in the water."

Naturally, our broker (who, like most brokers, was an eternal optimist) had a different perspective. "That's actually good news. If the Smedleys didn't think something could be worked out they wouldn't have bothered with a counteroffer. Get back to the Whimpsters right away. Tell them it's an encouraging sign, and work on reaching a compromise."

And there you have the two views of the negotiating process. The inexperienced salesperson tends to look upon any difference of opinion as a prelude to disaster—a sure sign that all efforts are about to go up in smoke and Junior's braces will have to be postponed for another year. The broker looks upon it as a necessary, and even stimulating, aspect of business life, and assumes that if folks weren't interested in striking a deal they wouldn't be talking.

Of course, the broker is right. Negotiation in real estate is simply the process of managing a transaction with the objective of reaching an agreement among the participants. It should make your adrenaline flow, not give you stomach cramps.

But enough of the heavy stuff. Let's lighten up a little.

## THE ULTIMATE, COSMIC DIFFICULT SITUATION

William Robert Dodd (or "Billy Bob," as he was known to his old friends) had died and gone to Heaven. Billy Bob had been a successful real estate broker on the Mississippi Gulf Coast for more than 40 years at Dodd's Bayside Realty. He passed on at a ripe old age, the way he always said he wanted to go. He was waiting to tee off on the ninth hole at the annual Realtor golf tournament at the country club. When Billy Bob got to Heaven, he found a long processing line at the Pearly Gates. It moved quickly, but when he reached the front of it the Angel in charge told him to step to one side and wait. "Your papers are still in escrow," she said, but quickly added, "Oh, that's just a little Heavenly joke. I am sure we will have everything straight in a moment." But Billy Bob was not amused, and he was definitely worried. Maybe they still held that 1968 tax return against him. Or maybe they didn't like his company slogan: "In Dodd You Can Trust." Or maybe . . . At that point St. Peter arrived, took Billy Bob by the arm and led him in. "Welcome to Heaven, Angel Dodd," St. Peter said. "Sorry for the delay, but you see you are the first real estate agent we have ever had up here."

# 11

# *Client Follow-Up and Referrals*

*Your Insurance Policy Against Lonely Days, Sleepless Nights, and a Penniless Old Age*

Traditionally, certain professions command a high degree of client loyalty. Real estate is not one of them.

Although it is entirely realistic for you to expect eventually to earn most of your money from repeat business and referrals, that idyllic situation won't just happen by itself. You will have to work hard at it and it will take time.

## FOLLOW-UP

Here are some things you can do to help you achieve your objective. When discussing this topic, I use the word "client" to refer to all past contacts, whether customers or clients.

### *Think Repeat*

1. *Do it right the first time.* By far the most important factor in determining whether people come back to you for their future real estate business, or whether they recommend you to their friends, is how well you handle their original transaction. Do a good job and it will then be mainly a matter of keeping in touch. Do a poor job and it won't make much difference what else you do.

2. *Make it the beginning of a beautiful relationship.* A broker from Ari-

zona got to the heart of the matter in this survey observation: "Too many agents view each closed transaction as the end of the relationship rather than as the start of it." When you automatically cross the street to chat with a former client you happen to see downtown (and he doesn't run when he sees you coming), you will know you are doing things right.

3. *Keep in touch.* In the business world, and most particularly in sales, out of sight is absolutely, definitely, unequivocally out of mind. That doesn't pump up the old ego, but it is a basic fact of life you have to accept. You need to let folks know on a regular basis that you are alive and well and still in business.

People like to be remembered by the professionals with whom they have worked, and they like to feel that their welfare is a matter of personal interest to those professionals. I am certain you would enjoy it if your physician sent you a personal note telling you he appreciated the confidence you had shown in him, and that he looked forward to your future relationship (assuming your heart could stand the shock of getting such a message). Doctors do not need to do things like that to prosper. Real estate agents do.

4. *Remember that the close is the opening.* The formal part of client follow-up starts at the closing. Sending a thank-you note and a small gift is a good way to begin. If I was working with a buyer, I tried to get a good color picture of the house they had purchased, enlarge it, and frame it in a nice wood frame. Another possibility would be to find an artist who would do a sketch of the house and present that, assuming you can find an artist who would do it for an affordable price and turn out a good product. I never did come up with the perfect gift for sellers, but they were generally so thrilled about receiving their check at the closing that it didn't seem to matter much.

### The Nitty Gritty

1. *Maintain closed-deal files.* By the time each transaction closes you will have a substantial amount of information. For listings, you will have your original market analysis, the formal listing agreement, copies of ads, multiple listing documents, pictures, your chronological log of actions taken, records of open houses, special promotional flyers, results of pest and dry-rot inspections, copies of offers, the opening of escrow, a preliminary title report, a closing statement, and a variety of other miscellaneous records. For buyers, the file may be somewhat less extensive, but will still contain vital documentation. It is important for you to keep each of these

files in one folder identified by the client's name and filed in a separate location called "closed deals." (Don't confuse this with the official "deal file" that the office will maintain. Yours will contain copies of all the essential documents, plus a great deal more informal personal information about the customers or clients, such as the composition of the family.)

These records form an integral part of your client follow-up program. Many times, a former client will simply call and tell you that they want you to list their home. Job transfers, health problems, changes in family relationships (discouragingly, divorces and separations alone generate a large amount of activity), a desire to move up or down in home size, and a host of related factors contribute to making ours a mobile society. When the call comes, if you can go to one source (your closed-deal file), it will save you an enormous amount of time. It is quite likely that in your real estate career you will sell the same property several times. Some houses will become old friends of yours.

2. *Keep them in suspense.* Enter your clients' names in whatever kind of "suspense" file that works best for you. There are several computer software programs that are designed to handle client follow-up, and it's possible your broker will have one that will handle the entire office. You should try to contact past clients at least three times annually, spaced throughout the year. The key is to make all contacts personal. Telephone calls are effective, but you should not use them exclusively.

I found that some of my most effective contacts occurred while I was driving around town previewing listings and showing property. Some meetings may occur on a random, unscheduled basis. Other times you may want to call ahead to see if it would be convenient if you dropped by for a few moments to visit. If you happen to be working with a prospective purchaser who is seriously interested in a home in an area where a previous client of yours lives, you may wish to arrange for a brief meeting between them to discuss the neighborhood. Make sure you have a satisfied former client before you try this one.

3. *Remember, you can hire help.* There are a number of national and regional firms that specialize in client follow-up programs. There are variations, and specific details change from year to year, but the principle is the same—someone else will handle your client follow-up for you, for a fee. For a time our real estate company used the services of two such companies, and we found them to be honest and reasonably efficient. Based upon my experience, however, my strong recommendation is that even if you subscribe to such a service, you still contact your former clients per-

sonally on a regular basis. You also need to do periodic checks to ensure the process is working as advertised. You have too much to lose not to give this job your close and constant personal attention.

## REFERRALS: THE EASIEST MONEY YOU WILL EVER MAKE

The term "referrals" covers not only the kind of informal referrals your former clients make to their friends and associates, but also the more formalized program that exists between real estate firms. There are two basic types: outgoing referrals and incoming referrals.

### Outgoing Referrals

Most people who sell their homes will buy another somewhere else. If that somewhere else is out of your service area, you have a potential referral, and if the referral results in a sale you will earn a fee. Early in the process of taking a listing, find out where your clients will relocate. Ask them for permission to refer them to a real estate company in that city. Even if they have not decided to buy, ask for their approval. Almost every real estate company has a packet of information about the local area, including maps, which a newcomer will find useful.

If you are part of a real estate franchise operation or if you are in an independent office with membership in one of the national referral companies, you will have no problem in deciding where to make your referral, and on what basis it will be made. Most franchises have an elaborate system that provides toll-free telephone numbers for a national coordinating agency and agreed-upon administrative procedures and referral fees.

If you are in a completely independent and unaffiliated office, you will have to decide to whom you wish to make the referral and what type of fee you expect. When doing that, refer to firms who are members of the National Association of Realtors, if possible, because they have agreed to be bound by a code of ethics in conducting their affairs.

There are some elaborate methods of determining referral fees, but we found it preferable to keep it simple. If we referred a prospect to another office, we expected 20 percent of the gross commission they received on any transaction resulting from the referral. (Ten percent is also common.) Remember, you get nothing if the referral does not result in a closed transaction at the other end. We telephoned the referral and secured verbal agreement to the terms before we provided the name and telephone number of the people being referred. We also asked that the referral be handled by a full-time agent with experience in handling referrals. We further requested that a copy of the official closing statement be sent to us upon the culmination of any transaction. (If you do not see the statement, you have no verifiable way of determining whether you are receiving the agreed-upon fee.) Most real estate brokers are delighted to receive referrals and will gladly agree to your fee, since these are bonus transactions for them.

If you are personally acquainted with an agent in the office to which the referral is being sent, and are satisfied that he or she will do an aggressive and professional job, make the referral to that specific individual, after coordinating with his or her supervising broker. Insist that within 24 hours of receiving the referral the agent call your clients on the telephone. Let the agent know when he or she can expect to catch them at home, and check to see that the contact has been made.

After each telephone conversation with the other agent, follow up in writing. Sometimes it may take months for a referral to pay off, so keep good records and keep asking for status reports for as long as the referral is active. In some instances, memories begin to fade when it is time to send you your check, so be ready to furnish written documentation of agreements.

Referrals can pay off for you. Let us assume that 15 of your listings sell each year, and that you refer 10 of the sellers to other real estate offices out of town. If five of those referrals result in closed transactions, your portion of the referral fees could go a long way toward paying MLS dues, postage, and any number of other items that have a way of increasing your overhead. There is a lot of money to be made for a minimal amount of effort and expense—and at the same time you will be performing a valuable service for your clients. Some offices even have a full-time relocation counselor paid for by the broker (from fees earned through referrals), who will handle all the administrative chores for you.

### Incoming Referrals

You have only limited control over how many incoming referrals you receive. Your broker will decide who gets them, but they are ordinarily distributed on some type of rotation basis. Many offices (including most national franchises) are very particular about who handles incoming referrals. It is not uncommon to use only agents who have closed a certain number of transactions and who have successfully completed specified in-house training courses. If that is the case where you work, proceed in all haste to qualify. Further, when you are at educational seminars out of town, particularly at Graduate Realtor Institute sessions, let agents from other offices in the state know that you appreciate referrals and that you will handle them efficiently.

Not all incoming referrals are of high quality so they need to be screened to make sure that they meet the following two minimum qualifications:

1. The people being referred know about, and approve of the referral. "Blind" referrals (made without the knowledge or permission of the clients) are not worth your effort, and can actually result in resentment on the part of the persons who are unsuspectingly referred.

2. Be sure you are given some background as to plans, timing, and financial qualifications of the people involved.

Incoming referrals are quite often blue-chip, gilt-edged prospects. With just a little experience, you will be able to quickly identify the most promising ones and react accordingly. Let's say that you have received a referral on a couple planning a house-hunting visit in the near future. How should you proceed?

1. *Call the prospects.* Do this the day you get the referral. If it is a weekday, you are more likely to catch them home after 7 P.M., their time. Your first order of business will be to identify yourself and relate your call to the agent who made the referral. Do not assume that you are the only agent with whom they will be in touch. Although that is often the case, you cannot depend upon it. Your goal will be to convince them that you can do the job for them better than anyone else. Further, do not assume that all of the information you have been given about them is correct. In a friendly way, try to verify what you were told.

The most important thing you will need to find out is whether their proposed trip is for house-looking or house-buying. If it is for the specific purpose of buying a home, you will need to arrange your schedule to stay with them for as long as necessary. To make their visit productive, you will need to know what they are looking for and what they can afford. Some people will tell you exactly the type of home they want and what they will pay, while others will be very noncommunicative. Do not press too hard if they seem reluctant. At this point you are just a voice on the phone, and some people find it awkward to discuss business matters with someone whom they have not met. If that's the case, you might get some insight by asking them about the house in which they are currently living, such as its size, style, location, and price range.

If they are making specific plans for the trip at the time you call, ask if they need help with motel or hotel room reservations. Determine what days they will be in town, how much time they will have for you, and when you will be able to first meet with them.

2. *Plan the visit.* Schedule your time to be as productive as possible. Try to meet with your prospects briefly in your office before you start showing them houses. It will give you a chance to get to know them and you can provide an overview of the schedule you have planned. If you have a map of the city on your office wall, you can tell them a lot about your town in a short time, including the location of schools, hospitals, shopping centers, and major residential areas. I always tried to introduce prospects to my broker since he was a very positive, gregarious person who always made newcomers feel at ease and relaxed. I also made it a point to introduce them to a few of the more impressive agents on our staff to emphasize our professionalism and team spirit.

When you start showing homes, you will have to be very flexible, for it might become immediately apparent that you have misjudged what the prospects really wanted. It is crucial that you have an intimate knowledge of properties in various price ranges and locations to be able to shift gears quickly. Most people will want time to themselves to explore the city and surrounding areas on their own. Make very sure that they understand that you can get them information on any property they see that has a real estate sign in front of it, for you do not want them calling other offices.

Buyers who are in town for only a short period rarely investigate homes for sale by the owner, but it happens on occasion. If it does, offer friendly general advice, wish them well, and keep in touch, for you want to make your association with them pleasant. Do not give them detailed suggestions on how to put together a specific offer or how to negotiate for you could be getting into a sensitive legal area.

In one instance, a young couple with whom I was working on a referral ended upon buying a house that was for sale by the owner. They were so distressed that I worked so hard with them and then got nothing, that they sent me Christmas gifts each year they were in town, and called me to list their home when they left. Not all stories like that have happy endings, so expect losses.

3. *Follow up.* If the visit results in a sale, you have accomplished your goal. If it does not, keep in close touch to be ready for the next visit or actual move. After having met and worked with the people, you should know exactly what they want and what they can afford. If something interesting comes on the market, immediately send them a picture along with descriptive information. Call them once every week or two to check on their status and to see if you can help in any way. If it will be several weeks or longer before they actually move, they may want to subscribe to your local paper. Send them the necessary forms. Some newspapers even have short complimentary subscriptions for prospective residents.

Keep the referring office fully informed. You may want to call the referring agent personally, for at that point he or she probably has better rapport with the people than anyone else, and may be able to help from that end in working with them.

## WHEN YOUR PAST CLIENTS GET AN ITCH

Let's say you move to a new city and shortly after you arrive you develop a terrific itch that just won't go away. You check with your new neighbors and get their recommendation for a local physician who specializes in skin ailments. The doctor prescribes an ointment that clears up your rash beautifully and in short order. On top of that, she seems like a decent, caring person. Chances are excellent that any time you develop a severe itch in the future you will go back to the doctor who treated you so well. You won't thumb through the Yellow Pages. You won't ask the service station attendant for his recommendations. You won't call Aunt Tillie, who is famous for her do-it-yourself home remedies. You won't even consult Cousin Fred, who sells ointments part-time when he isn't busy at the wrecking yard. Why should you? You know where to go to get professional service from someone you trust.

Any time anyone with whom you have worked develops even the slightest symptom of a real estate-related itch, you want to be the friendly professional that person calls. When that starts happening, you will know you are headed down the Yellow Brick Road.

# 12

# *Surviving*

## *Strategies for Staying Solvent and Staying Sane*

Certainly you will demand more from yourself and your career than mere survival. You will want to feel fulfilled in your work and earn an income that adequately reflects your abilities and rewards your efforts. But you have to get the basics under control first, before you can concentrate on doing the things that will really make your career take off.

Most of the threats to your job survival in real estate are simply variations of problems traditionally encountered in any profession. None are insurmountable, but taken in combination they can be formidable and you need to understand them. If you have previously been a successful business person operating in a highly competitive environment, particularly in sales, you may not need all the information I present. But keep an open mind. The survival techniques you learned in a related field may need some fine tuning.

### STAYING FISCALLY FIT

First, let's review the fundamental facts of life as a real estate agent. Whether you're an employee or an independent contractor, you are solely responsible for providing for your personal financial welfare. You will likely not be provided any company-paid medical, insurance, disability, or retirement benefits, although the brokerage may have plans in which you can enroll at your expense. These realities, plus the emotional pressures associated with any selling job, make it essential that you have a plan to keep your financial, physical, and mental health stable.

130

## LIFE ON A ROLLER COASTER

Managing on a fluctuating commission income is quite a challenge, since the rest of the world seems to operate on such an orderly basis. You, on the other hand, may earn several thousand dollars one month, and then not have a payday for two or three months.

The solution? When you are just getting started, you will need money to live on until the income starts. To be safe, you should have enough to last for several months. If you do not, you may quite understandably begin to let matters of survival cloud your judgment. As a recently licensed agent from Arizona expressed it in his survey: "You must be prepared to live without income for at least six months, or your integrity can be in jeopardy." Even if you make a sale the first day on the job (possible, but don't count on it), it generally takes 30 to 60 days or more for a transaction to close and for you to be paid. If you are married, it always helps to have a mate who is salaried. ("Get your husband a government job," was the sound advice from one survey participant.)

In rare instances, some affluent brokers may pay a new agent a monthly salary (called a "draw") while the agent is getting started; the amount is then deducted from later earnings. Many brokers who could easily afford this procedure don't do it because they do not feel it wise to place an individual in debt from the very start. I advise against it, except in a dire emergency.

Like it or not (and I hate it), budgeting is an absolute must. Over 75 percent of those who answered the survey said that *inability to budget personal finances to live on a commission income* was *very important* or *important* in contributing to failure (see Appendix A). Or, as a new agent from Missouri so aptly put it: "A fellow could starve to death!" The temptation is to assume that if you earn $4,000 in June you will earn at least half that much in July. That's not necessarily so. Most of us spend based upon what we earn and commit ourselves to debt based upon what we feel we *will* earn. Those who cannot discipline themselves to conserve their resources when paydays are frequent will find themselves scratching during the dry spells. (Real estate agents have been known to visit the local bank around April 15 of each year to borrow money for their Uncle Sam, who is totally unsympathetic to anything other than receiving, by the deadline, a good check for the total amount due.)

## GETTING PAID

Viewed from the outside, a job in residential real estate may appear to be glamorous, high paying, and not all that tough. That's how it looked to me. For example, most people know that, although commissions are negotiable, 6 percent is common. Let's see, sell just one $100,000 house per month and you'll gross a tidy $6,000, or $72,000 per year! You won't starve if you close one such sale a month, but it doesn't, in fact, put you in quite that high a tax bracket.

How does the commission system work? Let's illustrate by using the $100,000 sale. In most instances, you will sell another agent's listing. If that agent is from a different company, the commission will be split between offices, generally on a 50-50 basis. (It would work about the same if an agent from another office sold a listing of yours.) This means that the gross amount coming into your office will be $3,000.

Then there is the broker, who is providing everyone support and doing the best to make it all result in a profit so he or she can keep the doors open. Schedules differ, but a 50-50 split is common. That means that, of the $3,000, you personally gross $1,500. But remember, this is gross, not net.

From that, allocate roughly 15 percent as your cost of doing business. Automobile expenses, telephone calls, license fees, multiple listing fees, dues for professional affiliations, client relations expenses, clothing, business cards, postage, and office supplies all add up. Now consider federal, state, and local income tax, and Social Security. You should also plan to allocate a portion of your income to retirement plans. Most of these things will not be deducted from your check—you will have to budget for them.

After the dust has settled and the euphoria of receiving the check subsides (I took a picture of my first commission check), you can expect to net about $600 to $800 in spendable income, depending upon your individual situation. So you may have to sell a couple of houses and a listing or two each month to live in the style to which you would like to become accustomed. It has probably also occurred to you that the numbers would come out a lot better if you both listed *and* sold a piece of property. That's true. And that's how many of the most successful agents got that way and stay that way.

There is a fast growing concept in the real estate profession, referred to informally as the "One Hundred Percent" office, in which real estate licensees retain all of their commissions, pay a set fee to a broker, and handle all their other expenses. I will discuss this further in Chapter 13. While affiliating with such an office is a viable option for an experienced agent, it is not practical for the overwhelming majority of new licensees.

## BEING PREPARED FOR THE UNEXPECTED

### *When the Body Breaks*

The cost of medical care is astronomical, and it will only get worse. It is essential that you have insurance to avoid the economic ruin possible because of illness to you or a member of your family. If you have good insurance coverage of any type from a previous employer, or from a spouse's employer, hang on to it. Even if you decide to switch there is typically a waiting period to cover "preexisting conditions." There are a number of companies that sell policies, many of whom advertise widely in professional real estate publications. There are similarities in coverage, but there can be marked differences, particularly in responsiveness to claims. Your best bet is to investigate thoroughly by contacting several companies and comparing. If possible, talk to someone who is insured through the company. Find out how satisfied they are and how fairly and quickly claims are handled. You may also want to consider disability insurance to cover you if you are away from the job for an extended period.

### *When There Is an Untimely Demise*

If you never have anyone dependent upon you for financial support, you will have no need for life insurance. A life insurance policy is certainly not the best way to save money, although some do have cash value features, which simply means that eventually you could surrender the policy for cash or borrow against it. If you compare the premiums that you would pay over a number of years for a policy that does build cash value with what you could realize by simply putting the same amount in a savings account at the going interest rate, you will quickly get the picture.

It is not easy to get sound advice about life insurance, for any agent you talk to will have a vested interest. The larger the policy you buy, and the more money you pay, the better it is for the agent. Educate yourself as to the various forms of life insurance and decide which is best for you. You get the most for your money by purchasing decreasing term insurance (insurance that decreases in later years of the policy as your need for coverage declines). If an agent urges you to buy any other type, make sure it is to your advantage, not the agent's. These policies are widely available from companies affiliated with real estate professional associations. Investigate them first and use them as standards of comparison.

### When Ready Cash Is at Issue

You will also need to have cash for emergencies. The best approach is to open a savings account and to establish as your goal an amount equal to about two months income (that's been my goal now for about 30 years). The temptation will be to dip into this fund for non-emergency expenses, but the first time you have a real crisis you will appreciate being able to loan money to yourself, so to speak.

## PLANNING FOR RETIREMENT

If you are in your mid-twenties, it is hard to get excited about an event that might occur thirty-five or forty years in the future. But the mathematical reality is clear—the sooner you start saving for your retirement, the more financially secure you will be and the more flexibility you will have in determining your future lifestyle. Even if you are getting into real estate late in life, you need to plan for the day when you will retire completely. Here's how one veteran broker told me he advises his agents, young and old: "It's never too early to start and it's never too late, and no matter how much you save, you'll wish you had more."

The two major components to retirement planning are Social Security and do-it-yourself saving.

### Social Security

You have no choice—you have to participate. If you are an independent contractor, it will take a very sizable chunk out of your income; and if you are an employee both you and your broker will contribute. It would be extremely unwise, however, to depend upon Social Security as your sole source of retirement income. There are few issues of a more sensitive political nature than Social Security, and for that reason changes will be made slowly, but the evidence points to some drastic long-term revisions. Plan to have assets of your own.

You can get all the information you need about Social Security free from the Social Security Administration. Every city of any size has an office with an ample supply of literature that completely describes the program, and there are representatives who regularly visit smaller communities that do not have offices. It is essential that you formally check every two or three years on your official record of earnings, kept by the national Social Security Administration. Make certain you know exactly how your retirement entitlement is computed. The amount of your retirement check will be based upon your average earnings over a specified number of years that is determined by your date of birth. Know how long you will have to work to get maximum benefits. Social Security also has disability and survivor benefits features, as well as hospital and medical coverage for those over age 65. You should integrate these into your long-term estate planning.

### Do-It-Yourself Retirement Plans

To encourage individuals to provide for their own financial independence, the government has devised some very attractive programs. Details change, but the basic concept is likely to remain. You will be given substantial tax incentives to save for your own future. Currently, the two primary programs are individual retirement accounts (IRAs), for both employees and independent contractors, and Keogh plans, for independent contractors only. (The rules on who may open tax deductible IRAs are fairly selective, and change periodically, so keep up with them.) Subject to certain restrictions, money contributed to these plans is deducted from your reportable income for federal tax purposes. For example, if you invest $2,000 in an IRA, are in the 28 percent tax bracket, and are otherwise eligible, you will immediately have saved $560 you would have had to pay Uncle Sam. Further, federal tax on the interest you earn on your savings is then deferred until you withdraw the funds upon retirement.

Just to give you an idea as to what this kind of compounding does over a period of years, consider this. Assume that at age 25 you start contributing $2,000 each year to an IRA and that you continue doing so until you are 62, with interest on your money compounding at 10 percent per year. At age 62, you would have more than $600,000, and a tidy monthly income if you wished to start withdrawing it. If you left the money in until you were 67, it would top the $1 million figure! Since you can contribute even more to your Keogh, assuming you start earning a reasonable income, the figures in that instance would be even more impressive. Before you get too excited, however, consider what a loaf of bread might cost thirty-seven years from now.

The principle is sound, however, and as long as these programs exist, they form the most sensible approach possible for you to save money. Although savings plans account for a large portion of the money invested in IRAs and Keoghs there are other options, including the stock market. No-load mutual funds are a very popular choice. If you don't want to get fancy, there are now even several "index" funds that mirror the market as a whole. Even if you are older and plan to be in real estate for only a few years, IRAs and Keoghs are excellent investments.

## INVESTING YOUR MONEY

After you insure yourself, provide for emergencies, and establish a retirement plan, the next logical pillar in building your financial estate may be an investment in real estate.

### A Home of Your Own

If you are in the business of selling homes, it's a good idea to buy one of your own sooner or later—the sooner the better. You will be in a distinct minority among your peers if you do not. Among Realtor salespersons, 84 percent own their own homes. For Realtor brokers it is 90 percent.

If you've never owned a home, here is some basic guidance. You will have two major obstacles to overcome—the down payment and the monthly expenses. If you are fortunate enough to have a relative who will help you, fine, but most folks have to come up with the cash themselves. Use as a very rough planning factor 10 percent for a down payment and another 5 percent for closing costs, including loan fees. For a $90,000 house (you can adjust up or down for your area), you would need $13,500 cash at close. You may be able to reduce that if you are earning a commission on the transaction. You will have to finance the balance of $81,000. Assuming you got a mortgage at 10 percent fixed rate for 30 years, your monthly principal and interest payment would be $710.83, plus property tax and property insurance.

You can see that home ownership is not cheap, and that the hardest home to buy will be your first. The two variables that you need to keep up with are interest rates and property taxes. If interest rates were to drop to 6 percent (we can dream), your monthly payment would be $485.63. If you live in an area of high property taxes that seem to go up every year, you have a built-in payment escalator. On the positive side, there are substantial income tax advantages in owning a home, because interest and property taxes are deductible items, and there is always the possibility of a profit when you sell.

By the time you start looking at homes for yourself, you will be well versed in the house-hunting process, for you will have worked with others in satisfying their housing needs. But because this will probably be the most important investment you will ever make, it won't hurt to emphasize a few very significant matters.

1. *Get a firm handle on market value of the home.* You will become very good at this very quickly. Decide what outcome you want to achieve and establish your priorities. Make an offer that reflects your ideal outcome. Typically, that will be somewhat less than asking price. This does not apply if you, or your mate, have decided that, if you don't get that little charmer on Harmony Lane, the world as you know it will crumble around your feet and life will not be worth living. While you are playing real estate tycoon, the house might be sold to someone else! Just decide what it will take to buy it, and if you can afford it, make your first offer one that you know will be accepted. Even (gasp, groan) if that means a full-price offer? Yes. What is a couple of thousand dollars compared to twenty years of watery eyes or a mate with tight jaws every time you drive by that dream house on Harmony Lane?

2. *Be conservative.* Look at every house not only as a buyer, but as a seller, for that is what you will eventually be. If a property has a flaw, but it is one that does not particularly bother you, remember that it might very well bother others when it is time to sell. The most important factor for you to consider in choosing your home is—that's right—location! Everyone seems to know this, but it is startling how often it is ignored, even by real estate agents when they are buying a home for themselves. Insist upon property that is in a nice residential neighborhood, away from busy streets. If there is not a high pride of ownership in the neighborhood, as evidenced by well-cared-for homes, look elsewhere. If possible, do not buy the most expensive house in the neighborhood.

3. *Get an impartial inspection.* Make your offer contingent upon a satisfactory pest, dry rot, and structural inspection conducted by a licensed firm. In most areas, there are companies that specialize in generalized home inspections. It's worth paying for a professionally conducted inspection. By all means check out the home yourself as well. If the property is on a well, have it tested for potability and pressure. Take the water

sample yourself and have it analyzed. If there is a septic system, have it inspected by the county sanitarian or someone he or she recommends.

4. *Work to secure favorable financing.* Your first choice will be to assume a long-term fixed rate loan at an interest rate below the current market level. Assume a loan only with the concurrence of the mortgage holder. There are plenty of loans on the books that can be assumed, including older loans through FHA and VA. Just by keeping up with homes on the multiple listing service you will become aware of many. Do not take anyone's word that a loan may be assumed without checking yourself with the lender. Since there are frequently high equities involved in assumable loans (the difference between what the owner owes on the property and its market value), it is common for the seller to take back a second mortgage for a portion of that equity. Balloon payments, in which the entire balance due the seller is due to be paid in a few years, are also common. Be wary of these, particularly the ones that come due in just a year or so.

If you cannot find a loan to assume attempt to secure a fixed rate loan from either a conventional lender, the FHA, or VA. If you cannot qualify because the monthly payments are too high, it may be wise to wait and save more money for a larger down payment, as opposed to trying to find a "creative" solution to your problem. Agree to an adjustable rate mortgage only if you could live with the highest possible rate.

Once you own the house take care of it. A well-tended home in a nice neighborhood is always in demand. Protect your investment by not deferring maintenance on items such as painting and repairs. If your interests and talents tend toward working outside, so much the better, for the "curb appeal" of a home with an attractive yard can translate into thousands of dollars and a quick sale when the time comes.

5. *Remember that you are a licensed real estate agent.* The fact that you have specialized knowledge will make it incumbent upon you to be unusually open and forthright in all your dealings. Laws vary from state to state so you will have to check on local ground rules, but expect to have your personal dealings closely scrutinized. Keep your broker informed about everything you do, including buying your own home.

### Investment Properties

At some point, successful real estate agents seem inevitably drawn toward investing in income-producing property, usually residential property. Fifty percent of all Realtor salespersons, for instance, own investment real estate. Single family homes are the first choice (we're talking rentals here) at 28 percent, followed by vacant land at 17 percent, and multi-family units at 12 percent. Realtor broker statistics are even higher. There's a good reason for the interest in investment real estate. As an agent's income increases, so does the need for tax shelter, and few investments meet the need better than real estate (vacant land being an exception).

It is advisable, however, to enter your initial venture cautiously. First, do not be tempted to invest before you have a secure financial footing concerning your basic needs. Then, decide on the kind of investment with which you would be most comfortable. Is it a small rental cottage that you can drive by each day and admire? Or is it a duplex in a good rental area? In either case, are you prepared to deal with tenants and their inevitable problems? Could you withstand a downturn in your local rental market and prolonged vacancies? Finally, make absolutely certain that you are aware of all tax laws as they relate to rental property.

A nationally recognized author has sold thousands of copies of a book in which he outlines a system whereby he has turned a modest investment into millions in real estate. The plan is to buy old houses at bargains, fix them up, and sell them at huge profits. There is no question that money can be made by such an approach, but you can also lose your shirt. First, you have to have real expertise to judge whether a house is basically sound. Second, you must be able to estimate accurately how much work it will involve to make the repairs. If you are not handy and have to hire repairmen to do the work, it is most unlikely that the venture will be profitable (for you). And you must not only repair the house, you must also package a financing program that is attractive. Even experienced builders have difficulty putting an old house in order and selling it for a profit, so tread gently.

### Other Investments

There will be no shortage of other investment opportunities, from stocks and bonds to government securities to rare gems and metals. The more successful you become the more tempted you will be to invest in such ventures. Everyone must learn their own lessons, but the old pros (the survivors of good times and bad) offer these suggestions: stick to something you know (in your case, probably real estate), diversify, and be cautious.

## MAINTAINING YOUR PSYCHOLOGICAL BALANCE

In some professions you can leave your business concerns at the office at the end of the day, but that is just not the case in real estate. You will be under incredible self-imposed pressure to work late and put in extra time on weekends and holidays. There will always be some task that you could perform that might result in making more money. To compound matters, the more successful you become (the more sales in progress, the more listings) the greater will be the number of phone calls to you at home during your "off" hours.

## BURNOUT

"Burnout" is a term that has come into vogue in recent years, but the phenomenon was common in real estate long before there was a name for it. If you do not establish some personal behavior patterns and guidelines and stick to them, you will be a prime candidate for a "career readjustment" after three or four years, perhaps just at the point when you are becoming well-established and highly-paid. Here are a few suggestions to help you avoid that happening to you.

1. *Don't be a slave driver.* It is just as important to schedule time off as it is to schedule business appointments, and it is just as important to honor your commitment to yourself as to honor commitments to others. You may hesitate to follow this advice because of the nagging feeling that you may miss a phone call or that a detail on a pending transaction may not get taken care of. Because either of these events could mean literally thousands of dollars to you, the temptation is to consider yourself indispensable.

To allay your fears, one of your top priorities should be to establish a special working relationship with another agent in your office. Pick one who shares your personal business views and whom you trust implicitly. When you are out of town or on vacation that agent will handle your affairs and you will return the favor. It is the same kind of situation that exists when a physician is "on call" for an associate.

2. *Establish a communications system.* To avoid constantly worrying that you might be missing phone calls, you can do several things. First, for a nominal monthly fee you can have a "call waiting" feature installed on

your home phone. Here's how it works: if you are talking and another call comes in, you hear a signal. You can put the party to whom you are talking on hold, take the incoming call, and then finish your original conversation. If a wealthy out-of-town investor is at the airport and calls you about a $300,000 listing while you're on the phone discussing how to keep the bugs off of your begonias, you won't lose the caller to another agent. All members of your family need to be aware of how the system works and of the importance of courteously and effectively handling all calls.

You will also need an answering service or machine for periods when you are not available. Many individuals do not like using answering machines, and there are those callers who will not talk to one, but they are certainly better than nothing. Pocket paging devices are effective in maintaining contact when you are in the field. Finally, it would be good to have a phone in your automobile and fax machines are becoming as common as telephones with business professionals.

3. *Feel good and look good.* It is beyond the scope of this book or my expertise to offer detailed advice on diet and exercise, except to say that if you do not feel good physically and do not have a positive self-image, it will be hard for you to make the confident, successful impression that is so crucial.

It will be easy to fall into bad habits, for there will be so many occasions to celebrate and no shortage of frustrating experiences you would like to forget. If you do either by absentmindedly popping open a bag of candy (if life were fair, peanut M&Ms would be calorie-free), you'll find your spare tire gradually starting to inflate. It may be a constant battle, but the goal is to avoid becoming overly involved emotionally in your transactions and to vent your frustrations by exercising vigorously several times a week.

## A COMMERCIAL FROM THE SURGEON GENERAL

Smoking is not only a hazard to your health, it could be harmful to your career. As nonsmokers assert their rights more and more and as business owners begin to conclude that smoking in the workplace can be bad for business, the smoker's freedom is being inhibited. Some brokers do not permit agents to smoke in the office at all, and some have "thank you for not smoking" signs, even for customers. Smokers frequently seem unaware of the clinging nature of the smell of cigarette smoke. The aroma lingers on in the smoker's clothes long after the cigarette is gone. If you do smoke, be prepared for criticism and expect some unpleasant glances from non-smoking customers when they get a whiff of you. You could do your body and your career a great favor by giving it up. (You're right, there's nothing worse than a reformed sinner.)

## IT'S A FAMILY AFFAIR

You come home after a twelve-hour day in your real estate job. You spent the last six hours showing homes to people who finally confided that they were just browsing, and that, if they did see something they wanted, they would wait until nephew Clarence got his real estate license and buy through him. Your husband puts down his beer long enough to look up from the TV and complain that supper is late. Your daughter has had the phone tied up for forty-five minutes, even though she has been told repeatedly to "keep it short" so business calls can get through. Junior asks: "Sell anything today, mom?" Somehow it's not quite as much fun as you were led to believe it would be. The moral is clear. If you are part of a family, everyone has to understand how hard you work as a real estate agent and be prepared to make your job easier. The first $2,000 commission check or two you bring home should go a long way in getting their attention.

# 13

# *Where to From Here?*

*Long Term Options for Your Career*

To be a good general, you do not have to start as a private and work your way up through the ranks. But if you do, you will develop a perspective and understanding of your job not achievable by any other means. Likewise, you do not need to sell a lot of houses to succeed in the more specialized real estate jobs. However, the experience you will gain as a salesperson in face-to-face contact with the home-buying public will be of immense value to you and cannot be duplicated in any other way. Whether or not you ever want to do anything in your real estate career other than work in residential sales, it is good to at least know what the possibilities are down the road. There's no shortage.

## REMAINING IN GENERAL REAL ESTATE

Many agents spend their entire careers happily listing and selling residential property. They would not be content doing anything else, and would not really consider it "being in real estate." There are some advantages to limiting yourself primarily to residential sales. First, if you are good at it, you will be well paid and you will know what it takes (in terms of time and effort) to meet your financial expectations. Further, the longer you specialize, the better you will become, the more repeat business and referrals you will have, and the more control you will exercise over your business and personal life.

There are some negative factors. Although your income may be quite substantial, you will continually have to put together a large number of transactions, and despite the fact that you will control your activities more, your workload will always be large and demanding. Every buyer and seller is different, and each residential transaction will be unique, but there is just enough repetition to begin to bother some agents after a few years. And certain people simply need a new challenge to stay motivated.

If you do decide to remain in residential sales, let me suggest a goal that will add some zest to your professional life and provide the continuing stimulant you will need. Let's assume you've been in the business for about three years. You've become a Realtor and have achieved your GRI (Graduate Realtors Institute) designation. You earn a very decent living. You are looking for new horizons.

The National Association of Realtors has a program tailored for you. It is offered by NAR's Residential Sales Council. It is the professional designation Certified Residential Specialist (CRS), and represents the highest designation awarded to sales associates in the residential field. To earn it, you must have the GRI and meet other demanding professional requirements as well as completing several courses in such topics as: business development, listing strategies, sales strategies, career management, real estate investing, financial skills, computer application, and new home marketing. The courses are taught nationwide throughout the year by highly successful working professionals who have been down the same road you have. Don't wait to investigate this program. Know what the requirements are early in your career. If you are at all attracted to residential real estate sales, I can't imagine you not being turned on by this opportunity. For further information you may contact the Residential Sales Council at 430 North Michigan Avenue, Chicago, IL 60611-4092. Telephone: 1-800-462-8841.


## GREENER GRASS

If you conclude that you enjoy what you are doing, but would prefer doing it in another office under another broker, make *very* certain that you are actually improving your situation by moving. If you are making money where you are located, you are making money for your broker. You should be able to negotiate any reasonable changes you think might be necessary. Larger commission splits, more desirable office accommodations, increased broker support for high-producing projects, and more good-quality referrals are all possibilities.

Clearly, one of the most important factors in your success and contentment in real estate will be the personal and professional rapport you achieve with your broker. If you develop a good relationship, do not give it up without some very serious thought. Those who leave a company because they have become dissatisfied with the environment (as opposed to those who leave on good terms in order to take advantage of a more attractive professional opportunity), seem to make several such moves and have trouble achieving a satisfactory relationship anywhere.

## HAVING IT ALL

One special situation might tempt you to change offices even if you are happy where you are. We referred briefly in Chapter 12 to what is known generically as the "One hundred percent" concept, in which agents get 100 percent of all the commissions they earn. The broker provides the supervision required by law, acts as a general office manager, and supplies the necessary facilities support. In return, the agents pay a monthly fee for their office space, contribute to a salary for the broker, and are responsible for all of their own direct support, such as office supplies and postage, as well as personal advertising.

RE/MAX International Inc. (PO Box 3907, Englewood, CO 80155) is the leader in this concept. It is one of the most successful, vigorous franchises in North America. The typical RE/MAX sales associate has over ten years of experience and the average income for a RE/MAX agent typically exceeds the industry average by thousands of dollars (like several thousands of dollars). If it's such a great deal, why wait? Why not affiliate with a 100 percent office right away? I asked its co-founder and Chairman Dave Liniger if it was practical for a newly licensed agent to consider going to work for RE/MAX. The short answer is "probably not." There are a number of reasons, the most practical of which is that RE/MAX associates pay several thousand dollars per month for their share of office expenses. You would need to be awfully confident to commit to an annual overhead outlay of perhaps $20,000 before you even met a prospective client. Unless you are now highly successful in a directly related sales position with a lot of self assurance and a healthy bank account, file this one away for possible future reference.

## REAL ESTATE SALES MANAGEMENT

If a management career appeals to you, you have two basic options: you can work for someone else or you can start out on your own.

### Working as a Designated Broker or Sales Manager

A growing trend in the profession is for large real estate companies to hire one, or even two or more, brokers to run their offices. "Designated broker" is a widely used term. The concept is simple: you would be managing a real estate brokerage (alone, or with other brokers), while working for the owners of the company. Compensation would typically be in the form of a salary with other incentives for performance.

In large, active offices it is not unusual to encounter a sales manager whose job it is to supervise, train, and motivate the sales staff. The manager is generally paid a monthly or annual salary, as well as bonuses and incentives that are tied to the performance of the agents under him or her. In certain cases, the sales manager may do some selling, but the primary job is managerial.

If you are an outstanding salesperson, your broker (or another broker) might offer you such a position. It may be a tremendous opportunity, but do not automatically jump at it. On the plus side, you could expect to lead a more "normal" lifestyle (although, as a salaried employee, you are expected to be available whenever your salespeople need you, and that could be almost anytime). Your income will also be more stable, because you will not be entirely dependent upon putting deals together to get paid.

The mistake most brokers make is to assume that top sales agents automatically make top managers. That is not necessarily the case. You see the same thing in sports, where the superstar athlete often fails as a coach. It takes special skills and personality traits to become a good supervisor.

Top producers in real estate sales often achieve their success by being fiercely independent and employing highly individualistic business techniques. If you cherish your freelance status, a job as a sales manager is probably not for you. If, on the other hand, you think you might eventually like to be a broker, and the thought of supervising your current associates does not give you a sinking feeling in the pit of your stomach, becoming a sales manager could be a good move.

### Owning Your Own Brokerage

If you are suited for management, want to stay in the mainstream of general real estate, and don't want to work for someone else, you may want to own your own company. How do you know if you have leadership potential to risk it all and do it all on your own? It's not hard to tell. Consider your pre-real estate experience. Were you involved in leadership activities in school, in your previous job, or in civic groups? During your early years in real estate, were you active in professional organizations? Did you enjoy attending courses in professional education and react with particular enthusiasm to those classes that explained areas new to you? During the staff meetings at your office, did you contribute enthusiastically to group problem-solving sessions and did the other members of the group seem to particularly value your suggestions? Did you often wish that you were in a position to make the final decisions on how the office was run? Be very clear on the fact that not all good real estate agents have the potential to become good brokers. You have to have a burning desire to "be in charge," and the talent to do well when you are. If you are not certain, choose another course.

A logical way for you to learn more about the real estate profession and your own place in it is to get your broker's license. Doing so may involve additional course work covering office management, supervision, advanced financial and legal matters, and appraisal. As was the case when you got your salesperson's license, you will have to pass a test prescribed by the state licensing agency. Even if you decide that you do not wish to open your own office, having a broker's license is a logical career progression. You can still work in the same place under your current broker. Some organizations have several associate brokers. Having your broker's license opens the possibility of being able to take over and run a branch office of the company you work for; in this instance, you would operate in a separate physical facility, but you would still report to your broker.

If you decide you want to run your own company, you have two basic options. First, you can buy out an existing business. As you might expect, this approach will require some cash, sometimes quite a lot if there is real property involved in addition to the business itself. If you are buying into a franchise, the tab will be even higher.

More than any other factor, consider the reputation within the community of the company you are contemplating buying. If you buy a service station that has been poorly managed, you may be able to turn it around with new personnel and an aggressive, service-oriented approach. In real estate, however, public perceptions die slowly. If a company has a poor reputation, the bad rep is likely to persist despite the best efforts of new owners.

Another option is to start your own company from scratch. That does not necessarily mean you have to lease or buy your own office, purchase equipment and supplies, and secure agents. Some brokers start out as a one-person company, operating out of their own homes or in a very modest office. They expand as they gain confidence and capital.

Whether you opt for an existing company or start your own, you will eventually be in the position of recruiting sales agents. If you do a good job in this activity, it will be hard for you to fail. If you do a poor job, it will be nearly impossible for you to survive. If you don't think you are a good recruiter, be prepared to hire someone who is to work for you, for recruiting will be the key to your prosperity. For your really long range educational objectives, tuck away the fact that NAR's Real Estate Brokerage Manager's Council offers courses leading to the Certified Residential Broker (CRB) designation. You can get information by calling 1-800-621-8738.

## SPECIALIZED REAL ESTATE SALES

You may want to remain with the same company, but concentrate your efforts in a particular activity. Here are four possibilities.

1. *Exchanging.* You will recall from our discussion of investment property exchanges in Chapter 8 that there are exciting income possibilities in this activity. Larger transactions may include several different high-priced properties with a total value in the millions. There are exceptionally prosperous agents who work exclusively on property exchanges. If you close three or four exchanges per year (or perhaps only one or two), you can earn a whopping income and be fully occupied.

If you believe you would like to do exchanges full-time, your first step is to learn the basics. There are a number of books on the subject and professional organizations often sponsor educational sessions. If you are lucky, there may be a successful agent locally who specializes in real estate exchanges who teaches courses at your community college or university. If so, grab the opportunity. Make sure that any course you take is taught by someone currently active in exchanging and that the depth of instruction is adequate to get you beyond the initial overview stage.

There may be an Exchange Club organized through your local MLS. Members are typically agents who deal primarily or exclusively in exchanges and who meet on a periodic basis to trade information about specific properties. Meetings are an excellent source of contacts, and there are generally a handful of real pros in the group.

2. *Commercial and investment activities.* If you are fascinated by the prospect of dealing in commercial and investment transactions and you have genuine talent and true ambition, there is really no limit to your potential earnings. This is not the arena for the timid or faint of heart, so be ready for life in the fast lane to take you right to the high-rent district. A good starting point would be to contact the NAR affiliate, the Realtors National Marketing Institute, 430 North Michigan Avenue, Chicago, IL 60611-4092. Telephone: (312) 670-3780. The professional designation of Certified Commercial Investment Member (CCIM) is conferred upon those who meet stringent educational and experience standards.

3. *Farm and land sales.* I listed and sold two large farms while I was a general real estate agent. The experience convinced me that there was a great deal more to know than I had originally expected. If you did not grow up on a farm, you will be operating in a strange world with a bewildering language. Soil types, water and mineral rights, crop values, federal and state income tax and incentive programs, land leases, equipment valuation, and animal appraisal are just a few of the subjects with which you may have to become conversant. Farmers do not bluff easily and are exceptionally wary of anyone other than another farmer, so do not say more than you know. Although you can use many of the skills you develop while working in residential sales, the differences are so great that you would be foolish to try to compete with those agents who specialize in this without first preparing yourself.

The properties you will be trying to list or sell will not be located just around the corner, and they will ordinarily have a high price tag with comparatively few qualified buyers. You can easily spend a year marketing a listing, but if you earn a commission of $15,000 to $20,000 it is obviously worth it, particularly if you have more than one transaction going at one time. A good way to start is by contacting the Realtors Land Institute (RLI) at NAR's Chicago address and get a description of the professional courses they offer. Telephone: (312) 329-8446.

## DIFFERENT FOLKS, DIFFERENT STROKES

For some of you the overriding goal from your first day in the business will be to own your own real estate brokerage company. That's a noble and eminently achievable objective. The real backbone of the real estate industry in America has been the small "general store" office, looked over on a daily basis by a hardworking broker/owner. There are also tremendous brokerage opportunities available within the franchise systems, where many of the offices are independently owned and operated. Others of you will find your niche in an activity you knew about only vaguely before you became a licensed salesperson. Still others will continue in general sales and wonder why anyone would ever want to do anything else. It's hard to think of a profession in which you would have more options—all of them good.

You say you want more? There's plenty. Read on.

# 14

# *The Roads Less Traveled*

### *Other Real Estate Career Possibilities*

You will get a lot of mail as a real estate agent. Let me tell you about a packet I once received from an organization sponsoring an international conference on real estate. They were offering a one-week course in Geneva, Switzerland, for "the real estate professional who wants to become involved with the international real estate market." The faculty included people from the World Bank, Disney International, and Merrill Lynch Relocation Management International. The curriculum was intriguing: "International Manufactured Housing," "International Currency Hedging for the Real Estate Professional," and "A Case Study in Ecuadorian Real Estate Considerations." There was a hosted champagne mixer and reception dinner sponsored by the West Midlands Industrial Development Association. (You can bet that wasn't weenies and beans.) I still have the color brochure, complete with pictures of Swiss castles and quaint European villages. Unfortunately, I couldn't convince my broker to fund my trip.

## A VARIETY OF OPTIONS

You will have opportunities outside of general real estate brokerage that are just as exciting. During your early years, you will have a chance to decide whether or not they have potential for you. If you have established a favorable reputation as a residential agent, or if you have a background from a previous profession that is particularly appropriate for a specific activity, it is not at all unlikely that someone will be contacting you concerning a career change. Or you may simply get a brochure in the mail. However it comes, you will have the opportunity—or more than one opportunity—to explore a wide range of options. Some of these possibilities are the subject of this chapter.

### Real Estate Finance

One person with whom you will become very familiar is the loan officer. All lending institutions that make real estate loans, as well as certain government lending agencies, employ loan officers. Their job is to take loan applications, evaluate them, forward them to an underwriter for a final decision, and supervise the associated administrative work. When real estate is booming, there are tremendous opportunities in this field, but when times get tough and loan applications decrease, these specialists feel the pinch.

The job of mortgage broker is an interesting variation. A mortgage broker does not work for a specific lender. They take loan applications and place them with the lender that best meets the specific requirements and qualifications of the borrower. Not all lenders work with mortgage brokers, but enough do that they have a wide variety of possibilities to offer consumers. Their fee is typically paid by the institution making the loan (since having the loan application packaged for them saves them administrative costs), so it generally costs the borrower no more to work with a mortgage broker than it does to go directly to a lender. If you opt for the mortgage broker job, you will survive on a commission income rather than a set salary paid by a lending institution.

If you are excited by the challenges and opportunities of real estate finance and believe you would enjoy the lifestyle, develop other financial skills as well as your real estate expertise so your versatility will provide insurance against the upheavals caused by the inevitable downturns in the economy. A college degree, preferably in finance or business, is a necessity if you are thinking in terms of the higher echelons of management in a lending institution.

The Mortgage Bankers Association of America (1125 15th Street, NW; Washington, DC 20005) is a nationwide organization devoted to the field of real estate financing. Over 2,000 mortgage companies, savings and loan associations, commercial banks, life insurance companies, and others involved in mortgage lending belong. You may contact them for career information.

### Escrow and Title Insurance

In some areas of the country, real estate closings are handled by attorneys, who also perform title searches. In other places, the lending institutions themselves have an escrow department and hire an attorney to do the title search. Elsewhere, escrow and title companies perform both functions. The title search is done as a preliminary to issuing title insurance.

Both closings and title work should be performed by persons of intelligence who pay exceptional attention to detail. The escrow agent—the person who actually handles the closing—must be very adept in arithmetic functions and must have the ability to deal effectively with people who are in stressful situations. Real estate agents have the highest admiration for escrow (closing) officers, with whom they work closely. You see, if the escrow officers don't do their job properly, the agent never gets paid.

These are salaried jobs with more or less standard working hours. The best place to get additional practical information is your local title or escrow company. Community colleges quite often offer appropriate courses, as do some private schools. I typically have at least one or two students in my real estate salesperson licensing classes who are interested not in becoming a real estate salesperson, but learning more about the real estate profession in general to help them get a job in the escrow and title field.

The best book I have seen on the topic is *All About Escrow* by experienced California escrow officer Sandy Gadow (see "Real Estate Reference" in the References). Here is how she described the job to me: "Being an escrow officer is a combination of an accountant, a public relations personality, a legal assistant, and a salesperson." She suggested that an excellent way to get into the field and earn money at the same time would be to first attempt to secure a job as an "escrow assistant" or secretary in an escrow company, learn the ropes, and move up.

If you would like to know more about the title insurance field, a good contact is the: American Land Title Association (ALTA), 1828 L Street, NW; Suite 705, Washington, DC 20036. They are very active in producing educational material designed to make the intricacies of the field comprehensible to real estate professionals.

## *Appraising*

Fair or not (for the most part, not), appraisers got a lot of blame for the disastrous number of bad real estate loans that precipitated the Savings and Loan crash of the 1980s. The result, as might be expected, was federal intervention. By law, states must now regulate appraisal licensing, so if you are interested in this field, find out what the requirements are in your state.

If you enjoy doing the market analysis for a listing more than the other phases of listing and selling, you may be suited for appraisal. The real estate appraiser estimates, by as objective and scientific means as possible, the market value of real property.

In this field, you would have a number of options. Many appraisers are independent and either operate out of their homes or maintain an office. Some are salaried employees of government agencies, such as the county tax assessor's office, while others may be on the staff of financial institutions.

I should point out that there have been some predictions of dire downsizing of the appraising profession (more precisely, as it relates to the residential lending activity) based largely upon the impact of the computer. Lenders can now access real time information of comparable sales in seconds. Since their main concern is to verify that the property upon which they are considering making a loan has sufficient value, and since that is largely determined by what comparable properties are selling for, in many instances it is not necessary to hire an appraiser to do the research. They simply run the numbers and perhaps send someone out for a "drive by" to ensure the property is still in place and standing. You will want to keep close tabs on how this plays out if appraising is your choice of career fields.

Appraisal courses are widely available, and there are several organizations from which you can get additional information about the profession. Here are a few:

National Association of Independent Fee Appraisers, 7501 Murdoch Street, St. Louis, MO 63119.

Appraisal Institute, 875 North Michigan Avenue, Suite 2400, Chicago IL 60611-1980.

National Association of Real Estate Appraisers, 8383 East Evans Road, Scottsdale, AZ 85260-3614.

American Institute of Real Estate Appraisers, 430 North Michigan Avenue, Chicago, IL 60611-4088. An NAR affiliate.

National Association of Master Appraisers, PO Box 12617, San Antonio, TX 78212-0617.

In addition, the Henry Harrison Company, 315 Whitney Avenue, New Haven, CT 06511, publishes a wide variety of educational aids for appraisers, including a comprehensive book on how to pass appraisal exams titled *How to Pass Any General or Residential Appraisal Examination* (see the References under "Real Estate Appraisal").

### Real Estate Counseling

If you list and sell real estate, you are, in essence, a counselor. How good you are determines how well you will be paid, for until you produce results there is typically no compensation. Actual "real estate counselors," however, offer their counseling services for a fee, and if they are expert enough, people will gladly pay it. Particularly when considering investment properties, many prefer to get advice from paid counselors.

Practically speaking, it is difficult to see how you could establish credibility as a real estate counselor without first having achieved great success as an agent. The American Society of Real Estate Counselors, 430 N. Michigan Avenue, Chicago, IL 60611-4089, affiliated with the National Association of Realtors, is a leading professional organization. It awards the professional designation of Counselor of Real Estate (CRE) upon meeting predetermined standards. The National Association of Counselors, PO Box 12528, San Antonio, TX 78212, is another source of information.

### Corporate Real Estate

Many large corporations have developed an in-house real estate capability, since acquiring real estate, managing it, and disposing of it are functions of enormous magnitude for them. Job opportunities have increased as the trend toward corporate self-sufficiency has emerged.

The hiring process of any large business is tightly controlled, and as an applicant you must prepare and submit resumes, conduct interviews, and draw on your previous contacts. A college degree with a record of achievement and a demonstrated potential for future growth are minimal qualifications.

If the corporate world beckons, it would not be necessary to start by getting a real estate license, since as a corporate employee you would be exempt from normal licensing procedures. However, coupling your basic talents with several years of high-level performance in real estate sales, may help the corporate doors swing open.

There are several excellent master's degree programs in real estate at colleges and universities throughout the United States, if you already have your bachelor's degree. The expertise you would acquire in such a program, coupled with the personal contacts you would make, would be invaluable.

If you would like information about a possible career in the world of corporate real estate, an excellent source is the International Association of Corporate Real Estate Executives (NACORE is the acronym, based on their previous name—National Association of Corporate Real Estate Executives) 440 Columbia Drive, Suite 100, West Palm Beach, FL 33409. In a newsletter they publish, I read an article titled "How One Prepares for the Career" written by a young woman who was a Real Estate Asset Manager with the Burger King Corporation. She had received a Masters of Business Administration (MBA) in Real Estate and Construction Management (RECM) from the University of Denver. She was hired by Burger King upon graduation to help manage real estate holdings valued at over $1 billion. As she relates it, her job was to: "maximize return from the real estate portfolio through proactive asset management of approximately 200 properties." While no salary figures were mentioned, I'm guessing that such a job pays slightly more than that typically earned by the first year residential agent. If this lights your fire, contact NACORE for guidance and start checking around for MBA programs in real estate.

### International Real Estate

So, the conference in Geneva got your attention. Good. The organization that sponsored it is the International Real Estate Institute, 8383 East Evans Road, Scottsdale, AZ 85260. It's the largest international real estate association in the world with members in over 98 nations. They've had World Congresses in such exotic places as Copenhagen, Melbourne, Vienna, Athens, and London. Can interplanetary real estate and "Beam me up Scotty, I've got the listing agreement signed" be too far in the future?

### Planning

If you are interested in the kinds of activity that city, urban, and regional planners engage in, there are ample opportunities for you. But unless you have a bachelor's or master's degree in planning or a related discipline, the chances are slim that you would be able to secure meaningful employment. Government agencies and educational institutions (for faculty positions) are the primary sources of jobs, but some larger corporations have a staff of planners also. The emphasis on environmental and social factors as they relate to planning has spurred the development in this field. Almost every state has a university that offers a degree-granting program in some form of planning. For career information, contact: The American Planning Association (APA), 1776 Massachusetts Avenue, NW, Suite 400, Washington, DC 20036. It offers the AICP professional designation to candidates who fulfill association requirements.

### Property Management

There are enormous opportunities in property management. Owners of properties ranging from rented single-family residences to huge commercial complexes, such as shopping malls, are anxious to find reputable and efficient managers. The successful consummation of large real estate transactions sometimes turns on the quality of the firm that is to manage the property. General real estate firms often have a property management operation, so there is a chance that you will have gotten a taste of what is involved.

Management may involve specific bonding and licensing considerations so you need to investigate matters with your state licensing agency. Some enterprising real estate agents have formed their own residential property management companies and done quite well. The profit margin on each individual account is typically quite small; therefore, to be successful you must manage a large volume of properties or land a few big individual accounts, such as apartment complexes.

The Institute of Real Estate Management (IREM, 430 N. Michigan Avenue, Chicago, IL 60611-9966), a National Association of Realtors affiliate, is the largest of several professional organizations concerned with the needs and interests of property managers. They publish an annual catalog of publications, courses, and programs. If you believe managing a shopping mall has a certain glamour and appeal for you, the organization to contact for information is the International Council of Shopping Centers, 665 Fifth Avenue, New York, NY 10022.

### Land Development

The general term "land development" covers a wide spectrum. The first thing most people think of is the development of land for residential building purposes. The most common form would involve developing land into residential building lots and selling them to builders or private parties. If doing this interests you, it would be wise to start on a very small scale on an experimental basis before you cut yourself off from other income. Just locating and developing land for a very small residential subdivision could occupy much of your time and energy for months, and would no doubt test your business acumen in locating financing. Each state, county, and city has extensive requirements that must be satisfied before land can be converted to a residential subdivision. While these restrictions have served consumers well, they have made development an area where only the well-informed and astute players can prosper.

The American Resort and Residential Development Association (1220 L Street, NW, Suite 510, Washington, DC 20005) is a professional organization for those engaged in a wide range of land development activities.

### Home Building

If your idea of the typical home builder is one who turns out 200 or 300 homes a year, you share a common misconception. Although there are some giants, the average homebuilder in the prosperous 1970s constructed about 25 homes per year and in the 1990s it is much less than that. I am aware of several local builders who construct four or five homes per year and do quite well. Be advised, however, that this is a high-risk business, but one with tremendous opportunity.

Home builders, by and large, are entrepreneurs with a high tolerance for uncertainty and risk. If that describes you, investigate the opportunities. It is not exceedingly difficult to get started, assuming you have a buyer, have established yourself in the real estate profession, and have some cash plus good credit. It is generally easy to find a lot and the actual home building is primarily a managerial function. You must have the technical competence to judge the quality of the work being done and the supervisory skill to coordinate it, and it would be foolish to get involved unless you have some construction know-how, but your major tasks will be planning, organizing, controlling, and directing.

The National Association of Home Builders (NAHB), 1201 15th Street, NW, Washington, DC 20005, with over 150,000 members, is one of the most active of any of the professional associations in the country. Its membership is organized into state and local chapters that engage not only in professional development, but political action as well. They produce a catalog of products and courses that is available by writing them.

### Home Inspections

Because home buyers are typically eager to have a prospective purchase inspected before they O.K. the final deal, home inspection is a rapidly expanding profession. Sellers are often motivated to have their homes inspected and repairs made before they place the home on the market. Concern about such exotic potential problems as radon, lead, asbestos, buried gas tanks, dry rot, and bugs that eat wood have fueled the interest. I have a friend who was a former builder who now specializes in inspection and does extremely well at it. His wife, a very efficient and personable lady who sold real estate when I did, manages their prosperous family business. States are increasingly involved with licensing and bonding requirements, so check out any legalities. You can get some general career guidance by writing the American Society of Home Inspectors, 85 W. Algonquin Road, Arlington Heights, IL 60005.

### Real Estate Education

There are several possibilities if you decide you would like to teach real estate. The first, and one of the most popular, is to teach at a community college where career-oriented courses are emphasized. Those who instruct usually have master's degrees in business or a related field. Sometimes, however, real estate agents with acceptable academic credentials are hired to teach specific courses, so if you want to supplement your income while enhancing your own professional competence (and make some good contacts), explore this possibility. A broker from Texas summarized the advantages in his survey reply: "I teach part-time at the community college, which forces me to stay abreast of the current state of the art in real estate. It also provides a forum for recruiting bright new agents. Then, too, the prestige of being a 'prof' enhances my professional image and attracts more business to me as a result."

There are also a number of jobs in the various independent real estate schools. Since the content of the courses is strictly monitored by the state licensing authorities, and the academic and professional credentials of the instructors are carefully evaluated, you need excellent qualifications to qualify. This is a growth industry, for each time a state experiences some widespread consumer discontent with real estate licensees, a standard reaction is to increase the educational requirements for licensing, or to add to the continuing-education requirement.

Having taught real estate licensing in the evening adult education department at our local community college for several years, I can assure you that nothing you can do will keep your batteries charged more, or your ego in check better, than teaching prospective real estate licensees.

Another possibility is to present individual training seminars. Those who do are generally the real estate "fast burners," whose reputations for achieving staggering incomes ensures that when they speak, people pay to listen. Those who succeed in a big way, and command the big money, are generally dynamic public speakers who thrive on audience interaction. At another level, all of the franchises and many of the large independents have full-time trainers. These people typically instruct in the how-to techniques of real estate (listing and selling) and are ordinarily former agents (still with licenses) who were successful and who have a lively sense of communication. They may be on straight salary or on salary with incentive and bonus features.

The Real Estate Educators Association (REEA), located at 11 S. LaSalle Street, Suite 1400, Chicago, IL 60603-1210, is active in promoting communication and professionalism among real estate educators. It offers the opportunity to qualify for the professional designation of Designated Real Estate Instructor (DREI).

### Government Jobs

There are a number of jobs at the state and federal level in which a knowledge of real estate would presumably help. In each state, for instance, there is a real estate commission (or an equivalent) that oversees the entire real estate activity within the state, including licensing, education, inspection, and enforcement of rules and regulations. The combined work force across the nation is substantial, but entry is through competitive exams and state civil service channels.

### Other Possibilities

I know a broker who now spends almost all of his time producing weekly "Homes on Parade" magazines. He started by turning out one for the local company where he maintained his license. He did such a good job that he now produces them for dozens of other brokerages throughout the United States. Brokers send him photos and listing information, and he creates a finished product, prints it up, and sends copies back. If you have similar interests, there may be untapped opportunities worth exploring in your area.

## MORE?

You say you want even more? The possibilities are almost limitless, but I don't want to take away all the fun of discovery for you. Entrepreneurs are supposed to have great imaginations.

# 15

# Special Messages for Special People

## From Fast Trackers to Retirees

The real estate profession is truly a mansion with many rooms. No matter what your background there is definitely a place for you, if you want one. My purpose has been to give you the information you need to make a reasoned choice about your own career and much of what I have covered to this point should pertain to you no matter what your background. But there are challenges and opportunities that are unique to specific groups, so in this chapter I offer "special messages for special people."

### WOMEN IN REAL ESTATE

Well over half of all licensed real estate agents in the country are women and an increasing number are progressing to the broker ranks. Successful role models abound, and it would be difficult to find an occupation where you would encounter fewer barriers because of sex—it is an equal opportunity profession in the truest sense of the word.

Unfortunately, the opportunity for failure is just as great as the opportunity for success. Here are some questions it would be good to answer for yourself.

• *What is your motivation?* Here is a survey comment from an honest, if not tactful, broker: "Give me a woman who is divorced, supporting two kids, with house payments to make. Now *she* can sell real estate!"

Women come into the profession for widely different reasons. Many simply want to supplement the family budget. Others are looking for a meaningful challenge in their lives, with the money a nice, but incidental, feature. Many others need to earn a living, pure and simple. If they don't succeed, they don't survive—and they'll have to find another job. If you fall into this category, be very honest in assessing your talents and determination, and in recognizing the demands of the job. It is not nearly as easy as some successful women agents make it appear. Be certain, also, that you have the resources to see you through the predictably lean first six months.

- *What is your work experience?* When I was a new agent, my "big sister" was a woman who, many years before, had been a waitress. She was, and is, an outstanding real estate agent. We developed a close professional relationship and eventually covered for each other during absences. There are probably a lot of ex-waitresses who are earning very comfortable livings selling real estate. On the other hand, it has to be counted as a definite plus if you have had previous successful work experience in a more closely related job.

- *How tough are you?* When I was a corporal in the U.S. Air Force, the first sergeant of our outfit was a woman master sergeant (six stripes—the highest enlisted grade at that time). For those of you not familiar with the term, an old-time first sergeant was expected to be the toughest and meanest sergeant in the outfit, and could generally lick anyone in it. Our first sergeant certainly could have, although she never had to prove it. Her karate experience was a sufficient deterrent. She had come up through the ranks in World War II, and the image of her Sherman tank figure bulging in a too-small khaki uniform, with stripes running up and down her sleeves, is one that lives vividly in my memory. Now she was tough—physically and emotionally. I can't imagine a situation she couldn't handle, but she had the benefit of years of leadership training and experience.

How tough do you have to be in real estate? You certainly don't need to be a battle-hardened combat veteran with a karate chop that can shatter bricks, but you do have to be able to remain calm when things get tense. Let me give you a hypothetical situation (based on fact, embellished only slightly for dramatic impact) to stimulate your thinking.

### Take This Offer and . . .

Let's suppose that one of your first listings is a nice little three-bedroom home on five acres on a hillside in a peaceful country setting. The owner is a young, recently divorced working woman with two children.

You got the listing as a result of her calling your office one day when you were on floor duty. She explained that the place was too much for her to handle alone and that as soon as she sold it she would be looking for a small home to buy in town near her work. You do a thorough market analysis, ask several of the more experienced agents for their input, arrive at what you believe is a realistic price, meet with the young woman, and take the listing.

She assures you that her divorce is final and that the property is in her name alone. Your research confirms that to be the case. She mentions her ex-husband only once ("He was O.K. when he wasn't drunk."), but you learn from other sources that he spent time in jail for an incident in a barroom fight, and that he still visits on occasion.

You receive an offer on the property almost immediately. Although it is several thousand dollars below the asking price, it comes through a respected agent from highly qualified, motivated buyers. Indications are that they would be willing to negotiate and that a mutually satisfactory solution is entirely possible.

You make an appointment to present the offer, along with the other agent. The three of you are sitting around the kitchen table and have just about agreed upon the structure of a counteroffer at a substantially higher price, but with somewhat better terms for the buyers. The other agent says she is very confident that the proposal will be accepted.

Suddenly, from the back bedroom, stumbling and cursing, emerges one of the most thoroughly reprehensible-looking men you have ever seen. He is well over six feet tall and must weigh 250 pounds, or more. He is wearing a dirty tee shirt that smells of wine and beer, and looks as if he hadn't washed or shaved in days. The lady sweetly announces: "Ladies, this is my ex-husband, Linus."

Linus lurches toward the table where you are sitting, grabs the offer to purchase agreement out of your hands, and reads no further than the offering price. "So you're the little *bleep* who's trying to steal my wife's house," he screams in your face. "This place is worth twice this *bleeping* much. If you don't get your skinny *bleep* out of here, I'm going to stuff this where it won't never get no sunlight!"

To the woman you hastily mumble, "We'll talk later," grab your stunned associate by the hand, and get to the car as fast as possible. As you drive from the house, you see Mr. Wonderful in the rear-view mirror shouting at you and making obscene gestures. His snarling and barking German Shepherd escorts your car the quarter of a mile to the main road, doing his best to get at you through the car window.

Not every day in real estate will be that exciting (let's hope none will be), but you meet all types and you have to expect some rough-and-tumble situations. Not taking things personally, staying cool, and knowing when to retreat are valuable traits.

### What Do You Know About the "Business Birds and Bees?"

There is a certain element of glitz and glamour in the real estate business, and even an experienced girl's (or boy's) head could get turned. Agents understandably try to present the best possible appearance and attempt to stay psyched up when dealing with the public and associates. You will find yourself in situations, such as sales rallies and conventions, that promote socializing and revelry. You are also likely to meet a few super-salespeople who specialize in selling themselves. If you have a good grasp of who you are and clearly defined standards of conduct, you will find it all mildly amusing and view it with a friendly detachment.

If you are especially good-looking, you may find some of your male customers paying more attention to you than to the transaction at hand. (I've heard it works that way with male real estate agents and female customers too, but I have no firsthand knowledge.) Taking a friendly, no-nonsense attitude will keep things on an even keel.

Keep in mind that, in most home-buying situations with married couples, the woman quite often makes the final decision, or at least exercises veto power. Even if you are getting good vibes from the husband, remember that you have to sell them both, and a jealous wife is a mighty poor prospect to buy from you.

The Women's Council of Realtors (WCR) was formed to provide specialized guidance to women in their real estate careers. In its own words, the WCR mission is to "provide a referral network, provide programs and systems for personal and career growth, provide opportunities for increased productivity and financial security, and provide for the development of leadership skills." Their primary professional designation is the LTG (Leadership Training Graduate) awarded after completion of courses that emphasize communications, management, and leadership. They also sponsor a program on relocation, which leads to the professional designation RRC (Referral and Relocation Certification). Men are eligible to join. Information on WCR programs and products may be obtained by contacting them at: 430 North Michigan Avenue, Chicago, IL 60611-4093.

## HUSBAND-WIFE REAL ESTATE (OR HOW MUCH TOGETHERNESS CAN YOU TAKE?)

Real estate presents an ideal opportunity to work together with your spouse, if that's what you both want. There are several possible arrangements and a few important cautions.

In what may be the most common situation, both husband and wife work as licensed agents in the same office, but function independently. There are all sorts of variations possible. At one very successful local company the principal broker is a woman whose husband works there full time as an associate broker. If both partners are successful, there is the potential for a mighty healthy family income. Another advantage is that each can take pride in individual accomplishments.

The arrangement my wife and I had illustrates another possibility. We were both licensed agents in the same company and functioned as a team. I worked at it full time while my wife was part time. She developed some specialized prospecting programs and administered them, where I did most of the actual listing and selling. She was also relocation coordinator and on occasion listed property. As a matter of fact, she listed the most expensive piece of property (a large farm) that I ever sold. It was an arrangement with which we were both comfortable and which utilized our individual strengths.

There are some predictable problem areas. First, we are talking about a whole lot of togetherness, and, unless the relationship is exceptionally strong to begin with, a bad case of overexposure can develop. Second, each individual ego has to be delicately preserved. It is entirely possible that the woman may emerge as the more successful agent, so if you are a man with any male chauvinistic hang-ups you are in big trouble. In the same light, duties at home will have to be shared, which could come as a shock to some men. If you can handle these matters maturely, I can assure you that you will come to regard this phase of your married life as among your most cherished. The fact that all commission checks earned by both partners typically go into a joint checking account helps immeasurably.

## RETIREES AND REAL ESTATE

Many people look forward to retirement with eager anticipation and make a most satisfactory adjustment to it. A significant number, on the other hand, become bored. They may never admit it, but they actually miss working! Still others find that the Golden Years require slightly more gold than they have stored up, and they have to do something to earn extra cash.

There are a variety of excellent possibilities for retirees in real estate. There is sales, of course, and many seniors have become successful agents and continue to carry a full workload well into their seventies and beyond.

Two other possibilities exist that you might consider. One is property management. Pick up almost any newspaper in the country and you can generally find an ad that goes something like this: "Help wanted. Couple to manage apartment complex in exchange for rent and salary. Must be mature, dependable, and have experience with minor household maintenance and gardening." If you pursue this option, I strongly advise that you prepare by taking some of the property management courses offered by professional organizations. Some are generally available at the local level. Finally, if you are really good at household maintenance chores, such as fixing dripping faucets, repairing commodes, painting, unsticking doors, and replacing broken windows, you could earn a handsome income as "Fred, The Fix-it Man" or "Fern, The Fix-it Lady."

There is a negative stereotype or two about retirees that you will have to overcome. If you are considering real estate sales, your prospective broker may be worried that what you really want is a nice comfortable place to "hang your hat." The fact that a retiree probably already has a steady (albeit modest) income makes the motivation for entering real estate even more suspect.

It is best to meet the problem head on. Muster all the enthusiasm of a young college grad interviewing at IBM. Prepare a resume, buy new clothes, give it the works. Assure the broker that you have always carried more than your share of the workload and that you fully intend to do the same in real estate. Make a special point of telling the broker that you are definitely in it for the money, and not just to have a place to come when your golf game is rained out or your bridge game canceled.

A final suggestion. If you sold real estate several decades ago and have reactivated your license to give it another go, be very frugal with your advice and criticism. "That's not how we did it in the San Fernando Valley in '76," is not likely to win friends or influence brokers.

## REAL ESTATE FOR MILITARY RETIREES

If you are a military retiree with the right temperament, and you are willing to get out among the troops and hustle, a second career in real estate can turn out to be one of the most exciting and well-paying jobs you ever had. There are some features of the profession that ex-military people are typically quite enthusiastic about, along with a few that generally don't thrill them nearly as much.

First, the positive. In the military, your effectiveness was based largely upon subjective evaluation. That can be frustrating, for we all naturally think we do a better job than we are given credit for. In real estate, it is wonderfully simple. You are paid when you produce results. You are paid *every time* you produce results! For someone who is accustomed to receiving the same pay each month, regardless of how well or poorly you do, that is an exhilarating experience. There is even a danger that you can lose control and become a workaholic.

Then there is the excitement of being your own boss. You can come to work when you want, quit when you want, and dress how you like. Men, you can throw custom and caution to the wind and wear your hair long if that pleases you, and (may the Pentagon forgive you) even grow a beard and wear beads! As it turns out, the years of straight-arrow training will probably have left its mark, and you will no doubt continue to act like a good soldier should, but it is fun to have the option.

There are some potential frustrations. If you have spent 20 years or more getting to meetings on time, recognizing the chain of command, and generally following every accepted precept of good management and human relations ever conceived, the freewheeling, fiercely competitive nature of real estate can leave you perplexed. After the initial shock wears off, and after you get your nose pushed in the dirt once or twice, you will learn the ground rules and will be able to more than hold your own. Little things will always bother you, though. You will still grit your teeth when half the staff saunters in ten minutes late to a sales meeting, or someone clips his nails while the broker is talking. You will adjust.

You will also likely conclude that the level of professionalism among your new associates is not as high as that in the military. "My word is my bond" has no direct counterpart in the business world. But do not be too impatient. After a while, you will come to know who you can trust and who you would not leave alone in the supply room without an armed guard. Progress is being made on this front, particularly through the National Association of Realtors. You know how a really professional outfit should act, so pitch in and help them out with their efforts.

A cordial admonition is also in order. You will be happier if you accept the fact that you are starting over as a buck private in the rearmost rank. I have talked to dozens of ex-military people who are currently in real estate about their careers, and I have corresponded with many others. Their suggestion for success: Forget your rank. Or, as one ex-NCO put it: "RHIP-RIP (Rank Has Its Privileges–Rest in Peace)." Even if you had been the officer in charge of procurement at Humongous Air Force Base, and had handled multi-million-dollar projects so often that it all got a trifle dull, that will earn you no special privileges in real estate. You still have to deposit that $500 earnest money check the same as everyone else.

You will also have some negative stereotyping to overcome. Some of your coworkers are likely to see you as a saber-rattling automaton who will try to organize them into 0600 calisthenics every morning. You will eventually get most of the respect you deserve, but there is no rank insignia on your sleeves or shoulder to pave the way, and do not *ever* expect the same kind of courtesies and perks you enjoyed in the military, no matter how successful you become.

To make you feel welcome, here is a little story that is told about a former military man who went into real estate. A broker invited an ex-Army career type to join his real estate firm. The Army man seemed to be doing well enough, but it bothered the broker that the fellow did not show up for work until after 10 A.M. Finally, the broker could not stand it any more, and said, "Clyde, what did they say in the Army when you came in at mid-morning every day?" "Oh, not much," Clyde replied. "They just stood up and said, 'Good morning, Colonel.'"

### YOUR FIRST JOB?

If you are young and real estate is your first full-time job ever, you will find yourself in a distinct minority. If you are typical of other newcomers to the work place, you will bring with you a refreshing enthusiasm and an apparently inexhaustible supply of energy. Couple those admirable traits with the type of systematic and creative approach suggested in this book, and it will be only a matter of time until the paydays become frequent and predictable. What at first was bewildering and incomprehensible will start to fall into place, and in short order you will be one of the old-timers graciously offering advice and counsel to befuddled newcomers twice your age.

As you are getting started on the job, you will represent an extremely valuable asset to your broker in a way that you may not have anticipated. You will be reacting for the first time ever to the traditional ways things are done in the business world in general and the real estate business in particular. You will be unencumbered by a familiarity with the standard, the accepted, and the traditional. Because of this freshness, you will be an excellent sounding board. You will not have been conditioned by the old accepted arguments, and you were not around when "we tried that once before and it didn't work." If a policy or procedure seems questionable to you, do not be passive—express your reservations. If it doesn't seem to make sense or be fair, it probably poses problems for others also and it needs to be examined. You may even have to tell your Emperor Broker on occasion that he or she has no clothes on. The broker may not listen, but he or she deserves your honest opinion.

## THE "FAST TRACKERS"

There are some people in real estate who seem to be born to the profession. Everything they touch turns to gold. When I was very young, I had a short and undistinguished career selling the *Saturday Evening Post*. The standard procedure for most of us was to meet in front of J.C. Penney and wander amiably, but aimlessly, down Main Street, hoping someone would approach us and offer to buy one. Not my friend Reese. He had a system. He visited all the barber shops, doctors' offices, automobile dealers, restaurants—any place that might need a magazine each week. He also knocked on every door in the residential neighborhoods within biking distance of his home. Lord, that kid sold magazines. Reese was definitely several cuts above the rest of us as a salesman.

Be assured that if you are a fast tracker there are ample opportunities for you in real estate, and that the potential for material reward and emotional fulfillment are as great as any other in the business world.

## OPPORTUNITIES FOR TEACHERS

Because they have most of their summers free, and because the traits that make for good teachers also tend to make for good real estate agents, many educators are attracted to real estate.

Some work at it on weekends and holidays during the school year, and even after school. Many go into it on a full-time basis when they leave teaching.

One of my survey respondents, a high school social sciences teacher, described this arrangement: She was affiliated with a brokerage firm that was very active in new home sales. She spent most of her time when school was not in session in sales offices located in the model homes of various new-home subdivisions. She did not have to spend time prospecting, since her prospects came to her. She also taught several sections of personal finance at school, so she felt that the on-the-job experience she got in real estate gave her added credibility in the classroom.

Here is her brief comment about handling two demanding professions at the same time: "A lot of my friends are into skiing, stained glass, quilting, and other hobbies. Real estate gives me an emotional charge and it makes me a better teacher."

As a rookie real estate agent, I briefly shared office space with an ex-high school football coach who had left teaching to join our real estate company. It was an incredible experience, and it gave me an inferiority complex from which I had great difficulty recovering. His phone rang constantly. People called our secretary to make appointments just to talk to him on the phone. It seemed to me that everyone in that little community was beating down the doors to work with "the coach," while I was spending most of my time studying and getting ready to spring into action should the need ever arise. So if you have celebrity status, even if it is of the small-town athletic variety, it can be a big boost to your fledgling real estate career. Remember, though, that the initial contact with the prospect is only the first step in your lesson plan.

## MID-CAREER JOB CHANGERS

A prominent real estate educator from New York State made this comment when I asked her if she thought there was a need for the kind of real estate career guide I was writing: "Yes. Everyone and their brother thinks they can sell real estate."

It's true. There is a widespread fascination with the profession and there are probably thousands of people in the middle of other careers who would just love to chuck it all, get their real estate license, and start doing something they think they would really enjoy. A lot of people do just that. Almost 90 percent of all real estate agents were in another occupation before. While it's true that a small percentage of these people are retirees (notably from the military), and some were not actively engaged in their previous occupation when they came into real estate, there is still a goodly representation of people who simply got the real estate bug badly enough to change careers in midstream. You will have plenty of company if you make the same decision.

## NON-LICENSED INVESTORS

Over the past few years, an increasing number of students have enrolled in my real estate classes to learn more about how the profession operates with the objective of becoming more astute investors. They were interested in gaining the knowledge, but did not want to be burdened by the restrictions placed upon real estate licensees who buy for their own account. That involves mandatory disclosure and being held to a higher standard than non-licensees. One former student who followed this path has been particularly successful. He's in a type of service business that puts him in contact with many owners of real property who are planning repair work. Some are doing that in anticipation of selling. He's informed, articulate, and honest—and he's purchased a number of very good real estate investment properties by being there with "the fustest with the mostest."

## A LICENSE TO INVEST

There are also a handful of individuals who get their real estate license and affiliate with a broker with only one objective in mind—to find great real estate investment opportunities. No listing, no selling, no floor duty, no nothing but investing. Of course, there are some formidable hurdles. First, you would have to find a broker who would let you hang your license in his office. That would be tough. Next, you would have to disclose your license status in any transaction and your actions would be held to a high professional standard. The advantages would be that you would be on the ground floor of a lot of good opportunities and you would have your share of the commission to work with. Get a lot of guidance from seasoned pros before you even consider this one.

## GAME TIME

Game time approaches and you are chomping at the bit to go out there and "sell one for the Gipper." But hold on for just a minute. The grizzled old coach, who has been there himself and is obviously moved by the moment, has a few final inspirational words for you before kickoff.

# 16

# *A Final Encouraging Word*

### *How to Succeed in Real Estate by Really Trying*

Whoever observed "I've been rich and I've been poor—I'll take rich," said it for most of us. Although we may have never been really destitute and, at the same time, never aspired to be Rockefeller-rich, we are reasonably confident that there is no particular virtue in poverty.

Barring an unlikely run of dumb luck or the bequest of an affluent relative, becoming prosperous and staying that way takes a lot of hard work and an ability to manage success when it comes. In real estate, for example, there are those who are quite comfortable in administering a modest amount of achievement, but who start to lose control and confidence when things really start to hum and demands intensify. A major objective of this book has been to put you in the position to decide for yourself exactly how successful (and rich) you would like to be, based upon your priorities, the amount of effort you want to expend, and the lifestyle you want to lead. If it's fame and fortune you decide upon, here are a few final thoughts.

## YOUR PRESCRIPTION FOR PROLONGED PROSPERITY

You will likely attend a lot of megahype sales seminars and rallies during your real estate career. The search for the magic formula for success is endless. New marketing ideas will burst on the scene, remain in vogue for a while, and, mercifully, fade into well-deserved obscurity.

Some of them will truly boggle your mind. The most incredible I ever heard involved a form of hypnotism. ("When you hear the word 'blue' you will have warm and loving thoughts about the home on Tranquillity Circle and have an uncontrollable urge to buy it.") Most are not that bizarre and will have at least a few useful elements.

In reviewing my old course notes from the Realtors Institute, I came across the following comments of a now-forgotten (by me) speaker. "To get rich and be happy in real estate," I recall him saying solemnly to a suddenly attentive audience, "it will take a whole lot of perspiration and once in a great while a little inspiration. There is only one rule you ever need to worry about following. You will recognize it by its golden color." In response to a few scattered groans, he finished with something like, "Well, what do you want—originality or good advice?" In my notes, I wrote, "Hokey, but true." There is no magic formula for success, but I do have some suggestions I hope you will consider. If, as you read what follows, you think to yourself, "Hokey, but true," I'll be happy.

1. *Above all, keep in mind what creates the need for real estate agents.* As long as you have anything to do with residential real estate, remember that it is first, last, and always a people business. With all of the technical advances, organizational innovations, and intramural squabbles within the profession, it may be easy to lose sight of the primary reason real estate agents exist: to help people solve their housing problems. Those who stress service—honest, efficient, courteous, and above all, individualized—will have people lining up to see them. The same will apply in principle no matter where in real estate your career ultimately takes you.

2. *Develop an attitude.* Technology is changing the way real estate professionals do business. Virtual tours of homes from the comfort of the real estate office, computers that permit cross-country teleconferencing, entire training programs on one dinky little CD-ROM (whatever that is), software programs with bells and whistles for virtually your every real estate need are all part of the landscape. The future possibilities boggle the mind. It would be easy to become overwhelmed and intimidated, particularly for those of us who, as they say, have been around the block a few times. Keep an open mind and try out all the new stuff. Don't attempt to understand it all—just accept on faith that it's a miracle and develop the ability to sort out the useful from the glitzy.

3. *Take the long view.* When the nation's economy is healthy and the housing industry robust, folks tend to think and act like the good times

will roll forever. When interest rates skyrocket and unemployment soars, the doomsayers are sure things will never get better. But, whether times are good or bad, the urge for home ownership is so deeply ingrained in the American character that there will always be a need for true real estate professionals. One reason the dropout rate among agents is so high is that they allow themselves to ride an emotional roller coaster. Those who retain their enthusiasm, yet develop a sort of mature detachment born of a good grasp of historical perspective, will be the contented and prosperous survivors.

4. *Follow your heart.* It is highly unlikely that your plan to enter real estate is a result of your parents' lifelong dream to have a licensed salesperson in the family, and that they scrimped, saved, and made sacrifices for years just to pay for your training. It is much more probable that you are attracted to it because it sounds a little exciting and because you believe you will be good at it. In fact, you are much more likely to succeed if you *are* happy at what you are doing. If that means selling modest little homes in Topeka for the rest of your career, wonderful. On the other hand, if marketing condos on the French Riviera has a certain appeal to you, go for it. And someone has to be the first real estate agent in space, right?

5. *Listen to the little voice.* There are little voices, and then there are *little* voices. I am not talking about the one that whispers, "Sultan's Delight in the third at Pimlico." I am talking about your conscience. No matter how much we may try to bury it with rationalization or self-deception, it is always there, ready to tell us clearly what is right and what is wrong. So when you are showing the home to those nice people from out-of-state and the little voice says quietly, but firmly, "Better mention the lake in the basement," it is a good idea to pay attention.

6. *Forget the commission.* Forget the what!? You read correctly. Forget the commission. I can understand your confusion. But here's why I'm advising this drastic course of action.

Your success will be determined by how well you solve problems. Solve a lot of problems and you will make a lot of money. If you try to steer people toward solutions that result in the biggest payoff for you, as opposed to the best possible solution for them, you will become confused, ineffective, and transparent. People will lose confidence in you and you will lose respect for yourself.

Now, if a $400,000 farm you know about seems perfect for a rich Canadian who is looking for a ritzy horse set-up, you'll automatically spend a minute or two calculating what your potential earnings might be.

That's only natural. But, when you are making your decisions, the only question you should ask yourself is, "How well does this fit my customers or client's needs?"

Am I saying that, in deciding what properties to show a prospective purchaser, it should make absolutely no difference to you whether the commission is 5 percent, 6 percent, or 10 percent? Am I further saying that you should not even be influenced by such thrilling enticements as, "Sell this turkey and win a trip to Pango Pango on the luxury barge *Condemned?*" You have definitely got it. Solve the problems and the commissions will take care of themselves. It works that way. Trust me.

7. *Develop your network and keep it up-to-date.* Networking is really old wine in a new bottle. It simply means keeping in close contact throughout your career with those people on whom you know you can count to help you get a job done, and who can count on you to help them. Professional organizations provide potentially fertile ground. Start early and stay with it. Networking is absolutely critical; it pays incredible dividends.

8. *Let your little light shine.* I am not saying that if you think good thoughts, smile a lot, put in ten hours a day, and have good contacts you are sure to be hugely successful in real estate. Those are admirable traits, but it takes more in a highly competitive business. The phrase, "Early to bed, early to rise, work like hell—advertise," captures the spirit of the point I am making. I always sincerely felt that people were very fortunate to have me handling their real estate affairs. I knew what kind of a job I would do. I never felt even the slightest inclination to hide my light.

9. *Don't sell yourself short.* I thoroughly enjoy teaching real estate licensing courses at the local community college. It is disheartening, however, when I encounter a student with tremendous potential who is convinced that they are capable of only modest achievement. I have seen some of the great ones operate, in real estate and other professions. A rare few are gifted. Most are simply people of average abilities who are determined to succeed and who are, to resort to a cliché, "willing to dream the big dream."

10. *Do it all with a little class.* As a young U.S. Air Force officer I was stationed in Alabama when legendary coach Bear Bryant returned to his beloved alma mater to coach ("Mama called," said the Bear). Along with the rest of the state, I watched each Sunday afternoon during football season when Bear narrated the 'Bama game from the day before. On those infrequent occasions when the Tide lost or didn't win by as much as was expected, the inevitable question posed by the moderator was "what hap-

pened?" The typical growling response went something like this: "That was the sorriest job of coaching I've ever seen. We just have to suck it up and hunker down." No whining. No complaining. No looking for someone else to blame. Just work harder. Bear was, as they say, a class act, and one worthy of emulating in any profession, real estate included.

11. *Keep in touch with reality.* If you work in general residential real estate, you will have absolutely no difficulty staying humble. There is something about showing houses to the great American home-buying public that will tend to discourage any inclination you might have to develop a god-like image of yourself. And when a customer's child wets his pants on the back seat of your nice new car, you will be reminded that you are not in total control of even your own little universe. If you end up selling chalets to the beautiful people in Aspen, or shopping centers to oil-rich Middle Eastern sheiks, it is entirely possible that you may need to develop some other techniques of reminding yourself of your mortality. An honest mate or a very good friend are your best bets to perform that vital function.

12. *Remember, it's still the "land of opportunity."* There are so many "rags to riches" stories from real-life real estate that it's hard to know who to cite as the best examples. I'll mention just two very briefly.

One is Danielle Kennedy. She started selling real estate in 1972 at age 27 when she was six months pregnant with her fifth child and facing a personal crisis. Although she had very little formal sales training, she was driven by that most compelling of all motivations—to provide for her family. After a rocky start, she listed and sold over 100 homes yearly, which put her in the top one percent of all real estate professionals in the nation. She is currently one of the most successful real estate trainers, authors, and speakers in the country. (If you ever get the chance to listen to her, grab it. I've also included information on her educational material under "Real Estate Marketing" in the References.) In addition to her other remarkable achievements, she has handled with equal distinction and grace the demands of being a wife and the mother of eight children.

Another example is provided by Dave Liniger, the co-founder (with his wife) and now the Chairman of RE/MAX International Inc., whom I mentioned in Chapter Three. Liniger was a college dropout who joined the Air Force and taught ROTC at Arizona State University in the mid 1960s. While there, he started buying single family homes as investments, and is said to have owned twenty of them by age 24. He got a real estate license to save the commissions on his deals, and the rest, as they say, is history. The first company he worked for allowed agents to keep all of their commissions in exchange for a monthly fee. It was the inspiration for the 100 percent concept that he perfected and franchised. Under his leadership, RE/MAX has emerged as one of the largest, most prosperous, and vibrant real estate operations in the United States, Mexico, Canada, and other exotic locations around the globe. There are currently more than 2,600 RE/MAX offices worldwide with nearly 42,000 associates.

If you knew the personal history of the most successful local real estate brokers in your town, or if you were to examine the backgrounds of the top executives at any of the large franchises, I am certain you would find stories just as inspirational as those of Kennedy and Liniger. If you do not firmly believe that this is still the land of opportunity, where vision, persistence, and hard work will pay off for you, you simply have not been paying close attention.

13. *Get your priorities straight.* The story is told of two men who were attending the funeral of Andrew Carnegie, one of the wealthiest men in U.S. history. "How much did he leave behind?" asked one of the men. "He left it all," replied the other. How you order your life's priorities will be a very personal matter. This much, however, is incontestable: Unless your physical and emotional health are good, nothing else matters much. And if Mr. Carnegie couldn't take it with him, what chance do you think you have?

## WHEN YOU BECOME SUCCESSFUL BEYOND YOUR WILDEST DREAMS

As you are getting started, it will be hard for you to imagine that there will come a day when your biggest challenge will be to take care of all your business and still have time for a personal life of your own. That will happen if you've got the right stuff and you use it properly. When it does, be ready to make some changes in how you conduct your affairs. Here are two suggestions.

1. *It's about time.* First, you need to make a major adjustment in your attitude toward the value of your time. Just to give you a point of reference, assume that in your third year you net $100,000. (You did pay attention, didn't you?) Based upon a 40-hour week, with two weeks off for vacation, that means your net hourly wage would be roughly $50. You

may make less than that, or you could make more, but the concept is the same. The time you spend on any needless task costs you money.

It is not enough just to develop a general sensitivity to the fact that "time is money." Remember what a terrific deal you offer people. You can look listing prospects straight in the eye, for example, and honestly pronounce: "Folks, if I don't produce results you will owe me nothing. It makes no difference how much time I spend trying to help you solve your problem; if I don't deliver the goods to your satisfaction, I will thank you for allowing me to try, and we part friends, but no money changes hands." (Try asking your doctor, lawyer, CPA, or auto mechanic for that kind of guarantee.) I assume it is redundant to encourage you to be results oriented.

2. *Help wanted.* Beyond the normal things you can do to manage your time more effectively, there is another step you may want to consider— hiring help. I do not make this suggestion lightly. One of the exhilarating aspects of being a Lone Ranger Independent Contractor Real Estate Agent is that you are your own boss with no one else to worry about. You're in complete and total control of a dedicated, one-person operation—you. When you employ someone, you introduce all sorts of ugly words into the equation—words like overhead, span of control, bureaucracy, and employee relations (I had better stop—I don't want to stir up more snakes than I can kill).

Here's an example of how hiring an assistant can pay off. I once had a referral to make on a young couple who were heading to Montgomery, Alabama. I recalled a fellow I was associated with there when I was in the Air Force who had gone into real estate upon retirement. I called his office to place the referral and was put in touch with his administrative assistant, who, after screening my call, patched me in on the car radio to the Old Sarge himself. He handled the referral faultlessly, I received my fee, the couple found a home they were happy with, and Sarge earned a healthy commission. I learned from other sources that he had emerged as one of the most successful agents in the area. I'm sure he more than paid for his assistant's salary that month with my one referral.

The point is that you can vastly increase your earnings, and take a lot of pressure off of yourself, by paying someone to help you. More and more really successful agents—and those who wish to become really successful—are doing this. It takes a leap of faith, but the payoff can be substantial. (Remember, even the Lone Ranger eventually teamed up.)

You will find a reference in the References to the book *Multiply Your Success With Real Estate Assistants* by Monica Reynolds. Reynolds, who has emerged as the guru of the real estate assistant movement, was a top-producing real estate agent in her own right and then became an assistant to one of real estate's legendary superstars—Walter Sanford. Her book has deservedly emerged as the standard reference on the subject. It's full of practical guidance and would be a good starting point for you if I've convinced you that hiring help might be a wise move for you.

## ON PRIDE AND PROFESSION

Is real estate a profession that commands a high degree of public confidence and respect? If you believe Mr. Gallup and Mr. Roper, there's a great deal of room for improvement. It does not rate highly on public opinion surveys. In my own survey, 25 percent of the respondents thought that the *feeling that real estate is a field that lacks public respect* was *very important* or *important* in causing people to leave the profession. For that matter, is real estate really a profession? It all depends upon the criteria you establish. But that is not the point, nor is it really that critical where people place it on their hierarchy of respect. The important thing is *your* attitude toward what you do for a living. You will have every right to be as proud of your job in real estate as those in law, teaching, accounting, or medicine.

In our quiet little town alone, I can take you to any number of real estate licensees who are consummate professionals by any definition you wish to use. They observe the highest ethical standards in their business and personal affairs, they treat their clients and their competition with respect, and they keep up-to-date on the latest developments in the field. I am certain the same is true in all parts of the country. This does not mean that the overall level of professionalism within the industry cannot be raised. It needs to be, and you will be disappointed and discouraged by the conduct of some of your associates. At times, you will be appalled. But the foundation for improvement exists within organizations such as the National Association of Realtors and through state licensing agencies. Much more critical a task is the need to attract quality people into its ranks in the first instance. If you have come this far with me, I can assure you that you would fit in nicely.

## ALL THIS AND MONEY TOO

When I was getting started in real estate, another new agent in our office (who was having a little trouble earning that first commission) was fond of saying that real estate would be a lot of fun, if you only got paid for it. It is a lot of fun, and you can get paid for it—and paid extremely well. In the event your ultimate ambition is to be among the "soarers" of the real estate profession, I'll close with my "Top Ten Things to Remember If You Want To Soar Like an Eagle."

Good luck in *your* successful real estate career!

## TOP TEN THINGS TO REMEMBER
## IF YOU WANT TO SOAR LIKE AN EAGLE

10. You must conquer your fear of heights.

9. No matter how gross the vultures and other subspecies may act, emulate the actions of the highest and noblest soarers, and always conduct your affairs in a manner befitting a national symbol.

8. Don't be afraid to go out on a limb—after you've invested a few dollars in soaring lessons.

7. Keep your beak to the grindstone, but remember that longevity is enhanced by periodic flights of fancy somewhere over the rainbow.

6. Feather your nest for your post-soaring years.

5. Let the early birds fight over the worms—you go for more regal fare.

4. Map out a flight plan before you take off and learn to soar in both good weather and bad, but avoid tornadoes, hurricanes, lightning storms, and large airborne objects with "Boeing" written on the side.

3. Keep an eagle eye out for opportunities over distant horizons, but remember that hunting will likely be best in your own familiar domain.

2. Avoid associating with turkeys.

1. If at first you fail to soar—fly, fly again.

# Appendix A
# *Survey Results*

Question: Based upon your experience, please indicate how important you think each of the following is in causing people to leave the profession of real estate.

| | Very Important or Important | Neutral | Very Unimportant or Unimportant |
|---|---|---|---|
| 1. Lack of "self-starter" and "self-motivator" personality. | 91% | 5% | 4% |
| 2. Unrealistic income expectations. | 85 | 4 | 11 |
| 3. Unwillingness to work hard enough to produce results. | 84 | 10 | 6 |
| 4. Inability to budget to live on commission income. | 75 | 15 | 10 |
| 5. Lack of objective information about the career field before they entered it. | 73 | 18 | 9 |
| 6. Inability to plan and manage time. | 72 | 19 | 9 |
| 7. Inability to establish specific goals. | 70 | 18 | 12 |
| 8. Lack of long-term supervision and motivation by brokers. | 63 | 28 | 9 |
| 9. Inadequate preparation in practical real estate matters during pre-license activities. | 60 | 27 | 13 |
| 10. Pressures generated by problems typically associated with real estate transactions. | 56 | 31 | 13 |

*(continued)*

|  | Very Important or Important | Neutral | Very Unimportant or Unimportant |
|---|---|---|---|
| 11. Erratic and unpredictable work schedule | 53 | 11 | 36 |
| 12. Disenchantment with high-pressure sales techniques they were expected to use. | 43 | 38 | 19 |
| 13. Feeling that the real estate profession lacks public respect. | 25 | 40 | 35 |
| 14. Over-regulation of activities by state licensing agency. | 2 | 31 | 67 |

The purpose of the survey was to examine possible causes of attrition in real estate. Three hundred forty-nine active, licensed real estate salespeople and brokers participated. To show major trends, "very important" and "important" responses were combined, as were "very unimportant" and "unimportant."

# *Appendix B*

## *State Real Estate Commissions*

Alabama Real Estate Commission
1201 Carmichael Way
Montgomery, AL 36106
(334) 242-5544

Alaska Real Estate Commission
3601 C Street, Suite 722
Anchorage, AK 99503
(907) 563-2169

Arizona Department of Real Estate
2910 N. 44th Street, Suite 100
Phoenix, AZ 85018
(602) 468-1414

Arkansas Real Estate Commission
612 South Summit Street
Little Rock, AR 72201-4740
(501) 682-2732

California Department of Real Estate
2201 Broadway
Sacramento, CA 95818
(916) 227-0782

Colorado Division of Real Estate
1900 Grant Street, Suite 600
Denver, CO 80203
(303) 894-2166

Connecticut Real Estate Commission
165 Capitol Avenue
Hartford, CT 06106
(860) 566-5130

Delaware Real Estate Commission
P.O. Box 1401
Dover, DE 19901
(302) 739-4522, ext. 219

District of Columbia Real Estate
   Commission
P.O. Box 37200
Washington, DC 20013-7200
(202) 727-7450

Florida Division of Real Estate
400 W. Robinson Street
Orlando, FL 32801
(407) 423-6053

Georgia Real Estate Commission
Suite 1000—Cain Tower
229 Peachtree Street, N.W.
Atlanta, GA 30303-1605
(404) 656-3916

Hawaii Real Estate Commission
250 S. King Street, Room 702
Honolulu, HI 96813
(808) 586-2643

Idaho Real Estate Commission
P.O. Box 83720
Boise, ID 83720-0077
(208) 334-3285

Illinois Real Estate Commission
500 East Monroe Street, 2nd Floor
Springfield, IL 62701
(217) 782-9300

Indiana Real Estate Commission
IGCS, 302 W. Washington Street,
E034
Indianapolis, IN 46204-2700
(317) 232-2980

Iowa Real Estate Commission
1918 S. E. Hulsizer Avenue
Ankeny, IA 50021
(515) 281-3183

Kansas Real Estate Commission
Three Townsite Plaza, Suite 200
120 SE 6th Avenue
Topeka, KS 66603-3511
(913) 296-3411

Kentucky Real Estate Commission
10200 Linn Station Road, Suite 201
Louisville, KY 40223
(502) 425-4273

Louisiana Real Estate Commission
P.O. Box 14785
Baton Rouge, LA 70898-4785
(504) 925-4771

Maine Real Estate Commission
State House Station #35
Augusta, ME 04333
(207) 624-8516

Maryland Real Estate Commission
501 St. Paul Place, 8th Floor
Baltimore, MD 21202-2272
(410) 333-8124

Massachusetts Real Estate Board
100 Cambridge Street, Room 1313
Boston, MA 02202
(617) 727-2373

Michigan Real Estate Department
P.O. Box 30243
Lansing, MI 48909
(517) 373-0490

Minnesota Department of
    Commerce
133 East 7th Street
St. Paul, MN 55101
(612) 296-2488

Mississippi Real Estate Commission
1920 Dunbarton Drive
Jackson, MS 39126-5087
(601) 987-3969

Missouri Real Estate Commission
P.O. Box 1339
Jefferson City, MO 65102
(314) 751-2628

Montana Board of Realty Regulation
P.O. Box 200513
Helena, MT 59620-0513
(406) 444-2961

Nebraska Real Estate Commission
1200 N Street, Suite 402
Lincoln, NE 68508
(402) 471-2004

Nevada Real Estate Division
2501 E. Sahara Avenue
Las Vegas, NV 89158
(702) 486-4033

New Hampshire Real Estate
  Commission
State House Annex, Room 437
25 Capitol Street
Concord, NH 03301
(603) 271-2701

New Jersey Real Estate Commission
20 West State Street, CN-328
Trenton, NJ 08625
(609) 292-8280

New Mexico Real Estate
  Commission
1650 University Boulevard NE, Suite
490
Albuquerque, NM 87102
(505) 841-9120

New York Department of State
Division of Licensing
84 Holland Avenue
Albany, NY 12208
(518) 473-2728

North Carolina Real Estate
  Commission
P.O. Box 17100
Raleigh, NC 27619-7100
(919) 733-9580

North Dakota Real Estate
  Commission
P.O. Box 727
Bismarck, ND 58502-0727
(701) 328-9749

Ohio Division of Real Estate
77 South High Street, 20th Floor
Columbus, OH 43266-0547
(614) 466-4100

Oklahoma Real Estate Commission
4040 North Lincoln Boulevard, Suite
100
Oklahoma City, OK 73105
(405) 521-3387

Oregon Real Estate Agency
1177 Center Street, N.E.
Salem, OR 97310-2503
(503) 378-4170

Pennsylvania Real Estate
  Commission
P.O. Box 2649
Harrisburg, PA 17105-2649
(717) 783-3658

Rhode Island Real Estate Division
100 North Main Street
Providence, RI 02903
(401) 277-2255

South Carolina Real Estate
  Commission
1201 Main Street, Suite 1500
Columbia, SC 29201
(803) 737-0700

South Dakota Real Estate
  Commission
P.O. Box 490
Pierre, SD 57501-0490
(605) 773-3600

Tennessee Real Estate Commission
500 James Robertson Parkway
Suite 180, Volunteer Plaza
Nashville, TN 37243-1151
(615) 741-2273

Texas Real Estate Commission
P.O. Box 12188
Austin, TX 78711-2188
(512) 459-6544

Utah Division of Real Estate
P.O. Box 45806
Salt Lake City, UT 84145-0806
(801) 530-6747

Vermont Real Estate Commission
109 State Street
Montpelier, VT 05609-1106
(802) 828-3228

Virginia Real Estate Commission
3600 West Broad Street
Richmond, VA 23230
(804) 367-8552

Washington Real Estate Division
P.O. Box 9015
Olympia, WA 98507
(360) 586-6101

West Virginia Real Estate
  Commission
1033 Quarrier Street, Suite 400
Charleston, WV 25301-2315
  (304) 558-3555

Wisconsin Real Estate Bureau
P.O. Box 8935
Madison, WI 53708
(608) 267-7134

Wyoming Real Estate Commission
2020 Carey Avenue, Suite 100
Cheyenne, WY 82002-0180
(307) 777-7141

Source: Association of Real Estate
  License Law Officials (ARELLO)
    P.O. Box 129,
      Centerville, UT 84014-0129.

# *References*

Note: Four of the largest publishers of real estate career material are: the Real Estate Education Company (Dearborn Publishing), 155 N. Wacker Drive, Chicago, Ill. 60606-1719 (Orders/information: 1-800-621-9621); Gorsuch Scarisbrick Publishers, 8233 Via Paseo del Norte, Suite F-400, Scottsdale, Ariz. 85258 (Orders/information: 1-800-544-8398); Prentice Hall, 113 Sylvan Ave., Englewood Cliffs, N.J. 07632 (Orders/information: 1-800-947-7700); and John Wiley & Sons, 605 Third Ave., New York, N.Y. 10158-0012 (Orders/information: 1-800-225-5945). Many of the books below are available in general bookstores.

## REAL ESTATE LAW

Gibson, Frank; Karp, James; and Klayman, Elliot. *Real Estate Law*. 3rd ed. Chicago: Real Estate Education Company, 1992.

Irvin, Carol K. and Irvin, James D. *Real Estate Law*. Scottsdale, Ariz.: Gorsuch Scarisbrick, 1990.

Siedel, George J. *Real Estate Law*. 3rd ed. St. Paul, Minn.: West Publishing Company, 1993. Orders/information: 1-800-328-9352.

## REAL ESTATE FINANCE

Dennis, Marshall W. *Residential Mortgage Lending*. 4th ed. Englewood Cliffs, N.J.: Prentice-Hall Inc., 1995.

Garton-Good, Julie. *All About Mortgages*. Chicago: Real Estate Education Company, 1994. Other Garton-Good products/information: 1-800-445-8543.

Miller, Peter G. *The Mortgage Hunter*. New York: Harper Collins Publisher, 1996. This is the new title for the former *Common Sense Mortgage*.

Sirota, David. *Essentials of Real Estate Finance*. 8th ed. Chicago: Real Estate Education Company, 1996.
Wiedemer, John P. *Real Estate Finance*. 7th ed. Englewood Cliffs, N.J.: Prentice-Hall, Inc., 1995.


## REAL ESTATE MATH

Armbrust, Betty; Armbrust, John W; and Bradley, Hugh H. *Practical Real Estate Math*, 2nd ed. Scottsdale, Ariz.: Gorsuch Scarisbrick, 1995.
Sico, John, and Kovats, Frank W. *Nobody Ever Explained It Like That! A Real Estate Math Book*. Paramus, N.J.: Kovco Press, 1988. Orders/information: 201-843-9099.
Venetolo, William J. Jr.; Tamper, Ralph; and Allway, Wellington J. *Mastering Real Estate Mathematics*. 6th ed. Chicago: Real Estate Education Company, 1995.


## REAL ESTATE PRINCIPLES AND PRACTICE

(Note: The following are basic real estate texts in widespread use for licensing courses. Review any for good overview of what to expect in license training.)

Galaty, Fillmore W.; Allaway, Wellington J.; and Kyle, Robert C. *Modern Real Estate Practices*. 14th ed. Chicago: Real Estate Education Company, 1996.
Geschwender, Arlyne, *Real Estate Principles & Practices: A Contemporary Approach*. 5th ed. Scottsdale, Ariz.: Gorsuch Scarisbrick, 1997.
Harrison, Henry S. and Drisko, Barbara L. *Real Estate Principles & Practices*. New Haven, Conn.: H Squared Company, 1994. Orders/information: 1-800-243-4545.
Harwood, Bruce, and Jacobus, Charles J. *Real Estate Principles*. 6th ed. Englewood Cliffs, N.J.: Prentice-Hall, Inc., 1993.


## REAL ESTATE REFERENCE

Arnold, Alvin L. *The Arnold Encyclopedia of Real Estate*. 2nd ed. New York: Wiley, 1993 de Heer, Robert. *Realty Bluebook*, 31st ed. Chicago: Real Estate Education Company, 1995.

California Department of Real Estate, *Real Estate Law*. 1995. Orders/information: Department of Real Estate, Book Orders, P.O. Box 187006, Sacramento, Calif. 95818-7006. A variety of other very helpful products also offered. Write for Publications Request form.

Frascona, Oliver E. and Reece, Katherine E. *The Real Estate Book: The Ultimate Paper Trail*. Boulder, Colo.: Real Law Books 1995. Orders/information: 1-800-688-1555.

Gadow, Sandy. *All About Escrow*. 5th ed. El Cerrito, Calif.: ExPress, 1992. Orders/information: 510-236-5496.

Gross, Jerome S. *Webster's New World Illustrated Encyclopedic Dictionary of Real Estate*. 3rd ed. New York: Prentice Hall Press, 1987.

Harris, Jack C., and Friedman, Jack P. *Barron's Real Estate Handbook*. 2nd ed. Hauppauge, N.Y.: Barron's Educational Series, Inc., 1988.

Reilly, John W. *The Ultimate Language of Real Estate*. 4th ed. Chicago: Real Estate Education Company, 1993.

Reilly, John W. *Agency Relationships in Real Estate*. 2nd ed. Chicago: Real Estate Education Company, 1994.

Tosh, Dennis S., Jr. *Handbook of Real Estate Terms*. Englewood Cliffs, N.J.: Prentice-Hall, Inc., 1992.

Wurtzebach, Charles H., and Miles, Mike E. *Modern Real Estate*. 5th ed. New York: Wiley, 1994.

## REAL ESTATE ETHICS

Long, Deborah H. *Doing the Right Thing (A Real Estate Practitioner's Guide to Ethical Decision Making)*. Scottsdale, Ariz.: Gorsuch Scarisbrick, 1995.

Pivar, William H., and Harlan, Donald L. *Real Estate Ethics*. 3rd ed. Chicago: Real Estate Education Company, 1995.

## REAL ESTATE INDUSTRY STATISTICS AND HISTORY

Association of Real Estate License Law Officials (ARELLO), *1995 Digest of Real Estate License Laws*. Bountiful, Utah: ARELLO, 1995. (annual publication) Orders/information: 1-801-298-5572.

National Association of Realtors (NAR), *Membership Profile*. Washington,

D.C.: National Association of Realtors, 1994. One of a series of reports issued periodically by NAR.

National Association of Realtors (NAR), *Recruiting and Retaining the Best*. Washington, D.C.: National Association of Realtors, 1996. This is the report on "fast burner" Realtors. Very instructive if you are looking for role model characteristics.

Women's Council of Realtors, *Progress of Women in Real Estate*. Chicago: Women's Council of Realtors, 1988. Orders/information: 312-329-8483.


## EXAMINATION PREPARATION GUIDES

Beck, John A. and Ellis, John T. *Guide to the ASI Real Estate License Examinations*. 2nd ed. Englewood Cliffs, N.J.: Prentice-Hall, Inc., 1992.

French, William B.; Martin, Stephen J.; and Battle, Thomas E., III, *Guide to Real Estate Licensing Examinations*. 6th ed. Englewood Cliffs, N.J.: Prentice-Hall, Inc., 1992.

Garton-Good, Julie. *SuperCourse for Real Estate Licensing*, 2nd ed. New York: Simon & Schuster, Inc., 1995. For other Garton-Good products/ information: 1-800-445-8543.

Lindeman, J. Bruce and Friedman, Jack P. *Real Estate Examinations*. 5th ed. Happauge, N. Y.: Barron's, 1995.

Pivar, William H. *Real Estate Exam Guide for ASI Sales and Broker Exams*. 4th ed. Chicago: Real Estate Education Company, 1995.

Reilly, John W., and Vitousek, Paige Bovee. *Questions and Answers to Help You Pass the Real Estate Exam*. 4th ed. Chicago: Real Estate Education Company, 1992.

Sager, Lawrence. *Guide to Passing the PSI Real Estate Exam*. 2nd ed. Chicago: Real Estate Education Company, 1994.

Sterling, Joyce B. *Guide to Passing the AMP Real Estate Exam*. Chicago: Real Estate Education Company, 1996.

Tosh, Dennis S., and Ordway, Nicholas. *Real Estate Principles for License Preparation for the ASI Exam*. 4th ed. Englewood Cliffs, N.J.: Prentice-Hall, Inc., 1990.

Tosh, Dennis S., and Ordway, Nicholas. *Real Estate Principles for License Preparation for the ACT Exam*. 4th ed. Englewood Cliffs, N.J.: Prentice-Hall, Inc., 1990.

Tosh, Dennis S., and Ordway, Nicholas. *Real Estate Principles for License Preparation for the ASI Exam*. 4th ed. Englewood Cliffs, N.J.: Prentice-Hall, Inc., 1990.

van Reken, Randall S. *Preparation for the PSI Real Estate Exam.* Scottsdale, Ariz.: Gorsuch Scarisbrick, 1994.


## REAL ESTATE APPRAISAL

American Institute of Real Estate Appraisers. *The Appraisal of Real Estate.* 9th ed. Chicago: American Institute of Real Estate Appraisers, 1987.

Harrison, Henry S. *Appraising Residences & Income Properties.* New Haven, Conn.: H Squared Company, 1989. Orders/information: 1-800-243-4545.

Harrison, Henry S.; Martin, Stephen J.; and Battle, Thomas E. *How to Pass Any General or Residential Appraisal Examination.* New Haven, Conn.: H Squared Company, 1991. Orders/information: 1-800-243-4545.


## REAL ESTATE PROPERTY MANAGEMENT

Kyle, Robert C., and Baird, Floyd M. *Property Management.* 5th ed. Chicago: Real Estate Education Company, 1995.

Reed, John T. *How to Manage Residential Property for Maximum Cash Flow and Resale Value.* 2nd ed. Danville, Calif.: Reed Publishing, 1995. Reed also publishes a newsletter and other property management and income tax material. Orders/information: 1-800-635-5425.

Robinson, Leigh. *Landlording.* 7th ed. El Cerrito, Calif.: ExPress, 1994. Great practical reference.


## REAL ESTATE MANAGEMENT

Cyr, John, and Sobeck, Joan. *Real Estate Brokerage: A Management Guide.* 4th ed. Chicago: Real Estate Education Company, 1995.

Realtors; National Marketing Institute (RNMI). *Real Estate Office Management.* Chicago: RNMI, 1988.


## REAL ESTATE MARKETING

Allen, George. *How to Buy, Manage, and Sell a Manufactured Home Community.* New York: Wiley. 1996. Allen is the guru of manufactured homes. This is a great basic reference.

Hopkins, Tom. *How to Master the Art of Listing & Selling Real Estate.* Scottsdale, Ariz.: Tom Hopkins International, 1991. A wide variety of marketing products available. Orders/information: 1-800-528-0446.

Kennedy, Danielle. *Double Your Income In Real Estate Sales.* New York: Wiley, 1993. Kennedy also offers a series of real estate marketing products through her own company. Orders/information: 1-800-848-8070.

Knox, Dave. *The Mentor Series.* Minneapolis, Minn.: Dave Knox Seminars, 1994. This is a series of 5 videos on the basic topics of listing and selling. Knox has numerous other products. Orders/information: 1-800-533-4494.

Reynolds, Monica. *Multiply Your Success With Real Estate Assistants.* Chicago: Dearborn Financial Publishing, 1994.

Schwarz, Barb. *How to List Residential Real Estate Successfully.* Englewood Cliffs, N.J.: Prentice-Hall Inc., 1991. Schwarz markets a number of real estate career products through her own company. Call 1-800-392-7161.

## REAL ESTATE TAXES

Ayella, Albert J. *The Realtor's Bible of Personal Tax-Reduction Strategies.* Media, Pa.: ISU Publishers, 1996. Orders/information: 1-800-351-1031.

Hoven, Vernon. *The Real Estate Investors Tax Guide.* 2nd ed. Chicago: Real Estate Education Company, 1996.

Lank, Edith and Geisman, Miriam S. *Your Home As a Tax Shelter.* Chicago: Real Estate Education Company, 1993.

Reed, John T. *Aggressive Tax Avoidance for Real Estate Investors.* 15th ed. Danville, Calif.: Reed Publishing, 1996. Annual editions since 1981. Orders/information: 1-800-635-5425.

## REAL ESTATE PERIODICALS

*Today's Realtor.* National Association of Realtors, 430 North Michigan Avenue, Chicago, Ill. 60611. Official publication of NAR and included in membership.

*The Real Estate Professional.* Wellesley Publications, 1492 Highland Avenue, Needham, Mass. 02192. Subscription information: 1-617-729-0935.

# *Index*

# Paris-Underground

BY

## ETTA SHIBER

IN COLLABORATION WITH
ANNE AND PAUL DUPRE

NEW YORK

## Charles Scribner's Sons

1943

THIS BOOK IS
MANUFACTURED UNDER WARTIME
CONDITIONS IN CONFORMITY WITH
ALL GOVERNMENT REGULATIONS
CONTROLLING THE USE OF PAPER
AND OTHER MATERIALS

PRINTED IN THE UNITED STATES OF AMERICA BY H. WOLFF, NEW YORK

For

KITTY

## AUTHOR'S NOTE

*The basic facts in the book are a matter of record. Most of the names of the persons whose activities are described in this book have been changed, for obvious reasons. A few details, not already matters of record known to the Gestapo, have been recast, a few omitted, and the roles of various persons interchanged, in order to make it impossible for any use to be made of this book by the German authorities against anyone described in it.*

# Contents

# PARIS UNDERGROUND

doubt they felt as I did: that no relief was possible until we got out of German territory. We moved steadily ahead, through the pleasant countryside of France; but at every station we saw German uniforms and German faces, and we knew that we were still in the prison into which the Nazis have converted all of Europe.

Night fell, and the train rattled on, through a blacked-out countryside where no light relieved the gloom. I slept a little, dozing off for a few minutes at a time, and then being jerked into consciousness again as the train swayed and jolted over the bad road-bed. Our eyes were all still heavy with lack of sleep at seven in the morning, when the train pulled to a stop, and we saw the station sign through the windows: Hendaye—the Spanish border!

Faces brightened at once. Freedom seemed almost in sight, and already the universal suspicion which enshrouds every one in Nazi territory seemed to be lifting. I was asked to satisfy the general curiosity: why had the train stopped for me alone, in all France? I told them all I knew. I was an American, I had been in a Nazi prison, and I had been exchanged for some German prisoner in America.

An hour passed, then two. There was no sign of preparation to get our train under way again, to run it the few hundred yards that would get it out from under the shadow of the swastika. My fellow passengers began to show signs of nervousness. I became uneasy too. The Gestapo guards paced up and down beside the train. We were not yet out of their prison.

Finally a Gestapo agent came through the car and told us that the train would be delayed at Hendaye all morning. Any one who wished might get off and buy food in the station canteen, where either francs or dollars would be accepted.

There was consternation in my compartment. My neighbors had only brought enough food with them for the normal journey, and none of them would have any money until they got to Lisbon. I alone had money—about fifty dollars. I went into the canteen, bought enough food for all in my compartment, and came back. Some of it we shared with those in neighboring compartments.

The hours dragged slowly by. Morning became afternoon, and still there were no signs that we were going to move. All sorts of rumors began to crop up. Some persons said that Spain had refused to let any more refugee trains pass, and we would all have to go back to Paris. Depression settled over us again.

Some of the refugees spoke English, and after I had told my story, they took particular pains to be nice to me. I asked one of them if he would care to go to the canteen to buy us some more food. When he came back, he said:

"Mrs. Shiber, I found out why we are being held here. A French guard told me. It's because of you."

"Because of me?" I gasped, as the old fear that I should never be free again seized me once more.

"Yes, because of you. You're being exchanged, aren't you? Well, the Germans are waiting for the woman who was released in exchange for you, and she hasn't arrived yet. They're holding the whole train until she gets here. That's why we're all held up."

I could feel a stiffening in the attitude of those about me. They could hardly blame me, they knew it was not my fault—yet it was because I was with them that they were not yet certain of release, that they were still being held interminably in this train under the eyes of their jailers. I knew they wished I had not been with them. Their silent reproach seemed intolerable to me. But I could do nothing except sit in my place and pretend not to realize how ardently they wished me elsewhere.

Night came on again, and we slumbered uncomfortably in our crowded compartments. Morning dawned. Some of the men went to the canteen to ask news on our progress. They could learn nothing.

"How these people must hate me!" I thought. "I'm all that stands between them and freedom. Why don't the Germans take me off the train, and let it go on without me? They could send me on later, when the exchange prisoner arrives."

I hadn't the slightest idea whom I was being exchanged for, except that it was a woman.

About noon, the station was suddenly gripped in a feverish activity. The platform became crowded with every possible variety of German uniform. Down the road paralleling the tracks marched small units of various uniformed groups, all going in the same direction. Then a German military band appeared. Obviously, some ceremony was about to take place.

For more than an hour, we had not been permitted to go to the canteen. But the number of our guards had decreased. No doubt some of them were curious, and wanted to see what was going on themselves. It was not difficult to slip off the train without being seen. In company with a Czechoslovak who volunteered to go with me, I got off, and from behind a freight car watched the scene.

A train was crossing the international bridge from Spain and entering the station. As it arrived, the band burst into the *Horst Wessel Lied*, the soldiers on the platform snapped to attention, and dignitaries stepped forward on the swastika-decorated quay to greet the passengers on the train. From the appearance of the official-looking group which descended, I judged that they must be the German diplomats returning from the United States; but the most honored of the arrivals seemed to be a red-headed woman of about thirty-five or forty.

As she stepped from the train, the reception committee hurried to greet her. An enormous bouquet of flowers was thrust into her arms. I was too far away to hear what was said, but it was obvious that short formal speeches of welcome were being delivered to her, and that she was answering. She seemed to be in a hurry to get out of the crowd. With brusque arrogant movements, she burst out of the group surrounding her and hastened across the platform, while the reception committee trailed after her like the tail of a comet. She passed close to the car behind which I was standing. I heard the brutal exultant laughter with which she greeted some old friends, and had a close view of her rather coarse features and wrinkled brow. I knew I had seen her before, or at least her picture; but the name escaped me.

"Who could she have been?" I asked myself, as I got back into the car. "I wonder—could that be the woman for whom I was exchanged?"

It didn't seem unlikely. For hardly had I gotten back to my place again when our guards reappeared, drove every one back into the train, and slowly it rolled out of the station of Hendaye, across the international bridge, and onto the soil of Spain. We were free!

We were not yet, however, delivered from our guardian angels. I understood now why the Gestapo men on the train had worn civilian clothes. It took us two days to get through Spain and Portugal to Lisbon. During that time, neither Spanish nor Portuguese officials set foot in the train. Our Gestapo men travelled with us all the way through both countries.

At Lisbon, United States Consul Wiley found me in the train after a hurried search through car after car, during which, he confessed to me later, the idea occurred to him that perhaps the Germans had double-crossed the United States and hadn't really sent me out of the country.

He quickly discovered that I had been kept in complete ignorance of my own case.

"Then you don't even know whom you were exchanged for?" he asked.

"I haven't the slightest idea," I said, "except that it was a woman. I thought it might be a woman I saw in Hendaye—red-headed, arrogant in manner. Her face looked familiar."

"It should," Mr. Wiley said. "Her picture was in all the papers a few years ago. You must have seen it then. That was Johanna Hoffmann."

Johanna Hoffmann! I remembered now. She was the hairdresser of the German super-liner *Bremen*, taken off the ship by the F.B.I., and convicted of being a member of a dangerous German spy ring operating in the United States. She had been in jail in America since the autumn of 1938. Was what I had done, I asked myself, really worth such a price?

I felt that I was really safe at last when I crossed the gangplank from the dock in Lisbon to the deck of the *Drottningholm*. Every one aboard seemed to share in the same care-free feeling of joy in release from the anxieties which had beset them all for the last few months. The happy confusion aboard the ship was even greater than that which regularly accompanies the departures of ocean liners. All of us had waited months for the day of repatriation. Their common emotion made them friends at once, and I noted how utter strangers made friends of one another at sight, all alike jubilating in the thought: "At last! We're going *home!*"

An American newspaper correspondent stood beside me at the railing, watching the passengers board the ship.

"I was here when the *Drottningholm* came in with its Axis passengers," he said. "There was quite a difference. You should have seen them! They looked like pigs fattened for market. All of them had tremendous trunks, stuffed to the brim. The baggage master told me that Johanna Hoffmann brought along forty trunks and handbags. When she learned she could only take three trunks, she swore like a Prussian top-sergeant.

"But look at the Americans coming aboard. Don't they all seem ragged and starving? Look at their faces—lean and spare. And their luggage. There isn't much of it, and I'll bet that there's not much in those bags. What could they have brought from the places they're coming from?

"I think we missed a bet when we let the Axis people go. We should have made our exchange on the basis of weight. That way we would have gotten two Americans for every Axis national."

The Americans were underweight, certainly. But their faces were glowing with happiness. In a matter of minutes, the Swedish ship became a Little America, a piece of floating United States territory, of the gayest type. The decks, the bar, the salons were noisy with the jubilations of men and women. Even the children were unusually boisterous, as though they too sensed the removal of restriction. I could feel their elation more strongly perhaps than they did, for, so far as I knew, I was the only one who had reached this haven from a Nazi prison cell, escorted by watchful jailers of the Gestapo.

But I felt less like celebrating. The shadow of depression still hung over me, and inspired me with a sort of vague contentment, rather than a festive air. I found a quiet corner in one of the salons and sat down by myself. An official of the American Consulate of Lisbon saw me there, and came up to say good-bye.

"Hiding, Mrs. Shiber?" he laughed. "You mustn't do that. Every one on board knows about you. They want to hear your story. After all, you're the only passenger on this ship whom we had to dig out of a Nazi prison. Or are you having trouble forgetting about all that? It will pass, you know. Everything does. In a month or two you won't be able to believe that your adventures really happened to you instead of to some one else."

"I'm a little worried about one thing," I said. "This Johanna Hoffmann woman—she's dangerous. I can't forget how she was received at Hendaye, her self-importance, the air of a conquering hero which she assumed as she shook hands with the Gestapo officers. She even clicked her heels like a Nazi soldier. I'm sure she's back in Berlin already, setting to work to do us all the harm she can."

"Why should that depress you?"

"Well, I'm responsible for her being released. I'm afraid you've made a bad bargain. She's certainly more valuable to the Germans than I am to the United States."

"My dear Mrs. Shiber," he said. "Don't, for goodness sake, worry about that. The State Department knows very well what you did in Paris. I have looked through your record, and I know, too. Suppose the British government, in the last war, had had a chance to exchange Edith Cavell. Don't you think they'd have jumped at it? And you, after all, are the Edith Cavell of this war."

I couldn't let that pass unchallenged.

"No," I said, "you're wrong there. I am not the Edith Cavell of this war, but perhaps my dear friend Kitty was. Whatever merit there was in what we did belongs to her. I only followed where she led. And she alone has paid the price. She is still in the hands of the Gestapo, if she is alive; or dead, if the sentence passed on her has been carried out. Yes, Kitty Beaurepos may well have been the Edith Cavell of this war."

He had gone, and I remained seated in the corner of the salon, lost in my own thoughts. Most of the passengers had gone into the dining room, and from where I sat I could hear them exclaiming at menus such as most of them had not seen for many long months. That first dinner on the *Drottningholm* must have been a memorable feast for them. But I had no heart for their gaiety. I sat quietly in my corner, reliving my life in Paris, thinking of Kitty—was she still alive?

Suddenly the realization came to me that we were under way.

On deck, I leaned against the railing, and looked out over the dark water, unseeingly. Kitty's face haunted me. Her beautiful sad eyes seemed to be striving to emerge from the veil of the darkness of the sea and sky. The consular official had said that every one wanted to hear my story. Well, they should—my story and Kitty's. I would set it down while it was still fresh in my memory.

I went back to the salon again, settled myself before a writing table, and began to write. The account that follows is not my story alone. More than that, it is the story of my friend Kitty Beaurepos. This book is dedicated to her.

Kitty Beaurepos was the daughter of a London banker. She had received the traditional education of a young English society girl— a smattering of music and the arts, and a good deal of fine manners. She married young, went to live in Italy, had a son there. Then her husband died. Kitty moved to Paris, where she married a French wine merchant. After a while they decided to separate, on a thoroughly amicable basis.

Kitty loved Paris. She did not return to England, being financially independent as the result of an income received from her father's estate, which made it possible for her to live where she chose. But inactivity was impossible for her, and to keep herself occupied she opened a small dress shop in the Rue Rodier.

It was there that I met her, in 1925, when I visited Paris with my husband, William Noyes Shiber, on one of our annual three months' trips to France. Friends had told me of her shop, made to order for American clients like myself, of conservative tastes, and without inexhaustible pocketbooks. A deep sympathy developed between us immediately. I sensed a natural liking for me entirely unconnected with the desire of the shopkeeper to please a customer, and I reciprocated it. Thereafter I never failed to visit her on my yearly trips to Paris.

In 1933, I made the voyage to France without my husband, but with my brother Irving. His health had been bad, and the doctor had advised a cure at Aix-les-Bains. But the trip was a tiresome one, and my poor brother was not strong enough to stand it. He became so ill after reaching Paris that we could not go on to Aix.

In this emergency, Kitty was my greatest help. She secured the best medical care for my brother—but it was too late. When he died, Kitty saw at once how great the blow was to me. She not only relieved me of the care of making arrangements for the funeral, but actually came to live at the Hotel Bristol, in the Rue du Faubourg St. Honoré, where I was staying, to look after me. She let her business manage itself for a whole month, until my husband arrived.

In that crisis, I do not know what I should have done without Kitty, alone as I was in a strange city and a foreign country. I had always depended on my husband and my brother to look out for me; and without them I was lost. My husband realized at once, when he arrived, how important Kitty's aid had been to me. It seems today that he must have had a premonition when he said to her: "If anything ever happens to me, will you look out for Etta?"

Kitty laughed. "Of course I will," she said.

Three years later, in 1936, my husband died. I cabled to Kitty, informing her of his death. Within a few hours I had an answer. Kitty cabled to invite me to come to Paris and live with her. Her promise had not been lightly given. She had stretched out her strong arms to me in friendship across the ocean, as soon as she had learned that I was alone and troubled.

I read her cable with tears streaming down my cheeks. I answered in one word: "Coming."

Hardly a week later I got off the train at the St. Lazare station in Paris. Kitty was waiting for me on the platform. My first thought as I rushed towards her was: "How odd that I never noticed before how handsome Kitty is!"

She was forty then, tall, slender and wiry. As a young woman, she must have been very beautiful. Her most distinctive features were her eyes, large and brown, with a softness of expression which reflected the tenderness of her heart. Her wavy brown hair had become gently tinged with gray, which added to her air of breeding and distinction. I admired her as a woman of the world, as well as a person of kind and sympathetic character.

Kitty and I settled down together at 2, Rue Balny d'Avricourt, in an exclusive residential section of Paris near the Arc de Triomphe. It was a comfortable modern apartment of five rooms and bath on the sixth floor of a twelve-apartment building. Kitty had furnished it according to French taste, with a few modern pieces—a large divan with leather back and arms, comfortable armchairs, gay, warm, rosy colors in the living room. It was an ideal home, and I settled into it as in a haven.

Kitty and I spent three calm and happy years in that apartment. Not once was there the slightest disagreement between Kitty and myself. Her friendship never faltered. She took charge of our common existence with serene efficiency; and though she managed things so as to make me feel that I shared equally in her responsibilities, I knew that actually it was Kitty who directed the affairs of our household.

If Kitty had any problems of her own, business or personal, I never knew of them. She handled her life smoothly and without effort. The course of the rest of our days seemed assured, charming and calm, a pleasant existence for which our moderate means would suffice, spent partly in Paris and partly on the French Riviera. When we were in Paris, I made regular visits to my brother's grave. I envisaged the future as continuing indefinitely in this course, in which we two, no longer young, would end our lives in this quiet fashion.

I had counted without the war.

When Germany attacked Poland, Kitty said to me:

"This war is my war for two reasons. England is the country of my birth and France is the country of my choice. I am English by birth and French by marriage. I shall stay here. But you are an American, and your country is neutral. There is no reason why you should take the risks of war. I shall miss you if you go—but I think you ought to return to the United States."

I knew what Kitty had in mind. Every one was predicting immediate bombing of Paris as soon as the war began. She was protecting me, as she had always protected me, ever since we had first met.

"No, Kitty," I smiled back to her, "you can't get rid of me as easily as that. When I came to Paris, we entered into an unspoken compact to remain together. There was no three-year limit, and no special clause about wars. Let's forget about my going back to America. I'm legally a neutral, yes—but tell me what I can do to help your two countries."

The next day we both joined the Foyer du Soldat—the French equivalent of the U.S.O. We busied ourselves sending packages to soldiers, visiting their families, sitting with the wounded in the hospitals. We fell into a new routine, which in its turn became familiar and accustomed. The word "war" lost most of its terrors. Once again, we seemed to be caught up in a quiet enough pattern, one unlikely to lead us into perils or adventures. Even when the eight months of the "phony war" as you called it in America, or the *drôle de guerre*, as we described it in France, were suddenly ended by Germany's attack, we did not realize at once that the whole order of our existence was threatened. We were so busy, indeed, that we did not wake up to our danger until the Germans were actually hammering at the gates of Paris.

The end of our ivory tower existence came one day before the Nazis entered Paris, and here our real story begins—on the day of June 13, 1940.

## CHAPTER TWO

# Flight from Paris

FOR the third time, Kitty hung up the telephone with an air of resignation. For the third time, the repeated muffled ringing of the phone had told her that the friend she had called was not at home.

"All our friends seem to have left Paris already," she said. "We're the only ones left."

"I'll call the American Embassy," I said. "After all, I'm an American. They ought to be willing to tell me if the Germans are going to besiege Paris."

A startled voice answered me at the Embassy:

"Are you still in town? Don't you know that the government has moved to Tours? The Germans will be in Paris in a matter of hours —not days, hours! The city is being handed over without resistance."

For an instant, terror clutched at my heart. Then I hung up, and told Kitty what I had just heard. Pain and astonishment showed on her usually beautifully impassive features.

"No!" she cried. "No! It can't be! It's impossible! The French give up Paris without a battle! Why, only a few days ago Premier Paul-Reynaud said they would fight before Paris and defend every building, house by house. He begged the people not to flee, he told them not to listen to rumors, he said every one should stay where he was . . ."

"And meanwhile," I said, "he and his government have gotten away to Tours. That's proof enough that Paris has been abandoned to her fate. It's a pity they wouldn't tell the people. Don't they remember what the Germans did in Vienna, Prague, Warsaw—everywhere they set foot? Of course, a lot of people have gone already, but they went without really knowing what the situation was. We've just been handed over to the Germans, a million or two of us, without even being asked how we felt about it!"

I took Kitty's hand in mine, and went on:

13

"I don't intend to be handed over to the Nazis like that, Kitty! I didn't come to Paris from New York to live under German domination. Let's try to get out before they get here."

Kitty was efficiency itself. A few seconds were always enough for her to make a decision. Almost before the words were out of my mouth, she was on the way to the garage to get the car.

Left alone in the apartment, I moved from one room to another in hopeless despair. I pulled out a trunk and began to stuff our most valued possessions in it—the things I hated above all to leave to the Germans. But what to leave behind, what to take? The choice was difficult.

Our five-room apartment had long been too small for all our things. When Kitty decided to live apart from her husband, she had taken all her belongings with her, and after my husband's death, I brought all my movable property to Paris when I joined her. In the years we had lived together since, we had accumulated antique furniture, pictures, rugs, bric à brac—innumerable beautiful things which we had planned to spend the rest of our lives enjoying. Our closets and drawers were crammed with clothing, furs, linen, and jewelry.

I saw at once that we could not possibly take everything we treasured, and the impossibility of deciding what to leave behind soon brought me to a dead stop. I was standing before the almost empty trunk, staring into it stupidly, when the door was flung open with a bang and Kitty rushed in.

"Everybody's gone, Etta!" she cried. "Even the garage owner has disappeared. The only one left there was the old watchman. It was all I could do to get him to let me take the car."

She shot an accusing glance at the unfilled trunk.

"My God, haven't you started packing yet?"

And she dove into the closets like a whirlwind, throwing out a storm of clothing which I crammed into our bags. In a sort of blind frenzy we packed what we could, shoved everything else back into the closets, and pushed cherished personal belongings into the deepest recesses of bureau and secretary drawers, in a vague undefined hope that they would not be disturbed. Then we snatched up our three precious dogs, Winkie, Chinka and Mickey, and fled. We locked the door carefully behind us, and took the key along—though even then we had little hope that this would protect us from looting.

Our trunk, containing only jewelry and our most necessary clothing, was stowed away in the rear baggage compartment. Our bags shared the car with us. Kitty twisted the ignition key, stepped on the starter, threw in the clutch—and we were off, on a journey to nowhere in particular. Just away. Away from the Germans we could almost feel hurrying after us.

June 13, 1940, was a Thursday—but the deserted Paris streets through which we drove gave the city a feeling of Sunday. Hardly a car was to be seen. Only a few scattered pedestrians were in the streets. They looked nervous and apprehensive, hardly reconciled to the idea of living in Paris under German occupation.

But as we turned into the Boulevard Raspail from the Boulevard St. Germain, the impression of Sunday suddenly vanished. Ahead of us, the broad avenue leading towards the southern exits from the city was jammed with vehicles. The Boulevard Raspail had become a one-way street. Both roadways, on either side of the strip of green grass in the middle, were jammed with cars heading south, running an obstacle race with one another to reach the Porte d'Orléans.

Route Nationale No. 20, the broad highway which connects Paris with the south of France, was too narrow to accommodate the stream of frightened humanity which tried to flow along it to safety. In autos, on foot, on bicycles, thousands of refugees, as far ahead as we could see, blocked the road and struggled to advance. It was easy to understand now why the streets of Paris had been deserted. All Paris was on this highway.

Forward movement was confined to a few inches at a time. Rare traffic policemen were striving desperately to win an uneven struggle against chaos. They succeeded momentarily in lining cars up abreast, all facing the same way. They didn't have to worry about traffic coming in the opposite direction. No one was trying to get into Paris, from the south. The only movement towards the city was from the other side—that of the German Army, whose forward movement seemed to be communicated through space, by some mysterious process, to this civilian horde, and to furnish the impelling force which drove it forward.

Every sort of vehicle hemmed us in—limousines, horse-drawn carts, trucks, automobiles with household goods piled high upon their tops, all slowly oozing southward. On one side of us a typical middle-class Frenchman in city clothes was pushing a wheelbarrow full of his belongings. Behind him was a luxurious automobile, and that in turn was followed by a smart carriage, with a liveried footman sitting next to the coachman.

The noise was indescribable. Every driver was honking his horn continuously at those in front of him, and those who had no horns made up for it by shouting at the top of their lungs. Whenever a foot of clear space opened in the road there was a pellmell rush to occupy it, which usually ended in an inextricable tangle of the rival vehicles.

To one helpless traffic policeman standing impotent and bewildered in the middle of the road an irate driver near us shouted: "Why don't you let us go ahead? Why don't you *do* something?"

"Do? Do? What do you expect me to do?" the policeman shouted back. "It's like this all the way to Orléans. You're lucky if you can make three or four miles an hour."

Actually, that was much more than we made. We were a helpless unit in that endless, almost unmoving stream, which stretched ahead of us, we knew, for two hundred miles. Usually, we jarred forward a foot or two at a time. When we were lucky, we moved ahead as much as a few hundred feet, as the whole line hitched itself slowly forward before lurching to another stop. After each such movement, we would have to wait fifteen minutes or half an hour before we could budge again. Then the line would creep forward once more, and then stop. Hitch forward and wait, hitch forward and wait, over and over, interminably. It seemed that we had always been trapped in this monstrous glacier-flow, that we should never get out of it again.

Kitty looked at her watch.

"Five o'clock," she said. "We started at nine this morning, and we've covered about twelve miles. We'd have gotten farther walking.

We might as well have stayed in Paris. Every one on this road will be caught by the Germans."

Night fell. The endless line of cars was still crawling at snail's pace along the road to Orléans. Kitty hailed a motorcycle policeman who came along the edge of the road from the opposite direction, making difficult upstream progress against the flood of cars.

"*C'est impossible.* There's nothing to be done, Madame," he said in answer to her question. "The road is blocked all the way to Orléans. It will be days before it can be cleared."

"Then in that case the Germans are sure to catch up with us," Kitty murmured in despair.

The policeman shrugged.

"The Germans aren't gods either," he said. "How do you expect them to get over this road? They say it's General Weygand's idea to let refugees block this highway so that the Germans won't be able to catch up to the French Army before it has had time to organize a new line of defense."

He saluted, and put-putted off. We looked at each other in dismay. Then Kitty, to my surprise, suddenly broke into ironic laughter.

"Well," she explained, "this is a pretty kettle of fish! So it's we women and non-combatants who are supposed to hold back the Germans! I suppose that's all right for me. I'm English by birth and French by marriage. That makes me a belligerent, all right. But you're an American. You're supposed to be neutral. What do you mean by daring to oppose the German Army?"

And she went off into another peal of laughter—but it didn't sound much like mirth.

Morning dawned with the situation unchanged. We had spent it in the car on the highway, stopping sometimes for hours at a stretch. We dozed off fitfully once in a while, only to be awakened by a mad tooting of horns whenever a space opened up ahead of us.

That night was more unendurable than the day had been, although that had been tedious enough, because of our cramped, slow-moving progress. The hours were punctuated with unbearable sights and tales of suffering. They added to our misery as part of that tragic caravan, hungry, unkempt, aimless, travelling to an unknown destiny over impassable roads.

We heard those tales from hitch-hikers, pitiful bits of human flotsam, who crowded into the empty seats in our car and remained there until impatience drove them out to walk again, to be replaced at once by others. Under the stress of danger, they showed themselves in their true colors, without pretense—some selfishly thinking only of their own safety, others generous and kind, anxious to help those caught in the same dire straits as themselves.

The soldiers, in particular, were wonderful. I saw many of them giving bread and food from their packs to children, though they themselves were on emergency rations. Whenever a civilian car broke down—and they broke down frequently, overloaded and over-taxed as they were—there was always a soldier on hand to fix it, or try to fix it.

But during the night, there were few incidents to relieve the awful monotony of this interminable progress. We sat straight upright in the car, our dogs curled uncomfortably in our laps. Occasionally our tired eyelids would close, our heads drop forward—and the movement would jerk us back again to uncomfortable consciousness. No lights beckoned us forward, or helped us to find our way. The blackout was complete.

In the unfathomable darkness about us, we could hear the trudge of tired feet as thousands of refugees plodded doggedly by our motionless car, but we could see only those who brushed against it. Gradually, as the light grew stronger in the east, we began to make out their dim figures as they passed—mostly civilians, but some limping wounded soldiers, evacuated from the hospitals of Paris. If they wanted to escape the Germans, they had to do it on foot. Ambulances only had space for the gravely wounded.

Nine o'clock! We had been on the road for twenty-four hours—and we were still in the outskirts of Paris. We stopped at a roadside restaurant, and bought a small piece of Camembert cheese with bread and butter for the equivalent of 75 cents. I remember arguing with Kitty that it was a ridiculous price. She laughed at the idea that prices had any importance at such a time. We shared the food with the dogs. They were obviously hungrier than we were, and less worried.

We hitched forward again, start and stop, start and stop, for another half-mile or so. It brought us to an inn, in front of which an excited group was shouting and gesticulating.

"What is it?" called Kitty, as our car ground to one of its periodical stops. "What's happened?"

A man on the edge of the crowd answered.

"*C'est terrible!* The Germans are in Paris," he cried. "The radio has just announced it. That scoundrel Ferdonnet—you know, the traitor of Stuttgart—made the broadcast himself. He even had the nerve to apologize because it didn't happen on June 15, as he predicted a month ago, but on June 14, that the advance guard of the German Army entered Paris."

The line ahead of us hitched forward again, and though the Frenchman was still talking, we had to move on. I looked at Kitty. She had crouched down over the wheel and was looking intently ahead, her lips very tight. I didn't dare speak.

Instead, I tried to realize the news I had just heard, for though I had been prepared for it, I hadn't really let myself believe that it could come. Now it had happened, and the brutal fact was like a slap in the face. I tried to imagine what it would be like in Paris, the beloved Ville Lumière, under German domination, with Nazi soldiers goose-stepping down the Champs-Elysées. The very idea sent a cold chill down my back.

"And what's going to happen to us?" I asked myself.

For the first time, I realized that our situation was hopeless. We had left almost everything we owned behind us in Paris, and the Germans were already in possession there. We were slowly creeping along towards an unknown destination, and it did not even seem likely that we would reach it. If only we could proceed towards it, whatever it was, so long as it would take us out of reach of the Germans!

The long line had come to a standstill again. Some distance ahead of us, the highway curved to the right, and we could see a motionless line of vehicles stretching ahead of us for a mile or more. It was clear that an hour or two of tedious inching forward would be necessary to take us even as far ahead as we could see.

"My nerves won't stand much more of this," Kitty said suddenly. "The Germans are in Paris, and we aren't sixty miles from there. That means they can catch up to us in two or three hours."

"But how can they if the road is blocked?" I objected.

"You don't believe that stupid policeman, do you?" Kitty answered. "If I know the Germans, they're quite capable of using any means to sweep us off the road if they want to use it for their own troops and tanks."

"But what can we do?" I asked. "Hadn't we better leave the car, and go ahead on foot? At least we could get off the road then—if they come."

"No," Kitty said. "I've a better idea. The next time we come to a crossroad, I'm going to get off this accursed highway and try to cut through the country by the back roads."

As we were still motionless, Kitty got out her Michelin road map, and checked the routes. We found that besides the main National Road we were on, another chain of roads led south from Paris, almost parallel with it. From time to time, a crossroad connected the two. Although the other was indicated as a narrow country lane, probably in bad repair, we figured that it was likely to be jammed also, but not as congested as the main highway. In any case, it would be less likely to receive attention from the Germans. We thought that by shifting to this road, and perhaps criss-crossing from one to another as necessity demanded, we might be able to put another 150 miles between ourselves and the Germans in the next twenty-four hours. Then we could breathe freely again.

Kitty turned into the first crossroad, not much more than a dirt path winding between plowed fields on either side. A great feeling of relief seemed to affect not only us, but even the car, as for the first time it was able to speed forward unimpeded.

The deep ruts showed that this was a road ordinarily used only by peasant carts. But it was dry and hard, and as there were hardly any other cars on it, we were able to make forty miles an hour. We would have felt happier, though, if we had been making that speed southward, instead of in a direction which took us no farther from Paris.

We came shortly to another road leading southward, and on checking with the map, found it to be parallel to that which we had left. To our delight, no traffic was in sight. We turned into it and sped along, congratulating ourselves on finding this means of escape, and wondering why we had not thought of it before.

Rows of waving wheat rushed by us on either side. The road was bumpy, and we were pretty well shaken up, but we didn't care. Every minute carried us farther away from the Germans, and that was all that counted.

Our good luck didn't last long. After a few miles, the road turned to the left, and once again we were running in a direction which didn't take us away from Paris.

And then the blow came. Ahead of us, the road filled with automobiles—pouring *towards* us. As the first cars reached us, people shouted from them: "Turn back! Turn back! The Germans are behind us!"

Kitty applied the brakes, and the car stopped with a jerk. I pulled out the Michelin map, and set to studying it again. I found a road a little way back which took a southwesterly direction, and we decided to try that. But we had only been on it for a few moments when another horde of refugees came rushing towards us, crying once again that the Germans were behind them. By this time we had become quite bewildered, and even the map was no help to us. We neither knew where we were, nor in what direction we were going. All we could do was to follow the others. The next time we came to a highway sign, I checked with the map once more, and discovered that although our speedometer showed that we had covered 200 miles, we were only twelve miles south of the spot where we had left the main highway.

Night overtook us again, and as the complete darkness of the nationwide blackout covered us, we realized that we would have to abandon our plan. During the day we had been able to orient ourselves, but with darkness and the blotting out of landmarks, we lost our sense of direction completely. We were in deadly fear of turning in the wrong direction and running straight into the Germans.

We bowed to the inevitable. We decided to get back to the main highway while we still had a chance of finding it.

## CHAPTER THREE

# The English Pilot

IT WAS already dark when we reached the national road again, but we knew in advance we were coming to it, for we could hear the nerve-racking cacophony of the honking horns, at first faintly, and then louder and louder as we approached. We guided ourselves by the sound, for we had lost all sense of direction. We didn't know at what point we were rejoining the road, or how far we were from Paris.

We had reached a point about a hundred yards from the road when we heard a faint hum which rose swiftly in a fierce crescendo over our heads. With a jerk, Kitty stopped the car––so suddenly that I felt that she must have been expecting that sound and dreading it.

The hum became a roar, as the airplane passed by just ahead of us, and from the roar emerged the staccato tat-tat-tat of a machine gun. We could see the hulk of the plane in a denser black against the dark sky, and the flame spitting from the nozzles of its guns, as it swept over the crowded road, pouring death into the trapped ranks below.

In a matter of seconds, the crowded highway was emptied of its human freight. Terror-stricken drivers turned their cars off the road, into trees, into ditches, over the fields. Some of them overturned, and their occupants squirmed out and ran in panic from the road, or threw themselves into ditches. Only a few cars remained in the road, stalled, motionless. The figures in them were motionless, too. They had not joined the mad rush to get off the road because they were dead. They had been mowed down indiscriminately, men, women and children, by the sudden hail of death that had rained down upon them out of the sky.

Twenty minutes later several more planes swooped low over the road, but there was little for them to do. No one had attempted to get back on the highway. Only the stalled cars of the dead still remained for targets.

We had thrown ourselves into a roadside ditch with other refugees, and stayed there through the second attack. For some time, we didn't dare venture out. We remained lying in the dirt, apprehensively scanning the sky in the direction of Paris, wondering whether it was over, or whether more planes might suddenly roar down upon us if we emerged from our shelter.

I felt Kitty's hand squeeze mine. I looked towards her. Her eyes were wet with tears.

"Don't be afraid, Kitty," I said. "God will protect us."

Kitty shook her head.

"I'm not afraid. That's not why I'm crying. I can't help it when I think of those poor people—here, and in Poland, in Belgium, in Holland, the poor innocent refugees on whom the Boches turned their machine guns to clear the roads for their armies. I read about it in Paris, of course, but I didn't really believe it. I didn't want to believe it. I thought it was propaganda. I didn't think even German officers would be capable of ordering the massacre of innocent people. I didn't think German soldiers would be brutal enough to obey such orders. But it's true. We've seen it ourselves. We've seen them shooting down harmless, unarmed, helpless civilians!"

Kitty was silent for a moment. Then she added, almost under her breath, as though she were talking to herself:

"How does a young German flier feel, I wonder, when he opens fire on terror-stricken women and children—like us?"

All about us there was a ghostly silence. We knew that there were hundreds of people nearby, hugging the ground in fear like ourselves, but we might have been alone in this unknown open country. Then we heard a woman groaning somewhere in the dark, not far away. From her moans, we judged that she had been wounded. But no one offered to go to her aid. No one dared move.

It seemed ages before first one or two, then dozens of men and women began to creep cautiously out of the ditches. They stood up, looking first towards the sky, and began to collect their scattered belongings. Some of them stood aimlessly in the fields, as though at a loss what to do. They had been going somewhere, they didn't quite know where, running from a danger behind them. And now the danger had caught up to them. They stood still, trapped, de-

"That, Madame, is the way we are going. You will go back to Paris."

What else could we do? We turned our car into the highway, and started back over the same road we had taken southward, ages ago, it seemed, in another existence. Once again we were in the same congested stream of traffic. We moved once more at the same snail's pace, though in the opposite direction. But there was a difference now. No one seemed to be in any hurry to arrive. When the road was blocked, and there was a long wait, no horns tooted, no one shouted at those ahead to get going. Every once in a while, the motorcycle guards, obeying an order passed down the line, hustled us all off the road, into the ditches or the fields, and another motorized column would roar down the vacant lane we had left. Then we could turn back into the road again—those of us who had not broken axles or turned over in the process—and a few miles farther on repeat the same action all over again.

We passed a group of unarmed French soldiers standing by the roadside, guarded by Germans with fixed bayonets. They looked frightened, unlike fighting men. They had been taken one by one out of passing cars in which they had sought to escape.

A car ahead of us was stopped, and a squad of Germans pulled out a young man in civilian clothes. He protested:

"What are you taking me for? I'm not a soldier."

A German shouted at him coarsely:

"*Maul halten!* Do you think we're fools? You can't escape just by putting on civilian clothes, you know. Get over there with the others."

And he was shoved into the group of forlorn frightened French prisoners.

"Look," Kitty said suddenly. "*English* prisoners!"

It was a very small group, standing by the roadside, hemmed in by German guards. Three of them wore the uniform of the R.A.F. The car in which they had tried to escape was standing in the ditch at the side of the road.

By evening we reached the roadside inn where we had learned of the fall of Paris on the southward trip. We were exhausted, ready to drop. But when the innkeeper, standing in the doorway, saw us pull up and stop, he motioned us away.

"I have nothing to give you," he said, "nothing at all. A million people have been through here in the last two days. What can you expect? They have eaten everything. There is nothing left, nothing."

I started to climb wearily back into the car, but Kitty touched me on the arm. She was incomparable in such situations.

"A cup of tea will be enough for us," she said, turning her most winsome smile on the innkeeper.

"*Pensez-vous!* I have no sugar," the innkeeper said, none too graciously.

"That doesn't matter," said Kitty. "We'll take it without sugar." And she marched straight in and sat down.

It worked. The innkeeper led us into an inner room, locked the door carefully behind us, and produced not only tea, but the sugar he had denied having. Perhaps it was the effect of Kitty's disarming smile which caused him later to confess that he had a small piece of salami and a little cheese left that we might have also.

It was the first food we had tasted in thirty-six hours. We were so exhausted and so hungry that we had no thought of discussing our predicament until we had finished. But then we began to talk; and at our first words the innkeeper asked:

"You are English?"

"I'm English," Kitty answered, "but I'm a French citizen now, since I married a Frenchman. My friend here is American."

"Then you can do something for me," the innkeeper said. "I don't speak English myself, and I have some one here who speaks only English. I can't make him understand me. Could you talk to him for me? Ask him how long he intends to stay. Tell him that I am very sorry, I don't want to ask him to leave—but there are Germans all around, they are hunting for Englishmen, and—you understand —it is dangerous for me. I am likely to get into trouble if he stays. Wait here a minute. I will bring him to you."

He left the room. Kitty and I looked at one another.

"An English soldier, no doubt," Kitty said. "He hasn't a chance of escaping, of course. They're sure to get him."

When the innkeeper returned, he was followed by a tall young man with reddish blond hair wearing a leather coat, beneath which the gray-blue uniform of the R.A.F. was visible. He was very young —barely twenty, it seemed. He came up to our table, smiling as calmly as though he were surrounded by friends, miles from any danger. He sat down with us, and told us in a few words who he was and how he had come to be there.

His name was William Gray. A pilot caught at Dunkirk, he had been unable to get to the evacuating ships and return to England. But with the aid of French peasants, he had managed to work his way through the German lines and had set out for the south of France, hoping to get below the territory held by the Germans. But they had moved faster than he had, and here they had caught up with him.

"I don't want to trouble you ladies," he said apologetically, "but if you would just tell this chap for me to be patient, that I will go as soon as he can get me some civilian clothes, I will be able to take care of myself after that."

"My poor friend," Kitty said, "civilian clothes won't do you any good. We've just come from the south, and we saw the Germans taking young men out of automobiles, uniforms or no uniforms. They'll take any one of military age. And as for you, who don't know a word of French—why, you couldn't walk ten steps without being caught."

The young flier stared at us incredulously. His face reflected disappointment and dismay.

"You think there's no chance? How about cutting across the fields?"

"Oh, that's just childish!" Kitty exclaimed, almost angrily. "The Germans are searching everywhere. They'll get you before you even reach a village."

The innkeeper had been standing in the doorway during this conversation, straining his ears as though he could understand by listening more closely. Now he broke in.

"What does he say?" he asked. "Is he going to go? I'm very sorry, you know—but really, you see how it is. I can't keep him here. They may come any minute. It is very dangerous."

"Have you any civilian clothes you can sell him?" Kitty asked.

"Never in the world!" the innkeeper cried excitedly. "*Quelle folie!* Tell him he must not put on civilian clothes. I am a good Frenchman, I hate the Germans and I respect the English, but that is something I can't do for him. It will mean his death if they catch him!"

We looked at the innkeeper in bewilderment.

"But don't you understand?" he hurried on, impatiently. "Explain this to him: if he is caught wearing his uniform, he will be treated as a prisoner of war. If he is in civilian clothes, he will be considered a spy. They will simply shoot him at once."

Kitty translated. Gray sat still for a moment. He hadn't thought of that.

"I guess they've got me," he said finally. He rose, with an embarrassed smile.

"I'm sorry I disturbed you, ladies. Will you do one more thing for me? Find out how much I owe. I'd better get out of here as soon as I can. If I'm going to be caught anyway, I'd better not involve any one else."

No translation was necessary. The innkeeper saw the Englishman take out his purse, and realized that he was about to be rid of his dangerous guest. Too happy at this relief to be interested in money, he pushed aside the Englishman's hand, indicating by gestures that he wanted no payment. Also in gestures, William Gray expressed his thanks, and moved, with uncertain step, towards the door.

"What are you going to do?" Kitty asked.

He turned, still smiling, a forced smile through which his weariness and despair showed only too plainly.

"I don't know," he answered, "but please don't worry about me. I'll be all right. I hope you'll excuse me for intruding on you."

I pressed Kitty's arm.

"Don't let him go," I whispered. Kitty looked at me in surprise. "Haven't you noticed," I went on, "how much he looks like Irving —the same nose, the same chin? He looks exactly as poor Irving did when he was twenty."

Kitty had known my brother well, before that awful day when we buried him in the Père Lachaise cemetery in Paris.

"If only for the sake of Irving's memory, we can't let this boy go,"

I begged. "We've got to get him out of this. We can't let the Germans get him."

"That's all very well," said Kitty, "but how can we prevent it? What can we do?"

"I have an idea," I went on. "Our car is just outside . . ."

"But you're crazy!" Kitty exclaimed. "Don't you remember how they stopped all the cars? They'd pick him up before we got half a mile away. You don't think the German military police will let us cart him off right under their noses, do you?"

"Wait a minute, Kitty," I said. "I've thought of that. How about our luggage compartment? If we take the trunk out, he can hide there."

"All the way to Paris?"

"Yes," I said, "all the way to Paris. He'll have a better chance of giving the Germans the slip in a big city than here. We'll get him to Paris, and then figure out what to do with him there."

Kitty beamed on me with that enchanting smile which I had come to love so much in the years we had spent together. Automatically, she took over command again. I vaguely suspected her of having thought of the same plan before I uttered a word, and having simply left it to me to express what both of us desired. She hurried into the outer room, where William Gray was standing at the window, peering cautiously out towards the road.

"I say, Mr. Gray," she said, "come back here a moment. We want to talk to you."

And with that sentence, we were launched upon an adventure which a week earlier we would have dismissed as impossibly fantastic. Yet it had come about so naturally that neither Kitty nor myself realized that we had projected ourselves into a new course from which we would not thereafter be able to escape. We had closed the door on our calm unruffled existence.

## CHAPTER FOUR

# Running the Gauntlet

IT WAS no easy job for William Gray to stow himself away in the luggage compartment of our car, but he had to admit that it couldn't have been better arranged as a hiding place if it had been built especially for that purpose. It didn't open from the outside, like most luggage compartments. On the contrary, the opening was from the interior of the car, behind the back seats.

He was unfortunately tall, but luckily thin. He pulled himself in somehow or other, his long legs doubled up under him, and grinned at our expressions, which must have indicated our doubt that any one could ride long in so cramped a position.

"Now don't you worry about me," he assured us. "I'm quite comfortable. If by any chance the Germans find me here, you must swear up and down that you never saw me before in your lives, and don't know how I got in here. I'll say that I slipped in while you were in the inn eating. That way you won't get into any trouble on my account—in case."

We closed the luggage compartment on our passenger, and were on our way. The highway had cleared up somewhat now, and we made reasonable progress. There were guards all along the road, and three times before we reached the Porte d'Orléans, the point from which we had left Paris, we were stopped, and asked to show our papers.

We held them out with trembling hands, and our hearts were in our mouths as the guards peered into the car. But none of them made any motion to look into the luggage compartment and each time we drove on again, hearts thumping, but bursting with relief.

At the Porte itself, a more elaborate control had been set up. A German soldier assigned to inspect our car threw open the door, pushed our baggage aside and scrutinized the interior carefully, using a flashlight to illuminate every corner. His hand grazed the luggage compartment, and I held my breath. But he made no move to open it. He turned to us, and said in perfect French:

"Well, ladies, your wanderings on the French highways are over —at least, if you can prove you live in Paris. Have you your papers?"

We produced our identity cards, which gave our Paris address. Satisfied, he waved us on.

As soon as we were out of hearing, Kitty turned to me with a self-satisfied chuckle.

"Those efficient Germans aren't so smart, after all," she laughed. "Imagine! Four of them, and not one thought to look into the luggage compartment!"

"Thank God they didn't," I replied. "But after all, it's not so surprising. With a sentry every two hundred yards along the road watching every one who moves, it probably never occurred to them that any one would have an opportunity to stow some one away. Besides, the military police are only common soldiers. They've probably never seen a luggage compartment opening into a car before, and haven't any idea there would be room for a man to hide in it."

"There isn't much," Kitty said. "If we have to stop again, you'd better take a look at the poor fellow to make sure he hasn't suffocated."

A muffled voice reassured us from within the luggage compartment.

"I'm perfectly all right," William Gray said. "The only thing that worries me is that I might get you into trouble."

"Hush," Kitty warned him. "Not another word. Some one might hear you."

Although we had made better time coming back than going, still it had taken us all night to reach Paris. By the time we had cleared the bottleneck of the Porte d'Orléans, where thousands of returning refugees like ourselves were having their papers checked by the German military police, it was broad daylight. Once out of the congestion about the gate, we were able to speed along the outer boulevards at a normal pace, for the first time since we had started out. All about us we saw the signs of the German occupation.

It was with a constriction of the heart that I saw the Eiffel Tower again, for at its top, where the French Tricolor had always whipped proudly to the breeze, the Nazi swastika now flew.

German military cars rushed past us. When we reached the bridge we wanted to take across the Seine we had a long wait, until a German motorized regiment had passed over it. We went by the Louvre, and there, too, we saw the swastika flying where the Tricolor should have been.

But as we swung through the Place de la Concorde and into the Champs-Elysées, I could not restrain the feeling of joy at being back in Paris, even under the Germans, which always gripped me whenever I returned from a trip to look up that magnificent stretch towards the beautiful silhouette of the Arc de Triomphe, shining at the top of its hill against the clear blue sky.

Beneath its vault, I knew, lay the body of the Unknown Soldier, guarded by the Eternal Flame. From this point, every year, the great military parades which commemorated the storming of the Bastille, July 14, the day of French independence, took their start. I remembered how, nearly a year ago, I had seen the French Army in all its impressive might march down this broad avenue, followed by tanks which shook the ground and made the air vibrate with their roar, while from the sky behind the Arc, 600 planes swooped down above the procession. And now that mighty army had been defeated, and the avenue over which Louis the Fourteenth's horses had pelted to Versailles, the avenue over which Napoleon's victorious forces had marched into the city, was filled with hurrying German military cars, the swastika painted on their sides . . .

We circled the Arc, and a moment later the car ground to a stop in front of 2, Rue Balny d'Avricourt—home!

"At last," Kitty said, cutting the motor. "Very good. Very, very good indeed."

I was panic-stricken at the idea of getting out of the car. Somehow it had seemed safer to be sitting in it. It was our fortress.

"What do we do now?" I asked faintly.

"We must be very careful," Kitty said. "We must be discreet, and we must be on the alert every instant. Don't make any false moves —just act natural."

"Do—do I get out first?" I gulped.

I sensed imaginary Nazis everywhere, waiting to pounce upon me the moment I set foot on the ground. They might be watching us from behind lamp posts, or around the corner, or from any window in the street. They might even be waiting for us in the entrance, ready to trap us as we came in.

"Wait!" Kitty whispered tensely.

A German military guard came marching down the street, surrounding a French soldier. They have probably been searching the houses, I thought, looking for soldiers in hiding, and this is one of the poor chaps they caught.

We remained in the car, motionless. I looked at Kitty, and she seemed very pale. I wondered if she had just realized fully, as I had, at that very moment, that this adventure of ours could be very dangerous for ourselves, that William Gray was not the only one of us who risked being shot.

We waited for a few moments after the Germans had disappeared around the corner.

Kitty turned towards the luggage compartment.

"Mr. Gray! Can you hear me?" she called softly.

"Yes," came his muffled voice.

"We are going to get out now. Button up your leather coat over your uniform before you come out. I'll go first, then Etta, then you slip out, follow us into the house and get into the elevator right after us. Act naturally, and don't hesitate, whether we meet any one or not. Don't say anything now. The street is clear. Here we go!"

Briskly, Kitty opened the car door and stepped out. If I had worried about going first a moment ago, I was twice as frightened now at the prospect of being left behind. I sprang out of the car after Kitty and hurried across the sidewalk behind her. I heard the door of the car slam shut, and I knew William Gray was just behind me. I didn't dare look back. It was only a few steps across the sidewalk, but it seemed to take forever to cross it. Then we were in the familiar entry of our home, and I felt better. We were in luck. There was no one in the hall, and the elevator, of the self-service type common in French apartment houses, was, for once, empty, and waiting on the ground floor.

## CHAPTER FIVE

# "They Are Here"

IT WAS EASY enough for Kitty to say that we had to find some way of getting out of our predicament, but it wasn't so simple to do. Here we were, two middle-aged respectable women of sheltered background, with an English pilot on our hands, in enemy territory, and our problem was to find out how he could escape and get back to England. We knew it could be done, we knew that some persons had done it, but we had no idea how to go about it.

I remembered the "underground railway" of pre-Civil War days, which spirited runaway slaves into the free states. I supposed some similar organization existed to help hidden English soldiers—but how could we get in touch with it? It didn't seem likely that any one in our quiet circle would know anything about it. We were baffled, completely at a loss. We didn't know where to turn, how to begin.

Meantime the Gestapo was conducting its search for hidden soldiers with characteristic thoroughness. House to house searches yielded many Frenchmen of military age, hiding with friends or relatives or even with complete strangers, who had taken them in just as we had taken William Gray in. Once in a while they also got an English civilian or soldier. We heard that they relished such captures particularly; so we knew that our guest would strike them as a particular prize—if they caught him.

We lived for a week in an atmosphere of almost constant terror, expecting daily that the Gestapo would get around to us. We were as careful as we could be. William never went near the window, never answered the telephone. We even refused to let him smoke his pipe, lest the odor should give him away. It irked him that he couldn't shave, since, of course, he had had nothing with him, and we didn't dare to make the unexplainable purchase of a razor.

Whenever the doorbell rang, William dashed to the bathroom and locked himself in. But we realized that this would be no good

if the Germans really wished to search the apartment, and after a
while he gave it up.

The possibility of a search was a real danger, not a fancy conjured
up out of our fear. The Germans were doing it daily. They took a
block at a time, shut off all the streets leading to it, and then went
through it methodically, apartment by apartment, not forgetting the
cellars and roofs, searching every nook and cranny.

It was very clear that if such a search occurred in our block,
William would certainly be found—and we would be arrested along
with him. As the searches continued, it became daily more evident
that it was urgent to find a solution. Our immunity could not last
forever.

But where could we turn for help?

Both of us had many friends in Paris, but most of them seemed
to have gotten away earlier than we did, and were in the unoccupied zone. Kitty sat at the telephone for hours, dialling one number
after the other, but always the regular distant hum told her that no
one was at the other end of the line. Some of our friends had made
no attempt to leave Paris; but, perhaps not very curiously, those who
had been willing to stay behind though they knew the Germans
were coming were not the ones we felt we could trust with our
secret.

For by this time, the change had already taken place which split
the French people into two groups—those who were pro-British and
those who were anti-British, which was practically the same thing
as saying those who were anti-Vichy and those who were pro-
Vichy. Later, as the Germans taught the French to hate them, the
pro-British element increased greatly; but in the opening days of
the occupation, deceived by clever German propaganda and the
studied and ordered politeness of the Germans, which masked their
real intentions, many Frenchmen bowed to the act of Marshal Pétain
in concluding an armistice with the Germans.

A formidable propaganda campaign was begun, attacking the
pre-war régime of France, democracies in general, and the British in
particular. The newspapers and the radio, all under German control,
insisted day after day that the British were to blame for the defeat
of France, that Britain had forced France into the war and then

abandoned her to her fate when catastrophe threatened. The propagandists even went back into history, and brought out a popular-priced edition of the story of the trial of Jeanne d'Arc, to show that English perfidy had been exercised against France even then, when they burned a Frenchwoman who has since become a saint.

The continuous reiteration of this propaganda began to have its effect upon some Frenchmen. They had at first sought to explain the staggering blow which had been dealt them by some hitherto unsuspected military weakness of the French Army, or by the effect on the public morale of the broadcasts of Ferdonnet, the traitor of Stuttgart, who spoke nightly to France from Germany. But under the impact of German propaganda, Frenchmen began to discover a new scapegoat—the English. There were many of them who were ready to impute all the blame to them. And so France was divided into two camps, those who accepted this German theory which placed responsibility on the English, and those who fought against it.

Most of our acquaintances who had stayed in Paris belonged to the first group. Paris was still more or less deserted. Few persons had returned of their own free will. But once in a while we would meet some old friend in the street. If Kitty felt that he might prove sympathetic, she would hint that we had heard something about an English aviator in hiding, anxious to escape to England, hoping thus to find some one who might help us.

But the result was invariable. Always our friend's face would harden and his manner become cold. We would feel a sense of restraint between us. We knew that none of them would report us, but we knew also that they would do nothing to help us. They were afraid. We could understand that, for we were afraid too.

The only one who shared our secret was our Breton maid, Margot, who had been with Kitty for twelve years. We trusted her completely. When we returned to Paris, we sent word to her at her native village, to which she had gone some time before we left, and she returned to us immediately. She often heard our long conversations about the steps we thought of taking to help save William Gray. She never joined them, never mentioned him, but we knew she would not betray us.

Nothing useful came out of those long futile conversations.

Through them, we arrived at only one positive conclusion. That was that we had not only the Germans, but also a certain group of Frenchmen, to fear. We had to be careful everywhere, with every one. It was not safe to assume that every Frenchman was automatically the enemy of the Germans who had conquered his country.

Fearful though we were for ourselves during this period, we could not fail to be touched by the behavior of William Gray. He was so tactful, so inconsolable that his presence was causing us so much concern, and so worried, not for himself, but for us, at the fact that there seemed to be no solution to the situation, that we felt more strongly than ever that we had done right in bringing him to Paris. More than ever, we felt that we must find some way to save him.

Once we caught him tiptoeing out of the door, dressed to leave, trying to relieve us of our troubles by removing from us the risk of his presence. Kitty pulled his leather jacket off herself, and scolded him like a little boy caught in some naughtiness.

"Besides," she ended, after a torrent of scolding, "that wouldn't have solved anything. They'd have caught you before you could get off this street. Do you think it would have been hard for them to find out where you came from? No, it's just no good, my young man. And whatever you may think, it isn't courageous either. It's unworthy of you, and it's unworthy of us."

"But really," William protested, "it's cowardly of me to stay here while my very presence is endangering you every day I remain."

With typical energy, Kitty put him in his place at once.

"I never heard such nonsense!" she snorted. "Cowardly, indeed! We're perfectly safe as long as you don't leave here. Who would think to look here for a British soldier? What's the use of all the trouble we've gone to already if you're not going to let us finish the job? Ungrateful brat!"

And she smiled broadly at the boy she was berating.

"Now let that be the last of that. You're staying here until we find out how to get you out of reach of the Germans. I don't know whether it will take a week or a month or the duration, but I do know one thing—we're not going to let you out of here until we know the Germans won't get you."

There was nothing William could do except give in. He went to his room with a heart-rending smile of gratitude on his worried boyish face. As the door closed behind him, Kitty turned towards me. I had thought she was exaggerating her emotion for William's benefit, but now I could see that she was still deeply agitated, profoundly troubled by what had just happened.

"Etta," she said, "we just *can't* let him go. I wouldn't have any peace of mind for the rest of my life. I hadn't told you before, because I didn't want to worry you unnecessarily, but I hear they're shooting all the British soldiers they catch now. They treat them as spies."

"How do you know?" I asked.

"Mr. Vuillemin told me. Of course, I don't know whether he was telling the truth or not, but what reason would he have to lie? He told me about one case in Belgium where the Germans rounded up a company of French soldiers. There was a British soldier with them. He had his uniform on, but he had some civilian clothes in a bag. He had intended to use them to escape. They lined up the Frenchmen and marched them off as prisoners of war, but they charged the Englishman with having civilian clothes because he was a spy, and shot him on the spot."

A sickening wave seemed to pass through me as I imagined the bullets of a firing squad tearing into the skull of the gentle boy in the next room.

"But, Kitty, you don't think they could treat William that way?"

"I'm afraid they could," Kitty said. "That story has been haunting me like a nightmare ever since Mr. Vuillemin told it to me—and you know he isn't the sort of person to pass on mere rumors. Every time I think of it, I think of poor naïve William Gray, and I'm determined they shan't get the chance to murder him. That's why we mustn't let him slip out, Etta, even though he is willing to sacrifice himself for us. We've *got* to keep him from falling into the hands of the Germans."

But once again, it was easier said than done. Trains were running regularly now from Paris to the unoccupied zone, but there seemed to be no solution there. We could perhaps have gotten him a pass (for once the German administration established itself in Paris, anything could be had from it for a price, even a pass to the unoccupied zone), but an official pass was no guarantee he could get out. Inspection of papers at the border between the two zones was most severe, and the authorities did not hesitate to send a whole train back for the slightest irregularity. We heard of one train which was sent back to Paris three times before it was finally permitted to cross the border. And, of course, William did not speak French.

The more we heard about those trains, the surer we were that we dared not send him out of the occupied zone by that route. We learned that the Germans examined every compartment minutely, to make sure that nothing and nobody was hidden in it. Passengers were searched, uniformed female police being provided to inspect the women.

It was forbidden to carry any written document from one zone to the other, and the police made an especially rigid search for letters. They were described as arrogant, affecting contempt and disgust while they turned out the contents of trunks and handbags. They seemed to take special delight in ordering passengers to step off trains to the platform for further investigation when they reached the border at night, after every one had undressed and gone to bed in the sleepers. We were told that they showed a preference for ordering women in flimsy night dresses off the train in this fashion.

Even after inspections had been finished, trains were sometimes held for hours, without explanation, while the anxious passengers wondered what was wrong, and doubted if they would ever get safely out of German territory. Sometimes, though all papers were in order, the passengers would be told that the frontier was closed and the train couldn't go through. That usually meant a wait of several days.

That was the legal way of crossing the frontier. We were sure it would never do for William. He would have to get across it by stealth—and we had heard a thousand stories about that.

We had been told that persons crossing the demarcation line surreptitiously had to go on foot, being careful to avoid the guards on both sides of the border. At first, the penalty for being caught was only being returned to the zone you were trying to escape from. Then orders were given to open fire on any one seen trying to get from one region into the other. Some persons were killed in this fashion, and those who were only wounded were sentenced to long terms in prison.

Yet men still risked their lives to get out of German-held territory nightly. They had to sacrifice all their belongings, for of course they could carry no baggage on a trip which might oblige them to walk as much as ten miles across rough country in pitch darkness. There were volunteer guides who would take them across, and sometimes sentinels could be bribed. But here, too, caution was necessary. Sometimes a guide would lead his charges straight into the arms of the Germans and collect a reward for his services. Or a sentry would accept a bribe—and then fire on the refugees who had paid him. Nobody could be trusted.

Many ingenious ruses were used to cross the line. In one village, for instance, there was a cemetery whose main gate opened into unoccupied territory. But in the rear wall was an old forgotten door which had not served for years; and that was in unoccupied territory. Inhabitants of the village at first were surprised to note a sudden increase in the number of mourners at local funerals. But they noted also that fewer mourners returned from the cemetery than went to it; and the old-timers recalled the disused door and realized that it was serving once more.

Another story we heard was that of a doctor whose house happened to straddle the line of demarcation. His practice increased enormously—for after seeing his patients, he let them go out by either the front or back door, without inquiring by which they had entered.

But none of these stories helped us, for naturally by the time they had become common knowledge, the Germans knew them, too. They had already arrested those concerned and plugged the leaks in the frontier by the time we heard about them. We couldn't find any one who knew about any such means of getting across the border which hadn't yet been discovered. Day after day, we ran up against a blank wall in our attempts to find out how to get William Gray out of danger.

Kitty was late for supper. Margot had prepared what she could. It wasn't much. We had discovered from bitter personal experience the truth of what we had been told, that wherever the Germans appeared, food disappeared. We had an extra disadvantage. We had three ration cards in the house—but four mouths to feed.

When Kitty breezed in, I could tell at once from the look on her face that it was good news which had detained her.

"Imagine, Etta!" she burst out, before she had even taken her hat off. "I've found some one who can help us! Do you remember Chancel, of the Gueules Cassées?"

I remembered him very well. He was a big husky chap, who had suffered a face wound in the last war. The men disfigured in that fashion had formed their own association, and called it Les Gueules Cassées (The Broken Mugs). Chancel held some official position in this group, exactly what I don't remember. We had met him at the Foyer du Soldat, where we had both worked before our attempt to get out of Paris.

"I ran into him on the subway," Kitty said. "I couldn't say very much to him there, of course, for you can never tell who may be listening. They say some Gestapo agents do nothing except ride back and forth on the subways, listening to everything that's said. But the few words we exchanged gave me the impression that he can and will help us. I trust him. He's a real Frenchman, one who won't ever compromise with the Germans. I made an appointment to see him tomorrow afternoon."

We were all cheered up by even this faint glimmering of hope, and we treated our scanty meal as though it were a gala feast. For the first time, I saw a smile on William's face which wasn't distorted by some other emotion—fear, or worry, or anxiety for us. He had been particularly depressed during the last few days, and it was good to see him care-free for once.

We sat together in the living room after dinner drinking our last treasured coffee, which Margot had brought out because she sensed that this special treat would coincide with our holiday mood. We didn't talk. The silence seemed soothing, and we sat quietly, sipping our coffee, and thinking, all of us, of that interview next day which we hoped—no, which we believed—would end our troubles.

And then the doorbell rang.

Today, as I write these lines, that strident peal is months behind me, but I feel again the chill which seized my whole body and the cold perspiration which started from every pore. I don't know why that particular ring should have sounded like the trump of doom, unless it was because I knew, deep down inside me, that we were basing our happiness on the most fragile of hopes; and so an equally fragile interruption could destroy it, and plunge me back at once into the abyss of fear where I had dwelt for the past week. Or perhaps it was that there was a sharp, aggressive, urgent quality about that ringing, bequeathed to it by the finger which pressed upon the button, arrogant and unfriendly.

I can still see the pale frightened face of Margot as she slipped into the room and closed the door behind her. She almost whispered, in a colorless voice:

"The Germans are here."

Kitty was the first to recover from the icy terror which gripped all of us.

"Soldiers?"

"No, civilians."

"It must be the Gestapo," Kitty gasped.

There was an instant of silence so intense that I could hear Kitty's heavy breathing. Then she swung to me:

"Quick! Take Bill to your room. Try to hide him somewhere."

She cast a swift glance around the room.

"Take the third cup with you. Hurry!"

She shoved us in the direction of the door. As we went out, we heard her say, lifting her voice so that she could be heard outside, in a tone indicating impatience with a frightened servant:

"Don't be silly, Margot! Don't keep the gentlemen waiting. Bring them in here."

I was standing in the center of my room, straining my ears, trying to hear what Kitty was saying. I couldn't; but it seemed to me that they, in the next room, must be able to hear the beating of my heart. Each pulse sounded in my ears like the blow of a hammer.

William sat on the edge of the sofa, his head bent forward on his chest, his hands clenched. I wondered if he were praying. I remained standing only because I was petrified, my limbs too weak even to carry me to the sofa.

Kitty had told me to hide William? But how? Where? There wasn't even a closet in the room. The bathroom? Surely, if they searched at all, they would look there. What difference whether they found him here or there?

I stood still, immovable, thoughts and fears pursuing one another in my head in a mad torrent. Out of the vague indistinct familiarity of the objects about me, two of them suddenly took on sharpness and clarity as they caught my eye—the photographs, standing on my dresser, of the two men who had been dearest in the world to me—my husband, whom I had buried in New York, and my brother, who was resting here in Paris, in the cemetery of Père Lachaise.

In that ghastly moment, as if the two pictures had come to life, I could hear the very tones of their voices within me, and what they seemed to be saying was characteristic of what I had often heard them say in real life.

I imagined my husband's voice, as he would have said: "Well, Etta, you've gotten yourself into a pretty mess. But don't lose your head. There must be a way out."

And I seemed to hear my brother say, as he had said so often when he was alive:

"Don't worry, Etta. I'll fix everything up."

Even in my disarray, I could not help noticing again how much this picture of my brother looked like the young man sitting in anguish on the edge of the sofa, waiting for his executioners to come and lead him away to the firing squad. And suddenly I understood how my brother really was going to help us, how he was going to get us out of this dilemma.

I darted to the sofa, grasped William by the arm, started tearing at his clothes.

"Quick!" I whispered. "Get off your clothes, and into bed. Pretend you are very ill. Leave the talking to me."

Together we pulled off his outer clothing as I whispered my plan to him in quick short phrases. He was in bed in a matter of seconds.

I tied a towel around his head—just in time. For at that moment, I heard Kitty calling:

"Etta, where are you? This gentleman wants to see your room."

As I came into the living room, it seemed to me that the piercing glance of the Gestapo agent bored right through me. But I was strengthened for the part I had to play by the slight amusement I was able to feel, even through my terror, at the short moustache with which he had slavishly copied his master. Somehow that made him seem less terrifying, reduced the fear always induced by the word "Gestapo."

He was not alone. Two other plainclothesmen were standing in the doorway. Behind them I could see Madame Beugler, our concierge, her suspicious eyes watching every move of the German. It was easy to see that he would get no help from her.

I admired the calm with which Kitty was conducting herself. She introduced me with a smile which only one who knew her as well as I did could have realized was forced.

"This is my very dear American friend, Mrs. Shiber," she said. "She has been living with me in Paris, and finds herself an unwitting victim of the war, far from home—like yourself."

I steeled myself to be as natural as possible, while I said:

"Come this way if you want to see my room. You'll have to excuse its appearance. My brother is in bed. He's quite ill. I'm afraid he may have contracted intestinal flu, there's so much of it in town now. I hope you won't have to disturb him."

I could see surprise on the faces of both Kitty and the concierge, but fortunately the Gestapo agent wasn't looking at them. I evaded their eyes, for fear I'd betray myself, but turned towards my room and opened the door for the policeman.

He stepped across the threshold. William made a realistic invalid, with his unshaven face and the towel about his head.

"It's all right, Irving," I said soothingly. "Don't try to talk." I turned to the agent. "This is my brother," I said.

The Gestapo man darted a single swift glance at the bed.

"His papers, please," he said curtly.

I opened the drawer in my bureau where I kept all documents—

the drawer towards which it had seemed to me the eyes of my brother in the photograph were looking when, a few minutes ago, I had suddenly realized that there was a way out. I took out the red wallet which had remained undisturbed there ever since Irving's death, drew out his American passport and the green identity card issued to all foreigners in France by the police, and handed them over.

The Gestapo official flipped through the pages of the passport. He came to the picture of my brother, and flashed another quick glance towards the bed. I thanked God again for William's unshaven face, and also for the fact that the passport, issued some years back, carried a picture taken when Irving was nearer William's age.

The policeman closed the passport, and opened the identity card. "This card has expired," he said. "Why wasn't it renewed?"

"We intended to go back to America, because of the war," I said. "We would have gone long ago, if his health had been better. It didn't seem worth renewing it under the circumstances."

I knew that unrenewed identity cards were not unusual. So, apparently, did the German. He handed the card back without comment, and asked for my papers. Those, I knew, were in order, and I breathed more freely. He checked them, returned them with a frigid word of thanks, and left the bedroom. I breathed again. Our ordeal was over!

But there I was wrong. I had not counted on the methodical technique of the Germans.

Back in the living room, the Gestapo officer said to one of his aides:

"The list of tenants."

He took it, looked through it carefully. Then he turned towards Madame Beugler:

"I do not find the name of Madame's brother on this list."

I was thunderstruck. This was something I had not thought of. My knees weakened again. After all my acting, I thought, after we had apparently succeeded, were we to be tripped up by this minute detail?

It was Kitty's turn to save the situation. Mme. Beugler was obviously confused and frightened. Kitty spoke up:

"Goodness, it's no crime to forget a name, is it? Irving isn't a regular tenant here, anyhow. He has only been here since he was ill and needed some one to take care of him."

Mme. Beugler rose nobly to the occasion.

"I'm sorry, sir," she said to the policeman. "*Je suis idiote*—I forgot about the gentleman. He never asked me for a certificate of domicile, so he isn't on my list."

I held my breath for a few seconds which seemed like an age.

The Nazi sat down slowly at the table, took out his fountain pen, and put on a pair of glasses, which he drew from his pocket. This might have made him seem less formidable also—but I was too frightened to think of that at the moment. What did he intend to write, I wondered? Perhaps a warrant for our arrest?

What he did was to take the list of tenants, and add to it, in his own writing, the name of my brother Irving!

It had worked! We were saved! I wanted to shout with joy, but we were not yet alone. One of the two assistants looked perfunctorily into the closets and bathroom—and I rejoiced that I hadn't tried to hide William.

When they declared themselves satisfied that we were innocent of concealing anything or anybody, the Gestapo agent picked up his hat, and the procession started out, inspecting the entry on the way. The door closed behind them. Kitty instinctively sprang to it, and pushed the bolt.

Now I no longer had any desire to shout with joy. I had suddenly gone limp inside. Kitty leaned her back against the door, and we looked into each other's eyes in silence. Next door we heard the loud long peal of the doorbell.

In the doorway of my room appeared a pale-faced unshaven young man in his underwear, a towel tied around his head.

"What happened?" asked William Gray.

Not until we were sure the Gestapo men had left the building did we dare sit down again around the small table in the living room, from which, half an hour earlier, we had been precipitated in an instant from bliss to terror.

Without a word from us, Margot brought in a bottle of champagne and three glasses. We clinked them solemnly together as we drank a silent toast to our escape.

"How in the world did it ever occur to you to pass William off as your brother, Etta?" Kitty asked. "Had you thought of it before?"

"No," I said. "The idea had never entered my head. It must have been the danger that inspired me—or Irving. I think it was Irving. We have him to thank that we are not the prisoners of the Gestapo now."

And I told her of how Irving's photograph had caught my eye, and how I imagined that his voice had said he would help me.

"It's a miracle, Etta," Kitty said with conviction. "It's nothing short of a miracle. It's not so much that you thought of your brother's papers. The stupid thing is that we didn't think of that before, for you remember you were first attracted to William because he resembled your brother. The miracle is that that sharp-eyed Gestapo man didn't notice that the photograph on your bureau is a later picture of the man whose photo was on the passport—obviously a man twenty years older than William."

"I don't know how I looked," William said, "but I swear to you that while he was in the room I felt old enough to pass for my grandfather."

And with that, we all went off into peals of uncontrollable, almost hysterical, laugher, as our tortured nerves at last sought relief in merriment.

## CHAPTER SIX

# Plans for Escape

THIS experience provided us with a bitter, but a needed, lesson. Ever since we had returned to Paris with William, we had, of course, expected some such visit at any moment, but full realization of what it meant came only with the event itself. During those tense moments when we had felt the prison gates yawning before us, we understood as never before the danger we were running. They gave us new energy in our pursuit of a solution.

But at the same time that this incident goaded us on to greater efforts, it provided us with new problems. First of all there was the question of the concierge, who might now suspect our secret.

Madame Beugler had showed the greatest sympathy and friendship for Kitty ever since we had lived in the house, and we felt that we could count on her. A typical Frenchwoman, Mme. Beugler, we were sure, would be willing to help us even if Kitty told her the whole story, a part of which she must now suspect. But we thought it better not to involve her. We didn't know how much she might have believed of our story about my brother, but she would undoubtedly remember that I had buried a brother at Père Lachaise. She might have put two and two together and have penetrated our ruse, or she might have thought that I had another brother.

Whatever the case, we decided, after long debate, that we must make some explanation to Mme. Beugler.

"I tell you what I'll do," Kitty said. "I'm going to tell her that this is another brother of yours who has just arrived from Nice, and that we were hiding him because he got across the demarcation line surreptitiously. That will satisfy her. I'm sure she'll accept any explanation we choose to make."

That took care of Mme. Beugler; but another problem had now arisen, and this was one we couldn't do anything about. The Gestapo had access to French public records, and if they checked our statements against them, they would discover that the man whose papers they had inspected had been buried in Paris. It seemed evident that there was nothing we could do about that. It was rather unlikely that they would make such a check, and we decided that all we could do was to hope they wouldn't. For if they did, we hadn't a leg to stand on; we had hidden a person in our apartment by supplying him with the papers of a dead man. The proof would be clear in the municipal records and in that list of tenants with Irving's name on it.

So we gave that one up and turned to our third problem—the one which we had already found so hard to solve. How were we to get William out of the house and across the demarcation line? At least, it seemed, we had gained a little time in which to continue our efforts in this direction. William was now officially registered, under his borrowed name, as a tenant of this apartment, and it seemed temporarily safer to keep him there until we could find a legitimate reason to explain his leaving and have his name removed from the list.

If we now had more time, we had no easier problem, for we had said that my "brother" intended to leave for the United States. Suppose the Gestapo returned to demand proof that he had applied for a permit to leave, what would we do then? Or suppose the fact that he held an expired identity card were reported to the competent authorities, and a demand was made that he renew it? In that case, the discrepancies between William's appearance and the date of birth given on the identity card could hardly be missed. Close study of the photograph, too, might reveal that it wasn't a picture of William, particularly if he shaved. And for a few minutes we considered the idea of trying to change the photograph and the date of birth.

Kitty studied the identity papers carefully for some time, and then said, in a discouraged tone: "I'm afraid there's nothing we can do. It's not that I have any scruples about a bit of forgery in this case. I'd commit almost any crime short of murder to get William out of this. But we couldn't do a convincing job. For one thing, the official stamp on the card is printed partly over the photo, and we couldn't fake the stamp. All we can do now is to trust to luck."

So the upshot of our consideration of the new situation was that we must try to get William out of the apartment as soon as possible, to avoid any future comparisons between his papers and their originals; but that until we had arranged for him to get out of the occupied zone, he would probably be safer there than anywhere else.

The afternoon following our Gestapo visitation, we went to see Chancel. He lived in a modest little apartment near the Bastille, where he had remained during the period of panic when every one else was trying to get away. He was not afraid of the Germans, and judged that they would have no interest in him, a man too badly wounded in the first World War to fight again.

We took seats in his scrupulously clean typically French apartment and Kitty opened the conversation cautiously, approaching the subject with the greatest prudence; for even with Chancel, whom she trusted, she did not quite dare be too open. He sensed immediately the general trend of her talk, and smiled at her in the most friendly fashion imaginable.

"*Ma chère madame,*" he said, "you don't have to be so cautious with me. I didn't change my politics when the Germans came in. Now tell me—exactly what sort of a scrape have you gotten yourself into?"

"Well," Kitty gulped, "we're hiding an English pilot in our apartment!"

Monsieur Chancel whistled.

"Well!" he said. "That's quite an exploit for two ladies like yourselves, who certainly wouldn't be taken by any one for adventuresses! You've got one advantage. You certainly ought to be above suspicion."

"Oh, but we aren't!" Kitty said. "The Gestapo came last night!"

"The Gestapo?" Chancel exclaimed. "What do you mean?"

Kitty told him of the previous night's visit.

"Ah!" said Chancel. "That's better. It may not have been the Gestapo—just a routine check-up. You wouldn't have gotten off so easily if they had any reason to suspect you. . . . But now, tell me—how did you acquire this English pilot?"

So Kitty related the whole story—how we had first picked William up, our trip to Paris and our efforts to find a way for him to escape.

"You see our situation," she ended. "We haven't the slightest idea how to get William out of occupied territory, and there's no one we can turn to for help. In all the world, you're the only person we know who might possibly be able to assist us."

"As it happens," Chancel said, in a perfectly simple and natural tone, "I *am* in a position to help you."

Kitty and I looked at each other with a mounting hope that we both restrained until we could be sure that the words really had definite meaning, that they were a prelude to a solution of our problem and not simply an expression of sympathy.

"It's a pity you didn't come to me at once," Chancel went on. "You would have saved yourselves a great deal of worry—and last night's harrowing experience, for instance. Here is what we will do: Some very good friends of mine have transformed their home into a refuge for soldiers in hiding. They're not rich, but they're fairly well off just the same. They've got a roomy house on the Left Bank in a secluded street, very well placed for the purpose.

"Both of them wanted to do something to help the soldiers of this war. The man is a veteran of the last war—he was wounded then, and still has a slight limp. He and his wife lost their only son in this war. Through some of his acquaintances, they got word around to soldiers in hiding, who were looking for a chance to escape to join the Free French, that they would take care of them until they could be smuggled out. They've got a secret room for them in the cellar, with comfortable beds and furniture, well heated, where they stay for two or three days until some of our other friends can get them across the demarcation line."

Our hearts rose at these words. He was not, then, simply a sympathetic friend, but a man who belonged to the groups we knew to exist which helped soldiers to get away. Luck had put us on the right path.

"When can we take William there?" Kitty asked.

"Immediately," said Chancel. "I'll give you the address, and you can go there at once. . . . But just a minute. He's English, you say. Does he speak French?"

"Not a word," Kitty answered.

"Mm—that's bad," Chancel said slowly. "You see, what we do is to get travelling passes for these boys—there are ways of doing that, you know—and then we send them by train to a village on the frontier. There we have other friends who own an estate on the demarcation line, which passes right through it. We get them out through that estate. But if he doesn't speak French, that wouldn't work."

"It's worse than that," Kitty explained. "He's so typically Anglo-Saxon in appearance that the first German policeman who clapped his eyes on him would arrest him even if he talked French as well as Marshal Pétain himself. He's got to be kept out of sight. The only way to get him to the frontier is the way we brought him into Paris—in hiding."

She stopped for a moment, obviously turning something over in her mind.

"Give us the address of the frontier estate," she said. "I'll undertake to get him there in our car."

"That's not so easy now," Chancel objected. "According to the new German regulations, you know, you have no right to drive or even own a car. You can't buy gasoline. You might get some on the Black Market, of course, but even then you would have to be able to prove that you were operating your car in the public interest or in that of the occupying forces. And any German policeman can pick up your driver's license."

Chancel was silent for a moment. Suddenly he slapped his hand down hard on the table.

"I have it!" he said. "You ladies belonged to the Foyer du Soldat, where we met. It's still operating, you know, even under the Germans. They're perfectly willing to have some one else take part of the job of feeding the prisoners of war off their hands. Among other things, they're collecting food and other necessities for prisoners, and visiting wounded men in hospitals. Offer your services, and the use of your car, for these purposes, and you can put the Red Cross emblem on the auto, get Red Cross armbands, and be allowed ten gallons of gasoline a week. Besides, you'll have an excuse for moving about the country, visiting hospitals and camps for prisoners of war.

That's our solution! Just leave it to me. I'll make all the necessary arrangements."

Kitty must have felt like hugging Chancel, but she compromised by throwing one arm around me and squeezing me hard.

"You hear, Etta dear!" she cried. "If Monsieur Chancel manages to arrange that for us, we'll pop William back into the luggage compartment and we won't stop till we get to the border!"

## CHAPTER SEVEN

# William Escapes

THE actual escape of William Gray was so uneventful as to be almost disappointing.

Our first act was to shift him to the home of Monsieur Chancel's friends. It turned out to be a beautiful house, in which every piece of furniture was an antique of considerable value. He stayed there two days. During that time, Chancel procured a permit for William to use in Vichy territory. It was made out in the name of my brother, thus automatically regularizing the situation we had created on the night of the Gestapo visit, and ending our fears for the future.

But one problem still remained to be solved: How were we to get the gasoline for the trip? We had our identification papers from the Foyer du Soldat, and we had started visiting hospitals in the Paris region, but we had not yet received our gas ration coupons.

Kitty exhausted the small supplies of our friends—mostly doctors, who helped her out by sharing with her their own limited rations. But it didn't add up to enough for the trip. Kitty conceived a plan for getting some, which she kept to herself until after she had carried it out. Not until then did she tell me of her audacious method for getting gasoline.

Wearing the nurse's uniform in which she had worked in the American Hospital of Paris, Kitty drove boldly up to the entrance of the Invalides, where the German General Staff had established its headquarters. A young officer was in charge of the guards. She marched straight up to him, favored him with one of her most winning smiles, and said: "I've completely run out of gasoline. I wonder if you could let me have enough to get home?"

She had spoken in French, but the officer evidently recognized that her accent was not that of a native Frenchwoman.

"Do you speak English?" he asked.

Kitty wasn't sure just what lay behind that question.

"A little," she answered cautiously, in that language. "Do you?"

"I'd rather speak English," he said. "My French isn't very good."

"You speak English very well," Kitty said, exercising her smile again, as soon as she learned that his question had had no sinister intent behind it.

"Why shouldn't I?" he asked. "I lived in England until the war broke out—spent seven years there. I studied at Oxford, you see."

"Oh!" said Kitty. "When were you there?"

"1924."

"Did you by any chance know Anthony Faulkner?"

"Anthony Faulkner!" he exclaimed. "Don't tell me you knew Tony! Why, he was my best friend!"

"You know, Etta," Kitty said to me, when she reached this part of her story in telling it to me, "when he said that, I remembered the miraculous luck we had had up to now, and I was sure that some power was helping us! Imagine, out of the whole German Army, stumbling on some one who had a mutual friend!"

Kitty told the German that Anthony was her cousin, and he laughed. "So you speak English 'a little'," he said teasingly. "The truth is you're English yourself, aren't you?"

"Yes," Kitty admitted, "but I'm French by marriage."

"You know," the German said, "war or no war, it's nice to talk English again and remember England. I was very happy there. Won't you have dinner with me tonight when I go off duty? We can talk about Tony—and England."

"He was really rather nice, Etta," Kitty told me afterwards. "For a German, that is," she added hastily. "But I really couldn't accept. Somehow it would have seemed like an awful thing to do. I told him quite bluntly, though I was afraid it would lose me the gasoline. I said: 'You don't seriously think that I could dine with a German officer, do you?'"

Kitty's remark seemed to have hurt the German's feelings a little. He stiffened a bit, but remained friendly.

"I beg your pardon," he said. "I had forgotten for a moment the painful circumstances. I appreciate your frankness. Now tell me— do you really need gasoline?"

"I certainly do," Kitty answered.

The officer called his chauffeur, who was sitting in his car at the curb.

"Siphon off enough gasoline from my car to fill this lady's tank," he ordered. The chauffeur obeyed, and as Kitty, after thanking him, got into her car, the officer said, with what she felt to be a slightly ironical smile:

"I can only hope, Madame, that you will make good use of this gasoline."

"Oh, I will," Kitty laughed back at him. "I'll put it to better use than you could ever imagine."

And that night, with the German Army's gasoline powering our car, we were off to the south with William once more in the baggage compartment.

Our trip had every appearance of legitimacy. The insigne of the Foyer du Soldat was painted on our car, and we had parcels and gifts for a number of military hospitals in different sections of the country. Our itinerary was so arranged that the first stop was at the small town on the demarcation line which split France into two parts. We found Chancel's friends without trouble and handed William over to them after a sentimental farewell—and immediately put as much distance between ourselves and the line of demarcation as possible.

When we were finally back in Paris again, savoring the pleasure of being once more in our own home, and this time alone, without fear of the police, I sat down on the sofa beside Kitty and put my arm around her.

"Thank God we got out of this adventure so luckily," I said. "It might have ended very differently. We must have had a guardian angel watching over us. I didn't want to say so to you while William was still here, but I was constantly in deadly fear, every minute of the time. I noticed that you jumped every time the bell rang, too.

"Now that it's all over, let's be careful not to get into any more adventures like that one. Whatever we do, we must avoid anything that will bring the Nazis down upon us. You will be prudent, won't you, dear?"

Kitty looked into my eyes without answering for a moment. Then she sighed, and said: "I suppose you're right, Etta."

It was about a week later that Margot, usually the most self-effacing of maids, rushed into the living room with a triumphant yell, waving a postcard as if it were a battleflag. It was from William, and the postmark was Marseilles.

This was a pleasant surprise, for we had resigned ourselves to not knowing his fate; and indeed, there was only a period of some two weeks during which we could possibly have received word from him. When the Germans first came into Paris, all communication with southern France was cut off. On July 15, mail began to pass between the two zones once more, but a fortnight later, on August 1, the Germans ended all civilian and non-official correspondence between the two regions. It was during that brief period that William's card got through.

The complete shutting off of communications with the unoccupied zone was one of the greatest hardships for families which had been split between the two regions. After August 1, it was easier for a person in the unoccupied zone to get a letter from America than from Paris. Apparently the object of the regulation was to increase the division of the populations of the two zones, which the Germans hoped would weaken French resistance to the New Order, by pitting Frenchmen against each other instead of against the Nazis.

The two zones were not completely cut off from each other, for every night persons risked their lives to cross from one to the other carrying letters to be mailed after the border had been crossed. After six months of complete cessation of communications, the rule was relaxed to the extent of allowing ready printed cards to be sent across the line. These contained a number of stereotyped sentences (I am well, ill, better. I have received, not received, your letter, etc.), and the sender was allowed only to cross out the unwanted phrases. Some families discovered through these cards that though they had been separated for months, without news of absent members, they had been living all that time within a few miles of one another on opposite sides of the border.

But William's postcard arrived on July 31, the last day when such communications were allowed. He had naturally sent a cautious message, containing a sentimental greeting, and ending with the information that he had been reliably promised that he might soon "visit his parents."

I knew that meant England, and I was so happy that I felt that all our anguish had not been in vain. At the moment, I would have been almost willing to start a similar process all over again.

Kitty wasn't home when the card came. She had gone out early in the morning, and only came in late quite worn out. Ever since William had left, Kitty had spent most of her time out of the house, working her hardest for the Foyer du Soldat. In spite of her exhaustion, her face lighted up when I showed her William's card.

"Isn't that splendid!" she exclaimed. "That's the best news I've heard for a long time!"

"For him and for us, too," I said. "Now that we know he is safely across the frontier, we can be sure for the first time that there won't be any unpleasant repercussions for us from this affair. You remember we agreed that we must be careful not to get involved in anything like this again, don't you?"

"What have you got on your mind, Etta?" Kitty asked.

"I want to know what you've got on yours," I said. "I think you're keeping something to yourself. You might be able to hide something from other people, but not from me—not after four years of living together. Now today, for instance, you left home early in the morning, and you're only back now, obviously dead tired. You did the same thing yesterday. You aren't getting mixed up in any more adventures, are you?"

Kitty turned to me with a tired smile.

"Don't worry, Etta," she said. "I'm not doing anything dangerous. I just want to be helpful, to do something instead of sitting at home idly all day, fretting and fuming."

"Now, Kitty," I said, "you aren't deceiving me in the least. You're just trying to reassure me. You know I've never asked you what you were doing or how you spent your time in all the years we've lived together, but I'm worried about you now. I don't want you to get into any trouble. You've been up to something. What was it?"

"Oh, well," Kitty said, "I'll tell you, and you'll see it's perfectly harmless. I didn't say anything to you, because I didn't want to worry you about nothing—but if you're going to worry anyhow, I suppose I might just as well tell you what I've been doing the last two days.

"Do you remember that yesterday I drove Mme. Robert's 75-year-old mother to her home in the suburbs? Well, on the way back, I caught up with a young man trudging along the road. I had an idea he was another soldier dodging the Germans. It was the way he walked—in a hurry, but aimlessly, looking back over his shoulder every few steps. Besides he had on civilian clothes that didn't fit, and he looked tired, weak and hungry.

"I stopped beside him and asked if he wanted a lift. He noticed my English accent, and decided he could trust me. He told me he was a French officer, and that he had escaped from the prisoners' camp at Baune-la-Rolande. The clothes he had on were smuggled into the camp by a friend; that was how he got out. If he had run into any Germans on the road, he'd have been caught at once, but fortunately I met him first. So I popped him into the luggage carrier."

I let out a gasp that was almost a scream.

"Kitty! Don't tell me you've got him outside!"

"Don't be silly, Etta!" Kitty said. "I told you this was yesterday. As a matter of fact, I did think of bringing him here, but I remembered what you said about how you felt while we were hiding William, so I changed my mind. And I didn't even mention it to you for fear of upsetting you."

"What did you do with him?" I asked.

"I took him straight to Chancel, of course. Chancel got papers for him today, and now he's on his way—one more snatched out of the Germans' hands. Now are you satisfied?"

"It sounds all right," I said. "Are you sure there won't be any repercussions?"

"I don't see how there could be. Even if he should be caught, he doesn't even know who I am. I just picked him up and turned him over to Chancel. After all, it would be a pity not to take advantage of Chancel's organization when we have the chance. My heart aches when I think of all those English boys left behind at Dunkirk, still hiding somewhere in France. I'd like to find them and help them escape."

"Now Kitty," I said, alarmed, "you're not going to start hunting for escaped soldiers, are you?"

"Of course not, dear," she said. "Only, if I should happen to come across others, the least I can do for them is to take them to Chancel. It isn't likely to happen again, of course. You don't come across escaped soldiers every day."

"I certainly hope not," I said. "Look, Kitty. Let's be sensible about this. You say what you did yesterday wasn't dangerous. The boy doesn't know you. All right. But Chancel does. So do his friends on the border. They might get to them, and they might make them talk. They don't care how they do it, you know."

"They wouldn't give me away," Kitty said. "It would be easy enough for them to leave me out of it. Nobody saw me. It was so dark by the time I got into Paris that I could hardly find my way through the blackout."

"That's not the point," I said. "It's what might happen afterwards, whether you're seen or not. The Germans aren't going to let officers escape from prison camps without an investigation. They must be hunting for him right now. And if they get him, they'll move heaven and earth to trace every step of his escape and find every one who helped him. It was dreadfully dangerous, Kitty. You mustn't take chances like that. You're not the adventurous type. And you're up against a strong well-organized system. Just because a couple of sentimental impulsive women got out of one brush with it safely doesn't mean that it can be done again. It will take a well-organized French system to fight the Gestapo. It's too big a job for you, or for both of us. We were terrifically lucky the first time, Kitty, and we're not even sure we were up against the Gestapo. If the Gestapo really gets on our trail, we won't get off so easily. Remember what Chancel said! You mustn't risk your life again—because that's what you are doing, you know."

"You're a fine one to preach to me," Kitty said. "After all, you got me into this."

"I?"

"Yes, you." Her tone was serious, but she was still smiling, so I knew there was no blame behind her accusation. "Wasn't it you who suggested that we save William Gray?"

"Yes," I said, "and we've done it. Perhaps I wouldn't have had the courage if I had realized in advance what it meant. But now that chapter is closed, and I want you to promise not to get into another adventure of that kind."

Kitty had picked up a copy of *Paris-Soir* and pretended to be deeply immersed in it.

"Kitty," I repeated, "will you promise?"

"I did promise, didn't I?" Kitty said evasively. "Now, for goodness sake, let me read the paper. One would think I'd committed a crime!"

We were quiet for a time. Kitty turned the pages of her paper. I was reading a book. I had about decided that I was ready for bed when Kitty uttered a little exclamation, picked up a spoon from her saucer, and with its handle circled an item in the paper, pressing hard to leave a mark.

"Etta," she said, handing the paper to me, "isn't that interesting!"

She had been reading the "Missing Persons" column. It had become the most widely read part of the paper in France, for hardly any one was without a close friend or relative who had disappeared in the confusion of war. Six million persons had left northern France at the time of the invasion, and their only means of locating one another was through advertisements in the newspapers.

*Paris-Soir,* a pro-German paper since the Nazis had come in and taken it over, published several hundred such advertisements daily. The German censorship permitted it, for the Germans wanted civilians to return to their normal way of living in order that France might resume production—for Germany's benefit.

The announcement Kitty had marked read something like this: "Jonathan Burke is looking for his friends and acquaintances. Address Military Hospital, Doullens (Somme)."

"What's exceptional about that?" I asked. "I've seen hundreds like it."

"So have I," said Kitty. "But how about that name—Jonathan Burke? That can't be French. He must be English. Perhaps he's one of the boys from Dunkirk, trying to contact friends who could help him."

"There are Frenchmen with English names, you know," I said. "You're English, but you've got a French name."

"I married mine," Kitty said. "I doubt if he got his that way. I ask you, could a Frenchman possibly be named Jonathan? Burke, perhaps, but certainly not Jonathan. I've been looking at these advertisements for days, and this is the first time I've seen an English name. There are quite a few British soldiers scattered through hospitals and prison camps in northern France, you know. Besides, Etta, I *feel* that he's British. I'm sure of it. Why do you have to argue that he isn't?"

There was a tone of momentary exasperation in her voice. Then it changed.

"I'm sorry, Etta," she said. "I didn't mean to be rude."

But she was obviously agitated. She got up from her chair and walked into the next room. I was afraid I was displeasing her, but I was really worried now, for if she had been looking through the "Missing Persons" columns for English names day after day, it was obvious what was on her mind. She was searching for more William Grays. So I followed her, although I knew she was trying to escape from me, and sat down on our deep-seated divan beside her.

"I'm only insisting because I'm fond of you, Kitty," I said. "I don't want to see you get into serious trouble—and it looks to me as though you were looking for it. Suppose Jonathan Burke *is* an English boy. We're in no position to do anything for him. He's in a military hospital—that means under guard. Picking up a man on the road, by accident, is one thing; getting him out of a guarded hospital is another. Even if we worked out some brilliant scheme to help him escape, we'd probably be caught red-handed. You can't expect such luck as we had with William twice. The Nazis weren't born yesterday."

"They aren't supermen, either, even if they think they are," Kitty said. "Some of them are lax, some are stupid, and some are just plain indifferent." She adjusted a pillow behind her back and sank back into it. "Plenty of British soldiers have gotten out of the occupied zone since the armistice, and no one has been punished for it."

"You mean we don't know whether any one has been punished for it," I said. "There are other ways in which we can help, Kitty. We don't have to go to such extremes."

"Oh, I suppose you're right," she said. "But let me do just one thing, Etta. I won't unless you agree—but it's perfectly safe. Just let me answer Jonathan Burke's advertisement. I'll tell him that we'll bring him a package if he wants to see us. Now, don't look so startled! I said 'us' because I want you to come along. I want you to see for yourself that I'm not doing anything you wouldn't approve of.

"There's no harm in that, is there? I'm sure he's an English boy, and I want to do something for him. We're allowed to take packages to them, you know—in fact, at the Foyer du Soldat we're supposed to. What does it matter if we take one to a specific soldier, instead of to just any one?"

"All right," I said. "And I'll go with you—but just for one reason. That's to make sure you keep out of trouble."

And with that settled, I went off to bed. Kitty had seemed terribly tired herself, but she didn't go to bed at once. She had something she had to do before she could go to sleep. She stayed up long enough to write a letter to Jonathan Burke.

## CHAPTER EIGHT

# A Trip to Doullens

A FEW days later, Kitty dashed into my room before I was up. "He got my letter, Etta," she cried. "Look! Here's his answer!"

I didn't have to ask whose. I suddenly realized that I had been waiting almost as anxiously as Kitty for Jonathan Burke's reply.

She held the cheap, soiled envelope under my nose. The cramped, almost childish handwriting suggested that it had been written under difficult conditions—in Jonathan Burke's hospital cot, no doubt.

"Well, what does he say?" I asked.

Kitty seemed to hesitate a moment about opening the envelope. Then she tore it open, unfolded the single sheet within it, and scanned it rapidly.

"I *knew* he was English!" she exclaimed triumphantly.

"For goodness sake, read it!" I cried.

"He says," Kitty read: " 'Can you help? Well, I guess! I can use some food, that's sure, and it would be splendid to have some-one to talk to. Seems English is scarce around here, and I have nothing but time on my hands. You are wonderful to write to me, and I shall look forward to your visit.' . . . That's all," Kitty concluded, handing me the letter.

"Poor chap!" she went on. "There must be hundreds like him, not even able to talk to any one. How glad I am that I saw his ad! *Paris-Soir* is still good for something, even if it is a Nazi sheet. I'm sure we can manage to help the boy."

I looked at Kitty. She had a faraway look in her eyes that I had seen there before once or twice when she was particularly excited about the chances of freeing William Gray.

"Now, remember, Kitty," I said. "You promised. This is just a visit. We'll take him a package of food chat with him for a while, and that's all."

"Of course, of course," Kitty said impatiently.

"All right," I said. "That's settled, then. When shall we go?"

"We're on inspection duty at the Foyer du Soldat today," she said. "How about tomorrow?"

Tomorrow it was.

It was early in the morning of August 15 when we set out for the small town of Doullens. Our package for Lieutenant Burke contained several cans of sardines, some bread, cigarettes, and a few other things we thought he might like.

We were already in the car, about to start, when Kitty suddenly said: "I forgot something!"

She hurried back to the apartment and returned with a box covered with brown wrapping paper.

"Another gift?" I said. "What's in it?"

"It's not a gift," Kitty said. "Just something I want to leave at the Foyer on the way back."

She stepped on the starter, and we rolled through the streets of Paris. It was a beautiful day, and as we got out into the country, and moved swiftly along through fields bright with flowers, I felt elated about our errand. As we sped along, we speculated on Jonathan Burke's looks and character.

"I suppose he's wondering if we're coming at all," Kitty said. "Perhaps I should have answered his letter. He may have thought I had a momentary good impulse and then forgot all about him. He probably took me for a nosy old woman who wanted to pry into his troubles but wouldn't bother to do anything about them."

"The fact is that we couldn't do much about them," I reminded her uneasily. I sensed an air of determination, almost of recklessness, in Kitty's attitude which gave me an uneasy feeling.

We reached Amiens in good time. Doullens was about eighteen miles beyond it. Just before we reached the town, the road passed an old fortress, which we had visited on a pleasure trip two years earlier. Known as the Citadel, it dated from mediaeval times. We had been inside it, and seen its windowless cells, and the narrow slits through which its defenders had fired—the only openings through which the sun could penetrate.

It had never occurred to us that this building could possibly be put to any modern use, so we were astonished to see the Nazi swastika waving in the breeze over the Citadel, and helmeted German soldiers on guard at the entrance.

Kitty drew the car up beside a peasant woman standing by the side of the road.

"Why are the Germans guarding the Citadel?" she asked her.

Her face twisted with hate, the woman replied:

"God punish them, they've got our men in there. They've made a prison out of it. The men are shut up in those filthy holes where we wouldn't think of keeping our dogs. There's no sun, and they're all sick. There's not a day the priest isn't called in. Damn them all, I say!"

"You'd better be careful," Kitty said. "If they hear you, they're likely to arrest you too."

"I don't care if they do," said the old woman. "My two sons are in there. They had come home, they had civilian clothes on again, but the Boches came and took them away. My oldest son, that's Jean, was a sergeant. He had his discharge papers. He showed them, but they paid no attention to them. He came across the line, you see—slipped over without a pass. You understand—he couldn't get one, and he wanted to come home. I've been here since sun-up, trying to get a peep at them. But every time I get near the gate, the damned Boches chase me away."

"Poor woman," Kitty said, as we drove away. "Let's take a look at the Citadel while we're here."

She pulled up to the gate, picked up a few of the parcels we had brought with us for the hospital, and stepped briskly out of the car. "Come along," she said over her shoulder, and walked straight towards the gate. The sentry looked at our Red Cross armbands, and made no move to stop us.

Inside we passed through a low, arched hall, closed at the end by iron bars. Through it we could see the courtyard of the Citadel. It seemed to me the most sinister place I had ever seen in my life. Behind the high stone walls of the old fortress hundreds of prisoners were jammed together, surrounded by barbed wire barriers which seemed hardly necessary in addition to those thick walls and iron bars. Herded aimlessly together, the prisoners, some standing, some sitting, some lying on the ground, turned hungry, haggard faces towards the bars which separated them from us.

Kitty shuddered. "What a horrible place!" she said. "And all these people have done is to be on the losing side! No civilized country would keep the worst criminals in such a place!"

Heavy footsteps sounded in the dark corridor. A German sergeant came up to us, glanced at our Red Cross armbands, and said: "Let me see your papers, please."

He looked over them carefully. They carried the seal of the German Kommandantur, and stated that we were authorized to visit prison camps and hospitals to distribute gifts to the prisoners.

Kitty, with her disarming smile, said in German:

"We brought some packages for the prisoners. We would like to distribute them, and talk to some of the men."

The Nazi shook his head.

"You may leave the packages if you wish. Visiting the prisoners is strictly forbidden."

"But we are authorized to do so by the Commanding General," Kitty insisted. "See—it says so on our credentials."

The German still shook his head.

"The Commanding General himself has forbidden visits to the prisoners here," he said. "His order does not exempt you. Moreover, your credentials do not say that you may talk to prisoners— only that you may give them gifts."

And he shoved us towards the entrance, as though he were afraid to allow us even the brief glimpse we had had of the inside of the Citadel. In spite of our failure, I was glad to get out of the place. Kitty didn't say anything. We climbed into the car in silence, and continued toward Doullens.

The hospital was about a mile and a half from the Citadel, on the other side of the humble little town of Doullens.

We stopped in front of the hospital gate, under a spreading oak. Pulling our parcels out of the tonneau of the car, we walked towards the entrance, and passed through the arched stone gateway. Two helmeted German soldiers, standing stiffly at either side of the gate, appeared not even to see us. We learned later that the hospital, though operated by its French staff, was under the control of the German military authorities. Its patients were considered as prisoners of war, and on recovery would be confined to a prison camp—probably the Citadel.

To tell the truth, the hospital was not much of an improvement over the Citadel. It was filthy, dark and smelly, and infested with vermin. We even saw a rat scurrying through one dim passageway.

After making ourselves known to the director in charge, we wandered through the hospital on our own. No one had time to guide us, which suited us perfectly. We went into a number of rooms, talked with the soldiers, and left them the comforts we had brought.

In one room which I still remember vividly were two young Algerian soldiers, with badly wounded hands, which they were unable to use in any way. They were lying helpless and untended, on dirty mattresses, in their underclothes, without sheets or blankets. Over them swarmed hundreds of flies, not only on their bodies, but covering their faces like a living, stirring crust of black filth. They could not brush them away, and it was easy to see by the distortion of their features how intolerable was this slow, unavoidable parade of the insects over their helpless faces. They were literally gasping with thirst. Kitty and I found them some water, and made them as comfortable as we could, though there was little we could do. We brushed the flies away, but we knew they would return the instant we left.

In other rooms we found similarly bedridden men in much the same state. I was shaken by the sights I saw, gripped by the desire to help, but I knew very well that there was no way I could do much for these unfortunate men, condemned to escape from this horrible caricature of a hospital only to the more horrible caricature of a prison we had just seen—or to the grave.

Meanwhile Kitty was looking for Lieutenant Burke. She had refrained from asking for him in the prison office, not wishing to draw attention to our visit in connection with him. She had assumed that this hospital, like every other she had ever seen, would have a chart at each patient's bed, giving his name and a record of his condition. But there was nothing like that here. We were reduced to chance.

It was a relief to escape at last from the rooms and wards, and step out into the garden, where convalescent patients were allowed to roam about freely. We saw a number of them sitting about in the sun; and finally, in one corner, we noticed an English R.A.F. officer, in uniform, sitting by himself on a bench. Since most of the others we had seen were French, we judged this might be Lieutenant Burke, and we turned towards him.

He was about 27, lean, dark-haired with a small black mustache— a rather good-looking young man. His uniform was crumpled and faded, and he wore a bandage over his right eye.

As he saw us approaching, he seemed suddenly to come to life, like a puppet when the marionette master pulls the strings. A slow grin twisted his boyish mouth, and with a restrained gesture to his pale, emaciated hand, he invited us to sit down on a bench against the wall.

"How good of you to come!" he said at once, without even asking if we were the ones who had written him. "I hoped you would, but I didn't dare count on it. It's a long way from Paris, and, after all, I'm no kin of yours."

"You're a countryman of mine," Kitty reminded him.

"That doesn't always mean very much," said Lieutenant Burke, "though I guess it means more now than it did before we started fighting . . . I took a chance some one like you might see that ad when I put it in the paper. I didn't expect it to reach any one I knew already. I don't know anybody in Paris. I used to visit there in the old days—had a fine time: wonderful shows, marvelous night life. You know the sort of thing. But that was just during school vacations. I had no friends there."

As he talked, I watched him intently, and thought what a fine young man he seemed to be and how proud I would be to have a son like him. But I pitied his mother, for I knew that if I had been in her place I wouldn't be able to sleep for worry, knowing that my boy was shut up in this filthy place, under guard like a criminal . . . but perhaps she didn't know. That might be worse.

My feeling was so deep that when I asked, "Were you hurt

badly?" my voice was almost a whisper. I had to repeat the question before he understood me.

"I got a shrapnel wound at Dunkirk, Ma'am," he said.

"What a shame!" I exclaimed.

"I got off easy," Lieutenant Burke said grimly. "I left a lot of buddies back there who'll never see this world again—even with one eye."

"Did you lose your eye?" I almost moaned, but Kitty tactfully intervened to change the subject.

"We've been all through the hospital," she said quickly. "It's a filthy place. It's disgusting to think you have to stay here."

"Maybe it seems so to you," he said, "but I'm trying to stay here as long as I can. When I'm better they'll send me to the Citadel. You should see that!"

"We have," said Kitty.

"Well, then," he said, "you know there's worse places than this. I was there for two days before they brought me here. I don't want to go back there. I'd be back already if they weren't so slipshod here. They haven't found out yet that my wound's practically healed. Look!"

He pulled up the corner of his bandage. Underneath we could see a scar under the eye, completely healed. The eye itself seemed normal. He hurriedly pulled the bandage down again.

"You see," he said, "I'm perfectly fit to leave, but I'm stalling for time. There's hardly any guard—just the two men at the gate. I might be able to escape from here, but there isn't a chance of getting out of the Citadel. And I wouldn't get far in this uniform. I suppose they count on that—that, and our being weak. Otherwise they'd watch us more carefully."

Kitty got up from the bench. She walked a few steps nervously, then paced back towards us again. Suddenly she leaned over and said in a low voice into Lieutenant Burke's ear:

"Would you like me to take you to Paris?" (She seemed to have forgotten my very presence). "Will you risk it? I'm not afraid—but would you be? We can get you out of the occupied zone. We've done it before."

Lieutenant Burke clutched at Kitty's hand.

"Would I like you to take me to Paris!" he ejaculated, so loudly that he frightened me.

"Sh!" I warned him. "They'll hear us!" And I looked fearfully across the garden to the other convalescents; but no one was paying any attention to us.

"Would I be afraid?" Burke repeated. "Afraid? After this? After the Citadel I'd rather be rotting on the beach at Dunkirk, honestly dead, than rotting there while I'm still alive! What could happen to me any worse than being sent back to the Citadel? And that will happen any day now—the next time the commandant comes here to check on men well enough to go back."

"Has any one tried to escape from here before?" I asked.

"Everybody's thought of it," Burke said, "but there's not a chance. Three or four have actually gotten out of the hospital grounds— that's easy—but the highways are watched, and all of them have been picked up almost immediately. The punishment is going back to the Citadel, no matter how sick you may be. That's about the worst fate any of us here can imagine, so no one has tried to get away recently . . . You can't dodge the German motorcycle patrols. They run back and forth all the time over all the roads in the neighborhood.

"I'm willing to take any chance, Mrs. Beaurepos. I'll be back in the Citadel in a few days anyway, whether I do or not. But how can you manage it? After all, you're only a woman. I don't mean anything derogatory by that. But what can a woman do? . . . You remind me of my aunt Katherine—aristocratic, gentle, fine, wanting to help, but helpless. I know you *want* to help me. I'm sure you'd try. But, God, what can a woman do in times like these? You're just licked before you start."

The sound of his own voice seemed suddenly to embarrass him. He stopped short, and pressed his hand over the wound under his bandage, as though it itched. I noticed that his long fingers were trembling. His blue eyes seemed to gleam with the dry light of fever.

Kitty said softly:

"You are mistaken, Mr. Burke. We can get you by the motor-cycle patrols, and we will."

I looked at Kitty with admiration for her firm calm tone, but also with fear. I could feel the cold terror which had only left me with the safe departure of William Gray flooding me again. I didn't know whether I wanted more to help Lieutenant Burke or to get away without finding myself committed to another adventure like that from which we had so narrowly escaped.

Kitty had taken complete charge of the situation.

"You two wait here," she said. "I'll be back in a minute."

When she returned she had the brown parcel she had gone back to get before we started out. She handed it to Lieutenant Burke.

"There are a pair of overalls in this package," she said. "Get into them without being seen. You see the branches of that tree over there, on the other side of the wall? Our car is parked under it. There are bushes covering the wall at that point. Climb over the wall there. It's not high, and the bushes will hide you. The car is unlocked. Get into the back, and behind the back seat you will find the opening of a luggage compartment. Get into it, close it behind you, and wait."

Burke seemed a little doubtful. Kitty reassured him:

"There's been another English pilot in that cubby-hole before you," she explained. "He was taller than you are, but he was comfortable enough—especially after the trip was over."

Now for the first time, Kitty looked towards me. I suppose she expected a protest, for of course she knew that I must realize now that in spite of her half-promise, she had planned all this from the beginning. When she had brought the overalls with her, when she had chosen the spot to park the car, she was already preparing her plan.

But what could I say, with Burke beside us, visibly vibrating with hope? She saw that I was not going to say anything; and it was with a lilt in her voice which showed the relief she felt that she turned back to Burke:

"Don't forget to take off your bandage. Without that, and with these overalls, you'll be all right even if you're seen. If you get into the car unobserved, the battle's won. The motorcycle patrols won't stop us."

Burke nodded, without a word. He seemed too moved to speak.

"We'll go now. We don't want it to be noticed that we have talked with you longer than with other patients. Don't be nervous if we're slow coming. We'll stay at least ten or fifteen minutes more, and make sure of being seen with others just before we leave."

Kitty held out her hand. Burke took it, then shook hands with me also, as though we were saying a routine good-bye to him. As we walked away, I saw him fumbling with the package, as though trying to verify its contents by feeling it before opening it.

We passed by several groups of French officers, some bandaged, some apparently completely recovered. We shot sidelong glances at them, wondering if they had paid any attention to our conversation with Burke. If any of them had noticed us, they evidently intended to pretend they hadn't. They ignored us completely as we passed them.

One of the hardest things I ever did in my life was to enter the hospital building again, and walk through the wards, stopping to talk to patients as though nothing had happened. I tried to appear calm and natural, but I didn't feel as though I were succeeding. I forced a smile to my lips, where it seemed frozen in place; and then I found I didn't know how to stop smiling. It seemed to me that I must be walking through the wards like a hideous grinning gargoyle, the expression on my face felt so unnatural.

Kitty seemed cool as a cucumber. As far as I could see, she was acting just as naturally as before we had found Burke. I let her do the talking to the soldiers. I didn't trust myself.

The minutes dragged by like hours. As we left one ward, I clutched Kitty's arms, and whispered fiercely:

"We've waited long enough, Kitty. For God's sake, let's get out of here now."

"Not yet, Etta," Kitty said. "He hasn't had time to change his clothes yet. Better to allow too much time than too little. Keep your chin up, and don't look so terrified! That's better. Let's see who's in here."

And she turned into another ward. There was nothing to do but follow.

As we came out of this room into the dark corridor again, a

blond young man who seemed to have been lying in wait for us outside the door limped towards us, and whispered:

"I saw you with Burke. I'm English, too. I'm sure you're helping him get away from here. Please—get me out, too. I've *got* to get away from here!"

"What's your name?" Kitty asked.

"Corporal Lawrence Meehan. Lieutenant Burke will vouch for me."

Kitty stood silent for a moment, looking at the newcomer. Suddenly she seemed to come to the decision that he could be trusted.

"Why do you want to get out?" she asked.

"God, who doesn't? But I've a special reason. It's my leg. I'm not getting proper care here, not even rest and food. It's playing me the very devil. I know it would improve if I could get out of the Germans' hands, where I could have quiet and peace of mind. But it'll never get better here!"

He was trembling all over, and looked very ill. Drops of perspiration stood out on his forehead.

"But you have a fever," I objected.

"No, no, I'm not feverish at all—really. It's only the idea that perhaps I can get away. It's worked me up a little. I'll be all right the minute I get out of here."

"Look here, young man," Kitty said, "I'll make you a promise. If the Germans don't catch us, we'll come back for you next. But we can't take you now. We can only hide one at a time in our car. If you want to get out, your best bet is to keep us from being suspected of helping Burke; otherwise, of course, we couldn't ever come back here again for you. Now, is there anything you can do to keep them from noticing that Burke is missing—or at least from finding it out long enough so that they won't connect it with our visit?"

The corporal thought a moment.

"I could do this," he said. "At six every night, a clerk goes through the wards and calls the roll. I'm not in his ward (officers and non-coms are not put in the same ward, you know), but I can manage to be there and when his name is called, I'll say he's gone to the toilet. That will be all right at night, because they aren't very particular then; they don't expect escapes in daylight. But in the morning, the check is more careful, so they're sure to find he's missing then. They'll think he slipped out overnight."

"Perfect!" Kitty smiled. "That's all we need. You take care of that, and in two days we'll be back for you. Be ready."

And she swung around and strode off without a backward look. I hesitated. I thought I ought to say good-bye, or say something encouraging to Corporal Meehan. But as I saw Kitty's back retreating down the corridor, a feeling akin to panic came over me, and I hurried off after her like a stray kitten following a possible protector.

As we reached the gate, Kitty said loudly: "Wait here! I'll bring the car around to the gate for you."

I would have protested, but I didn't dare. Instead, I stood riveted with terror between the two German sentinels, and waited for an eternity. I heard the whir of the starter as Kitty pressed it, and the answering roar of the motor.

What, I wondered, had come into Kitty? Was it just bravado? Did she take pleasure in driving the car with Burke hidden in it right up to the sentries? As the car moved towards the gate, I started forward, to make her stop a little farther away. I was deathly afraid that it might occur to one of the sentries to look into the car, and perhaps even to think of opening the luggage compartment.

"Hop in," Kitty said, and then, to my terror, instead of starting up, she beckoned to one of the sentries.

He came over to the car.

"What time do you open the gates for visitors in the morning?" she asked calmly in German. He told her.

"We may have to make several trips here," she said coolly. "Have a cigarette?"

He accepted one, and another for his fellow sentry, and struck a light for her as she produced one for herself.

"*Danke schön,*" she said, and started the car.

I was about to upbraid her, when she spoke quietly, without looking towards me.

"I wanted to give him a chance to see that there was no one in the car except the two of us," she said. "Now even if they discover Burke's absence tonight, the sentry will swear up and down that our car was empty. In fact, since the other man saw him standing by it talking with us, he wouldn't dare voice a suspicion even if he had one. He'd be convicting himself of negligence."

"Kitty," I said "you're a wonder! But what would have happened if he had poked around inside the car and decided to open the luggage compartment?"

"He couldn't," Kitty said. "I locked it. And I certainly wouldn't have admitted that the key was any nearer than Paris."

## CHAPTER NINE

# Ten Thousand Englishmen

As we speeded out of Doullens, a German motorcycle patrol passed us, but didn't even pause to inspect our car, with its prominently displayed emblem.

From time to time, Kitty stopped, to ask Lieutenant Burke if he were comfortable. Each time the same reply echoed from the depths of the luggage compartment:

"More comfortable than I have been for weeks, thanks. How soon do we reach Paris?"

The drive was uneventful. The only incident occurred when we had to stop because the road was blocked by the car of a German official, who had crashed into a peasant's ox-cart. He was too busy shouting at the peasant and trying to extricate his car to bother about us; and as soon as he had backed out of his predicament, we sped on unhindered.

Arrived at our building, we re-enacted the same scene that had occurred when we reached there with William. This time the danger was less, for since Burke was in overalls, he would appear to be a workman entering the house if any one caught sight of him, whereas William had been marked by his uniform.

Once in the apartment, Kitty shot the bolt. We looked at one another like two tried and triumphant conspirators, and laughed.

"Practice makes perfect," said Kitty. "Remember how excited and worried we were the first time? I wasn't a bit frightened this time."

"Neither was I," I said, not quite truthfully.

But Lieutenant Burke was a new hand at this game. He was pale, and the perspiration was streaming down his face.

"Come, come," Kitty laughed banteringly, "don't show how little trust you have in us. We're past masters at this game, you know." She rang for Margot. "Is dinner ready?" she asked, when our maid appeared.

"Yes, such as it is, Madame," Margot answered, without showing the slightest surprise at the appearance of another young man. "I found a little cheese—not much, but very good. And we have some vegetables and bread."

We sat down to dinner, and during its course explained the next moves to our guest.

"Tomorrow morning we will take you to a very beautiful house across the Seine," Kitty told him. "You'll probably be there about two days. Then you will be moved down to the demarcation line, where friends of ours will get you across. I don't know whether you'll go by train, or whether we'll have to take you. It's a rather long trip to make in the luggage compartment—though our last visitor made it. The train would be more comfortable, but then you'd have to be able to pass for French. Do you speak French?"

"Yes—*un peu*," Burke said, "but not well enough to fool any one. No one would take me for a Frenchman."

"We'll let a Frenchman decide that tomorrow," Kitty said. "Our friend M. Chancel, who will arrange the details for getting you out, will tell us what to do. You can have complete trust in him."

After dinner we sat in the living room, and Jonathan told us about himself. He had been a civil engineer before the war. He described the hell of Dunkirk, but compared it favorably to that other inferno, Doullens, whose greatest torture was the hopelessness which gripped its inmates.

"I sat in the garden most of the time after they let me get up," he said, "worrying about the future and about my family—my mother and my sister, Mary. It was some of the others there—the French patients—who asked me why I didn't put an ad in the paper. Some of them had located relatives that way. I knew I wouldn't find any relatives, but I thought, 'What's the harm?' So I did."

He sighed.

"You're both wonderful," he said. "I guess the world hasn't gone to the dogs after all. No matter where you go or what happens, you always find good people everywhere."

He lapsed into silence. His face seemed to darken. It didn't look as though he were thinking pleasant thoughts.

"What's the matter, Jonathan?" Kitty asked. "Can we help?"

"I just thought, suddenly, of other English soldiers who haven't been as lucky as I. There are supposed to be about ten thousand of them, most of them escaped from the Dunkirk area, like myself. They're hiding in woods and caves in northern France, half-starved, tracked down like beasts. If they try to slip into the villages to get food, the Germans get them. They've organized special units to hunt for them. It's a miniature war, with well-armed well-fed German motorcycle police on one side, and starved, unarmed, broken, sick men on the other."

The figure Burke mentioned was roughly the estimate we had heard from Chancel, too. His organization had been trying to find some of these men, but without much luck. Obviously, it was not easy for those who wanted to rescue them to find their hiding places, especially while their enemies were also scouring the country in search of them.

After the Dunkirk evacuation (or, as Churchill called it, the miracle of Dunkirk), several thousand British soldiers were left in France. They were caught behind the lines of the German Army moving through France, without hope of escape. The Nazis captured many of them, but others took refuge in the woods, and it was these men the motorcycle patrols were trying to round up.

As the Germans moved southward, the British soldiers had followed close behind, hoping for a chance to break through some gap in the front and get out of German-occupied territory. Some of them had been seen as close to Paris as Chantilly, practically a suburb of the capital.

But their chances of breaking through were close to zero. As the Germans occupied Paris, signed the armistice, and moved down along the Atlantic coast to the Spanish border, the front became a frontier, and the English were trapped. Then the Nazis set to work to mop them up.

These were the men whose fate worried Burke.

"There's no way of saving them," he said gloomily, "no way at all. If we were all together, and had arms, we might be able to fight our way to the coast. I'm sure England would do the impossible to get boats over to us. But we're scattered all over the place. There's no way of getting together."

Burke went to bed early. Kitty and I sat in the living room. Margot, coming in with the coffee, found us sitting there silently. The unaccustomed quiet affected her, too, and she tiptoed about the table, clearing away the dishes, as though she were afraid to make a sound.

When she had left the room, Kitty turned to me with a look of determination, as though she were about to say something, then changed her mind, and began stirring her coffee with unnecessary vigor. Suddenly she seemed to come to a decision. She laid her spoon in her saucer with deliberation, and said to me:

"Etta, you will have to go back to America."

I was so surprised that I didn't know what to say. Kitty went on:

"There's no use arguing, Etta, I've decided. I can't simply remain here, taking things easy, while this cruel man-hunt is going on. I've got to help them—the thousands and thousands of William Grays and Jonathan Burkes, some of them wounded, half-starved, dying. I know you don't approve, and even if you did, I have no right to involve you. You're an American. These men aren't your countrymen. There's no reason why you should feel as I do about it. Besides, you're ten years older than I am. I can't drag you into danger with me. But I've got to help. So you'll have to go home, and leave me to do the work I feel I must do."

"This is the second time you have tried to send me away, Kitty," I said. "The first was when war was declared. And my answer is still the same. I won't leave you."

"This time you must," Kitty returned. "Because I'm going through with this whether you're here or not; and even if you have nothing to do with it, the consequences might be just as bad for you as for me. So you'd better go to the American Embassy to-morrow and tell them you want to leave as soon as it can be arranged."

I shook my head.

"No, Kitty," I said. "I'm going to stay with you. You gave me a helping hand at the most difficult period of my life, and after staying with you through the good times, I'm not going to desert you now that bad times have come.

"You may be worried about me, and want me to go because I might get into trouble—but I'm worried about you, and I intend to stay to keep you out of trouble. I'm afraid you're going to get yourself into a fatal mess if I leave you to your own devices. You're an incorrigible idealist, Kitty, and you've got to have some one to keep you from attempting the impossible.

"That's just what it is—the impossible! Don't you remember that Burke said only a few minutes ago that there was no way of saving those men? If an English officer thinks so, what could two weak women do?"

"Two weak women saved William Gray," Kitty said. "He was caught here after Dunkirk. Two weak women are saving Jonathan Burke. He's from Dunkirk, too. Their situation was just the same as that of the other ten thousand. What would have become of William Gray by now if it hadn't been for us? What was going to happen to Jonathan Burke? The lot of the others is no more desperate than theirs seemed to be. If we got them out of the hands of the Germans, why can't we do it again? After all, we know of a way of escape from occupied territory. I believe it was God who showed us that way. It would be sinful and criminal not to use our knowledge to save as many men as we can."

I looked at Kitty's flushed face, transformed almost with ecstasy. I realized I would never be able to convince her, or to turn her aside from the work she had chosen. But I made one more effort.

"But why should you alone do this, Kitty?" I asked her. "Isn't this more of a man's job?"

"Etta," Kitty said solemnly, "no one who knows how to help these men has any right to abandon the duty of aiding them to any one else. It's like seeing a drowning man, and looking around for some one else to save him for fear of getting your clothes wet."

She sat down next to me, and bent so close that I could feel the warmth of her feverish face against my cheek.

"It wouldn't be true if I told you that I am not afraid to die," she said. "I'm no braver than any other woman, and it horrifies me to think that my life might be snapped off brutally—before a firing

squad. When this horrible war is over, I'm looking forward to more
beautiful years like those we have already spent together. Like you,
I didn't know a peaceful moment while William was here, and
whenever the elevator stopped at our floor during the night, I woke
up at once. I'm really a coward. Yet if I were absolutely certain
that the Germans would execute me for harboring this boy, I still
wouldn't abandon him before I had made sure of his escape. And
even if I were absolutely certain that they would execute me for
continuing to try to save my countrymen, I would still do it—
because I have to. I couldn't hold up my head again if I didn't.
I couldn't enjoy a longer life gained at the expense of betraying
these poor fellows today. But I don't mean to be executed, Etta.
I'm going to be very careful, and I don't intend to get caught."

"All right, Kitty," I said. "If you're determined, I'll help you.
There's only one thing I won't do. That's to leave you to do this
alone. If you have to save soldiers, I have to stay."

## CHAPTER TEN

# The Gestapo Pounces

TELLING Kitty that I would help her cost me a night's sleep. Elated at my surrender, she insisted that we set to work at once to plan our campaign for helping the refugees from Dunkirk, and we talked until nearly dawn.

"The most difficult thing," Kitty began, "is how to contact these men. They have no addresses, they are living in the woods, and they are suspicious of every one. Chancel told me that his organization had tried to get food to them, but the men sent out to try to find them returned with the report that they hadn't been able to locate a single hidden soldier. They don't know, of course, whether persons looking for them are friends or enemies, so they hide from every one."

But Kitty thought she had found an answer for that.

"I've got an idea. Tell me what you think of it. I plagiarized from Lieutenant Burke, of course."

Her idea was to use the Missing Persons column, just as Burke had done. She assumed that the men in hiding would slip into villages when they could and get hold of newspapers to find out the progress of the war, and try to get some inkling of the most likely points at which to break out of occupied territory. Since they would have little to occupy their time, she thought also that they would probably read everything in any paper they got hold of. Thus they ought to see her advertisement.

"Now how about something like this, Etta?" Kitty asked, and she wrote:

"Jonathan Burke, formerly of Dunkirk, is seeking his friends and relatives. His present address is 2, Rue Balny d'Avricourt, Paris, 17."

"The way I figure it out," Kitty said, "is that all the men who were in Burke's unit will understand at once that Burke has found a means of escape, and will communicate with him. No doubt they'll pass the word on to others. When we get answers, we will go to

86

the places they indicate—that will be safer than putting anything in writing ourselves. If we only get one or two answers, we can get in touch with others by using their names, and so on."

I picked up the paper and read the wording of Kitty's advertisement carefully.

"I see two objections to this," I said. "The first is that we have to remember that not only English soldiers, but also Gestapo men will probably read this ad. It would be terribly dangerous to give our address—especially after the little experience we have had with the Nazis already. The second is that we can't use Burke's name. He's on record as a German prisoner. Suppose some one in the Doullens hospital sees it? They'll be down on us at once like a ton of brick."

"You're right," Kitty said, with disappointment in her voice. She thought for a moment.

"I have it!" she exclaimed. "We'll use William Gray's name. He's not on any German records anywhere, and he's safely out of occupied territory.

"As for the address, I know what we can do about that. There's a little café on the Rue Rodier, near where my shop used to be. It's a typical Paris *bistro,* and its proprietor is as French as they come. He's even named Durand." (What Kitty meant was that he had one of the commonest names in French, like Smith in English). "I ran into him the other day, and he rushed up to greet me with the words, 'In days like these, I'm happy to shake the hand of an Englishwoman.' I'm sure he'll let us give his address. He isn't responsible for what his customers do. In fact, he can always say that he doesn't even know who could have used it. Everybody here gives café addresses without even asking permission. I know we can trust him."

And with a sly chuckle, she added:

"Won't it be fun to help English soldiers to escape with the aid of the German-controlled newspapers?"

Kitty was so impatient to get to work that she rose early, in spite of our all-night conference, and went off to *Paris-Soir* to insert her advertisement. When she returned an hour later, she reported that she had even argued the advertising department into promising insertion of her ad in the last edition for the same day, in spite of the fact that the shortage of paper, which restricted *Paris-Soir* to two pages, often forced considerable delays in the appearance of advertisements.

She had also managed during her brief absence to talk with the café proprietor.

"It's all right," she told me. "He was wonderful. If the police make any inquiries, he is going to deny knowing who gave his address. If they leave any one there to watch who comes for that mail, he won't give it to us. We aren't to ask for it in any case. When we go there, we will simply sit down at a table and give an order, and if it's safe, he'll bring us letters without being asked. So that's all fixed."

We sat down to breakfast—for Kitty had been in such a hurry to get out that she hadn't waited for it. She prattled on happily to Lieutenant Burke about her plan, which he approved heartily.

After breakfast we were just putting on our hats to visit M. Chancel's Left Bank friends, to arrange for them to take Burke off our hands and start him on his trip out of France, when Chancel himself arrived.

The moment he entered the room, I sensed that he had bad news. He attempted to smile, but his expression was forced. It was obvious that he was laboring under some strain.

He sat down at our invitation, and we exchanged a few formal remarks while he seemed to be trying to decide just how to tell us what had happened. Finally, giving up any thought he may have had of breaking the news gently, he blurted it out.

"*C'est fini*. The Gestapo has discovered our little organization," he said.

We were thunderstruck.

"They raided my friend's house at 9 o'clock last night," Chancel continued. "They thought they were going to get all of us—and they would have if we hadn't been warned. They were just a little too late.

"A Frenchman—if you can call him a Frenchman—whom we

had trusted and let into our group betrayed us. He didn't know all of us, but he did know that we were meeting on the Left Bank last night. Fortunately one of the people he didn't know was our man in the Prefecture—the one who fixes up the exit visas for us. He warned us. Everybody got away in time, including the boys hiding there. They were the last ones to get out across the demarcation line through our route. It's no good any more, of course. The Nazis know about that, too . . . *malheureusement.*"

Chancel heaved a deep sigh.

"Now I've got to find some way of getting out myself," he said. "They know I'm in it. I didn't sleep at home last night, so they don't know where I am. I'm going to Salies de Béarn and see if I can get through there. Meanwhile, I came here to warn you not to go near my place or the Left Bank house. The Gestapo is watching both of them."

"Then they'll be here any minute!" I gasped.

"Oh, no!" Chancel answered. "You're all right. Our friend at the Prefecture is trusted completely by the Germans, and he knows everything they know. They've never heard of you, and don't know you're implicated. You're in no danger whatsoever."

Chancel rose, as though immobility irked him, and paced back and forward rapidly.

"It's too bad," he said. "Our organization is broken up, and just when it could have been most useful! In a few weeks, or a few months at the most, the Germans will have established such a perfect system of police, internment camps, and so forth, that we will find it difficult to help any one any more. In fact, by then they may have done such a good job of rounding up fugitives that there won't be any one to help. . . . Well, I'm going out, till this blows over, but I'll be back."

"You're going to risk that?" Kitty asked.

Chancel sat down again and smiled faintly:

"Yes, I'm coming back. I'll stay in the unoccupied zone just long enough to grow a beard to hide my face wounds, so the Germans won't be able to recognize me on sight. That will take three or four weeks, I suppose, and in the meantime I'll work on establishing a group to take care of men we get across the line, and smuggle them into Spain or Portugal. I'll get in touch with you when I come back."

"What a shame!" said Kitty. "And I was so hopeful of being able to get in touch with more English soldiers. I put an advertisement in *Paris-Soir* only this morning asking them to write me."

"You—what?" Chancel almost roared, as he leaped from his chair in the greatest excitement.

"I advertised for them in the paper," Kitty repeated.

"My God!" Chancel exclaimed. "That was terribly imprudent! What did you say?"

Kitty hurried to her desk, took the copy of her advertisement, and handed it to Chancel. He looked over it hastily, and said severely:

"You shouldn't have done this! Don't you realize that the Gestapo is going to read this even before the boys it's intended for? They read every line that appears in *Paris-Soir* before the paper is allowed to go to press. They're sure to spot this!"

Kitty was almost in tears. She made me think of a child whose newest toy has been taken away.

"When did you insert this ad? Is there still time to stop it?"

Kitty shook her head.

"No, it's in today's paper. They sent it to the printer while I was there. But is it really so dangerous? I've been very careful. I gave a false name and address at the paper. The address given in the advertisement is a café. I'm sure of the proprietor. He's prepared to deny he knows anything about it. I don't see how the Gestapo could possibly trace it to us."

Chancel read through the advertisement again, slowly and carefully this time.

"I beg your pardon," he said at last. "You can understand my excitement, under the circumstances. After all, this seems to be fairly safe. I must warn you of one danger, however. If replies come in, you will have no way of telling whether they are not from Gestapo agents. Therefore you must be extremely careful about answering them or acting on them. I've always been of the opinion myself that we tend to overestimate the cleverness and ingenuity of the Gestapo, but it would be a bad error to take them for idiots."

"Perhaps it isn't rescuing any more Englishmen that's our main problem just now," I interrupted. "Have you stopped to figure out what we're going to do with Lieutenant Burke?"

Kitty bit her lip. It was clear that in the excitement of plans for the future, she had forgotten entirely that we now had an unsolved problem of the past to worry about.

"Yes," she said. "I had forgotten. What advice can you give us about that, M. Chancel?"

"None," he said. "I'm sorry, but I'm temporarily unable to be of any use to you. I'm a fugitive myself now, and I don't know how I'm going to get over the frontier yet. You can be sure I'll do what I can. If I succeed in finding another way into the unoccupied zone, I'll see that you are informed. But it's very unlikely that you will have any word from me in less than a week."

He took his leave. With him, the slight courage his presence had given us evaporated. The atmosphere was funereal. We were back where we had been when we were hiding William Gray, and had no idea which way to turn to aid his escape. It seemed unlikely that the miracle of finding a Chancel would be repeated.

From the kitchen, in the deathly silence, we could hear Margot humming a Breton folk song. On the other side, we could hear Lieutenant Burke pacing back and forth. Perhaps he had sensed the predicament about which we still had to tell him.

Kitty's head turned towards the entrance. I didn't have to speak to her to know the meaning of that instinctive gesture. I, too, had heard the elevator. I realized that once again we would have to pass days of fear and trembling, when we would quiver each time the elevator stopped at our floor, or the door bell rang.

It was hardly with enthusiasm that Kitty unfolded the *Paris-Soir* when it arrived, and found our advertisement. She handed the paper to me, with a pitiful expression on her face.

"To think," she said, "that some poor fellows may answer this advertisement with the last feeling of hope they may ever experience —and we will be unable to help them."

She stared intently at the floor for a moment, as though she were discovering the design of the carpet for the first time.

"There is only one thing we can do, Etta," she said. "We must drive to the border, and find some French peasant living along the line who will agree to smuggle our protégés across. We'd better do it as soon as possible—tomorrow, if I can get gas."

Then she interrupted herself:

"We can't do it tomorrow! We have to get Corporal Meehan tomorrow. What in the world are we going to do with two of them? Goodness knows how long we'll have to keep them here!"

"But Kitty!" I protested. "You aren't going to bring Corporal Meehan here now, are you?"

Kitty looked at me in surprise.

"Why, Etta," she said, "how can you suggest that we should leave him there? We *must* go. We promised."

## CHAPTER ELEVEN

# "*Where Is Lieutenant Burke?*"

THAT night I dreamed that we drove up in our car to the hospital at Doullens. Before the gate stood the same Gestapo agent who had searched the apartment. He smiled with satirical courtesy, and said quietly: "We have been waiting for you for a long time." With that, two helmeted German soldiers raised their rifles and pointed them at us.

At this point, I awoke, so terrified that it took me nearly an hour to get to sleep again. Once more I went through the same nightmare, and woke up again at the same identical spot. I must have had that dream half a dozen times during the course of the night. When it finally came time to get up, I was worn and exhausted, hardly in shape to set out on another adventure.

But Kitty had apparently slept like a child. She had risen early, while I was still tossing through the last version of my bad dream, taken the car to the garage, and had it overhauled in preparation for the trip. When she joined me at the breakfast table, her eyes were bright and sparkling, and she was in excellent spirits. She saw at once that I was not, and said:

"If you don't feel well, Etta, you can stay home. I'll go to Doullens alone."

"I didn't sleep well," I explained. "I had a stupid recurring dream last night—that we were shot by the Germans at Doullens. You know I don't believe in dreams, but this one has started me thinking. Don't you agree that after smuggling Lieutenant Burke out of that hospital, it's suicidal for us to turn up there again, and repeat the performance?"

"Do you really think so?" Kitty asked, looking at me searchingly.

"I'm sure of it," I said. "It's quite possible they don't suspect us of having had anything to do with Lieutenant Burke's disappearance. In fact, perhaps it hasn't even occurred to them to put our visit and his escape together. But if we turn up there again, that will re-

mind them that we visited the hospital and talked to Burke just
before he disappeared. It may start them thinking. And then if
another soldier disappears, the fact that prisoners have escaped twice
just after our visits there is bound to seem suspicious. I'm afraid
we'll be arrested almost as soon as they find Meehan is missing.
And if they come here, they'll find the two men in the apartment.
We'll be caught in the act."

Kitty did not answer. She sipped her tea slowly, and I could see
that she was pondering what I had said. I knew how repugnant it
was to her to abandon Corporal Meehan after her promise to him.
I didn't like the idea either, but sober realities forced me to insist.

"Perhaps we'll be able to do something for him later," I reminded
her. "But I don't think we can succeed in helping him now. Instead,
we are going to imperil Lieutenant Burke, who isn't out of danger
yet. In trying to save one more, we may lose both. After all, you
know, in war it's often necessary to sacrifice individuals for the sake
of others. If we are caught trying to save Meehan, that means that
all your plans for helping many others will be destroyed."

Kitty put down her tea-cup and looked up at me.

"Etta," she said, "I can't answer you. Your arguments are perfectly sound. You are absolutely right. But I can't help it. I know it
isn't logical or sensible, but I can't desert the boy. I have to keep my
promise. I have no right to involve you. You see the danger clearly,
and don't want to risk it. I advise you to keep out of it. Remember,
I told you before I thought you ought to leave. If you don't feel as I
do about this, I still think you should go. I'm going to Doullens
today, and if I am caught, I don't want you to be the victim of my
decision."

She rose, and went into her room. I stepped into the kitchen, and
began to help Margot wrap up the gift parcels without which there
would have been no excuse for appearing at the hospital. The Foyer
du Soldat had supplied only a few parcels for Doullens and we had
distributed them at our last trip. We had to provide new ones ourselves.

Margot helped me wrap up the packages willingly, although she
had looked at us as though she thought we had taken leave of our
senses when we told her to get out the few cans of sardines and the

cheese we had in our pantry and make gift parcels of them. The food
shortage was beginning to assume tragic proportions. A can of
sardines brought a tremendous price on the Black Market, and
cheese, which we could only get through our ration books, was
limited to 100 grams (three and one-half ounces) per month. I felt
guilty as I helped Margot stow away the provisions she had secured
for us by standing patiently in line for hours. But this was all we
had to give, except a few packages of cigarettes, which we added to
the food.

Lieutenant Burke wandered into the kitchen. He seemed worried,
and I judged that he had overheard me talking to Kitty. His door
had been ajar.

"You heard what I said to Mrs. Beaurepos, I suppose," I said to
him. He nodded.

"Then why didn't you put in a word and help me out?" I asked.
"You agree with me, don't you? You must realize she is taking a
great risk."

"Yes," Burke said slowly, "I agree—but my own position is
very delicate. You got me out of Doullens, at great risk to yourself,
and I have no right to seek to dissuade you from doing as much for
some one else—particularly not on the grounds of my own personal
safety. Meehan has as much right to a chance to escape as I have.

"But it is true, I believe, that the danger is ten times greater on
the second attempt than on the first. That doesn't seem likely to
deter Mrs. Beaurepos. I don't think she's going to allow herself to
be dissuaded. If you can't stop her, let me give you a piece of advice.
Be very careful of Major Thibaud, the chief military physician
at Doullens. He's French, of course, but he's the typical military
man, who accepts the orders of his superiors without question, and
it makes no difference to him whether those superiors are French
or German. He has been following the instructions of the Germans
without a murmur. I think he would be perfectly capable of arresting you himself and turning you over to the Germans if he suspected anything."

I thanked him for the warning, picked up the parcels, and piled
them on the entry table. Then I put on my coat and went to Kitty's
room.

"Well," I said, "when do we start?"

"We?" Kitty exclaimed joyously. "Etta, do you mean you've changed your mind?"

"Not at all," I said. "I disapprove completely. I think you're taking an unnecessary risk and imperilling all your future plans—but if you're determined to go, I'm going with you."

Kitty threw her arms around me and kissed me on the cheek. Her brimming eyes were shining.

There was practically no traffic on the highway, and the trip to Doullens was a quick one. We passed a number of German military cars going north, but none of them showed any interest in us.

Just after we had passed Amiens, a large open truck appeared ahead of us. As we overtook it, we saw that it was full of English prisoners—about thirty of them crowded together in the body of the vehicle. Four German soldiers with fixed bayonets stood at the four corners of the truck, guarding them. They were dirty, ragged and unshaven. I judged they were some of the men who had been in hiding, and had been rounded up by the motorcycle patrols.

Kitty threw an almost panicky glance at me, and stepped on the accelerator, to get away from the distressing sight as quickly as possible.

"It's terrible," she burst out, "that Chancel's organization had to fail us at just this time, when there are so many to be helped! Did you see those poor men, worn-out and exhausted, packed into a truck without even a place to sit down, being moved about like cattle!"

She didn't speak again until the houses of Doullens came in sight. Then she said softly, almost as though she were speaking to herself:

"You said this morning, Etta, that sometimes it is necessary to sacrifice one individual for the sake of others. That is very true in times like these. How unimportant it would be to sacrifice one's own life if by doing so one could save a hundred or perhaps a thousand others!"

I looked at Kitty, but the words wouldn't come. She could read the emotion in my eyes.

"What's the matter, Etta?" she asked. "What's troubling you?"

"Nothing is troubling me," I said. "I was just admiring you."

"Oh, dry up," said Kitty. But she began humming contentedly as she guided the car through the narrow streets on the way to the hospital.

Kitty had timed our arrival so that we reached the hospital as the men were coming out into its garden after lunch. She parked the car under the same tree as before, gathered up the parcels, and we passed once more between the two sentries at the gate without a challenge.

As we walked slowly through the garden, we peered about for Corporal Meehan. We didn't want to ask for him, or even to be seen speaking to him if we could possibly avoid it. He wasn't in the garden, so we entered the building and started through the wards.

Finally we glimpsed him. He was in bed, looking very tired— much worse than when we had last seen him, but perhaps only because he was unshaven. His eyes lighted up at the sight of us, but he was clever enough to give no sign of recognition which others might have seen. We stopped at the bed of a French soldier next to his, and spoke to him for a few moments, pretending to pay no attention to Meehan. Then Kitty took my arm and steered me out into the corridor.

"We've got to distribute these parcels first," Kitty said. "Until we get rid of them, every one's eyes are going to be on us every second. Did you notice how those poor half-starved men stared at us, as though they were hypnotized? It's because they know we have food in these parcels."

We went to the main first-floor ward, and began to pass out our gifts. We had with us a ten-pound parcel which a relative of one of the patients had sent to the Foyer du Soldat for delivery to him. We found the boy to whom it was addressed, but his eyes were closed, and he seemed to be in a coma.

The man on the next bed stretched out a bony hand towards the parcel.

"It's no good giving it to him," he said. "He doesn't know what's happening, and doesn't care. He saw his brother killed at Dunkirk, and when he comes to, all he does is rave about joining him. It won't be long before he does. . . . The rest of us will go that way too unless you people can get us more packages. We can't recover our strength here because we get so little food—mostly dirty hot water they call soup. We're being starved to death."

Kitty helped him open the package and divide the contents among those in the ward—cake, chocolates and cigarettes.

When we had gotten rid of our parcels, and could move about without attracting so much attention, we passed through several wards on the way back to the one where we had seen Meehan, chatting with the prisoners, and doing our best to appear natural. Finally we got back to the room where we had seen Meehan. His bed was empty!

"How stupid!" I said. "Why didn't he wait for us? Or perhaps he went to the garden, expecting us to go there."

We went out into the garden. There was still no sign of him. By this time I, who had opposed coming in the first place, had become more anxious than Kitty seemed to be to find him. Without even thinking that this gave me an excuse to get Kitty away without letting her take the risk of engineering a second escape, I almost dragged her back through all the wards once more. Finally we gave up.

"We might as well go home, Kitty," I said. "He seems to have disappeared completely. We've wasted the whole day for nothing. And it's all his fault, the stupid fellow!"

We passed through the corridor on the way to the hospital office, where we had to sign out. "Perhaps he's in the office," I said to Kitty, as we approached it. "He might have been called there for some reason. That would account for our not finding him."

I reached for the doorknob; but just as I was about to put my hand on it, the door swung open. A man in the uniform of a major, with the emblems of the medical service on his tunic and cap, stood before us.

"*Ah, c'est vous*," he said. "Permit me to introduce myself—Major Thibaud."

It was the man of whom Lieutenant Burke had warned us!

"I believe you ladies have honored us with your visit before," he said slowly. "It is really very kind of you—extraordinarily kind, I might say—to take so much interest in so small a hospital."

Before either Kitty or myself had time to think of a reply, he bent over and said in a low confidential tone.

"I wonder if you would be kind enough to answer just one question for me? Would you be so good as to inform me where Lieutenant Burke is at this moment?"

I felt as though my heart had suddenly stopped beating. The scene seemed to be recreating my dream. Instead of the Gestapo agent, Major Thibaud was playing his part. But the end might very well be much the same.

Even in my terror, I could not fail to admire Kitty's self-possession.

"You must be a mind reader, Major," she said. "We have been through the whole hospital twice looking for him. Was he sent back to the Citadel?"

Major Thibaud did not answer at once. He scrutinized Kitty carefully. Then he stepped back through the door, saying, "Kindly come into my office."

The doctor's office was no more prepossessing than any of the rest of it—gray, dirty and foul-smelling. We sat down before Major Thibaud's desk in chairs which he designated to us with a wave of the hand. But he did not sit down. He clasped his hands behind his back, walked over to a small window and looked out for a moment, as though in deep thought. Then he paced back and forth slowly, once or twice. The silence and the tension of waiting were unbearable. Kitty, sitting close beside me, put her hand gently on my arm, and I felt a little more courageous. Major Thibaud turned, and stopped before us.

"Our conversation will be shortened," he began, "if you ladies will be intelligent enough not to deny the obvious fact that it was you who helped Lieutenant Burke to escape from this hospital. Since his disappearance, I have of course made a careful investigation. Your names appeared on our visitors' register for the day of Lieutenant Burke's escape, and it was simply a routine measure to check on you with the Foyer du Soldat. You, Mme. Beaurepos, are British-born. I can understand your sympathy with a British soldier, and it therefore does not surprise me that after your visit one of the very few English prisoners here should have been the one to escape. You, Mme. Shiber, are an American, and may be assumed to have a certain fellow feeling with another Anglo-Saxon also.

"I cannot, of course, criticize you ladies for desiring to help Lieutenant Burke to escape. However, we are not concerned here with human sympathies, but with decrees and ordinances. You happen to have violated the laws established by the High Command of the occupying forces."

Kitty, who had kept silent up to now, broke in at this point.

"But I assure you, Major, we know nothing about Lieutenant Burke's escape. We have just learned of it at this moment from you."

Major Thibaud lifted his hand to check her protests.

"Please," he said firmly. "I am not a fool, Mme. Beaurepos. That you helped Lieutenant Burke to escape is so obvious that I am not going to waste time even in debating the question. Perhaps you will realize the uselessness of your denial if I tell you that I happened to send for Lieutenant Burke to examine his eye twenty minutes after you had left the hospital. He had gone. So had you. There is really no sense in your denying that he went with you."

"Pardon me," Kitty retorted. "The fact that he may have disappeared at about the same time that we left the hospital doesn't necessarily mean that he went with us. He may have taken advantage of the distraction caused by our visit to get out; but he didn't get away with our help or knowledge."

"*Très bien,*" said the Major, in an irritated tone. "Persist in your denial, if you want. We both know what to think of it, of course. Now let me tell you what I am going to do."

He was silent for a moment, weighing his words. I could hear the sound of Kitty's breathing.

"You liberated a prisoner from this hospital," he said deliberately, raising his hand again to check another denial he saw forthcoming from Kitty. "It is my duty to hand you over to the authorities, which, in this region and at this time, means to the German Army. I am a soldier. It is my habit to obey orders."

He paused for another instant. My heart was beating madly.

A softened tone came into his voice.

"But I am not only a soldier, ladies," he said. "I am a Frenchman. That is why I have not yet reported the disappearance of Lieutenant Burke."

I sat bolt upright in my chair, thunderstruck at the unexpectedness of this development. I could see that Kitty, too, had suddenly realized that, after all, we were perhaps not yet lost.

"I have not yet decided," Major Thibaud was continuing, "just how to dispose of this case. The occupying authorities are, as you know, very meticulous, and the completeness of their records and of their controls does not make it easy for a man to disappear without being noticed. However, every system has its weaknesses, and that of completeness of records is afflicted with some of its own. It is, for instance, not impossible that in the multiplicity of papers concerned in receiving patients, discharging them, transferring them, and so forth, there might arise cases where it would require considerable research to discover just where a certain individual represented by those pieces of paper was supposed to be. It would take, perhaps, more trouble than it would be worth. This is simply an interesting observation which I have had occasion to make in the course of my work, and I would certainly not advise any one to trust any important practical measure to this possibility."

His dry tones suddenly became sharper, as though he were issuing an order.

"I must ask you ladies to leave this hospital at once, and not to return. If you had any intention of repeating your act, I must ask your formal promise that you renounce it. I might add that failure on your part to keep such a promise would very probably be fatal to yourselves. I advise you to forget this conversation as soon as you have left here. I am quite sure that I shan't remember it myself."

Kitty rose, and held out her hand.

"Thank you, Major," she said. "I am very happy to have met another real Frenchman."

Major Thibaud took her hand without answering her compliment.

"You will pardon me," he said drily, "if I take the precaution or escorting you to your car."

I was too exhausted by the emotional strain of the interview with Major Thibaud to speak until we were several kilometers outside of Doullens. The spell was broken by a German motorcycle patrol, which passed us with much shrill hooting, and enveloped us in whirling clouds of dust.

"I wonder what will happen to that poor corporal?" I said.

Kitty didn't answer.

"I'm afraid we'll just have to forget about him," I went on, afraid that she might not yet have abandoned the impossible task of rescuing Corporal Meehan. "We can't ever go back to the hospital again."

Kitty turned her head towards me and smiled.

"It won't be necessary," she said. "Corporal Meehan is in the luggage compartment."

## CHAPTER TWELVE

# Nach Paris

THE expression on my face was too much for Kitty. She started laughing so uncontrollably that she had to pull the car up to the side of the road. It was contagious. I had to join in, too, and there we sat by the side of the road, two women roaring with laughter, in a country where laughter had become rare.

"How do you know he's in there?" I asked when I could speak again. "You haven't had a chance to look."

"He is if he followed instructions," Kitty said. "Let's find out."

She leaned over the back of the seat, and called:

"Corporal Meehan! Are you all right?"

His muffled voice floated back to us.

"All right, thanks," he said, "except that I hurt my leg a little getting over that wall, low as it was."

"Don't worry about that," Kitty said. "We'll fix it up when we get home. We're off to Paris now."

As we swung out into the road again, I asked:

"But how did you do it, Kitty? We didn't even speak to him!"

"You showed me the way," Kitty said with a mischievous smile.

"I?"

"Yes, when you pointed out to me this morning how dangerous it would be if we were seen speaking to the second soldier to escape from Doullens. When I went into my room, I wrote down the same directions I had given Lieutenant Burke, and slipped them to Meehan while we were at the next bed. I never intended to speak to him."

"How could you, Kitty!" I said reproachfully. "All the time I was worrying myself to death looking for Meehan, you knew that he had already gone. Didn't you trust me?"

"Of course I did," Kitty said. "But let me ask you just one question: How did you feel in Major Thibaud's office when he accused us?"

"As though I were going to faint," I answered.

"Exactly," said Kitty, "and if you had known that Meehan was already in the car, you *would* have fainted—or maybe given him away. I thought you'd be less worried that way."

"But Kitty," I said, "what will happen now? Major Thibaud knows we took Burke out. When Meehan disappears too, what will he do? He can't protect us twice. Won't he denounce us?"

"I doubt it," said Kitty. "Just put yourself in his place. Suppose he reports Meehan's escape and says he suspects us. The Germans ask why. Does he say: 'Because the last time they were here, Lieutenant Burke escaped'? Of course not. Since he didn't report that as soon as it happened, he can't report it now. In fact, he's got to protect us from being suspected of Meehan's escape, because if they get us, they'll find out about Burke, and Major Thibaud will be for it too, for not having done anything about Burke's escape. I don't know how he'll get out of it—maybe he'll report that Meehan and Burke got away together overnight. That would put the responsibility on the sentries and the German motorcycle patrols instead of his own lack of vigilance about visitors, and set the Nazis on the wrong track in hunting for them. One thing is certain: he daren't take any chance of putting the Germans on the right trail. He'd be in trouble, too, if they caught us."

It sounded convincing, and I felt better—for a few minutes. Then, just as we were passing a German military post some 50 miles from Paris, there was a loud explosion, and the car skidded to a stop.

"Did they shoot at us?" I quavered.

Kitty laughed derisively.

"Silly! Just a tire," she laughed.

"Only a tire? What luck!" said a muffled voice from the compartment.

"Keep quiet!" Kitty warned. "Whatever you do, don't come out!"

I got out of the car, too, and together we took the spare tire off the back of the car. As we slid the jack under the axle, we heard Meehan's voice again:

"Hadn't I better get out and help? I can fix it in a minute."

Kitty leaned into the back of the car as though looking for tools, and said sharply: "For goodness sake, keep quiet! There's a German post only a few yards away."

Her warning came none too soon. A German officer strolled over from the military post, and stopped a few feet away, watching us with apparent enjoyment of our plight.

Kitty, tugging at the rim of the wheel, grunted between clenched teeth: "If that Fritz doesn't go away, I'll throw the jack at him."

"Be careful, Kitty," I whispered. "Don't forget we mustn't arouse their curiosity."

Kitty muttered in French something unladylike and unprintable about the German. Several times she turned to cast a contemptuous glance in his direction. He seemed to misread her meaning—or perhaps it was the picture Kitty presented, with the high color resulting from her effort enhancing her natural handsome charm. He walked over to the car, and bowed politely. I thought he might offer to help with the tire. But no!

"I beg pardon, ladies," he said. "I wonder if you would give me a lift to Paris? I have been waiting for my car for half an hour, and it hasn't arrived yet. You are French, I suppose?"

"No, Americans," I said. I hoped this might cause him to leave us alone. Unfortunately, it had exactly the opposite effect.

"Americans!" he said. *"Sehr interessant!"* And turning towards Kitty with a manner that made it quite plain that she was the one he was interested in, he said: "I am sorry I don't speak English, but I see that you speak French very well. Please excuse me for not offering to help you, but I thought you were French, and French women have been behaving very badly towards us. I could not, of course, risk a snub by offering to help. Since you are neutrals, Americans, I'm sure you'll allow me to aid."

He waved towards the post, and a soldier trotted across the road to us. The officer said a few words in German, the soldier saluted, and taking Kitty's place, began to wrestle with the recalcitrant tire.

"Well, well, Americans!" the German officer said again, as though Americans were rare objects. He launched into a dissertation evidently intended to be complimentary to us, about the charm of

American women and the brilliance of American moving picture stars.

I didn't pay much attention to what he said. I was anxiously scanning the road, hoping his car would appear. But the soldier finished changing the tire, saluted, and returned to his post, and no car had yet appeared.

"Well, *meine Damen*," the German smiled, "I'm afraid you're in for it. You'll have to accept my company to Paris—or rather to Chantilly. You can drop me off there."

And with that he opened the back door of the car. My heart was in my mouth. I knew that Meehan must have heard and would not speak, but to any one sitting in the back seat, the slightest movement or the lowest cough would be audible. Once again, Kitty's coolness saved the situation.

"Oh, don't sit back there all by yourself," she smiled. "Come in front with us. There's plenty of room for three."

Obviously the German was waiting for nothing better. He promptly got in the front seat, placing himself between us, with one arm resting along the back of the seat touching Kitty's shoulder.

The trip to Paris I thought would never end. The German, highly pleased with himself, sat jabbering away. Our only consolation was that as long as he continued to talk a steady stream he couldn't hear any noise from the luggage compartment. He seemed to be especially obsessed with the failure of French women to appreciate the merits of German officers.

"It's so stupid of the French not to invite us to visit their families," he said. "I should very much like to get to know Paris from the inside. We want only to be friendly. Yet these cold Frenchmen hold us at arm's length—and the women are even worse."

He tightened his grip on Kitty's shoulder a trifle, and went on:

"It's so sad to see Paris under these circumstances—Paris, so famous for its good living and its handsome, friendly women. *Ach,* Paris! *Ach,* French champagne! *Wein, Weib und Gesang!* At least, Madame, I can say that one woman has been charming to me in France."

Long before we had reached Chantilly, he was obviously paying court to Kitty. When at last, after what had seemed an interminable journey, we let him off in front of the German Kommandantur at Chantilly, he said: "I thank you heartily, ladies. I hope I may have the pleasure of meeting you again—perhaps of calling to pay my respects, if you will be good enough to give me your address?"

He produced a small notebook from his pocket, and without further ceremony copied Kitty's name and address from the plate on the dashboard, which complied with the French law that the owner's name and address must be displayed on every car.

"And if you should happen to find yourself in the neighborhood of the Rue St. Dominique, in Paris, I should be flattered if you would pay me a call. Please take my card—Captain Kurt Weber, special prosecutor of the Military Tribunal . . . *Auf Wiedersehen!*"

He saluted smartly, and walked briskly to the building of the Kommandantur, where he turned and favored us with another impeccable military salute before entering. We drove off hastily.

"Etta," Kitty said to me, "I thought I'd go mad! Honestly, there were moments when I thought of upsetting the car to get rid of him. Better take a look back there and see how our corporal is getting on."

I called softly but there was no answer. I listened, and heard what seemed to be the sound of snoring from the luggage compartment. My blood curdled at the thought: suppose he had fallen asleep and started snoring while the German was in the car. Now it didn't matter.

I turned back to Kitty.

"He's gone to sleep."

"Good," she said. Then, after a moment's pause:

"What in the world are we going to do if Captain Weber takes it into his head to call while we still have Burke and Meehan in the apartment? I think he has it in mind."

I thought he had also. He had harped throughout the drive on the cool reception he had had from French women. I had heard many stories about the boycott they had applied to the invaders, some of whom had been tactless enough to insist on being received in French families.

I had heard of one case, for instance, where a German officer had agreed to sign certain necessary papers for one lady only on condition that she receive him and members of his staff in her home and introduce them to some young French women. All the Germans desired, he explained, was to be able to enter into normal relations of friendship with French persons, and she would be doing her own people a service as well as the Germans by helping to promote better relations between them.

The papers which the French woman needed were authorizations freeing her husband from a prison camp. To get them, she consented. As agreed, the German officers arrived at her home, and were introduced to a number of her friends. Anticipating a pleasant evening, they set out to make conversation. One typical exchange began like this:

THE OFFICER: Paris is a beautiful city, isn't it?

THE LADY: Yes.

THE OFFICER: Parisian women are charming. Don't you think so?

THE LADY: Yes.

THE OFFICER: Don't you like us Germans?

THE LADY: No.

The Germans left twenty minutes after their arrival.

It was safe to say, the exceptions were so few, that French women were never seen in the company of Germans. Many German women had come to Paris to join their husbands, but most of the Germans were still completely deprived of feminine company, and hungered for it. To avoid incidents and public snubs which would tend to decrease the prestige of the German uniform, they were forbidden by their own regulations to approach French women in the streets of Paris during the daytime. But at night, under cover of the blackout, the soldiers were apt to show themselves highly aggressive.

It became very unpleasant for a woman to walk through the streets of Paris at night. They were pitch-black because of the stringent regulations, and it was possible to walk into a group of German soldiers without seeing them. They thought nothing of seizing a passing woman by the arm, and when they were in packs, they would often surround a woman, repeating over and over the only French phrase most of them knew: *"S'il vous plaît, Mademoiselle."*

There was usually no real danger. A woman had only to threaten resolutely to call an officer. The German soldiers were so well disciplined that the one word "officer" (which is the same in French and German) was sufficient to tame them completely. But with the officers themselves, that didn't work. One French woman told us her method for disarming them. That was to say, "You know, of course, that I'm Jewish."

The word was passed around among Parisian women that another way of embarrassing German officers was to gaze fixedly either at their collars or their feet. One friend of ours made successful use of this trick in a subway station, where she noticed a German officer staring at her in impertinent fashion, and thought it probable that he might annoy her. They were both standing at the center of the subway platform, where the first-class car of the subway trains stop. She began looking at his feet as though there were something curious about them. He quickly became aware of the direction of her gaze, and looked down at his shoes himself. He could hardly have seen anything abnormal about them, but as the young lady continued to stare at them, he became obviously ill at ease, and shuffled about as though trying to hide his feet. When the train pulled in, he hurried into the car in such haste that she was able to get into the following second-class carriage before he noticed that she had given him the slip.

## CHAPTER THIRTEEN

# The Wound

It was quite dark as we rounded the Arc de Triomphe, passing through the Place de l'Etoile. In other days, this circle had always blazed with light, and was one of the most frequented spots in Paris. Now it was dark, gloomy and deserted.

"There is only one thing to do," Kitty said, as we swung around the great bulk of the arch, dimly outlined in darkest black against a blue-black sky, "and that is to tell Margot that we are not at home to Captain Weber, and it is up to her to keep him out if he comes. We mustn't let him get inside the apartment."

She pulled up at the curb in front of our building.

"I'll go ahead to see if the coast is clear," she said. "Whatever you do, don't come up until I come back—just in case I've guessed wrong about how Major Thibaud will act. If I shouldn't come down at all, you'd better find some other place to spend the night."

But her fears were groundless. A few minutes later she was back.

"Everything's all right," she said. "Let's get him out of there."

We opened the baggage compartment. Corporal Meehan did not stir. Evidently he was still asleep.

Kitty reached in and shook him.

"Here we are, Corporal," she said. "Last stop. All change."

Still Meehan didn't budge.

"What's the matter with him?" I asked apprehensively. I was afraid some one would come along before we got him out. The street was deserted for the moment, but I knew a passerby might turn the corner at any instant.

There was a sort of moan from the luggage compartment, and Meehan stirred at last. He dragged himself out of his hiding place. He seemed to be having a good deal of difficulty in moving, which I attributed to his sudden awakening, and the cramped position he had been occupying. Kitty and I each took an arm and helped him out. We hobbled into the building, with Meehan between us, leaning heavily on our arms.

Kitty had left the elevator on the ground floor with the door jammed open, so that no one could call it before we got there. We helped Meehan in. His eyelids drooped, and he seemed about to fall asleep standing up, leaning against us and the wall.

"We'll have to get him into bed the minute we get in," Kitty whispered. "He can hardly stand. In his condition, the trip was probably too much for him."

Margot and Burke were both standing in the entry waiting for us when we opened the door. Both looked anxious.

"Everything go off all right?" Burke asked.

He got no answer. Kitty had let go of Meehan, and he had dropped heavily straight to the floor, and lay there, sprawled out and unmoving.

With an exclamation, Burke knelt down and bent over Meehan. He glanced up at us.

"He's fainted," he said. "What's the matter with him?"

"I don't know," Kitty said.

"Let's get him onto a bed," Burke said. He took hold of Meehan under the shoulders. Margot bent over to take his feet. But hardly had she touched him than she sprang up again with a scream.

"*Mon Dieu!*" she cried. "Blood!"

Sure enough, one leg of Meehan's trousers was soaked with blood. Burke was the first to realize what had happened.

"His leg wound must have reopened because of the cramped position and the jolting of the car," he said.

"Or when he climbed that wall," Kitty remarked. She turned to the maid.

"Margot," she ordered, "phone for a doctor at once." Then she suddenly checked herself as she realized the situation. "No, no," she countermanded, as Margot obediently moved towards the phone. "No! Don't! We can't call a doctor!"

"What shall we do?" I asked, thoroughly frightened now.

"First we'd better get him to bed," Burke said again, and bent over to lift him up. But the moment he moved him, great drops of blood dripped from the wounded leg to the floor.

"Guess we'd better let him lie still on the floor for the moment," Burke said. "He's lost too much blood already. Can't afford to lose more. The first thing is to stop the bleeding. I'll try to bandage the wound. Have you any bandages in the house?"

Kitty shook her head.

"Run to the pharmacy, Margot, and get some bandages. Whatever you do, don't tell what they're for."

Margot darted out the door.

"Etta," Kitty said, "get some towels from the bathroom—and a few handkerchiefs. They may help to bandage the wound temporarily until Margot gets back."

I turned to obey, when something happened which froze me in my tracks. The doorbell pealed, loudly and insistently.

We all stood stock still, silent and transfixed, as though we had been turned into statues. The bell rang again.

Kitty made a hopeless gesture with her hand.

"It's no use," she said. "We can't hide this. Etta, answer the door."

Never in my life have I performed any act with such reluctance as opening that door—but our fears were unfounded. Behind it was the answer to all our troubles.

I had expected to open to our visitor from the Gestapo, or perhaps to Major Thibaud, accompanied by the police. Instead, Henri Beaurepos, Kitty's husband, entered.

He stopped, astonished at the tense expressions of the little group that confronted him. Then his gaze swung downward to Corporal Meehan, lying on the floor, and he seemed to understand the whole situation in a flash, without need of an explanation. He took complete charge at once, and in a few minutes he had solved our problems like magic.

His first care was for Corporal Meehan. He phoned a doctor friend of his, whom he assured us could be trusted completely, and who had the further advantage of living close by. He was in our apartment in five minutes, and in fifteen Meehan was comfortably tucked away in bed, his wound washed and bandaged.

But the doctor did not hide from us that his condition was bad.

"He hasn't had proper care," he said, shaking his head disapprovingly. "Infection has set in, and it isn't going to be easy to treat at this stage. I'll come again in the morning, and decide whether I hadn't better have a specialist take a look at him."

When he left, Henri settled another problem for us. Kitty explained our activities, and Henri smiled at her description of our mental state, with two British soldiers on our hands, and no way to get them out of the occupied zone.

"So you let a little thing like that worry you, my dear?" he asked teasingly. "Why, it's child's play! Since the Germans established the demarcation line, I've crossed it secretly seven times. I have business at Bordeaux, and I've been going in and out to attend to it. I have a friend at Libourne—Tissier—you may have heard me speak of him; I buy his wine every year. His vineyards stretch across the line, and I pass through there. I can pass Lieutenant Burke across for you, and the wounded man too, whenever he's strong enough to travel. There's not the slightest difficulty about it."

Kitty threw an ecstatically happy look towards her husband.

"Mr. Tissier," Henri continued, "is an excellent Frenchman, and is delighted to let any one use his land to escape from the Germans. There's a slight charge, though—50 francs a person. That isn't the price Tissier puts on his services. It's a legitimate expense. It seems that the Herrenvolk, the Supermen, as they call themselves, like to make a little small change now and then. The New Order seems to bear a certain resemblance to the eastern system of government, which involves handing out frequent doles of bakshish. Tissier figures that tips to German sergeants work out at about fifty francs a head."

He grinned, and Kitty smiled back at him. I thought, as I had thought often before, that they were a curious couple. They seemed deeply in love with one another, although they had been separated for years. Ever since I had lived with Kitty, she had always talked of him most affectionately—yet much of the time she didn't even know his address. His business as a wine merchant required him to do a good deal of travelling, and sometimes months passed without his turning up, or even writing a letter. But whenever he did come to town, the day was a holiday for both of them. As far as I could see, there was no disagreement of any kind between them. They simply preferred, both of them, to live separately, and see each other only at intervals.

Henri was a fascinating companion, a good talker, who seemed to know a little about everything, and who always managed to learn what was going on within a few minutes of arriving anywhere. Although we lived in Paris, we knew very little of what was happening there. Henri, who had just come in, had heard all the news.

"I saw Goering this morning," he told us. "It seems that he and Himmler were not killed in the air raid. Too bad."

He was referring to an incident which had been whispered about Paris shortly before. A banquet had been given in a big hotel in Normandy to celebrate the arrival of Goering, at which several officers of the German General Staff had been present. For the sake of safety, no previous announcement of the banquet had been made —but the R.A.F., obviously well informed, arrived in good time to catch the party in full blast and did a little blasting of its own.

The day after, the swastika banners in Paris were draped with black. The word went around that the Germans were mourning some important persons killed at the banquet, but no one knew exactly who the victims were. Rumors were wild, as usual, some of them even suggesting hopefully that Hitler himself had been killed. Finally, they crystallized to the report that Goering and Himmler had been the victims, chiefly because Goering, always a conspicuous spectacle, hadn't been seen for several days. But here he had turned up again, alive and apparently unhurt! Henri said he had heard that the important victim had been, not Himmler, but Himmler's brother.

"I saw Goering in the Rue de la Paix," Henri said. "He was getting out of his car. He had on a light-colored eye-catching uniform, and he had brought along his field marshal's baton. I suppose he sleeps with it. When I first saw him, he was holding it in his outstretched arm like a choir boy afraid of being burned by his candle. It was a pretty ludicrous sight. I wondered that the officers with him were able to keep a straight face, but they managed. Perhaps they don't have the same sense for the ridiculous we have.

"He went into Cartier's. They tell me he bought an 8,000,000 franc necklace. I judge he can afford it. Money's no object to him. . . . He seems to prefer that his wife should wear French rather than German styles, in spite of the German claims that their fashions are sounder than our degenerate Paris modes. He goes to the best couturiers whenever he comes to Paris and personally picks out their most lavish creations for Madame Goering. He goes in heavily for silk pajamas. Incidentally, he buys them in such tremendous sizes that although Frau Goering is no lightweight, there's a suspicion that he wears those feminine pajamas himself."

The subject of Goering's purchases naturally led Henri on to the emptying of French shops by the Germans, which we had noticed vaguely, but hadn't paid much attention to, since we were too much preoccupied with our soldiers to think of clothes. Henri told us that the soldiers were buying women's clothing—particularly furs, stockings and cloth to make dresses—until most of the shops had been obliged to close for want of anything more to sell.

This was not only the result of individual purchases by German soldiers, supplied with plenty of occupation marks, but also of regular organized looting, Henri explained. It had not occurred to French citizens at first that private homes and apartments would be entered and stripped of their valuables. That, however, was what happened. Furniture, tapestries, art objects, and other valuables were taken from the homes of persons who had not returned to Paris. Specialists saw to their packing and transport to Germany. Linen was used to wrap up the confiscated objects, and thus went to Germany as well.

Henri told us one story of the caretaker of a château in the department of Seine-et-Marne who watched impotently while the building was so thoroughly cleaned out that he called to the Germans as they were leaving: "Wait a minute! You've forgotten to take the nails!"

Electric refrigerators seemed to be particularly welcome to the Nazis, Henri remarked. His refrigerator was one of the things which was missing when he returned to his home, where he found a Nazi officer had been billeted.

"I asked him," Henri said, "'Can I count on being allowed to keep the few things which have not yet been taken away?' The fellow wasn't embarrassed at all. It apparently struck him as quite a normal question. He said, 'I think so. The specialists have already been through here. They've probably taken everything they thought worth while.'

"The way it works, you know, is that they come in directly behind the fighting troops, and pounce before you have time to hide anything. They're very thorough; you know the Germans. You're lucky not to have had their visit here. Perhaps they ran out of transportation. That's the reason they've been giving for cutting down food parcels to the prisoners of war, you know—not enough trains to handle them. But they found trains for their loot, all right."

It was well after midnight. Henri looked at his watch, and rose to go.

"You'd better stay here," I said. "Don't you know that in Paris civilians can't use the streets at night? You might get picked up by a German patrol."

Henri smiled, and produced a pass with the seal of the German Kommandantur on it.

"Five hundred francs to a German sergeant-major for this," he said. "Good for fourteen days. Want one? I can get one for you."

He picked up his hat, and moved towards the door. With his hand on the knob, he turned.

"Oh, by the way," he said, "I'm dropping in at the Prefecture tomorrow morning. I know a man there who'll give us passes in French names for your two English friends. I'll see that they're taken to the train, and that some one goes with them all the way to Tissier's place to make sure there's no trouble. You needn't worry about them. I assure you they'll be all right."

As Kitty closed the door behind him, she turned slowly, and stood there, her back pressed against the closed door. I could see the tears in her eyes as she remained there, motionless.

"Why, Kitty," I said. "If that's the way you feel, why did you let Henri go? Didn't you realize that he would have liked to stay, if you had only uttered the slightest hint about it?"

"What a naïve little woman you are!" Kitty said, smiling through her tears. "Do you really think I'm crying about Henri? It's because what has happened is so beautiful! Only a few hours ago we thought our situation was hopeless, with Chancel's organization broken up, and no way of getting our boys out of German hands. And now we have a new means of escape for them—and for others!

"Etta! perhaps there will be answers to our advertisement tomorrow!"

## CHAPTER FOURTEEN

# Friends or Enemies?

EARLY in the morning—well before eight—the doorbell woke me. I knew Margot must have gone out at six to get into line at the grocery store (which meant that she would get in about noon), so I got up to answer the door myself.

A French boy who appeared to be about fifteen stood at the door.

"*Voici, Madame*," he said only, handing me three letters which he pulled out of his pocket, and immediately hurried towards the stairs.

"Wait a minute," I called after him. "Who are these from?" But he clattered down the stairs without answering.

I looked at the letters. They were addressed to William Gray at Durand's café. They must be replies to our advertisement, probably sent over to us by Monsieur Durand. I didn't like the boy's behavior, though, and as I went into Kitty's room to give her the letters, I told her about the curious way in which I had received them.

"Oh, don't worry about a little thing like that," Kitty laughed. "It's all right to be cautious, but don't let your imagination run away with you. The boy wasn't a Gestapo agent in disguise. He's probably Durand's errand-boy."

"Does Durand know our address?" I asked.

"Of course," Kitty said. "I gave it to him."

"I think that was a mistake, Kitty," I said. "We've got to work secretly, and no matter how much we may trust people, the best guarantee we can have that they won't give us away is not to let them know anything. I'd feel much more comfortable if Durand didn't know our address. He wouldn't betray us knowingly, no doubt, but suppose some one followed the boy?"

"You're right," Kitty said. "Perhaps that was incautious. But I'm sure Durand can be trusted. I'll check with him about the boy, and ask him not to send letters over any more. . . . Why don't you call in Lieutenant Burke while I open these letters? He'll be interested."

The first letter contained only this laconic message:

Should my name be familiar to you, kindly write to this address: Mlle. Lucie Beauvais, Bergasse, Somme.          JOHN HITCHCOCK.

"Do you know him?" Kitty asked, handing the letter to Burke. He looked at the letter carefully, and then shook his head.

"No," he said, "but that doesn't prove anything. Since you used William Gray's name, he's probably from his unit. For that matter, I wouldn't even recognize the names of every one in my own regiment."

Kitty took the letter back, and she stared at it intently, as though trying to wring some extra meaning from its single sentence.

"Bergasse must be a very small place," she said, "since the name of the village is the only address you need. Probably he's some English boy who found refuge in a peasant's home—too sick, perhaps, to continue to hide in the woods—or even wounded. We'd better write to him."

"Remember what Chancel said," I broke in. "He warned us that this was the dangerous moment. The Gestapo might be trying to trap us by answering the advertisement themselves. For all we know, the Gestapo wrote this letter. We must be very careful about answering it."

"For goodness sake, Etta," Kitty said, "how could you imagine that any one named John Hitchcock would be working for the Gestapo?"

"Would you expect a Gestapo agent writing a fake letter to sign with a German name?" I asked.

Kitty was silent for a moment. Then she burst out in exasperation:

"But what are we going to do? How are we going to tell? What's the use of all this effort if we're going to distrust the letters when they come in? William Gray isn't here. We can't check with him on these names! And see how cautiously this letter is worded. He's afraid of a trap, too. Would the Gestapo write that way?"

"They might if they were clever enough," I said. "They'd want to make it sound authentic. As for the name, perhaps they're using the name of a real soldier whom they've captured—just as we used William Gray's name. But what's in the next letter?"

It was even shorter than the other. It contained no message, only an address:

B. W. Stowe
12, Rue de la Gare
Reims

Kitty handed this too to Burke.

"What do you make of this?" she asked.

He studied it for a minute, then shook his head again.

"Not much," he said. "It seems a little odd that he should give an address in Rheims. That's a fairly large city. It's an unlikely place for a soldier to be hiding."

"It seems suspicious to me," I said.

"Oh dear," Kitty said, "Etta is going to see the fine hand of the Gestapo behind every one of these letters!"

"Make fun of me if you like," I said, "but let's not underestimate the Gestapo. I can't see any way to distinguish between genuine and fake letters, and this second one seems to me even more suspicious than the first. If you take my advice, you won't answer either of them."

"And perhaps abandon two English soldiers?" Kitty asked.

I didn't answer. I could see she was becoming irritated.

"Perhaps we can find some means of checking without giving ourselves away," Burke suggested. "Do you think you could locate some one trustworthy in Rheims, or even near that small village mentioned in the first letter, who could inquire cautiously and find out who wrote those letters?"

Kitty thought for a moment, her eyes half closed.

"Perhaps I could find some one at the Foyer du Soldat who has contacts in Rheims," she said, "but it won't be so easy for a small place like Bergasse. I think we ought to go there ourselves."

"I wouldn't do that if I were you," Lieutenant Burke said. "If two foreigners turn up in so small a place and try to make inquiries, they would be extremely conspicuous. If the Gestapo has set a trap there, you would be sure to be arrested and investigated; and if they checked back here, you'd be found out."

"Yes, you're right," Kitty said, with deep disappointment in her voice.

She was silent for a moment. Then she said:

"Under the circumstances, I'm afraid there wasn't much sense in publishing that ad at all. I did want to get in touch with English boys trying to escape—but if we don't dare communicate with them after they answer, what can we do for them? The whole scheme was no good. It has only caused us worry. I'm sorry I ever started it!"

Listlessly, she took up the third envelope and opened it. She read through it hastily, then looked up at me, her eyes shining again. She passed it to me, and said softly: "What do you make of this?"

It was in French, and rather long. It went:

Dear Sir:

I am the parish priest of the village of Conchy-sur-Conche, and I am writing to you at the request of a few of my parishioners, who seem to recognize an old friend in you. According to them, I can approach you with confidence on a matter very important from the point of view of my congregation.

Our church building, the pride of our congregation, is very much in need of urgent repairs, otherwise this beautiful product of the art of the Middle Ages, the church tower, will undoubtedly collapse.

Now that our country is bleeding from a thousand wounds, it might seem that there are scores of other things to save more important than an old church; but our restoration committee (of which I hope you will also become a member) has decided that it will immediately begin a campaign for a restoration fund, since a catastrophe may be expected any day, and irreparable, irreplaceable values would be lost with the collapse of our church.

I beg you, my dear sir, to inform me immediately when and where I could look you up, or when I can expect your visit. In case it is not easy for you to travel, perhaps you can send a representative with whom I could discuss the broadening of our collection campaign.

In order to avoid any misunderstanding, may I remark that I have already secured the permission of the church and the local authorities for my collection campaign.

Asking God's blessing upon you, I am,

Yours very faithfully,<br>
Father Christian Ravier<br>
Conchy-sur-Conche (Somme).

I ran through it, skipping a phrase here and there, and tossed it aside carelessly.

"Just an appeal for funds," I said, uninterestedly.

"Etta!" Kitty almost screamed. "Don't you get it? It might have been just an appeal for funds if it had come in our regular mail! But it was addressed to William Gray! It was in answer to our advertisement! It's written so that we will understand, but no one else."

"Of course!" I said. "How stupid of me!"

"Listen," Kitty said to Burke, and she translated the letter for him swiftly. Then, with mounting excitement, she went on:

"You see: 'a few of my parishioners seem to recognize an old friend in you.' He must be in touch with some men of William Gray's unit; that would be about the right place, too. Then he says 'according to them, I can approach you with confidence on a matter very important from the point of view of my congregation'—that is, of these men.

"He says himself, you see, that a church restoration, which is supposed to be what he is talking about, isn't very important these days; and yet he talks of the loss of something 'irreparable, irreplaceable' and says that a 'catastrophe' may be expected any day. It's easy to see what he means by a catastrophe; the men he has there—his 'congregation'—may be discovered and arrested.

"Let's see, now; what else? Ah, yes—he asks where he can look us up or if we can come to him; and he realizes that an English soldier couldn't move about very easily, so he asks if a 'representative' can come to see him—and about 'the broadening of our collection campaign'! Why, it's easy to see what that means—saving more soldiers! And I judge that when he talks about having the permission of the local authorities for his collection campaign, he means the French administration is helping him in getting English soldiers in his neighborhood together. Why, it's as plain as the nose on your face!" Kitty concluded triumphantly.

This time I could see no objection. When Kitty said, "Well, how about it, Etta? Do you think the Gestapo wrote that letter?" I answered: "No, I don't think so, Kitty. This one looks genuine."

"Now I tell you what I'll do," Kitty said. "I'll go to the office of the Bishop of Paris, and inquire if it is correct that a collection has been authorized for the restoration of the church at Conchy-sur-Conche. I imagine that if Father Christian was so careful to make his letter appear innocent, he probably actually has some such fund, so that in case of investigation he won't be suspected. If he has, we can use interest in restoring the church as an excuse for visiting him."

The doctor was back early the following morning to see Corporal Meehan—at seven o'clock. He brought a second man with him, whom he introduced as a professor of the medical faculty, and an eminent specialist. The two doctors went into Meehan's room, and Kitty, after waiting an hour for them to come out, grew too impatient to wait any longer, and set off for the office of the Bishop of Paris to check up on Father Christian.

I couldn't understand what the two doctors could be doing so long in Meehan's room. Eight-thirty, nine, nine-thirty—and there was still no sign from them, except the occasional murmur of their voices. Once I thought I heard a low moan from Meehan.

When Kitty returned, they were still there. I could see from her excited expression that her errand had been successful.

"It's all right," she said. "There *is* a fund for the restoration of Father Christian's church. If Henri hadn't promised to come and visit us, I would have started for Conchy-sur-Conche at once!"

In her enthusiasm, she had probably forgotten momentarily all about poor Meehan. But at this moment the door opened, and the two doctors came out. Excusing themselves for a moment, they stepped into the ante-room and launched into an animated discussion.

"Goodness!" Kitty exclaimed. "Have they been with Meehan all this time?" She looked at her watch. "Why it's almost ten o'clock!"

I nodded. We both strained our ears to catch the conversation going on in the ante-room; but what we could hear was so filled with medical terms that it did us little good. We exchanged uneasy glances. Apparently Meehan's state was worse than we had thought.

Lieutenant Burke entered the living room at the same time that the two doctors came back. His mind was filled with his projected departure with Henri Beaurepos, for which he had prepared, and naturally the first thing he said when he saw the doctors was:

"Well, what's the verdict? Will Meehan be able to come along with us?"

Kitty translated the question to them. They stared at her as if she were mad.

"Strong enough to travel?" our doctor repeated. "My dear lady, there's no question of that! He has a bad case of blood poisoning. We will do what we can—but the question is whether we shall be able to save his life."

When Henri arrived an hour later, he found us once again in the same state of terror as when he had first entered to find the unconscious corporal lying on the floor. The Professor had gone, but the doctor had remained. To Henri's incisive questions, the doctor repeated some of the things he had said to us.

"Of course," he said in answer to one of Henri's remarks, rather impatiently, I thought. "Naturally, he should be in a hospital. But it's too late now. I discussed all that with the Professor. He could have gotten him into a hospital bed, although it would have been very risky—we might all have been arrested by the Germans—but he can't be moved now. There's no choice. He must stay here.

"To tell you the truth, it's a miracle that he even got here. It seems impossible that he should have been able to walk out of the hospital, climb a wall, and survive the journey in that cramped position. Did you really get him here in the way you told me?"

We assured him that we had told the absolute truth. He shook his head wonderingly.

"It's astonishing what the human organism can do!" he murmured.

Kitty uttered a sentence which had been in my mind for some time, but which I hadn't dare phrase. It seemed difficult for her to say it. I had the impression that she was forcing the words out.

"Was it—dangerous—to move him from the hospital, doctor?" she asked. "Would it have been—better—to leave him there?"

"Judging from his condition," the doctor answered, "the great pity is that you didn't move him before. He's been very badly neglected . . . I suppose it wasn't their fault. They probably have no drugs and no equipment. Most of those military hospitals are like that . . . As it is, his condition is deplorable. *Pauvre garçon!* He may have taken so much risk only to come to Paris to die!"

"It's really as serious as that?" Kitty whispered, pallid.

The doctor nodded silently.

Lieutenant Burke, sitting with one elbow on the table, and his fist propping up his chin, compressed his lips, and as he saw me looking at him, shifted his gaze unhappily and stared steadfastly at the wall. No one spoke. The ticking of a wall clock suddenly entered my consciousness, sounding startlingly loud. The doctor cleared his throat.

"I wish I could avoid bringing this up," he said. "But do you realize the difficult situation which you may have to meet shortly? Frankly, I have very little hope. We weren't able to determine exactly how long the sepsis has existed. In his feverish condition, he was only able to give us vague answers. They weren't much help. We are using sulfa injections, but the result probably depends on whether or not the infection is relatively recent, and it appears to be fairly well established. To put it bluntly, you risk being left with a dead man on your hands. How are you going to explain his presence here?"

That was something I hadn't thought of. I had been worrying about Meehan's condition because of personal sympathy for him. Now I suddenly realized what a difficult problem would be created for us if he died!

Kitty jumped up from her chair with unusual violence.

"It's hateful!" she exclaimed. "I can't stand it! How can we sit here and discuss calmly how we're going to—what we're going to do if he dies, while he's still struggling for his life in there! It's heartless! It's cold-blooded. . . . I just don't believe it! He's not going to die! I won't discuss any clever plans for saving our skins if—" She sobbed suddenly, snatched at her handkerchief, pressed it to her eyes, and ran into her room.

Henri looked after her with a sigh.

"Well, that's Kitty all right," he said quietly. "Too much heart to giving up defending those she loves even when she knows she has lost . . . Doctor, perhaps it will be better for us to settle this before she comes back . . . It seems to me we'd better not try anything as dangerous as smuggling a body out of the house. Isn't there some way we could bury him from this apartment, under a false identity?"

"You can't simply give any name you happen to hit on, you know," the doctor said. "I can deliver you a death certificate, of course. But a city doctor will come here to check the death, and you will have to show the dead man's papers. He has to represent some real person."

"Why not use my brother's papers?" I asked. "That worked once before."

"It wouldn't work this time," Henri said. "That was just a routine check-up, and no comparison was made between the papers and official records. In the case of a death, papers are always checked with the official files. Besides that, all deaths are reported to the Prefecture of Police and entered in an alphabetical file. Simply in inserting the record of this death in its correct place, the authorities would be certain to notice that the same death had been reported before . . . Besides, there's likely to be more than a routine check-up. A death from a wound is a serious matter, you know."

"One thing is certain," the doctor said. "We can't report his death under his own name. If they learned that you had hidden an English soldier here, without reporting him until his death forced you to it, we'd all be arrested. . . . How about this: suppose I made a report now that you found this man in the street, took him in and then called me—we'd have to get your other Englishman out of the way first, of course. If we report him before he dies, instead of after, we might get away with it. And, after all, it can't make much difference to him whether he dies here or in a military hospital—if they dare move him to one."

"No, that won't do," I said quickly. "Suppose they find out his real identity—and in his present state he might tell them without realizing what he was doing. When they checked up, they would certainly discover that we had visited the hospital he escaped from, and we'd be caught just the same. . . . Besides, suppose he lives? We don't want to hand him back to his jailers if there's any chance of saving him."

"*Ma pauvre dame,*" said the doctor, "that chance is unfortunately very slight. However, I agree with you. I think we should try to find some other way, if only to give him every possible chance. And as you say, that probably wouldn't save you anyway."

"I think I have the answer," Henri broke in.

We all looked towards him.

"There is only one person who could die in this apartment without causing difficulties for you," he said. "That is myself."

"How do you mean?" I asked.

"It's very simple," Henri explained. "It's obvious we can't get away with a purely imaginary identity. We have to have the papers of some real person. Secondly, it can't be some one already dead. That would be sure to be discovered. Therefore we must borrow the identity of some living person.

"The person whose identity is borrowed would, of course, be legally dead from then on, which would be inconvenient at times, perhaps, but not exactly a terrible fate. In fact, in moments like these, it might occasionally be advantageous to have disappeared from the official records of the living. After the war, I'm sure the authorities will accept an explanation and rectify the error in the official files.

"Now to begin with, it might not be easy to find any one willing to deprive himself of civil rights for the duration, but as a matter of fact, there's no question of hunting around for some one else, for the circumstances make me the inevitable choice. If you found a stranger to lend you his identity, you'd still have to explain what he was doing here. But in my case it's simple. I am legally still Kitty's husband, and it would be quite natural for me to have stopped here, coming from the south. All we need to do is to think of some plausible excuse for my having gotten an infected wound. The doctor can testify that he was called to treat me for it, but it was too late. The only papers we will need will be my passport and the doctor's death certificate."

The doctor rose.

"I think that is the answer," he said. "You can count on me. If it is necessary, I will issue the certificate, and I believe there will be no trouble. And now, if you will excuse me, I have other cases to visit."

I thought that now that the discussion was over, it might be possible to tell Kitty what we had decided without hurting her too much. I went into her room, and found her sitting on the floor, beside her bed, one arm resting upon it. Her eyes were moist, and I judged that she had been kneeling by the bed praying.

In a few words, as gently as I could, I told her what we proposed to do if it should become necessary. This time she took it calmly enough, but with unshakable faith in the future.

"Henri is a fine fellow," she said. "It is splendid of him to offer. It might cause him more difficulties than he admits. Obviously, he doesn't need a passport for travelling, since he crosses the border illegally anyhow. But how about ration cards? How about unexpected developments in the future, in case he gets into trouble, and can't produce papers? . . . But he won't have to take that chance. Corporal Meehan is not going to die, believe me. I feel it so deeply that I know it must be true. He can't die . . . I know he can't."

The doctor came again the next day, and once more spent a long time in the corporal's room. When we asked for a report, he shrugged his shoulders.

"I don't know which way he will turn," he said. "There's no perceptible change today. I'm afraid he's suffering a little more, if anything. Still, in the condition he's in, every day he hangs on is so much gain. I haven't given up hope yet."

On the following day, the doctor came out of Meehan's room much sooner. He appeared relieved.

"It's remarkable!" he said. "These new sulfa drugs are amazing! His temperature is much lower. I think we're going to pull him through!"

I took Kitty's hand.

"Perhaps you were right after all, Kitty," I said.

She smiled back at me.

"I never doubted that he'd get better," she answered.

And she was right. In the next two days, Meehan improved with startling speed. He listened for hours to adventure novels which Burke read to him, and even became definitely gay. Henri, seeing that his passport wasn't going to be needed, made his postponed departure, but Burke stayed behind to keep an eye on Meehan while we went to Conchy-sur-Conche.

This was a concession to Kitty's impatience. When she suggested that we go to see Father Christian, I protested that Meehan still needed us.

"Well, there's Margot," Kitty said. "And the doctor comes every day. Anyhow, he's out of danger."

How well I understood what caused her to say that! So many of her countrymen were still in danger, that she couldn't wait to get back to the task of saving them. Meehan was out of danger now, so she had lost some of her interest in his case. The others now seemed more urgent to her.

But I insisted that Margot had to be out of the house much of the time, buying food; so Burke volunteered to stay until Meehan could leave with him. With that settled, we decided to leave for Conchy as soon as possible.

## CHAPTER FIFTEEN

# A Visit to Father Christian

IT TOOK us all the next day to arrange our trip to Conchy-sur-Conche. Our travelling permit from the German Military Command had expired and had to be renewed, and we had to find gasoline for the journey. Neither of these things was too simple to fix up, and it kept both of us trotting through various official bureaus until well along in the afternoon.

On our way home, Kitty suggested that we stop at Monsieur Durand's café to ask if there were any other replies to our advertisement.

"It's quite unnecessary for you to take the trouble of coming here for your letters," Monsieur Durand said. "If anything more comes, I'll send it over to you by Emile, as before."

"I wanted to speak to you about that," Kitty answered. "Are you quite sure the boy is absolutely trustworthy? When he brought the other letters he acted so queerly that Mrs. Shiber thought his behavior rather suspicious."

Monsieur Durand smiled.

"Don't give it another thought, ladies," he said. "The boy is quite all right. He's the son of the postman, whom I've known for years. In fact——"

Monsieur Durand looked carefully about, and then, bending towards us and whispering, although no one was in sight, continued: *"Le facteur, il est dans la combine aussi!"*

"The postman's in on it too?" Kitty echoed. "Why, what do you mean?"

*"Voici:* I told the postman to be very careful about these letters —that they weren't love letters, like most of the mail addressed to people at cafés. He spoke to the head of the sorting department at the post office, whom he knows very well, and he sees to it that these letters don't go through the German censorship. They don't try to read all mail, you know; they just check what they're interested in.

Now if they saw your adverisement, they may be looking for answers; but they won't find any, for our friend in the sorting department will keep all letters addressed to William Gray out of the mail sack that goes over to the German censorship. Well done, wasn't it?"

"Splendid!" Kitty agreed. But when we got outside, I couldn't refrain from saying:

"Kitty, doesn't it worry you to know that so many other persons of whom we know nothing are *dans la combine*, as Monsieur Durand puts it? Not only does he know what it is all about, but so does Emile, so does the postman, and so does his friend in the sorting department—at least four persons who share our secret, and for all we know there may be others. For instance, the mail sorter and the postman may not be on duty all the time. Do they pass on their information to their substitutes? You can say what you like, but I'm getting the cold shivers again. Suppose just one of these men, over a drink in Durand's café, for instance, says something about the *combine* loudly enough to be overheard by some other customer who may be working for the Gestapo—they're everywhere, you know. Just one little slip might be enough to doom us."

"Oh, don't be so nervous," Kitty said impatiently. "They're all patriotic Frenchmen, and old friends of one another. We can count on them. In fact, if we get into trouble, they may even help us out of it."

We started out to see Father Christian early the next morning. As usual, there was little traffic on the highways, and we made good time, leaving behind us one northern village after another whose names brought pangs to our hearts as we recognized in them places which had figured in the communiqués of a few weeks ago, when we had still believed that the French Army would be able to hold the Germans out.

We didn't talk much on the way. Kitty was no doubt busy with her own thoughts, as I was with mine. I was arguing with my fears, disputing within myself the distrust which I could not completely banish concerning Father Christian's letter.

There is no reason for worry, I said to myself. The letter was so convincing, so serene, so evidently honest, that it is next to impossible that it could be a Gestapo trap. But in the next instant, the response would come. But is it so impossible? Nothing is impossible when the Gestapo is concerned. Its members would be quite capable of conceiving such a trap.

"Look," said Kitty, pointing to the roadside sign: "Conchy-sur-Conche! And that must be the church steeple!"

It was my last chance to speak before we had committed ourselves. I couldn't resist telling Kitty of my apprehensions.

"There's no danger," Kitty said. "We haven't notified any one we're coming. Until we've seen Father Christian himself and have had a chance to size him up, our story is that we stopped only to have a look at the church as we were passing. Just leave everything to me."

She stopped the car in front of the church. We got out and looked up at its dilapidated steeple, with the air, we hoped, of curious and admiring tourists. The building was obviously many centuries old, and seemed to have been erected by pious artisans, inspired more by their devotion than by any knowledge of academic art. Perhaps that was why they had created a structure of lasting beauty, quite worthy of Father Christian's campaign for its restoration.

We walked about the church, hoping to encounter the priest; but no one appeared. We returned to the front.

"You get back into the car," Kitty suggested, "and keep a sharp watch for any one suspicious. I'm going inside."

But as I sat in the car on the main street of this small town of northern France, I saw nothing out of the ordinary. It was true that the town's aspect was not the same as it would have been in times of peace. Women, old men and children passed through the street, but it was immediately noticeable that no young men were visible. They, no doubt, were all in prison camps. Or were they, too, hiding in the forests like the Englishmen whom we were trying to aid?

Even middle-aged men were few. The only ones I saw were a postman and a gendarme, who passed slowly down the street as I sat in the car waiting for Kitty.

And then a young man appeared. But he was not a Frenchman. He was a German soldier. He carried no rifle, but his bayonet swung from his belt, which also supported a revolver. He walked with the uncertain gait of a man bored by inactivity, with no particular destination in mind. As he walked down the street, I noticed a curious phenomenon.

At every door, little groups were gathered, and many of the windows of the street were occupied by women, calling out the day's gossip to their neighbors. As the German moved along the street, the little groups seemed to dissolve, the heads disappeared from the windows. There was nothing conspicuous or demonstrative about this disappearance of the French before the lone representative of the invaders. They moved slowly, almost casually, so that one hardly noticed the movement itself. It failed to catch the eye. Yet one moment they were there, and the next they were not.

The progress of the German soldier along the street swept it clear of humanity as though an invisible broom were passing down the road before him. And behind him, the doors and windows filled again as he went by. He seemed to move through an automatically self-created vacuum. I could not help being deeply impressed by this silent demonstration of antipathy to the German, which consisted in refusing to remain even within his sight. The soldier himself, unless I imagined it, seemed to be sad, depressed, as though this avoidance of his person, as if he were a leper, had affected him deeply.

I had been waiting for perhaps a quarter of an hour when Kitty appeared in the church entrance with a priest by her side. I had expected from Father Christian's letter, I don't know just why, to meet a saintly old man, complete with long white beard. Instead, Father Christian turned out to be the first young man I had seen since our arrival at Conchy-sur-Conche, bright-eyed and energetic.

I judged him to be no more than twenty-eight. He was one of those Frenchmen whose classic profiles, passed through generation after generation down the centuries, remind the foreigner that France was once part of the great Roman Empire.

Kitty introduced me to Father Christian, and he suggested that we talk in the rectory, behind the church. From its architectural style, I surmised that it dated from about the same epoch as the church itself.

As we turned the corner of the building, I was astounded to see the German swastika flag waving above the entrance. Father Christian saw the expression on my face, and explained without waiting for a question.

"I'm sorry, but I can't do anything about that flag," he said. "I was in the army when the Germans entered the village. They took over the rectory for their headquarters then. I was captured before Paris, but I managed to escape, and came back here to resume my work. I asked them to hand back the rectory, but they refused. However, they did let me keep the rear part of the building, which they weren't using, and that's where I live now."

Father Christian led us through the garden into a side door towards the rear of the house. It let us into a small low-ceilinged room which looked like a warehouse compartment, for it was piled high with church paraphernalia, which, Father Christian explained, the Germans had thrown out of the rectory into the courtyard until he had moved it back into his own part of the rectory.

"We can talk safely here," Father Christian said. "The Germans are right over our heads, but they can't hear a word. Thick walls were the rule in the days when this building was put up. This room is completely sound-proof."

At first Father Christian did most of the talking. He told us that there were at least a thousand English soldiers hiding in the woods in the region of Conchy-sur-Conche, and that he maintained regular contact with them. But their hardships, he explained, were appalling.

"There isn't a day," he said, "when I am not called upon to bury one of them. They come at night, and leave the dead man beneath the cross at the entrance to the town, and there we pick the body up and give it Christian burial. And do you know, they are never marked by weapons! I have yet to see one who has died of wounds. The cause of death isn't even illness, for there are no traces of disease. The cause of death is simply exhaustion, debility. You might say that these lads in their twenties have died of old age, like men of eighty. They are completely worn out by the lives they lead, which saps their vitality before their time."

Father Christian sighed.

"There is so little we can do," he continued. "This is a small place, and even under the best of circumstances, it would be difficult for us to supply the needs of a thousand men. But today we are rationed ourselves; and besides, we must be careful not to attract the attention of the Germans. I try to keep body and soul together for these men, so far as my poverty permits. But even if we all gave up everything we possess, it would not be enough. I have already stripped every member of my congregation of clothing and food. I must say that they have all behaved admirably."

I thought of the scene I had witnessed when the German soldier passed down the street, and I mentioned it to Father Christian, adding that it seemed to me that the German looked sad, as though the ostracism to which he was subjected had made its mark on him.

"You are quite right," Father Christian said. "The Germans are depressed. Their attitude seems strange for a victorious people. It is only the very young soldiers who show a different spirit. They are arrogant and full of confidence. They try to convince the French officials, the only inhabitants who talk to them, because their duties oblige them to, that resistance to Germany is utterly foolish and futile because she will soon dominate the whole world. 'First we'll go to England,' they say, 'then to America.'

"But with the older men, it's a different story. It's already been a long and weary progress, they say, to Vienna, to Prague, to Warsaw, to Norway, to Amsterdam, Brussels and Paris. They are tired of fighting and want to go home. They tell us that England is next on the list, too. But as one of them said to me, 'And then what? I'm beginning to feel like another Wandering Jew—I'm a pure Aryan, you understand; it's just the idea that we are moving on ceaselessly from one country to another, and we can't stop. What would happen if we did?' He was afraid that if the succession of conquests ever ended, the conquered peoples would succeed in revenging themselves against the troops left to police them.

"He said to me: 'We really ought to massacre everybody, in self-defense, you understand, to make sure that some day we, ourselves, won't be massacred.'"

"What did you answer to that?" I asked.

"Oh," said Father Christian, with a grim smile, "I said, 'Cheer up. Perhaps there'll be an earthquake to wipe us all out together.'"

Kitty had obviously become impatient during this exchange.

"Let's go back to the English soldiers," she broke in. "How do they manage to keep from being caught?"

"They're very clever," Father Christian replied. "There have been several raids in this region by motorcycle patrols, but only a few men have been caught. They hide well, and they have learned to know every foot of the woods. They have a well-hidden headquarters in the forest, where they get news from the outside world by means of a radio which I smuggled in to them. Generally, the only catches the Germans make are of men so weak with starvation that they haven't strength to move.

"But I don't think they can remain hidden successfully very much longer. So far, there have been no systematic round-ups in this region, like those which have been going on north of us. There the method has been to surround whole counties with large forces, and simply close the circle. Any one hiding within it is pushed back as the lines tighten until finally the whole lot is captured without firing a shot. It's certainly only a question of time before they apply that method here, too.

"Now here is what I have done. I have made all the necessary arrangements to get these men out of here, a few at a time. I will take responsibility for getting them to Paris if you can take charge of them after that. I have already fixed it up to get identity cards for them, which will show that they have permission to go to Paris to take jobs in war factories there. This will enable them to take a train for Paris, and the chances are that they will meet with no difficulties.

"But it has to be remembered that very few of these men speak French, and therefore it is impossible to send them off alone. They must be escorted by some quick-witted person, able to speak up for them quickly in case of unforeseen circumstances. I plan to do that myself, unless it should be absolutely impossible, and I have to send some one else. I figure that it will seem much less suspicious if a priest is in charge of a group of three or four young men, handling their travelling passes, and so forth. Anyway, I will guarantee to deliver the boys to you in Paris if you can take care of them from then on. Can you do that?"

"We certainly can," Kitty answered enthusiastically, her flushed cheeks and sparkling eyes revealing her delight at the working out of her plans. "We have a five-room apartment in Paris. You can bring the boys directly to us, and we will let them rest there for a few days while we get them travelling papers to go to Bordeaux. From there we can send them across the line of demarcation through the estate of a Frenchman who is helping to get escaped soldiers out of occupied territory."

Kitty glanced at me, and continued:

"Of course, Etta, we will take care of the expenses—the railroad fares, and the 50 francs per person we will have to pay to get these men across the border."

I don't know which of the two seemed happier, Kitty or Father Christian. The young priest closed his eyes for a moment, and from the expression on his face, I thought he must be offering up an inward prayer of thanks.

"Preaching is my profession," he said finally, "and usually I don't have any difficulty finding words for what I want to say, but I'm at a loss to express the depth of my gratitude to you. If you knew the mental tortures I have suffered, as a helpless witness to the indescribable sufferings of these boys!—and then your advertisement appeared, out of nothingness, like an answer to my prayers! . . . When can I bring you the first batch?"

"When?" Kitty echoed. "Why, immediately, of course. There's no time to lose. Let them start tonight, and they can be at our place tomorrow."

"Goodness, Kitty," I interrupted. "Don't be so impatient. Remember, we have preparations to make, too. In the first place, we haven't heard yet from Libourne—from Monsieur Tissier. We have got to make arrangements with him for receiving these men and getting them over the border. Then we have to arrange with the Prefecture man about travelling passes. I think we will need at least a week to prepare."

"I'm afraid you're right, Etta," Kitty admitted with reluctance. "I think I had better go to Libourne myself, see Tissier, and prepare everything in advance. Then we'll notify Father Christian, and he can start sending the boys to us."

She paused for a moment, and then added gaily:

"But what's to stop us from taking one man back in the car with us now? How about it, Father? Do you think you could reach one of them in time to ask if he would like to come back to Paris with us?"

Father Christian smiled.

"Reaching them will be no difficulty," he said, "since there are four of them in the house now."

"In this house?" I stammered. "Here, under the same roof with the Germans?"

"Why, yes," said Father Christian simply. "What place is safer from search? They were all sick when I picked them up and brought them here. They're well again now, but I could hardly chase them back into the woods, could I?"

I was still astounded.

"Well!" I exclaimed. "I thought we were daring in taking escaped soldiers into our apartment. But you, under the very noses of the Germans! How in the world do you hide them?"

The priest rose.

"Come with me," he said. "I'll show you."

Remembering the age of the building, I imagined vaguely that we would be conducted into some mediæval hiding place, some crypt or secret dungeon, entered through a sliding panel or a secret staircase constructed hundreds of years ago. But the truth was much less romantic. Father Christian simply opened a door into a corridor, crossed it, and knocked on a door on the other side. It was opened by an elderly woman, whom Father Christian introduced as his cousin and housekeeper.

The room into which we were conducted, like Father Christian's, looked like a storeroom. The front part of the room contained an unencumbered strip hardly wide enough to stand in. Furniture removed by the Germans from the rest of the building filled the rest of it, piled up almost to the ceiling.

Father Christian closed the door carefully, and then, turning towards the mountain of furniture, said in slow and difficult English:

"Gentlemen, an English and an American lady have come to call on you."

To our astonishment, we heard the sound of movements in the

we were anxious to start him on his way for the sake of our own nerves.

It took us a week, however, to get in touch with Monsieur Valentin, the clerk at the Prefecture who had been recommended to us by Henri Beaurepos as the man who could supply us with travelling permits for our men.

Trusting in Henri's assurance that we could have perfect confidence in Valentin, we told him in detail what we were doing, and asked him to get us passes so that we could send the English soldiers from Paris to the frontier.

Monsieur Valentin listened to us gravely and attentively.

"What you are doing is very dangerous, ladies," he said, "very dangerous indeed. Possibly you don't realize quite how dangerous. I understand that the Germans intend to enforce new and drastic measures against any one who helps English soldiers to escape. However, if you two are not afraid of the possible consequences, I certainly should not be."

He told us that he would require a little time to get us the necessary papers. As a matter of fact, it took him a whole week—but when he provided the passes, we had everything we needed. He had succeeded in getting a large number of blank permits, duly signed, and stamped with all the necessary seals, so that we could fill in ourselves whatever names and details we wanted without having to make a special request to him each time we wanted to send men out.

I was the happiest person alive when the permits were at last in our hands, for Captain Handsby's nervousness had turned our peaceful home into a regular insane asylum. By now he had all of us tiptoeing about, starting at each other's movements, and imagining that Gestapo men were hiding behind every piece of furniture.

But we could not start him off yet, for we were still without word from Monsieur Tissier at Libourne; and we dared not ship the boys south until we knew that everything was ready for them at the frontier.

One morning during that waiting period Kitty and I were sitting at breakfast. She had picked up the paper, which she always read during the morning meal; but hardly had she glanced at it than she folded it hastily and made some inconsequential remark. I knew by

experience that this meant that Kitty had seen something in the
paper which she thought I had better not see, and I demanded to
know the bad news. I almost had to tear the paper away from her
to get it. As I unfolded it, Captain Handsby bent over to read it
across my shoulder.

It was impossible to miss the item which had caught Kitty's eye.
It was played up boldly on the front page, a German proclamation announcing that the death penalty would be imposed on any
persons discovered to be hiding English soldiers or aiding them to
escape.

"That means you," said Captain Handsby, turning deathly pale,
"and you can depend on it, the Germans will check first on all English residents of Paris to find out who is helping English soldiers
to escape. The Gestapo may be here any minute. We can't stay
another instant. Our presence is endangering your lives. I'm going
to leave at once. You'd better tell the others."

We were too stunned by the proclamation to stop him as he hurried
into his room to get ready to go. I looked at Kitty in dismay.

"There is only one thing to do," she said. "I must go to Libourne
to see Tissier at once. I'm afraid this order will frighten him out of
going through with it. This decree might very well be a catastrophe.
People like Tissier, who have been cooperating up to now, are likely
to stop through fear. You can't expect them not to react to a threat
of death."

"How about you?" I asked. "Are you forgetting that you are just
as much threatened as he is? Both of us are, in fact."

"But Etta, please!" Kitty answered. "I thought we had already
discussed that question between ourselves and settled it once for all.
We have already considered that risk, and decided to accept it. We
have been very careful up to now, and we shall be even more careful
in the future. We didn't get into this entirely of our own free will.
We were more or less led into it. But now that we are embarked
on this course, we've got to go ahead with it. We can't desert these
poor boys in the face of this threat, brutal as it is. We're up to our
necks in this business, anyhow. To begin with, we have three of
them here right now; and our first concern must be to get them out.
We have to continue at least to that extent. We have no choice."

She was silent for a moment. Then she added softly, as though speaking to herself:

"What can happen anyway? Nobody will find out."

Since we had travelling permits for our three refugees already, Kitty decided to kill two birds with one stone and take them to Libourne with her. I was a little worried about risking that, with no guarantee that Monsieur Tissier was still willing to get them across the line, but I'm afraid I didn't argue very firmly, for the prospect of getting them out of the apartment, especially the fidgety Captain, was so pleasant that I was really in favor of their going.

And I did enjoy to the full the unaccustomed peace and quiet that pervaded our apartment with the departure of our guests. For two days I neither read the papers nor listened to the radio. I locked the world and the war out of my mind and out of my home. I tasted again the quiet I had come to Paris to find, of which I had been brutally deprived by the war.

Kitty returned at the end of that time, fresh, youthful and buoyant. I didn't have to ask her to know that her trip had turned out well.

"This fellow Tissier is a wonderful old chap," she told me enthusiastically. "He's just a simple peasant, but he's got amazing common sense. In fact, he's even a philosopher of sorts. If all French peasants are like him, I don't wonder that they're supposed to be the backbone of this country.

"He hasn't swallowed the Vichy propaganda at all—just laughs when any one mentions Pétain's new political order. 'How was it possible for us to lose the war against Germany?' he asked me, and then went ahead and answered himself. 'It was like this,' he said, 'we got our carts going on the right road, but we couldn't get anywhere because some one was always poking a stick between the spokes of the wheels. Now who did that? It's easy to figure it out. It must have been the people who profited by it—the people who are running things in Vichy now.' That's the way he figures it out, and he tells me eighty per cent of the people he knows think the same thing."

"Did he know about the death decree?" I asked.

"Of course," Kitty said, "The Germans have posted it all over

Libourne. The walls and trees are covered with copies of it. When I mentioned it to him, he just spat. He said: 'I went through the 1914–1918 war. I might have keen killed a thousand times, but I got out of it. Now another war has passed over my head, and I'm still safe. I figure I'm that much ahead of the game already, and I can't lose.'"

For the next few days, Kitty and I were alone in the apartment together, as we had been in the happy days of peace. There was no need any longer to jump whenever we heard footsteps in the corridor outside, no need to fear the ringing of the doorbell. It was a blissful interlude—so blissful that I tried to prolong it by arguing with Kitty once more about the foolishness of continuing our activities now that the Germans had announced the death penalty. I remember that I said to her:

"Kitty, now that we have gotten rid of the three men we had to get across the border before we could get out of this dangerous business, there is no reason why we shouldn't stop. Remember what Captain Handsby said—that the very fact you are English-born gives the Gestapo a reason to suspect you. That ought to be enough to decide you to give up this work. It's only natural that the Germans should keep a more watchful eye on us, conspicuous because of our nationality, than on any particular Frenchman, indistinguishable from millions of other Frenchmen.

"Father Christian hasn't sent his first group along yet. There's still time to call it off. It would be only sensible to route these boys through some French family, less likely to be suspected than us."

Kitty looked at me angrily.

"Do you know of one? If you know a French family that will take them, that can get them travelling passes, that can get them across the border—in short, that can do what we are doing—*then* suggest that we turn the job over to them. But until you can find one, *we* have to do it."

But then, as always whenever she raised her voice in our discussions, she suddenly stopped, and a conscience-stricken look appeared on her face.

"Forgive me, Etta. I didn't mean to speak so rudely. But my whole heart is in this thing. I *must* keep on. One of the things that worries me most is that I am implicating you in everything I do. I would be so happy if you would only listen to me and go back——"

I knew what she was going to say. I broke in:

"It's no use, Kitty. That's one thing I won't do. You can have a clear conscience about my share of the risk, because I refuse, of my own free will, to go back to America and leave you alone. I'll stay with you whatever happens, and if I can't convince you that you're jeopardizing your life, I'll talk to Father Christian. Perhaps he will understand, after that decree, that you're not the proper person to continue this man-saving campaign, since you're English yourself, and likely to be suspected at once."

Kitty looked at me, troubled.

"Do you really think Father Christian would be capable of letting me down?" she asked.

I had no time to answer this strange rejoinder. Margot came into the room, and said: "There's a young priest asking for you. He says his name is Father Christian."

Father Christian's arrival was the result of a letter Kitty had written him from Libourne. With her customary impatience, the moment she had learned that Tissier was still willing to cooperate, she had sent Father Christian a letter in which she said that everything was ready to begin his collection campaign for the restoration of the church, and that she would be in Paris the following day, prepared to go ahead with it. This would have been unintelligible to any censor, but Father Christian understood at once, of course, that it meant he might begin to bring his boys to our place. So here he was with four of them.

His arrival created a problem. It was just about noon, and five unexpected guests for lunch were not easy to cope with in those days of restricted rations. Margot managed somehow to make a success of it, at the price of frightful inroads on some food we had recently succeeded in getting on the Black Market at outrageous prices.

The English boys were very quiet throughout the meal. They were much more subdued than the first ones we had rescued, which we supposed was a result of their having lived the lives of hunted beasts longer than their predecessors. We knew from the grateful smiles they directed at us during lunch, however, how much they appreciated our help. Their expressions weakened my determination to try to persuade Kitty of her danger, and I began to feel almost as strongly as she did the need to continue with what we were doing.

Nevertheless my more sober judgment could not let me forget that death decree, and I spoke to Father Christian about it, half hoping that he would remonstrate with Kitty. I couldn't very well ask him to directly, now that we had four English soldiers with us. But Father Christian, like Kitty, seemed not even to entertain the idea that this edict should make any difference to him. Instead, he discussed it impersonally, like an outsider unaffected by it.

"Judging from what I've heard," he said, "the Nazis are going to get just the opposite effect from what they expect by this brutal threat. Up to now, it's happened very often when I've spoken to French people about these boys that they've shrugged their shoulders and said, 'After all, if a million and a half of our boys can stand the German prison camps, why shouldn't the English be able to?' But I've noticed a change since the new order was issued. They're coming around to the belief that if it's as important as that for the Germans to stop the English soldiers from escaping, then it's the duty of all Frenchmen to help them get away.

"Apparently the Germans have had plenty of reason for taking drastic measures," Father Christian continued. "We seem by no means to be the only ones doing this sort of thing. I hear fantastic stories about escapes of English soldiers everywhere I go. It's impossible to tell which are true and which are not—but the fact that they're being told so widely in itself indicates how thoroughly people are aroused on this point.

"*Tiens!* Have you heard, for instance, any of the stories about the exploits of Englishmen wearing German uniforms? No? Well, one has practically become standard. It varies slightly in detail, but it always concerns two men in German officers' uniforms who turn up at a peasant's house and ask to spend the night. They always leave before dawn, and the peasant finds a note from them, sometimes with money, sometimes without, reading something like: 'Cheer up. You will soon be free again. Your English friends.' Possibly all the versions of this story come originally from the same source, or similar incidents may have occurred at different places.

"Then there's another story of a group of several soldiers in German uniform who marched into a hotel under command of an officer. The officer; apparently a typical Prussian, wearing a monocle and conducting himself in arrogant fashion, demanded accommodations for himself and his men. But the woman who kept the hotel noticed him looking at her fixedly, and realized she had seen him before somewhere. After a moment she recollected his face. It was that of an *English* officer who had stopped at her hotel during the war. He saw the light of recognition in her eyes, and with an apparently careless gesture, put his finger to his lips to warn her to keep quiet. She nodded, almost imperceptibly, to indicate she understood. He gave a stiff Prussian salute, and marched his men upstairs. The following day she found a note in his room with a single word on it: '*Merci!*' "

Father Christian chuckled.

"You know, all these stories have done the Germans a good turn," he said. "Germans who aren't known to be part of local garrisons often get a fairly cordial reception from the peasants these days, in the belief they may be Englishmen in disguise.

"They don't always figure it out, though. Here's a story I can vouch for, because I know the man it happened to. He owns a small delivery truck, which he is permitted to drive to transport food. He was stopped on the road by two men in German Luftwaffe uniforms, who asked him to drive them to the Villacoublay airfield, outside of Paris. When he refused, saying that he was going the other way, one of them drew a revolver and ordered him to take them to Villacoublay. My friend had a most unpleasant trip, with an occasional nudge in the back from the revolver to remind him to keep going.

"When they got to the airfield, the officers directed my friend to turn into a small road running towards a side entrance to the field. They got out of the car and handed him a sealed envelope. 'We'll want this again if we have to come back,' they said. 'You wait here for a few minutes. If we don't come back in a quarter of an hour, open it.'

"That naturally made my friend think something unusual was up, so he watched them through the wire fence. He saw them walk through the camp to the airfield, exchanging salutes as they marched along, then get into a plane and take off. He opened the letter. Inside was a thousand-franc note and a sheet of paper, on which was written: 'Thanks. R.A.F.'

"Since I know that story to be true," Father Christian concluded, "I don't find it hard to believe the others. They would explain why the Germans thought it necessary to decree the death penalty. Helping English soldiers to escape is getting to be quite a thriving industry."

Father Christian and the four boys stayed in the apartment until seven in the evening. Then, provided with the travelling permits which we filled out for them, they walked with Father Christian to the Gare d'Orsay, where he bought their tickets and saw them aboard the train.

We had the satisfaction of seeing them leave. We went over to the station ourselves a few moments before the train was due to pull out. We exchanged no words or gestures, of course, with either Father Christian or the boys; but we could see them through the window and our hearts went out to them as the train moved slowly away, taking them to freedom.

## CHAPTER SEVENTEEN

# An Old Friend

W E LIVED on pins and needles for two days after sending off Father Christian's first group of soldiers. Kitty had arranged with Tissier to notify us at once when the boys arrived, and to send us a second message when they had been smuggled safely across the border. But one day passed, and then another, and there was no word from Tissier. We began to fear that something had happened to our friends on the way when Tissier turned up himself.

He was the image of the French peasant making a visit to the city, attired uncomfortably in his black Sunday suit, and obviously rather ill at ease in it. His long drooping moustache, à la Clemenceau, was continually getting into the corners of his mouth. As a dweller in Paris, it was the first time I had met so typical a French peasant. And in talking with him, I acquired a deep respect for these simple, direct, unspoiled people whose sturdy character seems to me to represent the essence of all that is best in France. It remains an everlasting mystery to me how such a man, living in so isolated a community, could manage to be so accurately informed, and, on the basis of that information, could arrive at such accurate judgments concerning the situation in France. His native common sense served him much better than the more subtle minds of much cleverer persons.

His opinion of Marshal Pétain, for instance, was characteristic: "I'm not one of those who think the old man is a traitor," he told us. "After all, your wits can't be as sharp as you get along in life as they were in your prime. Now take me, for instance—I'm only seventy-three, much younger than the Marshal, but I often don't realize I'm being cheated in a deal until it's too late. That's what happened to this poor old fellow. They pulled the wool over his eyes. What do they expect of a man over eighty? He was fooled, and the whole country is suffering as a result. That's all there is to it."

In accordance with the habit of the French peasant, who considers it impolite to start a conversation with a blunt reference to the object of his visit, Monsieur Tissier covered most of the topics of the day before he came to the point.

"I came to Paris to do some shopping," he explained. "The stores in Bordeaux, where I used to do all my buying, never have anything any more. The Germans have cleaned them out. So as long as I had to come anyway, I decided to drop in on you ladies and tell you that you made a very bad mistake. In the future, whatever you do, don't let those boys travel without an escort."

We feared some mishap had occurred. Tissier quickly relieved our fears. But, as he pointed out, the English boys had only escaped arrest by a miracle, and we mustn't count on such good luck again.

What had happened was this:

Somewhere between Paris and Bordeaux, French gendarmes boarded the train to check the passengers. One of them spoke to one of our boys, who, of course, couldn't answer. When he discovered that there were four young men in the compartment, all provided with official French travelling permits, but none of them able to speak French, he was naturally suspicious. He ordered them off the train; but at this point the French passengers in the compartment intervened; and they were so violently indignant that the gendarme gave way, and the boys continued on their journey. But it was a close call, and they had had a good scare.

"You mustn't ever send them alone again," Tissier concluded vehemently. "Suppose an investigation were started to find out how they got travelling passes! It might lead back to your friends in the Prefecture and then to yourselves—and you know the penalty now. You must get French citizens to go with them. And you mustn't even let them sit together. Have one French boy with each English one, ready to speak up and answer questions. If you can't do that, it would be a crime to start them across France alone. The chances are against their ever getting to Libourne."

After Tissier had gone, Kitty was moody and thoughtful.

"Tissier is right," she sighed. "I hadn't thought of that difficulty before, but now that we know about it, what can we do? I have no idea where to find escorts for them. And Father Christian may arrive with more boys any day!"

Monsieur Tissier, who had arrived early, left about 11 o'clock. He hadn't been gone half an hour when Margot announced another caller—a Monsieur Corbier.

"I don't know any Monsieur Corbier," Kitty said, distrustfully. Unexpected visitors were not welcome at this period, when we feared that any moment might bring us an envoy from the Gestapo. "Did he say what he wanted?"

Monsieur Corbier spared Margot the necessity of answering. He simply opened the door, which Margot had closed behind her as she entered, and walked in. He looked rather like a doctor, for he had a black, uneven beard, a fashion still not uncommon among French doctors. He also wore thick-rimmed spectacles.

He stood still, one hand on the door knob, offering no explanation for his intrusion. Not unnaturally, we stared at him, expecting him to say something. His appearance seemed vaguely familiar to me, but I couldn't place him.

Finally he broke the silence.

"Well, my dear ladies," he said, "I think the test is conclusive. I am happy to see that you don't recognize me. I wasn't sure that these glasses and a three weeks' growth of beard would make that much difference in my appearance. But I see they do."

Kitty and I shouted almost in unison:

"Chancel!"

He chuckled at our surprise, and we had to smile, too. But Kitty, quickly becoming serious again, said: "You've come at the right time again. We've got another problem for you."

In the course of the next few minutes, Chancel explained his new activity to us. He was now working for a new organization, whose object was to smuggle out of France any Frenchmen who wanted to fight with the de Gaulle forces, and get them to England. He had come to ask us to work with him. But when Kitty explained our problem, he saw at once that he could adapt his plans to fit in with ours.

"Nothing is easier," he said, "than to get you French escorts for your boys, since I'll be sending Frenchmen out of the country just as you're sending Englishmen. Whenever you have any Englishmen to send out, let me know, and I'll provide the same number of French boys, on their way to join de Gaulle, to go with them. I suggest we conclude a sort of merger. You take care of getting the men to the frontier, and I'll have them picked up there and taken on to England. I don't know yet just which route we're going to use to do that— possibly across the Spanish frontier to Gibraltar or Lisbon, but more likely from some coastal village in southern France, where a fishing boat can take them out to an English ship. We might even send them the whole way across the Mediterranean to North Africa, and have them picked up and sent on from there."

Chancel's proposal fitted in perfectly with our needs. The problem of escorts was solved, and what was more, we would be spared the anguish of being left in doubt as to the fate of our boys after they crossed the frontier. Hitherto, we not only had no way of taking care of them after they got into the unoccupied zone, where, of course, they were still not entirely out of danger, and would be on their own in trying to get back to England, but there was not even any way by which they could let us know what had happened to them. We had given them letters of introduction to friends, and the addresses of other people they might be able to look up, but we had no reason for believing that any of them could get them out of the country. Now we had an opportunity to start the young men we wanted to help on a route of escape which would lead from the forests of northern France, not simply to the unoccupied zone, but all the way to England!

Chancel left with the promise to prepare escorts for our next group of English soldiers. He assured us that his men would be coached in advance on exactly how to meet all emergencies, so there would be no necessity of trying to make spur-of-the-moment explanations to their English comrades through the barrier of a foreign language.

"God must have sent you to us once again," Kitty said to him, as he was preparing to leave. "I was beginning to despair of the possibility of finding escorts to get our boys safely across France. You don't know what a load you've taken off my mind. Now everything will be all right."

Kitty's remark stuck in my mind. It was true, I thought, that we had experienced miraculous luck again and again. Was it all luck.

or was it the guiding hand of Providence? And could we always count on such good chance? Or were we perhaps being led deeper and deeper into actions from whose consequences there could be no escape, by a capricious fate which would turn against us only when we were completely enmeshed in its toils? I remembered the verse from Job: "Great things He does which we cannot comprehend."

It was on the following Friday that Father Christian arrived with another group of four young men. I noticed at once how tired he looked. He seemed to be near exhaustion.

"You look worn out, Father Christian," I said. "Aren't you overdoing it a bit? You might have sent some one else with this group, for instance—especially as it may seem odd that you should come to Paris twice in such a short time."

"Don't worry about that," Father Christian answered, with a smile. "I'm here this time with special German permission. I've got the Germans in Conchy very much interested in my campaign for restoration of the church. After all, they live in the rectory, which can stand a little repairing too, and they figure that if I do well, they may be able to ask for a few improvements to their living quarters. They would be delighted to have me come to Paris three times a week."

He paused a moment, and then added:

"As for sending some one else, that would be easy enough. Almost any one in the village would do it. But I think I'm the best one for the job as long as I can possibly manage it. My robes provide protection that a layman wouldn't have. The only thing that worries me is that something might happen while I'm away from home that would cause the Germans to discover the English lads hidden in the rectory."

Chancel was notified that we were ready to send four more Englishmen south, and it was arranged that they should start at seven o'clock. We watched from our window shortly before the hour set, and saw Chancel's escorts arrive. They came separately and with every appearance of nonchalance. The first one strolled slowly down the street, stopped to take out a cigarette, leaned casually against a lamp post as he lighted it, and then, putting his hands in his pockets, continued to lean against the post as he smoked it. A second arrived unfolding a newspaper, slowed up as he walked as though something particularly interesting had attracted his attention, and then stopped to read it better.

We didn't wait for all four of them to appear, for Chancel had instructed us to start the English boys down one at a time as soon as his men showed up. We watched them leave the building, and couldn't help admiring the technique of the French escorts. When the first English boy appeared, the man reading the newspaper appeared to finish the article he was looking at, folded it, and started off in the same direction, overtaking him gradually, but without appearing even to notice that he was on the street. The man leaning against the post made a casual sign to the second English boy who came out, as though he were an old friend he had been waiting for, and strolled slowly and nonchalantly across the street to join him. The third pretended to ask our man for a light. And we lost sight of the fourth as he was still walking along the street on the opposite side from the English lad he was to take in tow, with apparently no interest in him at all.

Kitty turned to me when we had watched this last pair out of sight.

"Chancel certainly knows his business," she said. "This is going to work beautifully."

And it did. The process of getting our protégés out of the country was reduced to a routine which operated with clockwork precision. By the end of October, we had sent about 100 English soldiers, accompanied by the same number of French soldiers, out of the country, usually in groups of four of each. We became so accustomed to it, that we hardly thought any more of the dangers we were incurring. But realization of them was not far below the surface, as we discovered on the one day during this period when we suffered a scare—or rather two scares, for oddly enough the only two untoward incidents which occurred at this time both came on the same day, a Monday towards the end of October.

Father Christian had arrived as usual with four young charges.

We were seated at lunch, which the half-starved men bolted ravenously under the benevolent smile of Margot, who seemed positively to delight in seeing the food which she could only procure by standing in line for hours disappearing in a matter of minutes.

Kitty said something to one of the boys, who had been quiet up to then. To our astonishment, he answered: "*Ich spreche nicht Englisch, gnaedige Frau.*"

A German! The thought flashed into my mind immediately: is he a spy, a Gestapo agent, perhaps, who has gotten among these boys to discover how they are escaping?

Kitty and I both cast startled glances towards Father Christian, who said calmly:

"I beg your pardon, ladies, I had completely forgotten to tell you that we have with us today Dr. Joseph Wandel, late of the German Army. Having decided that he was fighting on the wrong side, Dr. Wandel has, shall I say resigned? from the German Army, and he feels now that it would be highly advisable for him to move to some other country."

Well! He wasn't a spy—at least, Father Christian didn't think he was—but I hardly felt too happy to know that a German deserter was sitting at our table. This was even more serious than helping English soldiers to escape. Harboring a deserter would probably mean instant execution for any one caught at it.

Kitty's German is good, and I can manage with mine. We asked about Dr. Wandel's history, and he told us that he was an Austrian, who had been drafted into the German Army, but had firmly resolved to desert at the first favorable opportunity. He found it in France, and was hiding in the woods like the English soldiers when some of them stumbled on him.

"They treated me like a real comrade," Dr. Wandel said. "It was good of them to take an enemy in so freely. So I am in the same boat with them—or rather, I'm a little worse off. They might be shot as spies if they're captured—especially those wearing civilian clothes—but they can always hope to be treated as prisoners of war. I can have no such hope. If they get me, my most merciful end will be the firing squad. I was quite prepared not to be taken alive. But now I am in luck, for my good English friends told Father Christian about me, and he insisted on helping me to escape."

And he beamed good-naturedly around the table at all of us.

Of all the things that Dr. Wandel told us, the most interesting was that there had recently been an epidemic of suicides among German soldiers. It seemed hard to explain, for the German armies had been victorious everywhere, but Wandel thought it resulted from discouragement because soldiers who had been serving since long before the war had expected that with the fall of France, Britain would collapse, and they could go home; and now, after the momentary confusion which had followed the French debacle, the English were more determined than ever, and the end of the war was still not in sight.

Moreover, Wandel said, the Germans were in deadly fear of the reception they would get when they attempted to invade England. In August, the troops along the coast had seen thousands of German bodies washed up on the shore, horribly burned. They were quickly buried, and kept from the sight of most of the soldiers, but the story got around that the English had repulsed an invasion attempt by some horrible new weapon which had burned its victims alive.

We had heard rumors of this kind already from the French, but no one had been able to pin them down to much fact. Frenchmen as well as Germans had seen the burned bodies washed up on the coast, and some of them told of seeing great walls of flame rise suddenly from the waters of the Channel. There had been a vague and subtle reference to some repulse of an invading force in one of Churchill's speeches, which we heard surreptitiously on our radio, but that was all. We couldn't understand why, if the British had really thrown back the Germans, they had never publicized it; but talking with Wandel, we realized that perhaps secrecy was better, for German soldiers, not knowing the exact truth, had passed stories from mouth to mouth which must have been heavily exaggerated.

Wandel said that the German soldiers were never really sure whether an actual invasion attempt had been made or whether it was simply during practice maneuvers, but that they all had heard a story about the sea around the Nazi invasion barges suddenly bursting into flame. One theory was that the British had anchored oil drums off their coast and exploded them when the German boats reached them; but no one was quite sure how it had been done. All they knew was that at one instant they were moving forward over the sea, with the cool spray dashing in their faces; and at the next they were enveloped in a raging inferno of flames. Only those who hadn't quite reached the flaming area escaped with their lives.

After that, Wandel said, the German soldiers were so mad with terror that it was only by force that they could be persuaded to get into their boats for drill. Officers with drawn revolvers had to stand over them and threaten to shoot before they would obey. At some points along the coast, they were chained to the boats like galley slaves.

Father Christian confirmed what Wandel had said about the fear of the German soldiers whenever the invasion of England was broached. He told us that when some of the men stationed at Conchy were ordered to the coast, the younger ones wept, and kept repeating over and over a French phrase which had been shouted at them derisively by children: "*Chair à poisson, chair à poisson!*"—which means, food for the fish. One boy who had been billeted in a peasant's house, said as he left, "We'll never come back."

"But if they're so afraid," I asked Wandel, "why don't they revolt?"

"You don't know the German soldier," Wandel said. "His discipline is complete. He will permit himself to be chained into a boat which he believes is going to take him to a fiery death, or he will commit suicide to seek an easier end, but he will not revolt."

It was about five in the afternoon when we had our second shock of the day. Margot was preparing to serve tea when the doorbell rang. We had already told the boys what to do if this happened, and they hurried into my room, leaving Kitty and myself alone in the living room.

Margot went to answer the door. She returned in a moment, closed the door carefully behind her, and, deathly pale, whispered: "A German officer!"

Kitty looked quickly about the room to make sure that there were no telltale indications. Fortunately Margot had not yet set the table, and there was therefore no sign of the number of persons she expected to serve. She took me by the elbow, and said in a low voice:

"Come with me. We've got to keep him from coming in."

We went into the entry. There stood Captain Weber, the military prosecutor who had ridden into Paris with us, and had promised us, much to our dismay, that he would call.

He seemed very pleased with himself. He was rubbing his hands together in a self-satisfied manner as we came in. He had perfumed himself so strongly that we noticed the odor as soon as we entered the room. I had seen German humorous papers which depicted Prussian officers as preparing for romantic adventures by making lavish use of perfume, but I had thought it an exaggeration. Apparently it was not.

Screwing his monocle more tightly into place, Captain Weber stepped forward, all smiles, and said:

"*Ach,* my dear ladies . . . I was just passing this way, and I thought I would drop in for a moment. I hope I am not intruding."

And before we could think of some way to make plain to him that he was, he went on:

"What a beautiful place you have here! Real American atmosphere!"

And with that he stepped through the door and into the living room before either of us could think of any way of stopping him.

Kitty threw a despairing glance in my direction, and I understood what she wanted. I excused myself hurriedly, and went into my room, where I found the boys tensely straining their ears to catch the conversation. I could hear their heavy breathing, proof of their emotion.

"There's a German officer in the next room," I whispered. "I hope Mrs. Beaurepos will manage to get rid of him shortly. He probably won't look in here, because he hasn't come in any official capacity; but just to be safe, perhaps you had better tiptoe into the bathroom."

"Suppose he wants to go there?" one of the English boys asked.

At this point Dr. Wandel, who had gathered very little idea of what was going on from our whispered English, asked "*Was ist passiert?*"

I told him what had happened. He asked:

"Is he alone?"

I nodded.

"And you are sure he is not on official business? It is probable that no one knows he is here?"

"I can't be sure," I said, "but I think he has only come to pay a social call."

"*Ist in Ordnung*," he said, and a curious glint came into his eyes. "It is quite simple. If he comes into this room, he will not leave it alive. Do nothing. Just trust in me."

I was terror-stricken.

"But you mustn't—" I began.

"On the contrary, *gnaedige Frau*, I must. We have no choice. If he finds us here, I must kill him, otherwise we will all be killed ourselves. That is the only way out."

He spoke quite calmly, as though his proposal to murder Captain Weber were the most reasonable suggestion in the world. And before I could recover my poise sufficiently to translate to the English soldiers what he had said, he was trying to explain to them in his incredibly bad Engish:

"Do nothing. I do. I kill him. You—just look. I kill him *oder* he us kill."

I hurried into the kitchen, which I could reach from my room without going through the living room. Margot was there with her ear pressed to the door, trying to hear the conversation going on in the living room.

I walked over to the kitchen window, and pressed my forehead against the cold pane, trying to think of some means of getting Captain Weber out of the apartment. Suppose Kitty couldn't get rid of him? Suppose he should ask to be shown to the bathroom? Providence had gotten us out of tough spots before, I told myself; but would we get out of this one?

Providence was with us once more. While I was still in the kitchen, the bell rang again. It was Father Christian, back from a series of errands. I pulled him into the kitchen, and told him what had happened.

"Leave it to me, Mrs. Shiber," he said calmly. "I'll get rid of him for you." His eyes twinkled. "You will see the advantages of the cloth."

I led Father Christian into the living room. He stopped in pretended surprise at the sight of Captain Weber.

"Excuse me," he said. "Have I made a mistake? I thought it was today that we had our appointment."

"Oh, but it is!" Kitty cried, picking up her cue perfectly. "Captain Weber just happened to drop by."

And she introduced the two.

"I am so sorry to disturb you, Captain," Father Christian said politely, "but Madame Beaurepos, who has been very kind to some of my parishioners, has consented to go with me to see a needy family this evening. There are many sad cases at this moment, unfortunately."

Captain Weber, who had risen, showed obvious disappointment; but he tried to put the best face on the matter.

"Could I perhaps drive you somewhere?" he asked. "My car is outside."

"Thank you, Captain," Father Christian answered, "but I am afraid my parishioners would not understand if they saw me arrive with a German officer. You realize, of course, how they feel."

"Yes, indeed," said Captain Weber stiffly. "They do not yet understand that we have come to save their country from degradation." And he saluted stiffly, kissed Kitty's hand, and marched, rather than walked, out.

I followed him, and closed the door behind him. Margot, arriving uneasily from the kitchen caught me in her arms as I closed it. Otherwise, I believe I should have fallen to the floor in a dead faint.

## CHAPTER EIGHTEEN

# Check to the Gestapo

BY OCTOBER our wholesale traffic in escapes had run us into financial difficulties. The travelling expenses of the large number of men we had sent out of the country, including the fifty francs per head for getting them across the border, amounted to a substantial sum in itself; but even more expensive was feeding them while they were in Paris. We had only three food cards in the household, and as we often found it impossible to obtain even the amounts of food we were legally entitled to buy, we would have had to resort to the Black Market even for our own needs alone. In addition, everything the boys ate had to come from there. We had no trouble getting food in that way, but we paid through the nose for it.

The Black Market was supplied by truck drivers, who got produce through to the illegal vendors by turning half of each load over to certain German officials, who in turn saw to it that the truckmen got the gas and oil necessary to stay in business. The food which they brought in was sold at prices varying from ten to twenty times the legal rate fixed by the authorities. Often this legal rate was reasonable enough, but the commodities to which it applied couldn't be found. And the lower the rate, the greater was the incentive to divert foodstuffs to the more profitable Black Market.

The official theory was that no one in Paris was starving. Every one had his ration card, and the quantities of food it allowed were at least sufficient to sustain life. But in practice it wasn't possible to get the food your card called for unless you could give up a considerable part of your time looking for it. After standing in line for two or three hours, you might find there was no more of the article you wanted. You would try again the next day, and the next. Eventually, you would get what you wanted—if you could spare the time to wait for it. Margot did that job for us. Standing in line had become the major part of her work. But in many families, where every one worked, no one had time to wait for food, and these poor people often simply went without even the small quantity they were allowed.

The lucky ones were those who had places in the country, where they had accumulated stores of food. The only solution for the others was the Black Market, which did a flourishing business. It was a market where there were never any complaints. No one dared complain. Any protest at the high prices would have meant cutting off the only available source of surplus food. There were plenty of others ready to pay, more than could be accommodated.

The drain that purchases on the Black Market made on our small funds couldn't be remedied. Kitty's family fortune was in England, and there was no possible way she could draw on it. I had sent for money through the American Embassy, but none had yet reached Paris.

"I've got to look around for some money," Kitty said to me one day. "We'll have to give up our work for lack of funds if I don't get some assistance. I think I'll take a little trip to round up some help."

I shuddered at the thought of being left alone, and of having to take care of a group of English soldiers, perhaps, without her. But it was obvious that there was no other way. If Kitty could get to the Free Zone, she knew a number of well-to-do French families who would undoubtedly be glad to help. We had talked that possibility over several times, and Kitty was quite sure she could get contributions from them. But of course it couldn't be done by correspondence; she had to go herself.

"Very well, Kitty," I said. "I'm afraid I'll have to manage without you for a while. But don't stay away any longer than you absolutely have to. I'll be lost without you. And I think the sooner you start, the better. That will bring you back more quickly, perhaps before Father Christian turns up again."

That was a Thursday, and Father Christian's usual day for arriving was Friday. I figured that if Kitty left with the boys the following day, she might be back before the next lot arrived. It was so decided, and the next day she set off with our English soldiers, travelling in the same train, but pretending not to know them.

Left alone, I prepared to create for myself the same sort of arti-

ficial peace I had enjoyed the last time Kitty had left me alone—
no newspapers, no radio broadcasts, no links, as far as I could cut
them, with the world of war and politics. But this time, I was not
destined to remain undisturbed.

The very first night I remained alone, the air-raid sirens sounded.
I was undecided what to do, whether to stay in the apartment, or
seek shelter, when the concierge arrived to tell me that a very comfortable refuge had been fixed up in the cellar of the house next
door, and to suggest that I go there with her. I accepted—and that
gave me an opportunity to see the remarkable reaction of the French
people to an air raid by the British.

They came hurrying out of their apartments to the shelters, not
in fear, but with exaltation. Some of them were singing for joy.
Others embraced, with tears streaming down their cheeks. One man
shouted up at the sky: "Come on! Drop your bombs! We don't
care! We're on your side!" and some one else, up the street, called
through the darkness: *"Vive les Anglais!"*

It was only a few days before that the hated traitor, Marcel Déat,
had written in the *Oeuvre* that people were "naïve" who listened to
"false rumors" about the ability of British fliers to appear over
France. "Don't allow yourself to be misled," he wrote, "by this collective hallucination which seems to delude hundreds of Parisians
into believing that they have seen English airplanes over the city
every day. The German anti-aircraft is strong enough to see to it
that not one British plane will ever cross the Channel. Those who
say the contrary are liars."

It looked as though the Germans had joined the collective hallucination; for now the air-raid sirens were blowing away, as though
they too had decided that there was nothing imaginary about the
British planes.

It was, indeed, the real thing: not just planes, but bombs as well.
For two hours, we stayed in the cellar, while outside we could hear
the roar of airplane motors, the staccato barking of the machine
guns, and the distant explosions of bombs. Every time we heard the
dull crushing explosion of a bomb, the people in the cellar seemed
to take on new life and gaiety. They didn't seem to realize that they
might be killed or wounded themselves. They were too nappy about
this attack against the common enemy!

Some one in the shelter struck up *God Save the King,* and followed with *Tipperary.* Every one else joined in. A few knew the English words. The rest followed the tune wordlessly.

In the darkness of the cellar, where identification was difficult, and all felt free to talk, tongues were loosened, and pro-British and anti-German stories were told.

A woman sitting next to me leaned over and whispered in my ear: "See that man sitting by himself in the corner? He's the Gestapo's undercover man for this building. I'd like to see what kind of a report he'll hand in tomorrow."

Probably his report was corroborated by his fellows all over Paris. For the following night, though we heard the anti-aircraft guns open fire, and the distant sound of bombs, which we learned the next day had fallen on the airfields about Paris, the sirens did not sound; and the reason, we heard, was that the Germans had decided that it was unwise to allow Parisians to get together in the air raid shelters, where anti-German conversations could be carried on with impunity.

That night in the cellar was the first occasion when I had personally an opportunity to see how little effect the German anti-British propaganda had had. It seemed not to have registered at all on the little middle class people, the *petite bourgeoisie.* They revealed their sympathies spontaneously during that air raid.

But there had been other evidences, less striking, it is true, but significant. They were written on the walls.

Everywhere the Germans had put up anti-British propaganda posters. Again and again one passed remnants of such posters which some one had torn from the walls. Sometimes changes had been made in their inscriptions to change their meaning. For instance, one of the favorite placards showed a drowning French sailor, holding the flag of France above the waves. Its message was: "Don't Forget Oran." (That was, of course, where the British fired on the French fleet.) Very seldom could that poster be seen in its original form. Either some one would change it to "Forget Oran," or, more commonly, to "Don't forget!"

Another common poster showed a woman holding an emaciated baby in her arms in the foreground, while behind her could be seen a chubby Churchill, smoking his famous cigar, and smiling contentedly. This one was labeled "See what the blockade is doing to your children!" I once saw one of these posters with the original legend scratched out, and the substitution: "Tell us about our prisoners," while another one had been amended to read, with more appropriateness: "How about our potatoes?" (This was at the period when all the potatoes in the occupied zone had been requisitioned and sent to Germany.)

Then there was the poster which showed on a colored map the French colonies which had been taken under British control—meaning those ruled by de Gaulle. It read: "Frenchmen! Here is what the English have taken from you!" On one such poster I saw, scrawled in what looked like a child's hand, "And our bicycles?"

That referred to the fact that thousands of bicycles had been requisitioned by the Germans. They had a very simple way of doing it. They would simply stop a cyclist in the street, and ask him where he lived and where he worked. Then they would pull out their maps, demonstrate that he could get back and forth on the subway, and therefore didn't need a bicycle—and without further ado, they would make off with it.

In order to protect their posters from alterations, the Germans began to put them higher up on the walls. This made it harder to tamper with them—but it also made them harder to see. And on the space left free by their elevation, chalked inscriptions began to appear. Among the most common were "Vive de Gaulle!" "Down with Hitler!" "Death to the Boche!" and "God bless England!" Among more picturesque legends which I saw were "Doriot, you will be hanged!" (Doriot was an ex-Communist Fascist who put his terroristic anti-Semitic hordes at the service of the Nazis), "To see Venice, join the Greek Army," and "Napoleon, too . . ."

During the week I spent at home, I failed to enjoy the calm and quiet I had hoped for. Far from waiting until the following Friday to bring in his next group, Father Christian sent me three parties during the week, and three times I had to hand them over to Chancel's escorts, and start them on their way. But there were no difficulties. The system was working like a well-oiled machine.

The first two were brought to Paris by other guides than Father Christian himself, and so I assumed that he would no doubt arrive on his regular day, Friday, with a personally escorted convoy. He usually arrived at noon. So I was surprised, on answering the door a few minutes after nine Friday morning, to find it was Father Christian.

"Anything wrong?" I asked, apprehensively. His unusually early arrival seemed alarming.

"Don't worry," Father Christian smiled. "Nothing's wrong. I reached Paris with my boys last night, but I didn't bring them here because I didn't know if you could take care of so many overnight."

"Where are they now?"

"I put them up in a small hotel. I'll bring them over shortly."

I was alarmed at this change in method.

"Oh, dear," I said. "Do you think it was wise to do that—to put up English boys in a Paris hotel, where almost any one might be working for the Gestapo, from the proprietor to the guests? And how about the police registration form?"

"They didn't fill it out," Father Christian said calmly. "You needn't be alarmed. The proprietor of the hotel, Madame Henri, is one of us. We can trust her completely. She is only too happy to help."

"You mean she knows all about it, too?" I gasped. "How long have you known her?"

"Since yesterday," Father Christian answered imperturbably, and in answer to my anguished expression, hastened to add: "I assure you, Madame, there is no cause at all for worry. We priests, you know, are pretty good judges of people. I knew at once from the way she received us that we could depend on her. It was easy to see that she recognized at once that the boys were not French. I didn't have to explain anything. She understood at once. I didn't even ask, but she offered immediately to provide rooms whenever I came to Paris with young men in tow.

"It seems to me that the hotel would be a safer hiding place for us than this apartment. Comings and goings are more normal there. There is always danger that attention will be attracted to your house by the number of strange persons who go in and out. I came over now to suggest you come with me to meet Madame Henri, who is very anxious to make your acquaintance."

I shook my head decidedly.

"I'm sorry, Father," I said, "I don't want to make hers—nor extend knowledge of what we are doing to any one else. Kitty is out of town just now, so I don't know what she would say, but I hope she would agree with me on that. I think too many people are in the secret now. I certainly don't feel comfortable about any more learning it."

"But Madame Shiber," Father Christian protested, "what you don't realize is that all Frenchmen are with us! It is safe for us to ask *any one* to help. No one will betray us, unless we have the very bad luck of falling upon one of the very few persons who serve the Germans. I think, on the contrary, that we should try to gather about us more people who will be able to help us, so that we will have alternate courses of action to fit all possible future situations. From that point of view, it seemed to me that this woman, with her hotel, would be in an ideal position to cooperate with us."

"But we don't *need* any one else," I insisted. "We now have all the persons necessary to do what we want to do. Increasing the number of those who know about it won't help us any, and it will make it more likely that our secret will get out. We must keep the number of those who know it to the absolute minimum. It's the only safe way. I'm terrified whenever I think of the number of people who are in the know now. And now you want us to add Madame Henri to the list!"

"But why should you be so set against Madame Henri?" Father Christian asked, puzzled. "You don't even know her."

"Please don't misunderstand me, Father," I answered. "I have nothing against Madame Henri. How could I, since, as you say, I don't even know her? It's just the principle of the thing—the advisability of keeping knowledge of what we are doing in the smallest circle possible.

"No doubt Madame Henri is the staunchest of patriots—but if she should be arrested by the Gestapo, and if they should torture her to get information—and, you know, every one says they *do* do that—would she be able to keep silent to protect us? We will all be safer—you and I and Kitty—yes, and Madame Henri herself—if she doesn't know anything."

Father Christian seemed suddenly abashed.

"Perhaps you are right," he said. "I hadn't thought of it in that way. We are all taking risks, of course. But we are all in God's hand. I know I am doing his work. I put my trust in him, and I don't worry."

Father Christian's words calmed my fears, and the tranquillity they gave me lasted until after the new group of boys had been started on their way. Expecting no more visitors until Monday, I settled back in an easy chair, peaceful and unworried, and with the sense of satisfaction that comes from the accomplishment of good deeds. My blissful state was short-lived.

Margot came in hardly half an hour after the English soldiers had left, to tell me that a young boy had come to the door asking for Kitty. I recognized him at once. It was Emile, the boy whom Monsieur Durand had sent to our place with the letters which came to his café in answer to our advertisement.

"Well, what is it, Emile?" I asked him.

"Monsieur Durand says there is a Mr. Stove in the café who wants to talk to you, Madame."

Mr. Stove! What a queer name! I couldn't think of any one I knew, or Kitty knew, named Stove.

"What does he want?" I asked.

Emile didn't know. He hadn't seen the mysterious Mr. Stove. All he knew was that he had been told to bring me the message which he had already delivered.

Mr. Stove . . . Mr. Stove. . . . I repeated the name mentally—and then suddenly I saw the light. In French, "w" is pronounced like "v." What the boy was trying to say was "Mr. Stowe"—and that was the name which had been signed to one of the letters we had received in reply to our advertisement, which we hadn't dared answer for fear they were traps.

Hardly had I realized that when a second thought struck me like a blow in the face. How did this man know Kitty's name? The boy had said "Mr. Stove" wanted to speak to me, meaning Kitty, for he had asked for her, and assumed that I was she—yet our advertisement had contained only the name of William Gray!

For a moment, I was riveted to my chair as though I were paralyzed. I couldn't seem to gather my wits, to focus them on the problem of what to do next. I was afraid, as I have not been afraid before or since—no, not even when the Gestapo later came to arrest us. I suppose it was because I was alone, without Kitty to give me courage.

I must escape, I thought. Perhaps I could still catch the train the boys were to take, and get into the unoccupied zone, out of danger, with them. But with feminine intuition, I knew that I wouldn't do that. Suppose Kitty should return, perhaps within an hour or so, and find me gone? I began to grow calmer. After all, we had avoided other dangers before. Perhaps this one could be averted by other means than flight.

While all this was going on in my mind, Emile stood waiting before me. I thought he was beginning to show signs of impatience at my not having thought of an answer for Monsieur Durand. I got up, and said to him:

"Let's go, Emile."

I slipped on my coat and hurried away with the boy. Now that my decision was made, I wanted to get it over as quickly as possible.

I didn't accompany Emile all the way back to Monsieur Durand's café. I sat down at a table in a small restaurant a block away, and told Emile to tell Monsieur Durand to meet me there. I made it very clear that he was to give my message to Monsieur Durand without being overheard by Mr. Stowe, and that he was to tell Monsieur Durand to slip out without attracting any one's attention, that it was very important that he should not be seen.

Monsieur Durand arrived a few minutes later. Evidently Emile had done his job well. The café owner seemed both excited and surprised.

"Did you give our address to this Mr. Stowe?" I asked at once, as he sat down. It was the first thing that came into my head. It was what was worrying me most.

"Of course not," Monsieur Durand said. "Madame Kitty told me not to give the address to any one, so of course I didn't. But tell me, Madame, what has happened? What is the matter?"

"Just a minute, Monsieur Durand," I interrupted. "I'll tell you what I'm afraid of, but first I must know one or two things. How did he know Madame Beaurepos' name?"

"Oh, but he didn't!" Durand explained. "He asked for William Gray. I knew that meant you, of course, so I sent the boy around."

"But you didn't tell him who we were?"

Monsieur Durand showed his strong white teeth in a grin.

"*Pas si bête!*" (I'm not that stupid!)

I breathed again.

"Thank you, Monsieur Durand," I said. "You've done wonderfully. Now tell me all about it."

"It was like this," Durand began. "About an hour ago, this chap came in. I could see at once he wasn't a Frenchman. He beckoned to me, and I came over to his table. He asked me to sit down—said he wanted to talk to me. I sat down next to him, and he leaned over and began whispering. He said he had written a letter to William Gray and addressed it to him at my café, but that he had gotten no answer, and no one had come to see him. Now, he said, he had come here in the hopes of meeting Mr. Gray.

"I tried to pump him, and finally he confided to me, in an even lower whisper, that he was an Englishman. He said he was in great danger, and he didn't know how much longer he would succeed in keeping out of the clutches of the Germans. He said he wanted to find William Gray because he thought he might help him to escape."

"What did you say?" I broke in excitedly.

"You may be sure, Madame, that I'm not as stupid as I look," Durand answered. "I couldn't tell whether his story was true or not. I played safe. I told him that I didn't want to be mixed up in helping anybody to escape, that my customers' affairs were none of my business, and that anyway I didn't know any William Gray. I said people often gave the café as an address, and then came and asked if there were any letters for them, and that the name seemed vaguely familiar—I thought I had received some letters for a William Gray, but I wasn't quite sure. If he wanted to stay there, I told him, he was welcome to, and if William Gray came in to ask for mail, I would introduce him."

"And then you sent for me—that is, for Kitty?"

"Yes. I thought that if Madame Kitty came in, I could let her look at this fellow without his noticing her, and she could decide whether she wanted to talk to him or not."

I thought the situation over for a moment.

"What do you think of him, Monsieur Durand?" I asked finally. "You see all kinds in your café. You ought to be a good judge of people. Do you really think he's an English soldier trying to escape?"

Monsieur Durand scratched his forehead for a moment in evident embarrassment.

"That's hard to say," he said. "We talked French at first. His French wasn't bad, but he had a foreign accent. It didn't sound quite English—a little more like German. I told him he could speak English if he wanted, because I had learned some English in the United States. So he did speak a few words in English. Of course, I don't know the language very well—but it didn't sound quite right to me. And then he shifted back to French. He said he was afraid of attracting attention by speaking English—although his voice was so low no one could possibly have heard him. But that's all I—"

He stopped suddenly, his mouth ajar. Then he slapped his hand hard on his knee, and exclaimed: "*Diable! Que je suis stupide!* How idiotic of me only to remember now!"

"For goodness sake!" I said. "Stop calling yourself names and tell me—what's it all about?"

"I just remembered," Durand said. "I didn't notice it at the time, but I can see it now before my eyes just as plain as if it were lying on that table. That's the strangest thing!"

"Please, Monsieur Durand, before I go mad!" I pleaded. "*What's* the strangest thing?"

"It just struck me," Durand said. "He lit a cigarette while I was talking to him, and I remember now what the pack he took it from looked like. It was a German military cigarette—the kind they issue to soldiers. I'm sure of it. Now how would a British soldier get a pack of those cigarettes?"

I grasped Monsieur Durand's hand across the table.

"Sit tight, Monsieur Durand," I said. "Let me tell you something. Don't show too much surprise. Some one may be watching us. What you have just told me confirms my belief—your Mr. Stowe is a Gestapo man."

Monsieur Durand's healthy reddish face turned a dead white.

"Do you really think so?" he groaned.

"I certainly do," I said. "Just think it over. One of the letters we got for William Gray was signed by a Mr. Stowe. We thought it was a trap and didn't answer it. Now if this man were really a British soldier, he would be afraid of a trap, too. He would hardly walk into your café like this if he got no answer. He would be more cautious. Besides, if he could move about France so easily as to be able to come to Paris alone and hunt up your café, would he need help to escape? I'm sure he's a Gestapo man. You'd better be careful. If he doesn't find his William Gray, he may take it into his head to arrest you. He's been friendly so far, because he hopes to catch his prey by not arousing your suspicions. So he accepted what you said. But if he doesn't succeed, he'll certainly want to know more about your rôle in all this than you've told him."

"What shall I do?" Monsieur Durand asked helplessly. "What is going to happen now?"

"I'll tell you what you can do," I said. "I have travelling permits. You could go to the station now, just as you are, without returning to the café, and cross into the unoccupied zone. I can give you a travel permit and send you to a man who will get you across the border. And that will leave our Gestapo man at a dead end. He will know you were guilty, of course; but you will be out of reach, safe."

"I can't," Durand moaned, looking at me with a piteously terrified expression. "My wife, my children—they would arrest them. Besides, everything I have is here—my home, my business. No, I can't leave. . . . Perhaps it isn't as serious as you think. You may be exaggerating the danger. . . . I know what I'll do. I'm going straight back to the café, and if he's still there, I'll ask him to leave. I'll tell him I can't take the risk of having English soldiers in my place—that I don't know any William Gray, and that I don't want to have anything to do with him."

He said this with a great air of decision, as though his mind were made up. But he made no move to start. I could see that he hadn't convinced himself that he could get rid of his unwelcome customer so easily. Suddenly his face seemed to cloud over, as though he were grappling with an idea difficult to formulate; then it spread into a broad smile, and a cunning look came into his eyes. He said:

"There *is* a way out. A beautiful way. I'm surprised I didn't think of it before. I'm going to phone at once to Gestapo headquarters and report that there's a suspicious Englishman in my place. That clears me. They couldn't possibly suspect me after that."

And before I could say anything, he was in the phone booth at the other end of the room.

Hardly had Durand left the table than I was seized with fear that I had made a terrible mistake. Suppose this Mr. Stowe really were an English soldier? Then I would not only have failed to come to his help when he had turned to us, but I would have been responsible for his capture. I would have converted our advertisement into the trap which he might have feared it was.

I was so tortured by my conscience that I hardly acknowledged Monsieur Durand's good-bye as he hurried off to his café to receive the Gestapo when they arrived. I tried desperately to convince myself that I could have made no mistake. But, to my horror, the deductions which had seemed so unmistakable a moment before, when I had put them to Monsieur Durand, seemed to dissolve into nothingness, and I found myself arguing that he might very well be an Englishman after all.

Suppose Durand didn't think his English very good? After all, as he said himself, he was no judge. And the soldier might have been an Australian or a Yorkshireman. It was natural enough that a soldier in hiding wouldn't want to speak English in public. As for the pack of cigarettes—had Durand really seen them, or just imagined it afterwards? He hadn't noticed them at the time.

And about getting from Rheims to Paris—it wasn't so far, and it would be in the natural direction of escape anyway. If he were desperate, he might risk trying to get in touch with this William Gray, whose advertisement might have provided his only ray of hope.

The torture of these thoughts was too great for me to bear. I had to see what was happening, to reassure myself if I could. I walked to the café, and though it was rather chilly, sat down on the terrace to see what would happen.

I had only been there a few minutes when a German official car drove up. Three men in civilian clothes jumped out.

"That's it!" I thought. "That's the Gestapo!" And I writhed in internal anguish at the thought that I might have put them on the trail of an English soldier.

They couldn't have been in the café more than a minute, when the door opened and they emerged again. Two of the three men who had entered were on either side of another man whom I had not seen before, each one holding one arm. The third man followed behind, as though alert for any attempt to break away. My heart sank. It looked as if I had been wrong.

But as the door swung shut behind them, and they stepped from the terrace into the dusk of the street, the two men let go of the other's arms. All of them broke out into sudden boisterous laughter. They all climbed into the car, and "Mr. Stowe," still laughing, courteously offered the others cigarettes from a package which, I was quite sure now, was German military issue. And off they drove.

I felt better. I thanked God for allowing me to witness this scene, which set at rest a conscience which otherwise would have tormented me all the rest of my days.

## CHAPTER NINETEEN

# Made in Heaven

Kitty seemed tired and rather depressed when she returned from her trip to the unoccupied zone. I thought she must have failed in her mission. But I was wrong. Her first action was to open her bag, and pull out a sheaf of banknotes, which she tossed onto the table between us.

"Twenty-five thousand francs," she said. "That ought to keep us going for a while. And I've been promised more later if we need it."

The next two weeks were without incident. Father Christian arrived regularly with his young charges, without the slightest difficulties. Chancel called to tell us that he had received word that the first boys we had sent out had arrived in London. Our own troubles were eased by the contribution from Kitty's friend, which enabled us to feed the boys who arrived in Paris as well as any one could, through purchases made on the Black Market.

But though food was not too hard to obtain, given the necessary money, fuel was another matter. With the end of October, bitter cold set in; and Paris was universally unheated. The ration permitted was 55 pounds of coal per family per month—or enough to heat one room about two hours daily. Even this amount usually could not be found.

Persons calling on friends often carried blankets with them to keep themselves warm. I spent one evening at a friend's house sitting before a fireplace where there was no fire. My hostess had ironically tacked her coal card to the wall beside the fireplace, to represent the fuel to which she had a right, but which she couldn't find for sale.

The Germans were not bothered by the coal shortage. They had plenty. Their offices and their apartments were kept well supplied. The sight of coal trucks unloading their precious cargoes into the cellars of German-occupied buildings was one of the things which infuriated freezing Parisians the most.

We did not go out much. For one thing, two, and then three, days a week were pretty well occupied with taking care of Father Christian's boys. And on the days when we were free, we preferred to avoid contacts with other persons, in order to discourage visitors to our own place, who might come at the wrong time. If we didn't want people to come to see us, obviously we had to avoid as much as possible going to see them; and when invitations turned up which we couldn't possibly refuse, we made it a rule that only one would go, leaving the other behind in case of emergencies.

It still happened that close friends would drop in on us without notice occasionally, and in that case, our technique was invariable. If the doorbell rang when the boys were there, they made immediately for the bathroom, the safest hiding place in our apartment, and we did our best to keep the visitor from entering. We didn't expect that our old friends would dash to the police and denounce us even if they did catch us, of course, but we both felt that the fewer persons in our secret, the better. Taking unnecessary chances was not in our plans.

After a little experimentation, our evasive tactics boiled down to one of two methods. If we happened to go to the door dressed in anything suitable for street wear, we would say: "My dear, how glad I am to see you! I was just going out. Are you going my way?"

That occasionally let us in for unplanned walks, but in the frigid days of late October and early November, walking out of doors was a pleasant contrast to stationary freezing in the apartment.

When we were trapped in some costume distinctly impossible for street wear, we adopted our second subterfuge. Making no move to lead the way from the hall into the apartment, we would, as in the first case, express delight at seeing our friend, but then add in a whisper: "Keep your voice low. There's an inspector inside. He says he's come about our taxes, but you never can tell."

This usually got rid of the visitor with the greatest speed. In Paris in those days the ordinarily innocent word "inspector" evoked the image of the Gestapo for every one.

As a rule, whenever we achieved one of these oustings of an old friend, we had to promise a visit of our own; and our method for fulfilling these promises with the least strain on our schedule was to attend occasional gatherings where we knew a number of them would be together. Thus no one realized that we were leading a more secluded life than formerly. What difference there was in our habits they attributed to the changed conditions of war—lack of transportation, necessary preoccupation with securing food, and so forth.

On these sorties, I carried my blanket not only because of the heating problem, but also because I was obliged to spend the night wherever I found myself if I happened to stay too late to get home by ten. The Germans had decreed a rigorous curfew; and as a result, Parisians not only became quite accustomed to spending the night on sofas in strange apartments, but even hardened to sleeping on improvised beds made of two chairs.

Violators of this curfew (later extended to 11 o'clock) were made to sit up all night on the hard wooden benches of the nearest police station. In the morning they were set to work washing the corridors and lavatories of the barracks, polishing the shoes of the German soldiers, peeling potatoes in the military kitchens, and performing similar services until noon, and then released with warnings that a second offense would be more seriously punished. Second offenders were rare.

Under such conditions, social evenings naturally became fewer; and the subjects discussed at these gatherings were very different from those popular before the war. Typical was the first such gathering I attended that winter, at the invitation of so old and so close a friend that I felt I couldn't refuse. Her parties had always been renowned for their glitter and luxury, and the conversational brilliance of her guests. War and occupation had changed all that.

I went alone, of course, for Kitty had to stay home during my absence. The blackout was total, and as it grew dark early at this time of year, I groped my way to her house, my blanket clutched fearfully under my arm. I wasn't quite sure I was even ringing the right doorbell, but after a moment the door opened, and I was able to find my way in by the light of a minute lamp completely encircled in a blue shade.

"That's all the light we dare show," my hostess apologized. "If the German patrol saw the slightest glimmer from outside, we'd pay for it. We only dare keep enough light here to save you from breaking your neck."

When I entered, I found a group which looked quite different from the well-dressed society ordinarily to be found at my friend's house. All had their overcoats on, and the men were even wearing their hats. The women as a rule had their shawls or blankets wrapped around them like hoods.

It was freezing cold in the room, yet a glance at the big stove rigged up before the fireplace showed a faint gleam of fire. Through the transparent door, I could see that the glowing ashes were the remains of the paper balls with which Parisians were reduced to heating their apartments. They were made from newspapers, cardboard boxes and books whose literary value was considered inferior to their worth as fuel. The method was to soak them in water for 24 hours, until the paper turned into a sort of pulp which could be molded into balls. They were then dried, and made fair fuel for stoves—but unfortunately a fuel which burned too quickly to give much warmth.

"German stoves are white-hot compared to this one," a man was saying, as I entered the room. I recognized a well-known Parisian lawyer, who in other days would probably have been discussing the latest legal gossip. "Yet we can't even get the small rations we're entitled to! Of course, it's not enough to heat us even if we did get it. Perhaps that's why the Germans don't consider it worth while to give it to us."

"I met a friend today," some one else spoke up, "who's had a stroke of luck. A Gestapo agent has moved into his house."

"Luck!" a woman exclaimed. "I'd be afraid to sleep at night! What's lucky about it?"

"Why, don't you know?" said the first. "If even a single German state employee moves into an apartment building, the whole building gets enough coal to keep it warm—delivered to the door. Better pray for a German in your place."

That was a prayer I couldn't echo. I would have welcomed more heat in my place, but the last thing I wanted was to have a Gestapo man living in our building, apt to meet our protégés in the hall or the elevator. Heat so acquired, I decided, wasn't among my desires.

And so the conversation went on. Among these people, who on other occasions would have been discussing the arts, or sociological, scientific or professional matters, the level of conversation had been reduced to absorption in the attempt to satisfy the most primitive needs—food and shelter.

One man with a number of small children told how he had burned up all his wooden furniture to keep them warm. There was no longer a chair or a table in his house, he said, and they sat about on rugs like Orientals. A university professor told of gathering twigs in the public gardens to burn in his stove. We heard of a well-known writer who had burned up his valuable library because he could not stand the cold, and of a famous society figure who stayed in bed all day to keep warm.

From heat, the conversation turned to food, and from food to clothes. An exclusively feminine group huddled at one end of the room got started on clothes first—but this time their subject was not style and fashion. These women a few months ago had been among the smartest and best-dressed in the capital; today their conversation swung between the two extremes of meeting the problem of clothing themselves, no matter how, and of nostalgic regret for the luxuries they could find no longer.

There were no mentions of new dresses, as there would have been a few months earlier. The idea of a new dress had become something fantastic and unthinkable. The talk was of the insoluble problems of remodelling old dresses to keep them wearable. There were no thread on the market, no needles, no buttons, no clips. A sewing needle was an object so precious that the most generous woman hesitated to lend it to her best friend. Thread was obtained by unravelling completely worn cloth. Ribbons and loops were employed instead of buttons. The Parisienne's greatest asset was the same as always—her limitless ingenuity.

Many of the women there bewailed the lack of what in happier days they had looked upon as necessities of the toilet—cold cream, face powder, eau de Cologne, soap. Not even ordinary laundry soap was to be had, let alone the delicately perfumed brands to which these ladies had been accustomed.

One of the best known women of Parisian society lamented, almost in tears:

"If only I could get a bar of soap, any soap, that would actually dissolve in water and provide a lather—not the substitutes they give us nowadays, hard as rock and as difficult to dissolve! . . . I think more than anything else, more even than plenty of food, I would like a hot bath with lots of suds!"

And the women about her sighed in unison, moved by this evocation of something which had once seemed to them completely ordinary, but which now had taken its place among the greatest and most unattainable of luxuries.

Because we did not often go about to such gatherings, we were probably less well-informed than most inhabitants of Paris about what was going on in our own city, but we were better informed on the news of northern France in general. The boys Father Christian was bringing to us came from all parts of this region, and many of them had heard reports of the activities of the Germans and the extent of resistance in the various localities of the occupied zone, and even the prohibited zone—which was that part of the territory held by the Germans which was forbidden even to Frenchmen, unless they lived in it. This was composed chiefly of the coastal region, from which the Germans at first hoped to launch their invasion of England, and which later they guarded with equal, if not greater, strictness, for fear the British themselves would invade.

One of the letters we had received at the time of our advertisement in *Paris-Soir* had come from a town within this prohibited region, Bergasse. We had not dared answer it, and since it was in the prohibited region, we could neither visit it nor get any word there. Kitty thought this letter was a genuine one, and our failure to answer it weighed heavily on her conscience. She had mentioned the matter to me several times, but there was no way we could think of to inquire safely for the writer of the letter.

It was on a day when some of the soldiers were lunching at our apartment that Kitty was reminded of the letter from Bergasse by the fact that one of the young men with us that day had succeeded in getting out of the prohibited zone. The thought gave her hope; and she asked Father Christian:

"Tell me, Father, would it be possible for you to make contact with some one in Bergasse?"

"*Mais certainement,*" said the young priest. "Why not?"

"Don't forget that it's in the prohibited zone," Kitty warned.

"And don't forget," Father Christian smiled back, "that the servants of the Church are present wherever human beings gather. The priest of Bergasse is an old friend of mine. I am sure he would be willing to be of any service. And I believe I could get a message to him without any difficulty. What do you want in Bergasse?"

Kitty told him about the letter received from that point, and gave it to him, in the hope that he would be able to check on it in some way.

Three weeks passed. Father Christian didn't mention the matter again, and, to tell the truth, I had forgotten it.

It was a Friday, and we expected Father Christian with a group of the boys again. We planned a special lunch, for we were celebrating the saving of our 150th English soldier. It was Margot who had called attention to the number. On the previous visit of Father Christian, she had asked:

"Father, are you bringing four boys next time as usual?"

"I suppose so," he said. "Why?"

"Because if you are," she said, "I would like to bake a birthday cake. I have been counting up, and that will make exactly 150 we have sent away."

"That *is* an occasion, Margot!" Father Christian said gravely. "I will make it a point to bring four boys, and I will be sure to come with them myself, to help celebrate the occasion."

Even Kitty seemed surprised at the total we had reached. She threw a smile at me.

"Did you hear, Etta?" she asked. "One hundred and fifty boys! Almost a whole company! It mounts up fast, doesn't it?"

"Add the Frenchmen who escorted them out," I said, "and you've got more than your company. Of course, we can't claim full credit for those."

But Margot was thwarted of her desire to make a cake. Materials for it simply didn't exist. Not one of the necessary ingredients could be found—in fact, even candles for it wouldn't have been procurable, if we had ever gotten that far. However, she did get hold of two bottles of excellent Chateau-Neuf du Pape, and we had those on hand for our celebration.

When Father Christian arrived, Margot set the table in gala fashion for ourselves and the boys. She called his attention to the wine, and apologized for not being able to provide the cake.

"Well, never mind about that, Margot," Father Christian consoled her. "I have done a little something myself to provide a special note for this occasion. Mme. Beaurepos, Mme. Shiber, allow me to present Wing Commander John Hitchcock, of Bergasse."

Kitty gasped.

"Father Christian! Without saying a word . . .! Why, this is lovely! That's the most beautiful present I've ever had in my whole life! But how did you do it? Wasn't it terribly hard to get him out of the prohibited zone?"

"Oh, no, no," said Father Christian, deprecatingly. "It was easy enough. Nothing special, really."

The young R.A.F. man, who didn't look as though he could be over twenty, with his candid boyish face (one might almost have said girlish, if his expression had not borne the traces of the hardships he must have endured), disputed this.

"Nothing special!" he said. "I say! It was very special, if you ask me. Do you know what he did? He . . ."

But Kitty's conscience was still troubling her, and without even noticing that she was interrupting, it seemed to me, she burst out with her question.

"Tell me," she said, "when you didn't get any answer to your letter to us—weren't you—well, disappointed?"

His face clouded.

"Oh, yes . . . that letter," he murmured. "Well, to tell you the truth, I was rather down in the mouth when nothing happened. It had picked me up so, you know, when I saw your advertisement. . . . Well, perhaps I'd better tell you the whole story.

"I was at Dunkirk . . . couldn't get onto the boats. I was in the rear guard, and when we got too thin, of course, there was no holding them. They just broke through, and we split up, every man for himself, and took to the woods. I knew one thing, I wasn't going to be taken . . . but I wished I had been for a while, when I ran into a German patrol, and got a bullet in the shoulder. I gave them the slip all right, but then I went out . . . don't know how long. I may have been unconscious for a few hours or a few days. Woke up in a peasant's barn. Seems a peasant girl . . . good looker she was, too; not half bad . . . almost trod on me while she was out picking mushrooms. She told her father, he came out after dark, carried me in, and bedded me down in his hay loft. They got in a doctor, another good chap . . . he would have been for it, of course, too, if they knew what he did for me . . . and he patched me up fairly well. But then the question was, how to get out of there, and back to England.

"Then I saw your ad. I knew what it meant, at once. So I wrote. Then, of course, nothing happened. I'd pinned everything on that letter . . . only hope I had, as far as I could see, of ever getting away. When nothing happened, I had some pretty black days. Even thought of giving myself up, once or twice. But I thought, perhaps something will come of it yet. After all, if it had been a trap, something would have happened by now. It must have been all right. I'll wait. So I waited . . . and finally the Father appeared. He's a wonderful man, Father Christian. . . . But, Father," he said teasingly, "do you think it's right for a priest to make light of the marriage ceremony?"

"If you call it making light to combine a good match with a good deed, I certainly don't," said Father Christian, with a twinkle in his eye. "I'm thoroughly satisfied with everything that happened. And a fine young couple they make, too."

"For goodness sake," I said. "What's all this about a marriage? Did you have to dress up as a bride, Mr. Hitchcock?"

"Well, nearly," Hitchcock grinned. "It seems that Father Christian talked a girl in his village into marrying a peasant boy in Bergasse. Now in that part of the country, when a young man marries a girl from another village, a party goes to fetch her, a group of young men and girls, in gaily decorated carts. The church authorities arranged a collective pass for the party, and I went along to Conchy-sur-Conche as one of the wedding party."

"But didn't the Germans check up on the wedding party?" I asked. "Did you get by without question?"

"That's the best part of it," Hitchcock said, smiling at Father Christian. "They check up very carefully on men of military age, but they don't pay much attention to girls. So I dressed up as a girl, and went in their cart. The collective pass specified twelve girls. All the Germans did was count us. They looked at the individual papers of the men. And on the way back there were still twelve girls, of course; for the bride had taken my place."

"Well, Father Christian," Kitty said playfully, "I didn't think you would turn match-maker to rescue this young man."

"Oh, it wasn't that at all," said Father Christian. "I happened to know that the girl had been engaged to a young man in the Bergasse neighborhood since before the war—so when you mentioned Bergasse, that gave me an idea. I just told her that if she were going to get married, she might just as well do it right away, and she could perform a patriotic service at the same time. I'll guarantee that that marriage was one of the kind that's made in heaven."

## CHAPTER TWENTY

# Two Scares

ON NOVEMBER 23, Kitty received a letter from the Free Zone. It had been mailed in Paris, so that we knew at once how it had reached us. It was a common thing for people crossing the border secretly to carry mail for friends, posting it after they got into the other zone. It was the only way communication could be maintained between the occupied and unoccupied regions.

Kitty opened the letter, scanned it briefly, and announced:

"I'll have to take another trip."

She tossed it over to me. It was from the same friend who had given her 25,000 francs when she had made her last visit to the unoccupied zone. He wrote that he had succeeded in realizing his plans, and suggested that Kitty get in touch with him at once, since he was leaving soon for North Africa, where he had an estate.

"What does he mean by 'his plans'?" I asked.

"He told me before that he was trying to sell some property he has near the Italian border, and if he succeeded, he could let us have enough money to keep us going indefinitely," Kitty said. "I suppose he didn't want to make it too plain, but that must be what he meant. I had better go at once, if he's leaving the country."

"How long do you expect to be gone?" I asked.

"At least two weeks," she said, "and don't worry if I take three. As long as I'm crossing the border again, I'm going to clean up all our outstanding affairs. First I'll go to Marseilles to see the writer of this letter. Then I'll go to Lyons. Chancel told me yesterday that Captain Handsby—you remember him, the one who was so nervous —has been arrested by the Vichy police, and is being held there. I have some fairly influential friends in Lyons who may be able to do something for him. Then I want to go to Périgueux, where I know a wholesale grocer who has to travel a lot on business. He's offered to help get the boys around in the unoccupied zone."

I probably didn't look too happy at the prospect of being left alone for as long as three weeks, for Kitty added:

"I hope nothing unusual happens while I'm away. But in case anything unexpected does occur, you can always go to Chancel for help."

I tried to mask with a smile the fear I felt at looking forward to the three weeks when I would be left alone again. But I knew Kitty had to go, and there was no point in burdening her with my private fears.

"I'll be all right," I told her. "Everything is running like clockwork. Between Father Christian and Chancel, I'm almost unnecessary. Don't worry, take your time, and I'll manage."

Kitty left the next day, taking the same train as our latest batch of English soldiers. Once again I prepared to settle down to a comparatively calm period; once again I couldn't do it.

It was the Sunday after Kitty left, when I was alone in the apartment (Margot was taking a day off) that Monsieur Durand, the café owner, burst in, a paper in his hand and rage in his face. He slapped the paper down on a table and shouted:

"What are you two up to now? Have you both gone crazy?"

I couldn't imagine what was wrong. I answered calmly:

"Judging from your manner, Monsieur Durand, I should say that it is you who have gone crazy. Would you mind telling me what is the matter?"

Impressed by my tone, Durand became a little quieter; but it was still with considerable excitement that he pointed to the newspaper.

"Excuse me, Madame," he said, "but I think I have a right to be very much annoyed. After the incident of the other day, I thought you would have sufficient discretion not to involve me in your affairs again. But without even asking my permission, you have placed another advertisement. This time I certainly wouldn't have given my consent. It was too near a thing last time."

I read the advertisement on which he was holding a trembling finger. Sure enough, it seemed to be word for word the same as our previous announcement:

William Gray (formerly of Dunkirk) is looking for his friends and relatives. Address Café Moderne, Rue Rodier, Paris.

"Monsieur Durand," I said, puzzled, "I assure you that we didn't place this advertisement. It seems to be exactly the same as the other one, but we gave no orders that it should be repeated."

"Perhaps Madame Kitty did it without your knowledge," Durand suggested.

"Oh, I'm sure she didn't!" I cried. "In the first place, she would have told me. And in the second, she agreed with me after the other affair that we mustn't use your address again, and, in fact, had better not go near the café ourselves for a while. . . . Goodness! I hope you haven't led the Gestapo here! They must be watching your place! Monsieur Durand, I am afraid it is you who have committed the indiscretion by coming here, not us; for we didn't insert that advertisement."

"But if you didn't, who did?" Durand asked, uncertainly.

"The Gestapo!" I answered. I was certain of it. It had come to me like a flash when I remembered our decision not to go near the café again. "It must have been them. It couldn't have been any one else. We know already that they spotted the announcement and guessed at its meaning. They haven't dropped the case. This is their latest method. Perhaps they inserted that advertisement on purpose to see what you would do, who you would come to when you saw it."

"*Mon Dieu!*" said Monsieur Durand, "What have I done? What can I do now?"

"Nothing," I said. "If they followed you, the damage has already been done. But it may not have been for that at all that they had the ad reprinted. Perhaps they hoped to trap some English boys that way themselves. You may have some one representing himself as William Gray calling at your café for letters."

"And if I get any?"

"You are a good Frenchman, Monsieur Durand," I said. "If William Gray does receive any mail, I'm sure that you will see to it that it isn't delivered to the Gestapo."

Monsieur Durand left, apparently relieved. I had succeeded in convincing him that the Gestapo had wanted to catch English soldiers, not ourselves, and that, as he had previously cleared himself by denouncing their spy, they were probably not watching him. But

I hadn't succeeded in convincing myself. I pictured a Gestapo agent in Monsieur Durand's café watching him as he unfolded the paper, seeing the fear on his face, and following him as he rushed straight to my apartment. I sat at home, alone, quivering with fear, and expecting the peal of the bell at any instant. But as the hours passed I grew a little calmer. I reasoned that if Monsieur Durand had really been followed, we would both have been arrested by now. In fact, the most probable thing would have been that the Gestapo men would have burst in as we were talking together, to catch us red-handed.

Yet my heart was in my mouth all day, and when the bell rang at 9 o'clock, I jumped from my chair with a start, and stood motionless, in terror, for a moment, afraid to answer the door. But Margot had not yet returned from her day off, and there was nothing to do except go.

There were two young men standing outside the door. One of them said in French, "Where is Madame Kitty?"

I said she was not at home, and made no move to step aside to let them in. But the young man who had spoken simply shouldered me aside and entered, pulling his companion along after him.

Then, suddenly, I recognized him. At least, I thought, this wasn't the Gestapo—but I was almost as displeased to see him as if he had been a German agent. He was a young French seaman with whom we had had an unpleasant experience two weeks earlier. He was one of the escorts provided by Chancel for our English boys, but disregarding the instructions that had been given him to pick them up in the street, he had come to the apartment.

"Weren't you told to wait for our boys outside?" Kitty had asked.

"Of course I was," he said insolently. "But I was tired of wandering around with no place to go. I'd rather wait here."

"But that isn't the point," Kitty said. "It's dangerous for you to come up here. It's bad enough to have to smuggle the Englishmen into the house without any more persons coming in and out. It might give the whole thing away."

"Are you playing at soldiers, too?" the sailor asked. "I'm sick of orders and discipline. I'm doing what I want now, not what I'm told."

And he threw himself down on the sofa, stretched his legs comfortably out on it, and refused to be budged until the group left at 7 o'clock. Now here he was back again, and I was decidedly not pleased to see him, especially as I was alone in the apartment.

"How do you happen to be here?" I asked him. "Didn't you go to the unoccupied zone with the others?"

"I went all right," he said. "But I came back—with my friend here."

"You came back?" I repeated. "But how did you get across?"

"Same way I went," he grinned. "Your route . . . I couldn't see any sense in staying. Conditions are just as bad as here. No work anywhere."

"Work!" I said. "I didn't know that was why you wanted to cross the line."

"Listen, lady," he said. "Don't make me laugh. You don't think I was such a sap as to go to England to join de Gaulle, do you? The war's over, and I'm glad of it. I'm not fighting for any one, any more. Now—where's Madame Kitty?"

"I've told you that she's not here," I said, becoming angry at his manner. "And in any case, I'm sure there's nothing she wants to see you about."

"There's something I want to see her about, though," the sailor said. "She owes me some money, and I mean to have it."

I was stupefied. It had only begun to dawn on me that both men were drunk. In the ensuing conversation that became very plain, as both of them began to lapse into incoherence. Their argument, as nearly as I could make it out, was that Kitty should pay them for the valuable time they had consumed in escorting her English boys to the unoccupied zone, and also for the time they had "wasted" there. The claim made me furious.

"You're drunk, both of you," I shouted at them, quite beside myself with rage and the nervous tension I had been under all day; and I tried to push them out of the room. But drunk though they were, I hadn't the strength to move them.

Fortunately Margot arrived at this moment. By a combination of her brawn and a barrage of violent Breton French which she poured out at them, mingled with threats to call the police, she finally got them out into the hall, and bolted the door behind them. For a few minutes we could hear them outside, drunkenly cursing at us, and claiming that we owed them "damages"; but finally they went away.

I was a nervous wreck. This incident, coupled with Durand's visit, gave me the impression that a net was closing in around us. The two happenings of the day showed how unexpectedly dangers could arise from our situation. And now I was afraid that the two Frenchmen, who, if they hadn't been so drunk, would have realized very well that we didn't dare call the police, might take their revenge by informing on us. I began to wonder if I shouldn't have given them some money to get rid of them, to keep them quiet. But that would have opened up a prospect of continuous future blackmailing, and I was able to console myself with the realization that this would only have provided a momentary solution to our problem.

I went to bed without supper. I couldn't eat, although in these days of deprivation, I was almost constantly hungry. As usual, I read the paper before going to sleep—and that made sleep impossible.

In heavy display type, I came across this notice in it:

## 10,000 FRANCS REWARD!

Following the decree establishing the death penalty for all those who hide English soldiers or aid them to escape, the German High Command announces that it will pay 10,000 francs reward to any person providing names and addresses of those engaged in this criminal activity.

I dropped the paper with fear pounding away at my heart. Those two Frenchmen who had just left, I thought—they would turn Judases for the sake of the money they failed to get here. Suppose they see this announcement. Won't they denounce us at once?

I lay in bed with my eyes wide open, unable to sleep. I was too panicky to think intelligently. My mind ran a race with the same thoughts, over and over, never reaching any conclusion or finding any solution, but starting all over again, interminably, at the same point. At 2 o'clock, I gave up the attempt to sleep. I got up, and put some water on the electric grill to make tea. While it was heating, I prowled through the apartment, going through all the closets, opening every drawer, looking underneath even the heaviest pieces of furniture for anything that might be incriminating. I even tore out the fly-leaf from a volume of Byron, which one of the English boys had left behind him, after writing in it a dedication expressing his gratitude for what we had done for him, and burned it.

I drank my tea, and continued my hunt for tell-tale indications. It was 4 o'clock when I finished. Whether it was because I had exhausted myself with my efforts, or because the belief that I had destroyed all evidence against us had settled my mind, I fell into a heavy sleep as soon as I got into bed again.

## CHAPTER TWENTY-ONE

# The Arrest

IN SPITE of the late hour at which I had gotten to sleep, I was up before eight the next morning. According to my usual habit, I was eating my customary breakfast of coffee and toast standing. I never felt like taking the trouble to sit down to a table to eat breakfast if I were alone.

The door-bell startled me.

"Who could be ringing so early?" I asked myself. Margot had gone out to the market, so I went to the door myself to see who was there.

Two men were standing in the hall. They were in civilian clothes, but both carried briefcases. It had become the mark of their profession, the tell-tale stamp that replaced the uniform. I was sure at once what they had come for; but, oddly, I was not frightened. Meeting the emergency was less alarming than wondering when, and how, it would come.

One of them spoke to me in French:

"Where is Mme. Beaurepos?" he asked.

"She's not at home?" I said.

"Where is she?" he insisted.

"She's gone to Tours," I said. I don't know why I selected Tours. I knew I mustn't admit that she had left the occupied zone.

"When will she be back?" the man continued.

"Why are you asking all these questions about Mme. Beaurepos?" I asked—although I knew well enough. But he confirmed my suspicions by producing a badge, uttering at the same time the dread words:

"German Secret Police."

I was right. It was the Gestapo!

Somehow this scene was a disappointing anti-climax. Ever since the June day when we had first returned to Paris with William Gray hidden in our car, now five months past, I had lived in constant expectation of this scene. Not a single day had passed when I had not visualized it in some form or other. I had lived in constant dread of this moment, asking myself how I would behave, and if I would be able to keep my head. And now that it had come, I was calm and cool, as though it had been an everyday occurrence. Perhaps it was because the event seemed so much less spectacular than I had expected—simply two ordinary looking men, in civilian clothes and carrying briefcases, standing politely at the door of my apartment, like salesmen. Or perhaps it was because I had milked the situation dry of all its terrors in advance.

I remember that I looked into the small antique mirror hanging on the wall of the hall, and was surprised to find that I was smiling. "Perhaps I ought not to smile," I told myself. "It might annoy them, under the circumstances. I must be very careful now, and make no mistakes."

As I look back, it seems to me that I must have acted in the grip of some cold intensity, a sort of trance. I must have responded to the demands of the moment like an automaton or a somnambulist, my mind closed tight to thoughts of the future or to anything except meeting the immediate emergency. It was with complete composure that I let the two men in, and followed them into the living room, towards which they moved at once without waiting for me to indicate the way.

Either they assumed that I did not understand German, or they were indifferent to my hearing them. At least they seemed to be talking to one another with entire freedom, completely disregarding my presence.

"The Englishwoman probably guessed we were onto her," one of them said. "She's gotten out."

"Maybe not," said the other. "It's quite possible that she's only out of town, as her friend said, and will be back. How could she know we had anything on her?"

"Well, if she comes back, that will make it simple. Your job is to stay here and wait for her. Remember what Pietsch said. Don't leave the place for an instant, and, don't forget to answer the phone."

He looked about the room, as though reminded of something by his own words. Locating the phone, he walked across to it, and, with the air of one quite at home, called Gestapo headquarters. When he got the number, he said:

"This is Schulz. Give me Investigation, please. . . . Hello, Captain Pietsch. We're at the Englishwoman's place. Looks as if she smelled something. She's not here. Out of town, her friend says. . . . Yes, Mrs. Shiber. She was here all right."

He listened attentively for a moment.

"*Ja, ja,*" he repeated. "*Jawohl.* That's what I thought."

He hung up, and turned to me, switching back to French.

"You're coming along with me. Pack a few things in a bag. Be sure to put some warm clothing in."

The other man was already sitting at Kitty's desk, calmly and methodically beginning a search of her papers. I was glad I had destroyed everything incriminating that very night. He pulled out the middle drawer, emptied its contents onto the desk, and began going through the papers it contained one by one.

I went into my room and began to pack a suitcase. I put in some toilet articles, warm bathrobe, slippers, a nightgown and a few other things.

I had left the door open, and Schulz was standing in it, watching every move I made. Apparently, I wasn't quick enough for him; for suddenly he said, in English:

"Well, Madam, how long do I have to wait yet?"

"I'll be ready in a minute," I said.

I was trying desperately, as I dawdled with my packing, to think of some way of leaving a warning behind me. Father Christian was due to arrive at noon with four more English soldiers. Chancel hadn't been around for a week, and was likely to drop in at any time. Even Henri might turn up. I thought that if Margot came back in time, I might be able to give her a hint, so that she could keep people away—unless, as was highly probable, they made her a prisoner, too. I knew if I failed to find some way to keep Father Christian, at least, from coming to the apartment, he would simply walk into a trap; for that was what our lovely apartment had become now—a trap to catch any one who came to it.

All I could think of was the story of a man who had been arrested as I was being arrested now, and who informed his friends by writing the word "Gestapo" in soap on his bathroom mirror. But that wouldn't do any good this time, for I had to deliver my warning *before* any one entered the apartment, not after. I tried to think of some place where I might write a similar warning, on the door, perhaps, or in the elevator, but I couldn't think of any way of doing it without the knowledge of my jailer.

"Let's get going," said Schulz impatiently, as I finally closed my bag. I was still without a plan. As we started slowly downward in the self-service elevator, I hoped that we might meet the concierge in the hall, and that I might find some means of making her understand what had happened; but we reached the ground floor, and Madame Beugler was nowhere in sight.

We had reached the sidewalk when suddenly I remembered something—and simultaneously found an excuse for seeing the concierge.

"My dogs!" I gasped. "I forgot about them. I must ask the concierge to take care of them," and I turned and hurried back into the house so quickly that the Gestapo man was left standing alone, bewildered, on the sidewalk.

I almost ran to the concierge's *loge*, and pulled open the door. As luck would have it, Mme. Beugler was just behind it. I had just time to whisper to her, "Don't let any one go to my apartment. The Gestapo is there!" when Schulz appeared behind me. In a louder tone of voice, I said:

"Mme. Beugler—I am going to have to be away for a few days—I don't know how long. Will you take care of the dogs until I come back?"

Mme. Beugler nodded, looking a little bewildered. Schulz took me by the arm, and growled, as he led me out of the building again, "That's enough of this nonsense. You've got more important things than dogs to worry about."

I certainly had. For as Schulz had hurried me out, I had seen a man appear from behind the curtains that masked the doorway in the back of the *loge*; and his fellow resemblance to the two men who had called on me convinced me that he also was of the Gestapo; and that he was waiting there, hidden behind the curtains of the concierge's *loge*, to catch any one who might stop there before going to our apartment.

I got into the car waiting before the door, and Schulz sat down beside me. We started off in the direction of the Etoile. I was shaken by the sight of the third Gestapo man. I didn't know whether he had heard my whispered words to Mme. Beugler. I had spoken so softly, I thought, that probably he had not, and perhaps that was why he had come out of his hiding place.

But since he was there, since Mme. Beugler was being watched too, it seemed unlikely that she would be able to warn Father Christian, or tell any one else to warn him. The trap was still set. I had not been able to unspring it.

The car circled the Arc de Triomphe and stopped a few minutes later before the Hotel Matignon, on the Avenue Matignon.

Before the invasion of Paris, this historic building, which took its name from a former illustrious occupant, Marshal Matignon, had been the residence of the French Premiers. The Germans took it over after the invasion for Gestapo headquarters.

Schulz conducted me into the building between a number of helmeted guards, who flanked the entrance. We went up one flight, passed along a corridor, and finally stopped before a door bearing the name: "Captain Pietsch." He knocked, a voice growled, "*Herein*," and we entered.

The room looked as though it had been used for conferences by the French government, for a long table capable of seating some twenty persons or more stood in the center of it. I was told to sit down at one side of it. Two Germans were in the room, sitting at desks in one corner. One was in uniform, with a scar on his face probably gained from a student duel. Schulz addressed him as Captain Pietsch. The other was a mousy little man who looked like a schoolmaster, with his colorless hair brushed back in pompadour fashion and his tortoise-shell eye-glasses.

Schulz made his report to Captain Pietsch, and left the room. The two men paid no further attention to me. I sat there apprehensively as the minutes ticked by. From time to time one of them answered a phone. Messengers came in and out. Papers were attended to. Finally, Pietsch stepped over to the other man's desk, bent over, and said something to him in too low a tone of voice for me to catch it. The second man nodded, gathered up some papers, and the two of them came over to the table where I was sitting and took their places opposite me.

For what seemed to me several minutes, the two men sat staring at me in silence, as though I were an object of a nature which they couldn't quite understand without careful examination. I supposed this was their invariable technique, designed either to make me nervous (which it did) or to give them a chance to measure their victim and select the methods to use on me.

Finally Captain Pietsch stood up suddenly, fixed a monocle in his eye, and without any preface shouted in French, in so loud a voice that the window panes rattled:

"If you keep one single word from us, if you tell us one single lie, you'll learn how easily we can make suspects talk. Your life is no more important to us than a dog's—a mongrel cur's."

His face was livid with fury. He stared at me for a moment, then brusquely sat down again. Then the other man, whose name I learned later was Dr. Hager, spoke up. He used English, and, quite unlike Captain Pietsch, spoke in a low, almost caressing, voice.

"Mrs. Shiber," he said persuasively, "I really don't think there would be any point in your making matters any more difficult for yourself by denying anything. After all, we do not want to be obliged to imprison a citizen of your great country. Believe me, what we should like to do most of all is to be able to release you at once. If you are a sensible woman, you will simply tell us candidly everything that happened, and I assure you that we shall then be able to let you go."

All of this fitted in perfectly with what I had heard about Gestapo methods—alternation of threats with apparently sympathetic persuasion, the choice between the whip or freedom. The icy calm which had gripped me in my own apartment had disappeared after I had left those familiar surroundings. But it had still not been replaced by the kind of panic which had gripped me in anticipation of my arrest, on so many occasions. Instead, though I was, of course, apprehensive of what might happen to me, my mind was working clearly. I was thinking rapidly and easily. And my reaction to the tactics of my two inquisitors was to say to myself:

"Deny everything! Deny everything, even if they produce the most incontrovertible evidence!"

Dr. Hager was arranging a number of papers, official reports, apparently, before him. I could see some underscorings in red pencil under my name and Kitty's. With a friendly smile on his face, he said:

"All right, now, Mrs. Shiber, we will listen very attentively to your story. You may go right ahead. Tell us everything just as it happened. We know most of it anyway. We know that Mme. Beaurepos was carrying on her activities under cover of her work for the Foyer du Soldat. We know about her little trips. We know that she was smuggling English soldiers across the frontier. In short, we know the whole story, and all we want from you is information on some of the details of the case, which aren't particularly important, but which we want to put in the record for the sake of completeness. Who knows, you might produce some extenuating circumstances which would help your friend."

From the way in which Dr. Hager talked, I suspected that actually he knew nothing. Although to any one familiar with the facts, it sounded as though he had just described our activities, actually he had not shown knowledge of any point except that Kitty worked for the Foyer du Soldat and that she therefore moved about the country. They suspected, of course, that she was smuggling English soldiers out of the country, and had said that they knew it, in order to trap me into an admission. But if they had had more precise details, I was sure he would have mentioned them. It looked to me as though some one had denounced us, but that the Gestapo was not yet sure whether the denunciation was genuine, or whether some personal enemy, anxious for a reward, had made a false accusation.

The raid on our apartment and my questioning, I decided, was not evidence that the Germans had information, but that they wanted to get it. And I repeated to myself, "Deny everything. Perhaps by denying everything, I may still be able to save us; and it's certain that we're lost if I confess."

While these thoughts were going on in my mind, I must have remained silent for a minute or two after Dr. Hager had ceased talking, staring at him across the table. It was he who broke the silence, a little impatiently:

"Come, come, Mrs. Shiber, let's get this over with. Are you ready to tell us everything?"

"Tell you everything?" I repeated. "But I don't know anything. This is all new to me. I don't know anything about any activities of Mme. Beaurepos,, and I had no idea why you had me brought here today."

Captain Pietsch turned to Dr. Hager and whispered into his ear:

"I'll leave her to you. . . . Perhaps you're right. Perhaps she's a cultivated, intelligent American woman . . . but she sounds as though she's covering up to me. . . . Go ahead and try your humane methods, if you want to. But when you find you aren't getting anywhere with your sentimental nonsense, I'll take over. I'll guarantee to make her talk."

And with that he got up and left the room, without so much as a glance in my direction.

Although I knew very well how far the Gestapo was willing to go in its questioning of suspects, and so couldn't restrain a chill feeling about the backbone, I was sure this was all play-acting—not only because Captain Pietsch, while pretending to whisper, spoke loudly enough for me to overhear, but also because he spoke in French. I was certain that he wouldn't use this language to a German colleague, unless he wanted me to understand, too; for of course, he didn't know that I also knew German.

As the door closed behind Pietsch, Hager began again:

"I don't think we'll have any need of my colleague, Mrs. Shiber," he said soothingly. "You're an intelligent woman, and you realize that you can't protect your friend from the consequences of her ill-considered acts, so there's absolutely no reason why you should make trouble for yourself by concealment. Our reports show that you are not implicated in any way in this affair of smuggling English soldiers out of occupied territory, and the only charge we could bring against you would be that of failing to inform us of what was going on. I am quite sure our courts would be glad to overlook this matter, on the ground that you are a neutral and therefore on a somewhat different basis from a citizen of belligerent countries on either side—especially if you demonstrated that you were not an accomplice by your willingness to clarify these minor details on which we would like to check our own reports. . . . Now, Mrs. Shiber, on about what date did Mrs. Beaurepos first send English soldiers across the demarcation line?"

"I'm sorry," I said firmly, "but not only must I insist that I know nothing whatsoever about any such activity on the part of Mme. Beaurepos, but I refuse to answer any questions at all until I have the advice of a lawyer appointed by the American Embassy."

I was sure now that they knew very little, or Dr. Hager would not have said that I was not implicated in the escapes.

He looked at me and shook his head sadly.

"I don't know who could have advised you to adopt such a hostile attitude towards us," he said, in the voice of a mother disappointed in one of her cherished children, "but let me, in your own best interests, dissuade you from continuing in it. Perhaps you do not realize, Mrs. Shiber, how grave this case is, and how grave it might prove to be for yourself if your attitude convinced our courts that you were, not a neutral observer, but an approving witness, or even a participant, in the activity of Mme. Beaurepos.

"I am sure any lawyer with your interests at heart would give you the same advice as myself, but in any case, your request for a lawyer cannot be granted. Even if the American Embassy should send a lawyer here, he could not be admitted to this building. This is the headquarters of the German Secret Police, and no lawyers are permitted to meddle in our investigations.

"Your friend has committed a crime which may be punished by death. There is no such charge against you—yet. But if you try to save her, if you continue to maintain silence about what you must have seen while you were living with her, you may convict yourself of having been an accomplice, at least after the fact. And you may share her fate, without having contributed in the least towards helping her. . . . Now, Mrs. Shiber, about how many English soldiers in all did Mme. Beaurepos smuggle out of the country?"

"Deny everything," I repeated again to myself, and aloud I said:

"I'm sorry. With the best intentions in the world, I couldn't answer your question. I don't know the answer. I don't know anything about it. If Mme. Beaurepos was actually doing anything of that kind, it was in secret. I didn't know all her interests. We made it a rule not to interfere with each other's private activities. When I had a visitor, Mme. Beaurepos always retired inconspicuously, and when she had one, I did the same."

Across the room, I saw an electric clock on the wall. It was eleven o'clock. In an hour, Father Christian would be at the apartment. If he followed his usual habit, he would ring the bell, and when it opened would shout joyfully, as was his custom:

"I have a few hungry boys with me. May I bring them in to lunch?"

And, too late, he would notice that an unknown man had opened the door; or, if it was Margot who was sent to open it, that there was a Gestapo agent in the next room.

Dr. Hager changed tactics. He stopped asking direct questions about the English soldiers, and instead began to question me on our private lives. He sat there opposite me, never taking his eyes off me for an instant, and putting question after question on such minute details of our existence that it seemed ridiculous to take them seriously. I had to tell him everything about the beginning of my acquaintance with Kitty, the circumstances of my husband's death, and the reasons why I came to Paris.

It was just after 12 when Dr. Hager collected his papers, and rose from the table. His friendly smile had disappeared. He still looked like a schoolmaster, but now like a bad-tempered one, angry because his pupils had outsmarted him. I congratulated myself that I had been responsible for that. I had answered all of his questions, but whenever they began to get into dangerous waters, I had managed to avoid his traps. I was on my guard, and stubbornly determined that these people, who, I was now sure, knew very little about what we had been doing, should not learn a single name or a single useful fact through me.

The door opened, and Captain Pietsch entered.

"Well, how about it?" he asked. "Did the woman talk?"

To my amazement, Dr. Hager answered:

"Yes, she talked. I'm quite satisfied with the results. The interesting part was not what she said, but what she tried to conceal."

I looked at Dr. Hager with fear and stupefaction. Had I underestimated him? Instead of my outsmarting him, had he outsmarted me? Of course, I thought, he might have said that to confuse me; for though he spoke in German, he had learned from me during the questioning that I understood that language.

But then another thought struck me that drove everything else out of my head. He was talking before me as though he didn't care what I heard. Did that mean that he had no fear that I would ever be able to tell any one else of his methods? And did that mean that I would never be freed?

The Captain looked towards the clock, and mechanically I followed his look. It was ten minutes past twelve. Captain Pietsch put his hat on and went out. I was left alone with Dr. Hager, who was stuffing his papers into his briefcase, evidently preparing to leave also.

Ten minutes past twelve! Father Christian should have arrived at the apartment, but nothing had happened. Perhaps, after all, the concierge had managed to warn him. I began to regain courage once more.

The phone rang.

Dr. Hager picked it up, answered, listened for an instant, then lifted his head, gazed triumphantly at me, nodding his head significantly.

"Bring him here at once," he said finally, and then hastily corrected himself: "No, no! You mustn't move from there. You may have other visitors. I'll send some one over . . ." (he raised his head and looked steadily at me again as he finished) "for the priest."

I tried to show no emotion. I think I succeeded. I was prepared for what he thought might be a surprise, since I knew that Father Christian was expected, and I had already decided how to act if he should walk into the trap.

I heard Hager give orders for some one to go over to our apartment at once and bring over a priest who had been arrested there. Then turning towards me with a self-satisfied smile, he said:

"Have you ever noticed, Mrs. Shiber, that when a string of pearls breaks and one of them drops off, the others invariably follow, one after the other? It seems that we have broken the string."

While we were waiting for Father Christian to arrive, Dr. Hager again tried to impress upon me that the game was up, now that another one of us had been caught, and to urge me to save myself by telling him what I knew while there was still time. But I stuck to my denials.

When Father Christian was announced, Hager had a guard take me out, and at the same time told him to find Captain Pietsch and bring him in. Obviously, they wanted to talk to him alone, in an attempt to wring a confession from him, as they had tried to get one from me. I complained that I was hungry, and was given some ersatz coffee. About two o'clock, I was summoned back to the room. Father Christian was sitting where I had been. As I entered, he said, "How do you do, Mrs. Shiber?"

"Then you recognize her, do you?" Hager said.

"Of course," Father Christian said. "I was trying to call on Mme. Beaurepos and was arrested," he said to me. "I have no idea what this is all about."

That was all I needed to know. He had denied everything also. But, I wondered, what had happened to the boys? They couldn't have been arrested, or there would have been no possibility of Father Christian's denying his guilt. In the hours that followed, it became quite evident that, if Father Christian had brought them to Paris, they had in some way escaped the Gestapo, for there was no mention of them. Instead, we were plied again with question after question, sometimes separately, sometimes alone, sometimes by Dr. Hager, sometimes by Captain Pietsch, sometimes by both together. They tried to get us to contradict each other; but fortunately we both stuck to the simplest version of our relationship, indicated by Father Christian's opening remark to me when I was brought in. He said that he had come to see Mme. Beaurepos. I said the same, and added that I had only seen him in the apartment casually and knew little about him myself, except that Kitty was interested in a fund he was raising to restore his church. They tried to trip us up by asking such questions as when we had first met. Avoiding too great definiteness, I placed it at about the epoch when he had first come to Paris, and he did the same. I followed the system throughout, when I couldn't plead ignorance of a question, of keeping as close as possible to the truth.

That prevented my being contradicted either by ascertainable facts, or by Father Christian.

Again and again during that interminable afternoon, I heard him make virtually the same answer to many questions. He maintained that his connection with Mme. Beaurepos had to do with the church, and whenever the questioners touched on his reasons for coming to see her, he answered invariably:

"I am sorry, but as a member of a disciplined church, I can only account to my superiors for activity connected with my profession."

Although Captain Pietsch, his blood-shot eyes starting from his head, and the veins on his thick neck swelling, shouted at him that the Gestapo had ways of making stubborn people talk, Father Christian calmly refused to change his attitude.

They gave up at six o'clock. Dr. Hager summoned the policeman who had brought me to the Hotel Matignon, and said to him:

"The woman will remain under investigation."

Schulz told me to take my bag, which I had been carrying about with me all day, and come with him. As I left, I heard Dr. Hager reporting over the telephone—whether for our benefit or for his superiors, I wasn't quite sure.

"It seems to be a very well organized gang," he was saying. "They must have three leaders. One is no doubt working in northern France getting the men to Paris. The second, supervising the Paris headquarters, is in our hands." (That must mean me, I thought with a start, since I know they haven't caught Kitty). "The third, the one who helps them get over the frontier, is still at large."

That was all I heard as I was led out the door.

Once again we walked through the long corridor, and started to descend the stairs. Halfway down, I stopped short as a blood-curdling shriek reached my ears. Only a man in mortal terror of death could have uttered such a sound, I thought. I turned instinctively to my guide, my mouth, I think, open, and my face certainly wearing an expression of horror. He was stoical and unmoved.

"Come along," he ordered, taking me by the elbow and urging me on.

The shriek was followed by a succession of rapid screams, ending in a long wail that died suddenly away into nothingness. We had reached a side entrance leading into a courtyard before the terrifying noises stopped.

"Where are you taking me?" I asked, as we stepped out into the courtyard.

"Don't worry, Madame," he answered, with a broad grin. "We're going to a good hotel."

He motioned me to a waiting automobile, and got in beside me. Fifteen minutes later we drew up before the "good hotel." I recognized it at once.

It was the military prison of the Rue du Cherche-Midi.

## CHAPTER TWENTY-TWO

# *Prison*

THE SIGHT of the military prison carried me back in thought to the years of my past life, the peaceful, lovely years when Kitty and I had enjoyed Paris as only foreigners could, when we had looked upon it as a museum of history, not as a place where history was still being made—history in which we might become uncomfortably active pawns.

Kitty had brought back one day, from a prowl along the book stalls that lined the Seine, a pamphlet printed soon after the arrest of Captain Dreyfus, of the famous Dreyfus Case. On the title page an illustration showed the captain being led into the military prison on the Rue du Cherche-Midi.

"Let's visit this prison some day, Etta," Kitty said to me, as she showed me the picture. "I love to see the historic settings which are one of the things which make Paris so fascinating. There's hardly a street without some famous name connected with it here! You can live in the house where Molière wrote his plays, or take your coffee where Richelieu used to play chess—perhaps at the same table where Lenin and Trotzky also played three centuries later. I don't know any city where the past is involved with the present as much as in Paris."

So we made a pilgrimage to this famous prison. where we found a guide in a charming old Frenchman who was its warden. He apologized for not being able to show us around the section still used for military prisoners, although it was nearly empty. But he answered all our questions with enthusiasm. It was obvious that he had interested himself whole-heartedly in the past of the building that was in his charge.

"The prison was originally a convent," he told us. "A noble Frenchwoman, Madeleine Ciz, had it built when she was converted from the Protestant to the Catholic faith, and Louis XIV, the Sun King, contributed 1,500 livres to its construction. At the time of the

French Revolution, when the jails became overcrowded, the Revolutionary Committee requisitioned the convent and made it a prison. It's been one ever since."

"But where does it get its odd name?" Kitty asked. "From the street, I suppose—but what gave the street that name?" (Cherche-Midi means "search for noon.")

"On the contrary," said the warden, "the street gets its name from this building. When it was still a convent, the nuns used to provide food for the poor every day at noon. Early in the morning, beggars and destitute people would begin to turn up, and wait patiently in front of the building until the nuns brought out great kettles of soup at noon. So the building and the street got the name of 'the search for noon.'"

We walked about the part of the grounds to which we could be admitted, and admired its old-fashioned architecture, its thick walls and its arched entrances. I remembered particularly the amazing smallness of the windows, not much larger than a sheet of writing paper. That feature of the building depressed me; and I said to Kitty as we left: "How can the warden, a highly civilized man, appear so cheerful in spite of knowing that his prisoners are buried alive in this gloomy, airless tomb, almost without windows? It must be a horrible prison!"

Two years later, I myself entered this tomb.

I think humiliation is the dominant feeling of a prisoner received in a German jail. The absolute indifference to human dignity is horrible for a person used, like myself, to respect and deference through a lifetime. You no longer feel like a human being, like a person, but instead no more than an animal, without personality, whose feelings are considered worth no consideration from any one.

I was handed over first to indifferent women guards, who ordered me to strip to be searched. When I hesitated timidly, hoping that I might be allowed to keep on my last garments, they shouted rudely at me to hurry up, and fairly snatched my underwear from me, leaving me naked and shivering in the bitter cold of the unheated building.

After the minute search, I was taken to the photographer, where full face and profile pictures were taken, of the kind every one has seen on posters describing wanted criminals. I understood now why the faces in these pictures are always so stiff and the eyes of the hunted persons in them so full of fright. As the prison photographer fixed my head in a clamp that prevented me from moving it, I felt frightened and helpless too, and looked at the camera as though it were a gun trained upon me.

Before he took the picture, he pinned a number on my chest. I shall never forget that number. It was 1876. I was no longer Mrs. Etta Shiber, an American lady living in a comfortable apartment in the Etoile quarter, moving in a small and pleasant circle of loved friends and acquaintances. Now I was Number 1876, a record in a card catalogue, a statistic, an inmate of an institution where no one knew my name or cared to know it, where my friends could not find me. Indeed, they could not even know what had become of me. I felt myself cut off irrevocably from that other world in which I had lived, completely in the power of my captors.

The formalities of my reception lasted about an hour. Then the chief guard, a German sergeant major, rang a bell, and when a soldier of about fifty appeared, he said to him:

"Third floor."

I learned later that this was where all the woman prisoners were kept.

"Follow me, 1876," the soldier said.

This was the first time any one had called me by the number, and for a moment I didn't respond. He said roughly: "1876 is you. Don't forget it. Now come along."

We passed through a long corridor, where German soldiers were posted at every cross-corridor. They did not carry their rifles at shoulder arms, like sentries outside official buildings, but their bayonets were fixed, and they were on the alert, ready to use their weapons at a moment's notice.

We climbed winding stairways where nuns had once filed silently to their devotions. On every landing there was an armed sentry.

As we passed under an arched opening into a corridor on the third floor, a foul odor which I had begun to notice downstairs, and which I was sure was responsible for a splitting headache from which I was now suffering, thickened and became more intense.

My guide stopped before a heavy iron-bound door. He pulled open a little slide and looked through the small peep-hole it uncovered into the interior. Satisfied, he pushed a ponderous key into the lock, swung the door open, and unceremoniously shoved me in. The door swung to behind me, the lock clicked, and I was in my cell.

If the odor had been bad outside, it was suffocating here. I thought I would faint, or be violently sick, one or the other. In my first frightened glance about I saw four iron beds, taking up all the space of the cell, leaving barely room to press between them, except for the small area occupied by a table just big enough to support the tin canister standing on it. This was the source of the terrible smell— and again I was nearly sick as I visualized the hundreds of such utensils which must exist throughout this building, each one adding its stench to the horrible atmosphere in which I would have to live for I didn't know how long.

Three of the beds were occupied, although it was only a little after seven o'clock. The women in them turned frightened eyes towards me, but no one spoke. I sank down on the empty cot. I knew I should undress and get into bed, like the others, but I couldn't muster the strength to move. Except for the imitation coffee given me at Gestapo headquarters, I had had nothing to eat since my light breakfast early in the morning. But I didn't feel hungry. Indeed, if I had thought of food at that moment, before I had gotten accustomed to that awful smell, its very image would have revolted me.

The resistance I had maintained all day gave way, and I began to cry. The more I tried to restrain myself, from the last remnants of pride which forbade me to show my weakness before strangers, the more deeply I was shaken by my sobs. I had not wept so bitterly since my husband had died in my arms in New York and, before that, since my brother had died in Paris. But this time, I was weeping for myself.

A young girl in the next bed leaned towards me and whispered gently:

"Did they beat you? They beat every one before they bring them in here. They beat me, too."

I was immediately ashamed of myself. No one had beaten me— at least, not yet. What right had I to cry? The terrible pressure on my chest seemed to be lifted. I stopped weeping, wiped my eyes, and looked about.

My three cell-mates were all gazing at me. I didn't realize yet how much it means to a prisoner when some one else comes into his restricted world from outside, some one who can bring news and remembrance that something does exist outside of prison walls, some life of light and freedom, from which one is not necessarily cut off forever, with which some contact still remains. But I did feel instinctively that I had come into a new world, one entirely different from that which I had left. I began at once to feel a solidarity with these other three inhabitants of the new universe of which I was now also a citizen.

We began talking in low tones, huddled together so that we could hear one another without being audible ourselves outside of the cell, and in a few minutes we knew all about one another.

The young girl who had addressed those first sympathetic words to me was named Mary Bird. She was English, only twenty, and both beautiful and charming. She came from Guernsey, one of the Channel Islands, off the French coast, but belonging to England. The Germans occupied this island after taking the coast opposite it. Four weeks later Mary and twenty-seven other inhabitants of the island were arrested, charged with espionage on behalf of England.

I looked into her clear face and lovely blue eyes.

"Did you really do espionage work?" I asked.

Mary cast a frightened glance towards the neighboring bed, and protested: "Of course not. Neither did the others arrested with me. We did nothing of the kind."

The girl on the other side of me was a Spaniard named Lola. Her crime was having smuggled a French soldier over the Spanish frontier. He got over safely, but she was caught a few feet from the border and brought back.

"How many soldiers did you smuggle over the frontier?" I asked.

She looked at me in surprise.

"Why, only one of course—my boy—Gaston."

I realized at once that my own experiences had caused me to mistake a romantic flight for an organized effort to save soldiers from the Germans, like ours.

Lola's face took on an almost ecstatic expression as she added defiantly:

"They can keep me here as long as they want. Since I know he's safely out of their clutches, I don't care what happens to me. Nothing they can do can make me regret that I saved my man!"

The third occupant of the cell, whose bed was farthest from mine, was an Alsatian woman, Marthe Wenzinger. About thirty-five, she had probably been quite pretty when younger, but she had already lost her good looks. She was tall, with colorless hair and blue eyes. She had apparently managed to take good care of herself—her nails and skin showed that—but the clothes thrown over the foot of her bed seemed cheap and poor.

She told me that she had worked as a translator from French to German and vice versa in Paris. When the Germans came in, they arrested her, accusing her of espionage against Germany and for France before the war.

"Judging from your name, I imagine you must be of German-Alsatian descent," I said.

"That makes it worse. They hold it against me that in spite of my German descent, I was working for the French. But let me tell you something—it's safe for me to say it here, because there are only the four of us, and we're all in the same boat; we won't give one another away—because we Alsatians are of German descent, we understand the Germans better. And so I hate them more than any of you."

And she glared at me with an expression of concentrated hatred on her face. Then suddenly her features relaxed, and she smiled at me.

"And you, Madame. What are you here for?"

I began explaining myself to them—how I had come to Paris in search of a peaceful setting for the last part of my life, and how the war had swept me into its bewildering circle. I must have taken too long telling these preliminary facts, for the Alsatian woman interrupted impatiently:

"But what are you charged with?"

"Helping to smuggle English soldiers across the frontier," I said.

Mary Bird started as though in fright, and began:

"But for that—" and then interrupted herself suddenly, putting her clenched hand quickly to her mouth, as though to stifle what she had started to say. But I knew what the rest of the sentence would have been. She had meant to say: "But for that they can shoot you!"

"And did you really help English soldiers to get away?" the Alsatian woman asked.

I was tempted to answer: "Yes, more than 150 of them," when Mary Bird grasped my arm, saying swiftly: "Quiet! The guard is coming."

Sure enough, we could hear the tramp of heavy boots passing along the corridor. It was eight o'clock—the hour at which the guards checked on the prisoners, and extinguished the faint yellowish lights in the cells. The peep-hole in the door clicked open. Then it shut again, and the light went out. It was pitch dark, and I had not yet undressed or made my bed. I sat down on the side near Mary Bird and started to take off my clothes. Suddenly I felt an arm on mine, then the voice of Mary Bird whispered into my ear:

"Be careful of the Alsatian. She's a stool pigeon!"

## CHAPTER TWENTY-THREE

# First Day in Prison

I LAY on my back in bed, eyes open, gazing through the pitch dark towards the invisible ceiling. A deep silence had settled over the whole prison. I could hear only the heavy breathing of my three cell-mates. They had fallen asleep within a few minutes after the light had been put out. But in spite of my lack of sleep the night before, in spite of all the tiring experiences of the day, I could not sleep. The thoughts raced feverishly through my brain. Once in a while I dozed off for a moment, to start up from the beginning of some nightmare connected with the day's events.

So the Alsatian woman was a stool pigeon! How fortunate that Mary Bird had stopped me in time! I might have told her every-thing. It had never occurred to me that the Nazis would have placed spies even here, in these putrid cells, living under the same condi-tions as the prisoners, in order to deceive them into believing that they were their comrades. I saw that I must be more careful, that I must suspect everything and everybody.

But could Mary Bird be mistaken? Suppose this Alsatian woman were just another unfortunate, as miserable as ourselves, locked up either on a false charge, or because she actually had worked for her country against the enemy? Or could Mary Bird herself be a stool pigeon, trying to create confidence in me by accusing another? That, I thought, was completely incredible. I was sure this gentle girl was just what she seemed to be on the surface. But I made one resolve— not to admit the part I had played to any one, even the most sym-pathetic and the least suspect persons with whom I might come into contact.

I dozed off for a few seconds in the midst of these thoughts, and in a half-dream Father Christian's face floated before my eyes; and then suddenly the horrible screams I had heard in the Hotel Matig-non seemed to ring in my ears again, and I thought it was he who was screaming. I was jerked back to consciousness again, my nerves trembling with fright.

What is happening to him now? I wondered. Almost certainly he is in jail somewhere, too, perhaps in this very jail. Will they beat him, torture him? I asked myself. Of one thing I was sure. Whatever they did to him, they would never wring such a shriek of abject terror from his lips. He would die, I was sure, with the same high dignity as he had displayed when Captain Pietsch, his bloodshot eyes starting from his head, roared threats at him. He had made me feel then, unarmed and helpless as he was, that he was stronger than the Gestapo captain, with his revolver strapped to his belt and his henchmen within call.

Into my mind floated Dr. Hager's simile about the string of pearls. Who had broken that string, I wondered. Who had betrayed us?

Could it have been the two French soldiers I had ejected from the apartment? But what else could I have done? When Margot had threatened them with the police, perhaps she had given them the idea of going to the police themselves. Perhaps they had seen the offer of a reward. They wanted money. That was why they had come to our apartment. Maybe they had found another way to get it.

I told myself that this was impossible. The two men had been arrogant and insulting. If Margot had not returned, there is no telling what they would have done. But, after all, they were French. I couldn't imagine them betraying us to the Germans—at least, not intentionally. Perhaps that was it. Perhaps they had given us away without meaning to. They had been drinking. They were talking loudly, swearing; they were in no state to be cautious. Perhaps what they said had caused some prowling Gestapo agent to prick up his ears. Perhaps they had been arrested, and forced to talk . . . But if so, they couldn't have told much; for obviously, they knew more than the Gestapo seemed to know. They knew how the border was crossed, for they had crossed it. Perhaps they weren't the ones who had given us away; or perhaps they had held back all they could, after having betrayed us unwittingly.

That blood-curdling scream I had heard—could it have come from one of them?

Or would any one else have been willing to earn a 10,000-franc reward by denouncing us? The Gestapo agents had arrived only twenty-four hours after the prize was announced. But if so, who could it have been? So few persons knew, and none of them, it seemed, would be likely to have given us away.

Could it have been the owner of the hotel where Father Christian had stayed overnight with his boys? Or Emile, who brought the messages from Monsieur Durand? Or the letter carrier? Or the postal clerk who intercepted letters for "William Gray"? Or Monsieur Durand himself?

I couldn't believe that it was any of these—first of all, because all of them were French. All of them were fighting the same enemy as ourselves.

Then who, who, I asked my aching brain, who could have betrayed us?

I remembered that Dr. Hager had put one question to me again and again, in different forms: who was the person with whom we were in contact in the unoccupied zone? Who was the leader of that group? Could it be possible that our betrayal had originated there, on the other side of the border, from some one who had come into contact with men we had freed? Some one in Chancel's organization, perhaps? No, that seemed less likely, for then Chancel would have been the first to be arrested rather than ourselves.

But the unoccupied zone, we had been told, was full of Gestapo agents, and perhaps one of them had heard something from some of the boys themselves. They might very well have thought that once across the border, the danger was over, and with it the need for caution. They might have talked imprudently. Or it might have been some of the French escorts, rather than the English boys, who had given us away—perhaps in conversation with a friend in a café, a conversation loud enough so that some one could overhear. Especially if they had just reached the unoccupied zone, they might not have learned how well organized the Gestapo was there, too.

If the clue had come from the unoccupied zone, that would explain two things: why Dr. Hager was so obviously groping in the dark, and why he had showed such interest in our connections in the unoccupied zone. Our great mistake, I thought, might have been that we had failed to insist that every one of the boys should promise solemnly not to tell how he escaped until after the war; for even in England, there might be enemy ears listening, ceaselessly listening, to careless talk, everywhere, all the time.

But I had no way of coming to any conclusion. I only hoped that our betrayal had come in some such casual way as an overheard conversation in the unoccupied zone; for in that case, there might be no way in which the Gestapo could pursue its investigation any farther. They might come up against a blank wall, if only all of us remained firm in denial. Perhaps the other pearls would not drop off the string after all. Perhaps they could be, some day, restrung again.

And I dropped finally off to sleep.

Seven-thirty! The knuckles of a heavy hand beat loudly on the cell door. My companions hastily leapt from bed and began putting on their clothes.

I didn't move. I lay there for a moment, blinking, and trying to orient myself, after the deep sleep which had allowed me to forget, momentarily, where I was. Mary shook me by the shoulder, calling:

"Hurry, Mrs. Shiber, hurry, or you'll be punished."

"What do they do to you worse than keeping you penned up in a foul hole like this?" I asked, hurrying all the same, for I knew very well that the German genius for punishment was unlimited.

"They send you to the punishment cell," Mary said. "It's not a cell; it's a tomb. No window, no light, no furniture. They leave you there for days for the slightest offense."

"There must be a bed!" I exclaimed.

"No. There's a bare stone bench. That's all."

Ten minutes later the guard entered with a German officer, making the regular morning inspection. I was dressed, and my bed coverings were folded according to regulations, thanks to Mary's help. It was only when I put my bed in order that I discovered how filthy it was.

At eight A.M. they brought us a drink supposed to be coffee, foul to look at and foul to taste. With it we were supposed to eat bread saved from our ration of the supper of the day previous. But since

I had not been there the day before, I had no bread, and none was brought to me.

We had hardly finished, when the guard came again.

"Number 650," he called. "Examination!"

The Alsatian girl followed him out. As soon as she had gone, Mary Bird said:

"She's going to make her report. They'll ask her if she got anything out of you. I was frightened last night. I was afraid you were going to give yourself away. She doesn't admit it, but she knows English quite well. I said one or two things to make her start, just to find out. She knows Spanish, too."

I looked towards Lola.

"She's all right," Mary said. "You can trust her."

"But are you sure the Alsatian is a spy?" I asked.

"Certain. I've been here three weeks now, and I've noticed that she's always moved around, and whenever they shift her to another cell, a newcomer arrives just afterwards. There were four of us here yesterday. Two of them were shifted, and she was sent in just before you arrived. I was sure we were going to have a new cell-mate before you came, because of that. That's how I knew you were all right, too.

"This makes four times in three weeks that I've been in the same cell with her. I've heard her talk often enough to know that she tries to pump every one. She'll only stay here three or four days. If she hasn't got anything out of you by then, they'll move her somewhere else, to work on another new arrival.

"I could tell you a lot of things about her, but I'll wait till later. She may be back any minute, and before that, I want to tell you what really happened to me. I denied everything last night, of course, because she was listening."

In feverish haste, sometimes leaving a sentence unfinished and rushing on to the next in her anxiety to tell me her story before the spy returned, Mary Bird told me of the adventure of the little island of Guernsey.

Her island, she told me, lies in the Channel some thirty miles from France and eighty from England. It was a haven for English officers retired on pension and former colonial administrators, come there to pass the last years of their lives in calm and quiet.

"Well, we hope we can get it over as quickly as that. You see, it's all a question of finishing the investigation of this unfortunate case. Of course, if it takes us longer to get all the facts together—two or three months, say—we would have to hold you, because, you see, you're an important witness. They do that in your country, too, you know—hold what I believe you call material witnesses. The more quickly we can clean up this case, the more quickly we can let you go.

"Now I have been looking over the evidence, and I have come to the conclusion that you are actually quite innocent—that the principal actors took advantage of your good nature, and your unwillingness, as a neutral, to intervene or to denounce them. Actually, Mrs. Shiber, they were doing you a grave wrong, for without your realizing it, they were working, so to speak, under your unconscious protection. They counted on the fact that you were an American citizen to divert suspicion from them and perhaps to lighten the consequences if they were caught. No doubt they will try to implicate you in the hope that they will thus participate in the leniency which would naturally be extended to a neutral. They have acted shamefully towards you, in risking your liberty, even your life perhaps, for the sake of their own aims, and they certainly do not deserve any consideration on your part. They can hardly expect you to protect them by keeping silent—especially as it is in any case only a matter of time until we will have all the facts, and if you help us by giving us some information that will only mean shortening the investigation slightly, nothing more."

I could see very plainly now what he was getting at. I said nothing, though I thought he expected me to interrupt, and he continued.

"As I said, Mrs. Shiber, I am quite convinced of your own innocence, but I am afraid I cannot say the same for your friend, Mme. Beaurepos. She was the head of this group, but she managed to get away just in time. She knew we were after her. She told you she was going on a trip, but actually she was escaping and leaving you behind to take the punishment. If she had really been your friend, she would have taken you with her. Now do you see how badly you have been treated? Here you are, in prison, and she has escaped, rejoicing in her own liberty, and completely uninterested in your fate.

"Now, Mrs. Shiber, you see what the situation is. You have been the dupe of—I don't like to say this about an old friend of yours, but it happens to be the truth—an unscrupulous woman. Fortunately for you, we have been able to see through her schemes, and to realize that it is not you who are guilty, and so you will be freed as soon as we have completed our investigation. Now as I say, I hope that will only take a week or two; but it may take longer if we have trouble clearing up some of the minor details. So it rests only with you: give us your assistance on these points, and we will be able to do our work more rapidly, and consequently to release you sooner. I know this jail isn't a very pleasant place. I deeply regret the error that put you here in the first place. But now that you have been entered, I can't do anything about it. A discharge order has to be issued by my superiors before you can be freed, and in a case like this, no such order is ever approved until the investigation is completed. So, as you see, I am helpless. It depends only on yourself whether you will be out of here in, say, a week, or perhaps three or four months."

It was all very clear now; it was just what I thought he was leading up to. Dr. Hager was trying to persuade me to tell what I knew by dangling before my eyes the possibility of release. They had given me a little taste of prison in the hopes that the horrible prospect of remaining in jail would weaken my resolution. But I was surer than ever that they still knew very little about our case; otherwise, why would such elaborate measures be necessary to persuade me to talk? As for what they said about Kitty having abandoned me, that I knew simply could not be true. I had known her too long and too well to be taken in by that. It was this part of Dr. Hager's plea as much as anything else which convinced me that everything he said was false, carefully designed to make me betray my friends. Since I knew that could only be a ruse, I was certain the rest of what he said was untrue as well. He was trying to draw me out, I told myself; very well, I will try to draw him out.

"But Dr. Hager," I said, "I have told you I know nothing about this affair. What could I possibly tell you that would help?"

"We believe that your friend has escaped into the unoccupied zone," he said. "It would be natural for her to follow the route over which she sent the English soldiers if she believed she were about to be arrested. No doubt you have addresses of friends of hers there, with whom she might have made contact. Or perhaps you even have an idea what city she may be in. That would give us something to go on. Of course, we couldn't arrest her there. We have no authority in the unoccupied zone. So, if you still are reluctant to cause your friend any harm, even after what she has done to you, you can rest assured. If she is in the unoccupied zone, she is safe."

"But if she is safe there, if you can't arrest her in the unoccupied zone, why do you want to know where she is there?" I asked, with apparent innocence. As a matter of fact, I knew very well, from Henri and others, that the Gestapo operated in the unoccupied zone too, and that French police were often obliged to do their dirty work for them, arresting their own compatriots and handing them over to the Germans.

Dr. Hager shook his head slowly, like a schoolmaster disappointed in a stupid pupil.

"My dear Mrs. Shiber, don't you understand yet? I am trying to close this case, to get it over with—and incidentally, to get you out of here. I am not allowed to let the investigation drop until I have definitely accounted for all the suspects I have been ordered to follow up. Now I have accounted for all but one. Mme. Beaurepos' name is the only one against which we still have to place a question mark. If I can only report, 'Mme. Beaurepos has been located at Marseilles—'" he watched me narrowly as he mentioned the names of these localities, as though casually and at hazard, giving a rising inflection to each name, hoping, I was sure, that a light would come into my eyes at one of them—"'or Lyons—or Cannes—or Nimes—' then I can put down that she is beyond our jurisdiction, and that the investigation is ended."

I wondered how much of this might be true—had they actually arrested every one except Kitty? Were Tissier and Chancel perhaps in their hands? And frightened little bourgeois Monsieur Durand? He would be likely to tell anything he knew, not that he knew a great deal. I decided to make one more test of Dr. Hager.

"Dr. Hager," I said, "you told me a minute ago that you were willing to inform the American Embassy of your decision to release me, in my presence. Would you do that now?"

"Why, of course," Dr. Hager said. He picked up the desk phone, and said, "American Embassy, please."

He looked towards me, almost triumphantly, I thought, as though to say: "There! You didn't think I'd do it, did you?"

I couldn't hear the voice answer on the other end, though I strained my ears in the hope of catching it, but Dr. Hager said: "This is Dr. Hager of the German Secret Police talking. I wish to report the arrest of an American citizen. Would you be kind enough to connect me with the proper person?"

There was a pause. Then Hager identified himself again, and gave my name and address, as though to some one writing it down. Then he continued:

"We have been obliged to arrest and hold Mrs. Shiber in the military prison on the Rue du Cherche-Midi . . . yes, go ahead, take it down . . . Ready again? . . . on a charge of complicity in aiding English soldiers to escape from occupied territory . . . Yes, that's it . . . So far our investigation leads us to believe that Mrs. Shiber was an innocent victim of those actually guilty . . . We are obliged to hold her as a material witness, but we wished to inform you that she will be released as soon as our investigation has been completed . . . How long? We hope in a week or two . . . That depends partly on Mrs. Shiber herself. We think she could help us in locating the woman with whom she shared an apartment—a French citizen, British by birth—who was the ringleader of an organized gang, and as soon as we have discovered where she is, we will be able to close the case . . . Indeed? . . . Is that so? . . . I'm very happy to hear you say that. It is exactly the advice I have been giving Mrs. Shiber myself."

Still holding the phone close enough to his mouth so that any one at the other end could hear what he was saying, he said to me: "Mrs. Shiber, the Embassy tells me that in their opinion, as a neutral, you should avoid taking sides by withholding any information you may be able to give to the authorities in control of the territory on which you happen to live. They advise that you tell whatever you know."

I rose from my chair.

"I'd like to speak to them myself," I said.

Dr. Hager flashed a quick glance at the prison commander at the same time that he said, "Why, certainly, Mrs. Shiber," and rose as though to offer me his place.

The commander intervened quickly.

"I can't permit it, Dr. Hager," he said. "I'm sorry. I have already stretched a point in allowing you to call. Prison regulations are rigid on that point. Prisoners are not allowed to talk on the phone with any one at all. Even you yourself could not talk with a prisoner in that fashion. I am definitely unable to allow Mrs. Shiber to use the phone. It is strictly forbidden."

Dr. Hager shrugged his shoulders and made a gesture of impotence in my direction. He returned to the phone. "Hello . . . Hello," he said, then put down the phone. "They must have hung up," he said.

To me this little scene was conclusive. It had obviously been well rehearsed. I was certain Dr. Hager had not called the American Embassy. That meant that my suspicions were right, and his whole appeal was an elaborate attempt at deception. Once again, I said to myself: "Deny everything! You must continue to deny everything!"

"Well, Mrs. Shiber," said Dr. Hager, with a tone of great relief, as though everything were settled now, "let's get this annoying business over with. Now where do you think is the most likely place to look for Mme. Beaurepos?"

"I've told you already the only thing I know," I said, "that she was going to Tours."

"She didn't go to Tours," said Dr. Hager shortly. "That we know. That is in the occupied zone. Where would she go in the unoccupied zone? Where has she friends?"

"I have no idea," I said. "I told you that we lived completely separate lives. I didn't know her friends, and she didn't know mine."

I can't describe the look that Dr. Hager gave me. Mostly, it seemed to be disgust. There was anger in it, too. He had apparently been certain that he was about to reach his goal, and here he was, back where he started from. He stepped around the desk and exchanged a few whispered words with the prison commander. Then he turned towards me. His face was dark with rage.

"I have been wrong about you, Mrs. Shiber," he shouted at me. "I thought you were innocent. I thought you had been taken advantage of. But now I see that you are as guilty as the rest. That is the only reason you could have for hiding what you know. And such ridiculous excuses! Do you expect me to believe that you don't know the friends of Mme. Beaurepos, with whom you have been living for years? No, Mrs. Shiber! You are lying because you are in it as deep as all the rest! There is only one way out of this prison for you! That is to the scaffold! You know the punishment for your crime—death! You have just proved to me that you deserve it."

He stopped, and then suddenly shifted to a softer tone of voice, though his accents were still hard enough.

"Perhaps it is just that you do not realize the position you are in. Perhaps that is why you are so stubborn, not because you are guilty, or completely guilty, yourself. I will give you one more chance. I will give you until six o'clock this evening. If you haven't become reasonable by then, I will have no option. I shall have to record in my report that I consider you one of the guilty persons."

I can't pretend that I was not shaken at hearing myself threatened openly with the death penalty. But I managed to reply fairly steadily.

"I don't need until six o'clock tonight to make up some story to satisfy you," I said. "Perhaps it is stupid of me, not to try to secure my release by imagining some information which might deceive you into believing I was able to help. But I'm not cut out for such clever rôles. I can only repeat that I don't know anything."

Dr. Hager glared at me again, and the burning eyes behind his thick-lensed glasses frightened me. He rushed towards me, raising his right arm as he did so. Instinctively I backed away.

"Aren't you ashamed of yourself," I cried, "trying to strike a defenseless woman?"

A knock sounded on the door. Dr. Hager dropped his arm.

*"Herein,"* the prison commander growled.

The door swung open, and the guard announced:

"Mr. Marvel of the American Quakers."

## CHAPTER TWENTY-FOUR

# The Stool Pigeon

I LEARNED later that Mr. Marvel was a frequent visitor to the Cherche-Midi prison. As the Paris representative of the Quakers, he called systematically at the various camps for prisoners of war, the internment camps, and the prisons, and arranged for food and other comforts to be given to the inmates. For some reason, the Quakers had been particularly successful in securing permission from the Germans to carry on their work, and were able, for instance, to enter prisons like mine which even accredited diplomats found it almost impossible to visit. I suspected that one reason why the Germans allowed the American Quakers and certain other American organizations privileges refused to other groups was that the United States was still neutral, and the Germans hoped by cooperating with such non-official bodies to counteract to some extent their bad reputation in the United States.

It was apparent that Mr. Marvel was accustomed to considerable consideration in this prison. The prison commander offered him a chair with exaggerated courtesy, as Dr. Hager slipped unobtrusively out of the room. The guard entered to lead me back, but Mr. Marvel said:

"Excuse me, Major; isn't this Mrs. Shiber?"

"Yes," the commander answered.

"It's about her that I came today," he said. "May she stay?"

The commander ordered the guard to wait in the corridor, and Mr. Marvel turned to me, saying that as soon as he had learned that an American woman was in the prison he had hurried over to inquire about my situation.

"Did the American Embassy send you over?" I asked.

Mr. Marvel smiled.

"I'm sorry," he said, "but I am not allowed to talk to you about anything except your physical needs. That is the condition on which I am allowed here."

The German Major, who had suddenly stiffened in his chair when I had asked my question, relaxed again.

I was depressed at this rebuff. It seemed almost as though I were still shut off entirely from the world without, since I could not even communicate with this American who had succeeded in reaching me.

Mr. Marvel asked if I had brought enough clothing with me. I answered listlessly that I needed warm underwear, and he promised to send me some. At this point, the phone rang; and while the prison commander was talking, I ventured to say, in a low tone of voice:

"Did the Embassy send you because of a phone call from here this morning?"

"I don't know of any phone call," Mr. Marvel said. "The Embassy was told by a Monsieur Beaurepos that you had been arrested. I have been to several prisons looking for you. Tell me quickly what you are here for, so I can report to the Embassy."

I had only time to tell him the charge when the commander hung up, and Mr. Marvel shifted swiftly back to the subject of clothing and food. I was happy again, for I knew that if Henri had discovered what had happened, he would do his utmost to warn Kitty, and keep her from coming back to the apartment. And it also seemed probable that I had adopted the right course, for it was not Dr. Hager's phone call, as I had thought for a moment, which had brought Mr. Marvel to the prison; and so I was still convinced that it had been a fake. But now the Embassy knew of my plight, and I no longer felt abandoned and alone. Outside the prison walls, friends would be working for my release. I seemed to have grown suddenly much stronger; and for the first time since I had choked down that terrible ersatz coffee, I realized that I was very hungry.

Mr. Marvel said good-bye to me, and I was taken back to my cell. I stepped through the corridors almost light-heartedly. I felt that these horrible men who held me prisoner would no longer dare to raise a hand against me. I was protected now, shielded by the fact that my jailers knew that the great country of which I was a citizen had found out where I was, and would not permit them to mistreat me.

My cell-mates looked curiously at me when I returned, but the Alsatian woman was there again, so none of them asked me any questions. She, however, ignorant of course that I knew she was a spy, set herself to pump me. With a smile that was meant to appear sympathetic, but which had a particularly bad effect on me since it immediately called to mind Dr. Hager's similar expression, she said:

"Don't worry, Madame. America will come into the war soon, and then Germany will be finished. . . . Why did they call you to the office?"

It must have been the exaltation that had resulted from the visit of Mr. Marvel that caused me to answer as I did. The words poured from my mouth without my having thought them at all. It was an instinctive, an automatic reaction. It seemed to me that some power was talking through me, rather than that I myself uttered the words which I was surprised to find myself saying.

"If you are not afraid of earthly justice," I lashed out at her, "if you do not tremble with fear of punishment during your lifetime, for committing the foulest of all crimes, betraying the confidence of the miserable unfortunate persons in this jail, worming their secrets out of them and reporting them to their jailers, then you should fear the Hereafter and the implacable justice of God. What do you get for performing this hangman's job that makes you willing to appear on the Day of Judgment with so heavy a load of guilt upon your soul—money? Much money? Enough to make up for living in filth to do your filthy work, and dying in moral filth, and living in the memory of those who knew you as the lowest and the most abject of human beings?"

I shouted this out in a sudden torrent of white-hot rage and loathing, my eyes fixed on the Alsatian woman's face; and instead of terrifying her, I became terrified myself, as her cheeks flushed bright red, and then were drained suddenly of all their blood until they became dead white, creased with the shadows of her wrinkles. Her eyes took on the expression of a hunted animal, at bay and facing death, and suddenly, with a loud wail, she threw her arms around my neck and began weeping on my shoulder. Her entire body shook in spasmodic convulsions, and the sobs seemed to be wrenched from her by main force.

This sudden torrent of grief disarmed my other two cell-mates as well as myself. Mary and Lola sprang up, put their arms about her, and tried to console her.

We heard footsteps in the corridor. The cover was pulled aside from the peephole, the guard peered in, then indifferently snapped it shut again, and passed on. Only crying women! He had seen enough of that here. That was of no importance.

It was many long minutes before the Alsatian woman stopped crying. She sat on the edge of one of the beds, her face buried in her hands, and from time to time, after we thought she had finally finished, a great dry sob would rack her body. Then, without taking her hands from her face, she began in a low, broken, monotonous tone, to tell her story.

Part of what she had said already was true. An Alsatian speaking perfect French and German, and with an acquaintanceship with several other languages, she had worked up a prosperous little translation business in Paris. In the autumn of 1938, a year before the war broke out, a young German called at her place of business, and said that he had a confidential message for her. She took him into a private office, and without further formality, he said:

"I am in the service of the German Intelligence. We wish you to work for us."

"At first," the Alsatian woman continued, "I could not believe he was serious. It seemed absurd that the German Intelligence Service should recruit agents in so crude, even dangerous, a fashion. But he produced credentials, and quickly made it plain that the offer was a genuine one. I was indignant. I reached for the phone to call the police.

"With perfect assurance, the German said:

"'Don't do anything stupid, Fraulein. Before you use the telephone, read this letter.'

"He pulled a paper out of his pocket and handed it to me. I recognized my mother's handwriting at once. I had not heard from her for several weeks. She had gone to live in St. Polten, Austria, with my uncle, her brother, when my father died.

"The letter began:

"'My dear Marthe: I beseech you to comply with the wishes of the man who gives you this letter, for that will help to ease my terrible situation . . .' I read hastily through the rest of it. My mother was in the notorious Oranienburg concentration camp. I had read of its horrors in the French papers.

"What could I do? To refuse would have meant death or torture for my mother. To accept meant comparative happiness for her. I *had* to give in. I've been working for them ever since—two years that they have been absolute masters of my life, because it is in their power to mistreat my mother. They made me offer my services to the French espionage service, and when I succeeded in getting in, they made me work for them in the very heart of the French Army. Since they came into Paris, I have been assigned to this prison as a Nachrichten Agent."

She raised her face from her hands for the first time.

"No!" she cried, "I'm not doing this for money, or because I like it, or because I don't hate and despise myself every minute for doing it! I've thought of suicide—I've thought of it more than once. But then what would happen to my mother? There isn't any escape. I know. I've thought of everything. I'm condemned to do my work— and to do it well, for they watch me, they know I don't work for them willingly, and they know how to punish if I don't succeed. . . . Blame me if you want. You can't blame me more than I blame myself. But what would you have done? Would any of you have condemned her own mother? Wouldn't you have tried to save her, even at this awful cost?"

"Couldn't you escape?" asked Mary Bird.

"Escape! I could, yes, of course . . . but don't you understand yet how I am held to this work, even forbidden the last resort of leaving life itself? I could escape; but my mother can't escape. There is no escape from Oranienburg. If I saved myself, my mother would pay for it."

"Have you seen your mother since?" I asked.

"That is my chief reward," Marthe answered bitterly. "She is still in Oranienburg, but she is on a privileged regime—when I do good work—and I am allowed to visit her once every three months. She is a wonderful woman, a heroic woman," Marthe's eyes misted with tears again. "The last time I saw her, she urged me to try to get out of France, to go to some other country, America, perhaps, and leave her to her fate. 'I am 74,' she told me. 'I have not long to live anyhow. I no longer care what happens to me. I want to go to join your father. He was fortunate enough to die before this rule of anti-

Christ began.' But I couldn't do it. How could I? How can you condemn your own mother to shorten her life even by an hour?"

"If it were my mother," Lola said, "I should have accepted, just as you did; but I would have told them nothing useful. I would have lied to them. I would never have betrayed my cell-mates."

Marthe laughed scornfully.

"You are a baby," she said. "Do you think they are as naïve as that? Do you think they can be deceived so easily? I never know when a trap may be set for me, when some one may be testing me to make sure that nothing is held back. I don't know now whether one of you is not an *agent provocateur*. How do I know whether you, Mrs. Shiber, didn't attack me just now to make me say what I have just said? How do I know that you, or one of the others, won't report me, so that I will be punished, or my mother will suffer? Mrs. Shiber! How did you know I was a spy? Who told you? No one knows but the Germans. Did they send you here to trap me? Are you a spy, too? Are you another one of us?"

I gasped in amazement at the accusation. Marthe was almost hysterical.

"How can you think such a thing?" I exclaimed. "Don't you trust me?"

Marthe suddenly became more calm.

"I trust nobody," she said. "I suppose you're all right. But let me tell you what happened once. The first week I was here, I was put in a cell with a very young girl, who had been arrested for crossing the frontier illegally. She cried all night, and told me a pitiful story about how she had to escape because she had killed a German officer who had tried to assault her. She woke up in the night screaming, and said she saw the murdered man's face in her dreams. I took pity on her, and reported that I couldn't get anything out of her."

Marthe shook her head suddenly as though trying to free it of some hideous thought.

"Would you believe it?" she said. "That girl was an *agent provocateur*. She had been put in the cell to test me. I was confronted with her the next day, and asked why I hadn't reported her story. I tried to excuse myself by saying I had taken pity on her. 'We have no pity in this service,' I was told. They beat me and put me in the punishment cell. Three days later, the guard came and said, 'You are going to see your mother.' I was terrified. I thought perhaps they had killed her. But they had not. No, they had not killed her."

She buried her face in her hands again, and was silent for a moment. Then suddenly, half-crying, she shot out the rest of her story in a burst of sobs, talking at top speed as though to get it over with as quickly as possible:

"No, they hadn't killed her. I saw her in the camp hospital. She was recovering from the effect of solitary confinement in an un-lighted, unheated, dark cell. Think of it, an old woman of 74! They told her, 'This is a present from your daughter.' And now I hold nothing back—nothing!"

We looked at one another, Mary, Lola and myself, embarrassed, uneasy, at a loss how to help the tormented enigma of a woman weeping on the bed. But as we watched, her sobs stopped. She sat up, quite calm again, dried her streaming eyes, and said, "I'm sorry. I feel better now—relieved to get it all off my chest. I didn't mean what I just said. You can trust me now. I swear I'll never give any of you away."

But then she stopped and a cloud seemed to come over her face. She spoke hesitantly.

"But Mrs. Shiber . . . tell me . . . how did you know that I was a German agent? Did they tell you downstairs? During your ex-amination?"

I felt Mary's grip tighten on my arm. I knew what she meant. Be careful! Don't give me away!

"They didn't exactly tell me," I said. "I guessed from some things they said. Your name wasn't mentioned, though. . . . Do you know Dr. Hager?"

"Of course. He is assistant chief of the Gestapo investigation bureau."

"He tried to persuade me to help them," I said. "It was something like the offer they made you, but much less general, of course. He wanted me to provide them clues to help them find a friend of mine whom they haven't caught yet."

"And you refused?"

"Yes."

"You could refuse," Marthe said bitterly. "You don't have a mother locked up in a concentration camp. . . . I suppose they offered you some inducement?"

"They promised to free me. They said I could go back to America in a few weeks."

"Yes, yes," Marthe said musingly. "That's quite in the pattern. They wanted you to betray your friend, and they offered you freedom for it. . . . But you refused. How beautiful! . . . I wish I could have done the same! You knew where your friend was, but you wouldn't tell! I would have done the same, if I were free to act as I wanted."

She took my hand, and leaning towards me, said gently:

"Can I help you, Mrs. Shiber? I am allowed a free day tomorrow. I can come and go as I please. I could get word to your friend that she is in danger, that she must be careful. I can tell her where you are. . . . Would you like me to do that?"

I met Mary Bird's eye, and I saw a look of fright in it. What was Marthe really thinking? Did she want to help, or was this another trap? Which was her real self—the woman who had promised not to betray us, who was offering to help me now, or the German stool pigeon? Perhaps her whole story was a fiction. How did we know that she had a mother in a concentration camp? Suspicion and sympathy struggled in my mind, confusing me more and more. But I could see that there was only one safe course. I could not afford to take any risks. There was only one thing to say.

"Thank you, Marthe," I said, as gently as I could. "But the fact is that I don't know any way of getting into contact with my friend. What I told Dr. Hager was the truth. Her present whereabouts is a complete mystery to me."

"You don't trust me," Marthe said, turning away, and sinking onto the bed again. "I can't blame you. But I did think you believed me. I did think you understood."

"I will be perfectly frank with you, Marthe," I said. "I don't trust you. I do believe you. But you are not master of yourself. You have told us that. So I would not tell you anything even if I knew something. As it happens, I know nothing."

"Very well," Marthe snapped. "I suppose I should be grateful to you. You've saved me from committing a blunder—offering to help you. I might have been caught. I was risking more punishment for my mother. I shouldn't have done it. . . . But I was so happy to think some one believed in me again. . . . Oh, what's the use . . . let me alone, will you?"

Despite the rigid prison rule that no one was to lie on her bed during the day, she stretched herself out, pulled the blanket over her and closed her eyes. She seemed to be going off to sleep. But a few minutes later she jumped up from the bed without warning. She rushed at the door, and began kicking and striking at it with all her strength, so that the hollow sound of her feet and fists pounding on the iron resounded through the corridor. I heard the guard's running feet outside, the peephole clicked open. Then the door was flung ajar, the guard seized Marthe by the elbow, and pulled her out.

I never saw her again. But four months later, while our case was on trial, my lawyer told me that among some documents which he was allowed to see was her deposition. It was in my favor.

## CHAPTER TWENTY-FIVE

# Release!

THE DAYS dragged by in the prison of the Rue du Cherche-Midi with dreary monotony. Its beginning I have already described—wakening by the guard at 7:30, inspection ten minutes later, by which time we had to be dressed and have our beds made according to the prison regulations.

Our "coffee" was distributed at eight. It was black and nearly tasteless, which was fortunate, for what taste there was was unpleasant. What it was made of, I never succeeded in guessing, though I was told, vaguely, that German coffee was a mixture of four different ersatz products. It was sweetened with saccharine instead of sugar.

Lunch came at 11. It was always the same, day in, day out—whale soup. This was not a liquid, as its name indicated, but a sort of jellied mass inside which our meagre daily vegetable ration was included. It was supposed to be made from whale meat. With it came two slices of a rubber-like mass, the proud product of some branch of the German chemical industry, which looked like salami, but tasted like nothing in particular, and certainly had no meat in it at all.

The third and last meal of the day was handed to us at six in the evening. It consisted of a cup of ersatz tea, again sweetened with saccharine, and our daily bread ration, half of a very small round loaf of dark unappetizing bread. This we were supposed to distribute through the three meals of the day.

On this diet, we were constantly hungry.

Persons who have never skipped more than a meal or two can have no conception of the misery that comes with constant, unremitting hunger. Its very nature takes on a different quality. Ordinarily, hunger is a positive thing, which sharpens the appetite and causes a heartier approach to the next meal. But the hunger that fastens upon you when you eat insufficiently, day after day, is a negative feeling, an empty gnawing which is felt as a lack, but which creates no happier acceptance of the coming unpalatable meal, which doesn't contribute to make it more satisfactory—perhaps because you know in advance that it will not be enough, that the hunger which held you in its grip before you began eating will not diminish while you eat, and will still be as strong when you have finished.

It is almost with a sense of shame that I look back today to my prison experience, and realize that my thoughts, like those of my cell-mates, were almost exclusively preoccupied with food. Since there was nothing to do all day, and since four persons locked up together in a narrow room can't talk to each other all day long—particularly when they have no new experiences to talk about—I sat silent on my bed much of the time, day-dreaming and for half an hour or an hour, my thoughts would play with the idea of some simple dish, pork chops, for instance. I would imagine myself buying them in a store, carrying them home, preparing them for broiling, and the delicious aroma of broiling meat would seem to rise in my nostrils and awaken sharp pangs in my stomach. Indeed, there were times when I was not sure whether my imagination had not actually carried me to the point of hallucination, whether thinking of food had not progressed to the point where I actually saw it before my eyes.

The quantity of food the Germans gave us was perhaps one-third of that needed for the normal functioning of the human body. It was not so little that there was danger of dying of malnutrition, but it was not enough to permit ordinary activity.

This systematic starvation quickly deprived us of the greater part of our physical and mental energy. All we could do was sit on the edge of our beds, barely existing, not living. The slightest effort appeared enormous. Often we were too tired even to talk. If an object escaped our relaxed fingers, we would sit still for minutes, trying to muster enough energy to bend down and pick it up.

Was it the general shortage of foodstuffs throughout Europe which obliged the Germans to keep us on such short rations? That did not seem to be the answer. If that had been the only reason, our jailers would have permitted us to receive gifts of food from outside. The Quakers, for instance, wanted to supply us with extra food, but were not permitted to do so. The prison rules prohibited the sending of food to prisoners *while they were still under examination*—and that was the case of all those in the Cherche-Midi prison, none of whom had been tried and sentenced.

This made the German motive quite clear. They desired to weaken the prisoner, to reduce his will power, so that his powers of resistance would be less, so that his reasoning would be dulled. Thus he became clay in the hands of his inquisitors. It made it easier to extort information from him by such methods as those they had used against me. Perhaps if they had waited until I had been in prison two or three weeks, I wouldn't have seen through Dr. Hager's ruses. He made a mistake in tackling me too soon.

Similarly inhuman, it seemed to me, was the system which placed male guards over women prisoners, who had no privacy from them whatsoever. One never knew at what moment the peephole cover would be pulled back, and the guard would look into the cell. Indeed, the prison rules prescribed that guards should peep in at the inmates as often as possible, in order to know what they were doing at every hour of the day.

To me, the most disgusting necessity of all was that of being obliged to perform even the most private of physical functions in the presence of all my cell-mates. The canister I had so unpleasantly noticed when I was first imprisoned was our only toilet, and it was impossible to have any privacy in the use of it. Moreover, it remained in the cell all day long, being removed only at night, when the guard took it away, replacing it with an empty one.

In what other prison could such an incident have happened as that which I witnessed myself—an incident which happened to Lola? She was pregnant when she entered the prison. One morning she was incapable of getting up for the morning inspection. When the German officer arrived, she whispered to him, from white lips drawn tight in a pain-racked face:

"I am with child. I feel very ill."

"Don't lie to me," he snapped, and pulled the bed clothes off her to see for himself that she had spoken the truth.

I had never heard before of a prison whose inmates were not allowed a certain amount of exercise and fresh air daily, even if it was only half an hour in a courtyard. But in all the time I spent in

the Cherche-Midi prison, I never left my cell except when I was called to the warden's office.

We could not even walk back and forth in our cells, as wild animals may pace their cages, for the four beds which took up all the space made that impossible.

The ventilation slit in the cell—it didn't deserve to be called a window—was closed by glass, and so far as I know, couldn't be opened. At least, it never was. All day long we had to breathe the filthy air of the never-opened cell.

That was the atmosphere in which I lived, day after interminable day.

How did we spend our time? We spent it doing nothing; there was nothing for us to do. We could not read. We were allowed no books. We could not write. We were allowed no paper or pencils. Absolutely no occupation had been foreseen for the hapless prisoners who had to sit out the dreary hours, day after day, week after week, month after month. If starvation had not dulled our wits, this forced inaction would inevitably have done it sooner or later. The only breaks in the dull monotony were our three meals. In the morning, we drank our coffee, and then, like well-bred children, sat on the edges of our beds with our hands in our laps and waited for lunch.

At 11 o'clock, we had that meal, and then, once more sitting patiently on our beds, waited for supper. We strained our ears for the slightest sound in the corridor. The noise of the footsteps of the guard, passing the door, was an event, one of the few happenings which could distinguish any minute from any other. We knew the walk of every guard in our part of the prison. We usually knew when the peephole would open, for we could hear the guard coming. He would walk six steps, then stop. We would hear a slide click open and shut again. Six more steps. Click, click. Six more—and then it would be ours which would open.

The monotony became so unbearable that if we were left alone for two or three days at a stretch, we would begin to hope to be called for examination, even if a beating were likely to go with it. Anything was better than the unbroken procession of immeasurable time. But our greatest thrill, of course, was the arrival of a new cellmate. Only after I had been in prison for a while did I realize what

a great event my arrival must have been for my companions. Then I, too, began to long for the arrival of another prisoner. It didn't occur to me then that that meant I was also hoping that the Gestapo would catch new victims. All I could think of was that I needed desperately some event to break the monotony, something that my mind could take hold of, to prevent it from deserting me completely.

The 6 o'clock meal we saluted gladly, for it meant that we only had to sit idly for another hour. At seven we were permitted to go to bed; and an hour later the lights went out.

The first night I had spent in that awful atmosphere, with the black air pressing upon me, seemingly so heavy and so thick that I felt I could take it in my hand and squeeze it like rubber, had been horrible. But I came to long for the night, because then I could lie down, and if I couldn't sleep, at least I no longer saw the surroundings about me, and I could imagine, through the dark, other scenes than this bare prison cell.

About me in the dark I could hear my companions gasping for air in the putrid atmosphere, but still, in comparison with the day, the night sometimes seemed lovely, allowing me to lie in its silence and its blackness, as though enveloped in a heavy curtain, and float away in imagination, away from the stone walls, and iron-bound doors, and locks and keys of the prison.

In the lightheadedness provoked by insufficient food and lack of occupation to hold the mind down to any reality, it was not necessary to be asleep to dream. I could lie on my bed with my eyes open, staring into the impenetrable dark, and dream while I was still awake. Often, in this stage, halfway between sleep and wakefulness, I imagined suddenly that I was back in New York, and that I had just awakened from a nightmare. Sometimes the feeling would persist until I passed into a genuine dream, only to awake hours later; and sometimes it would pass at once, and I would realize, with despair in my heart, that it was the nightmare which was real, and the relief from it which was the dream.

Thus passed the endless days. Thus passed the welcome nights.

For some days after the disappearance of Marthe Wenzinger, there were only three of us in the cell. Then a new prisoner turned

up. This time the newcomer was a Polish girl, whose crime was trying to help members of the Polish Legion, hiding in France, to get to the unoccupied zone. I don't remember her name. She told me what it was more than once but I could never pronounce it, nor imagine how it might be spelled. It sounded as though it were all s's and z's.

She was an untamable girl, incurably optimistic, and though her refusal to accept defeat seemed unrealistic to us, who had become broken to prison life, it was a refreshing change to be in contact with this fighting psychology.

She had a freshly healed wound on her cheek. I asked her how she had gotten it. She smiled as she answered:

"That's a souvenir of the Hotel Matignon."

"The Hotel Matignon?" I repeated stupidly. I would have understood at once earlier, but by now my mental processes had been slowed up by starvation and inactivity.

"Well, wasn't that the route you took to get here?" she asked me. "You ought to know their methods. Of course, I asked for it. I fought back. I wasn't going to stand there like a cow being butchered while they beat me up. That awful Captain hit me and I hit him right back. It was no good, of course. I just got a terrible beating for it. The mark on my face is nothing. You should see my back."

Almost her first question to us was:

"What's the chance of escape?"

It was Mary Bird who answered:

"There isn't any."

The Polish girl was unimpressed.

"Huh!" she snorted. "Has any one ever tried?"

"I don't think so," Mary said. "I've been in five cells now, and seen quite a few prisoners. It's the first time I've heard any one even mention it. There's not a chance of getting out of this place."

"So that's your opinion, is it?" the Polish girl said, with more than a trace of sarcasm in her voice. "What have you done to find out? How about the guard? Have you tried him?"

"No," said Mary wearily. "It wouldn't do any good. The guard we had before this one carried some notes for me. They caught him. So they put a new man on.

"There, you see!" said the Pole, triumphantly. "German guards aren't unapproachable. If you managed to get away with something with the first one, I should think you would have tried again. Let me speak to him. I know the language his kind talks. . . . And how about the hospital? Did you ever play sick to get taken there? No, I can see by your faces none of you even thought of it! No wonder you think you can't escape. You haven't made the slightest effort, you haven't even considered how to go about it! You've just been sitting here like animals, hoping for good luck! Well, that's not my way. I'll show you that there's no such thing as an escape-proof prison."

Her attempt began next day. At lunch, she whispered something in the guard's ear. He didn't answer, but as he went out, our Polish friend sat down to eat her soup with an expression of great satisfaction. She never finished it. She was halfway through when the guard returned with the inspecting officer.

"Number 1902," he said. "Attempting to corrupt a guard. Ten days solitary confinement."

And the man to whom she knew how to talk hustled her away to the punishment cells. Her half-finished bowl of soup was left on the table behind her. As the door closed on her, we looked at one another with a common impulse. Then Mary picked up the bowl, and poured its contents into ours, dividing it as evenly as she could.

I had been arrested on November 26. On December 14, at 11 A.M., we heard the footsteps of the guard outside. It was lunchtime, and we expected him to enter with our soup. But when he swung the door open, he didn't have the pot he usually carried. Instead, he said:

"1876—come with me. You are to be released."

I stared at him stupidly for a minute.

"I—I—what?" I stammered.

"Come along. Hurry up," he ordered. "I've got to get lunch. I can't wait all day for you."

I hurriedly embraced my cell-mates, picked up my bag (it was always packed, for I had nowhere else to keep my few clothes), and followed him along the corridor.

"Are you sure I'm being freed?" I asked. "Isn't it only another examination?"

Release order which freed Mrs. Shiber from the Cherche-Midi prison for a short period before her trial.

My tone must have been almost a pleading one, but he gave no answer. He simply hurried along the corridor and then down to the ground floor until we reached the room where I had been received—where my fingerprints had been taken and where I had been searched.

There I was handed a release form which stated that I had been in the Cherche-Midi prison from November 26 to December 14, and on the latter date had been freed. I was told to sign a paper stating that I had been well treated in prison, that the food had been sufficient and of good quality, and that I had no complaint to make of the direction of the prison. I couldn't see any point in protesting. I signed.

Another guard took me to the office of the warden. The Major was standing behind his desk, smiling affably.

"Well, Mrs. Shiber," he said, "it gives me great personal satisfaction to be able to restore your freedom to you. I trust that you will not leave us with too bad an impression. The order to release you has just arrived, and though ordinarily, under prison regulations, all releases occur at 6 in the evening, I made a special exception in your case, in order to let you out at the earliest possible moment."

He picked up a bunch of keys from his desk. I recognized them at once as those which had been taken from me at the Hotel Matignon.

"Here are your keys," he said, handing them to me. "You are free."

Up to this moment, I had been dazed and suspicious. I expected another Nazi trick. But it seemed to be genuine. Still, I couldn't quite believe it yet.

"I'm free?" I murmured, talking to myself as much as to him.

"Yes, Madame. I have had no further instructions concerning your case—simply the order to release you."

"Could I leave the city, for instance?"

"Certainly, if you wish. You may do anything you could have done before your arrest."

He accompanied me to the door of his office, and opened it for me politely. I walked through the antechamber, between the stiff unmoving sentries, across the courtyard, and to the outer gate. An officer just inside looked at my release form, stamped it, and returned it politely. The heavy door was flung open, and, feeling as unreal as though it were all a dream, I walked out into the free air of the Rue du Cherche-Midi.

I stopped on the corner, my knees shaking. I felt I couldn't go any farther until I had had a minute to readjust myself to my new situation, to accustom myself again to free movement, to free exercise of my own will. I breathed in deeply, again and again, feeling the cold sweet air stab its way into the depths of my lungs. I looked about me at what others would have considered ordinary, everyday sights, completely uninteresting. But to me they were the fascinating stirrings of another world—people walking along the streets, moving wherever their own wills directed them; a rare automobile or two passing by; long lines in front of shops across the street; a man stepping from a corner café; a woman leaning out of an opened, unbarred window, shaking a dustcloth.

The scene wavered before my eyes. I could feel the tears welling up in them. I blinked them back, and turned in the direction of the Metro.

It was true. I was free.

## CHAPTER TWENTY-SIX

# Where Is Kitty?

I HAD turned mechanically towards the subway with the unconscious idea of going home, but then I stopped, wondering if that
was really what I wanted to do first. I must have looked drunk to
passersby, hesitating, wavering, and at the same time breathing in
deeply as though I had just made some great effort.

It occurred to me that I could go to a restaurant, where I would
eat as much as the rationing laws permitted me to buy. I could taste
at last some of those unattainable dishes I had dreamed of in prison.

And then the thought of another luxury came into my mind—a
bath! During all the time I had spent in that dreadful cell, I had
not been able to take one. We were without the simplest facilities
for keeping clean. A common washbasin served for all four of us
in the morning, and there was barely enough water to wet our
faces. And I could go to a hairdresser, too! All these possibilities
made me feel like a child looking ahead to Christmas.

And a newspaper! What had happened since I had been in jail?
We had been completely cut off from all news. I knew nothing of
what had happened while I was imprisoned. I wanted to catch up
with the progress of the world, too—even though I knew all French
newspapers were now controlled by the Germans.

I continued to walk indecisively towards the subway as I tried to
decide what to do first, and in the end it was habit rather than decision which took me home. I knocked on the door of Mme. Beugler's
loge. When she opened it, she seemed for a moment not to recognize
me. But then my dogs rushed forward, barking frantically. They
sprang up and licked my hands, making so much noise that neither
the concierge nor myself could make ourselves heard.

When they finally quieted down, Mme. Beugler's first words
were:

"My God, what have they done to you, Mrs. Shiber?" Only then
did I realize that the experiences of the past weeks must have

marked themselves deeply in my appearance. "But, thank God," the concierge added quickly, "at least you are free again."

"What happened to Margot?" I asked.

"They arrested her, too, but they let her go the next day. She came back here, but the two Germans living in your apartment advised her to look for another job. They told her that her employers probably wouldn't be back. So she went home to her family in Brittany."

"Oh, yes! Those Germans!" I said. "They aren't still there?"

"They left yesterday. They stayed there day and night—two of them in your apartment, and one man always down here in my *loge*. They were waiting for Mme. Kitty. They thought she would return, and they were going to arrest her. They must have decided it was no use, and moved out."

"How did you manage to warn Mme. Kitty's husband?" I asked.

The concierge was surprised.

"Monsieur Beaurepos? But I haven't seen him. It's lucky for him he didn't come here. They would have arrested him. They did arrest that good-looking young priest who used to come to see you."

"Yes, I knew that," I said. "But then—how in the world did Monsieur Beaurepos discover that I had been arrested? It was he who told the American Embassy."

I can't describe the joy I felt when I entered my apartment again after my irksome imprisonment. The first thing I did was simply to walk about from one room to another, unable to sit down calmly and rest. I turned the lights on and off, I tried the hot-water faucet to make sure that it was still working, and that I could actually enjoy the luxury of hot water whenever I wanted it.

The bell rang. I hurried happily to the door, wondering which of my friends would turn out to be my first caller.

When I opened the door and saw who it was, I had to steel myself suddenly to keep from fainting. It was Dr. Hager.

I had thought my nightmare was over. But here was the chief actor in it, and no doubt it was beginning again. My freedom was only an illusion, one more of their despicable tricks.

But Dr. Hager was wearing his sympathetic smile again, and using his softest voice.

"Goodness, Madame Shiber, don't look so frightened!" he said. "I only dropped in to ask if the two men who stayed here left everything in order. If they have done any damage, you will be reimbursed, of course. If anything is missing, don't fail to report it. . . . Do you mind if I have a look around to make sure everything is all right?"

He proved to be a thorough inspector. With my guidance, he poked into every closet, examined minutely all the rooms, even looked into the icebox.

"You must excuse my being very minute, Madame," he said to me at one stage in the proceedings. "I am responsible for any damage my men do."

"There doesn't seem to be any," I said, wondering what the real object of his search could be—for it obviously was a search.

"You're a very strange woman, Mme. Shiber," he said, still smiling, as he finished his inspection. "I expected you to ask me how it happened that you were released. One would say you aren't interested in your own case."

"I'm still a little dazed, I guess," I answered.

"That's not surprising, of course," Dr. Hager admitted. "Well, I can tell you, without giving away any official secrets, that the investigation of this case has been concluded—and, as I told you before, that was the only thing holding up your release. The criminals, except your friend, Mme. Beaurepos, are all in jail. The investigation demonstrated that you had taken no active part in any criminal activity, so you have been freed."

He walked to the door. With his hand on the knob, he paused and turned:

"And what do you plan to do now? Are you going to take my advice and go back to the United States?"

"I'd like to," I answered. "But can I? Do you think I would have any difficulties?"

"No, no, none at all," Dr. Hager protested, with a sweeping gesture. "You are entirely your own master. You can stay or leave, as you please. No one has any right to interfere with your plans. . . . Is there anything else I can tell you before I go?"

"Yes, I . . ." I hesitated a moment. "I wonder if you have found out what happened to Mme. Beaurepos?"

Dr. Hager made an impatient movement.

"Look here, Mme. Shiber," he said, "let me tell you something. The organization to which I belong is badly misjudged. Here in France, and in your country, too, you hear nonsense about the Gestapo taking revenge on persons. That's ridiculous. We have no interest in revenging ourselves on any one. An individual may stoop to that sort of thing, but an organization like ours has more serious purposes.

"No, we don't know where Mme. Beaurepos is, except that we know she has left the occupied zone. That's all we want. Our only purpose was to destroy her organization. We have succeeded. As far as we're concerned, it's entirely immaterial whether Mme. Beaurepos is ever apprehended or not. The case is closed."

He looked at me ponderingly for a moment before continuing.

"Of course, if Mme. Beaurepos should be so stupid as to make any effort to resume her old activity, that would be another matter. In that case, we would be obliged to arrest her. . . . I have a bit of advice for you, Mrs. Shiber. If you still think your friend deserves that you should help her, persuade her to go to America with you. It will keep her out of trouble. If she remains here, she may be tempted to commit a second offense—and I assure you, she would not escape us again."

When Dr. Hager had gone, I sat down and tried to imagine what had been the real purpose of his visit. I was sure that it wasn't to see if any damage had been done. He was certainly looking for something—but what? Surely his men must have inspected the apartment thoroughly while they were there; and I had only been back for a short time.

I gave the riddle up; but I couldn't get rid of the feeling of Dr. Hager's presence so easily. It seemed to me that I could sense him standing behind me, with that false smile of his on his face. For the first time, I was afraid to remain alone in my own apartment. I walked through it, putting the lights on in every room, even the kitchen.

"Goodness," I thought to myself, "I'm afraid of the dark! I'm acting like a child again. I'd better leave Paris. Not until I get as far away as possible can I be at peace again—far away, out of the reach of Dr. Hager and all his gang. I should have started to make arrangements to go today. Who knows—one lost day might still be fatal. The first thing tomorrow I'm going to see what I must do to get back home."

As soon as I got up the following morning, I collected all my documents, put them in my handbag, and set out for the American Embassy.

As I stepped from the elevator on the ground floor, I saw a French policeman in front of the concierge's *loge,* talking to Mme. Beugler.

"Why, here she is now," said Mme. Beugler, waving towards me. The policeman tipped his hat politely, and handed me a piece of paper. It was a request that I should come to the Prefecture at once concerning a traffic violation.

"There must be some mistake!" I objected. "I don't even own an automobile. My friend does, but it's in her name. I have nothing to do with it. I don't even drive!"

The policeman was firm.

"I can't help that, Madame," he said. "My orders are simply to bring you to the Prefecture to answer for this violation. Anything you have to say you will have to tell them there."

With a sinking heart, I preceded him to the door. I knew the charge of having committed a traffic violation while I was locked up in the Cherche-Midi prison was ridiculous, and I suspected that this might have some connection with Dr. Hager's visit of the night before. It was all an elaborate comedy. I had been released by the German police only to be taken over by the French police; and I had heard only too often how the French had been forced to do the dirty work of the Germans.

There had been cases, I knew, of French policemen discharged for refusing to carry out German orders, such as those to arrest Jews: and it was common knowledge that German instructions to the French police were often sabotaged by the very men appointed to carry them out, who might, for instance, warn those they were charged with arresting to get out of sight.

The French police themselves were not immune from feeling the weight of German displeasure. I had heard one story of an incident which occurred in a café on the Champs-Elysées, where two German officers had called the manager and demanded that a man at the next table, evidently Jewish, be told to leave. Obediently, the manager asked his Jewish customer to go to avoid trouble. Instead, he answered in a loud voice:

"Inform these officers that if my presence annoys them, their presence annoys me. I am a Frenchman. This is my country. If they don't like sharing it with those who belong here, we shall be very happy to have them leave."

One of the German officers, in a rage, told the manager that if the Jew did not leave in five minutes, the café would be closed permanently. On the manager's plea that his means of livelihood was being jeopardized, the customer got up and passed before the table of the officers; as he did so, he spat contemptuously on the ground. The officer who had threatened the manager, beside himself with fury, drew his revolver and killed him—and several hours later ten policemen were arrested at random in the district by German soldiers, and told that they would be punished because of the failure of the French police to keep order in that district. They were never heard from again.

I was myself inclined to be skeptical of stories like this one, but it was repeated throughout Paris, and believed by everybody.

Before the war, Parisians had always enjoyed jokes in which the police were held up to ridicule: but at the same time they had a good deal of liking for *monsieur l'agent* in most of his rôles. French police often had an easy and kindly manner. They seemed to represent the spirit of a free country. They were not required to salute Army officers—but when the Germans arrived, all that was changed. They were furnished with the white cuffs which distinguish German policemen and they were ordered to salute German Army officers and stand rigidly at attention when they passed by, or even when a German non-commissioned officer passed.

I witnessed one humiliating spectacle in the Place de l'Opéra, where a German sergeant took his revenge on a French policeman who had pretended not to see him when he passed. He ordered the unfortunate Frenchman to stand at attention, to salute him, and then to run three times around the Place. Parisians watched the representative of their law being put through these paces with expressions of the deepest shame. Finally, when the policeman finished his third round, out of breath, the German ordered: "About face!" and when the policeman obeyed, he gave him a hearty kick which sent him sprawling.

That was too much for the Frenchman. He sprang up and knocked the German over with one blow of his fist. But two sentinels, standing guard with fixed bayonets before the Kommandantur on the corner, ran over and seized the policeman. He was led away between them. I never heard what happened to him.

But most of the French police submitted to the German rules without rebellion—in fact, some of them even overdid it. Thus it was common, when Frenchmen crossed the street before traffic policemen who had been taught the new stiff German gestures, to find him exaggerating them, caricaturing them, in fact—sometimes with a sly wink for an obvious compatriot, as though to say: "This is the way *they* do it. Absurd, aren't they?"

But I knew that the French police had been forced nevertheless to obey the directives of the Germans, so I was sure, as I turned into the great gateway of the Prefecture with my escorting policeman, that it was really on the orders of the Germans that I was being summoned.

I showed my *convocation* at the doorway, and was directed to the traffic department on the second floor. A police lieutenant received me, studied the paper I handed him carefully for a minute, then asked:

"You are Mme. Shiber?"

"I am," I said.

"Can you prove your identity?"

That was easy, since I had all my papers with me. He glanced at them, rose from his desk, and opened a door in the rear wall; and with a polite gesture that would have done credit to a dancing master, said:

'This way, Madame, if you please."

I moved towards the door with a sinking heart, in spite of his courtesy, but as I entered the room, I could barely repress a scream of joy—for there stood Henri Beaurepos!

He stretched out both hands as he came towards me.

"My dear Etta," he said, "I'm so happy to see you again! I hope you weren't frightened by the means I used to get you here. You see, you are under constant observation. The only way I could think of to manage a meeting was to have you brought here by the police. The Germans no doubt know you are here, but if they ask why, we'll simply tell them that it was a mistake. . . . Now—did you know you were being watched?"

"No," I faltered. "No, I didn't. You mean . . . I'm not rid of them yet?"

"I'm afraid not, Etta," Henri said gravely. "That's one reason why I had you brought here—to warn you. I don't know what they told you, but I believe the only reason they gave you your freedom was in the hope that you would lead them to Kitty. They've done everything they could to find her—I know because some inquiries cleared through here—and they haven't succeeded. You're the decoy. They expect you either to lure her back by getting in touch with her, or to lead them to her.

"They're looking for me, too. Fortunately, as you see, my contacts are very good. I know that the Gestapo looked me up. They learned that I didn't see Kitty often, that I hadn't been in touch with her for some time, but just the same they want to arrest me, to find out if I know anything, and perhaps to use me as they want to use you, to help them find Kitty. So this was the only place I dared meet you. They would have been able to follow you anywhere else."

"But, Henri," I asked (this had been puzzling me ever since Mme. Beugler had denied seeing him), "how did you find out about my arrest? I thought at first that you had heard of it from the concierge, but she told me she hadn't heard from you."

"I did get the news from Mme. Beugler," Henri grinned, "only she didn't know it. I had a policeman inquire at your place preparatory to visiting you. . . . That's what we're reduced to nowadays. Before you make a surprise visit to a friend, you have to make sure he's still there, or you may meet a German policeman instead when you get to his apartment. It was when I read that the Germans were offering rewards for information about the escapes of English soldiers that I thought I had better begin taking precautions. It's fortunate that I did."

"What about Kitty?" I asked. "Where is she?"

"Don't you know?" he returned quickly. "I hoped you did. That was another reason why I wanted to talk to you."

I shook my head despairingly.

"Oh, Henri!" I almost wept. "You mean to say you haven't been able to tell her of my arrest—to warn her of her own danger? With all your cleverness, and resourcefulness, and influence—you haven't been able to locate her?"

"No," Henri said grimly. "That's just the trouble. She probably hasn't the slightest inkling that anything is wrong. She's likely to walk into their hands at any minute. While we're talking here, she may be going to the apartment now, under the eyes of the Gestapo man watching the building."

"But, Henri," I protested, feeling the blood leave my cheeks, "I must get back. We don't know what's happening there! I must be there to warn her . . ."

"Keep calm, Etta," Henri said soothingly. "You must keep your head. There's nothing you can do to warn her—in fact, you're one of the greatest dangers to her now, for they're watching every move you make. If she has gotten that far, she's lost anyway. . . . What we have got to try to do is to head her off in time. I have been scouring the unoccupied zone trying to find her—calling on friends of hers, trying every lead I could think of. I thought Marseilles might be a likely place, and I tried there, but no one we knew had seen her. What more could I do? I couldn't put an advertisement in the newspaper, warning her the police were after her. Anything that she would have understood would have been plain to the Gestapo, too."

"How terrible!" I said. "And to think that while you were in Marseilles, she may have been there, too! She said she was going there—and also to Lyons and Périgueux."

"You see, Etta," Henri exclaimed, "you can help me . . . I hope you didn't tell the Germans that?"

"Of course not," I said. "Do you think I'm out of my head? I told them I thought she had gone to Tours."

"Good!" said Henri. "Now—I went to Lyons; no trace there. But

Périgueux sounds like a good lead. That's a smaller place. It ought to be easier to find her, if that's where she is. . . . Now have you any idea who she might have seen?"

I told Henri the story of the friend at Marseilles who was financing our work whom she intended to see, but unfortunately I didn't know his name or address. Henri thought he knew who it might be. I also gave him some addresses of friends of Kitty's in Lyons, and particularly that of the person she intended visiting in Périgueux, which he seemed to think was the best clue of all.

Henri wrote down all the addresses, and put the paper carefully away in his wallet.

"If I have just a little luck," he said, smiling hopefully, "I may be able to catch up with her in time. . . . Now, Etta dear, pardon me for having been so engrossed with Kitty—what are your plans?"

I told him that I had been on my way to the Embassy to try to get back to America when his policeman had picked me up. I said also that I planned to try to get my Spanish and Portuguese visas that very day.

Henri frowned.

"I don't want to worry you unnecessarily, Etta," he said, "but I think you should be prepared for the probability that the Germans won't let you go. You can't leave without an exit visa from them— and they're watching you too closely for you to try to get out of the occupied zone illegally."

I could feel myself turning pale again.

"You mean they would refuse me a visa?" I asked.

"I don't think so—not outright. If I know the Germans, they won't refuse; you just won't get one. They'll put you off from day to day, on one pretext or another. But I don't think they intend that you shall get away. They want you to lead them to Kitty.

"Now this is my advice: Go to the American Embassy at once. Talk to them and ask what they think you should do. My guess is that you should try to get out of the occupied zone at once, if it's at all possible. We may be able to arrange something here, if it's necessary, but it would be easier in a few days, when they may have slacked off a little. I'm going to leave tonight to try to locate Kitty again, but you can come here and ask the officer who received you for assistance: and if it's wise to do so before I get back, he can probably help you get over the frontier. But consult the Embassy first, though perhaps you had better remember that they may be a trifle over-cautious. You know what diplomats are.

"Keep in regular touch with them anyway. If I were you, I'd arrange to check once a day, so that they can set to work to locate you if you fail to put in an appearance at the regular time. And again: you can come here with absolute confidence if you need any help—but don't write or telephone. This is where you will find me when I come back. It will be better for you to come, for we can't use that excuse of the mistaken summons again, very well."

He accompanied me to the door, and took leave of me with a warm handclasp.

"Good-bye, Etta, and good luck," he said. "Keep your chin up! And be on the watch for the Gestapo!"

I remembered his words as I left the Prefecture. I peered keenly about as I walked to the subway station of the Ile de la Cité. It was not too hard to identify my shadow. A young man was following close on my heels. When I got into the train, he entered the same car. When I got out, he followed.

Free? No. I was still a prisoner of the Gestapo. Only, for the moment, I was not supposed to know it.

## CHAPTER TWENTY-SEVEN

# Travels with a Shadow

I REALIZED now that I was still just as much a prisoner of the Gestapo as when I had been in jail. You can't call yourself free when you know some one is following your every step, charged with making a report on all your movements; and I know few things more nerve-racking than the consciousness that you are being spied on every minute.

During the rest of the day, I made several efforts to elude my shadow, but all of them were unsuccessful. For instance, when I left the American Embassy, which was my first port of call after the Prefecture, I slipped out of the side door on the Rue Boissy d'Anglas instead of the front door of the Avenue Gabriel. I looked about, and failed to see the Gestapo agent. Joyously, I hurried away—but I hadn't reached the next corner before I saw him again, following at a little distance.

They had not been very hopeful at the Embassy about the possibility of my being allowed to leave the occupied zone.

"I think it very improbable," one official there told me, "that they intend to let you get out of Paris. It seems pretty clear that they released you only in the belief that you would lead them to Mme. Beaurepos. You can't get out without a German exit visa, you know, and they aren't likely to give you one."

"In that case," I said, discouraged, "there's no point in bothering about Spanish and Portuguese visas."

"On the contrary," said the Embassy official, "get them, and go through all the other formalities necessary to go to the United States. In the first place, that deprives them of any excuse for refusing you an exit visa on the ground that your other papers are not complete. Secondly, it will demonstrate to them that your only desire is to return to the United States. But be very careful, Mrs. Shiber, that the Gestapo has no reason for deciding that you may be considering escaping into the unoccupied zone without an exit visa, for in that case they would undoubtedly arrest you at once."

Before leaving the Embassy, I inquired about Mr. Marvel. I said that I would like to call on him and thank him for his help.

"Don't do it," the official said, in alarm. "You might compromise his work. He is the only American who has permission to visit the prisons, and he manages it because the Germans are absolutely convinced of the conscientiousness with which he sticks to their restrictions on his activity—that he confine himself to the physical well-being of prisoners and refuse to discuss their cases. He is thus our only means of getting any information from the prisons, and if you called on him, they might suspect that he had exceeded his rôle, and bar him from the jails. We'll tell him, though, that you expressed your appreciation to us."

When my shadow reappeared behind me after I left the Embassy, I gave up the attempt to slip away from him up the Rue Boissy d'Anglas, and turned to come out on the Place de la Concorde—which, for me, was always the most beautiful square in the world. With their customary sensitivity, the French have classed it a *"monument historique,"* which means that no architectural innovations can be made in it without permission of the Fine Arts administration. Thus the harmony of the setting is preserved.

When the new American Embassy was built at one corner of the Place de la Concorde, it not only had to be designed to fit in with the rest of the square, but actually completed it as its first designer had laid it out; for he had planned a building on the site purchased by the Embassy in the same style as that opposite it, but it had never been built. The American Embassy thus brought to fruition at last the plan originally conceived for the square.

The aesthetic scruples of both the French and the American governments were not shared by the Germans. They moved into the Hotel Crillon, across the street from the American Embassy, and also took over the third of the three buildings forming the North side of the square, the French Navy Ministry. For their convenience, they then constructed a horrible temporary wooden bridge above the street connecting the two buildings, spoiling the whole harmony of the square.

Poor Paris! I thought as I passed it, with an inward shudder, what are you going to look like if the Germans honor you much longer with their presence?

I walked up the majestic Rue Royale, blocked at its far end by the Madeleine, turned into the Boulevard de la Madeleine and continued into the Boulevard des Capucines, one of the most lovely stretches of the Grands Boulevards. Once this street had been lively with traffic; now there were no automobiles to be seen, with the exception of an occasional German official car marked with the swastika. Instead of the brightly colored taxis, with their ebullient chauffeurs, there were bicycle taxis, powered by haggard perspiring human motors, pedaling away with all their might, in order to transport themselves and a passenger riding in a two-wheeled cart behind the bicycle. It made me think of the Chinese coolies and their jin-rikishas. I shuddered to see Europeans—Parisians—slaving away in this fashion, at a sort of labor against which Europeans in China had once objected on the ground that it was too degrading to human dignity.

I couldn't resist stopping at the Café de la Paix to rest for a few minutes in the spot where Kitty and I had spent so many happy hours in a time relatively near, but which seemed to have receded deep into the past. This had been one of our favorite spots—as it was, indeed, a favorite spot of all tourists, of whom few failed to visit this landmark of Parisian living, located at the corner where the Boulevard des Capucines opens into the Place de l'Opéra.

Apparently the Germans agreed with the other tourists, for they were there in force. They had invaded it as they had invaded France. The terrace was crowded with German officers and the Frauleins they had imported to do the office work of the many German government bureaus and business offices. It was easy to tell which ones were the Germans, even those who were not in uniform. They were loud, arrogant and boisterous, self-satisfied, impertinent, prosperous. Obviously they were, unlike the French, well fed and well paid. Here and there you would see an elderly gentleman, sitting quietly at a table, reading a paper. Those were the Frenchmen. They seemed almost to apologize for being there, tranquil islands of good taste and good manners in the tumultuous sea of noisy, self-assertive conquerors.

I suppose it was because the proportion of German customers was so high that the Café de la Paix had been able to get charcoal for its braziers. I always loved the tall cast-iron stoves which appeared in Paris with the first cold weather, set up behind glass screens, to make it possible to sit outside in spite of the temperature. I sat down next to one of them, feeling the pleasant warmth exuding from it, and watched, without displeasure, I must admit, my shivering shadow take up a position against a lamp post in the cold December wind that was whipping through the streets. In order to watch both entrances of the café, he had to post himself on the corner, exposed to all the breezes that blew through the Place de l'Opéra from the half-dozen streets that empty into it. He looked very uncomfortable, and I am afraid I sat there a little longer than I might have otherwise, trying to freeze him out. But he didn't budge, and he didn't come inside himself to watch me from warmer quarters. Perhaps he was afraid that I might slip out suddenly, leaving him to be intercepted by an indignant waiter if he tried to follow without taking time to pay his bill.

My next stop was the Louvre department store, where I made a few purchases. They were necessarily few, for there was almost nothing to be bought in the stores. Whatever one did succeed in buying had to be carried home, for there was no delivery service at all.

As I came out, a boy of 14 or thereabouts spoke to me.

"May I carry your parcels home for you, Madame?" he asked.

His manners were good, and he was obviously well brought up; but he seemed embarrassed, and I judged that offering himself for such services was still new to him.

"I'm sorry," I said, "but I'm not going straight home. I have to have lunch first."

"That doesn't matter, Madame," he said. "I can wait, if you want."

"How about you?" I asked. "Have you had lunch yet?"

He blushed, and answered shyly, "Not yet."

He was an appealing little chap, and I felt sorry for him; it seemed so obvious that he had been obliged, after a sheltered childhood, to seek this means of earning a little something to help out a diminished family budget.

"How would you like to have lunch with me?" I proposed.

He became a shade redder, and returned, confusedly:

"Well, you see, Madame . . . that is . . . I haven't any money. . . . I—"

"Oh, that's all right," I said. "I was inviting you. I don't like to eat alone. You can keep me company. . . . Only—do you know any place near here where it's possible to eat without ration cards?"

"Yes, Madame," he said, his eyes lighting up at the prospect of lunch. But then his voice took on a duller tone, as he continued. "But it's very expensive. All the cheaper places ask for cards."

"I think I can afford it," I said, smiling at the thought of how unlikely it was that he could suspect what I meant. "I haven't had to spend very much for food lately."

At the restaurant, my young friend got over his shyness. His eyes sparkling as he dug into a lunch probably much better than he had recently been accustomed to (for the restaurants which didn't bother about ration cards also violated the regulations by buying on the Black Market), he confirmed my suspicions. He did belong to a family which had been well-off before the war, but now had been ruined. His father, head of a manufacturing concern, could have been described as rich; but now he was a prisoner of war in Germany. The little fellow (Pierre was his name) lived alone with his mother, in their beautiful home in the luxurious residential district of Auteuil. Now it was bare of most of its objects of value, which had been sold at a fraction of their real worth, no doubt to be resold to Germans. Their only income was the few francs Pierre was able to make by such jobs as the carrying of parcels.

"Some of my friends sell newspapers," Pierre said. "There's more money in that. But I don't believe in it. It's spreading German propaganda."

He said it so stoutly that I looked at him with admiration, thinking that this fourteen-year-old lad could give lessons to many of his elders, who had accepted cooperation with the Germans because it promoted their businesses and their personal well-being. If Pierre is typical of the youngest generation, I thought, France is not yet lost. Her future will be assured by him and his fellows.

"Do you think, Madame," Pierre asked politely, with a grave concern beyond his age, "that these conditions can last much longer? I'm worried most about my father. What will he think when he comes home and finds out wnat we have been through? And how long will it be, do you think, before they will let him go? The war's over, isn't it? Why don't they send him home?"

"I'm sure he'll be home soon, Pierre," I consoled him, although actually I wasn't sure at all. It seemed plain by then that the Germans were deliberately holding the prisoners of war as a means of pressure on France—and also because that kept the birth-rate down and reduced the number of men she would have available to oppose to Germany in future years.

But Pierre took my assurance at its face value, and told me about his work as a carrier of packages. As a rule, he didn't try stores, he said, because there were few persons who came out of them with packages cumbrous enough so that they didn't want to carry them themselves. But railroad stations were profitable posts, for in the absence of taxis, arrivals had to go to their hotels on foot, and were glad to have some one help them with their luggage.

Pierre's chief trouble, he told me, was that he remained at the stations until closing time, and as many of his customers lived some distance away, he was often caught on the streets at the curfew hour, and had to dodge the German patrols on the way home.

"But it's easy," he told me. "You can hear them coming before you can see them, their heavy boots clump along so, and of course the blackout makes it easy not to get caught. When I hear a patrol, I ring the nearest doorbell. The concierges never mind opening when I tell them I'm hiding from the patrol."

He seemed to be turning something over in his little head for a moment. Then, with a grave smile, he said:

"It's funny, isn't it, Madame? Before the war, I couldn't go out in the streets alone, even in the daytime, without my governess or the chauffeur. Now I stay out alone, even at night, hiding from the German patrols. War makes changes in people's lives, doesn't it?"

"Yes, Pierre," I said, "war makes very great changes in people's lives."

Mme. Beugler came out of her *loge* to meet me when I returned home.

"Mme. Shiber," she said, "the concierge across the street told me something that might interest you. She says that some strange persons have moved into one of her apartments. They're Germans, and one of the things that struck her as odd is that they didn't bring any furniture in—only a sofa and two armchairs. She says they seem to do nothing except sit at the window all day, watching this house. I thought it might be about you."

"It probably is," I sighed, wearily. "They're having me followed, I know."

"Or perhaps it's for Mme. Kitty," the concierge suggested. "They don't want to leave any men here, so you won't suspect, but they still want to catch her if she should return."

I thanked her, and went up to my apartment. I sank into a chair and sought to organize my thoughts, to get a clear view of the situation. There could no longer be any doubt that I had been released simply because they still wanted to catch Kitty. All of Dr. Hager's talk about his lack of interest in catching individuals, about the case being closed, was intended only to pull the wool over my eyes.

It was plain now why he had advised that I should take Kitty to America. He thought that would send me to her at once, if I knew where she was. Then they would arrest her, and probably re-arrest me, too, as well. There was only one thing for me to do.

I must escape. I must get away while there was still time.

I went to the window and looked down into the street. The young man who had been following me all day was standing in front of the house. This time I felt almost sorry for him. He must have been cold. He kept his hands thrust deep into his pockets, except when, from time to time, he wanted to take his cigarette out of his mouth, or light another one.

I gazed across the street at the house opposite, trying to spot the Gestapo agents there, watching our building. I saw nothing suspicious. But then, I didn't even know which windows hid them. Were they perhaps on the same level with our apartment? Perhaps they had glasses with which they could actually look into my rooms, and see me moving about! I shivered, and closed the curtains.

Sunday morning I had a phone call from Mr. Marvel. He said that he was happy to learn that I had been released, and from the reserved manner in which he spoke I assumed that he realized that my phone had been tapped, and that the Gestapo was listening to whatever we said.

"I'd be very much obliged to you, Mme. Shiber," he said, "if you would be kind enough to return the warm clothing I brought to you at the prison. Fortunately, you don't need it any longer, but there are others who do, and our supplies are very limited."

"I'll be very glad, to do so, of course," I said. "Where can I bring it?"

I imagined that he wanted an excuse for meeting me, as well as to get the clothing back. By thus calling me on a telephone which he was sure was being watched, he was disarming any suspicions the Gestapo might have about our meeting in advance. We arranged to meet in the lobby of the Hotel Ritz at 7 o'clock that evening—not exactly the favorite place for delivering used clothing, perhaps, but in these wartime days no one bothered any longer about such inelegancies as carrying bundles into luxury hotels.

Hanging up the phone, I decided to go back to the Prefecture and see the officer to whom Henri had recommended me. I wanted to lose no time in getting away, and Henri had said that he might be able to slip me over the demarcation line in spite of the Gestapo shadowers.

As I left the house, I looked about for my faithful follower. He was standing in the doorway of the neighboring house, shabbily dressed as always, waiting patiently for my appearance. I don't know what got into me, but I couldn't resist walking over to him and saying: "To save you trouble, I might as well tell you that I'm going to take the subway to the Prefecture, and after that I'm coming back to the Place de la Concorde, to go to the American Embassy."

He looked startled. Embarrassed, he stammered:

"I—I—I don't understand, Madame. What . . . ?"

"Oh, never mind the play-acting," I said. "You've been following me ever since I was let out. You know the way. Come along."

And off I went, leaving him standing there. After a moment, I looked over my shoulder. There he was, padding along behind me, reminding me of a beaten dog following its master.

At the Etoile subway station, he sidled up to me in the waiting crowd, and whispered pleadingly:

"Excuse me, Madame . . . could I ask you, please . . . if you would be so kind . . . don't let my superiors know you spotted me?"

"Don't worry," I said. "I shan't mention it."

He looked immensely relieved. Inwardly, I felt a great desire to laugh. Yesterday, his presence had kept my nerves on edge. Now he had suddenly become ludicrous, even pitiful—a poorly paid hireling of the Gestapo, afraid that the person he was stalking would cause him to lose his job.

I found Henri's friend in the office I had visited before, in spite of its being a Sunday, and learned that Henri had, as planned, left for the unoccupied zone to look for Kitty. I told him that I had become convinced that I must try to get away as quickly as possible.

"Getting you across the demarcation line is simple enough," he told me. "The real job is to elude the people who are watching you. Once we have done that, the rest is easy. You can go by train to a certain town, where you will be met and taken across the border."

"I think there is only one man shadowing me when I move about town," I said. "I've identified him. He's outside now. But there are others watching the apartment from across the street, so it would be more difficult to start from there."

"The thing to do then," said the French police officer, "is to start you off from some point in your normal movements about town. You must leave just as you are, dressed in ordinary street clothes. Take no luggage. If you are seen leaving your house with a bag, you will never get out of the city. . . . Now as to your shadow. You say he's outside. . . . I could arrest him now, of course, for suspicious loitering about the Prefecture. . . . However, the train you want doesn't leave until nine tonight, and we couldn't hold him very long. He will have identification, of course, and though you could get away while we were checking and apologizing, all the stations would be watched before you could take a train. Besides, it would look a little too obvious; the Gestapo might be able to pin it on us. Let me see . . . what's the best way to work it?"

He rose, and walked across the room, his hands clasped behind his back. Then he turned, and said:

"It's always the same man who follows you? There's no likelihood that another man, whom you don't know, will be on the job say an hour or two before your train is due to leave?"

"I've only seen one," I said. "He was on duty all day yesterday, and he turned up again today."

"Good. Where will you be between seven and eight this evening?"

"I have an appointment in the lobby of the Ritz Hotel at seven," I answered. "I don't suppose it will last more than half an hour."

"Very convenient," said my officer friend, with satisfaction. "Here's what we'll do. When you've finished with your appointment in the Ritz, sometime between half-past seven and eight, say, pretend to notice that your purse has disappeared. Make a little agitation about it. Look about nervously for it, to collect a few witnesses. Then point at the man who is shadowing you, and say, 'I think that man stole it. He's been following me everywhere.' I'll have a couple of plainclothesmen there, and they will arrest him. At the same time, they will tell you that you must accompany them also.

"I don't think he'll protest in public, as long as he sees you are coming along, too. He will prefer to show his credentials in the privacy of the police station. We will stall him along as long as we can; and after he's identified himself, we'll do some long-winded apologizing. One way or another, I guarantee that he won't be able to give the alarm until after nine o'clock. By then you'll be on your way. We may be reprimanded for having been stupid enough to fall for your ruse, but that's about as far as they can go. I don't think they'll suspect us of anything more."

"Well," I said laughingly, "I'm not much of an actress; but since it's so important, I'm sure I'll be able to give a finished performance."

And I took my leave lighter in heart, and with confidence that I was as good as saved.

To allay the slightest suspicion of the Gestapo, I decided to make a second call at the German office on the Rue Galilée, where permits to go to the unoccupied zone were delivered. The day before I had made my application for an *Ausweis,* as these exit visas were called. I was sure I wouldn't get one, but I felt that it would seem less suspicious if I pretended to believe that I would.

There was a long line waiting to get exit visas, a group of the most motley sort, including almost all types and classes imaginable. What impressed me most was the silence of the crowd. These usually voluble Frenchmen had nothing to say to one another. I felt a sense of restraint, which I judged came from their consciousness of being within hearing of the enemy. Once in a while an impatient remark would reveal that some of them had been waiting for days or weeks or even months to get their permits to escape from German-ruled territory.

There was a Frenchwoman in line before me. At one refusal of a request, she turned to me and whispered that she also had little hope of getting the permit which she had been trying to get for two weeks. I was sympathetic, and she explained her case further. She said that she had asked for permission to visit her sick mother at Bergerac. She had been refused without explanation. Then, when she received news that her mother was dying, she had renewed her appeal, and had been told that she would have to present a medical certificate on her mother's condition before the *Ausweis* would be issued. She had learned that the only way to get this would be through the services of the Vichy government, since private communications were very limited, and when she tried to arrange for such a certificate, she was told that it would take weeks. Now her mother had died, and she was returning once more to ask permission to attend the funeral.

"I know what they'll say," she said resignedly. "They'll say there's no point in my going there, because she'll be buried before I arrive . . . They don't understand human feelings, these monsters!"

Behind me in the line was a Catholic priest. He had his identity card in his hand, and I saw on it a big letter "J." That meant that he was Jewish, and I was just trying to work up courage to ask a priest how he could be Jewish when the woman behind him did it before me.

"*Chère Madame,*" the priest explained, "my mother was Jewish. In the eyes of the Germans, that makes me Jewish as well, though I was born in the Catholic faith, and am a consecrated priest of the Catholic Church. I'm by no means the only Catholic priest in that situation. I know several others. If they introduce into France the same rule they have in Germany, that Jews must wear a yellow Star of David on their chests, then I will have to sew that on my priest's soutane. There's been talk of it."

"But how does that affect your work, *Monsieur le Curé?*" the woman asked.

"Not at all," he smiled. "I still remain the priest of my parish, in Passy—and I assure you, I have not lost one parishioner because of this stamp on my identity card. I am sure that I shan't lose one either if I should be obliged later to wear the Jewish star."

When I finally reached the head of the line, the official in charge thumbed through a card index file to find the record of my application. Looking at me in what seemed to me a curious fashion, he said: "Just a minute, Madame," and disappeared into an office in the rear, taking my papers with him—to consult a superior, I presumed. He came back immediately, and said:

"You must be patient, Madame. You only filed this application yesterday. Others have been waiting for weeks. We can't make exceptions, you know. You have to wait your turn."

"But I want to go to America," I said. "The boat won't wait."

The official shrugged his shoulders, and turned to the next applicant. But I refused to let him off so easily.

"When do you think I should come back?" I asked.

"I don't know. In a week or so."

I turned away, absolutely convinced that they would never give me an *Ausweis.*

It was 1 o'clock. The day was cold, but sunny. I decided to walk over to the Champs-Elysées, to see that beautiful avenue for the last time before leaving Paris. I wanted to carry the memory of it away with me. It was to be my good-bye to the beloved capital.

*"Paris sera toujours Paris."* That was what they had been singing only a few months ago—Paris will always be Paris. But how changed it seemed as I walked along! The exterior was the same, but the spirit had been crushed. The faces of the people looked strange, like the faces of dead friends, whose features remain the same, but give a different impression when the animation which inspired them has disappeared. Silent, and like mourners passing through a cemetery, the French passed sadly through their own streets. The

blue uniforms of their soldiers were no longer to be seen. The gray-green of Germany had replaced them. And there were more of those uniforms than there had ever been of French ones. They were everywhere one looked.

The Germans must have stationed enormous numbers of soldiers in Paris to keep its population under control. There must have been tens of thousands of them. They were everywhere. The big hotels and the luxurious apartment houses had been taken over by officers, who had no hesitation in ordering their owners to vacate without delay. Soldiers were quartered in barracks and in smaller hotels throughout the city.

Frenchmen were not even allowed to walk past the hotels occupied by German officers. Police or German soldiers stood guard before all of them. Certain streets, entirely given over to the Germans, were closed to traffic entirely—like the important Avenue Montaigne. Even trucks carrying their own soldiers were not allowed to pass here. It seemed that the noise might disturb the conquerors.

But there was a curious thing about the German private soldiers. They always seemed sad, depressed. Hitler, proud in his victory over France, had promised that every German should have a chance to see Paris. And thousands of German soldiers on leave took advantage of the occasion to visit the French capital, arriving daily to drive around the city in great sight-seeing buses. But they gazed stolidly and without visible pleasure at the spectacle about them. They never indulged in any of the gay pranks common to soldiers and sailors all over the world. I heard German soldiers singing only when ordered to do so on the march by their officers. By themselves, they never walked singing through the streets. Whether their air of constant melancholy came with them from their own country or whether it was produced by the hostile atmosphere about them, I had no idea.

I had reached the George V subway station (the one at which Frenchmen in occupied Paris always used to rise from their seats and stand at attention in tribute to the British), when I made an unexpected, and, in those circumstances, undesirable encounter.

Chancel came out of the subway entrance and moved towards me. My first reaction was joy. "So Chancel is still free!" I told myself exultantly. "It wasn't true when they said they had every one except Kitty. He is at large, too. Perhaps he can tell me where she is. Perhaps he can advise me about my present difficulties."

He had changed considerably since I had last seen him, but he was still recognizable. His beard, which had been only a scant growth when he first came back to Paris, was now thick and luxuriant. It changed his appearance considerably.

But immediately I remembered that I couldn't speak to him. My shadow, following dutifully behind, would certainly spot him and check up on him! I mustn't permit him to show recognition of me. I had become a danger to my old friends, walking about the city in this way, likely to draw unwelcome attention on any one I met. Thank God I would be out of it all in a few hours!

Chancel saw me. His eyes lighted up and he smiled. I turned aside a little as we approached, and whispered sharply as I passed:

"Careful! I'm being followed! Don't recognize me!"

And I swept by, increasing my pace a little with the intention of drawing my shadow along at greater speed, and giving him no time to pay any attention to Chancel, if he had noted his first signs of recognition. I hurried on for half a block, then looked back furtively over my shoulder. I couldn't see the man who had been following me; but a little crowd had suddenly gathered near the subway exit, and I heard a police whistle blowing.

I stood there, rooted to the spot, gazing towards the small knot of people, unable to approach, and unable to move away. A man left the group and walked in my direction. As he reached me, I couldn't help asking:

"What's happening?"

With a disgusted gesture, the man answered:

"Another Gestapo arrest. I don't know why."

I suddenly felt so weak that I had to stumble across the sidewalk and sit down at a café terrace. Poor Chancel! I had led them to him. They hadn't found Kitty through me, but they had got one fish in their net. It was the first reward for their release of me. I determined there shouldn't be another. I was going straight home, to stay there until it was time to keep my appointment with Mr. Marvel.

I spent the afternoon at home, growing increasingly more nervous as the minutes before the moment of escape moved slowly by. There was nothing in particular that I could do. There were no preparations to make, for I couldn't take anything with me. I mustn't arouse suspicions by leaving the house with any baggage, or even dressed for traveling. And I was too nervous to sit down and read a book.

I did, however, have to carry one package—warm underwear for Mr. Marvel. The Germans knew that I was supposed to meet him with these things, for they had heard my conversation with him over the phone. So I packed up the flannel underthings he had provided for me while I was in jail, and paced about waiting for the time to come to go to the Ritz and play the scene which I could not help rehearsing over and over in my imagination. I kept looking at my watch, sometimes at such short intervals that I had to watch the second-hand to convince myself that it hadn't stopped. At 6 o'clock my nervous tension was unbearable. I was then sitting, for a moment, in the living room. The dogs were lying at my feet, occasionally whining mournfully. They had sensed something was wrong with me.

I sprang suddenly to my feet. I would take the dogs for one last walk, before leaving them forever. They barked joyously as I put them on the leash and started out the door with them. The self-service elevator was rising in the shaft as I reached it. It stopped at my floor. Out of it stepped Schulz, the man who had arrested me before.

"Good evening, Mme. Shiber," he greeted me.

"What is it?" I asked, frightened.

"They want to see you at headquarters," he said. "You'll have to come along with me."

My bubble of hope collapsed. There went my chances for escape! Re-arrested already, just when I had expected to get away! But what could I do? Protests or a scene would have been useless. Silently, I opened the door of my apartment and led the dogs back in. They began whining again, disappointed of their outing, as I closed the door behind them. I picked up the parcel of warm underwear and took it along. I thought I might need it again.

But perhaps, I thought, as I got into the elevator with Schulz, perhaps I'm not going back to jail. Perhaps they just want to talk to me because of Chancel's arrest. If he said something that linked him with our case, they might have called me as a witness only. Perhaps I would still get another chance to escape.

But my hope was very slight as I left the building. I looked at my watch. Six-thirty. In half an hour, Mr. Marvel would be at the Ritz to meet me, in vain. In an hour, my friends of the French police would be there, ready to play the comedy whose heroine would be missing. And an hour later, the train that was to have taken me to freedom would puff out of the station, and I would not be on it.

At least, I hoped, my failure to appear should give the alarm. Mr. Marvel should realize what had happened.

## CHAPTER TWENTY-EIGHT

# Prison Again

ONCE AGAIN in the Hotel Matignon I faced Dr. Hager—this time in his third incarnation. I had already met the pleasant, sympathizing, smiling Dr. Hager and the angry, vituperative, threatening Dr. Hager. Now I made acquaintance with the ironic, superior Dr. Hager.

"Well, the comedy is over," he said, with a satiric smile, as he opened his examination of me. "We now have the last two members of the gang. We got Monsieur Corbier this afternoon, thanks to you, Mrs. Shiber. And I have just received word that Mme. Beaurepos was arrested in Bordeaux two hours ago. So there really wasn't any reason to allow you to wander around the streets any longer, was there?"

He smiled, as though with infinite appreciation of his own cleverness, and continued:

"You were not very wise, Mrs. Shiber. Do you remember when I told you that you might leave for America if you cooperated with us and told us what you knew? If you had not been so obstinate, you would be on your way to your own country now. As it is, you refused to accept the escape we offered you, and now it is too late. We are not going to make you any more such offers. You will have to stand trial now with the others."

One thing I noted with relief—they still did not know everything, since he had not mentioned Chancel's real name. But when he told me that Kitty had been arrested, the thought of Chancel was driven out of my head. So they had her at last—at Bordeaux; that must have been just after she crossed the line on her way back. Henri had failed to intercept her. Poor Kitty! What would become of her now?

My examination this time was very different from the first. There were no clever attempts to trick me, no veiled threats from Captain Pietsch (he wasn't even present). A clerk was called in to take down everything I said. This was to be my official deposition for the court records. Dr. Hager put precise questions, to which I was required to give precise answers. He showed no annoyance, one might almost say practically no interest, in the fact that I told the same story as before. I was still following my old principle: "Deny everything!" But he didn't seem to care. It frightened me and impressed me more than his previous examinations, which were meant to frighten and impress me, had done. His lack of insistence on confession made it seem clear to me that he no longer needed one. Now, I thought, he really knows something, so he no longer has to pretend he knows everything.

It took a long while to answer the hundreds of questions he put to me. At midnight, Dr. Hager called a recess while he sent out for refreshments for himself and the clerk. They gave me a cup of tea and a ham sandwich. It was the last decent food I was to have for seventeen months.

After this break, the questions and answers began again. I continued to take care to give nothing away, to say nothing that would be useful against Kitty, Father Christian, Chancel or any one else. When I had finished, there was a long wait while the deposition was typed, during which I half-dozed off from time to time. It was finally brought in for me to sign. I read it carefully—ten long single-spaced pages—fearing a trick, but everything in it was exactly what I had said. I signed my name to the bottom of each sheet. When I handed it back, it was nine in the morning.

Schulz was called in to take me back to the Cherche-Midi prison. As I prepared to leave, Dr. Hager addressed to me what I think was the cruelest sentence I had ever heard in my life.

It was this:

"It will be two or three months before your case comes up for trial, Mrs. Shiber. That isn't very long. Therefore I advise you to start preparing yourself. You should try to get accustomed to the idea that for the crime which you have committed, it is mandatory for the court to impose the death sentence. Good-bye, Mrs. Shiber."

And he bowed me out with a tooth-baring smile.

I followed Schulz in a daze. The death sentence *mandatory!* I had supposed that it was the maximum punishment! The subtle cruelty with which he had planted that poisoned barb in my prison, to torture me mentally for the weeks that would elapse before my trial, seemed to me more viciously sadistic than the brutal physical beatings which I knew some of his men administered to their helpless victims. Nor did I think any better of Dr. Hager after the trial, when I learned that he had not told the truth, and that the anguish he had inflicted on me was inspired by simple malice— his revenge, I suppose, for my failure to tell all he wanted to know.

My second arrest occurred on December 22, 1940. The process of entering the prison was less complicated than on the first occasion, for it was unnecessary to repeat some of the routine, such as the photographing. Indeed, the attitude of those who received me seemed to be that this was not a new imprisonment, but simply a continuation of the earlier one, which, indeed, it was. No doubt they had known very well that I would soon be back. The trick played on me had probably been used often enough before on others.

Somehow I did not feel this return to prison after my brief taste of liberty as bitterly as I would have expected if I had been told in advance what was going to happen. I seemed to re-enter immediately the atmosphere I had left. The intervening period was wiped away cleanly, as though by a sponge. Five minutes after I had set foot in the prison again, I felt as though I had never left it.

The three women who occupied the cell into which I was put this time were all French. One of them was a conspicuously beautiful girl, who had been cashier in the famous Paris restaurant, Chez Maxims, at the time of her arrest.

Maxims had become a favorite of German officers after the occupation, like most of the famous restaurants and places of entertainment in Paris. It quickly became known as the headquarters of a curious type of Black Market—that which dealt in prisoners of war.

Certain German officers who were able to secure the release of prisoners made their headquarters there, and it was possible to make deals with them for the freedom of relatives. Maxims was not the only place where this could be arranged; but it was the surest. At one or two other rendezvous, cut-rate bargains could be made. Releases were promised at from 20,000 to 50,000 francs. But there were numerous cases in which the amount was paid, and the prisoner was never freed. This never happened at Maxims, where more honorable corruption was the rule. But there the price ranged from 50,000 to 100,000 francs. Half the amount was paid at once, and the other half when the prisoner reached France.

The first problem of hapless French families with the price to ransom their relatives was to find the correct officer to approach. It would have been too bewildering simply to enter the restaurant and try to find the broker in human beings by guesswork; it was too thickly thronged with elegant officers in smartly-cut spick-and-span uniforms, which certainly did not look as though they had ever been exposed to the rigors of battle. It was necessary to know the password. Whispered to the headwaiter, it would lead to an introduction to the negotiator (not always the same officer), who would proportion his sympathy to the amount of money available as ransom. He would also explain very meticulously that in case the prisoner had already died, the money could not be returned.

The girl whose beauty had struck me when I first entered the cell was named Genevieve. Her father, she told me, was in a prison camp. She knew, of course, like all the employees of Maxims, who handled the liberation of prisoners, and she hoped to profit by the fact that she saw these officers every day (and often had to smile and show herself agreeable at their flirtatious sallies) to get a better bargain than was available to strangers. One of them finally agreed to secure her father's release at the rock-bottom minimum, not usually acceptable at Maxims, 20,000 francs, and to allow it to be paid in instalments of 2,000 francs at a time.

Her family had already paid five instalments when a letter which she had written to her father was returned with the word "Deceased" stamped across it. Some time later, the girl went to the German officer, told him that her father had died, and asked him, since her family was desperately poor, if he could return the 10,000 francs. He said he would do so the next day.

But the following morning, she was arrested and taken to the Cherche-Midi prison. No explanation was given her, and she only learned the reason later. The German officer, evidently unwilling to return the money, and equally unwilling to be embarrassed in his favorite restaurant by the sight of the girl who had dared ask for it, had simply reported that she was planning to cross the demarcation line surreptitiously to get to London via Lisbon. She left her mother in hysterics, in spite of an assurance from the police that she would be back in a few days, after questioning. She had now been there three months, without trial, and so far as she knew, without any likelihood of being tried—imprisoned on the simple unsupported denunciation of a corrupt Nazi Army officer!

The second of my three new companions was dark-haired, tall, sad-eyed Maria, a woman of 35, who wept most of the day and night, apparently unable, like the rest of us, to resign herself to prison life.

Her tale was one of almost continuous trouble. Her husband had fought in one of the international brigades in the Spanish civil war, and had suffered a spinal injury which paralyzed his legs. He had been returned to their small Paris home, and his wife went to work to take care of him and their two children, who were eight and ten.

When the Germans began closing in on Paris, Maria tried to arrange to take her husband south, out of their reach, but it was hard enough for a person in the best of health to get away at that time, and there was no way to transport a helpless person. So Maria sent her two children off with friends to stay in the south, and remained in Paris with her husband.

Shortly after the Germans arrived, an order was issued that all persons who had fought against Franco should report to the German authorities. Common belief was that they were to be turned over to Spain, for trial and punishment by her military courts. Sure that he would be discovered, the paralyzed man bowed to this last stroke of misfortune, and committed suicide by taking an overdose of the sleeping pills which were always left by his bed.

Her husband dead, Maria decided to try to get to southern France to rejoin her children. For weeks, she stormed the Rue Galilée, trying to get a permit. Then she received word that the younger child was seriously ill. She made for the demarcation line, and without help, without knowing how it might be crossed safely, tried to get across at night, alone. She was arrested, and it was for that banal offense that she was being held in prison. Her weeping centered about the fate of her children, especially the one who had been taken ill; for she had no way, of course, of knowing what had been its fate, nor did her friends know what had happened to her.

The last of the trio was also about 35. She looked as though she would have been very impressive in the elegant toilettes which were probably her accustomed costume, but was much less so in the dark-blue ski suit which she had been wearing when captured. She spoke a little English and very good German; but neither in those languages nor in her native French did she have anything much to say—though she was the most talkative of the group. She didn't seem to mind prison any more than the luxurious apartment which she said she had been occupying in the exclusive Avenue Henri-Martin, one of the most beautiful streets in Paris. Why she had been arrested she didn't seem to know, or very much care. She said only that she had been about to marry the man who had set her up in the de luxe apartment, and had been arrested while he was away in Vichy on business. She chattered incessantly, but the measure of how unimportant her talk was is the fact that today I can't remember what any of it was about. After three weeks, she was released, apparently with as little reason as she had been arrested.

Perhaps my failure to remember what she said was partly due, however, to my own mental condition. I spent ten weeks this time in the Cherche-Midi prison, and after only a few days of the old starvation rations and the monotonous routine of nothing to do, my mind became so blank that there were long stretches I couldn't remember at all. For instance, when I met Mr. Marvel recently in New York, he referred to a visit to me in my cell at the prison which I couldn't recall.

"You seemed very odd to me, Mrs. Shiber," he told me, trying to stir my recollection of the scene. "You sat there on your bed in a half stupor, your eyes neither quite open nor quite closed, hardly answering my questions. I had the feeling that you were there only in body, not in spirit."

But his prompting stirred no memory of the visit. It must have occurred at the period through which I moved like an automaton, going through the daily routine mechanically and without conscious volition. I sat for hour after hour in complete apathy, and though I was always tortured by hunger, my cell-mates often had to prod me to eat, or I would not have noticed that my food was there before me.

There is one period I remember clearly, however, which began with the very unusual distinction of a visit to my cell by the Major who was the warden of the prison. I don't suppose he came exclusively on my account; he seemed to be making a general tour of inspection. But he said to me: "It occurs to me that perhaps you would be more comfortable if I had you placed in the same cell with some other English-speaking person." I looked up at him in surprise, and indicated that I would like such a change. It was the only instance I had witnessed, or even heard of, in which any such trace of human feeling was evidenced by any of our jailors, and I didn't understand it. Was it perhaps that some one had reported my curious apathy, and the warden didn't want a conceivably important witness to lose her mind before trial?

However, the reason wasn't important, I thought. Any change was a welcome relief to the monotony. I was taken to the far end of the same corridor, and put in a cell with only one other occupant, an old woman whose features showed the strain of long mental torment.

When I entered the cell, I received a cold and suspicious reception which my experience with Marthe Wenziger enabled me to understand. But after a few minutes, she told me her name was Mrs. Syms, and I realized at once who she was—the mother of Mary Bird's fiancé. I told her about my previous experience as Mary's cell-mate, and she melted at once. Tears appeared in her eyes.

"Poor Mary," she murmured, "Do you think those beasts have told her what happened? . . . Oh, John, John . . ." And she burst into wild weeping, but almost without making a sound. It was more frightening than loud wails. Only the convulsive shaking of her fragile body betrayed the fact that she was sobbing hysterically, utterly unable to control herself. It took her some time to regain her calm, and then she told me what had happened.

John was her husband's name. He had been caught in the act of trying to signal to Mary, whom he had glimpsed from his window, and had been sentenced to a month in a dark cell.

He was already in bad physical condition. The prospect of a month alone in a windowless cell must have ended his hopes of survival; and he no doubt preferred that the end should come quickly. He succeeded in breaking the tin cover of his toilet pail over the stone bench, and drew the jagged end across his neck. They found him dead, his head resting on an open Bible, which, with a candle to read it by, was the one privilege allowed him to alleviate his month of solitary confinement. The remains of the candle, burned to the end, showed that he had placed it beside the book, where he had apparently sought final consolation as his life ebbed slowly away.

The suicide seemed to be considered a grave matter by the prison authorities, for though they showed so little consideration for their charges, it was their duty to keep them alive for eventual trial— this being a prison only for those who had not yet been permanently sentenced. It was considered bad for the morale of the other prisoners, and, besides that, a blot on the record of the prison administration. The warden himself came to Mrs. Syms' cell and told her what had happened. He even went so far as to express his sorrow.

"You needn't be sorry for me," she said. "If John thought that was the right thing to do, it must have been. He has always seen clearly, and he has always done what was right. My duty now is to follow him."

"When did you tell the warden that?" I asked.

"Today," she said, "not very long ago. It was only today that I heard . . ." She didn't finish the sentence.

Now I understood why I had been moved. The warden didn't want another suicide among his prisoners, and he counted on my presence to prevent Mrs. Syms from attempting to follow her husband. For once, I agreed with a German.

"My dear Mrs. Syms," I told her, taking one of her hands between mine. "You mustn't think of such things . . . Remember your son. He has lost one parent. You mustn't deprive him of the other. And how about Mary, who always talked of you with so much love and respect?"

Mrs. Syms did not answer at once. She looked into the hazy

dimness of the cell with unseeing eyes, and then murmured under her breath:

"I will have to go. John is calling me."

I spent two weeks with Mrs. Syms in our cell, laboring with her to rid her of the obsession of suicide. It was a benefit to myself which I hardly realized at the time. In reasoning with her, I forgot my own troubles—and I had an object at last, that of saving Mrs. Syms. It was almost with disappointment that on January 17, I heard the guard say to Mrs. Syms "You are to be released. Come with me."

"What about the others?" Mrs. Syms asked. "What about my son? What about Mary? Will all of them be freed?"

"No questions," the guard said shortly. "Get your things."

Mrs. Syms nervously gathered together her few possessions. Suddenly she straightened up, pointed her arm with outstretched finger straight at the guard, and said with an air of wonderful energy and authority:

"I demand an answer. What about the others?"

To my great surprise, her commanding attitude melted the guard. He answered obediently, if gruffly:

"All freed. Your son and his accomplice are prisoners of war. They will go to a prison camp. The rest of you can return home."

For once, it was the truth. I learned later through the prison grapevine that this was, indeed, the decision that had been made for the prisoners from Guernsey. We all thought that the suicide had precipitated this action.

With the departure of Mrs. Syms, I was again moved to another cell, and again I succumbed to the lethargy engendered by monotony and malnutrition. There were moments when my numbness turned into impotent rage, a sort of maniacal frenzy, and I could understand why maddened prisoners ran at their jailers and tried to strangle them, or beat their heads against the wall in desperate suicide attempts, as two of the inmates in our prison had done.

My greatest worry, in my more lucid moments, was that though I knew Kitty had been arrested. and was perhaps in this very jail, perhaps even in the next cell, only two feet away, I knew nothing of what had happened to her. Ignorance of her fate was one of my greatest tortures.

During this time, I received several visits from Mr. Marvel—visits which I did remember. Each time the guard opened the door for him, I hoped he would be able to give me some word from Kitty; but he was never allowed to enter the cell alone. He was always accompanied by two German soldier interpreters, one for English and one for French. Since Mr. Marvel spoke both languages perfectly, it was obvious that the "interpreters" were really listeners, sent along to make sure that he didn't transgress the rules restricting the subjects on which he could talk.

I thought he might try to convey some hidden message to me, and after each visit I would sit for hours, trying to remember his exact words and pondering on any hidden meaning they might have. It was a hopeless attempt, for he told me afterwards that they had none. But I think the effort helped save my sanity, for the fact of having some mental problem with which to struggle broke in on the awful sameness of my days. His visits were the only break in them. If I had not been able to look forward to them, I believe I would have collapsed, physically and mentally.

And then one day I got news of Kitty!

## CHAPTER TWENTY-NINE

# Kitty

M<small>Y FIRST</small> tidings about Kitty since my arrest were provided by the prison authorities, though they had no intention of assuaging my thirst for news about her—in fact, it certainly never occurred to them to consider the effect on me when they sent it out.

It happened at the evening distribution of food during the second month of my imprisonment. The guard gave us our evening measure of coffee and our portion of bread, but instead of handing over our daily ration of fat (so-called whale meat, which probably came from a chemical factory instead of a whale), he passed us a mimeographed notice, and went out, slamming the door behind him.

I looked at my cell-mates in dismay, for small as our fat ration was, we felt the need of it. The explanation for its absence was on the sheet of paper:

Prisoners will be deprived of their daily ration of fat today as punishment for the attempted escape of an Englishwoman, French by marriage, charged with helping English soldiers to escape from France. Her effort was foiled, and she has been sentenced to 30 days solitary confinement, as has her cell-mate, who failed to report her attempt. Prisoners are warned that any further escape attempts will be even more severely punished, and any prisoner undertaking such futile measures must realize that he is condemning his fellows to disciplining as well as himself.

I had no doubt from the description, and from my knowledge of her character, that this was Kitty, my indomitable Kitty, who refused to be confined even by the bars of a prison without trying to break through them. It made me wonder, too, if she hadn't become slightly maddened by confinement, for she had always had a tendency to claustrophobia. How often I had seen her moving about the room, throwing open one window after another, saying: "The air is so close, I feel as though I were in prison!" Now my poor Kitty, who loved air and freedom so much, *was* in prison, and sentenced to the worst imprisonment of all, a whole month, thirty endless days, in a dark tomb where she would feel herself buried alive!

I was beginning my third month in Cherche-Midi when I fell sick of some horrible infection. The inside of my mouth felt as though it were lined with canker sores. The German military doctor who served the prison took one look at it, and ordered me transferred to the hospital.

The order was the most welcome one I could possibly have heard. I dreamed in ecstasy of a clean hospital bed, of being able to wash, of better food, of the luxury of stretching out in bed in the daytime, instead of sitting rigid on its edge hour after hour. But the reality was not like that.

Though the prison was in the center of Paris, where there are dozens of fine hospitals, I was taken to the hospital of the prison of Fresnes, 70 miles away. I was placed on the driver's seat of a truck, on a cold windy day. Beside me, the driver sat stolidly, silent and sullen. Inside the truck, guarded from the full force of the cold, rode the two healthy men with me—a guard and an officer. I, the sick woman, was allotted the exposed cab of the truck.

I remember nothing of the ride except my constant discomfort and the fact that it seemed as though our journey would never end. I had a high fever, and I think I must have been a little out of my head. I had brought nothing with me from Paris so the prison hospital gave me one of their gowns, and put me to bed between sheets cold as ice.

The hospital was worse than the prison. I was in a cell, just as I had been before, but now I was alone, and the monotony was greater than ever. I saw the doctor once or twice. The sister who attended me washed out my mouth three times a day, and once in a while a cleaning woman came in. Otherwise, I saw no one.

I couldn't eat. The soup and coffee they offered me was execrable; I couldn't force it down, even after what I had been accustomed to in Cherche-Midi. The room was so cold I couldn't keep my hands over the covers, which were thin and inadequate.

...der committing Mrs. Shiber to the prison hospital of Fresnes for treatment. The slip ...es that she is suffering from running sores in the mouth. Note that the forms used in ... Paris prison taken over by the Gestapo are in German, imported from Leipzig, as ... printer's mark shows.

The only break in the monotony was the occasional opportunity to talk to the cleaning woman, who was an inmate of the prison. From her I learned that Kitty had been there a few days before. The black cell had been too much for her, and she had been brought to the hospital in a state of collapse before her month was up. She had made frantic efforts to obtain her transfer to a real hospital, offering to pay all costs if it could be arranged, but of course without success. She had asked for sleeping pills at night, but instead of taking them, had hidden them until she accumulated what she thought would be enough, and then had taken them all at once. It had made her very ill, and that was all. Shortly afterwards she had been returned to Cherche-Midi.

The pain in my mouth began to decrease. It must have run its course naturally, for the hospital was practically without medicine, and I couldn't see that they did anything for it, except to wash out my mouth with what seemed to be ordinary water. I begged to be returned to prison. So I rode back, locked in the Black Maria (the French call it *panier à salade*—salad basket).

When I got back to Cherche-Midi, I was so thin and weak that the guard had to help me up the stairs. I couldn't make it alone.

It was shortly after my return from the hospital that I was called to the warden's office, where I found Dr. Hager waiting for me.

"I have come to inform you," he said, "that your case has been put down for trial on March 7. You see that we have wasted no time. I said it might take three months, but we have done a little better than that. I have also come to give you a last warning. It appears that there is still time for you to modify your attitude and thereby, perhaps, to profit by the leniency of the court, which may be willing, after all, not to impose the supreme sentence . . . Mme. Beaurepos has made a complete confession, and therefore can expect to receive consideration from her judges. Your stubbornness in denial is likely to arouse their hostility. In any case, you cannot, under the circumstances, expect any clemency—unless, of course, you follow the example of your friend."

My instinct whispered to me: "Another trick! Deny everything!"

But Dr. Hager had come prepared. He opened his brief-case and drew out a bundle of documents.

INFIRMERIE CENTRALE

*Bulletin d'Excéat*

*La nommée Schiper Itta*
*actuellement en traitement à l'Infirmerie*
*centrale pour*
*peut rejoindre sa Maison d'origine.*

*Fresnes le 21 Août 1941*
*Le médecin*

Mrs. Shiber's discharge from the prison hospital of Fresnes. The personnel here was French, and the form is therefore in that language also. Misspelling her name as Itta Schiper (she was committed with a less marked error as Ettah Shiber), the prison doctor notes that she is to be returned to the prison she came from (maison d'origine).

"This is the prosecutor's brief," he said. "Would you like to see Mme. Beaurepos' confession?"

He looked through the documents, drew out one of 12 or 15 pages, and handed it to me.

I leafed through it. Each paragraph began with the words, "I confess . . ." and it seemed to contain a fairly complete account of our activities. I was thunderstruck. How could Kitty have done such a thing? How could she have handed us all over to the mercy of the Gestapo?

"Well, you see," said Dr. Hager, triumphantly, taking back the confession. "Mme. Beaurepos has saved herself. Now how about your confession?"

I remained silent. Dr. Hager raised his voice:

"Come, come, Mrs. Shiber, this is ridiculous! You will only provoke the anger of the court. I came here to save you from the result of your own stubbornness. These documents are to be sent to the court at once. It contains the deposition in which you obstinately deny all knowledge of this affair. It was very childish of you to adopt so obviously false an attitude. If you wish to change it, there is still time. I can replace it by your confession, and I assure you, it will increase your chances immensely at the trial. You will be considered by the judges as cooperative, rather than hostile. I am acting only in your own interest."

Dr. Hager would have done better if he had omitted that last sentence. I thought I knew him too well to believe that, and it convinced me that he was still playing a double game. He seemed to have all his evidence, so what more did he want of me? Whatever it was, I was sure it would be to my disadvantage. I said simply: "I have nothing to add to my original deposition."

Dr. Hager shrugged his shoulders with the air of washing his hands of the whole affair, and stuffed his papers back into his brief-case. I was led back to my cell.

At 8 o'clock on the morning of March 7, the guard ordered me to accompany him for trial. I followed him through the long corridors till we came to the head of the staircase. There he stopped, peered through the peephole into a cell, jerked open the door, and called:

"Number 2017—for trial!"

A woman appeared in the door of the cell. It was Kitty.

My heart bounded suddenly in my chest and then began thumping so hard it seemed to me that it must be audible. Kitty had hardly changed at all during her ordeal of imprisonment. She had on the same coat she had been wearing when she left for the unoccupied zone, when I had last seen her. Her face was pale, and there were deep shadows under her eyes; but she did not seem broken either in body or spirit.

She looked towards me, and I thought I detected the shadow of a smile as she said softly, "Hello, Etta."

"Silence!" the guard roared. "Prisoners must not talk."

And so, forbidden to say anything to my old friend to ease my bursting heart, I walked silently with her to the ground floor, and out into the courtyard, where we were turned over to other guards.

We heard a car draw up outside the gate, and then it was thrown open. A green-painted convict transport van stood at the curb. The guard opened the door and Kitty got in. I followed her. The door was locked behind us, and with a lurch the van started.

Alone with Kitty, I raised my arms to hug her, but I let them fall in astonishment when she looked at me reproachfully as she said: "How could you have given us all away, Etta? How could you have had the weakness to tell everything to those people?"

"I . . . I . . . ?" I stammered, so taken back that I couldn't get the words out before she continued:

"They must have terrorized you, Etta . . . but you should have been firm. I ought to be angry at you. God knows you deserve it. But I just can't be angry at you. Anyway, what does it matter now?"

"But, Kitty," I exclaimed, recovering my power of speech, "I didn't tell them anything—not a thing. I swear to you that I have always denied everything—even a few days ago, when Dr. Hager came to the jail and urged me once more to confess."

"But, Etta," Kitty protested, "I saw your confession with my own eyes. It was a ten-page deposition, signed by you. I recognized your handwriting."

"I made a ten-page deposition," I said, "and I signed it, but it was a denial, not a confession. If you saw anything else, it was a forgery."

"My God!" said Kitty. "I believed in it—and I *did* confess."

"Tell me," I asked, "when Dr. Hager showed you my forged confession, did he tell you that there was no sense in continuing your denials, that I had earned the clemency of the court, and that you should do likewise?"

"Something like that," Kitty said.

"That was what he said to me," I said, "when he showed me your confession. But I didn't trust him. I continued to deny it."

Hastily we compared dates and notes. As nearly as we could make out, Dr. Hager had tried the same trick on both of us on the same day, one after the other. I had come first, so that the confession I had seen had also been a forgery—but then Kitty had failed to see through the ruse and had given him a real one.

"It's awful, awful," Kitty moaned. "I was the one who gave us away! And I accused you! Oh, how could I have been so stupid?" I put my arm around her shoulder.

"It wasn't your fault, Kitty," I said. "That devil would have tricked any one."

"What are we going to do now?" Kitty asked.

"What I have been doing right along," I said. "Deny everything." Kitty shook her head slowly.

"It's too late, Etta," she said. "What they put in the forged confessions may have been fairly complete, but the confession I made has everything in it—everything! They questioned me for hours. They have fifteen pages of the most minute details—names, dates, places, everything. It wouldn't do any good for me to stand up now and say that I made it all up. With the information I gave them, they will be able to verify everything. We're lost, Etta, lost . . . and it was all my fault!"

The car jolted to a stop, Kitty threw her head up proudly, brushed her hair back with her hand, and smoothed out the wrinkles of her dress.

"Heads up, Etta!" she said. "Don't let these Germans see we're afraid of them! Don't give them that satisfaction, whatever happens."

We heard the key turn in the lock, and the door of the van was swung open. I saw where we were at once—in the Rue St.

Dominique, in front of the military tribunal, established in an 18th century mansion of the St. Germain quarter.

I got out, and Kitty followed. Dr. Hager was standing at the door. When he saw us he rushed towards us, and seizing the guard by the collar of his tunic, began shaking him in a rage, twisting his collar till the guard's bobbing face became crimson, and shouting at him in the most violent German abuse:

"You fool! You idiot! You dog! What do you mean by leaving these two women alone together before the trial? Why weren't you sitting inside with them? . . . You're through being a guard, my fine fellow, but you're not through with prisons. I'll see that you find out what prisons are for."

And suddenly he aimed a vicious kick at the guard, then stalked off into the courtroom.

The guard, dropping his head like a beaten dog, led us around to a side entrance. He was too dispirited to object when we whispered to each other.

"Kitty," I said under my breath, "how long do you think we'll get?"

"A year or two, perhaps," she said, "but the war may end sooner, and then we'll get out."

"But, Kitty!" I protested. "The death sentence!"

"Oh, Etta," Kitty said. "Don't be melodramatic. How can they condemn two women to death? Don't worry. There's no chance of that."

## CHAPTER THIRTY

# The Trial

Our guard led us up one flight, past files of helmeted sentinels. Two stiff-faced German soldiers also stood at either side of the courtroom door.

The room itself was a magnificent 18th century salon with tapestried walls, priceless draperies and sparkling crystal chandeliers. It looked as though it had been a ballroom, and, indeed, there was still a grand piano standing majestically in one corner of this high-ceilinged room. "This looks as if we had been invited to a reception, not a trial," I said to myself as we entered. But the disposition of the rest of the furniture was more businesslike.

In the center of the room was a long table, behind which were several high-backed chairs, for the judges. On it lay thick bundles of documents, tied with cords. They were, I assumed, the papers concerning our case.

Opposite this table was a long bench for the defendants. We were seated there, and a moment later Monsieur Tissier was brought in. He was dressed in his Sunday best, as he had been when he called on us in Paris. But how different it looked now! During his long imprisonment, his suit had become wrinkled and torn. It had lost the air of having just been removed from the mothballs which it had so plainly worn when we had seen it before.

When he spied us, Tissier stopped uncertainly, apparently wondering whether he would be allowed to greet us. Then he made up his mind to risk it, stepped up to us, and held out his hand. We both shook hands with him, and then he sat down at the edge of the bench, first dusting it off carefully. After all, this was still his Sunday suit.

Next to appear in the courtroom door, accompanied by a guard, was Father Christian. He strode forward quickly and firmly, apparently unaffected by his months of imprisonment. He seemed fresh and alert, and his eyes moved quickly over the room with evident interest in the scene. He greeted us with a faint smile as he sat down beside Tissier. It was the first time the two men had met, but they could hardly be in doubt of each other's identity. They shook hands.

Chancel was the last to arrive. He took his place between Father Christian and myself, greeting us only with a slight nod, as a well-bred person sitting down beside strangers might have done. He gazed grimly at the floor, and when I threw a sidewise glance in his direction, he looked quickly away. I thought he might be angry with me, that perhaps he attributed his arrest to me—which would have been accurate enough, except that it was not my fault. That, however, was not his reason. I was to find out later why he adopted this attitude.

I watched the door anxiously, expecting to see Monsieur Durand enter at any moment. But no one else appeared. "Good," I thought, "they didn't get him."

Next to arrive were our lawyers. The Germans had permitted us each to select a lawyer, but it was an empty formality. Before the German Military Court lawyers were not permitted to examine witnesses, and they were therefore little more than spectators of the proceedings. They could not even talk to their clients. They were, however, allowed to sum up at the end of the trial.

Mr. Marvel had procured a lawyer for me—no simple task, for in the first place it was necessary to find a Frenchman who knew perfect German, and also, to satisfy the requirements of the court, one who could prove that none of his four grandparents were Jewish.

It was exactly ten by the bronze grandfather's clock which stood against one of the walls when the judges entered the courtroom. They were preceded by their president, a man of about 50, wearing a colonel's uniform. His eyes were a cold, icy blue, and his face seemed to have been chiseled from granite.

Two officers of lower rank, the so-called "voting judges," followed their presiding officer. Both wore eye-glasses, and looked as though they had been poured from the same mold. They were blond, color-less, and with a tendency to stoutness.

Last to enter was the prosecutor.

I could hardly restrain a shriek when he entered the room.

Kitty nudged me inconspicuously, and I realized that she had recognized him too.

It was Captain Weber, the German officer who had ridden back with us, when we were traveling from Doullens to Paris with a soldier in our luggage carrier, who had later come to our apartment with an obvious interest in getting better acquainted with Kitty. He walked in a calm, dignified manner to the left end of the long table, where a chair had been placed for him, and sat down. He glanced in our direction, but showed no surprise. I judged that he had already gathered from the documents in our case who we were. He had had plenty of time to prepare for this encounter; but for us it was an unexpected shock. How would his presence affect our case? Would he be better, or worse, disposed to us than a complete stranger?

There was no way of telling. After his single glance in our direction, Captain Weber became immersed in the documents before him and paid us no more attention.

It was then that we were astounded by an almost comic spectacle. Six German privates marched stiffly into the room. I noticed, with the curious fixity on unimportant detail that sometimes seizes upon one at such moments, that their broad leather belts had round buckles on which was inscribed, *Gott mit uns*. Behind them came an interpreter.

The six marched up to the judges' table, halted before it, right-faced towards the judges, saluted, and shouted, "Heil Hitler" in unison. An oath was read to them, which I suppose was the equivalent of our own swearing in of a jury. They saluted again, left-faced back into single file, marched solemnly to a rank of six chairs standing at one side of the room, swung around simultaneously, and plumped down on their chairs in unison. The whole thing was so well-drilled that it was obvious that it must have been rehearsed with the greatest of care. This was our "jury," and it was clear that they could be counted on not to upset any of the calculations of the court.

I couldn't help smiling at this catering to democratic ideas by a burlesque of a jury trial. As I was to discover later, their rôle was to sit there, listening to proceedings like any genuine jury, and after the trial, when the judges left the room to confer, to march out also in the unlikely case, I supposed, that the judges should desire to ask their opinion. But the sight of them sitting there, in the correct attitude prescribed by military regulations, each with his cap balanced at an identical angle on his right knee, was sufficient to convince any one that they would hardly presume to disagree with the colonel and the two captains sitting at the judges' bench. My impulse to laugh at this parody of a court of justice was quickly checked by the realization that it held my life in its hands.

I looked towards Kitty, wondering if this spectacle had affected her in the same way. The expression on her face didn't accord with the encouraging words she had uttered to me as we entered the building. I had seen it before, stoical and fixed, but only when she was in grave trouble. I tried to analyze my own feelings, and found I didn't seem to have any. I was stonily calm, even indifferent.

"Frau Kitty Beaurepos," the presiding justice called.

A guard touched Kitty on the elbow. She rose, and was led before the long table.

The first questions put to her were the usual formal ones: name, address, age, place of birth, nationality, religion, and so forth. Then the presiding judge put the first real question to her:

"Do you feel conscious of your guilt?"

"Certainly not," Kitty answered. "I should have felt guilty to have acted in any other way. I am an Englishwoman. My conscience told me that it was my duty to help English soldiers."

"Permit me to inform you," the judge said in a cutting tone, "that no account of these proceedings will be published in the newspapers. It is therefore unnecessary to make speeches. If your diatribe was addressed to England, it was quite futile. It will not reach that far. If it was your aim to convert the prosecutor or myself to Anglophilia, I think I can assure you that in that also you are hardly likely to succeed."

He picked up one of the papers in front of him, and said:

"Moreover, you are not an Englishwoman. You married a French citizen, Henri Beaurepos. You are therefore French."

Turning towards the prosecutor, he added:

"Why is this man Beaurepos not among the prisoners? Has anything been done to apprehend him?"

Kitty answered first.

"I married Monsieur Beaurepos ten years ago. We have not lived together for the last five years. I have taken steps in Lyons to divorce him."

This last I knew was untrue. Kitty was evidently trying to prevent any suspicion from being shed on Henri. She did not know, of course, that the Germans were looking for him, but that his caution, and his friends in the French police, had saved him from capture.

Somewhat to my surprise, neither the judge nor the prosecutor added anything to this—the latter, perhaps, because Kitty had saved him from confessing a failure on the part of the police. The judge consulted his papers again, and said:

"Frau Beaurepos, you are charged with having conspired with Mme. Shiber, Monsieur Christian Ravier, Monsieur Tissier and Monsieur Corbier for the purpose of smuggling English soldiers out of the country."

"That is inexact," said Kitty, in a clear voice.

"Indeed!" said the judge sarcastically. "That is very curious, considering that I have your signed confession before me. I presume you intend to retract it. I fear you are going to cause us to waste valuable time. Who gave you the very bad advice to deny what you have already admitted?"

"I have had advice from no one," Kitty said steadily. "I am not retracting my confession. But there is no reason why these others should be here with me. They were not involved in my activities."

"In the course of my duties as a military judge," the German colonel said, "I have heard a number of curious and, shall I say, incredible, stories told by prisoners, but few as difficult to believe as that Frau Shiber, for instance, who occupied the same apartment with you, failed to notice that it was a sort of way station for escaping soldiers. She must have been singularly obtuse."

"Nevertheless," Kitty insisted, "she knew nothing of my activities. I was careful to keep them secret from her. My greatest crime is that I have involved an innocent woman in this affair."

"Ah, yes," said the judge, still in that same sarcastic tone, "And Monsieur Tissier? I note that you used his estate to cross the boundary line. That was accomplished while he was looking the other way, I presume?"

"We did not ask his permission," Kitty said. "We picked it because of its position. Then we simply crossed it. That was all."

"Better and better," said the judge. "Now, Monsieur Ravier. What interesting excuse have you prepared for him?"

"I used him as a cloak," Kitty said. "He thought I was traveling about the country to help him collect funds for the restoration of his church. That pretext was valuable to me to explain my movements."

I listened to Kitty with mingled admiration and pity. It was splendid of her to try to save the rest of us, at her own expense, but her story was so pitifully thin that it couldn't possibly have stood up, even before a less biased court than this one.

"Well, we have one left," the judge said. "What about Monsieur Corbier?" And immediately, without waiting for her to answer, he continued, mimicking her voice, "Monsieur Corbier is completely innocent, and I met him only to discuss with him the present death agonies of the British Empire."

Captain Weber broke into raucous laughter, followed quickly by the other judges and the interpreter. The six soldiers of the "jury" seemed a little disconcerted. They stared at one another for a moment, then, deciding that when a colonel makes a joke, a private should laugh, they burst out simultaneously into a sort of snort, stopping short with the same unison with which they had begun. It couldn't have been more exact if it had been rehearsed.

When the merriment had subsided, Kitty answered quietly:

"I do not know Monsieur Corbier."

I realized that she had spotted the same detail that I had. Chancel was still being addressed as Corbier. That explained why he had pretended not to know us. The Gestapo, which had sought him before as Chancel, and no doubt was still seeking him, now had him in their power without realizing his real identity. It was probable that they knew less about his activities than about ours.

"You are very noble," the judge said, with an even heavier overlay of sarcasm than before, "but, of course, childish and clumsy.

Your efforts to save your co-defendants will be of no avail, and I am surprised that you should have been so stupid as to make the attempt. As far as you yourself are concerned, you have admitted the crimes charged against you. You made a confession, and you have just stated that you do not retract it. That is all we need hear from you. We will allow the others to convict themselves, as you, Frau Beaurepos, have just done."

He made a gesture of dismissal, and Kitty was led back to her seat. He called the next name

"Frau Etta Shiber!"

It was my turn. I took my place before the table, and went through the preliminary questions. Then came the first important one.

"You know the charges against you," the judge said. "Are you guilty?"

"I am guilty . . ." I said.

The judge looked up startled.

"Another curious one!" he said. "The first confesses her guilt in 15 pages, and then claims she has committed no crime—and that when she committed the crime she says she didn't commit, nobody helped her." He looked around, but got only a titter from Captain Weber. "Now this woman, who has declared in 10 pages that she is innocent admits at once that she is guilty."

"I hadn't finished," I said. "I started to say that I am guilty only of not persuading my friend to come to America with me when the war broke out. She was emotionally disturbed by the fact that thousands of soldiers from her country were in danger. I should have realized that she was not capable of understanding the situation clearly, and should have persuaded her to come away."

Captain Weber rose from his place.

"Mr. President," he said, "is this a conspiracy to make a mockery of this trial? Are we to sit here while the defendants make speeches defending one another!"

"Do not be alarmed, Mr. Prosecutor," the judge said. "The court has not yet heard anything which impresses it as being describable as a defense. The reactions of the prisoners are curious, but not effective . . . Frau Shiber, I see, is by way of being an amateur lawyer. She is filing an insanity plea for Frau Beaurepos. I regret to inform you, Frau Shiber, that insanity is not considered as alleviating, but as aggravating, the offense in this court. In the degenerate democratic system lunatics may be considered as comparatively desirable members of the community, and thus worth saving from punishment, but we do not regard the matter from quite the same viewpoint. However, it's quite evident that Frau Beaurepos is in full possession of her senses . . . I may add that you are in deep water yourself, Frau Shiber, so that you would do better to attend to your own defense than to seek excuses for your friend. Her hearing is over. We are on yours now. Suppose we keep to the subject. Do you recognize your guilt of the crimes with which you are charged?"

"I am innocent," I said.

"So you intend to continue denying everything?" the judge asked.

"It is not a question of denying anything," I said. "I am innocent. There's nothing to deny."

The judge turned his cold steely eyes on me for a minute, without moving or speaking. Then suddenly he thumped his fist on the table before him so hard that the piles of papers jumped from the wood.

"Nonsense!" he roared. "Innocent! How dare you claim to be innocent! Why, this business went on before your eyes, under your nose. The apartment where you lived was constantly filled with escaping soldiers. This dastardly secretive activity went on in your presence. Of course, you were second in command of this band of criminals! Of course, you took part in every activity of Frau Beaurepos! You participated in every discussion! You accompanied your friend on her clandestine trips! You are guilty, Frau Shiber! There is no use trying to hide it! The court will take note of your attitude!"

He had roared all this out in a single breath, in a paroxysm of fury. I stood transfixed, hypnotized by his gaze and his words.

"If that is all you came to tell us today, Frau Shiber," the judge ended, resuming a calmer tone, though still a severe one, marked by only a trace of his habitual sarcasm, "you might as well have stayed in your cell. I have already read your deposition. I knew already that you claimed to be as innocent as a newborn lamb. If you have nothing to add to that statement, you might as well take your seat."

I stumbled back to the bench. If I had had any hope after Kitty's testimony, it had disappeared now. This court was not going to worry about proof. It was true, of course, that I was guilty; but it was quite evident that if I had been innocent, the result would have been the same. As long as they believed I was guilty, that was enough. The tribunal was not going to waste time making the prosecution establish guilt.

## CHAPTER THIRTY-ONE

# Captain Weber Speaks

WHEN MONSIEUR TISSIER in his turn moved up to the long table and stood before his judges, I experienced a curious reaction. For a split second, the scene before me seemed to flatten out, as though it were a painting on a flat surface—a painting by Daumier. I seemed to see before me, as I might have seen it on a canvas, in the deep shadows which Honoré Daumier would have given it, this pathetic-grotesque picture of a humble old man facing the leering faces, not of his prosecutors, but of his persecutors. Then the sudden perception of how this scene might have been transmitted to canvas by one of the most savage of France's painters vanished, and I was again part of the scene, not a spectator of it, in a courtroom, not looking at a painting of it.

But I remained impressed by the symbolism of the scene. This dignified old man, in the shabby, wrinkled, black suit which had been his Sunday best, humble and helpless, confronting those implacable judges who were unwilling to forgive even the conquered, seemed to me to represent France, beaten and despoiled. The simple innate dignity which animated him seemed also to have been felt by the presiding judge, who resented it, and sought to break it down by a petty attack on the old man.

During his study of the documents in the case, he had noticed one detail which, he thought, gave him a chance to heap ridicule on Tissier; and as soon as the preliminaries had been disposed of, he hastened to take advantage of it.

"I notice that you signed your deposition with a cross instead of your name," he said. "Is it possible that you can't write your own name?"

"No," said Tissier calmly, "I cannot."

"Well, well!" said the judge sarcastically. "How very revealing! In this country which prides itself on its literacy, a man who, as his papers show, has been elected mayor of his community three times in succession, can't even sign his name! What ignoramuses the others must be! No wonder a country which chooses illiterates to lead it is too weak to defend itself! Don't you think, Monsieur Tissier, that there should be schools in France to teach mayors how to read and write?"

"I did not say I do not know how to read and write," Tissier said. He raised his right arm and held it out before him.

"I know how to write," he said, "but I cannot hold a pen because a German bullet tore my hand on the Marne in 1914 and my fingers have been paralyzed ever since."

As Tissier held out his hand, with its stiff, bent fingers, it was obvious what he must be saying, and the judge, his face reddening, hastily put the next question without waiting for the interpreter to translate. Tissier's examination was short. He admitted that he had allowed any one who wanted to do so to cross his estate, because, he said, he did not admit the right of foreigners to make regulations binding Frenchmen in France.

Father Christian followed Tissier. I wish I had a stenographic record of his testimony, for, ignoring legal questions, he put our moral defense in clear, simple terms more eloquent than any reproduction of them which I can set down here from memory. As nearly as I can remember, the way he summed up his attitude was this:

"France is still at war with Germany. The generals surrendered to you, but the people did not. The war is still being fought, not on military fronts this time, but in the cities, the towns, the villages, in the homes of humble individuals. What we did was to fight one of the minor skirmishes in that war. You have won this skirmish, but you have not won the war, and you will never win the war. How many are you in France? A million? Two million? There are *forty* million against you!

"When a soldier fights in battle, he knows that he may be killed. But he knows that as long as the fight continues, his death may not be in vain. We knew, too, that we might be killed in this battle. But we know also that our deaths will not be in vain. You cannot stamp out resistance by imprisoning or executing the few individuals you surprise here and there. Their fellows will only be inspired to avenge them.

"I am a priest, but in this war I have been a soldier, and a soldier who has not surrendered. For I was fighting for more than a military decision between two powers, rivals for control over the same parcel of land. I was fighting for justice, and in this war, I could see only one kind of justice, a justice partaking at the same time of the human and the divine. I do not expect to find that justice, or any justice, in this court. But I know that in the end, divine justice will prevail; and the verdict of God will be pronounced, not against us, but against you, who presume to judge us."

I was surprised that Father Christian was allowed to talk so long, uninterruptedly, pausing after each phrase while the interpreter translated it—quite faithfully, as far as my own imperfect German allowed me to judge. Dr. Weber had stepped behind the presiding judge's chair and was whispering to him. Perhaps it was absorption in their conversation which caused him to allow Father Christian to continue, or perhaps his speech was the subject of their whisperings. I imagined that Weber was urging him to cut Father Christian off, and that the judge, perhaps, was saying: "Let him talk. He's only convicting himself."

Last to be called was Chancel, and once more he was addressed under the name of Corbier. It was obvious now that the Germans actually did not know whom they had in their power, that they were ignorant of the fact that the man they had sought even before our activities began was actually before them. Kitty must have been overjoyed to realize that she had taken the right line in denying that she knew Chancel, when he said, in answer to the judge's stock question as to whether he were guilty:

"Of course not. I have never seen the other defendants before, and have no connection with them."

"You seem to forget," the judge said, "that you were arrested because you were seen to greet Mme. Shiber."

"I greeted no one," Chancel said. "I recall that just before I was arrested, the lady whom I learned here today is Mme. Shiber came towards me on the street. From a little distance, she looked like a friend, and I started to lift my hat. But as she came closer,

I realized I had mistaken her for some one else. I told that to the Gestapo any number of times. Is it a crime to make a mistake in identity these days?"

"It is a crime to have things like this in your possession," the judge rapped out suddenly, and drew out a picture postcard from the documents before him. "This was found in your apartment! A caricature of the Fuehrer, with, *'Vive la France! A bas les Boches!'* written on it! That stamps you as an enemy, of the same vile type as the other defendants! How do you explain that?"

I was astounded at the sudden anger displayed by the judge at the production of this exhibit, which he must nevertheless have seen several times before. He seemed as irate as if he had just come upon it for the first time. I could only explain it by the rage with which the Germans always encountered the word "Boche," which they considered the worst term that could possibly be applied to them.

"There must have been thousands of cards like that in circulation," Chancel said. "I received that one in the mail. I can't help what people send me. It might have been posted by your own police to manufacture evidence against me, since they hadn't anything else. How do I know?"

"But you kept it!" the judge roared. "You kept it! That is the proof of your guilt. That is all we need to know! That is enough for us! You are stamped as an enemy of the Reich! And for our enemies we have no pity! You may sit down!"

Chancel turned and walked back to his place. As his eyes met mine, I saw in them a quick flash of recognition, as though he wanted to tell us, "Thanks. I can't say more now."

It was the prosecutor's turn. I wondered what he could have to do, for it seemed to me that the judge had played his rôle for him already. It turned out that there was to be no further examination of witnesses. The Gestapo had done all that. The records of their researches had been placed before the judges, and that was all that was necessary. It was not even considered important that we should know what testimony had been given against us, or who had given it. The few questions the judge had asked us constituted our entire trial. Now the prosecutor was to ask that we be sentenced, in the name of Hitler.

Unnecessary though it seemed, Captain Weber was not going to miss the opportunity to make a long speech. He arranged a heap of documents before him, poured a glass of water from a bottle and gulped it down, and then proceeded to launch himself into an amazing and jumbled discourse, in which known facts were thrown together with guesses and possibilities, without the slightest distinction being made among them. The mere assertion of any detail by the prosecutor seemed to be considered by him as sufficient evidence of its truth—an assumption in which the court evidently concurred.

"Sitting here before us," Weber began, "caught red-handed in their felonious activity in behalf of the enemy who attacked our peaceful nation without provocation and is now being justly punished for it, are the members of an English spy ring. The unceasing vigilance of our military authorities and of the Gestapo has foiled their criminal plans. We have here all the principal traitors to our Fuehrer with one exception—the tailor Chancel, who is still a fugitive, but who will not escape us.

"Mme. Beaurepos took the vilest advantage of our good nature and our clemency towards the conquered, whose treachery in attacking us we were so willing to forget, by operating under the veil of a charitable organization which we permitted to function among our prisoners. She brought English soldiers—our sworn enemies—to her Paris apartment, and returned them to England, together with French soldiers, that they might take up arms against us again, and destroy the lives of Germans. She is as much a murderer as if she herself had fired the shots into the defenseless backs of our brave men. She gave tools and explosives to others to permit them to sabotage our efforts to restore peace and calm to this territory which we hold by the right of conquest."

I looked at Kitty as he said this, an entirely new charge which hadn't been hinted at before. She simply lifted her eyebrows and shrugged her shoulders slightly, as though to say, "What's the use?"

"According to the data in my possession," Weber continued, waving vaguely to the papers before him, "more than 500 English soldiers were returned to service in England. These men were transported to Paris by Christian Ravier, who abused his priestly robes by using them as a shield for the men he brought to the apartment of

Mme. Beaurepos. By this act, he has himself defiled the office he holds, and deserves no consideration because of it.

"Chancel, the fugitive, transported these men to the estate of Tissier, who smuggled them across the border into the free zone. Mme. Shiber supplied the money necessary to carry on this work. Monsieur Corbier was one of the liaison men of this organization. That is the general outline of their rôles. I will now explain their exact activities, one by one."

And he did so for nearly an hour, mingling correct details with pure imagination in the most fantastic manner. I found myself again and again listening to his account as if it had been a story told of other persons, it had so little relation to the facts. I judged that actually they had been able to find out little except what Kitty had confessed; for all the details he mentioned which were exact were such as she might have confessed, incriminating herself, but involving the rest of us only as she was forced to give explanations of our relations with her.

In dealing with Kitty, Weber laid emphasis on the assertion that she was a spy, for which, of course, there was no shred of evidence, and couldn't be, for the accusation was completely untrue. The English soldiers she had sent back to England, he asserted, had carried information about the strength of German garrisons in the towns she had visited, maps showing the emplacement of gun positions, photographs of war plants for the use of the R.A.F.

Father Christian was described first as a dangerous anarchist, then as a Communist. Tissier was set down as an avaricious old man who charged 50 francs a head for smuggling prisoners out of occupied territory. (Who gave them that detail, I wondered? That didn't sound like Kitty). Besides, Tissier wanted to revenge himself on Germany because of his crippled hand, which was a light punishment for his crime of having fought against Germany once before.

At one point, Weber admitted by implication how flimsy was the chain of evidence by depicting Chancel as one of the ringleaders and predicting that when he was caught, much more would be known about our operations. But when he came to Corbier in his speech, being completely without facts, he dwelt upon his diabolical cunning in refusing to admit the known fact that he had shown signs of recognizing me on the street, and that he had succeeded in destroying all evidence against himself except, by a fatal oversight, that damning postcard—"this evidence, gentlemen, that he was a personal enemy of our Fuehrer, Adolf Hitler!"

But what astounded me most was his description of myself.

"And now we come to Mrs. Shiber," he thundered, "an American millionaire, the perfect product of the Anglo-Saxon pluto-democracies, where the rich grind the faces of the poor into the ground, and fatten on their sweat and their labor. By the ill-gotten gains of the sweat-shops that furnished her with her millions, Mrs. Shiber was able to live a life of sybaritic luxury in Paris, far from the harsh and uncivilized atmosphere of the United States. And to what use did she put those millions? To the succor and comfort of our enemies. Seventeen million francs were consumed in these evil machinations——"

I gasped. I couldn't help myself. I had no idea how many dollars were represented by 17,000,000 francs, but I was certain it was more money than I had ever seen in my life. Somehow the precision of this particular lie impressed me more strongly than the curious description of myself which had preceded it.

Dr. Weber took time out to swallow another glass of water. Then he launched into the peroration of his speech.

"But what," he demanded, "is the greatest crime of these defendants? Is it that they have been responsible for the loss of more lives of the soldiers of the Fuehrer? No. That is grave, but it is not the gravest of all. The Fuehrer's soldiers are happy to give their lives that the world may be reborn, strengthened and regenerated, that the New Order may reign for a thousand years to come, under the benevolent guidance of our blessed German nation! The great sin of these defendants is that they have tried to dam the wave of the future, that they have ignorantly and viciously tried to rob the whole world and all its people of the blessings of the future realm of strength and joy for which we Germans have been ready to sacrifice everything.

"This criminal opposition to the great projects of Adolf Hitler is the greatest of all crimes. It is that principle which clarifies the issue before us. What does it matter if we have no complete record of the connection of the defendant Corbier with the others? That would attest only to his minor crime, to his crime of detail. The postcard we found in his house is the proof of his major crime, the crime which transcends all others, his unalterable enmity to the great revolution of our time, to the greatest revolution of history. And of all these others, too, we know—we have heard from their own lips— that they, too, would stand in the way of this great regeneration of a corrupt world. What if they have been clever enough to hide their traces here and there? Must the guilty be freed because we cannot prove exactly when and where and how they sinned, though we know that they are the enemies of the human race? No, *meine Herren!* The guilty must accept their punishment, without equivocation, without quibbling! What right have they to demand that we prove in detail their ignominious acts, into which we deign to pry too far, for fear of coating ourselves with the mire in which they live! They must be lopped off, like diseased members, from the body of the community which they would infect, because they are the bitter enemies of mankind, of Germany, of our great leader, Adolf Hitler!"

He sat down. Judges, attendants, guards, "jury"—every one except ourselves—raised their arms in unison, and shouted, "Heil Hitler!" Weber rose again, a piece of paper in his hand. From it, he read:

"I demand the sentence of death for Frau Beaurepos, Frau Shiber and Herr Ravier. I demand seven years at hard labor for Herr Tissier. I demand three years at hard labor for Herr Corbier. In my opinion this is the just penalty they merit under the law."

## CHAPTER THIRTY-TWO

# The Sentence

I DIDN'T hear the lawyers for the defense, who were allowed to speak for fifteen minutes apiece. I couldn't follow what they were saying, for the words kept echoing through my head, "I demand the sentence of death for . . . Frau Shiber!"

It wasn't so much that I was frightened, at the moment, or even surprised, for I had been more or less prepared; it was just that this thought monopolized my attention to the exclusion of everything else. I told myself that I would prefer death to years in such a prison as that which I had left. After all, I was no longer young. I had nothing to look forward to except death in prison, or perhaps being freed after my sentence, broken in health, and able to do nothing except await the release of death.

But I had to adjust myself to this idea, which had suddenly become more real than ever before. My mind seemed to be trying to struggle out of a sort of apathy to a new arrangement of values and outlook.

Through the confusion of conflicting ideas which struggled within my brain to reach a new clarity, I remember noticing Captain Weber, sitting at the end of the table, his chin on his hand, and then the presiding judge, and remarking that both seemed cut out of the same pattern, as though one were only another incarnation of the other. What Weber had asked, it seemed to me, the judge would certainly grant. They were too much alike to disagree. One had demanded the death sentence. The other would pronounce it.

I looked towards Kitty. She, too, seemed not to be hearing the drone of the defense lawyers. There was a faraway look in her eyes, and I realized that she must be struggling as I was to bring this new idea into the focus of reality.

I cannot recall a word of what any of the defense attorneys said. I did not even realize when they stopped speaking, for I was only brought back to awareness of the scene about me by the sharp raps of his gavel with which the presiding judge announced that he and his two associates would retire to discuss the verdict. But just as they rose to leave the room, the door opened, and Dr. Hager appeared, out of breath, and apparently highly excited. He went straight up to the presiding judge, opening his brief-case as he approached him. Arrived at the table, he pulled out a folder containing some papers, and handed it to him, talking rapidly, but in a low voice, as he did so.

The judge beckoned to Weber. He and the other two judges put their heads together for a moment. Then there was a great nodding, as though a group of automatic figures had been set in motion all at the same time, and every one sat down again. The judge rapped once more with his gavel.

"I declare this trial reopened," he said. "Important new evidence has just been brought to the attention of the court . . . Monsieur Chancel, stand up!"

Chancel! Then they had discovered whom they had captured!

I had to admire Chancel's presence of mind. He remained perfectly motionless at this unexpected pronouncing of his name. But he was the only one who was not trapped. All our heads swung around towards him.

"Dear me, Herr Chancel," the judge said ironically, "I see that if you have forgotten your name, your friends have not. And I notice that they *do* seem to know you, suddenly. You might as well abandon the comedy, Herr Chancel—or Herr Corbier, if you prefer."

I bit my lip. My only consolation was that I had not been the only one to be caught. In any case, I told myself, the game was up. They knew his identity anyway. It really made no difference, now.

Chancel rose and walked again towards the table. Dr. Hager beamed as he approached. He was obviously very much pleased with himself.

"So it appears that we did have the other ringleader, after all," said the judge. "It seems, Herr Chancel, that you were incautious enough not to destroy your genuine papers, and also to leave them, together with some in the name of Corbier, with one of your friends, who has had the misfortune to be apprehended. Would you like to modify your statement that you don't know the defendants and had nothing to do with their activities?"

"If you are so well informed already," said Chancel, "it seems unnecessary that I should add anything."

"Perhaps you are right," said the presiding judge. "It is quite unnecessary. We know already what your attitude is. Nothing you could say would be likely to change our opinion. It is a matter of indifference to this court whether you admit or continue to deny your obvious connection with this criminal conspiracy."

Captain Weber rose:

"I should like to modify my recommendations to the court," he said, "to include the name of Herr Chancel among those for whom the death penalty is demanded."

"The alteration is noted," the judge said. "You may sit down, Herr Chancel."

Chancel's defense attorney immediately sprang to his feet. The incident had restored my ability to pay attention to what was going on, and this time I listened to the plea, which was based on the fact that Chancel was a member of the Gueules Cassées, the group composed of men wounded in the face during the last war. Chancel's lawyer appealed to the court as a military body to show the respect paid by one soldier to another who had performed his duty and sacrificed his well-being for his country, and pointed out the deference which the German government had often shown towards this organization. For this reason, he concluded, he asked the court not to pronounce the death sentence.

He spoke in German, a language which Chancel did not understand. While his lawyer was speaking, Chancel sat quietly on the bench, staring blankly in front of him, as though indifferent to the whole proceedings.

With the end of his speech, the interrupted program was resumed. The judges filed out of the room, followed, with the same military precision with which they had entered it, by the "jurors." For the first time, now that the case was over, our lawyers were allowed to talk to us. They moved over to our bench, and we talked over the case, at the same time munching some sandwiches and drinking a little red wine, for which one of them sent out. I could hardly refrain from tearing at my sandwich, the first decent food I had seen since my re-arrest, but the first sip of the wine, to which I had become completely unaccustomed, made me dizzy, and I didn't dare take any more.

Chancel, the moment the proceedings were over, turned to us, and said, "Permit me, ladies and gentlemen, to apologize for my tardiness in greeting you. I know that you all understood why."

Father Christian seemed unmoved by the sentence of death asked against him.

"I am quite happy," he told me, "because they didn't get the boys who were with me when I was arrested. I saw them as the Gestapo car which took me away rounded the corner, waiting in different doorways, where I had left them. They looked to me as though they wanted to spring on the car and wrest me away from the Gestapo. Perhaps they would have, if they'd had time to think. But of course we were gone almost as soon as they saw us."

"What happened to them, do you think?" I asked.

"I'm sure they're all right," said Father Christian, "I had given them precise instructions in case of such an accident."

"You mean," I said, "that you had expected that some day you would ring our bell, only to be arrested?"

"Of course," he said. "Why, otherwise, would I have taken the precaution to come first without the boys? We are all in the hand of God, and his ways are mysterious. I had not to question the fate he might decree for me. But in the meantime, 'God helps him who helps himself,' and so I took my precautions."

"What did you tell the boys to do?" I asked.

"They were instructed to go to the hotel where we stayed one night—the one of which I told you," he said. "Its proprietress is a clever woman. I'm sure they're out of the country, like the others."

Monsieur Tissier sat beside us on the bench, saying nothing. His hands were clasped in his lap, and he seemed pondering deeply. I felt guilty for his fate, responsible that he was now in this courtroom, waiting to hear his doom. I turned towards him, and began to try to tell him how sorry I was that we had gotten him into this fix.

"It's not your fault, Madame," he said. "Please don't disturb yourself about me. I assure you, I am not worried about myself."

"But you are so silent," I said. "You seem so downcast."

"I was thinking about my vines," he said. "It is March. I should be trimming the stalks. And the roots should be covered with earth, and channels cut so that the melting snow will drain off the land and not flood my vines. There are a thousand things to do in a vineyard, Madame. I wonder who will care for mine?"

Our lawyers got into an argument among themselves about the probable sentences. One of them said pessimistically, forgetting probably that we were within hearing, that no doubt the sentences had been decided upon before court convened, and that probably the prosecutor's requests would be granted.

"On the contrary," my lawyer said, "I don't think there will be any death sentences at all. I don't believe they will dare sentence Mrs. Shiber to death, since she's an American citizen. The Germans don't want to take any action which would irritate the United States. And if Mrs. Shiber is not given a death sentence, it won't be easy to impose one on any one else. Father Christian would probably escape the death punishment, too, as a priest."

"Yes, but how about my client?" asked Kitty's lawyer.

"Well, the fact that she was born English and is French by marriage ought to help," my lawyer answered. "If she were either all English or all French, it would probably be worse."

"That," Kitty whispered in my ear, "is about the thinnest argument I've ever heard. If that's the only hope he has for me, I might as well give up."

The minutes dragged by, and the judges did not reappear. Conversation died down, and we all sat nervously on our bench, our eyes on the door. One of the lawyers looked at his watch.

"They've been out an hour," he said.

"It couldn't have been any previously prepared sentence, then," one of the others said. "They must really be discussing the case."

But at that moment Chancel's lawyer, who had gone out to see what was happening, came back and dispelled that illusion.

"They aren't discussing the sentence," he said. "They're having lunch. I saw them from the corridor. They left the door half-open. They're stuffing themselves like pigs, and having a high old time while they're about it."

It was two o'clock when the doors opened and the judges filed ceremoniously back into the courtroom. It couldn't have taken more than a few seconds for them to take their places again, but to me it seemed hours before the presiding judge rose from his seat, picked up a sheet of paper, and read the sentences. They were:

For Kitty, death; for Father Christian, death; for Chancel, five years at hard labor; for Tissier, four years at hard labor; for myself, three years at hard labor.

The thought of three more years of prison surged through my mind and overcame me with horror. I half-opened my mouth to cry: "Kill me, too—but not three more years of that terrible prison. I'll die there!"

But Kitty caught me by the arm, and whispered into my ear:

"Control yourself, Etta. Don't let these Germans see us lose our dignity. Don't cry. You don't want them to have the satisfaction of making an American cry."

I was at once profoundly ashamed of myself. I had received the lightest sentence of all, and when it was pronounced, I had for a moment thought only of myself. And Kitty—Kitty, who had just heard herself condemned to death—was consoling me, encouraging me! I squeezed her hand hard, and choked down the sobs I had felt welling up within me.

Now that the trial was over, no one worried any more about our being together, and once more we were locked into the prison van together, without a guard, for the trip back to the Cherche-Midi. Both of us realized that this would probably be the last time we would ever see each other, in this jouncing, evil-smelling vehicle in which we were being carried back to jail like freight. I broke down, and laying my head on Kitty's chest, wept bitterly, but this time it was more for her than for myself, and for sorrow at our parting. Kitty smoothed my hair, and said:

"Cry now, Etta, if you like. You'll feel better for it. But promise me to be strong before the Germans. Never weep where they can see you. If you must cry, hold your tears back until night, when no one will hear or see you. That is what I did in prison, Etta. I was not weeping for myself, but because I had brought you into this fatal adventure. I should have made you go home when there was still time. Believe me, your sentence hurts me more than mine.

"Don't worry about me. Promise me that you will never think of me sadly. I am not sad. I did what I had to do. I knew the price, and I am willing to pay it. I have given England back 150 lives for the one she is losing now. Think of that when you think of me. Remember that I was not one who failed, but who succeeded, who won a 150-to-one victory against the Germans. Smile when my name comes to your mind, as you used to smile at me in the old days. Forget the troubles and the worries of the past months, and remember only the strong young boys with the brave hearts whom we sent home again . . .

"There was a time when I was terrified at the thought of death; but not now. I have become accustomed to that thought now. Millions will have died before this war is over, and one more death will make little difference—especially when by that death I have purchased renewed life for so many others . . . Perhaps death comes easier if it comes unexpectedly, in action, when a bullet strikes without even being noticed. But even though its coming has been announced to me in advance, I can look it in the face and not be afraid. I have done my task. I have earned my rest."

She was silent for a moment, and then she smiled sadly, and said to me, so softly that I could hardly hear her over the noise of the van, as though she were speaking to herself:

"And when the war is over, go to England, and walk along the embankment of the Thames, in the spring, where I always used to walk. I will be with you . . . See if you can find some of the boys we sent to England. Tell them that as I once helped them, now they must help me. They must carry on the work I can no longer do by continuing to be what they have always been—the loyal and unwavering defenders of England."

The van came to a clanking stop. We had reached the prison.

## CHAPTER THIRTY-THREE

# Cut Rate for Freedom

I REMAINED in the Cherche-Midi prison until May 16, when I was sent, with twenty-five other women who had been sentenced to prison terms, to the prison of Fresnes—the same whose hospital had appeared so horrible to me.

It was a large jail, five stories high, which reminded me of pictures I had seen of Sing Sing. It surrounded a small courtyard, where I learned that prisoners were allowed to spend two hours each day in the afternoon, and I looked forward to getting the air which had been denied me at Cherche-Midi. But I was to have no such luck.

My sentence, which called for hard labor, should actually have worked out in practice to solitary confinement, for there was in fact no hard labor which a woman of my age could perform at Fresnes. But the warden found it impossible even to keep me in solitary confinement, for the prison was too crowded to allow a single prisoner to have a whole cell to herself. All he could do, therefore, was to rule that I must remain indoors when the others went out.

Although I missed the opportunity to get fresh air and to move about a bit, I nevertheless found the two hours when I was left to myself the pleasantest of the whole day. Continuous solitary confinement would no doubt have had a very bad effect on me; but since I was cooped up day and night with other cell-mates, the two hours when I was left alone provided a blissful change. I cannot hope to describe the intense yearning for a few minutes' privacy which besets prisoners forced to live day in, day out in the constant presence of other persons, as I had to do at Cherche-Midi. My daily two hours alone in the cell were so welcome to me that I was actually afraid I might be permitted to go out into the courtyard with the others. It was worth the loss of exercise and fresh air. I was very careful never to admit to any one how I felt about it, for fear my routine would be changed.

Fresnes had one advantage over Cherche-Midi—a prison for women alone, it had women guards. But the food was simply indescribable—much worse than at Cherche-Midi, a thing which I would have thought impossible before I made the change. I could hardly choke it down, though I was always hungry. In quantity, the rations here, as at Cherche-Midi, were starvation portions—certainly not enough to keep an adult healthy for any considerable period.

"Breakfast" came at 8:30 A.M. It consisted of a coffee substitute made from barley. Lunch was at eleven—a colorless liquid concoction with a nauseating odor, accompanied by ice-cold smelly potatoes. The first time I tasted that soup, I promptly threw it up. I had a chance to try again at five in the afternoon. That was the last meal of the day, and it consisted also of the vile-tasting soup.

I do not think that I could have survived six months at Fresnes if it had not been for the Quakers, who managed to get me extra items of food from time to time. Realizing that something was wrong when I failed to meet him at the Ritz, Mr. Marvel had traced me again, and during all the time I was at Fresnes, he saw to it that I received parcels from his organization. I am sure that I owe my life to that aid. It was malnutrition, certainly, which was responsible for the high death rate at Fresnes. Almost daily I heard the bells of the tiny prison chapel toll for funerals. Very often, in moments of depression, I heard that sound and told myself that one day it would sound for me, that I would never leave Fresnes alive.

There was only one bed in my cell, for three of us. Because I was the oldest, I was allowed to sleep in it. The other two had to sleep on the floor.

One of my two inmates was a rather remarkable woman, Mme. Berthet, tall, blonde and with expressive blue eyes. She was about forty-five, with an American mother and an Alsatian father. She had been born in Alsace while it was under German rule, but her thinking was French, not German. She told me that it was because of a cousin that she found herself in jail. He had been a prisoner of war in Germany, and had succeeded in escaping. She hid him, and both were arrested. She got two years for aiding an escaped prisoner.

Mme. Berthet was a woman of exceptional accomplishments. She had studied law in Germany, and had practised as a consulting lawyer in Paris. She was also a legal interpreter, being equally conversant with French, German and English.

She had already served eleven months of her sentence when I arrived at Fresnes, and had hopes of being released shortly. She told me that her husband had influential connections with important German officials, and, indeed, either she or he must have had some friends in high places, for the first Friday I spent in jail, she said to me, "Well, I'll see you Monday. I'm going home for the week-end."

"What?" I exclaimed incredulously.

"Oh, I always spend the week-ends at home," she said lightly. "I'm the only prisoner in Fresnes who takes the week-ends off."

I thought she was joking, but a few minutes later a guard came for her, and sure enough, she didn't return until Monday morning.

When she returned, I couldn't refrain from expressing my surprise at such a curious procedure.

"I know one thing," I said to her, "and that is that the Germans don't allow any one such privileges unless they get something in return for it. I don't know what you do in exchange for your week-ends of freedom—but I've had an experience like this before, and I know what I suspect."

Mme. Berthet looked at me teasingly, apparently not in the least perturbed by what I had said.

"Well, now," she said mockingly, "what do you suspect?"

I told her about Marthe Wenzinger, "an Alsatian like yourself," I explained. Mme. Berthet listened with an amused smile on her lips, and burst into a little chuckle when I had finished.

"So you think I'm a spy, too, do you, Mrs. Shiber?" she laughed. "To begin with, you've already been sentenced. Why should the Gestapo bother about wasting a spy's time on you now? You're dead right about one thing, though. The Germans don't hand out any privileges without compensation. I pay for my week-ends out—or rather my husband does; but it's not the kind of transaction you think. It's just an ordinary business arrangement. He pays cash."

"You mean your husband pays somebody to let you spend the week-ends at home?" I gasped.

"Exactly," said Mme. Berthet. "Everything has its price, you know, especially in Nazidom. You may remember how we used to hear about the incorruptibility of Nazi civil servants? Don't believe it. They'll sell anything. It's costing my husband a pretty penny now for my weekly vacations, and he's trying to settle the matter once and for all by buying me out of here entirely. I imagine he'll succeed."

She was right. Only two weeks later she was released, and I said good-bye to her, thinking that I wouldn't see her again.

But some ten days after she had left, a guard came to the cell and told me there was a visitor to see me. She took me, not to the usual visitors' room, where wire screens separated the prisoners from those who came to see them, but to a small office, where she left me alone with—Madame Berthet! She was completely transformed, now that she was no longer a jail-bird, elegantly dressed, her hair elaborately arranged, and in appearance quite a different person from my former cell-mate.

"I don't imagine you expected to see me, Mrs. Shiber," she said, "but you see, I haven't forgotten you. How would you like to get out of here?"

"Of course I'd like to get out," I said. "But how?" I was suspicious of her again. There was something curious about all this, and about her ability to arrange a private interview with me so easily.

"The same way I did," Mme. Berthet said. "I've been talking to my husband about your case. He thinks it can be arranged."

"I don't know what to say," I said confusedly. "Just what is your husband's means of influence with the Germans? How does he arrange all this? What do they want me to do?—for I'm sure that I won't be allowed out of jail for nothing."

"Oh, dear, Mrs. Shiber!" Mme. Berthet said. "You still suspect me of trickery, don't you? Well, now, I'll tell you how my husband got his influence. It's a long story and it has nothing to do with the case; but you asked for it, so here it is. You'll see that you needn't worry.

"My husband owned a factory making agricultural machinery before the war. Shortly after the occupation, he was visited by a representative of a German concern which asked him if he would consider selling his factory. He refused; and immediately he began to find it impossible to operate. He couldn't get raw materials, of which the supply was controlled by the Germans; work was constantly being hampered by visits of officials for 'inspections,' followed by impositions of irksome regulations; his workers were subjected to pressure to move to other employment; and he found himself facing the prospect of having to shut up shop. The Germans let him taste about a month of this treatment, and then their man came back again. There was nothing else to do. He sold out. Incidentally, all this occurred about the time I was arrested, and perhaps my sentence would have been lighter if they hadn't been working on him at the time.

"You have to give them credit for one thing—they paid a good price. They have plenty of money, of course; they get it from us for nothing. . . . Well, there was my husband, an active man all his life, left with nothing to do. He was chafing at his inactivity, and finally he hit upon a plan.

"I suppose it was what had happened to himself that gave him the idea. He paid particular attention to the effort the Germans were making to acquire majority interests in all French business. The object was pretty plain. While they had unlimited amounts of money at their disposition, and unlimited means of coercion, the Germans planned to buy up all French businesses, in perfectly legal form and according to French procedure. Thus, after the war, when the occupation of France will have to end, Germany will *own* France. She will have economic control over the country which can't be broken. Even if she loses the war, she will still have won France."

"But certainly, if Germany loses the war, she will have to give back what she has taken," I objected.

"How?" Mme. Berthet asked. "It may seem easy to you, Mrs. Shiber, but remember that all these transactions were perfectly legal ones, under French law. The businesses will have been bought and paid for. Ownership of stock often can't be traced, because most French stocks, unlike your American ones, are made out to the bearer, not to any particular person. Sometimes French citizens are used to represent the Germans, who are the real owners of a business that seems to be in French hands. And remember that every one of these changes will have been consecrated by further contracts and developments made since on the faith that the first transfers are valid. To try to untangle the structure after the war might mean wrecking the whole economic system of the country, or tearing down the legal principles on which the forced exchanges were based.

"Now my husband reasoned that the Germans needed Frenchmen to act as agents, and dummy owners, and acquirers of stock in these affairs, so he offered his services. That is the origin of his influence with the Germans. He has done them great services in securing important transfers of French businesses to German ownership. He receives heavy commissions for each such transaction, and has amassed quite a considerable fortune. This activity has also put him in touch with many influential Nazis, and that is how he was able to find the right persons to approach, first to let me get out of jail during week-ends, and finally to buy me out of prison altogether. He may be able to do the same for you."

"I am afraid," I said coldly, "that I would prefer not to have any dealings with a man who is selling out his own countrymen to the enemy."

"Oh, come now," Mme. Berthet laughed, "don't be so stiff-necked. My husband says some one is going to do it, so it might as well be he."

"Not long ago," I said, "I met a fourteen-year-old boy who had to support himself and his mother because his father was a prisoner in Germany. He refused to sell papers, the easiest way for him to make money, because it was spreading German propaganda. He could have made the same excuse as your husband."

Mme. Berthet glanced furtively about the room. Then she came closer, and whispered, as though she were afraid of being heard outside the room.

"Mme. Shiber," she said, "I think I can trust you. I must tell you the real reason why my husband is doing this. He is keeping duplicate records of every transaction with which he is concerned, and of the means of coercion used to force sales. After the war, it will be easier to annul the sales he has handled than most of the others. He is pretending to help the Germans in order to be able to undo their work afterwards. He will be one of the principal witnesses against the Germans when these transactions are reviewed later. Now do you understand, Mrs. Shiber?"

She looked straight into my eyes with those clear expressive eyes of her own, and I was convinced, for the moment at least, that she was telling the truth.

"Yes," I said, "now I understand. But what do you think you can do for me?"

"I spoke of your case to my husband," she said, "and he took it up with some of his German connections. They said yours is not nearly as simple as mine, partly because you are a foreigner, partly because political considerations are involved, partly because your offense was much graver. But he finally got them to name a price. To get me out, he paid 100,000 francs. They will free you for one million."

"A million francs!" I said. "Goodness! That sounds like a lot of money! What is it in dollars?"

"At forty francs to the dollar, just $25,000."

"I could never raise that much," I said. "All I have in the world is a few thousand francs in the prison office, and $1,000 which was sent to me at the American Embassy while I was in jail."

"That doesn't matter," Mme. Berthet said. "My husband would be glad to advance you the million francs. All you need do is deposit $25,000 in his name in an American bank."

"You don't understand," I explained. "I haven't $25,000 in America or anywhere else. I've never in my life had that much money at one time."

"You must be joking!" Mme. Berthet said. "My husband made inquiries, and the Germans told him you spent millions financing the escapes of the English soldiers. You surely don't expect me to believe that you haven't $25,000 to free yourself?

"Look! I'll put all my cards on the table. It wasn't only because of interest in your case that I took the trouble of trying to arrange this way out for you. My husband, as I told you, has plenty of money now—in francs and in Paris—but who knows what it will be worth after the war? He's very anxious to find some way to convert some of it into dollars, in a New York bank—and this provides a means. Now don't you see, Mrs. Shiber, how advantageous this will be for all of us? You get your freedom, my husband is enabled to insure our future. I'm sure it's worth $25,000 to you to be out of this hole."

She opened her bag and drew out a sheaf of papers.

"Here," she said, "everything is prepared. All you have to do is to sign this document authorizing your bank to transfer $25,000 to an account in my husband's name—we have left a blank here, where you can fill in the name of the correct bank—and we will have you out of here in a few days."

"But, really, I'm telling you the truth," I protested. "I'm not a millionaire, whatever the Germans said. I haven't that much money."

Mme. Berthet looked at me for a moment with a curious twisted smile. Then she lifted her eyebrows, sighed, and stuffed the papers back into her bag.

"Oh, well," she said, "I see how it is. You think the price is too high. You are saying to yourself, I suppose, that since my husband wants dollars in New York, he has no interest in beating the Germans down. I assure you, Mrs. Shiber, you can't bargain with these people. They set their price, and that's all there is to it. We can't do any better for you.

"Think it over. If you change your mind, you will be allowed to communicate with me through the prison officials. They will send for me if you ask them to. I will give you a few days before my husband has to tell the officials with whom he dealt that you value your money more than your freedom. It may create some difficulties for us. I'm sure we wouldn't have gone so far if we had dreamed that you wouldn't be anxious to accept and grateful to us for helping you.

"But I advise you not to hesitate too long. People are saying that America may enter the war soon. In that case, you won't be able to get out, at any price."

I went back to my cell in a daze. Mme. Berthet's proposition had left me in a curious frame of mind. I couldn't make out where, in her curiously mixed character, self-interest ended and a genuine desire to be helpful began. She had evidently carried away a very false idea of me, too, since she believed that I had plenty of money, but would rather stay in jail than part with it. How happy I would have been to pay the last penny I owned to leave this prison! But when she said $25,000, she might as well have said a million. One was as impossible for me to get as the other.

Was it really true that America might enter the war? Then what would happen to me? The American Embassy would close, Mr. Marvel and the Quakers would no longer be able to help me—and I would be alone and a prisoner in an enemy land!

Mme. Berthet's visit certainly did not cheer me up.

## CHAPTER THIRTY-FOUR

# *Micheline*

M Y OTHER cell-mate at Fresnes was Micheline Seurat, a widow of thirty, pretty and frail, now serving her second sentence. Both had been for the same offense—referring to the Germans as "Boches." The first time they had given her six months. This time it was a year.

"But, Micheline," I asked her, "after you had gone to jail for using that word once, why weren't you more careful thereafter?"

Micheline shrugged her little shoulders.

"*C'était plus fort que moi.* I couldn't control myself. It just escaped me. You would have done the same. It was at that Gaumont-Palace affair."

"What Gaumont-Palace affair?" I asked. I hadn't heard anything about it. I knew the Gaumont-Palace, of course, the largest moving picture theatre in Paris, holding some five to six thousand people.

"Why, it was in all the papers," Micheline said. "But then, you must have been in jail at the time. It was like this. I went to see a picture there one evening and there was a newsreel which consisted of nothing but pictures of Hitler—the Fuehrer visiting the front lines, the Fuehrer pinning the Iron Cross on a soldier's tunic, the Fuehrer inspecting a munitions plant, the Fuehrer surrounded by school children, the Fuehrer this and the Fuehrer that. It was disgusting! Let the Germans make a God of him if they want to, but why should they try to ram him down our throats? Naturally every one began whistling and booing." (In France, it should be explained, whistling is a sign of disapproval, not of approval). "The film was stopped, the lights were put on, and a Gestapo officer came out on the stage and said the film would be shown again, from the beginning, and if there were any further disturbances, we would have to take the consequences. So they started again, and the whistling began again. The show was stopped, and the audience told to leave.

"We all filed out, most of us not at all put out at not seeing the rest of the show. We were pleased with having stopped the Hitler picture. But as we came out of the theatre, we found German police at every exit. They were arresting every fiftieth person to come out, man, woman or child, to be punished for the insult to the Fuehrer.

"It was really terrible. There they had us pinned in, in single file, between two lines of Germans, and at the head an officer was counting the people as they filed out, to himself, so you couldn't guess how near you were to the fatal number. He would say, '*Fünfzig*,' and the guards would pull the fiftieth person out of the line and hustle him off to one side. I would have been all right, for they took a young man just three places in front of me, so I couldn't possibly have been caught, but I got angry when they pulled him away, and said, '*Sales Boches*,' just a little too loud. So here I am."

A few weeks in the same cell with Micheline, and I became almost a member of her family. She told me all the gossip about her relatives, which ones were nice, which were not, who had money, who had divorced. I shared her admiration of some and her indignation of others. And naturally, in my turn, I began to tell her about my own past life, and my friends—chiefly, of course, Kitty. I told her often how painful it was not to have had any news of her, not to know whether she was still alive or whether the sentence of execution had already been carried out. One day, when I was talking of Kitty, Micheline said,

"I have been thinking about your friend, and I believe I have thought of a scheme to get news of her."

"How?" I asked.

"Well, since she was not transferred here when you were, she probably stayed at the Cherche-Midi prison. Now, whenever any of their prisoners are ill, they send them to the hospital here."

"I know," I said. "I was here once myself."

"Well, if we could get in touch with any prisoners from Cherche-Midi, we might be able to find out something about your friend. There are almost always some of them here. The cleaning in the hospital is done by woman prisoners. At the exercise hour, I will try to find one of them who may be able to ask a few questions for us."

But it was only three days later that Micheline succeeded in locating one of the cleaning women.

"You should see the girl I found," Micheline said. "I don't believe you could understand a word she says, though. She's as tough as they come, a *fille du milieu* from Montmartre, and she talks underworld slang exclusively. She's been here since before the war. Her gang murdered an informer and she got four years as an accomplice. Her name is Titi. She'll see what she can find out, and all she asks is that you get her some '*mégots.*'"

"Some what?" I asked.

"I told you you wouldn't understand her," Micheline said triumphantly. "That means cigarettes."

"I'd be glad to," I said, "but how can I?"

"Oh, you can get them all right," Micheline said. "Ask the guard to buy you some out of your money in the prison office. Then I'll take them to Titi. Of course, you'll have to pay Black Market prices, and throw in a good tip for the guard."

For the next week there was no news. Micheline returned every day from the exercise period to report that no one in the hospital knew anything about Kitty. There were a dozen Cherche-Midi patients there at the time, and I thought it an ominous sign that with so many of them at Fresnes, none had even heard Kitty's name.

But finally, Micheline returned triumphant.

"I've good news for you," she said. "Your friend is still at Cherche-Midi. And do you know what Titi is doing? Really, you should get her a mountain of cigarettes! She is trying to arrange a meeting between you!"

"A meeting!" I said. "How can that be?"

"One of the patients in the hospital here now works in the Cherche-Midi laundry," Micheline explained. "She is returning in a few days. She was the one who knew Kitty was there, because she distributes the laundry to the prisoners. She will take a message to Kitty to pretend to be ill so that she can be sent here, and then you will pretend to be ill also, and have to go to the hospital as well. Titi will see to it that you are put in adjoining beds. What do you say?"

"I'd love to see Kitty again," I said with a sigh. "But I doubt if it will work. You have to be much more than really sick to be sent to the hospital here. If the prison doctor were concerned about his charges, I would be there now. My health is bad as it is. I've always had high blood pressure, and I can feel that my heart is not functioning well now."

This was the strict truth, for the bad food and my emotional reactions to prison life had had a deleterious effect on my health. I often lay awake all night, because of the irregularity of my heartbeat. I had not complained of it, because my experience with the hospital had been that it was no improvement over a cell, but now, I thought, if by any chance Kitty should be brought here, I would have a real illness to complain of, and perhaps I could see my dearest friend once more.

I went to sleep that night quite happy. I thought Titi's scheme fantastic and impractical, but even the little ray of hope it gave me tranquilized me: and for the first time for several nights, I went easily off to sleep, to dream that Kitty and I were back together in our beloved apartment, before the shadow of war had fallen over it.

## CHAPTER THIRTY-FIVE

# A New Cell-Mate

M R. MARVEL paid me another visit, bringing with him a welcome
parcel containing several cans of food, potato salad, tuna fish,
bread and sugar. He was accompanied by a snub-nosed bespectacled
German, whose job was to listen to everything he said, to make sure
that he didn't exceed his privileges.

The German's presence infuriated me, for there were two questions I particularly wanted to ask. One was whether he knew anything about Kitty. The other was if it were true that America was
about to enter the war.

I asked outright about Kitty, but the German immediately intervened.

"You know you have no right to ask such questions," he said.
"You should not bother Mr. Marvel with them."

I looked in despair towards Micheline, and it seemed to me that
I saw her lips pouting to pronounce the fatal word. I frowned sternly
at her.

A few minutes later I tried to phrase my second question so that
the German wouldn't realize what I was trying to find out.

"Thank you again for coming to see me, Mr. Marvel," I said. "Do
you expect to stay on even if America enters the war?"

But the German was on the alert.

"If you persist in putting improper questions to Mr. Marvel," he
said sternly, "we cannot permit him to continue to visit you."

We could hardly wait for the cell door to close before we pounced
upon the food Mr. Marvel had brought, wolfing it down glut-
tonously.

"Thank you for that murderous look," Micheline murmured
through a full mouth, as soon as the excitement of getting real food
had subsided a bit. "I was just going to say 'Boche' once more.
They're so stupid! What harm would it do for you to know what

has happened to your friend? Is that going to upset their sacred Fuehrer?"

At the exercise period that day, Micheline's talk with Titi brought real news. As soon as she had been locked into the cell again with me, she threw her arms around my neck and whispered in my ear: "Guess what? A message from your friend!"

"No!" I squealed. "What did she say?"

"She's going to try to get into the hospital here!" said Micheline.

"Oh, if only she can!" I said fervently. Looking back, I don't know why I wanted so strongly to see Kitty again, under the circumstances. But I did. It wasn't reasonable, perhaps, but then sentiment rarely is.

"How did you find out?" I asked.

"A new patient from Cherche-Midi had a message from the laundry woman," Micheline explained. "The laundry woman saw Kitty and told her of the plan, and Kitty said that she would do her best if—Oh!"

Micheline's little exclamation told me at once that she had stopped herself just as she was about to say something she hadn't intended I should hear. It wasn't difficult to imagine what it would have been. Kitty would try to do it if her sentence wasn't carried out in the meantime.

I began figuring how much time had elapsed since the trial. It was almost exactly three months after March 7, the date of our trial. I knew the death sentence had to be approved by the military Kommandantur of Paris, and if Kitty's lawyer were energetic, I assumed that he might be able to appeal her case all the way up to Berlin. Even so, considering how cavalierly the Germans dealt with procedure, it seemed that Kitty couldn't count on much more time.

And as I made this calculation, suddenly, without warning, I burst into a spasm of weeping. The thought of Kitty's execution, which had gradually passed into the background of my mind, again occupied the first place in my thoughts. The hope of seeing her again had suddenly been routed by the realization that at any moment, even now, she might be paying the supreme penalty for her acts. And in addition to the sorrow for Kitty which swept over me like a wave, I was overcome by a feeling of guilt because I had given so little thought to her plight since I had been in prison. Once again, I had been pitying myself, the luckiest of all of us.

Micheline sat beside me on our one bed, and put her arm around my shoulders.

"Don't cry for the evil that is going to happen," she said softly. "Perhaps it may never come. My mother always used to tell me, when I was a little girl, and cried in anticipation of something I feared, that it was soon enough to meet trouble when it came, and that there was no point in crying ahead of time, for there would be plenty of opportunity for tears when the bad news really came . . . Besides, I don't think your friend is going to be executed. The Germans don't wait three months to carry out their sentences. If they had meant to kill your friend, they would have done it already."

"Do you really think so, Micheline?" I asked. "You aren't saying that only to console me?"

"No, it's true," she said. "I was in Lille when some persons were sentenced to death at noon, and we heard the firing squads an hour later."

On Mr. Marvel's next visit, he had with him, not only the German guide, but also a Frenchman, whom he introduced to me by saying:

"As I am obliged to return to the United States, I wanted to present to you Mr. Maurice Fleury, who will take over my work. He will come to see you from time to time, just as I did, on behalf of the Quakers."

This announcement was a heavy blow to me. Mr. Marvel represented not only my sole contact with the outside world, but also, to me, America. No matter how assiduous his French successor might be, he could not possibly mean as much to me as one of my own countrymen. While Mr. Marvel was still visiting me, I could tell myself that I was not entirely cut off from my own country, a prisoner in a foreign land. But with his departure I would feel deserted and alone.

I saw that my expression had made him realize how much his announcement had affected me, but he could say nothing to console me, for the German was actually watching our lips, ready to pounce upon us for uttering unpermitted thoughts even before they had been made audible. Nor could I ask the question which rose in my mind immediately: What of America and the war? This time, however, it was hardly necessary. I could guess the answer from the news I had just heard. America could not yet be at war, or Mr. Marvel would not be able to return to the United States; but that event was probably considered imminent, or he would not be leaving.

All we could do was to exchange sympathetic glances. Then the three men left the cell, and I remained alone with my thoughts, for it was the exercise hour, and the other prisoners were all in the courtyard.

For a brief moment, I was seized by a giddy feeling of panic. America is preparing to enter the war, I thought, and all Americans are returning home. The American Embassy, my last hope, the final refuge to which I might cling, will close. Even the faint moral support its existence gave me will disappear now. I will be entirely in the power of the enemy. Who knows how long the war will last? If it goes on longer than my term, I will remain a prisoner. I will never escape alive from the horrible captivity, I told myself in despair.

But then the thought of Kitty came to my mind, and once more gave me strength.

"Why am I complaining," I said to myself, "when she is bearing so bravely a lot much more desperate than mine?"

Perhaps it was because I had lost hope of early release that I set to work now to compile my prison almanac. All the prisoners had their private calendars, on which they checked off the days they had served, but so far I had not made one. I had a sort of unexpressed superstitious belief in some miracle, which would bring about my release suddenly and unexpectedly. With the departure of Mr. Marvel and my fear that soon all Americans would have left France, that naïve hope faded away; and I accepted resignedly the conclusion that I would have to serve my full term.

I therefore prepared my prison calendar, with a line for each day of the three years I would have to serve, and each night crossed off one of the lines. Micheline saw me at it, and one day glanced idly at my calendar.

"You've shortened your sentence by one day, my friend," she observed, tossing it back to me.

"How?" I asked, as dismayed by the prospect of one day more in jail as though it made much difference in the dreary reach of three long years.

"Because," said Micheline, "you are unlucky enough to be serving until March 7, 1944. And 1944 happens to be a leap year, so that February will have twenty-nine days."

Silently, I added one more line to my calendar, making it 1,096 days I would have to serve instead of 1,095. I felt, as I did it, an absurd resentment at the judge who had cheated me of an extra day of freedom, by making my sentence extend just one week beyond that extra day.

Thirty days had been crossed off on my calendar since the message from Kitty, and there had been no further news. Had she been unsuccessful in her attempt to simulate sickness? Or—but I didn't dare think of the possible alternative.

Day after day Micheline returned from the exercise period only to report that Titi had no more news. Prisoners from the Cherche-Midi jail arrived constantly at the Fresnes hospital, but none of them had any word from her.

"Perhaps," I said to Micheline one day, "the Germans discovered that messages could be carried between the two prisons. Or it may be that the laundress was moved to other work, and can't keep in touch with the other prisoners any more."

"I tell you what I'll do," Micheline said. "When I see Titi this afternoon, I'm going to ask her to try to get word back by some other patient returning to Cherche-Midi. If our laundress has failed us, perhaps we can get another messenger."

I waited anxiously for her return, but when the exercise period ended, Micheline did not return. I heard the other prisoners entering their cells at four, as usual, but my cell-mate did not come back. I could hardly take my eyes off the door, and I jumped at the slightest noise outside. But at six, Micheline was still missing.

When the guard came in with the big pot full of the disgusting liquid referred to in the prison as soup, I couldn't refrain from asking about Micheline.

"My cell-mate didn't come back from her afternoon exercise," I said. "Do you know what happened to her?"

The guard looked at me stolidly as she ladled my portion of soup out into my bowl, picked up her pot and walked out without a word. I wanted to throw the bowl of soup after her, I was so furious.

I didn't sleep all night, worrying about Micheline's fate, and also because her disappearance, if it was permanent, meant cutting me off from Titi and possible news from Kitty. At seven in the morning, when a key grated in the lock, I was still awake. I jumped up quickly, thinking Micheline was being brought back. Perhaps she had been overheard talking to Titi and had spent a night in the punishment cell.

But no! The door opened, and the guard pushed a strange woman into the cell, then came in behind her, and began gathering up Micheline's few poor belongings—a nightgown, a thin cloak, some underwear, a few toilet articles. She tied them up into a bundle, and went out without a word. Obviously Micheline was not coming back; and I was left alone in the cell with the stranger.

How I hated my new cell-mate! It was not her fault, but the resentment I felt against the sudden disappearance of Micheline, at this moment when I was torn with anxiety about Kitty and counted desperately on her to get me news, was transferred to the woman who had had the bad luck to replace her.

The new arrival was about 50. She sat down easily on the end of my bed, as though she felt quite at home in prison. I decided that she had not just entered it, for her hair had been dyed blond, but since the last opportunity she had had to care for it, some two inches of a grayish-dark layer had grown beneath the dyed portion. Her face was worn and flabby, and there were heavy pockets under her eyes. She looked like a woman worn out by a hectic and probably none too savory past.

She cast a glance at my calendar, which I had attached to the wall. "Three years, *hein*?" she said. "What was that for—stealing?"

I was indignant. Then it occurred to me that, after all, it wasn't particularly surprising that a jail-bird should be suspected of theft. I didn't feel like confiding in her, either. So I simply said, "No, not stealing."

"Embezzlement?"

"No."

"Well, don't tell me," she said sarcastically, "I love to play guessing games."

She looked me over carefully, then inspected the clothes I had hung against the wall, and said, disappointedly:

"I get it now. You're just one of those politicals they've got crowding the prisons these days. Right?"

I nodded. The tone of her voice indicated that she considered me an impostor, practically without any right to be in jail at all. She obviously had nothing but contempt for "politicals," who got into jail fraudulently, without committing any of the crimes more honest criminals had to perpetrate to gain admission.

And Louise Dallon was, indeed, familiar with prisons. She had already, she told me, served six sentences, totalling twelve years. She specialized in a particular type of stealing. She would take a job as a cook under a false name in some wealthy household, and at the first favorable opportunity would make off with everything valuable she could carry away.

"I got off easy this time, considering my record," she said casually. "Only a year. I'm sure if I'd worked it a little more cleverly I could have gotten off entirely. They've got so many politicals like you in the jails, they haven't any room for us any more. You'd be surprised how many people up on light charges are acquitted just because there's no place to put them."

She shook her head wonderingly.

"These are funny times," she said. "You don't meet the same kind of people any more. You politicals aren't so much fun, if you don't mind my saying so. Sort of stuffy. . . . Now take the Black Maria that brought me here from Rouen. Six of us there were in it. And would you believe it, I was the only legitimate one? Mine was the usual—I cleaned out an apartment. But the others! No business to be there at all. Babes in the wood, all of them! We were all one-year people. I did something for it. I had a right to be there. But the others! Well, I wouldn't let them put any airs on with me—calling themselves prisoners! One of them had drawn capital V's on the walls of houses; another one had shouted, 'Vive de Gaulle!' Then there was a woman who had some English leaflets dropped from airplanes in her house, and another who was arrested for listening to the London broadcasts. The most desperate criminal in the lot was a woman who refused to serve a German soldier in a grocery store! What's the country coming to when people like that can call themselves criminals?"

And without the slightest transition, she switched to:

"How's the grub here?"

"Terrible," I said. "But I get special parcels every once in a while, and I'll share with you, if you'll do something for me."

The idea had come to me while she was talking that an old hand at jail life like herself might make an even better go-between than Micheline. If there was any way to get around prison regulations, she ought to know it.

I told her that I wasn't allowed to leave the cell, and that I wanted her to find out for me what had happened to Micheline, and to get in touch with Titi again for me.

"Titi?" she exclaimed. "Which Titi? Not Titi of the Place du Tertre?"

"I don't know," I said. "All I know is that she's from Montmartre, and got four years because she belonged to a gang that killed a man."

"That's the one!" she said. "That's Titi, all right."

And just as I thought everything was working out beautifully, and that she would be the ideal person to get in touch with an old acquaintance, she exploded:

"*Eh non, madame! Jamais!* Talk to Titi of the Place du Tertre! Never! I wouldn't stoop to speak to her if she were the last person on earth. The likes of me speak to the likes of her! I ought to scratch your eyes out for asking it."

I shrank back, half-terrified and half-bewildered at the rigidity of the criminal hierarchy. But then Louise laughed hoarsely.

"Oh, well, you don't know any better," she said. "You're only a political. But talk to Titi for you! *Non, ma 'tite 'dame. Ça, jamais!*"

## CHAPTER THIRTY-SIX

# Louise Clears Up a Mystery

IN THE next few days, my conversations with Louise gave me a glimpse into a strange new world, whose conceptions were very different from those I had been used to, but which was no less hemmed in by rigid conventions than my own. One of the most astonishing features of her underworld thinking to me, who had been accustomed to think of criminals as persons who had rejected ordinary morality, was that, on the contrary, her moral scruples remained, and even, one might say, were enhanced, by the fact that in justifying her own way of living she was obliged to assert her own blamelessness all the more violently.

Thus, when I ventured to ask her if she believed in religion, she almost jumped down my throat, violently insulted that I had even presumed to suggest that she might not be deeply religious. She informed me that she never missed church on Sunday.

"Well, then," I said, "you must believe in the Ten Commandments."

"Of course I do," she answered aggressively. "Why?"

"Even the seventh commandment?" I asked.

"Which one is that?" she asked suspiciously.

"Thou shalt not steal," I reminded her.

"I see what you're driving at," she said. "You're like the lawyers. You call it stealing, what I do. Well, it isn't stealing. The rich people only call it that because they've got the law on their side. But how did they get their fine things? By cheating other people, didn't they —people who weren't smart enough to protect themselves? They call that business. Well, I call it business, too. If they aren't smart enough to be careful who they're hiring, or to keep watch on what they've got—well, that's their bad luck. They don't have to take me in. That's their mistake. I'm out to do them, like they're out to do other people in business. They ought to be careful. If they aren't, they deserve to lose out. When I lose out, what happens? They put

335

me in jail. Do I go whining around about it? Not on your life. That's the game we're playing.

"I'll tell you what stealing is. If I took things for my own use, because I liked them, that would be stealing. But I don't. It's straight business with me. I don't take anything that can't be turned into cash. Even if I pick up something I take a fancy to, I don't keep it. That wouldn't be right. I stick to business. I'm a serious, dependable person.

"There's all kinds make their living that way, Madame, just as there's all kinds in your set. Take that Titi, for instance. There's a bad one, that'll do you a mean trick any time she gets the chance. But you ask any one that knows me, and they'll tell you you can count on Louise. They'll tell you I never told a lie in my life."

"Is that why you spent twelve years in prison?" I asked her.

"Oh my God," said Louise. "You still don't know what I'm talking about! You're thinking of what I tell the police or the judge. I tell 'em anything I think they'll believe. What else can you do? That's not lying. That's part of the job. You have to keep out of jail if you can. They know you're trying to do that, anyway. They don't expect you to give yourself away—wouldn't believe you if you did. That doesn't count. I'm talking about my private life. I wouldn't tell a lie to a friend, not for a million francs. That's the kind I am."

Louise, I discovered, was resentful at the presence of "politicals" in the jails. She seemed to feel about us in much the same way that steerage passengers feel about the gay parties from first class who sometimes go slumming in their part of the ship in evening dress after a good dinner. She classed us with "the high class dames" who occasionally got into prison before the war for kleptomania, whose mental processes she heartily condemned. What she did wasn't stealing, from her moral viewpoint, but what they did was, because it didn't serve any useful purpose. It wasn't business with them. It was plain, simple, inexcusable vice. As for those of us who were foolish enough to get put into jail for expressing their political opinions, well— "Couldn't they keep to their place and stay out of here?" Louise asked hotly.

"But there's a war on," I said. "All of us are fighting it now."

"Not me," said Louise. "That's the bunk. War is for big shots. It's got nothing to do with us."

"But, Louise," I said. "You're a Frenchwoman. The Germans have invaded your country. Don't you want to see them out of here?"

"What difference does it make to me whether I get chased by French cops, or German cops?" Louise asked. "I end up in the same jail, don't I? What difference does it make to the big shots either? You don't think this is a real war, do you? Maybe it was different last time, but you can't make me think the German army pushed us over in six weeks. It was all fixed in advance. Some of the rich people fixed it up. It's their racket. I steal a little silverware here and there, and you try to preach to me. The big shots steal the whole country, and you think you ought to get into trouble trying to save it. Wake up, kiddo. You weren't born yesterday, were you?"

Set a thief to catch a thief, I remembered. Maybe Louise wasn't so far wrong. Maybe some persons inside the French state had done what she did from inside a family. The same thing on a bigger scale. Getting away with the furniture. Only the furniture of a state included not only its resources and its political power, but things like liberty and justice. Thieves had gotten away with those.

It was curious, I thought, how a woman could drift into Louise's sort of life, and still retain all the conventional moral principles. All she had to do was to readjust her thinking to persuade herself that she wasn't violating them, and she could continue to apply them strictly to every one else. I remembered how the street-girls of Paris used to be called *lorettes* because there was a special early-morning mass for them at the little church of Notre Dame de Lorette. They didn't feel either that their way of living made them moral outlaws. Perhaps, I thought, criminals often just happen. Perhaps Louise slipped as unconsciously into her way of life as I had slipped unconsciously into helping Kitty smuggle her English soldiers out of the country. After all, though I didn't agree with the law that called me a criminal, and did agree with the law that called her one, our legal positions were just the same. We were both considered equally guilty of crime, and the proof was that we were in the same cell. In fact, my fault was considered the more heinous, for I had been sentenced to three times as long a term as Louise. I didn't feel myself a criminal,

I didn't regret what I had done—but then, neither did she. Had I, I asked myself, any right to take a superior attitude towards Louise? Wasn't it perhaps bad luck rather than immorality that had shaped her lot?

Once or twice I tried again to bring up the question of speaking to Titi, but Louise was so violent on that subject, that I never dared press the matter. Finally, one day, I managed to get far enough to explain how anxious I was to try to arrange a meeting with my friend in the hospital.

"What's so important ‚about that?" Louise asked. "There's no hurry, is there? How long's she in for?"

"She was sentenced to death," I said.

Louise stared at me, terrified. I was astounded at the effect the words had on her. Apparently, to this hardened frequenter of jails, a death sentence was still highly impressive.

"Death!" she repeated. "Death?" Then: "Why didn't you tell me before. That's different. All right, I'll talk to Titi for you. She's not in my class, mind, but if that's the only way you can get in touch with your pal, all right. Tell me about it. What's Titi got to do with it?"

I explained to her what had gone on up to then.

"I'll try to locate her this afternoon, and find out what goes," Louise said. "I dunno if she's around. I ain't seen her since I got here."

Louise came back from the courtyard. As the door clanged shut behind her, she dropped onto the bed, and said: "Well, I found out what happened. I told you that Titi was a louse."

"Why," I said, "what did she say?"

"She didn't say anything," Louise said, with satisfaction. "She's in solitary. That's why I ain't seen her. Thirty days! So's your old cell-mate."

"Micheline?" I exclaimed.

"Yeh," Louise said. "Hair pulling. They got into a fight. On account o' you and your friend. Plenty of the girls heard what it was all about. I got the whole story."

"On account of me!" I echoed. "Louise—tell me what happened!"

"Titi got sore because Micheline was nagging her about not getting any more news from your friend," Louise reported. "Finally she said, 'Quit worrying me about her. They took her away from Cherche-Midi three weeks ago.' Micheline asked why she hadn't told her before. She said, 'Would your American have given me any more cigarettes if she knew her friend wasn't there any more? I wanted to keep on getting them.' That made Micheline so mad she slapped Titi. And that Titi—she's a bad one. She shouldn't have hit her. She jumped at Micheline, and they had a terrible fight. The girls told me they never saw nothin' like it. So they both got thirty days."

I hardly heard the last words.

"Kitty!" I gasped. "They took her away! Then they've executed her! She must be dead by now!"

Even Louise seemed shaken by the expression on my face.

"Wait a minute, Madame," she begged. "Don't take it so hard. I don't think they took her away to be executed. They just moved her to another prison."

"Why do you think so?" I asked faintly.

"They did more talking than I told you yet before the fight broke out," Louise said. "Titi told her that some German police took her away. They took all her things with her, and a day's rations. They wouldn't do that if they were going to shoot her. They do their shooting at Vincennes. That's only in the suburbs. They wouldn't need a day's rations to go there. Besides, they took two other women with her who had long sentences, but not death. Titi thought they might have moved them to the prisons at Nancy or Dijon."

I was saddened at the thought that Kitty was again out of reach, but at least I felt better at the thought that she was probably still alive.

"Thank you, Louise," I said. "Would you do something else for me? See if you can find out anything about Kitty—maybe from new prisoners coming here from Cherche-Midi."

"I'll try," Louise said. "More likely we might find out if any one is transferred here from whatever other jail they sent her to. It used to be pretty easy in the old days. Even in St. Nazaire, we could find out in a couple of weeks anything we wanted to know about any other pen. But since the Germans took over it's been tougher. I'll send out the grapevine call for your friend though. Maybe we'll get something."

## CHAPTER THIRTY-SEVEN

# A New Prison

THE first cold snap of winter came suddenly. The thermometer dropped to freezing overnight, and the steel and cement man-trap of Fresnes turned into a refrigerator. Remembering the misery caused by the cold at Cherche-Midi, I looked ahead with apprehension to the prospect of passing another winter in prison—and in a jail that seemed likely to be colder than Cherche-Midi had been.

Cherche-Midi was a medieval building. Its walls were a yard thick, and the minute windows which gave so little light did have the advantage of keeping the cold out, too. Huddled together, four in a cell, we could at least warm the air slightly with the heat of our bodies. But Fresnes was a modern prison, a structure whose cells, tier on tier, were steel cages apparently suspended from the girders above, planned to be kept at a livable temperature by its central heating system. And Louise had brought back the news, gleaned at the exercise period, that there would be no coal for the furnaces. Even the warden's office, and the quarters for the German members of the prison staff, would be heated only by small stoves.

Louise, muffled up in her overcoat, a shawl knotted around her neck, her gloves on her hands and her hands in her pockets, said grimly, "There's no doubt about it, *ma p'tite dame,* we'll just freeze to death here unless some miracle happens."

It seemed to me that the cement floor and the iron door and bars, far from providing any protection from the cold, actually transmitted it. I followed Louise's example, putting on all the clothes I had, and sitting muffled up in the biting cold of the cell, praying for Louise's miracle.

The afternoon exercise period, hitherto Louise's delight, because of the opportunity it afforded her to talk to the other prisoners, now became a source of terror, and she envied me the regime which made it unnecessary for me to go out. She came back from the cold breezes of the courtyard with blue lips and chattering teeth, gazing longingly at the cot into which she was not allowed to get during the daytime.

"If only I dared slip under the bed covers to get warm!" she said. "But if they catch me, I'll go to the punishment cell, and that will be worse. . . . If this cold keeps up, I'm going to pretend I'm sick and get sent to the hospital. At least I can cover myself up in bed there."

During these freezing days, Louise and I usually huddled up together, sometimes with our arms around one another, for warmth. I hadn't entirely abandoned my idea of trying to reform her, and I tried to persuade her that honest work would be preferable to the kind of life she led. I actually got her to the point where she wouldn't interrupt me impatiently at the first few words, and I did my best to convince her that there was more satisfaction in the accomplishment of a given task than in outwitting an unsuspecting employer, and that the world was a pleasanter place to live in if it wasn't necessary always to be dodging policemen.

I finished one such lecture with no interruption, but at the end, Louise said sarcastically:

"And what do I live on?"

"Live on what you can make honestly," I said. "When you get a job as a cook, work at it. Instead of robbing the place, stay there and do what you are hired to do."

"Huh!" Louise snorted. "Work from seven in the morning till eleven at night for 400 francs a month, when I can make fifty times that in a few days, and take life easy for three or four months until it's time to do another job? Take orders from a stupid woman who's never satisfied? Live in a little cubbyhole up under the roof, and have the family prying into my private business all the time? No, thank you! None of that for me. And what else can I do, especially at my age, with no education? I live better the way I manage now."

"Do you call this good living here?" I asked her.

Louise shrugged her shoulders.

"I don't always get caught," she said. "And when I do, it don't last forever."

My efforts to shift Louise's point of view were so little successful that on the one occasion when I thought I had made some progress, I was quite taken aback to discover what she really had in mind. One day, when we had been sitting side by side for some time without saying anything, she said suddenly, out of a blue sky:

"Madame, how would you like to teach me English?"

"I'd be glad to," I said. "We can start right away if you want Why?"

I hoped she would say that she wanted to learn the language because it might increase her ability to earn an honest living.

"I want to go to America," she said. "I hear there are a lot of rich people there—and that they like French cooks. If I got into one of those families, I could make a real haul. . . . And they tell me the prisons are better, too, if you get caught. Yes, I'd like to go to the United States."

"Well, there's not much chance of your getting there," I said, "even if the war ends. They don't let people with prison records into the country."

"Why not?" asked Louise. "Americans get put in prison too, don't they?"

Early in November, a German commission arrived to inspect the prison. They looked into every cell, and I felt like an animal being sized up for slaughter by butchers under their searching, unfriendly glances. We didn't know what the inspection was all about, but that it was something very much out of the ordinary seemed indicated by the suppression that day of the regular exercise period.

Louise came back from the courtyard with the answer the next day.

"Remember I told you it would take a miracle to get us out of this icebox?" she asked. "Well, the miracle has happened. We're all going to be transferred to other prisons. The Gestapo finds the Cherche-Midi prison too small. It's going to take over this one, too. We'll be split up among the different provincial prisons. I hope they send me to Dijon. That's a fine place. No trouble about heat there. They keep the men working in the forest all day, cutting wood. The women don't do anything except sit in nice warm cells. . . . I might come across your friend Kitty there. If I do, and if we're sent to different places, I'll get word to you somehow. Trust me to find a way."

"Do you think that's where she is?" I asked.

"How should I know? . . . But I tell you what. We can probably get a message to her wherever she is. Since we're probably all going to different places, I'll just spread the word around, and one of us will be sure to reach the same prison. She can tell your friend where you are, if they let us know before we go. I'll pick out some girls who know the ropes and tell them what to do."

A week later, I left the prison of Fresnes. There was no previous official notice. At seven in the morning, we were told to assemble in the courtyard, each with all her belongings in a bundle. We knew at once that that meant we wouldn't be returning to our cells. I took down my calendar from the wall, and put it in my bundle. It was the only souvenir I carried away from Fresnes.

In the courtyard, the prisoners were lined up in long rows. I looked about for Micheline, and finally caught a glimpse of her in a group already passing out of the gate under the escort of French gendarmes. She waved to me, and I waved back. That was all we could do. I would have given anything to have been able to say good-bye to her properly.

Apparently no arrangements had been made to send any particular individuals to any special prison, for instead of forming the groups by name, the officer in charge simply moved down the line counting. When he had reached 200, he ordered those prisoners to keep together, and said to a guard beside him:

"This group is for Troyes. Line them up in fours, and start them off. You only have an hour before the train leaves."

Louise and I were in this group. When Louise heard where we were going, she said: "Troyes? I'm not going there. There's no prison there—only the county jail attached to the court house. They can't be planning to put 200 people there. I'm not taking any of their makeshift accommodations. I'll take my chances with some other group."

"How will you manage that?" I asked.

Louise winked.

"Just keep your eye on me," she said.

The gendarmes bustled about, trying to get us into fours. Louise became separated from me in the process. She seemed to be falling towards the rear, purposely I imagined. They finally got us into some semblance of order, and with gendarmes in front, behind, and on both sides, we started to move towards the gate. I heard little screams behind, and turned. A woman was lying on the ground. I wasn't surprised to see that it was Louise. Two of the gendarmes tried to get her up, but she hung limp and relaxed in their arms. The German officer in charge beckoned to a woman not yet included in any group.

"Get in there," he said, pointing to the place left vacant by Louise; and to a guard, "Call the doctor."

We started forward again, leaving Louise behind. She had won. She wasn't going to Troyes. But what made her think, I wondered, that the place she would draw instead would be any better?

I realized what a sorry sight we must present from the faces of the people we met in the streets. Some of their expressions seemed shocked, others terrified. We must have been a pitiful caravan, women young and old, thin and gaunt from our existence in prison, trudging through the streets with our bundles, surrounded by gendarmes.

I think the people who saw us realized that most of us were not ordinary criminals, for there seemed to be too much sympathy in their eyes for that.

Reaching the railroad station, we passed through lines of German soldiers surrounding it. It was clear that they had no intention of letting any one escape in the confusion of boarding the train.

Three cars were waiting for us on a siding. I climbed into one of them, a third-class coach with hard wooden benches. Some of the gendarmes got aboard also. They warned us not to try to attempt to escape, for if any one did, they would be obliged to fire. Not trusting to talk alone, they locked the doors and windows.

Our cars were hooked onto a train, and we pulled slowly out of the station. The bleak November countryside seemed to coincide with the hopelessness of our situation, as our moving jail cut across the land. Through the window I saw the leafless trees bending before the strong, cold wind. I felt more a prisoner than ever, because I could see the outside world from which I was shut away. Somehow it was worse to pass across it, to have it before one's sight, and to know that one couldn't enter it, than to be shut away from it behind stone walls, and know only in one's mind that it was there, nearby but unattainable.

To make it worse, our coaches had been attached to an ordinary passenger train, and as we stopped at the different stations (it was a local, which seemed to stop every few minutes), we could see passengers getting freely in and out of the ordinary passenger coaches. At each station, the gendarmes posted themselves at the doors of our coaches, locked though they were. It was obvious that the train service wasn't anywhere near equal to the demands on it, for there were crowds at even the smallest stations, and almost everywhere, some of them were left standing on the platform, unable to get aboard, when we pulled out. We saw them again and again storm the locked doors of our coaches, only to be waved back by the gendarmes standing behind them. Most of them looked up puzzled at the windows behind which we were imprisoned as they sought places elsewhere.

As we paused at these stations, I thought—and so, I soon discovered, did many of the others—that we would never be likely to have so good a chance of escape as now. If only one of the doors were left unlocked! If only the gendarmes failed to guard it! I didn't dare express my thought out loud—but others did.

"What a shame," a woman near me said suddenly, loud enough to be overheard by the gendarme seated at the end of one of the benches of our compartment, "that French police should be set to guarding French people, sentenced by the Germans! How can they do their dirty work for the Boches, I'd like to know?"

An elderly gray-haired woman of cultured appearance, sitting across the way, said: "It's disgraceful! If I were a man in the place of any of these gendarmes, I'd leave the door open at the next station."

The gendarme sat silently in his place, looking down at his feet, as though he hadn't heard. But the woman sitting next to him nudged him violently, and said: "Aren't you ashamed of yourself—you, a Frenchman—acting as a German stool pigeon? I'd rather beg than make my living taking orders from the Germans. You're not a Frenchman!"

The gendarme turned towards her.

"What am I to do, Madame? I have a wife and three children. I have been a policeman all my life. I don't know how to do anything else. How could I get a new job today, in times like these? This isn't my regular job. I work for the French government, not for the Germans. I have to do what I am ordered to do."

"The French government! Vichy! Phew! It has to do what it's ordered to do, too—by the Boches," some one else cried.

"*Mesdames*! Please! This is doing you no good," the gendarme pleaded, very much on the defensive. "I don't want to report you. I'm a Frenchman, too. I'm only doing my duty."

"You call yourself a Frenchman!" said the woman next to him again, "but you take us to jail when you know very well we've been sentenced by the Germans."

"Don't forget," said the gendarme. "Some of you have been condemned by the Germans; but there are common criminals here too. I'm not the judge. I can't decide which of you are political prisoners and which aren't."

"All of us here are political prisoners," one woman said, and jumped up. "Ladies—if there are any of you who are not political prisoners, hold up your hands."

One woman alone raised her hand. She didn't look like a criminal. She was a modest looking woman in her thirties, and she seemed embarrassed.

"And what did you do, Madame?"

In an almost inaudible voice, she confessed:

"I forged a food ration card—but it was for my baby."

"That's not what I mean," the first woman said. "You're no criminal. Is there any one here for theft, or robbery, or assault?"

No one raised her hand. Perhaps there may have been some ordinary criminals among us who didn't choose to admit it, but no one was in a frame of mind to go into that. The fury broke on the unfortunate gendarme from all sides. Another one hurried along the corridor to our compartment.

"What's going on here?" he demanded sternly.

His colleague tried to tell him, not without difficulty, for by now the shouting women threatened to drown out his voice entirely.

As soon as the newcomer had seized the situation, he bellowed above the tumult: "Ladies! Ladies! You forget we would be punished if we let you escape!"

"Come with us," one of them shouted. "Let your job go!"

And realizing that this half-hearted defense was almost a compliance, the women redoubled their efforts. This time they shifted their tactics, praising the men as real Frenchmen, unwilling to see French women jailed by the invader. The second gendarme gazed at the women for a moment, then walked slowly to the front of the coach, unlocked the door, and then beckoned to his fellow, who walked with him to the back, leaving the open door unguarded.

Almost unable to believe in their success, the women gazed at each other with wide open mouths, in silence. Then they began hastily gathering up their bundles, and crowding into the corridor, ready to get out as soon as the next station was reached.

It was none too soon. I could see that we were nearing Paris. The next stop would probably be the last before the capital, for we were in its suburbs.

I was thinking feverishly myself. As soon as I got off the train, I told myself, I must get to the Paris Prefecture in some way, and get in touch with Henri's officer friend. This time no one would be following me, and he ought to be able to get me across into the unoccupied zone.

The train was slowing up. I left my bundle in the luggage rack. It would only be an incumbrance, and a dangerous distinguishing mark. I took my place in the corridor with the others.

The women in front had pulled open the door before the train quite came to a stop. There was a forward surge—and then a backward wave. From where I stood, I couldn't see what was going on. "Why didn't they get off?" I wondered.

Those in front pushed violently to the rear again. I slipped back into the compartment to escape the crush. Through the window I saw the answer. The platform was filled with German police. As the disappointed women were shoved back into the car, a German officer leaped aboard and began berating the French gendarmes for their carelessness. They had come to take over before we reached Paris, figuring, no doubt, that that would be the most dangerous place from the point of view of escapes. Our opportunity had passed. We sat depressed and silent while our coaches remained on a siding in Paris, and while they were attached to the train for Troyes. And hardly a word was spoken before our arrival there at three P.M.

## CHAPTER THIRTY-EIGHT

# Prison at Troyes

WE WERE tired after our long journey, but no one thought of suggesting any rest for us after the trip. We had no sooner alighted from the train than we were lined up and marched towards our destination. It was two miles, and all of us, weakened by the privations of prison life, were exhausted when we reached our new home. When we saw it, we looked at one another in dismay.

The building was still unfinished. Scaffolding covered it, and piles of brick lay about on the ground. One of us, who came from the region, identified it as a building originally intended for a hospital. Work had been interrupted on it when the war came, but the Germans had used it to house internees temporarily until their permanent internment camps were ready. Now it was to be our prison.

Inside it was even more evident than outside that the building was only half-finished. We climbed the stairs single file, clinging close to the naked unplastered walls in order not to fall off the narrow winding staircase, which had no banister. Most of the walls showed the bare brick. The only sign of plumbing I saw was one unconnected pipe projecting from a wall.

What about heat? was my first thought.

There was no sign of any heating system as we filed through the corridors, nor did I see any means of heating the room into which I was pushed with four others. There was no furniture—just five sacks of straw heaped up in a corner. These, laid on the floor, were to be our beds.

Louise was right, I thought, as I gazed with dismay about this cheerless cell. I was far from changing my mind a little later when I laid my straw sack on the floor, and tried to make myself as comfortable as I could under the single thin blanket which had been given me in the meantime.

At Fresnes, when the cold weather began, I had longed for the stuffy but warmer air of Cherche-Midi. Here I yearned for the bed I had slept in at Fresnes. In spite of my exhaustion, I lay awake half the night; the other half was filled with nightmares from which I kept awaking with a start, my body protesting at the hardness and coldness of the cement floor, which I could feel clear through the straw.

"This must be temporary," I thought. "They'll do something about this tomorrow. Even the Germans can't expect any one to live in such conditions."

But nothing was done on the morrow, or the next day, or the next. Our jailers seemed quite satisfied that they had done their full duty towards us. There was not the slightest heat in the prison, and every day the weather grew colder. We had one pitcher of water a day in our cell which was supposed to serve five of us for both drinking and washing—but as the water in it was customarily frozen, and we had no means of melting it, we had to do without both.

It must have been because they realized there was danger of our dying from cold that we were allowed here one privilege which had not been permitted elsewhere. We could stay in bed all day if we wanted—if you could call resting on the straw sack under the scanty blanket staying in bed. What we did on the coldest days was to place the sacks side by side, so that the five of us could lie on three of the sacks, keeping as close together as possible for warmth, with the other two sacks over us as well as the five blankets and all the spare clothing we had, including even the cloth bags one or two of us kept their clothes in. We got into this communal bed fully dressed, of course, and with shawls or towels tied around our necks and feet, or transformed into improvised mittens. During the coldest spells, we spent most of the twenty-four hours of the day in this fashion, clambering out only when we had to, to get our food or for other reasons, and scurrying shivering back into our artificial burrow as quickly as we could.

We were more avaricious of heat than the primitive peoples who never let their fires go out because they have no means of kindling new ones. The only heat we had to conserve was that manufactured by our own bodies, and we were misers about that. If one of us carelessly disturbed a blanket so that a little cold air came in, she was due for immediate simultaneous scolding from the other four. We regarded the heat generated by each one of us as common property, which no one had a right to waste.

One of the minor annoyances that preyed on us at Troyes was that for weeks at a time, though there was a large window in our cell, we could not see out of it. It was covered with an impenetrable layer of frost. This increased our idle boredom. There was nothing to distract us, nothing to do except lie all day on our sacks. The afternoons seemed endless, and the nights interminable.

Usually, when a guard appeared with our food, on the cold days when we were huddled together under our pile of clothing, only one of us would creep out to get it—and she would be assailed by a stream of complaints if her manner of getting out of our bed let too much air in. The unlucky person who had to get out served the others, who thus enjoyed the questionable luxury of taking their meals in bed.

Under these conditions, it can hardly be said that we lived individual lives. We were all units in one life, and that no very eventful one, like the microscopic animals which live in colonies, the smaller individuals constituting one larger one. Perhaps it was partly to maintain our sense of individuality in spite of this that we talked to each other so much about ourselves, and about our pasts. Lying in the heap of straw and clothing, I learned quickly the life stories of all my companions.

The intellectual of our group was Mme. Ragomin, an Argentine of Spanish origin who had lived in Paris for many years. A dentist by profession, she was also somewhat of a linguist, speaking English, French and German besides her native Spanish. She didn't speak them too well, however.

It took a good listener to get all the details of Mme. Ragomin's stories, for she mixed up her languages, and whatever she had to say came out in a mixture of all four. Her conversation always made me think of a juggler keeping a number of objects in the air at the same time. That was the way she tossed her four languages about.

Her first confession gave me a shock. She admitted that she had worked for the German Intelligence Service. When she saw the effect produced on us, she went on (I'm not going to try to reproduce her mixed language):

"Don't be afraid. Haven't you ever heard of an *agent double?* That's what I was. I was sending information to the British Intelligence Service all the time. That's the only reason why I was working for the Germans. I had to do it to get inside information for the British. The Germans got suspicious, set a trap for me, and I was caught, red-handed. I didn't have a chance of getting out of it. . . . What I can't understand is why they didn't shoot me. That's what usually happens to a spy who works for the wrong side."

Also on the intellectual side was Mme. Santot, a bony-faced French spinster of about fifty, who had been a school-teacher all her life, and looked it. She was bitter, not against the Germans, but against the Vichy government. It was Vichy that had sentenced her, because she refused to follow the instructions given her to conduct her classes in the spirit of the new directives of Marshal Pétain, who replaced the splendid motto of France, "Liberté, Egalité, Fraternité," by "Travail, Famille, Patrie" (Work, Family, Country).

Mme. Santot evidently had the obstinacy that characterizes many spinsters, who become increasingly uncompromising as the years roll on, unshared with any one with whom some mental accommodation might be necessary. When she received the new instructions, she read them to her pupils, and then attacked Pétain for replacing liberty by the sort of work which amounts to slave labor; the unselfish ideal of fraternity, which implies that all men are brothers, by the narrower concept of family, which concentrates on the self-interest of a small unit; and equality by country, because he desired blind obedience to the sort of country he was creating, in which equality would no longer have any place. For that, she had been sentenced to a year in prison.

"One year?" echoed Mlle. Blanc, a young woman of 22, when Mme. Santot told us her story. "Why, I got a year for only—well, see for yourself."

In spite of the cold, she crept out from under the blanket, unbuttoned the overcoat she was wearing, and pulling her chemise out from under her blouse, showed us a small pin, like those so common before the occupation—crossed French and British flags.

"I got a year just for wearing this," she said, "or rather, for wearing another just like it. They took away the one I had on my coat. But I had another in my bag, and I have always managed to keep them from finding it. I had it pinned on my underwear while the judge was sentencing me for wearing it. And I wear it still."

Climbing back under the covers, she told us the details of her arrest. It was shortly after the German occupation when a German soldier spoke to her on the street, telling her, she realized afterwards, to take off the pin. But as she knew no German, she didn't understand him. He called a patrol and she was arrested. Not until she appeared before a military court, one of whose officers spoke French, forty-eight hours later, did she discover that it was her pin that had caused all the trouble.

"I was so angry at being kept in a dirty cell for 48 hours just because of a pin," she said, "that I lost control of myself. I called them some names, I guess. I told them it was idiotic to keep any one locked up for two days for such a trifle. Well, I should have held my tongue. Instead of two days, I got three hundred and sixty-five."

The fifth person in the cell was the woman who had confessed in the train to having forged a food ticket. She still seemed to have a sense of guilt about it, for she didn't tell us her story until she had been urged by all of us. She was a humble person, who seemed to think that we were all heroines of romantic legends, while for herself she accepted the thesis of her judges that she had committed an ignominious crime. But after she had told us what she had gone to jail for, we all felt, in spite of her protestations, that she was the best of us all.

Her name was Mme. Otto. She had six children. Her husband was a prisoner of war in Germany, and she was left alone to struggle with the problem of getting food for her family in a country where even the wealthiest found it difficult to get enough to eat. In an attempt to increase her children's meagre portions of food, she had applied for a ration card in her husband's name—one more ration, she hoped, to divide among the six. Her deception was discovered, and she was sentenced to six months in jail.

She cried softly as she told us her story, particularly when she spoke of her children, whose fate she didn't know. She had been allowed no news of them since she had been in jail. And yet, with her mother's heart torn daily by anxiety over the fate of her children, she had remained uncomplaining, unembittered, feeling herself almost justly punished for a guilty attempt to gain food rations which, perhaps, she thought, might have been needed more badly by some one else than by her own starving brood.

"You can't have much longer to serve now," I said. "When will you get out?"

"About Christmas," Mme. Otto said. "I was sentenced June 23."

"And what's the date today?" Mme. Ragomin demanded.

None of us could figure it out. I reached for my calendar and started to check the days.

"How can any one remember the date," said the school-teacher, "when the days are all the same, when nothing special ever happens to distinguish one from the others."

And as I worked it out, she continued, "Today is a dead, dull, drab day like the others, which will pass like all the other meaningless days on which nothing has happened into the well of history and be forgotten."

I had finished my calculation.

"Today," I said, "is December 7, 1941."

## CHAPTER THIRTY-NINE

# Pearl Harbor: Axis Report

THE guard who brought our "breakfast" the next morning was not the usual one. Instead of stopping in the door, measuring out our portion of the ominous-looking liquid referred to as coffee, and then moving on without speaking, she actually came into our cell, and filled the cups there. Then, advancing towards us, she said: "Which one of you is the American?"

"I am," I answered, wondering why in the world she wanted to know. I didn't like her expression. It boded me no good.

"Oh, so it's you, is it?" she answered, and regarded me for what seemed an eternity. It was obvious that she had something to say, and obvious also that she was in no hurry to say it.

Finally she decided to speak.

"I've got news for you," she said. "America is in the war."

All of us started. To the others, that meant one thing: the certain defeat of Germany. Europeans had all clung to that hope. They remembered that the entry of the United States had been the beginning of the end before. They were sure it would be that way again. I suppose the others looked happier about it than I did; for to me, it meant, of course, that the awful aloneness that I had anticipated had become a fact.

"Yes," said the guard slowly, "America's in the war—and they say she's out again, already."

"Out again?" I gasped. "What do you mean?"

"Out! Knocked out! She's lost the war already, that's what I mean," she said.

"It's not possible!" Mme. Ragomin spoke up.

"Oh, yes it is!" the guard retorted. "How can she fight without a navy? And she hasn't got any navy, any more. It was all sunk—all of it. The Japs attacked Pearl Harbor, and didn't leave a single ship afloat. What are the Yankees going to do now?"

She picked up her pot of coffee and stalked to the door.

355

"The radio says they're expecting Roosevelt to ask for peace terms any hour now," she said, and slammed the door behind her.

We looked at one another in dismay. We were so upset we forgot to drink our coffee, which usually we gulped down as soon as we got it, in order not to lose any of its precious heat.

"It can't be true," Mlle. Blanc said. "How could the Americans be surprised like that?"

"Of course it isn't," Mme. Ragomin chimed in. "It's just one more of their Nazi lies. Don't you think so?" she asked the school-teacher.

Mme. Santot was less certain.

"I never believe more than half they say," she said. "No doubt it's exaggerated. But they must have some basis for it. What do you think, Mrs. Shiber?"

"If it's only half true, that would be terrible," I said. "It wouldn't surprise me if America has entered the war—but if the Japanese sunk the fleet, or even half of it, that would be an incredible tragedy. I don't believe we could have been caught napping like that."

We talked of little else all morning, and when a call came for Mme. Otto to report to the prison office, she volunteered at once to try to find out if it were true. She jumped out of bed and went through the curious reverse process we had to follow if we left the cell—instead of dressing to go out, we undressed; that is, we took off the odd garments we might be wearing over our regular clothes for warmth.

She was gone about half an hour. When she returned, there was a curious expression on her face. She seemed worried and uncertain. In fact, I had almost the impression that she was afraid of us when she entered.

Thinking only of what the guard had told us that morning, I said at once: "What's the matter? Bad news?"

"No," she said, "on the contrary. Rather good news, I think."

And as all of us turned to her expecting some report on America's entry into the war, she came out with something entirely different. "I am being released at once."

This was an event, and for the moment we forgot about Pearl Harbor, too.

"Released?" Mme. Ragomin cried. "Then why look so sad about it? You ought to be happy. Or are you going to miss our collective bed so much?"

"No," Mme. Otto said miserably. "It's not that. It's—well, I'm not going home. I've got to go to Germany. I don't know—if I'll like it there.

"I have to join my husband," Mme. Otto explained. "You see, he's a machinist. He makes precision instruments. It seems they need skilled workers in their factories. They offered to let him out, and me, too, if he'd go to work for them. So he said, Yes. . . . We'll have the children with us, you know."

She proffered the last sentence apologetically, as if in extenuation.

"So you're going?" said Mlle. Blanc. There was a touch of scorn in her voice.

"What else can I do?" Mme. Otto said helplessly. "It doesn't depend on me. My husband arranged it all. . . . We get the same food rations as the Germans do. . . . That will be better for the children."

"When do you go?"

"Right away. They're preparing my release papers. I just came back to get my things."

She started to gather up her few pitiful belongings and make a bundle of them.

"I think your husband is just a rotten collaborationist," said Mlle. Blanc, aggressively.

"Please!" said Mme. Otto, plaintively, as though some one had struck her in the face. Tears welled slowly from her eyes and began running down her cheeks.

"Perhaps the poor man was thinking of the children," Mme. Ragomin said, coming to her defense. "Perhaps he wanted to get his wife out of jail. You can't blame him for that."

"Nonsense!" said Mme. Santot sharply. "She was getting out in two or three weeks anyway. He's selling himself for bigger rations, that's all. Probably making a bad bargain, too—out of a prison camp into slavery. The man's a fool as well as a traitor! I'd starve before I'd work for the Germans!"

Mme. Otto timidly said: "Please!" again. The tears were flowing faster now, but she was not sobbing. They seemed to be streaming out of her eyes and running down her cheeks of their own volition, without her knowledge.

"He's a good man," she said. "He doesn't mean any harm. He doesn't know what it's like in France—what they've done here."

But Mme. Santot was not the sort to relent.

"You agree with me yourself, don't you?" she pursued her victim. "That's why you looked so sad when you came in, isn't it? You don't approve, do you?"

Mme. Otto shook her head slowly through her tears.

"I wish he hadn't done it," she said. "But how do I know why? It must have been for the children."

She gathered up her belongings and moved slowly to the door. Then she stopped, and, with the tears still flowing down her cheeks, she said:

"Mrs. Shiber—I almost forgot. It's true what they said. There was a radio on in the office. It said the Japanese had sunk the whole American fleet."

The key grated in the lock, and the door opened.

"Come on," said the guard.

"Good-bye," said Mme. Otto timidly. I answered her, and so did Mme. Ragomin. The other two were silent. Mme. Otto cast them an anguished look, and the tears fell faster as she passed out of the door.

Mme. Otto's news, on top of the intense embarrassment and pity I had felt at the scene which accompanied the departure of this simple, humble little woman, threw me into the deepest depression. My cell-mates seemed to react in the same fashion.

"What's going to happen to France?" Mme. Santot asked. "Our only hope since our defeat has been America's intervention. If America has been beaten already . . ." her voice trailed away.

"We can't be beaten already," I said. "I'm sure of that. Even if we have lost all our fleet, I know my countrymen. They won't accept defeat. It will make it harder. But I'm sure we'll win all the same, in the end, fleet or no fleet. We've never lost a war yet! And think of all our factories! Think of the planes, and the tanks, and the guns we can build! How could we be beaten so easily? The British weren't beaten after Dunkirk were they—or even after the fall of France? If they could hold on, almost alone, for a year and a half, why should America give up so easily? No, Mme. Santot, I'm sure of one thing—if America is in the war, America will win it."

"After all," said Mme. Ragomin, "there's no more reason for believing the radio than the guard. It tells more lies than she could ever imagine."

The enervating prison regime began to tell on me, and again, as once before in Cherche-Midi, I began to lose track of what was going on around me. I remained for hours, even days, in a state of half-consciousness, something like the waking sleep which sometimes precedes real slumber, in which dream and reality merge inextricably into each other. It was during this period that Mme. Santot and Mme. Ragomin fell out. How their quarrel originated, I never could make out. Probably the source of it was nothing else than irritation at being confined so long together; but whatever started it, they quarreled all day long, from the moment they woke up until we all went to sleep.

Mlle. Blanc and I tried to reduce the argument by occupying the two middle places in the common bed, but their tart remarks were then only fired back and forth over our heads, in a constant barrage of verbal machine gun fire. Most of it I heard only intermittently, as a sort of dull distant chatter which made no sense, as I lay with closed eyes, sometimes losing consciousness of my surroundings for an hour or more, sometimes achieving a sharper focus again, when my invariable thought was: "Thank goodness; there's a little more of my time gone without my noticing it."

I could feel again that there was great irregularity in my heartbeat, and from the discomfort it caused me, I knew that my blood-pressure must again be dangerously high. I wondered if I should report sick, and if so, what kind of treatment I could expect. If it were like the hospital at Fresnes, it wouldn't be worth troubling about. I needed a warm room, food fit to eat, facilities for keeping clean. Would I get them? I was so apathetic that my doubt about this possibility was sufficient to keep me from making any, decision, affirmative or even negative, about asking for the doctor.

But as I lay long hours in my cell, while the constant battle of my two cell-mates went on over my head, I began to accept as a certainty the idea that I would not live through the more than two years which still remained of my sentence. So far, I had survived on the residue of the strength built up in the years of good living. Now there was no reserve left. I felt as if all strength had been drained from me.

Now, I thought, the parcels from the Quakers will probably stop coming. They were all that kept me going. And these long spells of semi-consciousness could mean only one thing—the approach of the end.

I put my hand on my thumping heart, and its irregular beat convinced me that it would be the first of my organs to give way. Perhaps it would stop some day quite suddenly and unexpectedly, and my two quarrelsome neighbors would continue their dispute over my unhearing ears, until suddenly they would discover with horror and surprise that one of their companions had escaped forever.

## CHAPTER FORTY

# A New Arrival

A FEW days before Christmas, a new prisoner was assigned to our cell to replace Mme. Otto. When the guard shoved her in and slammed the door behind her, she took a few faltering steps towards us, and then stopped in obvious amazement.

I could understand her surprise. To us, our system of huddling together in our common bed had become habitual and quite commonplace, but to a newcomer it must have seemed odd to find us all bundled up together under our pile of variegated coverings. She stood staring at us, and our four pairs of eyes looked up at her. We saw a really beautiful woman of about 35, with the noble profile and the jet-black hair which denoted Mediterranean origin. Her excellent figure was set off by well-cut clothes of good quality—in fact, she presented an elegant appearance, of a nature to which we were no longer accustomed.

She broke the silence first.

"Do you lie there on your backs like that all day?" she asked.

"We do," said Mme. Ragomin, "and you'd better put on everything you've got and join us if you don't want to freeze to death. There's no heat in this place."

"That's not my idea of a solution for that problem, ladies," said the newcomer. (Her name, we learned shortly, was Marguerite Moyat). "You aren't planning to spend all winter in that attitude, are you? It's only December now; it will be colder before it's warmer, and it won't be warm until April at the earliest. You must insist on heat."

"Don't be ridiculous," Mme. Santot snorted. "You must be very green to talk about insisting on anything."

"Pardon me," said Marguerite, "but may I ask you one question: has it occurred to any one of you to protest against the lack of heat?"

We looked at one another in amazement.

"Protest!" Mlle. Blanc repeated. "What's the good of that? The Germans have all the coal. A lot they care whether we freeze or not."

"And I don't care whether they care or not," Marguerite said. "I just insist on the regulations. We were sentenced to prison, but not to a cold cell . . . I'm not as green as you think. I've already served three months, and I've got things out of the Germans that no one else ever dared ask. You don't know how to go about it. If you ask for any favors, if you ask for any human treatment, you won't get it. Don't ask. Demand. They understand that. Tell them freezing isn't in the rules. They have an unholy respect for the rules. Threaten them. Tell them you intend to report them to their superiors. Do you know they won't dare refuse you the right to do it? Browbeat them! It's the only way. They have no sympathy for the weak, but they're afraid of the strong. . . . So you admit you haven't tried protesting? All right, I'm going to protest!"

"That's all very interesting," said Mme. Ragomin, "but how are you going to make your protest? The guard won't even answer our questions. How are you going to persuade her to take your complaint to the warden or the German commander?"

"Persuade? I'm not going to persuade any one. I'm going to order her. She doesn't have to answer me. An order doesn't require an answer. She'll take my message to the warden. You'll see. I happen to know that prison regulations oblige the warden to receive the complaint of any prisoner who wishes to make one. And if the prisoner isn't satisfied with the result, he can appeal to the military commander of the region in which the prison is located. . . . So I'm going to file a complaint in my name at least. Do you authorize me to make it in yours also?"

We consulted one another, and agreed that it was worth taking the risk. We told her she might speak for all of us—if she got a chance to speak at all.

While we were waiting for the next round of the guard, Marguerite told us her story. She had been the secretary to a manufacturer of canned food. When the Germans came in, her employer got away to unoccupied territory, leaving her behind to keep an eye on the business.

Not long after the occupation, she received a letter from him, carried in by a messenger who had crossed the demarcation line surreptitiously. In it, her employer informed her that he wanted to begin manufacturing in North Africa, and asked if it would be possible for her to get out with the company's funds, so that he could resume business. Marguerite started to collect the firm's assets in preparation for following these instructions, and had turned several million francs into cash, ready to take them out with her, when the Germans arrested her. Her employer's letter, which she had foolishly failed to destroy, was evidence of her intention of getting the money out of the occupied zone, so she was sentenced to 18 months.

The guard arrived not long after she had finished telling her story, and Marguerite put her theories to the test.

"Guard," she said peremptorily. "You will tell the warden that I wish to see him or the German commander at once to make a complaint in accordance with the general prison regulations governing prisoners' rights."

And she turned her back immediately and walked to the other side of the cell, as though that ended the matter.

The guard remained imperturbable as usual, and clanked away with her soup pot without making any answer.

"See?" said Mlle. Blanc. "That's the last of that."

"I will make you a little bet," Marguerite said, "or I would if either of us had anything to bet, that that is not the end of that. The guard won't dare not to report to the warden a request made according to the rules."

And sure enough, half an hour later the guard returned, and said gruffly:

"The commander will see you now."

Marguerite left the cell with a triumphant glance in our direction.

"She can look like that now," said Mlle. Blanc, "but how will she come back? Or will she come back? Have they got punishment cells here?"

But Marguerite was back, and in fifteen minutes.

"It was easy!" she said. "You know who commands this place— an Austrian! I spotted his accent the moment he opened his mouth. His place is so hot I could hardly stand it. When I told him the cells were freezing, I looked hard at the big stove in the middle of his office—and he started apologizing! He told me he had already made a report about it, but he couldn't fix up anything because the building had been designed for central heating and had no fireplaces or chimney outlets in the separate rooms. He said it's impossible to get enough stoves for the cells—but he's trying to get a few for the corridors, to dry out the walls—if he can get coal for them. Anyway, he's promised to get us heavier blankets by Christmas."

We all brightened up; all, that is, except Mlle. Blanc, who wasn't willing to give up yet.

"You got promises," she said, "but I'll wait till I see something done before I celebrate. What good will stoves in the corridors do? No heat will get into these ice-boxes. As for blankets—remind me when we get them."

And she turned out to be right. The blankets never came. Nor did we ever get any stoves, even in the corridor.

On that first day, Marguerite continued to brave the cold outside our common nest. She only joined us in bed at night; and in the morning, she alone crept out and picked up the water pitcher. When she saw the water in it was frozen, she gave up, and came quietly back into bed with the rest of us. From that time on, we were five once more in our share-the-heat community.

Marguerite's place in the bed was next to me, and as she talked rather good English, we got into the habit of talking together in that language, becoming close friends. I quickly discovered the one weakness in her intellectual armor. She believed the future could be foretold from playing-cards. She had managed to bring a dog-eared pack in with her, somehow or other, and she could consume hours reading the cards. No one discouraged her, for it helped pass the time, but when I tried to argue with her about it, and showed that I did not really take her results seriously, she became quite heated.

"Oh, I know you sceptics!" she snorted. "You take a very superior attitude about the cards, but what explanation do you advance for unusual happenings? You have a mystic idea of your own, which is so familiar to you that it never occurs to you how odd it is. You ascribe everything to an unknown force you call 'accident.' If a brick happens to fall on your head, it's an accident. If a bridge collapses when you walk over it, it's an accident. But why did the brick drop at the precise instant when you passed by, and not a second sooner or later? Why did the bridge collapse just when you happened to be passing over it, and not some one else? You can believe that's all caused by your mysterious 'accident,' if you want. I believe there aren't any accidents. Everything is planned ahead, everything is foreordained. And if that is so, why shouldn't we be able to look into the future? I know the cards tell us what is to come, because they have told me, many times, and they have been right!"

"But that's just coincidence," I said. "They must have been wrong pretty often, too."

"Not at all," said Marguerite, hotly. "All the things I've read in the cards haven't happened yet—but it takes time for everything to be fulfilled. Your 'coincidence' is just 'accident' again, under another name. . . . Wait! I'll prove to you that the cards don't lie. I'll ask them about your immediate future. Then wait and see if it doesn't turn out as they say."

She took an unconscionable time with her cards this time, laying them out, studying them, and then beginning the whole process again, until finally she turned to me with the greatest seriousness, and said, "Mrs. Shiber, you are going to be released soon."

I shook my head doubtfully.

"But it must be so!" Marguerite said. "I did it three times. I got the same result each time. I tell you, you will be out of here soon."

I thought it was no use continuing the argument about the validity of fortunes told by playing cards. I just said:

"It sounds impossible. I have more than two years to serve still, and I don't see any possibility of release."

"I don't see any likelihood of it either," Marguerite said. "But I know you will be released. It's in the cards. They say you will be released before me. . . . Look! I am going to give you the address of my cleaning woman. She has the keys to my apartment. You can stay there when you get out."

I didn't try to argue with her. She wrote a note then and there to her *femme de ménage,* acting at once on what she thought she had seen in her cards. I took it as though I believed in it, too, tucked it away in a pocket, and promptly forgot about it.

My first bad heart attack came in February.

It was signalled by a sharp pain, and the sensation that a giant fist was squeezing my heart inexorably. I suppose it was because of my weakness as a result of privation that I lost consciousness almost immediately, which was a relief, for it freed me from the pain. When I came to, my cell-mates were bending over me, their faces absolutely colorless.

That was the first of a series of spasms, which were spread over a period of twenty-four hours. Almost always I lost consciousness. The prison doctor was called in three times, but didn't order my transfer to the hospital, because there was no one who could watch me constantly, while in the cell the others could take care of me.

When the series of attacks passed, and I showed signs of feeling better, Marguerite said,

"You frightened the others. They thought it was the end. But I knew you couldn't die here, because the cards promised you freedom."

"Perhaps that's what they meant," I said. "There's more than one kind of release, you know."

Marguerite shook her head decidedly.

"No, that's not possible," she said. "If it were death, the cards would have showed it. The ten of spades is the death card. It never appeared in your fortune. You watch!"

And she went through her rigmarole again, laying out her cards in the prescribed pattern. Sure enough, the ten of spades did not turn up among them.

Perhaps it was because I had ceased to argue with Marguerite about her belief in cards that she dared resort to them once again on my behalf. I had talked with her often about Kitty, expressing the fear that haunted me that she must have been executed by now.

"Would you like to know what has happened to her?" Marguerite asked.

"Of course," I said, wondering how she proposed to get that information. But then she produced her cards, and my hopes sank. However, I was too tired of the subject to continue to argue the point, so I made no protest. Finally, after Marguerite had laid out her cards and studied them, she turned to me and said, "Your friend is alive!"

No doubt she expected me to express joy, but when she saw that the news had no effect on me, she realized at once why that was.

"I see you still don't believe in my cards," she said. "All right! You will some day. Remember, when you get out of here—and it can't be very long now; the cards say so—remember that I read it here. Then, perhaps, you will believe also that the cards were right when they told me that your friend is still alive."

Spring came late that year. Not until the middle of March was it warm enough for us to abandon our common bed. From our cell window, we could see the fields turning green. We opened the windows, and breathed in the spring air, with its scent of young grass and of fresh-turned earth in the ploughed fields we could see between the bars. We heard the chirping of the birds outside. Even in prison, spring seemed to mean an awakening, a refreshing, a rebirth of life.

My periods of lethargy lessened. I felt once again that, after all, I might not die in prison. I might still live to be able, one day, to walk through the green fields unhampered, to move about at my own will, as freely as the birds which played outside our window in the first warm sunshine.

## CHAPTER FORTY-ONE

# *Spring*

SPRING brought a welcome change into the lives of the cooped-up inmates of Troyes. A space behind our building was fenced off with barbed wire, and we were allowed to spend two hours daily in the fresh air, walking about or sunning ourselves. This time, I was anxious, after so long a period of indoor life, to get out and enjoy the warm weather. Fortunately, the prohibition against my joining the other prisoners had apparently been lost sight of between Fresnes and Troyes. When the first exercise period was announced, I lined up with the others, and no one prevented me from going out with them.

It was the middle of April. The trees were showing the tender green of their first leaves. There was a fragrant warm breeze, with only the slightest touch of chill in it, refreshing and invigorating. I walked briskly up and down, enjoying the air—enjoying it, perhaps, too much. I was conscious of my heart pounding away, but I was too happy to pay much attention to it.

I must have overdone it. Halfway up the stairs, I suddenly collapsed, losing consciousness immediately. It's a wonder I was not killed, for I might have pitched right over the unprotected edge of the banisterless stairs. Mme. Ragomin told me afterwards that she caught me as I was falling, or I might have done so.

When I came to, I was back in my cell. The prison doctor, who was French, was standing over me, which didn't surprise me, but what was astonishing was that the Austrian Major who commanded us was there too. He smiled at me sympathetically—which put me at once on my guard. So far, it had never boded me any good when a German showed signs of sympathy.

"*Gott sei dank,*" he said. "I am happy to see that you are better. The doctor tells me that you have had these attacks before. Why did you not report them to me? I could have seen to it that you were allowed certain privileges which would improve your state of health."

I looked towards the French doctor in astonishment. I assumed that he had reported my previous attacks as a matter of routine, and I was surprised to hear the Major profess ignorance of my condition —and quite as surprised at his solicitude, which, after my previous experiences, rang very false. There had been one occasion when the prison doctor had sent to Troyes for a specialist to examine my heart. Surely the warden must have known of that! And if he had allowed me to go untended during those freezing winter months, why was he so suddenly concerned now?

His next remark surprised me even more.

"Don't you know, Madame," he asked, "that prison regulations permit you, in consideration of the state of your health, to petition for parole in order to get private treatment until you are completely recovered? All you require is a certificate from the prison doctor that your state of health necessitates it. What is your opinion on that, doctor?"

"I think definitely," the French doctor said, "that Madame is in no condition to remain here."

"How long a leave do you think she would require to recover normal health? Three months, perhaps?"

The doctor considered for a moment. Then he shook his head.

"Six, I should say."

"*Meinetwegen,* six months it is then. . . . You doctors are incorrigible—always taking the part of the prisoners against the administration. Well, then, doctor, if you will be good enough to prepare the medical certificate, I will send the petition through the Kommandantur. I hope, Madame, that you will shortly be able to enjoy a little vacation."

He smiled so broadly that the sunlight filtering through the window sparkled on his gold teeth, and left the cell followed by the guard, who had been standing stiffly at attention in the doorway during this conversation.

The doctor remained behind, and as soon as the door had closed, I said to him:

"Please tell me, doctor, just how bad my condition is. You are a

Frenchman so I can say to you that I am surprised at so much solicitude from the Germans. Is it because he's afraid I might die on his hands?"

"Not at all, Madame!" the doctor said. "Don't alarm yourself unnecessarily. This regime is very bad for your health. That goes without saying. But living a normal life, with proper care, you have nothing to worry about. You have many long years ahead of you. But since you're lucky enough to get this chance of clemency, by all means, take it."

"Clemency!" I said. "It's the *mot juste,* doctor! But why is clemency being offered to me, in particular? It's not a German habit, you know. And why now, when conditions are improving, after I spent all winter freezing here? What's behind it all, doctor?"

The doctor made a helpless gesture.

"How should I know, Madame? I'm not in their confidence. I'm only the doctor—and French to boot. They don't tell me what their motives are. . . . It's not usual, I know that. But it's fortunate for you, and I see no reason in the world why you shouldn't take advantage of it."

The moment the doctor left, Marguerite said, "Well, Mrs. Shiber, what do you think of the cards now? Weren't they telling the truth?"

"What I'd like to know," I answered evasively, "is whether the Germans are telling the truth. Is it only because they're so concerned with my health that they're willing to let me go?"

"What other reason could they have?" asked Mlle. Blanc. "Unless, of course, they want to be lenient with you because you're an American."

"She was an American last December, too," Mme. Santot broke in drily, "when we were all lying here like corpses in a morgue ice-box—if you'll permit the comparison. She didn't become an American this afternoon. Besides, now that America is in the war, there's less reason than ever for her to get special treatment. I admit I don't understand it."

"It's quite simple," Mme. Ragomin opined. "There's no sense hunting for complicated explanations. Today's attack on the staircase—in public, where it made more of an impression than those you had in here—has frightened the commander. He likes to submit a good report at the end of the year, and the fewer deaths on it, the better. He probably thinks your condition is much worse than the doctor says it is, and he prefers to have you out of here."

"I don't believe it," the school-teacher said. "They don't care that much about deaths. That may have been true of pre-war civilian prisons, but not of these German military jails. There's a woman on the third floor with asthma so bad she can hardly breathe. She has frequent bad attacks, and the doctor has asked her transfer to a hospital several times, but she's still there. Here on our own floor there's a woman with a bad case of tuberculosis, with a recurrent high fever. She hasn't been offered any parole either. There's something funny about this, but I certainly can't figure it out. I'm going to talk to some of the more experienced prisoners tomorrow and see if any one can explain it."

I found it difficult to go to sleep that night. I lay awake, thinking of the joy of returning to my apartment once more. . . . But then, I wondered, what will happen when the six months are up? It will be November then. Will I have to go back to finish my term, just at the worst time of year? Can I perhaps get an extension? And is the six months considered as part of my term, or will I have to spend six months more in jail when I return to make up for it?

Mlle. Blanc was lying on the sack next to me.

"Mme. Shiber," she whispered, "are you still awake?"

"Yes," I said. "Why?"

"Would you do me a great favor?" she asked. "You will be going to Paris soon. Would you go to see my mother when you get there?"

"Of course, my child," I said. I reached over to pat her cheek. It was wet. She had been crying.

"Certainly I will," I said. "What do you want me to tell her?"

"Just that I am very lonely without her, and that I think of her constantly . . . and that I have taken her advice. Can you remember that?"

"Yes," I said. "Where does she live?"

"3, Rue Washington," she said. "Mme. Blanc, of course. . . . You won't forget it?"

"I'll write it down in the morning," I said, "to make sure. Remind me then."

"No, no," she said. "Please don't wait until morning. Memorize it now. Do you remember it still?"

"3, Rue Washington," I said. "Now are you happy?"

"Yes," she said, very softly. "Now I am happy. . . . You're sure you won't forget it before morning?"

"I'm sure I won't," I said. "Now try to go to sleep, dear. You need rest."

"Yes," she said. "I do need rest. I'm going to sleep now."

Poor child, I thought, prison life has been harder on her than on any of the rest of us—perhaps because she is younger, and less able to resign herself placidly to her fate. I had noticed she had grown thinner and paler in the weeks we had been together. I wondered if she didn't really need a parole more than I did.

It must have been the result of having been out in the open air for the first time in months the previous day that accounted for none of us waking until the guard banged on the door with our morning "coffee."

We sprang sleepily out of our blankets, and had our cups filled with the hot liquid. Mlle. Blanc still lay quietly under the covers.

Mme. Santot bent over her.

"Wake up before your coffee gets cold," she called, and shook her by the shoulder, then jerked her hand away as if she had been stung.

"She's so cold," she exclaimed, "and stiff! I think she's dead!"

We froze suddenly in our tracks. I remember noticing that Mme. Ragomin, who was just about to drink her "coffee," stopped with the cup poised in mid-air, as though unable either to continue the motion, or put the cup down.

Summoning up all her courage, Mme. Santot turned the girl over. We could all see the rigidity of her body now. She pulled up an eyelid. It did not close. One eye remained open, staring blankly and horribly at us.

It was too much for Marguerite. She ran to the door and began pounding on it, shouting for the guard. We could hear her come running down the corridor, the pot banging against her knees as she ran. She jerked the door open.

"What's going on in here?" she demanded harshly. Then, catching sight of the motionless figure on the bed, she asked, *"Morte?"*

Mme. Santot nodded.

"Touch nothing," she ordered. "I'll get the doctor."

She was back in an instant with the same physician who had cared for me. The doctor gave one glance at the body, and nodded.

"Probably before midnight last night," he said. "Hmm!"

He bent over swiftly, looked closely at the girl's lips and chin, then sniffed the air sharply. Then, kneeling beside the sack, he started hunting through the bed-clothes. In a moment he straightened up. He had a small phial in his hand. There was still a little of a colorless liquid in it.

"Now where in the world did she get that?" he asked himself. He turned to the guard.

"Get some one to take the body to the morgue," he said. "Notify the commander. I'll wait here till you get back."

The guard went out. The doctor turned to us.

"Did she have any special reason for committing suicide?" he asked. "Do any of you know why she did it?"

Mme. Santot shrugged her shoulders.

"She was young and she was in prison," she said.

"But she had only eighteen months to serve!" said Mme. Ragomin. "Couldn't she have stood it that long?"

"She was murdered by the spring," Marguerite said. "I think it was the contrast between the fresh breeze, and the green outside, and her own imprisonment."

I didn't say anything. I could hear her soft voice, with a little note of pleading, saying to me in the night: "3, Rue Washington. . . . Please don't wait until morning. . . . Now I am happy. . . . I'm going to sleep now."

## CHAPTER FORTY-TWO

# *Parole*

MME. SANTOT was as good as her word. She succeeded in finding out the reason why parole had been offered me, through one of the inmates who had been a stenographer and had been put to work in the prison office.

According to her, she had seen a letter in the files from the Kommandantur of Paris, informing the warden that there was a possibility that I might be exchanged for a very important German prisoner held in the United States. Immediately after she had seen that letter, the commander had called the doctor in, and said:

"I see that Mme. Shiber has had several heart attacks. In your opinion, doctor, how bad is her condition?"

"It is not grave," the doctor said, "but naturally prison regime is particularly hard on a woman in her condition."

"But there is no danger of death?"

"I couldn't answer for that if she remains in prison," the doctor had answered. "Under normal conditions, with a reasonable amount of food, rest and comfort, she would be quite all right."

That was the morning of the day when I fainted on the stairway. It was easy to piece the rest of it together; the commander, impressed by the fact that I might be of value to the Germans for an exchange, and fearing from the doctor's statement that I might die if I remained in prison, had suggested the parole in order to make sure that I would be on hand if and when I would be useful to them.

"Now I understand," I said, when Mme. Santot had finished. "I didn't think the Germans would worry about the death of a prisoner unless they saw some advantage in keeping her alive. . . . But I don't see why I should be important enough for any one to be exchanged for me. . . . Probably the whole thing will fall through. I'm not going to believe it until it happens. That way I won't be disappointed."

But it did happen, and the very next day. When the guard came in as usual in the morning, and doled out our portion of "coffee," I had no reason for thinking that this would be the last time I would have to swallow that horrible potion. When the sergeant of the guard arrived in the middle of the morning, this unexpected interruption raised my hopes for a moment, but he motioned four men into the cell. They searched it minutely, going over the straw sacks especially, inch by inch. We guessed what they were hunting for—they wanted to find out if any more poison were hidden in the cell. But they found nothing. We heard them go into the next cell after ours. Apparently Mlle. Blanc's suicide had stimulated a prison-wide search.

When the door opened at the usual hour for lunch, I was expecting nothing out of the ordinary. But the guard entered without her pot of soup, and said to me, "Come to the office, please."

I stared at her. It was the first time I had ever heard her, or any of the guards, say, "Please." She didn't even shout at me to hurry. Instead, she went on, "And bring your belongings."

"Bring your belongings!" It's true, I thought, they must be letting me out! I hastily gathered up my things, saying as I did so:

"My friends! Perhaps my petition for a parole has been granted! Don't you think so?"

"Don't hope for too much yet, Mme. Shiber," Mme. Ragomin said kindly. "There's hardly been time for action on that. They are probably moving you to the ground floor so you won't have to walk up and down stairs. We'll see you in the yard this afternoon. . . . *Au 'voir.*"

"*Au revoir,* ladies," I said, and followed the guard. Mme. Ragomin's explanation was probably correct, I told myself. Forty-eight hours wasn't time enough for my parole to have been granted. But still that "please" of the guard stuck in my mind, and I still hoped.

I went down the banisterless stairway very slowly and cautiously, and the guard patiently slowed her step to accommodate mine. I hoped with all my pounding heart that it would be release, not transfer, which would mean that I would have to adjust myself to a new set of cell-mates, very probably much less congenial than those I had grown to like in the hard days we had spent together.

The guard stopped with me outside the door of the warden's office. The sentry told her to wait; the Major was busy for the moment.

Also standing outside the door was an elegantly dressed woman, wearing an expensive coat and a fashionable hat, a veritable fashion plate. She was evidently in the custody of the French gendarme who stood beside her. I didn't recognize her until she spoke:

"Mme. Shiber, I believe," she said. "We have met before."

It was Mme. Berthet, from Fresnes!

"What are you doing here?" I asked. "Did you have anything to do with getting me paroled?"

"I?" she laughed. "Goodness, no! I'm going back to jail myself. . . . I ought to be very angry with you. It's all your fault."

"*My* fault?" I echoed, surprised.

She glanced at the gendarme. He seemed to have no objection to our talking, and my guard, for once, was courtesy itself.

"Yes, because if you had accepted my proposal, I wouldn't have tried to smuggle some of my husband's money out into Switzerland. They caught me. They got the money and I got a year."

"You don't have to worry," I said to her. "Your husband will no doubt be able to get you out once more—or at least get you weekends off again."

"My husband!" she exclaimed harshly. "That stinker! Do you know what he testified at the trial? That I had stolen the money from him, and was trying to get away with it! And do you know what I said?"

I never found out what Mme. Berthet had said. At that moment the door opened, and the guard motioned to me to come in.

The Commandant rose politely when I entered.

"Won't you sit down, Mrs. Shiber?" he said, and sat down again himself only after I had done so.

"Mrs. Shiber," he began with unction, "I have good news for you. I have received a favorable answer to your petition for a six months' parole. You see that we lose no time here. I had a special messenger take the petition to Paris, and I received an answer by telegraph. . . . Now, Madame, you understand that since you are still technically in custody, we must keep tabs on you. Therefore, I must ask you where you desire to pass this time?"

"In Paris," I said.

"That is quite permissible," the major returned. "But you understand that your freedom is conditional, and that you must comply with certain regulations. If you violate them, we will be obliged to bring you back here. I do not think you will find them very onerous. On arriving in Paris, you will report to the Kommandantur, and you must not go elsewhere without securing prior permission. During your residence in Paris, you must present yourself in person daily, and report any changes of address."

"Every day?" I asked, rather surprised at this requirement.

"Yes," he answered, somewhat stiffly. "I think this privilege should be worth that much to you. . . . And now, Madame, a pleasant journey to you, and better health, I hope."

The momentary stiffness gone, he accompanied me to the door and opened it for me to pass through. My guard took me over again and conducted me to the quartermaster's office, where I was given a release certificate stating the conditions of my parole, and asked to sign for an envelope containing the money I had had with me when I entered.

"We have made certain deductions for items you were allowed to buy during your imprisonment," I was told. "You will find an accounting for them with the money."

"Yes, yes," I murmured. "That's perfectly all right."

I was too anxious to get outside the prison gates even to look in the envelope. I signed the receipt, and a moment later the doors swung out before me. For the second time I tasted the ecstatic joy of freedom after imprisonment.

The railroad station was, I knew, some two miles from the prison. I remembered the direction from which we had come on arriving, and started out on foot. But I had overestimated my strength. I was able to walk only a couple of hundred yards when I felt so tired that I didn't dare continue. I sat down on a boulder by the side of the road, and waited for some vehicle to pass. The first arrival turned out to be a peasant with an ox-cart. When I told him I wanted to get to Troyes, but was too weak to walk, he helped me up onto the low cart, and walked along beside me, guiding the oxen with occasional light blows from a long stick he carried.

"Coming from there?" he asked, jerking his thumb back over his shoulder towards the prison.

"Yes," I said, suddenly ashamed for the first time of having been in prison, before some one who didn't know why.

"How'd they treat you there?"

"Well," I said, "it's run by the Germans but the guards are French. They treated us all right—no worse than they treat any one else, I suppose."

"You're a foreigner, aren't you?" he asked, suspiciously.

"I'm an American."

"American!" he said, and stopped short. So did the oxen, no doubt habituated to copying his movements. Then he started forward again, the oxen obediently resuming their slow placid gait.

"I don't suppose there's any chance of your getting back to America now?" he said.

"I don't know," I said. "There may be. I think that's why they let me out. I hope they're going to exchange me."

The peasant seemed to have gained new energy.

"Listen, Madame," he said, "if you get back to your country, give your countrymen this message from an old French peasant—and tell them he knew that he was speaking for forty million Frenchmen. Tell them not to delay. Tell them not to wait too long. Tell them they needn't bother to put off their coming until they are able to do the job all alone. For they won't have to do it alone. We will fight with them, just as we did last time. We expect them. We are biding our time. But we are ready. We have our arms. They are hidden—well hidden. We are waiting for your countrymen to come to bring them out. And then, together, we'll drive the Boche out of *la belle France* as we did once before. . . . But tell them to hurry. Tell them that we are weakening every day. The sooner they come, the stronger we will be to help them. . . . Will you tell them that, Madame?"

"I will tell them," I said. "I won't forget."

The railroad station was a bewildering place for me, with crowds hurrying back and forth, free to move in any direction, unregimented and, so it seemed after prison, disorderly. It is going to take me some time, I thought, before I will be able to resume my normal place in society and get used to people again.

I went into the ticket office to get a ticket for Paris, and for the first time opened the envelope that contained my money. It had held 12,000 francs when I had handed it over. Now there were only about 8,000 left.

I sat down on a bench to examine the document listing the *Gebühren*—the "deductions." I had been charged for the one or two small items I had been allowed to buy through the prison office—a comb, pins, and other trifles—at a ridiculous rate, and there was even a charge for the doctor who had been called in for me from town (quite without my knowledge, for I was unconscious at the time). But the heaviest charge was for "medicine," and for a moment I was puzzled. Then I realized suddenly what it must be. It was under that form that the cigarettes I had bought for Titi were entered.

At the ticket window, I stood before a man smoking a cigarette. I caught a whiff of the smoke, and immediately my head began to turn and I felt giddy—although before my arrest, I had often smoked as many as twenty a day. It was, I supposed, partly lack of habit and partly the weakness resulting from malnutrition.

I learned as I bought my ticket that there would be no train for Paris for another hour. I wandered aimlessly across the street and walked into the first small restaurant I came across, thinking to eat something before taking the train—for I had left the prison without lunch—not that that would have made much difference.

It was like every little French restaurant, run, I assumed, by a man and his wife, the former waiting on the customers, the latter doing the cooking. As I entered it I glanced at a mirror hanging on the wall near the entrance and stopped short. We had had no mirrors in prison, and I had not seen my own face for months. I didn't recognize myself.

My unkempt hair had grown stringy and was now almost all white. My face was yellow and sickly, and lined with wrinkles. And my clothes! The hat which had come from one of the best shops of Paris was a formless mass of felt and cloth. My tailored suit, of excellent material and perfect cut—well, it looked as if it had been slept in, not once, but every day for months—as it had.

The proprietor saw my startled look when I glanced into the

mirror. Putting it together with my disheveled appearance, he said, politely and with an understanding smile:

"I suppose, Madame, you come from the hospital—that is, from the prison."

"Yes," I said. "I would like something to eat, but of course I have no ration card."

"Naturally," he said. "It is too bad, but—really, Madame, I can't serve you without a card. You realize my situation. I would do it gladly, but if I am caught, they would close me up."

"I understand," I said dully. "It's not your fault, of course."

"From your accent, Madame, I should judge you were English or American?" he pursued.

"American," I said.

"American?" he repeated. Then, switching to not bad English, he went on, "So they had an American in jail there! Look, Madame —I was a waiter for a while on the French Line—the *paquebots,* you know. Then I worked for a little while in New York. I am very fond of Americans, Madame. I cannot sell you anything—but perhaps if you would like to be my personal guest? They cannot prevent me from sharing my own rations with you."

I tried to protest, politely, though it was only a gesture. I was too anxious to change from prison fare to be too meticulous about not depriving any one else of their rations. I let him lead me through the kitchen to his private apartment.

"Sit down," he said, pushing a chair up to the table. "Excuse me just a minute." And I heard him back in the kitchen, saying excitedly to his wife: "*Figurez-vous!* An American in their dirty jail! Watch the dining room while I get her something to eat."

He returned with what to me was a banquet—a piece of roast meat, salad, cheese. There was even a small piece of butter for the bread. The proprietor sat with me, drinking a glass of red wine—I didn't dare touch it yet—and talking with me, chiefly about the last war.

"You remember, Madame," he said, "what your General Pershing said when he arrived in 1917 'Lafayette, we are here!' The Americans saved France then, and we know they will save us again. That is our last hope, and our only hope, Madame—your country. We know she will not fail the people of France."

## CHAPTER FORTY-THREE

# Father Christian

IT WAS 9 o'clock in the evening when I reached Paris. I stepped from the *Gare de l'Est* into the street with a feeling of apprehension. So many times before I had come out of this station into the gayly lighted square before it, with its rows of brilliant cafés and the happy, laughing crowds thronging their terraces. Now it was gloomy and deserted, and the few persons hurrying by wore expressions which convinced me that the city was feeling the oppression of the invader even more bitterly than when I had last left it.

I went at once to my apartment. This time it was I who almost failed to recognize Mme. Beugler. She had lost weight, and now the bones of her head showed plainly under the sunken flesh of her once plump face.

"Have you been ill?" I asked, after we had exchanged greetings.

"No," she said, with a tired smile. "I know I've changed. I'm much thinner than when you saw me last. It's the food situation. It's very bad here now. Much worse than when you were here. One of the tenants was calculating the other day that the French people altogether have lost 400,000,000 kilograms in weight. That's figuring an average loss of 10 kilos per person—and I've lost 15 myself. I used to weigh 65, now I weigh 50[1] . . . Has Mme. Kitty been released also?"

The question pained me so much, I couldn't explain completely at once. I said only:

"I don't know, Mme. Beugler. You see, we haven't been together."

"What a pity! I always supposed you were in the same cell, and could console one another."

I couldn't bring myself to tell her of Kitty's death sentence; and I had learned already from what she had said that she knew nothing of what might have happened to her. I changed the subject·

"What happened to our dogs?"

[1] A kilogram is 2.2 pounds.

"They aren't here any more," Mme. Beugler said uneasily. "I don't know if you noticed, Madame. There isn't a dog in Paris any more. When there isn't even enough to eat for human beings, what can you do about dogs?"

"You didn't *eat* them, did you?" I almost screamed.

"Goodness, no!" Mme. Beugler said vehemently. "No, Madame, that isn't what I meant. I wouldn't do a thing like that—although, I tell you, there are people who ate their dogs. That's a fact. Their cats, too. . . . I couldn't feed the dogs, Madame. What could I do? I had to turn them over to the Society for Prevention of Cruelty to Animals. They put them out of the way painlessly. I assure you, Madame, it was the best way."

"I suppose it was," I answered wearily, saddened by this news, though on my already dulled senses it fell with less of an impact than it would have done at other times. "I'm tired. I think I'll go to bed." And I reached out mechanically to the board where our keys used to hang.

"But, Madame," the concierge said, surprised. "Surely you didn't expect to find your apartment intact when you returned!"

"Why, yes . . . I did," I faltered. "I hadn't thought about it. . . . You mean . . . it's not mine any more?"

"*Voilà!* In March, the Germans came with a big moving van. They said you had been convicted of smuggling English soldiers out of the country, and your property was to be confiscated. They took everything away—everything! You never saw anything like it. They even pulled nails out of the walls, and saved them. I had to telephone the landlord to keep them from taking the curtain rods and other fixtures that belonged to the building."

"Then it's empty!" I said. "Our things are gone!"

"Wait!" said Mme. Beugler. "You haven't heard the oddest thing of all yet. Two days afterwards they came back, and showed me an order that your apartment was to be turned over to a German officer. And they brought back the identical furnishings they had taken out. Your own things! And moved them right back in again! Now what kind of sense does that make, I ask you? If the Germans were going to hand the apartment over to one of their officers, why did they move everything out and then back again?"

"So a German officer is living with all our lovely things now!" I said, feeling as though I were likely to burst into tears at any moment.

"Yes," Mme. Beugler answered. "A military prosecutor—Captain Weber is his name."

Weber! Now I understood the curious story Mme. Beugler had told about the removal and return of our furniture. I remembered Weber looking about and complimenting us about the taste with which we had fixed up our apartment. No doubt the furniture had been taken out while he was arranging to get our place for himself, and was put back in at his request.

"Thank you, Mme. Beugler," I said. "I'm very tired. I must find a place to sleep before curfew. *Au 'voir.*"

I walked out into the dark streets. I felt as though I had just been present at the funeral of my past.

Finding a place to sleep was not too easy. I tried one or two small hotels and found them filled. It was after 10. If I failed to find a place before 11, I would be picked up by the patrol, and would spend my first night outside of prison in the police station! Suddenly I remembered the hotel where Father Christian had left his boys one night. He had given me its address when he tried to get me to come to visit the proprietress. I determined to go there.

As I entered the hotel, I found myself in a sort of lobby deserted of all guests. The only person in sight was a middle-aged woman at the hotel desk, working at the books. As I approached, she gave a fleeting glance at my bedraggled clothes, and said coldly:

"Sorry. We have no vacant rooms."

"Please," I said, "try to squeeze me in somehow. I'm very tired and it's nearly curfew. I don't blame you for finding me rather unprepossessing, but I can't help my appearance. You see, I've just come out of a German prison."

She took off her glasses and looked at me without them, with a more human interest, I thought.

"A German prison?" she repeated. "Why were you there?"

"You're Mme. Henri, aren't you?" I asked, without answering her question.

"Why, yes. How do you know my name?"

"Father Christian told me," I said. "I am Mrs. Shiber."

"Mrs. Shiber! The American? The one who wouldn't come to see me?"

"I'm afraid so," I said. "I didn't want to let any more people than I could help in on our secret. As you see, I had reason to be afraid."

"I don't hold it against you," said Mme. Henri, smiling broadly. "I understand. But now you trust me more, *n'est-ce pas*?"

"Father Christian guaranteed that you could be depended upon," I said, "so I came here when I found that they had confiscated my apartment."

"*Les cochons!*" Mme. Henri exclaimed. Then suddenly, a look of distrust came into her eyes. "Excuse me," she said, "but can you prove you are Mrs. Shiber?"

I showed her my papers and my prison discharge.

"Excuse me, Mrs. Shiber," she said. "I just happened to think suddenly—after all, I do not know her, and it could be a trick. . . . It is 11. Just a minute. I must close."

She locked the door. I thought that in hundreds of thousands of other buildings at the same moment, Paris was simultaneously locking itself up for the night. Animation was suspended now until morning.

Mme. Henri led me to a room, with a little embarrassment at having to admit that she had intended to bar me at first on the grounds of my appearance, which did not, I confess, make me appear a desirable guest. It was clean and cozy, with a tiny bathroom attached to it. Not many months ago I would have found it ordinary enough, but now, after the prison of Troyes, it seemed the height of luxury. I even reveled in the wall-paper, of that curious purple violence found only in low-priced French hotels.

An hour later, fresh from a bath, my hair combed, and my face feeling clean for the first time in months, I was reclining in my soft bed, ravenously devouring a slice of cold meat which Mme. Henri had brought up to me. She was sitting on the edge of the bed, questioning me on my prison experiences. I told her of the last report I had had from Kitty—that she had been transferred from the Cherche-Midi prison, but that I didn't know where.

"If only I knew!" I exclaimed. "Perhaps then I could find out whether she is . . . I mean, what has happened to her."

"From what I have heard," Mme. Henri said, "she has probably been moved to Germany. I'm afraid that makes it impossible to expect to get any news of her."

"Germany?" I exclaimed. "But how did you learn that?"

"Father Christian told me."

"Father Christian!" I almost shouted. "You have seen Father Christian? How? Where? When?"

"Two weeks ago, in this room."

"I don't understand," I said. "He was condemned to death, too."

"Of course, you couldn't know, just coming from prison," said Mme. Henri. "It was stupid of me. I should have told you at once. But I was so busy asking you questions that I forgot what you would like to know. Here's what happened. Four weeks after he was sentenced, the prison was notified that officers from the Château de Vincennes would call for him on a certain day, his execution having been set for dawn the day after. Sure enough, two officers arrived with an order for his delivery, signed a receipt taking over his custody, and took him away. . . . There must have been a fine scene at the prison an hour or so later when the *real* officers arrived."

"Then the men who got him were—?"

"From the British Intelligence Service! They had learned the exact time when the transfer was to be made, and called themselves just an hour earlier."

"But that was a long while ago," I said. "You say you saw him only two weeks ago. Didn't he get away to England then?"

Mme. Henri laughed.

"Not he," she said, "not Father Christian. That was the idea of the Englishmen who got him out, but he said, 'I was resigned to the fact that my life was over, and so this extra life I have been granted is clear gain; in risking it, I risk nothing. Besides, God has snatched me from death once, and he can do it again, if he so wills.' And he went back to smuggling soldiers out of the country. That isn't all. He's also working with friends, publishing secret papers, sending information to the British, and so forth. He's a brave man, Father Christian!"

"I would so like to see him again," I said. "Do you think it would be possible?"

"Perhaps," said Mme. Henri, "but we had better be very careful.

We must make sure first that you are not watched, for instance. I don't know how to reach him, but he communicates with me fairly regularly, and I will tell him about you. But he will probably know already that you have been released. Through his underground connections, he has followed the fate of all those who were convicted with him. That was how he learned that Kitty had been sent away to Germany."

"Has he told you anything about the others?" I asked. "Chancel and Tissier, I mean?"

"Both in the prison of Dijon. Chancel could have gotten out. The Gueules Cassées interceded for him, and he was offered his liberty if he would sign a guarantee never to oppose the Germans again. He refused to sign, so he's still in jail."

I left Mme. Henri's hotel the next morning, for I was obliged to report my address to the police, and I thought it would be better not to stay there, since they might check up to find out if my new address had any connection with my past activities. I told her that I would not come back to the hotel for several days, in order to have time to discover whether or not I was being followed, and that if I were, I wouldn't come back at all. But I arranged with her to have dinner at the same restaurant every night, where she was to come also whenever she heard from Father Christian. There we agreed that we would strike up a conversation as though we were strangers, in order to communicate with one another without being suspected, in case I should be provided, once more, with a shadow.

## CHAPTER FORTY-FOUR

# Last Days in Paris

IT WAS only when I put my hand into my coat pocket as I left the hotel and touched a slip of paper that I remembered something which had completely slipped my mind the previous day—I had Marguerite's note to her *femme de ménage* telling her to let me occupy her apartment. I went to the address it gave, fearing that it, too, might have been taken over by the Germans, but this time I was in luck. Before noon, I found myself established in a pleasant little Left Bank studio. My first care was to make my required appearance before the police, where I was given something very necessary—ration books. My next act was to get some new clothes. I found it almost impossible to find anything very attractive. The stores were bare of merchandise. But it wasn't hard to improve on what I was wearing, and I felt that I had regained some of my self respect when I was able at last to change the garments which I had worn day after day for so many months (and during the winter, without ever taking them off).

My first visit was to 3, Rue Washington, to keep the promise I had made to poor little Mlle. Blanc. I was very nervous as I rang the bell. I knew I had a painful ordeal before me, and as I waited at the door, I tried to phrase the sentences in which I would have to tell Mme. Blanc of the last hours of her daughter.

In the end, I am afraid I blurted it out rather badly, but Mme. Blanc helped me by maintaining an iron composure. There was a tightness on her face and a hardness in her voice which betrayed the grip she was holding on her soul to prevent her emotions from breaking through, but she reined herself in before the stranger who had entered her life once, briefly, to bring her evil tidings.

When I repeated her daughter's message: "Tell her that I am lonely without her, that I think of her constantly, and that I have taken her advice," Mme. Blanc said quietly, but with that curious tautness in her voice: "That was not the way I foresaw it."

I tried to frame an apology for us, her cell-mates, and especially for myself, who had not realized her intention, in spite of the strange way she had spoken to me. If we had dreamed that she had poison, I said, we would have taken it from her. But who would have imagined that she could have gotten it in prison?

"She took it with her," her mother said. "I gave it to her." Her voice was dull and without inflections.

"*You* gave it to her?" I repeated, thunderstruck.

"Yes," said Mme. Blanc, still in that expressionless monotone. "Perhaps you will not understand me. I may have been wrong. I did not want to let the Germans take her away without giving her the means to escape if what they might do became unbearable to her. How could I tell what might happen to her? They might have beaten her. They might have tortured her. You see, I was thinking of helping her to escape ill-treatment. I didn't think that it would happen like that—that the drab days, and the privation, and the confinement would be too much for her . . . and the time so short until she could have come back to me. . . ."

For the first time, her voice quavered.

"Thank you, Mrs. Shiber," she said. "Would you mind going now? I'd like to be alone."


It was ten nights before Mme. Henri appeared at the restaurant where I had dined faithfully day after day, arriving with the first customers and leaving with the last. She came up to my table, and saying to me, "*Permettez-vous?*" as though she were a complete stranger asking if she might sit at the same table, she took a seat and continued to act as though she did not know me.

I could see that she was purposely dragging out the meal, and I did the same. Once or twice, she asked me to pass the salt, or hand her the bill of fare. She was still playing the part of the stranger, but paving the way by these routine remarks to be able to speak to me naturally later.

By the time she thought it safe, there was no one left but the proprietor and a lone waiter who evidently wished that we would get out and let him go home. Mme. Henri waited until the last customer had gone, and then, still taking the precaution of appearing to be addressing me casually, she said, "I have seen Father Christian."

"Wonderful!" I exclaimed. "When can I see him?"

"Not at all, I'm afraid," she replied. "He asked me to say to you that he regrets it deeply, but that he has reason to believe from underground reports that although you do not seem to be shadowed regularly, they are keeping close tabs on you. It would be dangerous to both of you for you to try to see him. He would be recognized, no doubt, and it would appear as though you intended to resume your old activities. He said to tell you that he hopes to see you again after the war, when there will be no more Germans in Paris."

"Did you ask him about Kitty?"

"Yes; but he knows nothing new. He says he does not believe she has been executed yet, because they would probably have learned of that. They have agents even in Germany, and they are still trying to find out what happened to her. He suggests that you ask permission to write to her at the Kommandantur. If she has already been executed, they will probably tell you so. If not, they may even give you the prison address."

I was at the Kommandantur at noon. I handed my release papers to the officer in charge to have him stamp it with the date, as he did daily, and was about to ask if I could send a letter to Kitty, when he said:

"So you are Mme. Shiber? We have just sent a messenger to your apartment to look for you."

"What's the matter?" I asked, with a sinking feeling. Once again, I thought, my temporary freedom is illusory. I am going back to jail again. Is it because of my meeting with Mme. Henri? Have I led the German police to another victim, and am I being returned again, now that I have served my purpose as a danger to all who meet me?

"Nothing's the matter, Madame. You must leave Paris today, that's all."

"Today? But why?"

"You are going to America, Madame," he said, and a broad grin appeared on his face. I imagined that he had enjoyed my evident fear, and had amused himself for a few seconds by delaying this announcement.

I was conducted to the office of a German colonel, who informed me that in accordance with an agreement between the United States and Germany, I was about to be exchanged. He told me that I was to return to my apartment, pack anything I wanted to take with me, and wait there for a Gestapo escort who would take me to Juvisy, where I would board a train for Lisbon at 5 o'clock that afternoon.

I listened in a daze, but in spite of my bewilderment and elation, I didn't forget my anxiety for news of Kitty.

"May I make one request, Colonel?" I asked. "I would like to send a farewell message to my friend who was arrested with me before I leave Europe. She is in prison, but I do not know where."

"What is her name?"

"Kitty Beaurepos," I breathed.

"Excuse me a moment," he said politely, and stepped into the outer office. I waited tensely for the result. In a few moments he was back.

"Yes," he said. "You can write to Mme. Beaurepos. Address the letter to her at the *Politische Zivil Gefangenen Stelle,* and it will be forwarded."

"Then she's still alive!" I couldn't help exclaiming. "Thank God for that!"

The Colonel looked at me with a quizzical smile.

"So that was what you wanted to know," he said. "Why didn't you say so? I could have told you that here in Paris we have no way of knowing that. All we have here is that address. You can send your letter there, and it will be forwarded—if she is still alive. But whether she is or not, I am afraid we cannot guarantee."

And so I come to the end of my story. You know the rest—how I was exchanged for Johanna Hoffmann, how I boarded the refugee train at Juvisy, the journey to Lisbon, and finally my return aboard the *Drottningholm* to the free soil of my own country. In this new atmosphere of a country which, though at war, had not yet tasted nor realized what war meant, the experiences I have related receded into a distance which each day seemed to grow more unreal and more dreamlike. At times, it seemed to me quite impossible that all this should have happened to me, that I should have been caught up into these toils—I, an ordinary woman with no particular taste for adventure.